P9-CFW-197

XML

IN A NUTSHELL

Other XML resources from O'Reilly

Related titles

.NET and XML
Content Syndication with
    RSS
Java and XML
Learning XML
Learning XSLT
Office 2003 XML
Practical RDF

RELAX NG
XForms Essentials
XML Hacks
XML Pocket Reference
XML Publishing with
    AxKit
XML Schema

XML Books Resource Center

xml.oreilly.com is a complete catalog of O'Reilly's books on XML and related technologies, including sample chapters and code examples.

O'REILLY
XML.com

XML.com helps you discover XML and learn how this Internet technology can solve real-world problems in information management and electronic commerce.

Conferences

O'Reilly brings diverse innovators together to nurture the ideas that spark revolutionary industries. We specialize in documenting the latest tools and systems, translating the innovator's knowledge into useful skills for those in the trenches. Visit *conferences.oreilly.com* for our upcoming events.

O'REILLY NETWORK
Safari Bookshelf

Safari Bookshelf (*safari.oreilly.com*) is the premier online reference library for programmers and IT professionals. Conduct searches across more than 1,000 books. Subscribers can zero in on answers to time-critical questions in a matter of seconds. Read the books on your Bookshelf from cover to cover or simply flip to the page you need. Try it today with a free trial.

XML

IN A NUTSHELL

Third Edition

*Elliotte Rusty Harold
and W. Scott Means*

O'REILLY®

Beijing • Cambridge • Farnham • Köln • Paris • Sebastopol • Taipei • Tokyo

XML in a Nutshell, Third Edition

by Elliotte Rusty Harold and W. Scott Means

Copyright © 2004, 2002, 2001 O'Reilly Media, Inc. All rights reserved.
Printed in the United States of America.

Published by O'Reilly Media, Inc., 1005 Gravenstein Highway North, Sebastopol, CA 95472.

O'Reilly books may be purchased for educational, business, or sales promotional use. Online editions are also available for most titles (*safari.oreilly.com*). For more information, contact our corporate/institutional sales department: (800) 998-9938 or *corporate@oreilly.com*.

Editor:	Simon St.Laurent
Production Editor:	Marlowe Shaeffer
Cover Designer:	Ellie Volckhausen
Interior Designer:	Melanie Wang

Printing History:

January 2001:	First Edition.
June 2002:	Second Edition.
September 2004:	Third Edition.

Nutshell Handbook, the Nutshell Handbook logo, and the O'Reilly logo are registered trademarks of O'Reilly Media, Inc. The *In a Nutshell* series designations, *XML in a Nutshell*, the image of a peafowl, and related trade dress are trademarks of O'Reilly Media, Inc.

Many of the designations used by manufacturers and sellers to distinguish their products are claimed as trademarks. Where those designations appear in this book, and O'Reilly Media, Inc. was aware of a trademark claim, the designations have been printed in caps or initial caps.

While every precaution has been taken in the preparation of this book, the publisher and authors assume no responsibility for errors or omissions, or for damages resulting from the use of the information contained herein.

 This book uses RepKover™, a durable and flexible lay-flat binding.

ISBN: 0-596-00764-7
ISBN13: 978-0-596-00764-5
[M]

Table of Contents

Part II. Narrative-Like Documents

Part III. Record-Like Documents

Part IV. Reference

Preface

In the last few years, XML has been adopted in fields as diverse as law, aeronautics, finance, insurance, robotics, multimedia, hospitality, travel, art, construction, telecommunications, software, agriculture, physics, journalism, theology, retail, and comics. XML has become the syntax of choice for newly designed document formats across almost all computer applications. It's used on Linux, Windows, Macintosh, and many other computer platforms. Mainframes on Wall Street trade stocks with one another by exchanging XML documents. Children playing games on their home PCs save their documents in XML. Sports fans receive real-time game scores on their cell phones in XML. XML is simply the most robust, reliable, and flexible document syntax ever invented.

XML in a Nutshell is a comprehensive guide to the rapidly growing world of XML. It covers all aspects of XML, from the most basic syntax rules, to the details of DTD and schema creation, to the APIs you can use to read and write XML documents in a variety of programming languages.

What This Book Covers

There are thousands of formally established XML applications from the W3C and other standards bodies, such as OASIS and the Object Management Group. There are even more informal, unstandardized applications from individuals and corporations, such as Microsoft's Channel Definition Format and John Guajardo's Mind Reading Markup Language. This book cannot cover them all, any more than a book on Java could discuss every program that has ever been or might ever be written in Java. This book focuses primarily on XML itself. It covers the fundamental rules that all XML documents and authors must adhere to, from a web designer who uses SMIL to add animations to web pages to a C++ programmer who uses SOAP to exchange serialized objects with a remote database.

This book also covers generic supporting technologies that have been layered on top of XML and are used across a wide range of XML applications. These technologies include:

XLink
>An attribute-based syntax for hyperlinks between XML and non-XML documents that provide the simple, one-directional links familiar from HTML, multidirectional links between many documents, and links between documents to which you don't have write access.

XSLT
>An XML application that describes transformations from one document to another in either the same or different XML vocabularies.

XPointer
>A syntax for URI fragment identifiers that selects particular parts of the XML document referred to by the URI—often used in conjunction with an XLink.

XPath
>A non-XML syntax used by both XPointer and XSLT for identifying particular pieces of XML documents. For example, an XPath can locate the third address element in the document or all elements with an email attribute whose value is elharo@metalab.unc.edu.

XInclude
>A means of assembling large XML documents by combining other complete documents and document fragments.

Namespaces
>A means of distinguishing between elements and attributes from different XML vocabularies that have the same name; for instance, the title of a book and the title of a web page in a web page about books.

Schemas
>An XML vocabulary for describing the permissible contents of XML documents from other XML vocabularies.

SAX
>The Simple API for XML, an event-based application programming interface implemented by many XML parsers.

DOM
>The Document Object Model, a language-neutral, tree-oriented API that treats an XML document as a set of nested objects with various properties.

XHTML
>An XMLized version of HTML that can be extended with other XML applications, such as MathML and SVG.

RDDL
>The Resource Directory Description Language, an XML application based on XHTML for documents placed at the end of namespace URLs.

All these technologies, whether defined in XML (XLinks, XSLT, namespaces, schemas, XHTML, XInclude, and RDDL) or in another syntax (XPointers, XPath, SAX, and DOM), are used in many different XML applications.

This book does not provide in-depth coverage of XML applications that are relevant to only some users of XML, such as:

SVG
> Scalable Vector Graphics, a W3C-endorsed standard XML encoding of line art.

MathML
> The Mathematical Markup Language, a W3C-endorsed standard XML application used for embedding equations in web pages and other documents.

RDF
> The Resource Description Framework, a W3C-standard XML application used for describing resources, with a particular focus on the sort of metadata one might find in a library card catalog.

Occasionally we use one or more of these applications in an example, but we do not cover all aspects of the relevant vocabulary in depth. While interesting and important, these applications (and thousands more like them) are intended primarily for use with special software that knows their formats intimately. For instance, most graphic designers do not work directly with SVG. Instead, they use their customary tools, such as Adobe Illustrator, to create SVG documents. They may not even know they're using XML.

This book focuses on standards that are relevant to almost all developers working with XML. We investigate XML technologies that span a wide range of XML applications, not those that are relevant only within a few restricted domains.

What's New in the Third Edition

XML has not stood still in the two years since the second edition of *XML in a Nutshell* was published. The single most obvious change is that this edition now covers XML 1.1. However, the genuine changes in XML 1.1 are not as large as a .1 version number increase would imply. In fact, if you don't speak Mongolian, Burmese, Amharic, Cambodian, or a few other less common languages, there's very little new material of interest in XML 1.1. In almost every way that practically matters, XML 1.0 and 1.1 are the same. Certainly there's a lot less difference between XML 1.0 and XML 1.1 than there was between Java 1.0 and Java 1.1. Therefore, we will mostly discuss XML in this book as one unified thing, and only refer specifically to XML 1.1 on those rare occasions where the two versions are in fact different. Probably about 98% of this book applies equally well to both XML 1.0 and XML 1.1.

We have also added a new chapter covering XInclude, a recent W3C invention for assembling large documents out of smaller documents and pieces thereof. Elliotte is responsible for almost half of the early implementations of XInclude, as well as having written possibly the first book that used XInclude as an integral part of the production process, so it's a subject of particular interest to us. Other chapters throughout the book have been rewritten to reflect the impact of XML 1.1 on their subject matter, as well as independent changes their technologies have undergone in the last two years. Many topics have been upgraded to the latest versions of various specifications, including:

- SAX 2.0.1
- Namespaces 1.1
- DOM Level 3
- XPointer 1.0
- Unicode 4.0.1

Finally, many small errors and omissions were corrected throughout the book.

Organization of the Book

Part I, *XML Concepts*, introduces the fundamental standards that form the essential core of XML to which all XML applications and software must adhere. It teaches you about well-formed XML, DTDs, namespaces, and Unicode as quickly as possible.

Part II, *Narrative-Like Documents*, explores technologies that are used mostly for narrative XML documents, such as web pages, books, articles, diaries, and plays. You'll learn about XSLT, CSS, XSL-FO, XLinks, XPointers, XPath, XInclude, and RDDL.

One of the most unexpected developments in XML was its enthusiastic adoption for data-heavy structured documents such as spreadsheets, financial statistics, mathematical tables, and software file formats. Part III, *Record-Like Documents*, explores the use of XML for such applications. This part focuses on the tools and APIs needed to write software that processes XML, including SAX, DOM, and schemas.

Finally, Part IV, *Reference*, is a series of quick-reference chapters that form the core of any Nutshell Handbook. These chapters give you detailed syntax rules for the core XML technologies, including XML, DTDs, schemas, XPath, XSLT, SAX, and DOM. Turn to this section when you need to find out the precise syntax quickly for something you know you can do but don't remember exactly how to do.

Conventions Used in This Book

`Constant width` is used for:

- Anything that might appear in an XML document, including element names, tags, attribute values, entity references, and processing instructions.
- Anything that might appear in a program, including keywords, operators, method names, class names, and literals.

`Constant width bold` is used for:

- User input.
- Emphasis in code examples and fragments.

`Constant width italic` is used for:

- Replaceable elements in code statements.

Italic is used for:

- New terms where they are defined.
- Emphasis in body text.
- Pathnames, filenames, and program names. (However, if the program name is also the name of a Java class, it is written in constant-width font, like other class names.)
- Host and domain names (*cafeconleche.org*).

 This icon indicates a tip, suggestion, or general note.

 This icon indicates a warning or caution.

Significant code fragments, complete programs, and documents are generally placed into a separate paragraph, like this:

```
<?xml version="1.0"?>
<?xml-stylesheet href="person.css" type="text/css"?>
<person>
   Alan Turing
</person>
```

XML is case-sensitive. The PERSON element is not the same thing as the person or Person element. Case-sensitive languages do not always allow authors to adhere to standard English grammar. It is usually possible to rewrite the sentence so the two do not conflict, and, when possible, we have endeavored to do so. However, on rare occasions when there is simply no way around the problem, we let standard English come up the loser.

Finally, although most of the examples used here are toy examples unlikely to be reused, a few have real value. Please feel free to reuse them or any parts of them in your own code. No special permission is required. As far as we are concerned, they are in the public domain (although the same is definitely not true of the explanatory text).

Request for Comments

We enjoy hearing from readers with general comments about how this book could be better, specific corrections, or topics you would like to see covered. You can reach the authors by sending email to *elharo@metalab.unc.edu* and *smeans@ewm.biz*. Please realize, however, that we each receive several hundred pieces of email a day and cannot respond to everyone personally. For the best chance of getting a personal response, please identify yourself as a reader of this book. Also, please send the message from the account you want us to reply to and make sure that your reply-to address is properly set. There's nothing so frustrating as spending an hour or more carefully researching the answer to an interesting question and composing a detailed response, only to have it bounce because the correspondent sent the message from a public terminal and neglected to set the browser preferences to include their actual email address.

The information in this book has been tested and verified, but you may find that features have changed (or you may even find mistakes). We believe the old saying, "If you like this book, tell your friends. If you don't like it, tell us." We're especially interested in hearing about mistakes. As hard as the authors and editors worked on this book, inevitably there are a few mistakes and typographical errors that slipped by us. If you find a mistake or a typo, please let us know so we can correct it in a future printing. Please send any errors you find directly to the authors at the previously listed email addresses.

You can also address comments and questions concerning this book to the publisher:

O'Reilly Media, Inc.
1005 Gravenstein Highway North
Sebastopol, CA 95472
(800) 998-9938 (in the United States or Canada)
(707) 829-0515 (international or local)
(707) 829-0104 (fax)

We have a web site for the book, where we list errata, examples, and any additional information. You can access this site at:

http://www.cafeconleche.org/books/xian3/

Before reporting errors, please check this web site to see if we have already posted a fix. To ask technical questions or comment on the book, you can send email to the authors directly or send your questions to the publisher at:

bookquestions@oreilly.com

For more information about other O'Reilly books, conferences, software, Resource Centers, and the O'Reilly Network, see the web sites at:

http://www.oreilly.com
http://xml.oreilly.com
http://www.xml.com

Acknowledgments

Many people were involved in the production of this book. The original editor, John Posner, got this book rolling and provided many helpful comments that substantially improved the book. When John moved on, Laurie Petrycki shepherded this book to its completion. Simon St.Laurent took up the mantle of editor for the second and third editions. The eagle-eyed Jeni Tennison read the entire manuscript from start to finish and caught many errors, large and small. Without her attention, this book would not be nearly as accurate. Stephen Spainhour deserves special thanks for his work on the reference section. His efforts in organizing and reviewing material helped create a better book. We'd like to thank

Matt Sergeant, Didier P. H. Martin, Steven Champeon, and Norm Walsh for their thorough technical review of the manuscript and thoughtful suggestions. James Kass's Code2000 and Code2001 fonts were invaluable in producing Chapter 27.

We'd also like to thank everyone who has worked so hard to make XML such a success over the last few years and thereby given us something to write about. There are so many of these people that we can only list a few. In alphabetical order we'd like to thank Tim Berners-Lee, Jonathan Borden, Jon Bosak, Tim Bray, David Brownell, Mike Champion, James Clark, John Cowan, Roy Fielding, Charles Goldfarb, Jason Hunter, Arnaud Le Hors, Michael Kay, Deborah Lapeyre Keiron Liddle, Murato Makoto, Eve Maler, Brett McLaughlin, David Megginson, David Orchard, Walter E. Perry, Paul Prescod, Jonathan Robie, Arved Sandstrom, C. M. Sperberg-McQueen, James Tauber, Henry S. Thompson, B. Tommie Usdin, Eric van der Vlist, Daniel Veillard, Lauren Wood, and Mark Wutka. Our apologies to everyone we unintentionally omitted.

Elliotte would like to thank his agent, David Rogelberg, who convinced him that it was possible to make a living writing books like this rather than working in an office. The entire IBiblio crew has also helped him to communicate better with his readers in a variety of ways over the last several years. All these people deserve much thanks and credit. Finally, as always, he offers his largest thanks to his wife, Beth, without whose love and support this book would never have happened.

Scott would most like to thank his lovely wife, Celia, who has already spent way too much time as a "computer widow." He would also like to thank his daughter Selene for understanding why Daddy can't play with her when he's "working" and Skyler for just being himself. Also, he'd like to thank the team at Enterprise Web Machines for helping him make time to write. Finally, he would like to thank John Posner for getting him into this, Laurie Petrycki for working with him when things got tough, and Simon St.Laurent for his overwhelming patience in dealing with an always-overcommitted author.

—Elliotte Rusty Harold
elharo@metalab.unc.edu

—W. Scott Means
smeans@ewm.biz

XML Concepts

Introducing XML

XML, the Extensible Markup Language, is a W3C-endorsed standard for document markup. It defines a generic syntax used to mark up data with simple, human-readable tags. It provides a standard format for computer documents that is flexible enough to be customized for domains as diverse as web sites, electronic data interchange, vector graphics, genealogy, real estate listings, object serialization, remote procedure calls, voice mail systems, and more.

You can write your own programs that interact with, massage, and manipulate the data in XML documents. If you do, you'll have access to a wide range of free libraries in a variety of languages that can read and write XML so that you can focus on the unique needs of your program. Or you can use off-the-shelf software, such as web browsers and text editors, to work with XML documents. Some tools are able to work with any XML document. Others are customized to support a particular XML application in a particular domain, such as vector graphics, and may not be of much use outside that domain. But the same underlying syntax is used in all cases, even if it's deliberately hidden by the more user-friendly tools or restricted to a single application.

The Benefits of XML

XML is a metamarkup language for text documents. Data are included in XML documents as strings of text. The data are surrounded by text markup that describes the data. XML's basic unit of data and markup is called an *element*. The XML specification defines the exact syntax this markup must follow: how elements are delimited by tags, what a tag looks like, what names are acceptable for elements, where attributes are placed, and so forth. Superficially, the markup in an XML document looks a lot like the markup in an HTML document, but there are some crucial differences.

Most importantly, XML is a *metamarkup language*. That means it doesn't have a fixed set of tags and elements that are supposed to work for everybody in all areas of interest for all time. Any attempt to create a finite set of such tags is doomed to failure. Instead, XML allows developers and writers to invent the elements they need as they need them. Chemists can use elements that describe molecules, atoms, bonds, reactions, and other items encountered in chemistry. Real estate agents can use elements that describe apartments, rents, commissions, locations, and other items needed for real estate. Musicians can use elements that describe quarter notes, half notes, G-clefs, lyrics, and other objects common in music. The X in XML stands for *Extensible*. Extensible means that the language can be extended and adapted to meet many different needs.

Although XML is quite flexible in the elements it allows, it is quite strict in many other respects. The XML specification defines a grammar for XML documents that says where tags may be placed, what they must look like, which element names are legal, how attributes are attached to elements, and so forth. This grammar is specific enough to allow the development of XML parsers that can read any XML document. Documents that satisfy this grammar are said to be *well-formed*. Documents that are not well-formed are not allowed, any more than a C program that contains a syntax error is allowed. XML processors reject documents that contain well-formedness errors.

For reasons of interoperability, individuals or organizations may agree to use only certain tags. These tag sets are called *XML applications*. An XML application is not a software application that uses XML, such as Mozilla or Microsoft Word. Rather, it's an application of XML in a particular domain, such as vector graphics or cooking.

The markup in an XML document describes the structure of the document. It lets you see which elements are associated with which other elements. In a well-designed XML document, the markup also describes the document's semantics. For instance, the markup can indicate that an element is a date or a person or a bar code. In well-designed XML applications, the markup says nothing about how the document should be displayed. That is, it does not say that an element is bold or italicized or a list item. XML is a structural and semantic markup language, not a presentation language.

 A few XML applications, such as XSL Formatting Objects (XSL-FO), are designed to describe the presentation of text. However, these are exceptions that prove the rule. Although XSL-FO does describe presentation, you'd never write an XSL-FO document directly. Instead, you'd write a more semantically structured XML document, then use an XSL Transformations stylesheet to change the structure-oriented XML into presentation-oriented XML.

The markup permitted in a particular XML application can be documented in a *schema*. Particular document instances can be compared to the schema. Documents that match the schema are said to be *valid*. Documents that do not match are *invalid*. Validity depends on the schema. That is, whether a document is valid or invalid depends on which schema you compare it to. Not all documents need to be valid. For many purposes it is enough that the document be well-formed.

There are many different XML schema languages with different levels of expressivity. The most broadly supported schema language and the only one defined by the XML specification itself is the *document type definition* (DTD). A DTD lists all the legal markup and specifies where and how it may be included in a document. DTDs are optional in XML. On the other hand, DTDs may not always be enough. The DTD syntax is quite limited and does not allow you to make many useful statements such as "This element contains a number," or "This string of text is a date between 1974 and 2032." The W3C XML Schema Language (which sometimes goes by the misleadingly generic label *schemas*) does allow you to express constraints of this nature. Besides these two, there are many other schema languages from which to choose, including RELAX NG, Schematron, Hook, and Examplotron, and this is hardly an exhaustive list.

All current schema languages are purely declarative. However, there are always some constraints that cannot be expressed in anything less than a Turing complete programming language. For example, given an XML document that represents an order, a Turing complete language is required to multiply the price of each order_item by its quantity, sum them all up, and verify that the sum equals the value of the subtotal element. Today's schema languages are also incapable of verifying extra-document constraints such as "Every SKU element matches the SKU field of a record in the products table of the inventory database." If you're writing programs to read XML documents, you can add code to verify statements like these, just as you would if you were writing code to read a tab-delimited text file. The difference is that XML parsers present the data in a much more convenient format and do more of the work for you so you have to write less custom code.

What XML Is Not

XML is a markup language, and it is only a markup language. It's important to remember that. The XML hype has gotten so extreme that some people expect XML to do everything up to and including washing the family dog.

First of all, *XML is not a programming language*. There's no such thing as an XML compiler that reads XML files and produces executable code. You might perhaps define a scripting language that used a native XML format and was interpreted by a binary program, but even this application would be unusual. XML can be used as a format for instructions to programs that do make things happen, just like a traditional program may read a text config file and take different actions depending on what it sees there. Indeed, there's no reason a config file can't be XML instead of unstructured text. Some more recent programs use XML config files; but in all cases, it's the program taking action, not the XML document itself. An XML document by itself simply *is*. It does not *do* anything.

 At least one XML application, XSL Transformations (XSLT), has been proven to be Turing complete by construction. See *http://www.unidex.com/turing/utm.htm* for one universal Turing machine written in XSLT.

Second, *XML is not a network transport protocol*. XML won't send data across the network, any more than HTML will. Data sent across the network using HTTP, FTP, NFS, or some other protocol might be encoded in XML; but again there has to be some software outside the XML document that actually sends the document.

Finally, to mention the example where the hype most often obscures the reality, *XML is not a database*. You're not going to replace an Oracle or MySQL server with XML. A database can contain XML data, either as a VARCHAR or a BLOB or as some custom XML data type, but the database itself is not an XML document. You can store XML data in a database on a server or retrieve data from a database in an XML format, but to do this, you need to be running software written in a real programming language such as C or Java. To store XML in a database, software on the client side will send the XML data to the server using an established network protocol such as TCP/IP. Software on the server side will receive the XML data, parse it, and store it in the database. To retrieve an XML document from a database, you'll generally pass through some middleware product like Enhydra that makes SQL queries against the database and formats the result set as XML before returning it to the client. Indeed, some databases may integrate this software code into their core server or provide plug-ins to do it, such as the Oracle XSQL servlet. XML serves very well as a ubiquitous, platform-independent transport format in these scenarios. However, it is not the database, and it shouldn't be used as one.

Portable Data

XML offers the tantalizing possibility of truly cross-platform, long-term data formats. It's long been the case that a document written on one platform is not necessarily readable on a different platform, or by a different program on the same platform, or even by a future or past version of the same program on the same platform. When the document can be read, there's no guarantee that all the information will come across. Much of the data from the original moon landings in the late 1960s and early 1970s is now effectively lost. Even if you can find a tape drive that can read the now obsolete tapes, nobody knows what format the data is stored in on the tapes!

XML is an incredibly simple, well-documented, straightforward data format. XML documents are text and can be read with any tool that can read a text file. Not just the data, but also the markup is text, and it's present right there in the XML file as tags. You don't have to wonder whether every eighth byte is random padding, guess whether a four-byte quantity is a two's complement integer or an IEEE 754 floating point number, or try to decipher which integer codes map to which formatting properties. You can read the tag names directly to find out exactly what's in the document. Similarly, since element boundaries are defined by tags, you aren't likely to be tripped up by unexpected line-ending conventions or the number of spaces that are mapped to a tab. All the important details about the structure of the document are explicit. You don't have to reverse-engineer the format or rely on incomplete and often unavailable documentation.

A few software vendors may want to lock in their users with undocumented, proprietary, binary file formats. However, in the long term, we're all better off if we can use the cleanly documented, well-understood, easy to parse, text-based formats that XML provides. XML lets documents and data be moved from one system to another with a reasonable hope that the receiving system will be able to make sense out of it. Furthermore, validation lets the receiving side check that it gets what it expects. Java promised portable code; XML delivers portable data. In many ways, XML is the most portable and flexible document format designed since the ASCII text file.

How XML Works

Example 1-1 shows a simple XML document. This particular XML document might be seen in an inventory-control system or a stock database. It marks up the data with tags and attributes describing the color, size, bar-code number, manufacturer, name of the product, and so on.

Example 1-1. An XML document

```
<?xml version="1.0"?>
<product barcode="2394287410">
  <manufacturer>Verbatim</manufacturer>
  <name>DataLife MF 2HD</name>
  <quantity>10</quantity>
  <size>3.5"</size>
  <color>black</color>
  <description>floppy disks</description>
</product>
```

This document is text and can be stored in a text file. You can edit this file with any standard text editor such as BBEdit, jEdit, UltraEdit, Emacs, or vi. You do not need a special XML editor. Indeed, we find most general-purpose XML editors to be far more trouble than they're worth and much harder to use than simply editing documents in a text editor.

Programs that actually try to understand the contents of the XML document—that is, do more than merely treat it as any other text file—will use an *XML parser* to read the document. The parser is responsible for dividing the document into individual elements, attributes, and other pieces. It passes the contents of the XML document to an application piece by piece. If at any point the parser detects a violation of the well-formedness rules of XML, then it reports the error to the application and stops parsing. In some cases, the parser may read further in the document, past the original error, so that it can detect and report other errors that occur later in the document. However, once it has detected the first well-formedness error, it will no longer pass along the contents of the elements and attributes it encounters.

Individual XML applications normally dictate more precise rules about exactly which elements and attributes are allowed where. For instance, you wouldn't expect to find a G_Clef element when reading a biology document. Some of these rules can be precisely specified with a schema written in any of several languages, including the W3C XML Schema Language, RELAX NG, and DTDs. A document may contain a URL indicating where the schema can be found. Some XML parsers will notice this and compare the document to its schema as they read it to see if the document satisfies the constraints specified there. Such a parser is called a *validating parser*. A violation of those constraints is called a *validity error*, and the whole process of checking a document against a schema is called *validation*. If a validating parser finds a validity error, it will report it to the application on whose behalf it's parsing the document. This application can then decide whether it wishes to continue parsing the document. However, validity errors are not necessarily fatal (unlike well-formedness errors), and an application may choose to ignore them. Not all parsers are validating parsers. Some merely check for well-formedness.

The application that receives data from the parser may be:

- A web browser, such as Netscape Navigator or Internet Explorer, that displays the document to a reader
- A word processor, such as StarOffice Writer, that loads the XML document for editing
- A database, such as Microsoft SQL Server, that stores the XML data in a new record
- A drawing program, such as Adobe Illustrator, that interprets the XML as two-dimensional coordinates for the contents of a picture
- A spreadsheet, such as Gnumeric, that parses the XML to find numbers and functions used in a calculation
- A personal finance program, such as Microsoft Money, that sees the XML as a bank statement
- A syndication program that reads the XML document and extracts the headlines for today's news
- A program that you yourself wrote in Java, C, Python, or some other language that does exactly what you want it to do
- Almost anything else

XML is an *extremely* flexible format for data. It is used for all of this and a lot more. These are real examples. In theory, any data that can be stored in a computer can be stored in XML. In practice, XML is suitable for storing and exchanging any data that can plausibly be encoded as text. It's only really unsuitable for digitized data such as photographs, recorded sound, video, and other very large bit sequences.

The Evolution of XML

XML is a descendant of SGML, the Standard Generalized Markup Language. The language that would eventually become SGML was invented by Charles F. Goldfarb, Ed Mosher, and Ray Lorie at IBM in the 1970s and developed by several hundred people around the world until its eventual adoption as ISO standard 8879 in 1986. SGML was intended to solve many of the same problems XML solves in much the same way XML solves them. It is a semantic and structural markup language for text documents. SGML is extremely powerful and achieved some success in the U.S. military and government, in the aerospace sector, and in other domains that needed ways of efficiently managing technical documents that were tens of thousands of pages long.

SGML's biggest success was HTML, which is an SGML application. However, HTML is just one SGML application. It does not have or offer anywhere near the full power of SGML itself. Since it restricts authors to a finite set of tags designed to describe web pages—and describes them in a fairly presentation oriented way at that—it's really little more than a traditional markup language that has been adopted by web browsers. It doesn't lend itself to use beyond the single application of web page design. You would not use HTML to exchange data between incompatible databases or to send updated product catalogs to retailer sites, for example. HTML does web pages, and it does them very well, but it only does web pages.

SGML was the obvious choice for other applications that took advantage of the Internet but were not simple web pages for humans to read. The problem was that SGML is complicated—very, very complicated. The official SGML specification is over 150 very technical pages. It covers many special cases and unlikely scenarios. It is so complex that almost no software has ever implemented it fully. Programs that implemented or relied on different subsets of SGML were often incompatible with each other. The special feature one program considered essential would be considered extraneous fluff and omitted by the next program.

In 1996, Jon Bosak, Tim Bray, C. M. Sperberg-McQueen, James Clark, and several others began work on a "lite" version of SGML that retained most of SGML's power while trimming a lot of the features that had proven redundant, too complicated to implement, confusing to end users, or simply not useful over the previous 20 years of experience with SGML. The result, in February of 1998, was XML 1.0, and it was an immediate success. Many developers who knew they needed a structural markup language but hadn't been able to bring themselves to accept SGML's complexity adopted XML whole-heartedly. It was used in domains ranging from legal court filings to hog farming.

However, XML 1.0 was just the beginning. The next standard out of the gate was Namespaces in XML, an effort to allow markup from different XML applications to be used in the same document without conflicting. Thus a web page about books could have a `title` element that referred to the title of the page and `title` elements that referred to the title of a book, and the two would not conflict.

Next up was the Extensible Stylesheet Language (XSL), an XML application for transforming XML documents into a form that could be viewed in web browsers. This soon split into XSL Transformations (XSLT) and XSL Formatting Objects (XSL-FO). XSLT has become a general-purpose language for transforming one XML document into another, whether for web page display or some other purpose. XSL-FO is an XML application for describing the layout of both printed pages and web pages that approaches PostScript for its power and expressiveness.

However, XSL is not the only option for styling XML documents. Cascading Style Sheets (CSS) were already in use for HTML documents when XML was invented, and they proved to be a reasonable fit to XML as well. With the advent of CSS

Level 2, the W3C made styling XML documents an explicit goal for CSS. The pre-existing Document Style Sheet and Semantics Language (DSSSL) was also adopted from its roots in the SGML world to style XML documents for print and the Web.

The Extensible Linking Language, XLink, began by defining more powerful linking constructs that could connect XML documents in a hypertext network that made HTML's A tag look like it is an abbreviation for "anemic." It also split into two separate standards: XLink for describing the connections between documents and XPointer for addressing the individual parts of an XML document. At this point, it was noticed that both XPointer and XSLT were developing fairly sophisticated yet incompatible syntaxes to do exactly the same thing: identify particular elements in an XML document. Consequently, the addressing parts of both specifications were split off and combined into a third specification, XPath. A little later yet another part of XLink budded off to become XInclude, a syntax for building complex documents by combining individual documents and document fragments.

Another piece of the puzzle was a uniform interface for accessing the contents of the XML document from inside a Java, JavaScript, or C++ program. The simplest API was merely to treat the document as an object that contained other objects. Indeed, work was already underway inside and outside the W3C to define such a Document Object Model (DOM) for HTML. Expanding this effort to cover XML was not hard.

Outside the W3C, David Megginson, Peter Murray-Rust, and other members of the *xml-dev* mailing list recognized that third-party XML parsers, while all compatible in the documents they could parse, were incompatible in their APIs. This led to the development of the Simple API for XML, or SAX. In 2000, SAX2 was released to add greater configurability and namespace support, and a cleaner API.

One of the surprises during the evolution of XML was that developers adopted it more for record-like structures, such as serialized objects and database tables, than for the narrative structures for which SGML had traditionally been used. DTDs worked very well for narrative structures, but they had some limits when faced with the record-like structures developers were actually creating. In particular, the lack of data typing and the fact that DTDs were not themselves XML documents were perceived as major problems. A number of companies and individuals began working on schema languages that addressed these deficiencies. Many of these proposals were submitted to the W3C, which formed a working group to try to merge the best parts of all of these and come up with something greater than the sum of its parts. In 2001, this group released Version 1.0 of the W3C XML Schema Language. Unfortunately, this language proved overly complex and burdensome. Consequently, several developers went back to the drawing board to invent cleaner, simpler, more elegant schema languages, including RELAX NG and Schematron.

Eventually, it became apparent that XML 1.0, XPath, the W3C XML Schema Language, SAX, and DOM all had similar but subtly different conceptual models of the structure of an XML document. For instance, XPath and SAX don't consider CDATA sections to be anything more than syntax sugar, but DOM does treat them differently than plain-text nodes. Thus, the W3C XML Core Working Group began work on an XML Information Set that all these standards could rely on and refer to.

As more and more XML documents of higher and higher value began to be transmitted across the Internet, a need was recognized to secure and authenticate these transactions. Besides using existing mechanisms such as SSL and HTTP digest authentication built into the underlying protocols, formats were developed to secure the XML documents themselves that operate over a document's entire life span rather than just while it's in transit. XML encryption, a standard XML syntax for encrypting digital content, including portions of XML documents, addresses the need for confidentiality. XML Signature, a joint IETF and W3C standard for digitally signing content and embedding those signatures in XML documents, addresses the problem of authentication. Because digital signature and encryption algorithms are defined in terms of byte sequences rather than XML data models, both XML Signature and XML Encryption are based on Canonical XML, a standard serialization format that removes all insignificant differences between documents, such as whitespace inside tags and whether single or double quotes delimit attribute values.

Through all this, the core XML 1.0 specification remained unchanged. All of this new functionality was layered on top of XML 1.0 rather than modifying it at the foundation. This is a testament to the solid design and strength of XML. However, XML 1.0 itself was based on Unicode 2.0, and as Unicode continued to evolve and add new scripts such as Mongolian, Cambodian, and Burmese, XML was falling behind. Primarily for this reason, XML 1.1 was released in early 2004. It should be noted, however, that XML 1.1 offers little to interest developers working in English, Spanish, Japanese, Chinese, Arabic, Russian, French, German, Dutch, or the many other languages already supported in Unicode 2.0.

Doubtless, many new extensions of XML remain to be invented. And even this rich collection of specifications only addresses technologies that are core to XML. Much more development has been done and continues at an accelerating pace on XML applications, including SOAP, SVG, XHTML, MathML, Atom, XForms, WordprocessingML, and thousands more. XML has proven itself a solid foundation for many diverse technologies.

2

XML Fundamentals

This chapter shows you how to write simple XML documents. You'll see that an XML document is built from text content marked up with text tags such as <SKU>, <Record_ID>, and <author> that look superficially like HTML tags. However, in HTML you're limited to about a hundred predefined tags that describe web page formatting. In XML, you can create as many tags as you need. Furthermore, these tags will mostly describe the type of content they contain rather than formatting or layout information. In XML you don't say that something is italicized or indented or bold, you say that it's a book or a biography or a calendar.

Although XML is looser than HTML in regard to which tags it allows, it is much stricter about where those tags are placed and how they're written. In particular, all XML documents must be well-formed. Well-formedness rules specify constraints such as "Every start-tag must have a matching end-tag," and "Attribute values must be quoted." These rules are unbreakable, which makes parsing XML documents easier and writing them a little harder, but they still allow an almost unlimited flexibility of expression.

XML Documents and XML Files

An XML document contains text, never binary data. It can be opened with any program that knows how to read a text file. Example 2-1 is close to the simplest XML document imaginable. Nonetheless, it is a well-formed XML document. XML parsers can read it and understand it (at least as far as a computer program can be said to understand anything).

Example 2-1. A very simple yet complete XML document

```
<person>
  Alan Turing
</person>
```

In the most common scenario, this document would be the entire contents of a file named *person.xml*, or perhaps *2-1.xml*. However, XML is not picky about the filename. As far as the parser is concerned, this file could be called *person.txt*, *person*, or *Hey you, there's some XML in this here file!* Your operating system may or may not like these names, but an XML parser won't care. The document might not even be in a file at all. It could be a record or a field in a database. It could be generated on the fly by a CGI program in response to a browser query. It could even be stored in more than one file, although that's unlikely for such a simple document. If it is served by a web server, it will probably be assigned the MIME media type application/xml or text/xml. However, specific XML applications may use more specific MIME media types, such as application/mathml+xml, application/xslt+xml, image/svg+xml, text/vnd.wap.wml, or even text/html (in very special cases).

 For generic XML documents, application/xml should be preferred to text/xml, although many web servers come configured out of the box to use text/xml. text/xml uses the ASCII character set as a default, which is incorrect for most XML documents.

Elements, Tags, and Character Data

The document in Example 2-1 is composed of a single *element* named person. The element is delimited by the *start-tag* <person> and the *end-tag* </person>. Everything between the start-tag and the end-tag of the element (exclusive) is called the element's *content*. The content of this element is the text:

```
Alan Turing
```

The whitespace is part of the content, although many applications will choose to ignore it. <person> and </person> are *markup*. The string "Alan Turing" and its surrounding whitespace are *character data*. The tag is the most common form of markup in an XML document, but there are other kinds we'll discuss later.

Tag Syntax

Superficially, XML tags look like HTML tags. Start-tags begin with < and end-tags begin with </. Both of these are followed by the name of the element and are closed by >. However, unlike HTML tags, you are allowed to make up new XML tags as you go along. To describe a person, use <person> and </person> tags. To describe a calendar, use <calendar> and </calendar> tags. The names of the tags generally reflect the type of content inside the element, not how that content will be formatted.

Empty elements

There's also a special syntax for *empty elements*, elements that have no content. Such an element can be represented by a single *empty-element tag* that begins with < but ends with />. For instance, in XHTML, an XMLized reformulation of standard HTML, the line-break and horizontal-rule elements are written as <br /> and

<hr /> instead of <br> and <hr>. These are exactly equivalent to
</br> and <hr></hr>, however. Which form you use for empty elements is completely up to you. However, what you cannot do in XML and XHTML (unlike HTML) is use only the start-tag—for instance <br> or <hr>—without using the matching end-tag. That would be a well-formedness error.

Case-sensitivity

XML, unlike HTML, is case-sensitive. <Person> is not the same as <PERSON> or <person>. If you open an element with a <person> tag, you can't close it with a </PERSON> tag. You're free to use upper- or lowercase or both as you choose. You just have to be consistent within any one element.

XML Trees

Let's look at a slightly more complicated XML document. Example 2-2 is a person element that contains more information suitably marked up to show its meaning.

Example 2-2. A more complex XML document describing a person

```
<person>
  <name>
    <first_name>Alan</first_name>
    <last_name>Turing</last_name>
  </name>
  <profession>computer scientist</profession>
  <profession>mathematician</profession>
  <profession>cryptographer</profession>
</person>
```

Parents and children

The XML document in Example 2-2 is still composed of one person element. However, now this element doesn't merely contain undifferentiated character data. It contains four *child elements*: a name element and three profession elements. The name element contains two child elements of its own, first_name and last_name.

The person element is called the *parent* of the name element and the three profession elements. The name element is the parent of the first_name and last_name elements. The name element and the three profession elements are sometimes called each other's *siblings*. The first_name and last_name elements are also siblings.

As in human society, any one parent may have multiple children. However, unlike human society, XML gives each child exactly one parent, not two or more. Each element (with one exception we'll note shortly) has exactly one parent element. That is, it is completely enclosed by another element. If an element's start-tag is inside some element, then its end-tag must also be inside that element. Overlapping tags, as in this common example from HTML, are prohibited in XML. Since the em element begins inside the strong element, it must also finish inside the strong element.

The root element

Every XML document has one element that does not have a parent. This is the first element in the document and the element that contains all other elements. In Examples 2-1 and 2-2, the person element filled this role. It is called the *root element* of the document. It is also sometimes called the *document element*. Every well-formed XML document has exactly one root element. Since elements may not overlap, and since all elements except the root have exactly one parent, XML documents form a data structure programmers call a *tree*. Figure 2-1 diagrams this relationship for Example 2-2. Each gray box represents an element. Each black box represents character data. Each arrow represents a containment relationship.

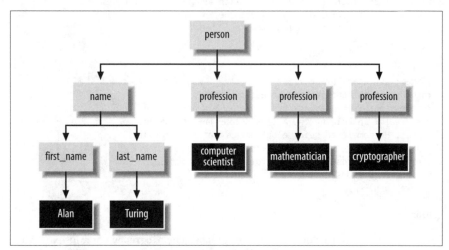

Figure 2-1. A tree diagram for Example 2-2

Mixed Content

In Example 2-2, the contents of the first_name, last_name, and profession elements were character data; that is, text that does not contain any tags. The contents of the person and name elements were child elements and some whitespace that most applications will ignore. This dichotomy between elements that contain only character data and elements that contain only child elements (and possibly a little whitespace) is common in record-like documents. However, XML can also be used for more free-form, narrative documents, such as business reports, magazine articles, student essays, short stories, web pages, and so forth, as shown by Example 2-3.

Example 2-3. A narrative-organized XML document

```
<biography>
  <paragraph>
  <name><first_name>Alan</first_name> <last_name>Turing</last_name>
  </name> was one of the first people to truly deserve the name
  <emphasize>computer scientist</emphasize>. Although his contributions
  to the field are too numerous to list, his best-known are the
```

Example 2-3. A narrative-organized XML document (continued)

```
eponymous <emphasize>Turing Test</emphasize> and
<emphasize>Turing Machine</emphasize>.
</paragraph>

<definition>The <term>Turing Test</term> is to this day the standard
test for determining whether a computer is truly intelligent. This
test has yet to be passed. </definition>

<definition>A <term>Turing Machine</term> is an abstract finite
state automaton with infinite memory that can be proven equivalent
to any other finite state automaton with arbitrarily large memory.
Thus what is true for one Turing machine is true for all Turing
machines no matter how implemented.
</definition>

<paragraph>
<name><last_name>Turing</last_name></name> was also an accomplished
<profession>mathematician</profession> and
<profession>cryptographer</profession>. His assistance
was crucial in helping the Allies decode the German Enigma
cipher. He committed suicide on <date><month>June</month>
<day>7</day>, <year>1954</year></date> after being
convicted of homosexuality and forced to take female
hormone injections.
</paragraph>

</biography>
```

The root element of this document is biography. The biography contains paragraph and definition child elements. It also contains some whitespace. The paragraph and definition elements contain still other elements, including term, emphasize, name, and profession. They also contain some unmarked-up character data. Elements like paragraph and definition that contain child elements and non-whitespace character data are said to have *mixed content*. Mixed content is common in XML documents containing articles, essays, stories, books, novels, reports, web pages, and anything else that's organized as a written narrative. Mixed content is less common and harder to work with in computer-generated and processed XML documents used for purposes such as database exchange, object serialization, persistent file formats, and so on. One of the strengths of XML is the ease with which it can be adapted to the very different requirements of human-authored and computer-generated documents.

Attributes

XML elements can have attributes. An attribute is a name-value pair attached to the element's start-tag. Names are separated from values by an equals sign and optional whitespace. Values are enclosed in single or double quotation marks. For example, this person element has a born attribute with the value 1912-06-23 and a died attribute with the value 1954-06-07:

```
<person born="1912-06-23" died="1954-06-07">
  Alan Turing
</person>
```

This next element is exactly the same, as far as an XML parser is concerned. It simply uses single quotes instead of double quotes, puts some extra whitespace around the equals signs, and reorders the attributes.

```
<person died = '1954-06-07'  born = '1912-06-23' >
  Alan Turing
</person>
```

The whitespace around the equals signs is purely a matter of personal aesthetics. The single quotes may be useful in cases where the attribute value itself contains a double quote. Attribute order is not significant.

Example 2-4 shows how attributes might be used to encode much of the same information given in the record-like document of Example 2-2.

Example 2-4. An XML document that describes a person using attributes

```
<person>
  <name first="Alan" last="Turing"/>
  <profession value="computer scientist"/>
  <profession value="mathematician"/>
  <profession value="cryptographer"/>
</person>
```

This raises the question of when and whether one should use child elements or attributes to hold information. This is a subject of heated debate. Some informaticians maintain that attributes are for metadata about the element while elements are for the information itself. Others point out that it's not always so obvious what's data and what's metadata. Indeed, the answer may depend on where the information is put to use.

What's undisputed is that each element may have no more than one attribute with a given name. That's unlikely to be a problem for a birth date or a death date; it would be an issue for a profession, name, address, or anything else of which an element might plausibly have more than one. Furthermore, attributes are quite limited in structure. The value of the attribute is simply undifferentiated text. The division of a date into a year, month, and day with hyphens in the earlier code snippets is at the limits of the substructure that can reasonably be encoded in an attribute. An element-based structure is a lot more flexible and extensible. Nonetheless, attributes are certainly more convenient in some applications. Ultimately, if you're designing your own XML vocabulary, it's up to you to decide when to use which.

Attributes are also useful in narrative documents, as Example 2-5 demonstrates. Here it's perhaps a little more obvious what belongs to elements and what to attributes. The raw text of the narrative is presented as character data inside elements. Additional information annotating that data is presented as attributes. This includes source references, image URLs, hyperlinks, and birth and death dates. Even here, however, there's more than one way to do it. For instance, the footnote numbers could be attributes of the footnote element rather than character data.

Example 2-5. A narrative XML document that uses attributes

```
<biography xmlns:xlink="http://www.w3.org/1999/xlink/">

  <image source="http://www.turing.org.uk/turing/pi1/busgroup.jpg"
  width="152" height="345"/>

  <paragraph><person born='1912-06-23'
  died='1954-06-07'><first_name>Alan</first_name>
  <last_name>Turing</last_name> </person> was one of the first people
  to truly deserve the name <emphasize>computer scientist</emphasize>.
  Although his contributions to the field were too numerous to list,
  his best-known are the eponymous <emphasize xlink:type="simple"
  xlink:href="http://cogsci.ucsd.edu/~asaygin/tt/ttest.html">Turing
  Test</emphasize> and <emphasize  xlink:type="simple"
  xlink:href="http://mathworld.wolfram.com/TuringMachine.html">Turing
  Machine</emphasize>.</paragraph>

  <paragraph><last_name>Turing</last_name> was also an
  accomplished <profession>mathematician</profession> and
  <profession>cryptographer</profession>. His assistance
  was crucial in helping the Allies decode the German Enigma
  machine.<footnote source="The Ultra Secret, F.W. Winterbotham,
  1974">1</footnote></paragraph>

  <paragraph>
  <last_name>Turing</last_name> committed suicide on
  <date><month>June</month> <day>7</day>, <year>1954</year></date>
  after being convicted of homosexuality and forced to take female
  hormone injections.<footnote source="Alan Turing: the Enigma,
  Andrew Hodges, 1983">2</footnote>
  </paragraph>
</biography>
```

XML Names

The XML specification can be quite legalistic and picky at times. Nonetheless, it tries to be efficient where possible. One way it does that is by reusing the same rules for different items where possible. For example, the rules for XML element names are also the rules for XML attribute names, as well as for the names of several less common constructs. Collectively, these are referred to simply as *XML names*.

Element and other XML names may contain essentially any alphanumeric character. This includes the standard English letters *A* through *Z* and *a* through *z* as well as the digits *0* through *9*. XML names may also include non-English letters, numbers, and ideograms, such as ö, ç, Ω, 串. They may also include these three punctuation characters:

_ The underscore

- The hyphen

. The period

XML names may not contain other punctuation characters such as quotation marks, apostrophes, dollar signs, carets, percent symbols, and semicolons. The colon is allowed, but its use is reserved for namespaces as discussed in Chapter 4. XML names may not contain whitespace of any kind, whether a space, a carriage return, a line feed, a nonbreaking space, and so forth. Finally, all names beginning with the string "XML" (in any combination of case) are reserved for standardization in W3C XML-related specifications.

> The primary new feature in XML 1.1 is that XML names may contain characters only defined in Unicode 3.0 and later. XML 1.0 is limited to the characters defined as of Unicode 2.0. Additional scripts enabled for names by XML 1.1 include Burmese, Mongolian, Thaana, Cambodian, Yi, and Amharic. (All of these scripts are legal in text content in XML 1.0. You just can't use them to name elements, attributes, and entities.) XML 1.1 offers little to no benefit to developers who don't need to use these scripts in their markup.
>
> XML 1.1 also allows names to contain some uncommon symbols such as the musical symbol for a six-string fretboard and even a million or so code points that aren't actually mapped to particular characters. However, taking advantage of this is highly unwise. We strongly recommend that even in XML 1.1 you limit your names to letters, digits, ideographs, and the specifically allowed ASCII punctuation marks.

XML names may only start with letters, ideograms, or the underscore character. They may not start with a number, hyphen, or period. There is no limit to the length of an element or other XML name. Thus these are all well-formed elements:

- `<Drivers_License_Number>98 NY 32</Drivers_License_Number>`
- `<month-day-year>7/23/2001</month-day-year>`
- `<first_name>Alan</first_name>`
- `<_4-lane>I-610</_4-lane>`
- `<téléphone>011 33 91 55 27 55 27</téléphone>`
- `<персна>ГаЛнна°Nванов</персна>`

These are not acceptable elements:

- `<Driver's_License_Number>98 NY 32</Driver's_License_Number>`
- `<month/day/year>7/23/2001</month/day/year>`
- `<first name>Alan</first name>`
- `<4-lane>I-610</4-lane>`

References

The character data inside an element must not contain a raw unescaped opening angle bracket (<). This character is always interpreted as beginning a tag. If you need to use this character in your text, you can escape it using the *entity reference* <, the *numeric character reference* <, or the *hexadecimal numeric character reference* <. When a parser reads the document, it replaces any <, `, or < references it finds with the actual < character. However, it will not confuse the references with the starts of tags. For example:

```
<SCRIPT LANGUAGE="JavaScript">
  if (location.host.toLowerCase().indexOf("ibiblio") &lt; 0) {
    location.href="http://ibiblio.org/xml/";
  }
</SCRIPT>
```

Character data may not contain a raw unescaped ampersand (&) either. This is always interpreted as beginning an entity reference. However, the ampersand may be escaped using the & entity reference like this:

```
<company>W.L. Gore &amp; Associates</company>
```

The ampersand is code point 38 so it could also be written with the numeric character reference &:

```
<company>W.L. Gore &#38; Associates</company>
```

Entity references such as & and character references such as < are markup. When an application parses an XML document, it replaces this particular markup with the actual character or characters the reference refers to.

XML predefines exactly five entity references. These are:

<
> The less-than sign, a.k.a. the opening angle bracket (<)

&
> The ampersand (&)

>
> The greater-than sign, a.k.a. the closing angle bracket (>)

"
> The straight, double quotation marks (")

'
> The apostrophe, a.k.a. the straight single quote (')

Only < and & must be used instead of the literal characters in element content. The others are optional. " and ' are useful inside attribute values where a raw " or ' might be misconstrued as ending the attribute value. For example, this image tag uses the ' entity reference to fill in the apostrophe in "O'Reilly:"

```
<image source='oreilly_koala3.gif' width='122' height='66'
      alt='Powered by O&apos;Reilly Books'
/>
```

Although there's no possibility of an unescaped greater-than sign (>) being misinterpreted as closing a tag it wasn't meant to close, > is allowed mostly for symmetry with <.

 There is one unusual case where the greater-than sign does need to be escaped. The three-character sequence]]> cannot appear in character data. Instead you have to write it as]]>.

In addition to the five predefined entity references, you can define others in the document type definition. We'll discuss how to do this in Chapter 3.

Entity and character references can only be used in element content and attribute values. They cannot be used in element names, attribute names, or other markup. Text like & or < may appear inside a comment or a processing instruction. However, in these places it is not resolved. The parser only replaces references in element content and attribute values. It does not recognize references in other locations.

CDATA Sections

When an XML document includes samples of XML or HTML source code, the < and & characters in those samples must be encoded as < and &. The more sections of literal code a document includes and the longer they are, the more tedious this encoding becomes. Instead you can enclose each sample of literal code in a *CDATA section*. A CDATA section is set off by <![CDATA[and]]>. Everything between the <![CDATA[and the]]> is treated as raw character data. Less-than signs don't begin tags. Ampersands don't start entity references. Everything is simply character data, not markup.

For example, in a Scalable Vector Graphics (SVG) tutorial written in XHTML, you might see something like this:

```
<p>You can use a default <code>xmlns</code> attribute to avoid
having to add the svg prefix to all your elements:</p>
<pre><![CDATA[
        <svg xmlns="http://www.w3.org/2000/svg"
            width="12cm" height="10cm">
          <ellipse rx="110" ry="130" />
          <rect x="4cm" y="1cm" width="3cm" height="6cm" />
        </svg>
      ]]></pre>
```

The SVG source code has been included directly in the XHTML file without carefully replacing each < with <. The result will be a sample SVG document, not an embedded SVG picture, as might happen if this example were not placed inside a CDATA section.

The only thing that cannot appear in a CDATA section is the CDATA section end delimiter,]]>.

CDATA sections exist for the convenience of human authors, not for programs. Parsers are not required to tell you whether a particular block of text came from a CDATA section, from normal character data, or from character data that contained entity references such as < and &. By the time you get access to the data, these differences will have been washed away. No code you write should depend on the difference between them.

Comments

XML documents can be commented so that coauthors can leave notes for each other and themselves, documenting why they've done what they've done or items that remain to be done. XML comments are syntactically similar to HTML comments. Just as in HTML, they begin with <!-- and end with the first occurrence of -->. For example:

```
<!-- I need to verify and update these links when I get a chance. -->
```

The double hyphen -- must not appear anywhere inside the comment until the closing -->. In particular, a three-hyphen close like ---> is specifically forbidden.

Comments may appear anywhere in the character data of a document. They may also appear before or after the root element. (Comments are not elements, so this does not violate the tree structure or the one-root element rules for XML.) However, comments may not appear inside a tag or inside another comment.

Applications that read and process XML documents may or may not pass along information included in comments. They are certainly free to drop them out if they choose. Do not write documents or applications that depend on the contents of comments being available. Comments are strictly for making the raw source code of an XML document more legible to human readers. They are not intended for computer programs. For this purpose, you should use a *processing instruction* instead.

Processing Instructions

In HTML, comments are sometimes abused to support nonstandard extensions. For instance, the contents of the script element are sometimes enclosed in a comment to protect it from display by a nonscript-aware browser. The Apache web server parses comments in *.shtml* files to recognize server-side includes. Unfortunately, these documents may not survive being passed through various HTML editors and processors with their comments and associated semantics intact. Worse yet, it's possible for an innocent comment to be misconstrued as input to the application.

XML provides the *processing instruction* as an alternative means of passing information to particular applications that may read the document. A processing instruction begins with <? and ends with ?>. Immediately following the <? is an XML name called the *target*, possibly the name of the application for which this processing instruction is intended or possibly just an identifier for this particular processing instruction. The rest of the processing instruction contains text in a format appropriate for the applications for which the instruction is intended.

For example, in HTML, a robots META tag is used to tell search-engine and other robots whether and how they should index a page. The following processing instruction has been proposed as an equivalent for XML documents:

```
<?robots index="yes" follow="no"?>
```

The target of this processing instruction is robots. The syntax of this particular processing instruction is two pseudo-attributes, one named index and one named follow, whose values are either yes or no. The semantics of this particular processing instruction are that if the index attribute has the value yes, then search-engine robots should index this page. If index has the value no, then robots should not index the page. Similarly, if follow has the value yes, then links from this document will be followed; if it has the value no, they won't be.

Other processing instructions may have totally different syntaxes and semantics. For instance, processing instructions can contain an effectively unlimited amount of text. PHP includes large programs in processing instructions. For example:

```
<?php
   mysql_connect("database.unc.edu", "clerk", "password");
   $result = mysql("HR", "SELECT LastName, FirstName FROM Employees
      ORDER BY LastName, FirstName");
   $i = 0;
   while ($i < mysql_numrows ($result)) {
      $fields = mysql_fetch_row($result);
      echo "<person>$fields[1] $fields[0] </person>\r\n";
      $i++;
   }
   mysql_close( );
?>
```

Processing instructions are markup, but they're not elements. Consequently, like comments, processing instructions may appear anywhere in an XML document outside of a tag, including before or after the root element. The most common processing instruction, xml-stylesheet, is used to attach stylesheets to documents. It always appears before the root element, as Example 2-6 demonstrates. In this example, the xml-stylesheet processing instruction tells browsers to apply the CSS stylesheet *person.css* to this document before showing it to the reader.

Example 2-6. An XML document with a processing instruction in its prolog

```
<?xml-stylesheet href="person.css" type="text/css"?>

<person>
   Alan Turing
</person>
```

The processing instruction names xml, XML, XmL, etc., in any combination of case, are forbidden in order to avoid confusion with the XML declaration. Otherwise, you're free to pick any legal XML name for your processing instructions.

The XML Declaration

XML documents should (but do not have to) begin with an *XML declaration*. The XML declaration looks like a processing instruction with the name xml and with version, standalone, and encoding pseudo-attributes. Technically, it's not a processing instruction, though; it's just the XML declaration, nothing more, nothing less. Example 2-7 demonstrates.

Example 2-7. A very simple XML document with an XML declaration

```
<?xml version="1.0" encoding="ASCII" standalone="yes"?>
<person>
  Alan Turing
</person>
```

XML documents do not have to have an XML declaration. However, if an XML document does have an XML declaration, then that declaration must be the first thing in the document. It must not be preceded by any comments, whitespace, processing instructions, and so forth. The reason is that an XML parser uses the first five characters (<?xml) to make some reasonable guesses about the encoding, such as whether the document uses a single-byte or multibyte character set. The only thing that may precede the XML declaration is an invisible Unicode byte-order mark. We'll discuss this further in Chapter 5.

The version Attribute

The version attribute should have the value 1.0. Under very unusual circumstances, it may also have the value 1.1. Since specifying version="1.1" limits the document to the most recent versions of only a couple of parsers, and since all XML 1.1 parsers must also support XML 1.0, you don't want to casually set the version to 1.1.

Don't believe us? First answer a couple of questions:

1. Do you speak Cambodian, Burmese, Amharic, Mongolian, or Divehi?
2. Does your data contain obsolete, nontext C0 control characters such as vertical tab, form feed, or bell?

If you answered no to both of these questions, you have absolutely nothing to gain by using XML 1.1. If you answered yes to either one, then you may have cause to use XML 1.1. XML 1.0 allows Cambodian, Burmese, Amharic, etc. to be used in character data and attribute values. XML 1.1 also allows these scripts to be used in element and attribute names, which XML 1.0 does not. XML 1.1 also allows C0 control characters (except null) to be used in character data and attribute values (provided they're escaped as numeric character references like &#x07;), which XML 1.0 does not. If either of these conditions applies to you, then you might want to use XML 1.1 (although realize you're limiting your audience by doing so). Otherwise, you really should use XML 1.0 exclusively.

The encoding Attribute

So far, we've been a little cavalier about character sets and character encodings. We've said that XML documents are composed of pure text, but we haven't said what encoding that text uses. Is it ASCII? Latin-1? Unicode? Something else?

The short answer to this question is "Yes." The long answer is that, by default, XML documents are assumed to be encoded in the UTF-8 variable-length encoding of the Unicode character set. This is a strict superset of ASCII, so pure ASCII text files are also UTF-8 documents. However, most XML processors, especially those written in Java, can handle a much broader range of character sets. All you have to do is tell the parser which character encoding the document uses. Preferably, this is done through metainformation, stored in the filesystem or provided by the server. However, not all systems provide character-set metadata, so XML also allows documents to specify their own character set with an *encoding declaration* inside the XML declaration. Example 2-8 shows how you'd indicate that a document was written in the ISO-8859-1 (Latin-1) character set that includes letters like ö and ç needed for many non-English Western European languages.

Example 2-8. An XML document encoded in Latin-1

```
<?xml version="1.0" encoding="ISO-8859-1" standalone="yes"?>
<person>
  Erwin Schrödinger
</person>
```

The encoding attribute is optional in an XML declaration. If it is omitted and no metadata is available, the Unicode character set is assumed. The parser may use the first several bytes of the file to try to guess which encoding of Unicode is in use. If metadata is available and it conflicts with the encoding declaration, then the encoding specified by the metadata wins. For example, if an HTTP header says a document is encoded in ASCII but the encoding declaration says it's encoded in UTF-8, then the parser will pick ASCII.

The different encodings and the proper handling of non-English XML documents will be discussed in greater detail in Chapter 5.

The standalone Attribute

If the standalone attribute has the value no, then an application may be required to read an external DTD (that is, a DTD in a file other than the one it's reading now) to determine the proper values for parts of the document. For instance, a DTD may provide default values for attributes that a parser is required to report, even though they aren't actually present in the document.

Documents that do not have DTDs, like all the documents in this chapter, can have the value yes for the standalone attribute. Documents that do have DTDs can also have the value yes for the standalone attribute if the DTD doesn't change the content of the document in any way or if the DTD is purely internal. Details for documents with DTDs are covered in Chapter 3.

The standalone attribute is optional in an XML declaration. If it is omitted, then the value no is assumed.

Checking Documents for Well-Formedness

Every XML document, without exception, must be well-formed. This means it must adhere to a number of rules, including the following:

1. Every start-tag must have a matching end-tag.
2. Elements may nest but may not overlap.
3. There must be exactly one root element.
4. Attribute values must be quoted.
5. An element may not have two attributes with the same name.
6. Comments and processing instructions may not appear inside tags.
7. No unescaped < or & signs may occur in the character data of an element or attribute.

This is not an exhaustive list. There are many, many ways a document can be malformed. You'll find a complete list in Chapter 21. Some of these involve constructs that we have not yet discussed, such as DTDs. Others are extremely unlikely to occur if you follow the examples in this chapter (for example, including whitespace between the opening < and the element name in a tag).

Whether the error is small or large, likely or unlikely, an XML parser reading a document is required to report it. It may or may not report multiple well-formedness errors it detects in the document. However, the parser is not allowed to try to fix the document and make a best-faith effort of providing what it thinks the author really meant. It can't fill in missing quotes around attribute values, insert an omitted end-tag, or ignore the comment that's inside a start-tag. The parser is required to return an error. The objective here is to avoid the bug-for-bug compatibility wars that plagued early web browsers and continue to this day. Consequently, before you publish an XML document—whether that document is a web page, input to a database, or something else—you'll want to check it for well-formedness.

The simplest way to do this is by loading the document into a web browser that understands XML documents, such as Mozilla. If the document is well-formed, the browser will display it. If it isn't, then it will show an error message.

Instead of loading the document into a web browser, you can use an XML parser directly. Most XML parsers are not intended for end users. They are class libraries designed to be embedded into an easier-to-use program, such as Mozilla. They provide a minimal command-line interface, if that; this interface is often not particularly well documented. Nonetheless, it can sometimes be quicker to run a batch of files through a command-line interface than loading each of them into a web browser. Furthermore, once you learn about DTDs and schemas, you can use the same tools to validate documents, which most web browsers won't do.

There are many XML parsers available in a variety of languages. Here, we'll demonstrate checking for well-formedness with the Gnome Project's *libxml*, which you can download from *http://xmlsoft.org*. This open source package is written in fairly portable C and runs on most major platforms, including Windows, Linux, and Mac OS X. (It's preinstalled in many Linux distros.) The procedure should be similar for other parsers, although details will vary.

libxml is actually a library but it includes a program called *xmllint* that uses this library to check files for well-formedness. *xmllint* is run from a Unix shell or DOS prompt like any other command-line program. The arguments are the URLs to or filenames of the documents you want to check. Here's the result of running *xmllint* against an early version of Example 2-5. The very first line of output tells you where the first problem in the file is:

```
% xmllint 2-5.xml
2-5.xml:5: error: Unescaped '<' not allowed in attributes values
  <person born='1912/06/23'
                           ^
2-5.xml:5: error: attributes construct error
  <person born='1912/06/23'
                           ^
2-5.xml:5: error: error parsing attribute name
  <person born='1912/06/23'
                           ^
2-5.xml:5: error: attributes construct error
  <person born='1912/06/23'
                           ^
2-5.xml:5: error: xmlParseStartTag: problem parsing attributes
  <person born='1912/06/23'
                           ^
2-5.xml:5: error: Couldn't find end of Start Tag image line 3
  <person born='1912/06/23'
                           ^
```

As you can see, it found an error. In this case the error message wasn't particularly helpful. The actual problem wasn't that an attribute value contained a < character, it was that the closing quote was missing from the height attribute value. Still, that was enough information to locate and fix the problem. Despite the long list of output, *xmllint* only reports the first error in the document, so you may have to run it multiple times until all the mistakes are found and fixed. Once we fixed Example 2-5 to make it well-formed, *xmllint* simply printed the file it read:

```
% xmllint 2-5.xml
<biography xmlns:xlink="http://www.w3.org/1999/xlink/">

  <image source="http://www.turing.org.uk/turing/pi1/busgroup.jpg"
  width="152" height="345"/>

  <paragraph><person born='1912-06-23'
  died='1954-06-07'><first_name>Alan</first_name>
  ...
```

Now that the document has been corrected to be well-formed, it can be passed to a web browser, a database, or whatever other program is waiting to receive it. Almost any nontrivial document crafted by hand will contain well-formedness mistakes, which makes it important to check your work before publishing it.

3

Document Type Definitions (DTDs)

While XML is extremely flexible, not all the programs that read particular XML documents are so flexible. Many programs can work with only some XML applications but not others. For example, Adobe Illustrator can read and write Scalable Vector Graphics (SVG) files, but you wouldn't expect it to understand a Platform for Privacy Preferences (P3P) document. And within a particular XML application, it's often important to ensure that a given document adheres to the rules of that XML application. For instance, in XHTML, li elements should only be children of ul or ol elements. Browsers may not know what to do with them, or may act inconsistently, if li elements appear in the middle of a blockquote or p element.

XML 1.0 provides a solution to this dilemma: a document type definition (DTD). DTDs are written in a formal syntax that explains precisely which elements may appear where in the document and what the elements' contents and attributes are. A DTD can make statements such as "A ul element only contains li elements" or "Every employee element must have a social_security_number attribute." Different XML applications can use different DTDs to specify what they do and do not allow.

A validating parser compares a document to its DTD and lists any places where the document differs from the constraints specified in the DTD. The program can then decide what it wants to do about any violations. Some programs may reject the document. Others may try to fix the document or reject just the invalid element. Validation is an optional step in processing XML. A validity error is not necessarily a fatal error like a well-formedness error, although some applications may choose to treat it as one.

Validation

A valid document includes a *document type declaration* that identifies the DTD that the document satisfies.* The DTD lists all the elements, attributes, and entities the document uses and the contexts in which it uses them. The DTD may list items the document does not use as well. Validity operates on the principle that everything not permitted is forbidden. Everything in the document must match a declaration in the DTD. If a document has a document type declaration and the document satisfies the DTD that the document type declaration indicates, then the document is said to be *valid*. If it does not, it is said to be *invalid*.

There are many things the DTD does not say. In particular, it does not say the following:

- What the root element of the document is
- How many of instances of each kind of element appear in the document
- What the character data inside the elements looks like
- The semantic meaning of an element; for instance, whether it contains a date or a person's name

DTDs allow you to place some constraints on the form an XML document takes, but there can be quite a bit of flexibility within those limits. A DTD never says anything about the length, structure, meaning, allowed values, or other aspects of the text content of an element or attribute.

Validity is optional. A parser reading an XML document may or may not check for validity. If it does check for validity, the program receiving data from the parser may or may not care about validity errors. In some cases, such as feeding records into a database, a validity error may be quite serious, indicating that a required field is missing, for example. In other cases, rendering a web page perhaps, a validity error may not be so important, and a program can work around it. Well-formedness is required of all XML documents; validity is not. Your documents and your programs can use validation as you find needful.

A Simple DTD Example

Recall Example 2-2 from the last chapter, which described a person. The person had a name and three professions. The name had a first name and a last name. The particular person described in that example was Alan Turing. However, that's not relevant for DTDs. A DTD only describes the general type, not the specific instance. A DTD for person documents would say that a person element contains one name child element followed by zero or more profession child elements. It would further say that each name element contains exactly one first_name child element followed by exactly one last_name child element. Finally it would state that the first_name, last_name, and profession elements all contain text. Example 3-1 is a DTD that describes such a person element.

---

* The document type declaration and the document type definition are two different things. The abbreviation DTD is properly used only to refer to the document type definition.

Example 3-1. A DTD for the person element

```
<!ELEMENT person      (name, profession*)>
<!ELEMENT name        (first_name, last_name)>
<!ELEMENT first_name (#PCDATA)>
<!ELEMENT last_name  (#PCDATA)>
<!ELEMENT profession (#PCDATA)>
```

This DTD would probably be stored in a separate file from the documents it describes. This allows it to be easily referenced from multiple XML documents. However, it can be included inside the XML document if that's convenient, using the document type declaration we discuss later in this section. If it is stored in a separate file, then that file would most likely be named *person.dtd*, or something similar. The *.dtd* extension is fairly standard although not specifically required by the XML specification. If this file were served by a web server, it would be given the MIME media type application/xml-dtd.

Each line of Example 3-1 is an *element declaration*. The first line declares the person element, the second line declares the name element, the third line declares the first_name element, and so on. However, the line breaks aren't relevant except for legibility. Although it's customary to put only one declaration on each line, it's not required. Long declarations can even span multiple lines.

The first element declaration in Example 3-1 states that each person element must contain exactly one name child element followed by zero or more profession elements. The asterisk after profession stands for "zero or more." Thus, every person must have a name and may or may not have a profession or multiple professions. However, the name must come before all professions. For example, this person element is valid:

```
<person>
  <name>
    <first_name>Alan</first_name>
    <last_name>Turing</last_name>
  </name>
  <profession>computer scientist</profession>
  <profession>mathematician</profession>
  <profession>cryptographer</profession>
</person>
```

This person element is also valid because profession elements are declared to be optional:

```
<person>
  <name>
    <first_name>Alan</first_name>
    <last_name>Turing</last_name>
  </name>
</person>
```

However, this person element is not valid because it omits the required name child element:

```
<person>
  <profession>computer scientist</profession>
```

```
    <profession>mathematician</profession>
    <profession>cryptographer</profession>
  </person>
```

This person element is not valid because a profession element comes before the name:

```
<person>
  <profession>computer scientist</profession>
  <name>
    <first_name>Alan</first_name>
    <last_name>Turing</last_name>
  </name>
  <profession>mathematician</profession>
  <profession>cryptographer</profession>
</person>
```

The person element cannot contain any element not listed in its declaration. The only extra character data it can contain is whitespace. For example, this is an invalid person element because it adds a publication element:

```
<person>
  <name>
    <first_name>Alan</first_name>
    <last_name>Turing</last_name>
  </name>
  <profession>mathematician</profession>
  <profession>cryptographer</profession>
  <publication>On Computable Numbers...</publication>
</person>
```

This is an invalid person element because it adds some text outside the allowed children:

```
<person>
  <name>
    <first_name>Alan</first_name>
    <last_name>Turing</last_name>
  </name>
  was a <profession>computer scientist</profession>,
  a <profession>mathematician</profession>, and a
  <profession>cryptographer</profession>.
</person>
```

In all these examples of invalid elements, you could change the DTD to make these elements valid. All the examples are well-formed, after all. However, with the DTD in Example 3-1, they are not valid.

The name declaration says that each name element must contain exactly one first_name element followed by exactly one last_name element. All other variations are forbidden.

The remaining three declarations—first_name, last_name, and profession—all say that their elements must contain #PCDATA. This is a DTD keyword standing for *parsed character data*—that is, raw text possibly containing entity references such as & and <, but not containing any tags or child elements.

Example 3-1 placed the most complicated and highest-level declaration at the top. However, that's not required. For instance, Example 3-2 is an equivalent DTD that simply reorders the declarations. DTDs allow forward, backward, and circular references to other declarations.

Example 3-2. An alternate DTD for the person element

```
<!ELEMENT first_name (#PCDATA)>
<!ELEMENT last_name  (#PCDATA)>
<!ELEMENT profession (#PCDATA)>
<!ELEMENT name       (first_name, last_name)>
<!ELEMENT person     (name, profession*)>
```

The Document Type Declaration

A valid document includes a reference to the DTD to which it should be compared. This is given in the document's single document type declaration. A document type declaration looks like this:

```
<!DOCTYPE person SYSTEM "http://www.cafeconleche.org/dtds/person.dtd">
```

This says that the root element of the document is person and that the DTD for this document can be found at *http://www.cafeconleche.org/dtds/person.dtd*.

The document type declaration is included in the prolog of the XML document after the XML declaration but before the root element. (The prolog is everything in the XML document before the root element start-tag.) Example 3-3 demonstrates.

Example 3-3. A valid person document

```
<?xml version="1.0" standalone="no"?>
<!DOCTYPE person SYSTEM "http://www.cafeconleche.org/dtds/person.dtd">
<person>
  <name>
    <first_name>Alan</first_name>
    <last_name>Turing</last_name>
  </name>
  <profession>computer scientist</profession>
  <profession>mathematician</profession>
  <profession>cryptographer</profession>
</person>
```

If the document resides at the same base site as the DTD, you can use a relative URL instead of the absolute form. For example:

```
<!DOCTYPE person SYSTEM "/dtds/person.dtd">
```

You can even use just the filename if the DTD is in the same directory as the document:

```
<!DOCTYPE person SYSTEM "person.dtd">
```

Public IDs

Standard DTDs may actually be stored at multiple URLs. For example, if you're drawing an SVG picture on your laptop at the beach, you probably want to validate the drawing without opening a network connection to the W3C's web site where the official SVG DTD resides. Such DTDs may be associated with public IDs. The name of the public ID uniquely identifies the XML application in use. At the same time, a backup URL is also included in case the validator does not recognize the public ID. To indicate that you're specifying a public ID, use the keyword PUBLIC in place of SYSTEM. For example, this document type declaration refers to the Rich Site Summary DTD standardized by Netscape:

```
<!DOCTYPE rss PUBLIC "-//Netscape Communications//DTD RSS 0.91//EN"
                "http://my.netscape.com/publish/formats/rss-0.91.dtd">
```

A local catalog server can convert the public IDs into the most appropriate URLs for the local environment. The catalogs themselves can be written in XML, specifically the OASIS XML catalog format (*http://www.oasis-open.org/committees/entity/spec.html*). In practice, however, PUBLIC IDs aren't used very much. Most of the time, validators rely on the URL to actually validate the document.

Internal DTD Subsets

When you're first developing a DTD, it's often useful to keep the DTD and the canonical example document in the same file so you can modify and check them simultaneously. Therefore, the document type declaration may contain the DTD between square brackets rather than referencing it at an external URL. Example 3-4 demonstrates.

Example 3-4. A valid person document with an internal DTD

```
<?xml version="1.0"?>
<!DOCTYPE person [
  <!ELEMENT first_name  (#PCDATA)>
  <!ELEMENT last_name   (#PCDATA)>
  <!ELEMENT profession  (#PCDATA)>
  <!ELEMENT name        (first_name, last_name)>
  <!ELEMENT person      (name, profession*)>
]>
<person>
  <name>
    <first_name>Alan</first_name>
    <last_name>Turing</last_name>
  </name>
  <profession>computer scientist</profession>
  <profession>mathematician</profession>
  <profession>cryptographer</profession>
</person>
```

Some document type declarations contain some declarations directly but link in others using a SYSTEM or PUBLIC identifier. For example, this document type declaration declares the profession and person elements itself but relies on the file *name.dtd* to contain the declaration of the name element:

```
<!DOCTYPE person SYSTEM "name.dtd" [
  <!ELEMENT profession (#PCDATA)>
  <!ELEMENT person (name, profession*)>
]>
```

The part of the DTD between the brackets is called the *internal DTD subset*. All
the parts that come from outside this document are called the *external DTD
subset*. Together they make up the complete DTD. As a general rule, the two
different subsets must be compatible. Neither can override the element declarations the other makes. For example, *name.dtd* cannot declare the person element
because the internal DTD subset already declares it. However, entity declarations
can be overridden with some important consequences for DTD structure and
design, which we'll see shortly when we discuss entities.

When you use an external DTD subset, you should give the standalone attribute
of the XML declaration the value no. For example:

```
<?xml version="1.0" encoding="UTF-8" standalone="no"?>
```

 Actually, the XML specification includes four very detailed rules
about exactly when the presence of an external DTD subset does
and does not require the standalone attribute to have the value no.
However, the net effect of these rules is that almost all XML documents that use external DTD subsets require standalone to have the
value no. Since setting standalone to no is always permitted, even
when it's not required, it's simply not worth worrying about the
uncommon cases.

A validating processor is required to read the external DTD subset. A nonvalidating processor may do so, but is not required to, even if standalone has the
value no. This means that if the external subset makes declarations that have
consequences for the content of a document (for instance, providing default
values for attributes), then the content of the document depends on which parser
you're using and how it's configured. This has led to no end of confusion.
Although some of the earliest XML parsers did not resolve external entities, most
of the parsers still being used can do so and generally will do so. You should read
the external DTD subset unless efficiency is a major concern, or you're very
familiar with the structure of the documents you're parsing.

Validating a Document

As a general rule, web browsers do not validate documents but only check them
for well-formedness. If you're writing your own programs to process XML, you
can use the parser's API to validate documents. If you're writing documents by
hand and you want to validate them, you can either use one of the online validators or run a local program to validate the document.

The online validators are probably the easiest way to validate your documents.
There are two of note:

- The Brown University Scholarly Technology Group's XML Validation Form at *http://www.stg.brown.edu/service/xmlvalid/*
- Richard Tobin's XML well-formedness checker and validator at *http://www.cogsci.ed.ac.uk/~richard/xml-check.html*

First, you have to place the document and associated DTDs on a publicly accessible web server. Next, load one of the previous URLs in a browser, and type the URL of the document you're checking into the online form. The validating server will retrieve your document and tell you what, if any, errors it found. Figure 3-1 shows the results of using the Brown validator on a simple invalid but well-formed document.

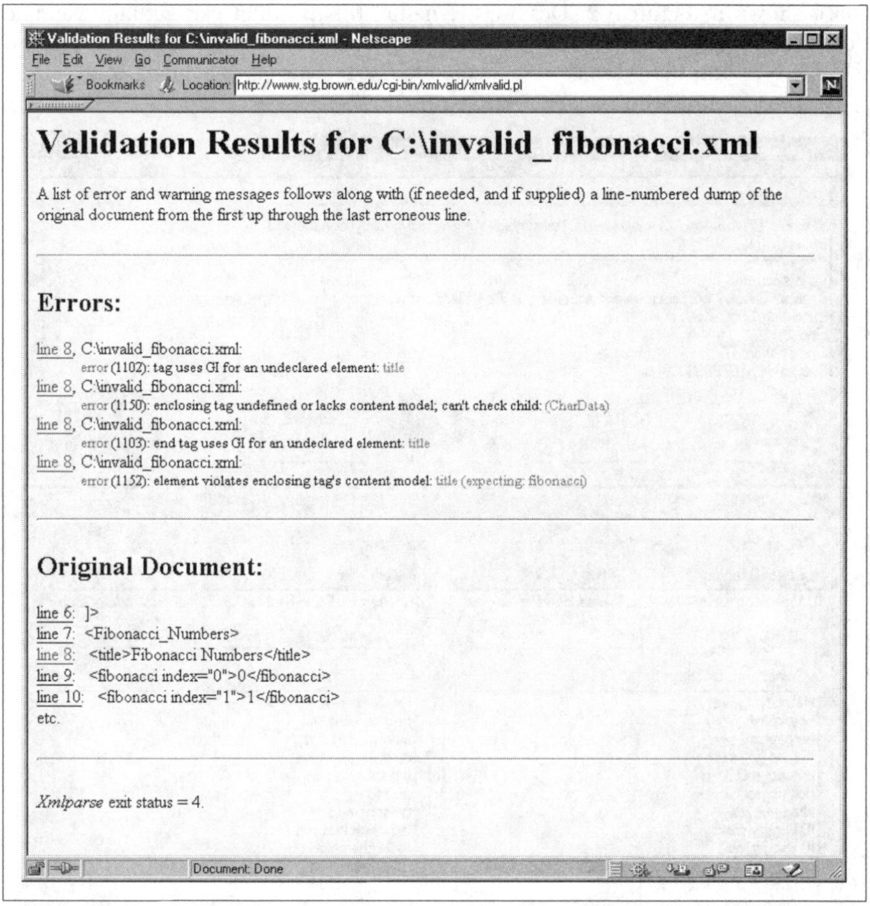

DTDs

Figure 3-1. Validity errors detected by the Brown University online validator

Most XML parser class libraries include a simple program you can use to validate documents if you're comfortable installing and using command-line programs. With *xmllint*, use the --valid flag to turn on validation. (By default, *xmllint* only checks for well-formedness.) Then pass the URLs or filenames of the documents you wish to validate on the command line like this:

```
% xmllint --valid invalidhotcop.xml
invalidhotcop.xml:3: validity error: Element SONG content does not follow
the DTD
Expecting (TITLE , COMPOSER+ , PRODUCER* , PUBLISHER* , LENGTH? , YEAR? ,
ARTIST+), got (TITLE PRODUCER PUBLISHER LENGTH YEAR ARTIST )
</SONG>
       ^
```

You can see from this output that the document *invalidhotcop.xml* has a validity error that needs to be fixed in line 3.

There are also some simple GUI programs for validating XML documents, including the Topologi Schematron Validator for Windows (*http://www.topologi. com*), shown in Figure 3-2. Despite the name, this product can actually validate documents against schemas written in multiple languages, including DTDs, RELAX NG, and the W3C XML Schema Language, as well as Schematron.

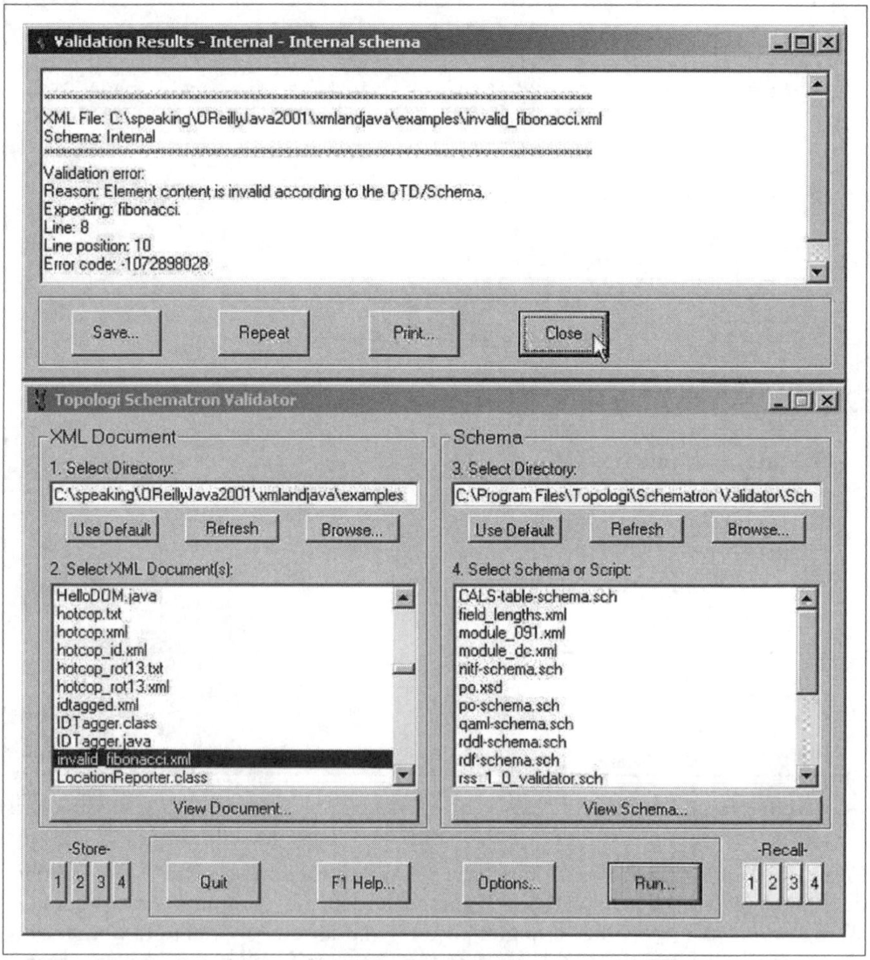

Figure 3-2. Validity errors detected by the Topologi Schematron Validator

Element Declarations

Every element used in a valid document must be declared in the document's DTD with an element declaration. Element declarations have this basic form:

```
<!ELEMENT name content_specification>
```

The name of the element can be any legal XML name. The *content specification* indicates what children the element may or must have and in what order. Content specifications can be quite complex. They can say, for example, that an element must have three child elements of a given type, or two children of one type followed by another element of a second type, or any elements chosen from seven different types interspersed with text.

#PCDATA

The simplest content specification is one that says an element may only contain parsed character data, but may not contain any child elements of any type. In this case the content specification consists of the keyword #PCDATA inside parentheses. For example, this declaration says that a phone_number element may contain text but may not contain elements:

```
<!ELEMENT phone_number (#PCDATA)>
```

Such an element may also contain character references and CDATA sections (which are always parsed into pure text) and comments, and processing instructions (which don't really count in validation). It may contain entity references only if those entity references resolve to plain text without any child elements.

Child Elements

Another simple content specification is one that says the element must have exactly one child of a given type. In this case, the content specification consists of the name of the child element inside parentheses. For example, this declaration says that a fax element must contain exactly one phone_number element:

```
<!ELEMENT fax (phone_number)>
```

A fax element may not contain anything else except the phone_number element, and it may not contain more or less than one of those.

Sequences

In practice, a content specification that lists exactly one child element is rare. Most elements contain either parsed character data or (at least potentially) multiple child elements. The simplest way to indicate multiple child elements is to separate them with commas. This is called a *sequence*. It indicates that the named elements must appear in the specified order. For example, this element declaration says that a name element must contain exactly one first_name child element followed by exactly one last_name child element:

```
<!ELEMENT name (first_name, last_name)>
```

Given this declaration, this name element is valid:

```
<name>
  <first_name>Madonna</first_name>
  <last_name>Ciconne</last_name>
</name>
```

However, this one is not valid because it flips the order of two elements:

```
<name>
  <last_name>Ciconne</last_name>
  <first_name>Madonna</first_name>
</name>
```

This element is invalid because it omits the last_name element:

```
<name>
  <first_name>Madonna</first_name>
</name>
```

This one is invalid because it adds a middle_name element:

```
<name>
  <first_name>Madonna</first_name>
  <middle_name>Louise</middle_name>
  <last_name>Ciconne</last_name>
</name>
```

The Number of Children

As the previous examples indicate, not all instances of a given element necessarily have exactly the same children. You can affix one of three suffixes to an element name in a content specification to indicate how many of that element are expected at that position. These suffixes are:

?   Zero or one of the element is allowed.

*   Zero or more of the element is allowed.

+   One or more of the element is required.

For example, this declaration says that a name element must contain exactly one first_name, may or may not contain a middle_name, and may or may not contain a last_name:

```
<!ELEMENT name (first_name, middle_name?, last_name?)>
```

Given this declaration, all these name elements are valid:

```
<name>
  <first_name>Madonna</first_name>
  <last_name>Ciconne</last_name>
</name>
<name>
  <first_name>Madonna</first_name>
  <middle_name>Louise</middle_name>
  <last_name>Ciconne</last_name>
</name>
```

```
<name>
  <first_name>Madonna</first_name>
</name>
```

However, these are not valid:

```
<name>
  <first_name>George</first_name>
  <!-- only one middle name is allowed -->
  <middle_name>Herbert</middle_name>
  <middle_name>Walker</middle_name>
  <last_name>Bush</last_name>
</name>
<name>
  <!-- first name must precede last name -->
  <last_name>Ciconne</last_name>
  <first_name>Madonna</first_name>
</name>
```

You can allow for multiple middle names by placing an asterisk after the middle_name:

```
<!ELEMENT name (first_name, middle_name*, last_name?)>
```

If you wanted to require a middle_name to be included, but still allow for multiple middle names, you'd use a plus sign instead, like this:

```
<!ELEMENT name (first_name, middle_name+, last_name?)>
```

Choices

Sometimes one instance of an element may contain one kind of child, and another instance may contain a different child. This can be indicated with a *choice*. A choice is a list of element names separated by vertical bars. For example, this declaration says that a methodResponse element contains either a params child or a fault child:

```
<!ELEMENT methodResponse (params | fault)>
```

However, it cannot contain both at once. Each methodResponse element must contain one or the other.

Choices can be extended to an indefinite number of possible elements. For example, this declaration says that each digit element can contain exactly one of the child elements named zero, one, two, three, four, five, six, seven, eight, or nine:

```
<!ELEMENT digit
  (zero | one | two | three | four | five | six | seven | eight | nine)
>
```

Parentheses

Individually, choices, sequences, and suffixes are fairly limited. However, they can be combined in arbitrarily complex fashions to describe most reasonable content models. Either a choice or a sequence can be enclosed in parentheses. When so enclosed, the choice or sequence can be suffixed with a ?, *, or +. Furthermore, the parenthesized item can be nested inside other choices or sequences.

For example, let's suppose you want to say that a circle element contains a center element and either a radius or a diameter element, but not both. This declaration does that:

```
<!ELEMENT circle (center, (radius | diameter))>
```

To continue with a geometry example, suppose a center element can either be defined in terms of Cartesian or polar coordinates. Then each center contains either an x and a y or an r and a θ. We would declare this using two small sequences, each of which is parenthesized and combined in a choice:

```
<!ELEMENT center ((x, y) | (r, θ))>
```

Suppose you don't really care whether the x element comes before the y element or vice versa, nor do you care whether r comes before θ. Then you can expand the choice to cover all four possibilities:

```
<!ELEMENT center ((x, y) | (y, x) | (r, θ) | (θ, r) )>
```

As the number of elements in the sequence grows, the number of permutations grows more than exponentially. Thus, this technique really isn't practical past two or three child elements. DTDs are not very good at saying you want n instances of A and m instances of B, but you don't really care which order they come in.

Suffixes can be applied to parenthesized elements, too. For instance, let's suppose that a polygon is defined by individual coordinates for each vertex, given in order. For example, this is a right triangle:

```
<polygon>
  <r>0</r>   <θ>0</θ>
  <x>0</x>   <y>10</y>
  <x>10</x>  <y>0</y>
</polygon>
```

What we want to say is that a polygon is composed of three or more pairs of x-y or r-θ coordinates. An x is always followed by a y, and an r is always followed by a θ. This declaration does that:

```
<!ELEMENT polygon
    (((x, y) | (r, θ)), ((x, y) | (r, θ)), ((x, y) | (r, θ))+)>
```

The plus sign is applied to ((x, y) | (r, θ)).

To return to the name example, suppose you want to say that a name can contain just a first name, just a last name, or a first name and a last name with an indefinite number of middle names. This declaration achieves that:

```
<!ELEMENT name (last_name
               | (first_name, ( (middle_name+, last_name) | (last_name?) )
               ) >
```

Mixed Content

In narrative documents, it's common for a single element to contain both child elements and un-marked up, nonwhitespace character data. For example, recall this definition element from Chapter 2:

```
<definition>A <term>Turing Machine</term> refers to an abstract finite
state automaton with infinite memory that can be proven equivalent
to any any other finite state automaton with arbitrarily large memory.
Thus what is true for one Turing machine is true for all Turing
machines no matter how implemented.
</definition>
```

The definition element contains some nonwhitespace text and a term child. This is called *mixed content*. An element that contains mixed content is declared like this:

```
<!ELEMENT definition (#PCDATA | term)*>
```

This says that a definition element may contain parsed character data and term children. It does not specify in which order they appear, nor how many instances of each appear. This declaration allows a definition to have 1 term child, 0 term children, or 23 term children.

You can add any number of other child elements to the list of mixed content, although #PCDATA must always be the first child in the list. For example, this declaration says that a paragraph element may contain any number of name, profession, footnote, emphasize, and date elements in any order, interspersed with parsed character data:

```
<!ELEMENT paragraph
  (#PCDATA | name | profession | footnote | emphasize | date )*
>
```

This is the *only* way to indicate that an element contains mixed content. You cannot say, for example, that there must be exactly one term child of the definition element, as well as parsed character data. You cannot say that the parsed character data must all come after the term child. You cannot use parentheses around a mixed-content declaration to make it part of a larger grouping. You can only say that the element contains any number of any elements from a particular list in any order, as well as undifferentiated parsed character data.

Empty Elements

Some elements do not have any content at all. These are called *empty elements* and are sometimes written with a closing />. For example:

```
<image source="bus.jpg" width="152" height="345"
       alt="Alan Turing standing in front of a bus"
/>
```

These elements are declared by using the keyword EMPTY for the content specification. For example:

```
<!ELEMENT image EMPTY>
```

This merely says that the image element must be empty, not that it must be written with an empty-element tag. Given this declaration, this is also a valid image element:

```
<image source="bus.jpg" width="152" height="345"
       alt="Alan Turing standing in front of a bus"></image>
```

If an element is empty, then it can contain nothing, not even whitespace. For instance, this is an invalid image element:

```
<image source="bus.jpg" width="152" height="345"
       alt="Alan Turing standing in front of a bus">
</image>
```

ANY

Very loose DTDs occasionally want to say that an element exists without making any assertions about what it may or may not contain. In this case, you can specify the keyword ANY as the content specification. For example, this declaration says that a page element can contain any content, including mixed content, child elements, and even other page elements:

```
<!ELEMENT page ANY>
```

The children that actually appear in the page elements' content in the document must still be declared in element declarations of their own. ANY does not allow you to use undeclared elements.

ANY is sometimes useful when you're just beginning to design the DTD and document structure and you don't yet have a clear picture of how everything fits together. However, it's extremely bad form to use ANY in finished DTDs. About the only time you'll see it used is when external DTD subsets and entities may change in uncontrollable ways. However, this is actually quite rare. You'd really only need this if you were writing a DTD for an application like XSLT or RDF that wraps content from arbitrary, unknown XML applications.

Attribute Declarations

In addition to declaring its elements, a valid document must declare all the elements' attributes. This is done with ATTLIST declarations. A single ATTLIST can declare multiple attributes for a single element type. However, if the same attribute is repeated on multiple elements, then it must be declared separately for each element where it appears. (Later in this chapter you'll see how to use parameter entity references to make this repetition less burdensome.)

For example, ATTLIST declares the source attribute of the image element:

```
<!ATTLIST image source CDATA #REQUIRED>
```

It says that the image element has an attribute named source. The value of the source attribute is character data, and instances of the image element in the document are required to provide a value for the source attribute.

A single ATTLIST declaration can declare multiple attributes for the same element. For example, this ATTLIST declaration not only declares the source attribute of the image element, but also the width, height, and alt attributes:

```
<!ATTLIST image source CDATA #REQUIRED
                width  CDATA #REQUIRED
                height CDATA #REQUIRED
                alt    CDATA #IMPLIED
    >
```

This declaration says the source, width, and height attributes are required. However, the alt attribute is optional and may be omitted from particular image elements. All four attributes are declared to contain character data, the most generic attribute type.

This declaration has the same effect and meaning as four separate ATTLIST declarations, one for each attribute. Whether to use one ATTLIST declaration per attribute is a matter of personal preference, but most experienced DTD designers prefer the multiple-attribute form. Given judicious application of whitespace, it's no less legible than the alternative.

Attribute Types

In merely well-formed XML, attribute values can be any string of text. The only restrictions are that any occurrences of < or & must be escaped as < and &, and whichever kind of quotation mark, single or double, is used to delimit the value must also be escaped. However, a DTD allows you to make somewhat stronger statements about the content of an attribute value. Indeed, these are stronger statements than can be made about the contents of an element. For instance, you can say that an attribute value must be unique within the document, that it must be a legal XML name token, or that it must be chosen from a fixed list of values.

There are 10 attribute types in XML. They are:

- CDATA
- NMTOKEN
- NMTOKENS
- Enumeration
- ENTITY
- ENTITIES
- ID
- IDREF
- IDREFS
- NOTATION

These are the only attribute types allowed. A DTD cannot say that an attribute value must be an integer or a date between 1966 and 2004, for example.

CDATA

A CDATA attribute value can contain any string of text acceptable in a well-formed XML attribute value. This is the most general attribute type. For example, you would use this type for an alt attribute of an image element because there's no particular form the text in such an attribute has to follow.

```
<!ATTLIST image alt CDATA #IMPLIED>
```

You would also use this for other kinds of data such as prices, URLs, email and snail mail addresses, citations, and other types that—while they have more structure than a simple string of text—don't match any of the other attribute types. For example:

```
<!ATTLIST sku
 list_price              CDATA #IMPLIED
 suggested_retail_price  CDATA #IMPLIED
 actual_price            CDATA #IMPLIED
>
<!-- All three attributes should be in the form $XX.YY -->
```

NMTOKEN

An XML *name token* is very close to an XML name. It must consist of the same characters as an XML name; that is, alphanumeric and/or ideographic characters and the punctuation marks _, -, ., and :. Furthermore, like an XML name, an XML name token may not contain whitespace. However, a name token differs from an XML name in that any of the allowed characters can be the first character in a name token, while only letters, ideographs, and the underscore can be the first character of an XML name. Thus 12 and .cshrc are valid XML name tokens although they are not valid XML names. Every XML name is an XML name token, but not all XML name tokens are XML names.

The value of an attribute declared to have type NMTOKEN is an XML name token. For example, if you knew that the year attribute of a journal element should contain an integer such as 1990 or 2015, you might declare it to have NMTOKEN type, since all years are name tokens:

```
<!ATTLIST journal year NMTOKEN #REQUIRED>
```

This still doesn't prevent the document author from assigning the year attribute values like "99" or "March", but at least it eliminates some possible wrong values, especially those that contain whitespace such as "1990 C.E." or "Sally had a little lamb."

NMTOKENS

A NMTOKENS type attribute contains one or more XML name tokens separated by whitespace. For example, you might use this to describe the dates attribute of a performances element, if the dates were given in the form 08-26-2000, like this:

```
<performances dates="08-21-2001 08-23-2001 08-27-2001">
  Kat and the Kings
</performances>
```

The appropriate declaration is:

```
<!ATTLIST performances dates NMTOKENS #REQUIRED>
```

On the other hand, you could not use this for a list of dates in the form 08/27/2001 because the forward slash is not a legal name character.

Enumeration

An enumeration is the only attribute type that is not an XML keyword. Rather, it is a list of all possible values for the attribute, separated by vertical bars. Each possible value must be an XML name token. For example, the following declarations say that the value of the month attribute of a date element must be one of the 12 English month names, that the value of the day attribute must be a number between 1 and 31, and that the value of the year attribute must be an integer between 1970 and 2009:

```
<!ATTLIST date month (January | February | March | April | May | June
   | July | August | September | October | November | December) #REQUIRED
>
<!ATTLIST date day (1 | 2 | 3 | 4 | 5 | 6 | 7 | 8 | 9 | 10 | 11 | 12
   | 13 | 14 | 15 | 16 | 17 | 18 | 19 | 20 | 21 | 22 | 23 | 24 | 25
   | 26 | 27 | 28 | 29 | 30 | 31) #REQUIRED
>
<!ATTLIST date year (1970 | 1971 | 1972 | 1973 | 1974 | 1975 | 1976
   | 1977 | 1978 | 1979 | 1980 | 1981 | 1982 | 1983 | 1984 | 1985 | 1986
   | 1987 | 1988 | 1989 | 1990 | 1991 | 1992 | 1993 | 1994 | 1995 | 1996
   | 1997 | 1998 | 1999 | 2000 | 2001 | 2002 | 2003 | 2004 | 2005 | 2006
   | 2007 | 2008 | 2009 ) #REQUIRED
>
<!ELEMENT date EMPTY>
```

Given this DTD, this date element is valid:

```
<date month="January" day="22" year="2001"/>
```

However, these date elements are invalid:

```
<date month="01"      day="22" year="2001"/>
<date month="Jan"     day="22" year="2001"/>
<date month="January" day="02" year="2001"/>
<date month="January" day="2"  year="1969"/>
<date month="Janvier" day="22" year="2001"/>
```

This trick works here because all the desired values happen to be legal XML name tokens. However, we could not use the same trick if the possible values included whitespace or any punctuation besides the underscore, hyphen, colon, and period.

ID

An ID type attribute must contain an XML name (not a name token but a name) that is unique within the XML document. More precisely, no other ID type attribute in the document can have the same value. (Attributes of non-ID type are not considered.) Each element may have no more than one ID type attribute.

As the keyword suggests, ID type attributes assign unique identifiers to elements. ID type attributes do not need to have the name "ID" or "id", although they very commonly do. For example, this ATTLIST declaration says that every employee element must have a social_security_number ID attribute:

```
<!ATTLIST employee social_security_number ID #REQUIRED>
```

ID numbers are tricky because a number is not an XML name and therefore not a legal XML ID. The normal solution is to prefix the values with an underscore or a common letter. For example:

```
<employee social_security_number="_078-05-1120"/>
```

IDREF

An IDREF type attribute refers to the ID type attribute of some element in the document. Thus, it must be an XML name. IDREF attributes are commonly used to establish relationships between elements when simple containment won't suffice.

For example, imagine an XML document that contains a list of project and employee elements. Every project has an ID type attribute named ID, and every employee has a social_security_number ID type attribute. Furthermore, each project has team_member child elements that identify who's working on the project. Since each project is assigned to multiple employees and some employees are assigned to more than one project, it's not possible to make the employees children of the projects or the projects children of the employees. The solution is to use IDREF type attributes like this:

```
<project id="p1">
  <goal>Develop Strategic Plan</goal>
  <team_member person="ss078-05-1120"/>
  <team_member person="ss987-65-4320"/>
</project>
<project id="p2">
  <goal>Deploy Linux</goal>
  <team_member person="ss078-05-1120"/>
  <team_member person="ss9876-12-3456"/>
</project>
<employee social_security_number="ss078-05-1120">
  <name>Fred Smith</name>
</employee>
<employee social_security_number="ss987-65-4320">
  <name>Jill Jones</name>
</employee>
<employee social_security_number="ss9876-12-3456">
  <name>Sydney Lee</name>
</employee>
```

In this example, the id attribute of the project element and the social_security_number attribute of the employee element would be declared to have type ID. The person attribute of the team_member element would have type IDREF. The relevant ATTLIST declarations look like this:

```
<!ATTLIST employee social_security_number ID    #REQUIRED>
<!ATTLIST project id                      ID    #REQUIRED>
<!ATTLIST team_member person              IDREF #REQUIRED>
```

These declarations constrain the person attribute of the team_member element to match the ID of something in the document. However, they do not constrain the person attribute of the team_member element to match only employee IDs. It would be valid (though not necessarily correct) for a team_member to hold the ID of another project or even the same project.

IDREFS

An IDREFS type attribute contains a whitespace-separated list of XML names, each of which must be the ID of an element in the document. This is used when one element needs to refer to multiple other elements. For instance, the previous project example could be rewritten so that the team_member children of the project element could be replaced by a team attribute like this:

```
<project project_id="p1" team="ss078-05-1120 ss987-65-4320">
  <goal>Develop Strategic Plan</goal>
</project>
<project project_id="p2" team="ss078-05-1120 ss9876-12-3456">
  <goal>Deploy Linux</goal>
</project>
<employee social_security_number="ss078-05-1120">
  <name>Fred Smith</name>
</employee>
<employee social_security_number="ss987-65-4320" >
  <name>Jill Jones</name>
</employee>
<employee social_security_number="ss9876-12-3456">
  <name>Sydney Lee</name>
</employee>
```

The appropriate declarations are:

```
<!ATTLIST employee social_security_number ID     #REQUIRED
<!ATTLIST project  project_id             ID     #REQUIRED>
                   team                   IDREFS #REQUIRED>
```

ENTITY

An ENTITY type attribute contains the name of an unparsed entity declared elsewhere in the DTD. For instance, a movie element might have an entity attribute identifying the MPEG or QuickTime file to play when the movie was activated:

```
<!ATTLIST movie source ENTITY #REQUIRED>
```

If the DTD declared an unparsed entity named X-Men-trailer, then this movie element might be used to embed that video file in the XML document:

```
<movie source="X-Men-trailer"/>
```

We'll discuss unparsed entities in more detail later in this chapter.

ENTITIES

An ENTITIES type attribute contains the names of one or more unparsed entities declared elsewhere in the DTD, separated by whitespace. For instance, a slide_show element might have an ENTITIES attribute identifying the JPEG files to show and the order in which to show them:

```
<!ATTLIST slide_show slides ENTITIES #REQUIRED>
```

If the DTD declared unparsed entities named slide1, slide2, slide3, and so on through slide10, then this slide_show element might be used to embed the show in the XML document:

```
<slide_show slides="slide1 slide2 slide3 slide4 slide5 slide6
                    slide7 slide8 slide9 slide10"/>
```

NOTATION

A NOTATION type attribute contains the name of a notation declared in the document's DTD. This is perhaps the rarest attribute type and isn't much used in practice. In theory, it could be used to associate types with particular elements, as well as limiting the types associated with the element. For example, these declarations define four notations for different image types and then specify that each image element must have a type attribute that selects exactly one of them:

```
<!NOTATION gif  SYSTEM "image/gif">
<!NOTATION tiff SYSTEM "image/tiff">
<!NOTATION jpeg SYSTEM "image/jpeg">
<!NOTATION png  SYSTEM "image/png">
<!ATTLIST  image type NOTATION (gif | tiff | jpeg | png) #REQUIRED>
```

The type attribute of each image element can have one of the four values gif, tiff, jpeg, or png but not any other value. This has a slight advantage over the enumerated type in that the actual MIME media type of the notation is available, whereas an enumerated type could not specify image/png or image/gif as an allowed value because the forward slash is not a legal character in XML names.

Attribute Defaults

In addition to providing a data type, each ATTLIST declaration includes a default declaration for that attribute. There are four possibilities for this default:

#IMPLIED
> The attribute is optional. Each instance of the element may or may not provide a value for the attribute. No default value is provided.

#REQUIRED
> The attribute is required. Each instance of the element must provide a value for the attribute. No default value is provided.

#FIXED
> The attribute value is constant and immutable. This attribute has the specified value regardless of whether the attribute is explicitly noted on an individual instance of the element. If it is included, though, it must have the specified value.

Literal
> The actual default value is given as a quoted string.

For example, this ATTLIST declaration says that person elements can but do not need to have born and died attributes:

```
<!ATTLIST person born CDATA #IMPLIED
                 died CDATA #IMPLIED
>
```

This ATTLIST declaration says that every circle element must have center_x, center_y, and radius attributes:

```
<!ATTLIST circle center_x NMTOKEN #REQUIRED
                 center_y NMTOKEN #REQUIRED
                 radius   NMTOKEN #REQUIRED
>
```

This ATTLIST declaration says that every biography element has a version attribute and that the value of that attribute is 1.0, even if the start-tag of the element does not explicitly include a version attribute:

```
<!ATTLIST biography version CDATA #FIXED "1.0">
```

This ATTLIST declaration says that every web_page element has a protocol attribute. If a particular web_page element doesn't have an explicit protocol attribute, then the parser will supply one with the value http:

```
<!ATTLIST web_page protocol NMTOKEN "http">
```

General Entity Declarations

As you learned in Chapter 2, XML predefines five entities for your convenience:

<
> The less-than sign, a.k.a. the opening angle bracket (<)

&
> The ampersand (&)

>
> The greater-than sign, a.k.a. the closing angle bracket (>)

"
> The straight, double quotation marks (")

'
> The apostrophe, a.k.a. the straight single quote (')

The DTD can define many more entities. This is useful not just in valid documents, but even in documents you don't plan to validate.

Entity references are defined with an ENTITY declaration in the DTD. This gives the name of the entity, which must be an XML name, and the replacement text of the entity. For example, this entity declaration defines &super; as an abbreviation for supercalifragilisticexpialidocious:

```
<!ENTITY super "supercalifragilisticexpialidocious">
```

Once that's done, you can use &super; anywhere you'd normally have to type the entire word (and probably misspell it).

Entities can contain markup as well as text. For example, this declaration defines &footer; as an abbreviation for a standard web page footer that will be repeated on many pages:

```
<!ENTITY footer '<hr size="1" noshade="true"/>
<font CLASS="footer">
```

```
<a href="index.html">O&apos;Reilly Home</a> |
<a href="sales/bookstores/">O&apos;Reilly Bookstores</a> |
<a href="order_new/">How to Order</a> |
<a href="oreilly/contact.html">O&apos;Reilly Contacts</a><br>
<a href="http://international.oreilly.com/">International</a> |
<a href="oreilly/about.html">About O&apos;Reilly</a> |
<a href="affiliates.html">Affiliated Companies</a>
</font>
<p>
<font CLASS="copy">
Copyright 2004, O&apos;Reilly Media, Inc.<br/>
<a href="mailto:webmaster@oreilly.com">webmaster@oreilly.com</a>
</font>
</p>
'>
```

The entity replacement text must be well-formed. For instance, you cannot put a start-tag in one entity and the corresponding end-tag in another entity.

The other thing you have to be careful about is that you need to use different quote marks inside the replacement text from the ones that delimit it. Here we've chosen single quotes to surround the replacement text and double quotes internally. However, we did have to change the single quote in "O'Reilly" to the predefined general entity reference '. Replacement text may itself contain entity references that are resolved before the text is replaced. Self-referential and circular references are forbidden, however.

General entities insert replacement text into the body of an XML document. They can also be used inside the DTD in places where they will eventually be included in the body of an XML document, for instance in an attribute default value or in the replacement text of another entity. However, they cannot be used to provide the text of the DTD itself. For instance, this is illegal:

```
<!ENTITY coordinate  "((x, y) | (y, x) | (θ, r) | (r, θ))" >
<!ELEMENT polygon (&coordinate;, &coordinate;, &coordinate;+)>
```

Shortly, we'll see how to use a different kind of entity—the parameter entity—to achieve the desired result.

External Parsed General Entities

The footer example is about at the limits of what you can comfortably fit in a DTD. In practice, web sites prefer to store repeated content like this in external files and load it into their pages using PHP, server-side includes, or some similar mechanism. XML supports this technique through external general entity references, although in this case the client, rather than the server, is responsible for integrating the different pieces of the document into a coherent whole.

An external parsed general entity reference is declared in the DTD using an ENTITY declaration. However, instead of the actual replacement text, the SYSTEM keyword and a URL to the replacement text is given. For example:

```
<!ENTITY footer SYSTEM "http://www.oreilly.com/boilerplate/footer.xml">
```

Of course, a relative URL will often be used instead. For example:

```
<!ENTITY footer SYSTEM "/boilerplate/footer.xml">
```

In either case, when the general entity reference &footer; is seen in the character data of an element, the parser may replace it with the document found at *http://www.oreilly.com/boilerplate/footer.xml*. References to external parsed entities are not allowed in attribute values. Most of the time this shouldn't be too big a hassle because attribute values tend to be small enough to be easily included in internal entities.

Notice we wrote that the parser *may* replace the entity reference with the document at the URL, not that it must. This is an area where parsers have some leeway in just how much of the XML specification they wish to implement. A validating parser must retrieve such an external entity. However, a nonvalidating parser may or may not choose to retrieve the entity.

Furthermore, not all text files can serve as external entities. In order to be loaded in by a general entity reference, the document must be potentially well-formed when inserted into an existing document. This does not mean the external entity itself must be well-formed. In particular, the external entity might not have a single root element. However, if such a root element were wrapped around the external entity, then the resulting document should be well-formed. This means, for example, that all elements that start inside the entity must finish inside the same entity. They cannot finish inside some other entity. Furthermore, the external entity does not have a prolog and, therefore, cannot have an XML declaration or a document type declaration.

Text Declarations

Instead of an XML declaration, an external entity may have a text declaration; this looks a lot like an XML declaration. The main difference is that in a text declaration the encoding declaration is required, while the version attribute is optional. Furthermore, there is no standalone declaration. The main purpose of the text declaration is to tell the parser what character set the entity is encoded in. For example, this is a common text declaration:

```
<?xml version="1.0" encoding="MacRoman"?>
```

However, you could also use this text declaration with no version attribute:

```
<?xml encoding="MacRoman"?>
```

Example 3-5 is a well-formed external entity that could be included from another document using an external general entity reference.

Example 3-5. An external parsed entity

```
<?xml encoding="ISO-8859-1"?>
<hr size="1" noshade="true"/>
<font CLASS="footer">
  <a href="index.html">O'Reilly Home</a> |
  <a href="sales/bookstores/">O'Reilly Bookstores</a> |
  <a href="order_new/">How to Order</a> |
  <a href="oreilly/contact.html">O'Reilly Contacts</a><br>
```

Example 3-5. An external parsed entity (continued)

```
 <a href="http://international.oreilly.com/">International</a> |
 <a href="oreilly/about.html">About O'Reilly</a> |
 <a href="affiliates.html">Affiliated Companies</a>
</font>
<p>
 <font CLASS="copy">
  Copyright 2004, O'Reilly Media, Inc.<br/>
  <a href="mailto:webmaster@oreilly.com">webmaster@oreilly.com</a>
 </font>
</p>
```

External Unparsed Entities and Notations

Not all data is XML. There are a lot of ASCII text files in the world that don't give two cents about escaping < as < or adhering to the other constraints by which an XML document is limited. There are probably even more JPEG photographs, GIF line art, QuickTime movies, MIDI sound files, and so on. None of these are well-formed XML, yet all of them are necessary components of many documents.

The mechanism that XML suggests for embedding these things in documents is the *external unparsed entity*. The DTD specifies a name and a URL for the entity containing the non-XML data. For example, this ENTITY declaration associates the name turing_getting_off_bus with the JPEG image at *http://www.turing.org.uk/turing/pi1/busgroup.jpg*:

```
<!ENTITY turing_getting_off_bus
        SYSTEM "http://www.turing.org.uk/turing/pi1/busgroup.jpg"
        NDATA jpeg>
```

Notations

Since the data in the previous code is not in XML format, the NDATA declaration specifies the type of the data. Here the name jpeg is used. XML does not recognize this as meaning an image in a format defined by the Joint Photographs Experts Group. Rather this is the name of a notation declared elsewhere in the DTD using a NOTATION declaration like this:

```
<!NOTATION jpeg SYSTEM "image/jpeg">
```

Here we've used the MIME media type image/jpeg as the external identifier for the notation. However, there is absolutely no standard or even a suggestion for exactly what this identifier should be. Individual applications must define their own requirements for the contents and meaning of notations.

Embedding Unparsed Entities in Documents

The DTD only declares the existence, location, and type of the unparsed entity. To actually include the entity in the document at one or more locations, you insert an element with an ENTITY type attribute whose value is the name of an unparsed entity declared in the DTD. You do not use an entity reference like &turing_getting_off_bus;. Entity references can only refer to parsed entities.

Suppose the image element and its source attribute are declared like this:

```
<!ELEMENT image EMPTY>
<!ATTLIST image source ENTITY #REQUIRED>
```

Then, this image element would refer to the photograph at *http://www.turing.org.uk/turing/pi1/busgroup.jpg*:

```
<image source="turing_getting_off_bus"/>
```

We should warn you that XML doesn't guarantee any particular behavior from an application that encounters this type of unparsed entity. It very well may not display the image to the user. Indeed, the parser may be running in an environment where there's no user to display the image to. It may not even understand that this is an image. The parser might not load or make any sort of connection with the server where the actual image resides. At most, it will tell the application on whose behalf it's parsing that there is an unparsed entity at a particular URL with a particular notation and let the application decide what, if anything, it wants to do with that information.

DTDs

 Unparsed general entities are not the only plausible way to embed non-XML content in XML documents. In particular, a simple URL, possibly associated with an XLink, does a fine job for many purposes, just as it does in HTML (which gets along just fine without any unparsed entities). Including all the necessary information in a single empty element such as <image source = "http://www.turing.org.uk/turing/pi1/busgroup.jpg" /> is arguably preferable to splitting the same information between the element where it's used and the DTD of the document in which it's used. The only thing an unparsed entity really adds is the notation, but that's too nonstandard to be of much use.

In fact, many experienced XML developers, including the authors of this book, feel strongly that unparsed entities are a complicated, confusing mistake that should never have been included in XML in the first place. Nonetheless, they are a part of the specification, so we describe them here.

Parameter Entities

It is not uncommon for multiple elements to share all or part of the same attribute lists and content specifications. For instance, any element that's a simple XLink will have xlink:type and xlink:href attributes, and perhaps xlink:show and xlink:actuate attributes. In XHTML, a th element and a td element contain more or less the same content. Repeating the same content specifications or attribute lists in multiple element declarations is tedious and error-prone. It's entirely possible to add a newly defined child element to the declaration of some of the elements but forget to include it in others.

For example, consider an XML application for residential real estate listings that provides separate elements for apartments, sublets, coops for sale, condos for sale, and houses for sale. The element declarations might look like this:

```
<!ELEMENT apartment (address, footage, rooms, baths, rent)>
<!ELEMENT sublet    (address, footage, rooms, baths, rent)>
<!ELEMENT coop      (address, footage, rooms, baths, price)>
<!ELEMENT condo     (address, footage, rooms, baths, price)>
<!ELEMENT house     (address, footage, rooms, baths, price)>
```

There's a lot of overlap between the declarations, i.e., a lot of repeated text. And if you later decide you need to add an additional element, available_date for instance, then you need to add it to all five declarations. It would be preferable to define a constant that can hold the common parts of the content specification for all five kinds of listings and refer to that constant from inside the content specification of each element. Then to add or delete something from all the listings, you'd only need to change the definition of the constant.

An entity reference is the obvious candidate here. However, general entity references are not allowed to provide replacement text for a content specification or attribute list, only for parts of the DTD that will be included in the XML document itself. Instead, XML provides a new construct exclusively for use inside DTDs, the *parameter entity*, which is referred to by a *parameter entity reference*. Parameter entities behave and are declared almost exactly like a general entity. However, they use a % instead of an &, and they can only be used in a DTD, while general entities can only be used in the document content.

Parameter Entity Syntax

A parameter entity reference is declared much like a general entity reference. However, an extra percent sign is placed between the <!ENTITY and the name of the entity. For example:

```
<!ENTITY % residential_content "address, footage, rooms, baths">
<!ENTITY % rental_content      "rent">
<!ENTITY % purchase_content    "price">
```

Parameter entities are dereferenced in the same way as a general entity reference, only with a percent sign instead of an ampersand:

```
<!ELEMENT apartment (%residential_content;, %rental_content;)>
<!ELEMENT sublet    (%residential_content;, %rental_content;)>
<!ELEMENT coop      (%residential_content;, %purchase_content;)>
<!ELEMENT condo     (%residential_content;, %purchase_content;)>
<!ELEMENT house     (%residential_content;, %purchase_content;)>
```

When the parser reads these declarations, it substitutes the entity's replacement text for the entity reference. Now all you have to do to add an available_date element to the content specification of all five listing types is add it to the residential_content entity like this:

```
<!ENTITY % residential_content "address, footage, rooms,
                                baths, available_date">
```

The same technique works equally well for attribute types and element names. You'll see several examples of this in the next chapter on namespaces and in Chapter 9.

This trick is limited to external DTDs. Internal DTD subsets do not allow parameter entity references to be only part of a markup declaration. However, parameter entity references can be used in internal DTD subsets to insert one or more entire markup declarations, typically through external parameter entities.

Redefining Parameter Entities

What makes parameter entity references particularly powerful is that they can be redefined. If a document uses both internal and external DTD subsets, then the internal DTD subset can specify new replacement text for the entities. If ELEMENT and ATTLIST declarations in the external DTD subset are written indirectly with parameter entity references, instead of directly with literal element names, the internal DTD subset can change the DTD for the document. For instance, a single document could add a bedrooms child element to the listings by redefining the residential_content entity like this:

```
<!ENTITY % residential_content "address, footage, rooms,
                                bedrooms, baths, available_date">
```

In the event of conflicting entity declarations, the first one encountered takes precedence. The parser reads the internal DTD subset first. Thus, the internal definition of the residential_content entity is used. When the parser reads the external DTD subset, every declaration that uses the residential_content entity will contain a bedrooms child element it wouldn't otherwise have.

Modular XHTML, which we'll discuss in Chapter 7, makes heavy use of this technique to allow particular documents to select only the subset of HTML that they actually need.

External DTD Subsets

Real-world DTDs can be quite complex. The SVG DTD is over 1,000 lines long. The XHTML 1.0 strict DTD (the smallest of the three XHTML DTDs) is more than 1,500 lines long. And these are only medium-sized DTDs. The DocBook XML DTD is over 11,000 lines long. It can be hard to work with, comprehend, and modify such a large DTD when it's stored in a single monolithic file.

Fortunately, DTDs can be broken up into independent pieces. For instance, the DocBook DTD is distributed in 28 separate pieces covering different parts of the spec: one for tables, one for notations, one for entity declarations, and so on. These different pieces are then combined at validation time using *external parameter entity references*.

An external parameter entity is declared using a normal ENTITY declaration with a % sign just like a normal parameter entity. However, rather than including the replacement text directly, the declaration contains the SYSTEM keyword, followed by a URL to the DTD piece it wants to include. For example, the following ENTITY declaration defines an external entity called "names" whose content is taken from the file at the relative URL *names.dtd*. Then the parameter entity reference %names; inserts the contents of that file into the current DTD.

```
<!ENTITY % names SYSTEM "names.dtd">
%names;
```

You can use either relative or absolute URLs. In most situations, relative URLs are more practical.

Conditional Inclusion

XML offers the IGNORE directive for the purpose of "commenting out" a section of declarations. For example, a parser will ignore the following declaration of a production_note element, as if it weren't in the DTD at all:

```
<![IGNORE[
  <!ELEMENT production_note (#PCDATA)>
]]>
```

This may not seem particularly useful. After all, you could always simply use an XML comment to comment out the declarations you want to remove temporarily from the DTD. If you feel that way, the INCLUDE directive is going to seem even more pointless. Its purpose is to indicate that the given declarations are actually used in the DTD. For example:

```
<![INCLUDE[
  <!ELEMENT production_note (#PCDATA)>
]]>
```

This has exactly the same effect and meaning as if the INCLUDE directive were not present. However, now consider what happens if we don't use INCLUDE and IGNORE directly. Instead, suppose we define a parameter entity like this:

```
<!ENTITY % notes_allowed "INCLUDE">
```

Then we use a parameter entity reference instead of the keyword:

```
<![%notes_allowed;[
  <!ELEMENT production_note (#PCDATA)>
]]>
```

The notes_allowed parameter entity can be redefined from outside this DTD. In particular, it can be redefined in the internal DTD subset of a document. This provides a switch individual documents can use to turn the production_note declaration on or off. This technique allows document authors to select only the functionality they need from the DTD.

Two DTD Examples

Some of the best techniques for DTD design only become apparent when you look at larger documents. In this section, we'll develop DTDs that cover the two different document formats for describing people that were presented in Examples 2-4 and 2-5 of the last chapter.

DTDs for Record-Like Documents

DTDs for record-like documents are very straightforward. They make heavy use of sequences, occasional use of choices, and almost no use of mixed content. Example 3-6 shows such a DTD. Since this is a small example, and since it's easier to understand when both the document and the DTD are on the same page, we've made this an internal DTD included in the document. However, it would be easy to extract it and store it in a separate file.

Example 3-6. A DTD describing people

```
<?xml version="1.0"?>
<!DOCTYPE person [
  <!ELEMENT person (name+, profession*)>
  <!ELEMENT name EMPTY>
  <!ATTLIST name first CDATA #REQUIRED
                 last  CDATA #REQUIRED>
  <!-- The first and last attributes are required to be present
       but they may be empty. For example,
       <name first="Cher" last=""> -->
  <!ELEMENT profession EMPTY>
  <!ATTLIST profession value CDATA #REQUIRED>
]>
<person>
  <name first="Alan" last="Turing"/>
  <profession value="computer scientist"/>
  <profession value="mathematician"/>
  <profession value="cryptographer"/>
</person>
```

The DTD here is contained completely inside the internal DTD subset. First a person ELEMENT declaration states that each person must have one or more name children, and zero or more profession children, in that order. This allows for the possibility that a person changes his name or uses aliases. It assumes that each person has at least one name but may not have a profession.

This declaration also requires that all name elements precede all profession elements. Here the DTD is less flexible than it ideally would be. There's no particular reason that the names have to come first. However, if we were to allow more random ordering, it would be hard to say that there must be at least one name. One of the weaknesses of DTDs is that it occasionally forces extra sequence order on you when all you really need is a constraint on the number of some element.

Both name and profession elements are empty so their declarations are very simple. The attribute declarations are a little more complex. In all three cases, the form of the attribute is open, so all three attributes are declared to have type CDATA. All three are also required. However, note the use of comments to suggest a solution for edge cases such as celebrities with no last names. Comments are an essential tool for making sense of otherwise obfuscated DTDs.

DTDs for Narrative Documents

Narrative-oriented DTDs tend be a lot looser and make much heavier use of mixed content than do DTDs that describe more database-like documents. Consequently, they tend to be written from the bottom up, starting with the smallest elements and building up to the largest. They also tend to use parameter entities to group together similar content specifications and attribute lists.

Example 3-7 is a standalone DTD for biographies like the one shown in Example 2-5 of the last chapter. Notice that not everything it declares is actually present in Example 2-5. That's often the case with narrative documents. For instance, not all web pages contain unordered lists, but the XHTML DTD still needs to declare the ul element for those XHTML documents that do include them. Also, notice that a few attributes present in Example 2-5 have been made into fixed defaults here.

Example 3-7. A narrative-oriented DTD for biographies

```
<!ATTLIST biography xmlns:xlink CDATA #FIXED
                              "http://www.w3.org/1999/xlink">

<!ELEMENT person (first_name, last_name)>
<!-- Birth and death dates are given in the form yyyy/mm/dd -->
<!ATTLIST person born CDATA #IMPLIED
                 died CDATA #IMPLIED>

<!ELEMENT date    (month, day, year)>
<!ELEMENT month   (#PCDATA)>
<!ELEMENT day     (#PCDATA)>
<!ELEMENT year    (#PCDATA)>

<!-- xlink:href must contain a URL.-->
<!ATTLIST emphasize xlink:type (simple) #IMPLIED
                    xlink:href CDATA   #IMPLIED>

<!ELEMENT profession (#PCDATA)>
<!ELEMENT footnote   (#PCDATA)>

<!-- The source is given according to the Chicago Manual of Style
     citation conventions -->
<!ATTLIST footnote source CDATA #REQUIRED>

<!ELEMENT first_name (#PCDATA)>
<!ELEMENT last_name  (#PCDATA)>

<!ELEMENT image EMPTY>
<!ATTLIST image source CDATA   #REQUIRED
                width  NMTOKEN #REQUIRED
                height NMTOKEN #REQUIRED
                ALT    CDATA   #IMPLIED
>
<!ENTITY % top_level "( #PCDATA | image | paragraph | definition
                      | person | profession | emphasize | last_name
                      | first_name | footnote | date )*">

<!ELEMENT paragraph  %top_level; >
<!ELEMENT definition %top_level; >
<!ELEMENT emphasize  %top_level; >
<!ELEMENT biography  %top_level; >
```

The root biography element has a classic mixed-content declaration. Since there are several elements that can contain other elements in a fairly unpredictable fashion, we group all the possible top-level elements (elements that appear as immediate children of the root element) in a single top_level entity reference. Then we can make all of them potential children of each other in a straightforward way. This also makes it much easier to add new elements in the future. That's important since this one small example is almost certainly not broad enough to cover all possible biographies.

Locating Standard DTDs

DTDs and validity are most important when you're exchanging data with others; they let you verify that you're sending what the receiver expects and vice versa. Of course, this works best if both ends of a conversation agree on which DTD and vocabulary they will use. There are many standard DTDs for different professions and disciplines and more are created every day. It is often better to use an established DTD and vocabulary than to design your own. However, there is no agreed-upon, central repository that documents and links to such efforts. The largest list of DTDs online is probably Robin Cover's list of XML applications at *http://www.oasis-open.org/cover/siteIndex.html#toc-applications*.

The W3C is one of the most prolific producers of standard XML DTDs. It has moved almost all of its future development to XML, including SVG, the Platform for Internet Content Selection (PICS), the Resource Description Framework (RDF), the Mathematical Markup Language (MathML), and even HTML itself. DTDs for these XML applications are generally published as appendixes to the specifications for the applications. The specifications are all found at *http://www.w3.org/TR/*.

However, XML isn't just for the Web, and far more activity is going on outside the W3C than inside it. Generally, within any one field, you should look to that field's standards bodies for DTDs relating to that area of interest. For example, the American Institute of Certified Public Accountants has published a DTD for the Extensible Financial Reporting Markup Language (XFRML). The Object Management Group (OMG) has published a DTD for describing Unified Modeling Language (UML) diagrams in XML. The Society of Automotive Engineers has published an XML application for emissions information as required by the 1990 U.S. Clean Air Act. Chances are that in any industry that makes heavy use of information technology, some group or groups, either formal or informal, are already working on DTDs that cover parts of that industry.

4

Namespaces

Namespaces have two purposes in XML:

1. To distinguish between elements and attributes from different vocabularies with different meanings that happen to share the same name

2. To group all the related elements and attributes from a single XML application together so that software can easily recognize them

The first purpose is easier to explain and grasp, but the second purpose is more important in practice.

Namespaces are implemented by attaching a prefix to each element and attribute. Each prefix is mapped to a URI by an `xmlns:prefix` attribute. Default URIs can also be provided for elements that don't have a prefix. Default namespaces are declared by `xmlns` attributes. Elements and attributes that are attached to the same URI are in the same namespace. Elements from many XML applications are identified by standard URIs.

In an XML 1.1 document, an Internationalized Resource Identifier (IRI) can be used instead of a URI. An IRI is just like a URI except it can contain non-ASCII characters such as é and π. In practice, parsers don't check that namespace names are legal URIs in XML 1.0, so the distinction is mostly academic.

The Need for Namespaces

Some documents combine markup from multiple XML applications. For example, an XHTML document may contain both SVG pictures and MathML equations. An XSLT stylesheet will contain both XSLT instructions and elements from the result-tree vocabulary. And XLinks are always symbiotic with the elements of the document in which they appear since XLink itself doesn't define any elements, only attributes.

In some cases, these applications may use the same name to refer to different things. For example, in SVG a set element sets the value of an attribute for a specified duration of time, while in MathML, a set element represents a mathematical set such as the set of all positive even numbers. It's essential to know when you're working with a MathML set and when you're working with an SVG set. Otherwise, validation, rendering, indexing, and many other tasks will get confused and fail.

Consider Example 4-1. This is a simple list of paintings, including the title of each painting, the date each was painted, the artist who painted it, and a description of the painting.

Example 4-1. A list of paintings

```
<?xml version="1.0" encoding="ISO-8859-1" standalone="yes"?>
<catalog>

  <painting>
    <title>Memory of the Garden at Etten</title>
    <artist>Vincent Van Gogh</artist>
    <date>November, 1888</date>
    <description>
      Two women look to the left. A third works in her garden.
    </description>
  </painting>

  <painting>
    <title>The Swing</title>
    <artist>Pierre-Auguste Renoir</artist>
    <date>1876</date>
    <description>
      A young girl on a swing. Two men and a toddler watch.
    </description>
  </painting>

  <!-- Many more paintings... -->

</catalog>
```

Now suppose that Example 4-1 is to be served as a web page and you want to make it accessible to search engines. One possibility is to use the Resource Description Framework (RDF) to embed metadata in the page. This describes the page for any search engines or other robots that might come along. Using the Dublin Core metadata vocabulary (*http://purl.oclc.org/dc/*), a standard vocabulary for library catalog–style information that can be encoded in XML or other syntaxes, an RDF description of this page might look something like this:

```
<RDF>
  <Description
     about="http://www.cafeconleche.org/examples/impressionists.xml">
    <title> Impressionist Paintings </title>
    <creator> Elliotte Rusty Harold </creator>
```

```
    <description>
      A list of famous impressionist paintings organized
      by painter and date
    </description>
    <date>2000-08-22</date>
  </Description>
</RDF>
```

Here we've used the Description and RDF elements from RDF and the title, creator, description, and date elements from the Dublin Core. We have no choice about these names; they are established by their respective specifications. If we want software that understands RDF and the Dublin Core to understand our documents, then we have to use these names. Example 4-2 combines this description with the actual list of paintings.

Example 4-2. A list of paintings, including catalog information about the list

```
<?xml version="1.0" encoding="ISO-8859-1" standalone="yes"?>
<catalog>

  <RDF>
    <Description
        about="http://www.cafeconleche.org/examples/impressionists.xml">
      <title> Impressionist Paintings </title>
      <creator> Elliotte Rusty Harold </creator>
      <description>
        A list of famous impressionist paintings organized
        by painter and date
      </description>
      <date>2000-08-22</date>
    </Description>
  </RDF>

  <painting>
    <title>Memory of the Garden at Etten</title>
    <artist>Vincent Van Gogh</artist>
    <date>November, 1888</date>
    <description>
      Two women look to the left. A third works in her garden.
    </description>
  </painting>

  <painting>
    <title>The Swing</title>
    <artist>Pierre-Auguste Renoir</artist>
    <date>1876</date>
    <description>
      A young girl on a swing. Two men and a toddler watch.
    </description>
  </painting>

  <!-- Many more paintings... -->

</catalog>
```

Now we have a problem. Several elements have been overloaded with different meanings in different parts of the document. The title element is used for both the title of the page and the title of a painting. The date element is used for both the date the page was written and the date the painting was painted. One description element describes pages, while another describes paintings.

This presents all sorts of problems. Validation is difficult because catalog and Dublin Core elements with the same name have different content specifications. Web browsers may want to hide the page description while showing the painting description, but not all stylesheet languages can tell the difference between the two. Processing software may understand the date format used in the Dublin Core date element, but not the more free-form format used in the painting date element.

We could change the names of the elements from our vocabulary, painting_title instead of title, date_painted instead of date, and so on. However, this is inconvenient if you already have a lot of documents marked up in the old version of the vocabulary. And it may not be possible to do this in all cases, especially if the name collisions occur not because of conflicts between your vocabulary and a standard vocabulary, but because of conflicts between two or more standard vocabularies. For instance, RDF just barely avoids a collision with the Dublin Core over the Description and description elements.

In other cases, there may not be any name conflicts, but it may still be important for software to determine quickly and decisively which XML application a given element or attribute belongs to. For instance, an XSLT processor needs to distinguish between XSLT instructions and literal result-tree elements.

Namespace Syntax

Namespaces disambiguate elements with the same name from each other by assigning elements and attributes to URIs. Generally, all the elements from one XML application are assigned to one URI, and all the elements from a different XML application are assigned to a different URI. These URIs are called *namespace names*. The URIs partition the elements and attributes into disjoint sets. Elements with the same name but different URIs are different types. Elements with the same name and the same URIs are the same. Most of the time there's a one-to-one mapping between namespaces and XML applications, although a few applications use multiple namespaces to subdivide different parts of the application. For instance, XSL uses different namespaces for XSL Transformations (XSLT) and XSL Formatting Objects (XSL-FO).

Qualified Names, Prefixes, and Local Parts

Since URIs frequently contain characters such as /, %, and ~ that are not legal in XML names, short prefixes such as rdf and xsl stand in for them in element and attribute names. Each prefix is associated with a URI. Names whose prefixes are associated with the same URI are in the same namespace. Names whose prefixes are associated with different URIs are in different namespaces. Prefixed elements and attributes in namespaces have names that contain exactly one colon. They look like this:

```
rdf:description
xlink:type
xsl:template
```

Everything before the colon is called the *prefix*. Everything after the colon is called the *local part*. The complete name, including the colon, is called the *qualified name*, *QName*, or *raw name*. The prefix identifies the namespace to which the element or attribute belongs. The local part identifies the particular element or attribute within the namespace.

In a document that contains both SVG and MathML set elements, one could be an svg:set element, and the other could be a mathml:set element. Then there'd be no confusion between them. In an XSLT stylesheet that transforms documents into XSL formatting objects, the XSLT processor would recognize elements with the prefix xsl as XSLT instructions and elements with the prefix fo as literal result elements.

Prefixes may be composed from any legal XML name character except the colon. The three-letter prefix xml used for standard XML attributes such as xml:space, xml:lang, and xml:base is always bound to the URI http://www.w3.org/XML/1998/ namespace and need not be explicitly declared. Other prefixes beginning with the three letters xml (in any combination of case) are reserved for use by XML and its related specifications. Otherwise, you're free to name your prefixes in any way that's convenient. One further restriction namespaces add to XML is that the local part may not contain any colons. In short, the only legal use of a colon in XML is to separate a namespace prefix from the local part in a qualified name.

Binding Prefixes to URIs

Each prefix in a qualified name must be associated with a URI. For example, all XSLT elements are associated with the http://www.w3.org/1999/XSL/Transform URI. The customary prefix xsl is used in place of the longer URI http://www.w3.org/1999/XSL/Transform.

 You can't use the URI in the name directly. For one thing, the slashes in most URIs aren't legal characters in XML names. However, it's occasionally useful to refer to the full name without assuming a particular prefix. One convention used on many XML mailing lists and in XML documentation is to enclose the URI in curly braces and prefix it to the name. For example, the qualified name xsl:template might be written as the full name {http://www.w3.org/1999/XSL/Transform}template. Another convention is to append the local name to the namespace name after a sharp sign so that it becomes a URI fragment identifier. For example, http://www.w3.org/1999/XSL/Transform#template. However, both forms are only conveniences for communication among human beings when the URI is important but the prefix isn't. Neither an XML parser nor an XSLT processor will accept or understand the long forms.

Prefixes are bound to namespace URIs by attaching an xmlns:*prefix* attribute to the prefixed element or one of its ancestors. (The *prefix* should be replaced by the actual prefix used.) For example, the xmlns:rdf attribute of this rdf:RDF element binds the prefix rdf to the namespace URI http://www.w3.org/TR/REC-rdf-syntax#:

```
<rdf:RDF xmlns:rdf="http://www.w3.org/TR/REC-rdf-syntax#">
 <rdf:Description
    about="http://www.cafeconleche.org/examples/impressionists.xml">
    <title> Impressionist Paintings </title>
    <creator> Elliotte Rusty Harold </creator>
    <description>
     A list of famous impressionist paintings organized
     by painter and date
    </description>
    <date>2000-08-22</date>
 </rdf:Description>
</rdf:RDF>
```

Bindings have scope within the element where they're declared and within its contents. The xmlns:rdf attribute declares the rdf prefix for the rdf:RDF element, as well as its descendant elements. An RDF processor will recognize rdf:RDF and rdf:Description as RDF elements because both have prefixes bound to the particular URI specified by the RDF specification. It will not consider the title, creator, description, and date elements to be RDF elements because they do not have prefixes bound to the http://www.w3.org/TR/REC-rdf-syntax# URI.

The prefix can be declared in the topmost element that uses the prefix or in any ancestor thereof. This may be the root element of the document, or it may be an element at a lower level. For instance, the Dublin Core elements could be attached to the http://purl.org/dc/ namespace by adding an xmlns:dc attribute to the rdf:Description element, as shown in Example 4-3, since all Dublin Core elements in this document appear inside a single rdf:Description element. In other documents that spread the elements out more, it might be more convenient to put the namespace declaration on the root element. If necessary, a single element can include multiple namespace declarations for different prefixes.

Example 4-3. A document containing both SVG and XLinks

```
<?xml version="1.0" encoding="ISO-8859-1" standalone="yes"?>
<catalog>

 <rdf:RDF xmlns:rdf="http://www.w3.org/TR/REC-rdf-syntax#">
   <rdf:Description xmlns:dc="http://purl.org/dc/"
     about="http://www.cafeconleche.org/examples/impressionists.xml">
    <dc:title> Impressionist Paintings </dc:title>
    <dc:creator> Elliotte Rusty Harold </dc:creator>
    <dc:description>
     A list of famous impressionist paintings organized
     by painter and date
    </dc:description>
    <dc:date>2000-08-22</dc:date>
   </rdf:Description>
 </rdf:RDF>
```

Example 4-3. A document containing both SVG and XLinks (continued)

```
<painting>
  <title>Memory of the Garden at Etten</title>
  <artist>Vincent Van Gogh</artist>
  <date>November, 1888</date>
  <description>
    Two women look to the left. A third works in her garden.
  </description>
</painting>

<painting>
  <title>The Swing</title>
  <artist>Pierre-Auguste Renoir</artist>
  <date>1876</date>
  <description>
    A young girl on a swing. Two men and a toddler watch.
  </description>
</painting>

<!-- Many more paintings... -->

</catalog>
```

A DTD for this document can include different content specifications for the dc:description and description elements. A stylesheet can attach different styles to dc:title and title. Software that sorts the catalog by date can pay attention to the date elements and ignore the dc:date elements.

In this example, the elements without prefixes, such as catalog, painting, description, artist, and title, are not in any namespace. Furthermore, unprefixed attributes (such as the about attribute of rdf:Description in the previous example) are never in any namespace. Being an attribute of an element in the http://www.w3.org/TR/REC-rdf-syntax# namespace is not sufficient to put the attribute in the http://www.w3.org/TR/REC-rdf-syntax# namespace. The only way an attribute belongs to a namespace is if it has a declared prefix, like rdf:about.

In XML 1.1 there's one exception to the rule that unprefixed attributes are never in a namespace. In XML 1.1/Namespaces 1.1, the xmlns attribute is defined to be in the namespace http://www.w3.org/2000/xmlns/. In XML 1.0/Namespaces 1.0, the xmlns attribute is not in any namespace.

It is possible to redefine a prefix within a document so that in one element the prefix refers to one namespace URI, while in another element it refers to a different namespace URI. In this case, the closest ancestor element that declares the prefix takes precedence. However, in most cases, redefining prefixes is a very bad idea that only leads to confusion and is not something you should actually do.

 In XML 1.1, you can also "undeclare" a namespace by defining it as having an empty ("") value.

Namespace URIs

Many XML applications have customary prefixes. For example, SVG elements often use the prefix svg, and RDF elements often have the prefix rdf. However, these prefixes are simply conventions and can be changed based on necessity, convenience, or whim. Before a prefix can be used, it must be bound to a URI like http://www.w3.org/2000/svg or http://www.w3.org/1999/02/22-rdf-syntax-ns#. It is these URIs that are standardized, not the prefixes. The prefix can change as long as the URI stays the same. An RDF processor looks for the RDF URI, not any particular prefix. As long as nobody outside the *w3.org* domain uses namespace URIs in the *w3.org* domain, and as long as the W3C keeps a careful eye on what its people are using for namespaces, all conflicts can be avoided.

Namespace URIs do not necessarily point to any actual document or page. In fact, they don't have to use the http scheme. They might even use some other protocol like mailto in which URIs don't even point to documents. However, if you're defining your own namespace using an http URI, it would not be a bad idea to place some documentation for the XML application at the namespace URI. The W3C got tired of receiving broken-link reports for the namespace URIs in their specifications, so they added some simple pages at their namespace URIs. For more formal purposes that offer some hope of automated resolution and other features, you can place a Resource Directory Description Language (RDDL) document at the namespace URI. This possibility will be discussed further in Chapter 15. You are by no means required to do this, though. Many namespace URIs lead to 404-Not Found errors when you actually plug them into a web browser. Namespace URIs are purely formal identifiers. They are not the addresses of a page, and they are not meant to be followed as links.

Parsers compare namespace URIs on a character-by-character basis. If the URIs differ in even a single normally insignificant place, then they define separate namespaces. For instance, the following URLs all point to the same page:

> *http://www.w3.org/1999/02/22-rdf-syntax-ns#*
> *http://WWW.W3.ORG/1999/02/22-rdf-syntax-ns#*
> *http://www.w3.org/1999/02/22-rdf-syntax-ns/*
> *http://www.w3.org/1999/02/22-rdf-syntax-ns/index.rdf*

However, only the first is the correct namespace name for the RDF. These four URLs identify four separate namespaces.

Setting a Default Namespace with the xmlns Attribute

You often know that all the content of a particular element will come from a particular XML application. For instance, inside an SVG svg element, you're only likely to find other SVG elements. You can indicate that an unprefixed element and all its unprefixed descendant elements belong to a particular namespace by attaching an xmlns attribute with no prefix to the top element. For example:

```
<svg xmlns="http://www.w3.org/2000/svg"
     width="12cm" height="10cm">
  <ellipse rx="110" ry="130" />
  <rect x="4cm" y="1cm" width="3cm" height="6cm" />
</svg>
```

Here, although no elements have any prefixes, the svg, ellipse, and rect elements are in the http://www.w3.org/2000/svg namespace.

The attributes are a different story. Default namespaces only apply to elements, not to attributes. Thus, in the previous example, the width, height, rx, ry, x, and y attributes are not in any namespace.

You can change the default namespace within a particular element by adding an xmlns attribute to the element. Example 4-4 is an XML document that initially sets the default namespace to http://www.w3.org/1999/xhtml for all the XHTML elements. This namespace declaration applies within most of the document. However, the svg element has an xmlns attribute that resets the default namespace to http://www.w3.org/2000/svg for itself and its content. The XLink information is included in attributes, however, so these must be placed in the XLink namespace using explicit prefixes.

Example 4-4. An XML document that uses default namespaces

```
<?xml version="1.0"?>
<html xmlns="http://www.w3.org/1999/xhtml"
      xmlns:xlink="http://www.w3.org/1999/xlink">
  <head><title>Three Namespaces</title></head>
  <body>
    <h1 align="center">An Ellipse and a Rectangle</h1>
    <svg xmlns="http://www.w3.org/2000/svg"
         width="12cm" height="10cm">
      <ellipse rx="110" ry="130" />
      <rect x="4cm" y="1cm" width="3cm" height="6cm" />
    </svg>
    <p xlink:type="simple" xlink:href="ellipses.html">
      More about ellipses
    </p>
    <p xlink:type="simple" xlink:href="rectangles.html">
      More about rectangles
    </p>
    <hr/>
    <p>Last Modified May 13, 2000</p>
  </body>
</html>
```

The default namespace does not apply to any elements or attributes with prefixes. These still belong to whatever namespace their prefix is bound to. However, an unprefixed child element of a prefixed element still belongs to the default namespace.

How Parsers Handle Namespaces

Namespaces are not part of XML 1.0. They were invented about a year after the original XML specification was released. However, care was taken to ensure backward compatibility. Thus, an XML parser that does not know about namespaces should not have any trouble reading a document that uses namespaces. Colons are legal characters in XML element and attribute names. The parser will simply report that some of the names contain colons.

A namespace-aware parser does add a couple of checks to the normal well-formedness checks that a parser performs. Specifically, it checks to see that all prefixes are mapped to URIs. It will reject documents that use unmapped prefixes (except for xml and xmlns when used as specified in the XML or "Namespaces in XML" specifications). It will further reject any element or attribute names that contain more than one colon. Otherwise, it behaves almost exactly like a non-namespace-aware parser. Other software that sits on top of the raw XML parser—an XSLT engine, for example—may treat elements differently depending on which namespace they belong to. However, the XML parser itself mostly doesn't care as long as all well-formedness and namespace constraints are met. Many parsers let you turn namespace processing on or off as you see fit.

Namespaces and DTDs

Namespaces are completely independent of DTDs and can be used in both valid and invalid documents. A document can have a DTD but not use namespaces or use namespaces but not have a DTD. It can use both namespaces and DTDs or neither namespaces nor DTDs. Namespaces do not in any way change DTD syntax nor do they change the definition of validity. For instance, the DTD of a valid document that uses an element named dc:title must include an ELEMENT declaration properly specifying the content of the dc:title element. For example:

```
<!ELEMENT dc:title (#PCDATA)>
```

The name of the element in the document must exactly match the name of the element in the DTD, including the prefix. The DTD cannot omit the prefix and simply declare a title element. The same is true of prefixed attributes. For instance, if an element used in the document has xlink:type and xlink:href attributes, then the DTD must declare the xlink:type and xlink:href attributes, not simply type and href.

Conversely, if an element uses an xmlns attribute to set the default namespace and does not attach prefixes to elements, then the names of the elements must be declared without prefixes in the DTD. The validator neither knows nor cares about the existence of namespaces. All it sees is that some element and attribute names happen to contain colons; as far as it's concerned, such names are perfectly valid as long as they're declared.

Parameter Entity References for Namespace Prefixes

Requiring DTDs to declare the prefixed names, instead of the raw names or some combination of local part and namespace URI, makes it difficult to change the prefix in valid documents. The problem is that changing the prefix requires changing all declarations that use that prefix in the DTD. However, with a little forethought, parameter entity references can alleviate the pain quite a bit.

The trick is to define both the namespace prefix and the colon that separates the prefix from the local name as parameter entities, like this:

```
<!ENTITY % dc-prefix "dc">
<!ENTITY % dc-colon ":">
```

Namespaces

The second step is to define the qualified names as more parameter entity references, like these:

```
<!ENTITY % dc-title       "%dc-prefix;%dc-colon;title">
<!ENTITY % dc-creator     "%dc-prefix;%dc-colon;creator">
<!ENTITY % dc-description "%dc-prefix;%dc-colon;description">
<!ENTITY % dc-date        "%dc-prefix;%dc-colon;date">
```

Do not omit this step and try to use the dc-prefix and dc-colon parameter entities directly in ELEMENT and ATTLIST declarations. This will fail because XML parsers add extra space around the entity's replacement text when they're used outside another entity's replacement text.

Then you use the entity references for the qualified name in all declarations, like this:

```
<!ELEMENT %dc-title; (#PCDATA)>
<!ELEMENT %dc-creator; (#PCDATA)>
<!ELEMENT %dc-description; (#PCDATA)>
<!ELEMENT %dc-date; (#PCDATA)>
<!ELEMENT rdf:Description
  ((%dc-title; | %dc-creator; | %dc-description; | %dc-date; )*)
>
```

Now a document that needs to change the prefix simply changes the parameter entity definitions. In some cases, this will be done by editing the DTD directly. In others, it may be done by overriding the definitions in the document's internal DTD subset. For example, to change the prefix from dc to dublin, you'd add this entity definition somewhere in the DTD before the normal definition:

```
<!ENTITY % dc-prefix "dublin">
```

If you wanted to use the default namespace instead of explicit prefixes, you'd redefine both the dc-prefix and dc-colon entities as the empty string, like this:

```
<!ENTITY % dc-prefix "">
<!ENTITY % dc-colon  "">
```

5

Internationalization

We've told you that XML documents contain text, but we haven't yet told you what kind of text they contain. In this chapter we rectify that omission. XML documents contain Unicode text. Unicode is a character set large enough to include all the world's living languages and a few dead ones. It can be written in a variety of encodings, including UCS-2 and the ASCII superset UTF-8. However, since Unicode text editors are not ubiquitous, XML documents may also be written in other character sets and encodings, which are converted to Unicode when the document is parsed. The encoding declaration specifies which character set a document uses. You can use character references, such as θ, to insert Unicode characters like θ that aren't available in the legacy character set in which a document is written.

Computers don't really understand text. They don't recognize the Latin letter Z, the Greek letter γ, or the Han ideograph 鵡. All a computer understands are numbers such as 90, 947, or 40,821. A *character set* maps particular characters, like Z, to particular numbers, like 90. These numbers are called *code points*. A *character encoding* determines how those code points are represented in bytes. For instance, the code point 90 can be encoded as a signed byte, a little-endian unsigned short, a 4-byte, two's complement, a big-endian integer, or in some still more complicated fashion.

A human script like Cyrillic may be written in multiple character sets, such as KOI8-R, Unicode, or ISO-8859-5. A character set like Unicode may then be encoded in multiple encodings, such as UTF-8, UCS-2, or UTF-16. However, most simpler character sets, such as ASCII and KOI8-R, have only one encoding.

Character-Set Metadata

Some environments keep track of which encodings particular documents are written in. For instance, web servers that transmit XML documents precede them with an HTTP header that looks something like this:

```
HTTP/1.1 200 OK
Date: Sun, 28 Oct 2001 11:05:42 GMT
Server: Apache/1.3.19 (Unix) mod_jk mod_perl/1.25 mod_fastcgi/2.2.10
Connection: close
Transfer-Encoding: chunked
Content-Type: text/xml; charset=iso-8859-1
```

The Content-Type field of the HTTP header provides the MIME media type of the document. This may, as shown here, specify which character set the document is written in. An XML parser reading this document from a web server should use this information to determine the document's character encoding.

Many web servers omit the charset parameter from the MIME media type. In this case, if the MIME media type is text/xml, then the document is assumed to be in the US-ASCII encoding. If the MIME media type is application/xml, then the parser attempts to guess the character set by reading the first few bytes of the document.

Since ASCII is almost never an appropriate character set for an XML document, application/xml is much preferred over text/xml. Unfortunately, most web servers including Apache 2.0.36 and earlier are configured to use text/xml by default. If you're running such a version you should probably upgrade before serving XML files.*

We've focused on MIME types in HTTP headers because that's the most common place where character set metadata is applied to XML documents. However, MIME types are also used in some filesystems (e.g., the BeOS), in email, and in other environments. Other systems may provide other forms of character set metadata. If such metadata is available for a document, whatever form it takes, the parser should use it, although in practice this is an area where not all parsers and programs are as conformant as they should be.

The Encoding Declaration

Every XML document should have an *encoding declaration* as part of its XML declaration. The encoding declaration tells the parser in which character set the document is written. It's used only when other metadata from outside the file is not available. For example, this XML declaration says that the document uses the character encoding US-ASCII:

```
<?xml version="1.0" encoding="US-ASCII" standalone="yes"?>
```

This one states that the document uses the Latin-1 character set, although it uses the more official name ISO-8859-1:

```
<?xml version="1.0" encoding="ISO-8859-1"?>
```

---

* You could fix Apache's MIME types instead of upgrading, but you really should upgrade. All versions of Apache that are old enough to have the wrong MIME type for XML also have a number of security holes that have since been plugged.

Even if metadata is not available, the encoding declaration can be omitted if the document is written in either the UTF-8 or UTF-16 encodings of Unicode. UTF-8 is a strict superset of ASCII, so ASCII files can be legal XML documents without an encoding declaration. Note, however, that this only applies to genuine, pure 7-bit ASCII files. It does not include the extended ASCII character sets that some editors produce with characters like ©, ç, or ".

Even if character set metadata is available, many parsers ignore it. Thus, we highly recommend including an encoding declaration in all your XML documents that are not written in UTF-8 or UTF-16. It certainly never hurts to do so.

Text Declarations

XML documents may be composed of multiple parsed entities, as you learned in Chapter 3. These external parsed entities may be DTD fragments or chunks of XML that will be inserted into the master document using external general entity references. In either case, the external parsed entity does not necessarily use the same character set as the master document. Indeed, one external parsed entity may be referenced in several different files, each of which is written in a different character set. Therefore, it is important to specify the character set for an external parsed entity independently of the character set that the including document uses.

To accomplish this task, each external parsed entity should have a *text declaration*. If present, the text declaration must be the very first thing in the external parsed entity. For example, this text declaration says that the entity is encoded in the KOI8-R character set:

```
<?xml version="1.0" encoding="KOI8-R"?>
```

The text declaration looks like an XML declaration. It has version info and an encoding declaration. However, a text declaration must not have a standalone declaration. Furthermore, the version information may be omitted. A legal text declaration that specifies the encoding as KOI8-R might look like this:

```
<?xml encoding="KOI8-R"?>
```

However, this is not a legal XML declaration.

Example 5-1 shows an external parsed entity containing several verses from Pushkin's *The Bronze Horseman* in a Cyrillic script. The text declaration identifies the encoding as KOI8-R. Example 5-1 is not a well-formed XML document because it has no root element. It exists only for inclusion in other documents.

Example 5-1. An external parsed entity with a text declaration identifying the character set as KOI8-R

```
<?xml version="1.0" encoding="KOI8-R"?>
<стих>Была ужасная пора,</стих>
<стих>Об ней свежо воспоминанье...</стих>
<стих>Об ней друзья мои, для вас</стих>
<стих>Начну свое повествованье.</стих>
<стих>Печален будет мой рассказ</стих>
```

External DTD subsets reside in external parsed entities and, thus, may have text declarations. Indeed, they should have text declarations if they're written in a character set other than one of the Unicode's variants. Example 5-2 shows a DTD fragment written in KOI8-R that might be used to validate Example 5-1 after it is included as part of a larger document.

Example 5-2. A DTD with a text declaration identifying the character set as KOI8-R

```
<?xml version="1.0" encoding="KOI8-R"?>
<!ELEMENT стих(#PCDATA)>
```

XML-Defined Character Sets

An XML parser is required to handle the UTF-16 and UTF-8 encodings or Unicode (about which more follows). However, XML parsers are allowed to understand and process many other character sets. In particular, the specification recommends that processors recognize and be able to read these encodings:

UTF-8	UTF-16
ISO-10646-UCS-2	ISO-10646-UCS-4
ISO-8859-1	ISO-8859-2
ISO-8859-3	ISO-8859-4
ISO-8859-5	ISO-8859-6
ISO-8859-7	ISO-8859-8
ISO-8859-9	ISO-8859-JP
Shift_JIS	EUC-JP

Many XML processors understand other legacy encodings. For instance, processors written in Java often understand all character sets available in the Java virtual machine. For a list, see *http://java.sun.com/products/j2se/1.4.2/docs/guide/intl/ encoding.doc.html*. Furthermore, some processors may recognize aliases for these encodings; both Latin-1 and 8859_1 are sometimes used as synonyms for ISO-8859-1. However, using these names limits your document's portability. We recommend that you use standard names for standard encodings. For encodings whose standard name isn't given by the XML 1.0 specification, use one of the names registered with the Internet Assigned Numbers Authority (IANA), listed at *ftp://ftp.isi.edu/in-notes/iana/assignments/character-sets*. Knowing the name of a character set and saving a file in that set does not mean that your XML parser can read such a file, however. XML parsers are only required to support UTF-8 and UTF-16. They are not required to support the hundreds of different legacy encodings used around the world.

Unicode

Unicode is an international standard character set that can be used to write documents in almost any language you're likely to speak, learn, or encounter in your lifetime, barring alien abduction. Version 4.0.1, the current version as of June, 2004, contains 96,447 characters from most of Earth's living languages as well as several dead ones. Unicode easily covers the Latin alphabet, in which most of this book is written. Unicode also covers Greek-derived scripts, including ancient and modern Greek and the Cyrillic scripts used in Serbia and much of the former Soviet Union. Unicode covers several ideographic scripts, including the Han character set used for Chinese and Japanese, the Korean Hangul syllabary, and phonetic representations of these languages, including Katakana and Hiragana. It covers the right-to-left Arabic and Hebrew scripts. It covers various scripts native to the Indian subcontinent, including Devanagari, Thai, Bengali, Tibetan, and many more. And that's still less than half of the scripts in Unicode 4.0. Probably less than one person in a thousand today speaks a language that cannot be reasonably represented in Unicode. In the future, Unicode will add still more characters, making this fraction even smaller. Unicode can potentially hold more than a million characters, but no one is willing to say in public where they think most of the remaining million characters will come from.*

The Unicode character set assigns characters to code points; that is, numbers. These numbers can then be encoded in a variety of schemes, including:

- UCS-2
- UCS-4
- UTF-8
- UTF-16

UCS-2 and UTF-16

UCS-2, also known as ISO-10646-UCS-2, represents each character as a two-byte, unsigned integer between 0 and 65,535. Thus the capital letter *A*, code point 65 in Unicode, is represented by the two bytes 00 and 41 (in hexadecimal). The capital letter *B*, code point 66, is represented by the two bytes 00 and 42. The two bytes 03 and A3 represent the capital Greek letter Σ, code point 931.

UCS-2 comes in two variations, big endian and little endian. In big-endian UCS-2, the most significant byte of the character comes first. In little-endian UCS-2, the order is reversed. Thus, in big-endian UCS-2, the letter *A* is #x0041.† In little-endian UCS-2, the bytes are swapped, and *A* is #x4100. In big-endian UCS-2, the letter *B* is #x0042; in little-endian UCS-2, it's #x4200. In big-endian UCS-2, the letter Σ is #x03A3; in little-endian UCS-2, it's #xA303. In this book we use big-endian notation, but parsers cannot assume this. They must be able to determine the endianness from the document itself.

To distinguish between big-endian and little-endian UCS-2, a document encoded in UCS-2 customarily begins with Unicode character #xFEFF, the zero-width nonbreaking space, more commonly called the *byte-order mark*. This character has the advantage of being invisible. Furthermore, if its bytes are swapped, the resulting #xFFFE character doesn't actually exist. Thus, a program can look at the

---

* After a few beers, some developers are willing to admit that they're preparing for a day when we're part of a Galactic Federation of thousands of intelligent species.

† For reasons that will become apparent shortly, this book has adopted the convention that #x precedes hexadecimal numbers. Every two hexadecimal digits map to one byte.

first two bytes of a UCS-2 document and tell immediately whether the document is big endian, depending on whether those bytes are #xFEFF or #xFFFE.

UCS-2 has three major disadvantages, however:

- Files containing mostly Latin text are about twice as large in UCS-2 as they are in a single-byte character set such as ASCII or Latin-1.
- UCS-2 is not backward- or forward-compatible with ASCII. Tools that are accustomed to single-byte character sets often can't process a UCS-2 file in a reasonable way, even if the file only contains characters from the ASCII character set. For instance, a program written in C that expects the zero byte to terminate strings will choke on a UCS-2 file containing mostly English text because almost every other byte is zero.
- UCS-2 is limited to 65,536 characters.

The last problem isn't so important in practice, since the first 65,536 code points of Unicode nonetheless manage to cover most people's needs except for dead languages like Ugaritic, fictional scripts like Tengwar, and musical and some mathematical symbols. Unicode does, however, provide a means of representing code points beyond 65,535 by recognizing certain two-byte sequences as half of a surrogate pair. A Unicode document that uses UCS-2 plus surrogate pairs is said to be in the UTF-16 encoding.

The other two problems, however, are more likely to affect most developers. UTF-8 is an alternative encoding for Unicode that addresses both.

UTF-8

UTF-8 is a variable-length encoding of Unicode. Characters 0 through 127, that is, the ASCII character set, are encoded in one byte each, exactly as they would be in ASCII. In ASCII, the byte with value 65 represents the letter A. In UTF-8, the byte with the value 65 also represents the letter A. There is a one-to-one identity mapping from ASCII characters to UTF-8 bytes. Thus, pure ASCII files are also acceptable UTF-8 files.

UTF-8 represents the characters from 128 to 2,047, a range that covers the most common non-ideographic scripts, in two bytes each. Characters from 2,048 to 65,535—mostly from Chinese, Japanese, and Korean—are represented in three bytes each. Characters with code points above 65,535 are represented in four bytes each. For a file that's mostly Latin text, this effectively halves the file size from what it would be in UCS-2. However, for a file that's primarily Japanese, Chinese, Korean, or one of the languages of the Indian subcontinent, the file size can grow by 50%. For most other living languages, the file size is close to the same as it would be in UCS-2.

UTF-8 is probably the most broadly supported encoding of Unicode. For instance, it's how Java *.class* files store strings, it's the native encoding of the BeOS, and it's the default encoding an XML processor assumes unless told otherwise by a byte-order mark or an encoding declaration. Chances are pretty good that if a program tells you it's saving Unicode, it's really saving UTF-8.

ISO Character Sets

Unicode has only recently become commonplace. Previously, the space and processing costs associated with Unicode files caused vendors to prefer smaller, single-byte character sets that could only handle English and a few other languages of interest, but not the full panoply of human language. ISO, the International Standards Organization, has standardized 15 of these character sets as ISO standard 8859. For all of these single-byte character sets, characters 0 through 127 are identical to the ASCII character set, characters 128 through 159 are the C1 controls, and characters 160 through 255 are the additional characters needed for scripts such as Greek, Cyrillic, and Turkish.

ISO-8859-1 (Latin-1)
: ASCII plus the accented letters and other characters needed for most Latin-alphabet Western European languages, including Danish, Dutch, Finnish, French, German, Icelandic, Italian, Norwegian, Portuguese, Spanish, and Swedish.

ISO-8859-2 (Latin-2)
: ASCII plus the accented letters and other characters needed to write most Latin-alphabet Central and Eastern European languages, including Czech, German, Hungarian, Polish, Romanian, Croatian, Slovak, Slovenian, and Sorbian.

ISO-8859-3 (Latin-3)
: ASCII plus the accented letters and other characters needed to write Esperanto, Maltese, and Turkish.

ISO-8859-4 (Latin-4)
: ASCII plus the accented letters and other characters needed to write most Baltic languages, including Estonian, Latvian, Lithuanian, Greenlandic, and Lappish. Now deprecated. New applications should use 8859-10 (Latin-6) or 8859-13 (Latin-7) instead.

ISO-8859-5
: ASCII plus the Cyrillic alphabet used for Russian and many other languages of the former Soviet Union and other Slavic countries, including Bulgarian, Byelorussian, Macedonian, Serbian, and Ukrainian.

ISO-8859-6
: ASCII plus basic Arabic. However, this character set doesn't have the extra letters needed for non-Arabic languages written in the Arabic script, such as Farsi and Urdu.

ISO-8859-7
: ASCII plus modern Greek. This set does not have the extra letters and accents necessary for ancient and Byzantine Greek.

ISO-8859-8
: ASCII plus the Hebrew script used for Hebrew and Yiddish.

ISO-8859-9 (Latin-5)
: Essentially the same as Latin-1, except six Icelandic letters have been replaced by six Turkish letters.

ISO-8859-10 (Latin-6)
> ASCII plus accented letters and other characters needed to write most Baltic languages, including Estonian, Icelandic, Latvian, Lithuanian, Greenlandic, and Lappish.

ISO-8859-11
> ASCII plus Thai.

ISO-8859-13 (Latin-7)
> Yet another attempt to cover the Baltic region properly. Very similar to Latin-6, except for some question marks.

ISO-8859-14 (Latin-8)
> ASCII plus the Celtic languages, including Gaelic and Welsh.

ISO-8859-15 (Latin-9, Latin-0)
> A revised version of Latin-1 that replaces some unnecessary symbols, such as 1/4, with extra French and Finnish letters. Instead of the international currency sign, these sets include the Euro sign, €.

ISO-8859-16, (Latin-10)
> A revised version of Latin-2 that works better for Romanian. Other languages supported by this character set include Albanian, Croatian, English, Finnish, French, German, Hungarian, Italian, Polish, and Slovenian.

Various national standards bodies have produced other character sets to cover scripts and languages of interest within their geographic and political boundaries. For example, the Korea Industrial Standards Association developed the KS C 5601-1992 standard for encoding Korean. These national standard character sets can be used in XML documents as well, provided that you include the proper encoding declaration in the document and the parser knows how to translate these character sets into Unicode.

Platform-Dependent Character Sets

In addition to the standard character sets discussed previously, many vendors have at one time or another produced proprietary character sets to meet the needs of their specific platform. Often, they contain special characters the vendor saw a need for, such as Apple's trademarked open apple or the box-drawing characters, such as ⊦ and ⊣, used for cell boundaries in early DOS spreadsheets. Microsoft, IBM, and Apple are the three most prolific inventors of character sets. The single most common such set is probably Microsoft's Cp1252, a variant of Latin-1 that replaces the C1 controls with more graphic characters. Hundreds of such platform-dependent character sets are in use today. Documentation for these ranges from excellent to nonexistent.

Platform-specific character sets like these should be used only within a single system. They should never be placed on the wire or used to transfer data between systems. Doing so can lead to nasty surprises in unexpected places. For example, displaying a file that contains some of the extra Cp1252 characters ‹, ‰, ˆ, , ", †, ..., ‡, œ, Œ, •, ', ', ", ", –, —, Ÿ, š, ™, ›, and ~ on a VT-220 terminal can effectively disable the screen. Nonetheless, these character sets are in common use and often seen on the Web, even when they don't belong there. There's no absolute rule that says you can't use them for an XML document, provided that you include the proper encoding declaration and your parser understands it. The one advantage to using these sets is that existing text editors are likely to be much more comfortable with them than with Unicode and its friends. Nonetheless, we strongly recommend that you don't use them and stick to the documented standards that are much more broadly supported across platforms.

Cp1252

The most common platform-dependent character set, and the one you're most likely to encounter on the Internet, is Cp1252, also (and incorrectly) known as *Windows ANSI*. This is the default character set used by most American and Western European Windows PCs, which explains its ubiquity. Cp1252 is a single-byte character set almost identical to the standard ISO-8859-1 character set—indeed, many Cp1252 documents are often incorrectly labeled as being Latin-1 documents. However, this set replaces the C1 controls between code points 128 and 159 with additional graphics characters, such as ‰, ‡, and Ÿ. These characters won't cause problems on other Windows systems. However, other platforms will have difficulty viewing them properly and may even crash in extreme cases. Cp1252 (and its siblings used in non-Western Windows systems) should be avoided.

MacRoman

The Mac OS uses a different, nonstandard, single-byte character set that's a superset of ASCII. The version used in the Americas and most of Western Europe is called MacRoman. Variants for other countries include MacGreek, MacHebrew, MacIceland, and so forth. Most Java-based XML processors can make sense out of these encodings if they're properly labeled, but most other non-Macintosh tools cannot.

For instance, if the French sentence "Au cours des dernières années, XML a été adapte dans des domaines aussi diverse que l'aéronautique, le multimédia, la gestion de hôpitaux, les télécommunications, la théologie, la vente au détail et la littérature médiévale" is written on a Macintosh and then read on a PC, what the PC user will see is "Au cours des derni?res annžes, XML a žtž adapte dans des domaines aussi diverse que l'ažronautique, le multimždia, la gestion de h™pitaux, les tŽžcommunications, la thžologie, la vente au džtail et la littžrature mždižvale," not the same thing at all. Generally, the result is at least marginally intelligible if most of the text is ASCII, but it certainly doesn't lend itself to high fidelity or quality. Mac-specific character sets should also be avoided.

Converting Between Character Sets

The ultimate solution to this character set morass is to use Unicode in either UTF-16 or UTF-8 format for all your XML documents. An increasing number of tools support one of these two formats natively; even the unassuming Notepad offers an option to save files in Unicode in Windows NT 4.0, 2000, and XP. Microsoft

Word 97 and later saves the text of its documents in Unicode, although unlike XML documents, Word files are hardly pure text. Much of the binary data in a Word file is not Unicode or any other kind of text. However, Word 2000 and later can actually save plain text files into Unicode. To save as plain Unicode text in Word 2000, select the format Encoded Text from the Save As Type: Choice menu in Word's Save As dialog box. Then select one of the four Unicode formats in the resulting File Conversion dialog box. In Word 2003, select the plain text format. When you save, Word will pop up a dialog box that prompts you for the encoding. Choose Other Encoding and then select one of the four Unicode formats in the list box on the right.

Most current tools are still adapted primarily for vendor-specific character sets that can't handle more than a few languages at one time. Thus, learning how to convert your documents from proprietary to more standard character sets is crucial.

Some of the better XML and HTML editors let you choose the character set you wish to save in and perform automatic conversions from the native character set you use for editing. On Unix, the native character set is likely one of the standard ISO character sets, and you can save into that format directly. On the Mac, you can avoid problems if you stick to pure ASCII documents. On Windows, you can go a little further and use Latin-1, if you're careful to stay away from the extra characters that aren't part of the official ISO-8859-1 specification. Otherwise, you'll have to convert your document from its native, platform-dependent encoding to one of the standard platform-independent character sets.

François Pinard has written an open source character-set conversion tool called *recode* for Linux and Unix, which you can download from *http://recode.progiciels-bpi.ca/*, as well as GNU mirror sites. Wojciech Galazka has ported recode to DOS. You can also use the Java Development Kit's *native2ascii* tool at *http://java.sun.com/j2se/1.4.2/docs/tooldocs/win32/native2ascii.html*. First, convert the file from its native encoding to Java's special ASCII-encoded Unicode format, then use the same tool in reverse to convert from the Java format to the encoding you actually want. For example, to convert the file *myfile.xml* from the Windows Cp1252 encoding to UTF-8, execute these two commands in sequence:

```
% native2ascii -encoding Cp1252 myfile.xml myfile.jtx
% native2ascii -reverse -encoding UTF-8 myfile.jtx myfile.xml
```

The Default Character Set for XML Documents

Before an XML parser can read a document, it must know which character set and encoding the document uses. In some cases, external metainformation tells the parser what encoding the document uses. For instance, an HTTP header may include a Content-type header like this:

```
Content-type: text/html; charset=ISO-8859-1
```

However, XML parsers generally can't count on the availability of such information. Even if they can, they can't necessarily assume that it's accurate. Therefore, an XML parser will attempt to guess the character set based on the first several bytes of the document. The main checks the parser makes include the following:

- If the first two bytes of the document are #xFEFF, then the parser recognizes the bytes as the Unicode *byte-order mark*. It then guesses that the document is written in the big-endian, UTF-16 encoding of Unicode. With that knowledge, it can read the rest of the document.

- If the first two bytes of the document are #xFFFE, then the parser recognizes the little-endian form of the Unicode byte-order mark. It now knows that the document is written in the little-endian, UTF-16 encoding of Unicode, and with that knowledge it can read the rest of the document.

- If the first four bytes of the document are #x3C3F786D, that is, the ASCII characters <?xm, then it guesses that the file is written in a superset of ASCII. In particular, it assumes that the file is written in the UTF-8 encoding of Unicode. Even if it's wrong, this information is sufficient to continue reading the document through the encoding declaration and find out what the character set really is.

Parsers that understand EBCDIC or UCS-4 may also apply similar heuristics to detect those encodings. However, UCS-4 isn't really used yet and is mostly of theoretical interest, and EBCDIC is a legacy family of character sets that shouldn't be used in new documents. Neither of these sets are important in practice.

Character References

Unicode contains more than 96,000 different characters covering almost all of the world's written languages. Predefining entity references for each of these characters, most of which will never be used in any one document, would impose an excessive burden on XML parsers. Rather than pick and choose which characters are worthy of being encoded as entities, XML goes to the other extreme. It predefines entity references only for characters that have special meaning as markup in an XML document: <, >, &, ", and '. All these are ASCII characters that are easy to type in any text editor.

For other characters that may not be accessible from an ASCII text editor, XML lets you use *character references*. A character reference gives the number of the particular Unicode character it stands for, in either decimal or hexadecimal. Decimal character references look like њ; hexadecimal character references have an extra x after the &#; that is, they look like њ. Both of these references refer to the same character, њ, the Cyrillic small letter "nje" used in Serbian and Macedonian. For example, suppose you want to include the Greek maxim "σοφός εαυτόν γιγνωσκει" ("The wise man knows himself") in your XML document. However, you only have an ASCII text editor at your disposal. You can replace each Greek letter with the correct character reference, like this:

```
<maxim>
  &#x3C3;&#x3BF;&#x3C6;&#x3CC;&#x3C2;
  &#x3AD;&#x3B1;&#x3C5;&#x3C4;&#x3CC;&#x3BD;
  &#x3B3;&#x3B9;&#x3B3;&#x3BD;&#x3CE;&#x3C3;&#x3BA;&#x3B5;&#x3B9;
</maxim>
```

To the XML processor, a document using character entity references referring to Unicode characters that don't exist in the current encoding is equivalent to a Unicode document in which all character references are replaced by the actual characters to which they refer. In other words, this XML document is the same as the previous one:

```
<maxim>
    σοφός εαυτόν γιγνωσκει
</maxim>
```

Character references are only recognized and replaced in element content and attribute values. They may not be used in element and attribute names, processing instruction targets, or XML keywords, such as DOCTYPE or ELEMENT. Character references can appear in comments and processing instruction data, but the parser does not recognize them there. They may be used in the DTD in attribute default values and entity replacement text. Tag and attribute names may be written in languages such as Greek, Russian, Arabic, or Chinese, but you must use a character set that allows you to include the appropriate characters natively. You can't insert these characters with character references. For instance, this is well-formed:

```
<λογος>
&#x3C3;&#x3BF;&#x3C6;&#x3CC;&#x3C2;
</λογος>
```

This is not well-formed:

```
<&#x3BB;&#x3BF;&#x3B3;&#x3BF;&#x3C2;>
    &#x3C3;&#x3BF;&#x3C6;&#x3CC;&#x3C2;
</&#x3BB;&#x3BF;&#x3B3;&#x3BF;&#x3C2;>
```

Chapter 27 provides character codes in both decimal and hexadecimal for some of the most useful and widely used alphabetic scripts. The interested reader will find the complete set in *The Unicode Standard Version 4.0* by the Unicode Consortium (Addison Wesley, 2003). You can also view the code charts online at *http://www.unicode.org/charts/*.

If you use a particular group of character references frequently, you may find it easier to define them as entities and then refer to the entities instead. Example 5-3 shows a DTD defining the entities you might use to spell out the Greek words in the previous several examples.

Example 5-3. A DTD defining general entity references for several Greek letters

```
<!ENTITY sigma             "&#x3C3;">
<!ENTITY omicron_with_tonos "&#x3CC;">
<!ENTITY phi               "&#x3C6;">
<!ENTITY omicron           "&#x3BF;">
<!ENTITY final_sigma       "&#x3C2;">
<!ENTITY epsilon_with_tonos "&#x3AD;">
<!ENTITY alpha             "&#x3B1;">
<!ENTITY lambda            "&#x3C3;">
<!ENTITY upsilon           "&#x3C5;">
<!ENTITY tau               "&#x3C4;">
<!ENTITY nu                "&#x3BD;">
<!ENTITY gamma             "&#x3B3;">
<!ENTITY iota              "&#x3B9;">
<!ENTITY omega_with_tonos  "&#x3CE;">
<!ENTITY kappa             "&#x3BA;">
<!ENTITY epsilon           "&#x3B5;">
```

These entities can even be used in invalid documents, provided that the declarations are made in the document's internal DTD subset, which all XML parsers are required to process, or that the parser reads the external DTD subset. By convention, DTD fragments that do nothing but define entities have the three-letter suffix *.ent*. These fragments are imported into the document's DTD using external parameter entity references. Example 5-4 shows how the maxim might be written using these entities, assuming they can be found at the relative URL *greek.ent*.

Example 5-4. The maxim using entity references instead of character references

```
<?xml version="1.0" encoding="ISO-8859-1" standalone="no"?>
<!DOCTYPE maxim [
 <!ENTITY % greek_alphabet SYSTEM "greek.ent">
 %greek_alphabet;

]>
<maxim>
  &sigma;&omicron;&phi;&omicron_with_tonos;&final_sigma;
  &epsilon_with_tonos;&alpha;&upsilon;&tau;&omicron_with_tonos;&nu;
  &gamma;&iota;&gamma;&nu;&omega_with_tonos;&sigma;&kappa;&epsilon;&iota;
</maxim>
```

A few standard entity subsets are widely available for your own use. The XHTML 1.0 DTD includes three useful entity sets you can adopt in your own work:

Latin-1 characters, http://www.w3.org/TR/xhtml1/DTD/xhtml-lat1.ent
 The non-ASCII characters from 160 up in ISO-8859-1

Special characters, http://www.w3.org/TR/xhtml1/DTD/xhtml-special.ent
 Letters from ISO-8859-2 (Latin-2) that aren't also in Latin-1, such as Œ and various punctuation marks, including the dagger, the Euro sign, and the em dash

Symbols, http://www.w3.org/TR/xhtml1/DTD/xhtml-symbol.ent
 The Greek alphabet (though accented characters are missing) and various punctuation marks, mathematical operators, and other symbols commonly used in mathematics

Chapter 27 provides complete charts showing all characters in these entity sets. You can either use these directly from their relatively stable URLs at the W3C or copy them onto your own systems. For example, to use entities from the symbol set in a document, add the following to the document's DTD:

```
<!ENTITY % HTMLsymbol PUBLIC
    "-//W3C//ENTITIES Symbols for XHTML//EN"
    "http://www.w3.org/TR/xhtml1/DTD/xhtml-symbol.ent">
%HTMLsymbol;
```

Since these are fairly standard DTDs, they have both Public IDs and URLs. Other groups and individuals have written entity sets you can use similarly, although no canonical collection of entity sets that covers all of Unicode exists. SGML included almost 20 separate entity sets covering Greek, Cyrillic, extended Latin, mathematical symbols, diacritical marks, box-drawing characters, and publishing marks. These aren't a standard part of XML, but several applications including

DocBook (*http://www.docbook.org/*) and MathML (*http://www.w3.org/TR/ MathML2/chapter6.html#chars_entity-tables*) have ported them to XML. MathML also has several useful entity sets containing more mathematical symbols.

xml:lang

Since XML documents are written in Unicode, XML is an excellent choice for multilingual documents, such as an Arabic commentary on a Greek text (something that couldn't be done with almost any other character set). In such multilingual documents, it's useful to identify in which language a particular section of text is written. For instance, a spellchecker that only knows English shouldn't try to check a French quote.

Each XML element may have an `xml:lang` attribute that specifies the language in which the content of that element is written. For example, the previous maxim might look like this:

```
<maxim xml:lang="el">
  &#x3C3;&#x3CC;&#3C6;&#3BF;&#3C2; &#x3AD;&#3B1;&#3C5;&#3C4;&#x3CC;&#x3BD;
  &#x3B3;&#x3B9;&#x3B3;&#x3BD;&#X3CE;&#x3C3;&#x3BA;&#x3B5;&#x3B9;
</maxim>
```

This identifies it as Greek. The specific code used, el, comes from the Greek word for Greek, ελληνικά .

Language Codes

The value of the `xml:lang` language attribute should be one of the two-letter language codes defined in ISO-639, "Codes for the Representation of Names of Languages," found at *http://lcweb.loc.gov/standards/iso639-2/langhome.html*, if such a code exists for the language in question.

For languages that aren't listed in ISO-639, you can use a language identifier registered with IANA; currently, about 20 of these identifiers exist, including i-navajo, i-klingon, and i-lux. The complete list can be found at *ftp://ftp.isi.edu/in-notes/ iana/assignments/languages*. All identifiers begin with i-. For example:

```
<maxim xml:lang="i-klingon">Heghlu'meH QaQ jajvam</maxim>
```

If the language you need still isn't present in these two lists, you can create your own language tag, as long as it begins with the prefix x- or X- to identify it as a user-defined language code. For example, the title of this journal is written in J. R. R. Tolkien's fictional Quenya language:

```
<journal xml:lang="x-quenya">Tyalië Tyelelliéva</journal>
```

Subcodes

For some purposes, knowing the language is not enough. You also need to know the region where the language is spoken. For instance, French has slightly different vocabulary, spelling, and pronunciation in France, Quebec, Belgium, and Switzerland. Although written identically with an ideographic character set, Mandarin and Cantonese are actually quite different, mutually unintelligible dialects of Chinese. The United States and the United Kingdom are jocularly referred to as "two countries separated by a common language."

To handle these distinctions, the language code may be followed by any number of subcodes that further specify the language. Hyphens separate the language code from the subcode and subcodes from each other. If the language code is an ISO-639 code, the first subcode should be one of the two-letter country codes defined by ISO-3166, "Codes for the Representation of Names of Countries," found at *http://www.ics.uci.edu/pub/ietf/http/related/iso3166.txt*. This xml:lang attribute indicates Canadian French:

```
<p xml:lang="fr-CA">Marie vient pour le fin de semaine.</p>
```

The language code is usually written in lowercase, and the country code is written in uppercase. However, this is just a convention, not a requirement.

ATTLIST Declarations of xml:lang

Although the XML 1.0 specification defines the xml:lang attribute, you still have to declare it in the DTDs of valid documents. For example, this information declares the maxim element used several times in this chapter:

```
<!ELEMENT maxim (#PCDATA)>
<!ATTLIST maxim xml:lang NMTOKEN #IMPLIED>
```

Here I've used the NMTOKEN type, since all legal language codes are well-formed XML name tokens.

You may declare the xml:lang attribute in any convenient way. For instance, if you want to require its presence on the maxim element, you could make it #REQUIRED:

```
<!ATTLIST maxim xml:lang NMTOKEN #REQUIRED>
```

Or, if you wanted to allow only French and English text in your documents, you might specify it as an enumerated type with a default of English like this:

```
<!ATTLIST maxim xml:lang (en | fr) 'en'>
```

Unless you use an enumerated type, the parser will not check that the value you give it follows the rules outlined here. It's your responsibility to make sure you use appropriate language codes and subcodes.

Internationalization

II

Narrative-Like Documents

XML as a Document Format

XML is first and foremost a document format. It was always intended for web pages, books, scholarly articles, poems, short stories, reference manuals, tutorials, textbooks, legal pleadings, contracts, instruction sheets, and other documents that human beings would read. Its use as a syntax for computer data in applications such as order processing, object serialization, database exchange and backup, and electronic data interchange is mostly a happy accident.

Most computer programmers are better trained in working with the rigid structures one encounters in record-like applications than in the more free-form environment of an article or story. Most writers are more accustomed to the more free-form format of a book, story, or article. XML is perhaps unique in addressing the needs of both communities equally well. This chapter describes by both elucidation and example the structures encountered in narrative documents that are meant to be read by people instead of computers. Subsequent chapters will look at web pages in particular, then address technologies—such as XSLT, XLinks, and stylesheets—that are primarily intended for use with documents that will be read by human beings. Once we've done that, we'll look at XML as a format for more or less transitory data meant to be read by computers, rather than semipermanent documents intended for human consumption.

SGML's Legacy

XML is a simplified form of the Standardized General Markup Language (SGML). The language that would eventually become SGML was invented by Charles F. Goldfarb, Ed Mosher, and Ray Lorie at IBM in the 1970s and developed by many people around the world until its eventual adoption as ISO standard 8879 in 1986. SGML was intended to solve many of the same problems XML solves in much the same way as XML solves them. It was and is a semantic and structural markup language for text documents. SGML is extremely powerful and achieved some success in the U.S. military and government, in the aerospace sector, and in other domains that needed ways of efficiently managing technical documents that were tens of thousands of pages long.

SGML's biggest success was HTML, which was and is an SGML application. However, HTML is just one SGML application. It does not have anything close to the full power of SGML itself. SGML has also been used to define many other document formats, including DocBook and TEI, both of which we'll discuss shortly.

However, SGML is complicated—very, very complicated. The official SGML specification is over 150 very technical pages. It covers many special cases and unlikely scenarios. It is so complex that almost no software has ever implemented it fully. Programs that implement or rely on different subsets of SGML are often incompatible. The special feature that one program considers essential is all too often considered extraneous fluff and omitted by the next program. Nonetheless, experience with SGML taught developers a lot about the proper design, implementation, and use of markup languages for a wide variety of documents. Much of that general knowledge applies equally well to XML.

One thing all this should make clear is that XML documents aren't just used on the Web. XML can easily handle the needs of publishing in a variety of media, including books, magazines, journals, newspapers, and pamphlets. XML is particularly useful when you need to publish the same information in several of these formats. By applying different stylesheets to the same source document, you can produce web pages, speaker's notes, camera-ready copy for printing, and more.

Narrative Document Structures

All XML documents are trees. However, trees are very general-purpose data structures. If you've been formally trained in computer science (and very possibly even if you haven't been), you've encountered binary trees, red-black trees, balanced trees, B-trees, ordered trees, and more. However, when working with XML, it's highly unlikely that any given document matches any of these structures. Instead, XML documents are the most general sort of tree, with no particular restrictions on how nodes are ordered or how or which nodes are connected to which other nodes. Narrative XML documents are even less likely than record-like XML documents to have an identifiable structure beyond their mere treeness.

So what does a narrative-oriented XML document look like? Of course, there's a root element. All XML documents have one. Generally speaking, this root element represents the document itself. That is, if the document is a book, the root element is book. If the document is an article, the root element is article, and so on.

Beyond that, large documents are generally broken up into sections of some kind, perhaps chapters for a book, parts for an article, or claims for a legal brief. Most of the document consists of these primary sections. In some cases, there'll be several different kinds of sections; for instance, one for the table of contents, one for the index, and one for the chapters of a book.

Generally, the root element also contains one or more elements providing metainformation about the document—for example, the title of the work, the author of the document, the dates the document was written and last modified, and so forth. One common pattern is to place the metainformation in one child of the root element and the main content of the work in another. This is how HTML documents are written. The root element is html. The metainformation goes in a head element, and the main content goes in the body element. TEI and DocBook also follow this pattern.

Sections of the document can be further divided into subsections. The subsections themselves may be further divided. How many levels of subsection appear generally depends on how large the document is. An encyclopedia will have many levels of sectioning; a pamphlet or flier will have almost none. Each section and subsection normally has a title. It may also have elements or attributes that indicate metainformation about the section, such as the author or date it was last modified.

Up to this point, mixed content is mostly avoided. Elements contain child elements and whitespace, and that's likely all they contain. However, at some level it becomes necessary to insert the actual text of the document—the words that people will read. In most Western languages, these will probably be divided into paragraphs and other block-level elements like headlines, figures, sidebars, and footnotes. Generic document DTDs like DocBook won't be able to say more about these items than this.

The paragraphs and other block-level items will mostly contain words in a row—that is, text. Some of this text may be marked up with inline elements. For instance, you may wish to indicate that a particular string of text inside the block-level element is a date, a person, or simply important. However, most of the text will not be so annotated.

One area in which different XML applications diverge is the question of whether block-level items may contain other block-level items. For instance, can a paragraph contain a list? Or can a list item contain a paragraph? It's probably easier to work with more structured documents in which blocks can't contain other blocks (particularly other instances of the same kind). However, it's very often the case that a block has a very good reason to contain other blocks. For instance, a long list item or quotation may contain several paragraphs.

For the most part, this entire structure from the root down to the most deeply nested inline item tends to be quite linear; that is, you expect that a person will read the words in pretty much the same order they appear in the document. If all the markup were suddenly removed and you were left with nothing but the raw text, the result should be more or less legible. The markup can be used to index or format the document, but it's not a fundamental part of the content.

Another important point about these sorts of XML documents: not only are they composed of words in a row, they're composed of *words*. What they contain is text intended for human beings to read. They're not numbers or dates or money, except insofar as these things occur as part of the normal flow of the narrative. The #PCDATA content of the lowest-level elements of the tree mostly have one type: string. If anything has a real type beyond string, it's likely metainformation about the document (figure number, date last modified, and so on) rather than the content of the document itself.

This explains why DTDs don't provide strong (or really any) data typing. The documents for which SGML was designed didn't need it. XML documents that are doing jobs for which SGML wasn't designed, such as tracking inventories or census data, do need data typing; that's why various people and organizations have invented a plethora of schema languages. However, schemas really don't improve on DTDs for narrative documents.

Not all XML documents are like those we've described here. Not even all narrative-oriented XML documents are like this. However, a surprising number of narrative-oriented XML applications do follow this basic pattern, perhaps with a nip here or a tuck there. The reason is that this is the basic structure narratives follow, which has proven its usefulness in the thousands of years since writing was invented. If you were to define your own DTDs for general narrative-oriented documents, you'd probably come up with something a lot like this. If you define your own DTDs for more specialized narrative-oriented documents, then the names of the elements may change to reflect your domain—for instance, if you were writing the next edition of the Boy Scout handbook, one of your subsections might be called MeritBadge—however, the basic hierarchy of document, meta-information, sections and subsections, block-level elements, and marked-up text would likely remain.

TEI

The Text Encoding Initiative (TEI, *http://www.tei-c.org/*) is an XML (originally SGML) application designed for the markup of classic literature, such as Vergil's *Aeneid* or the collected works of Thomas Jefferson. It's a prime example of a narrative-oriented DTD. Since TEI is designed for scholarly analysis of text rather than more casual reading or publishing, it includes elements not only for common document structures (chapter, scene, stanza, etc.) but also for typographical elements, grammatical structure, the position of illustrations on the page, and so forth. These aren't important to most readers, but they are important to TEI's intended audience of humanities scholars. For many academic purposes, one manuscript of the *Aeneid* is not necessarily the same as the next. Transcription errors and emendations made by various monks in the Middle Ages can be crucial.

Example 6-1 shows a fairly simple TEI document that uses the "Lite" version of TEI, a subset of full TEI that includes only the most commonly needed tags. The content comes from the book you're reading now. Although a complete TEI-encoded copy of this manuscript would be much longer, this simple example demonstrates the basic features of most TEI documents that represent books. (In addition to prose, TEI can also be used for plays, poems, missals, and essentially any written form of literature.)

Example 6-1. A TEI document

```
<?xml version="1.0" encoding="UTF-8" standalone="no"?>
<!DOCTYPE TEI.2 SYSTEM "xteilite.dtd">
<TEI.2>
```

Example 6-1. A TEI document (continued)

```
<teiHeader>
  <fileDesc>
    <titleStmt>
      <title>XML in a Nutshell</title>
      <author>Harold, Elliotte Rusty</author>
      <author>Means, W. Scott</author>
    </titleStmt>
    <publicationStmt><p></p></publicationStmt>
    <sourceDesc><p>Early manuscript draft</p></sourceDesc>
  </fileDesc>
</teiHeader>

<text id="HarXMLi">

  <front>
    <div type='toc'>
      <head>Table Of Contents</head>
      <list>
        <item>Introducing XML</item>
        <item>XML as a Document Format</item>
        <item>XML on the Web</item>
      </list>
    </div>

  </front>

  <body>

    <div1 type="chapter">
      <head>Introducing XML</head>
      <p></p>
    </div1>

    <div1 type="chapter">
      <head>XML as a Document Format</head>
      <p>
        XML is first and foremost a document format. It was always
        intended for web pages, books, scholarly articles, poems,
        short stories, reference manuals, tutorials, texts, legal
        pleadings, contracts, instruction sheets, and other documents
        that human beings would read. Its use as a syntax for computer
        data in applications like syndication, order processing,
        object serialization, database exchange and backup, electronic
        data interchange, and so forth is mostly a happy accident.
      </p>

      <div2 type="section">
        <head>SGML's Legacy</head>
        <p></p>
      </div2>
```

Example 6-1. A TEI document (continued)

```
          <div2 type="section">
            <head>TEI</head>
            <p></p>
          </div2>

          <div2 type="section">
            <head>DocBook</head>
            <p>
              DocBook (<hi>http://www.docbook.org/</hi>) is an
              SGML application designed for new documents, not old ones.
              It's especially common in computer documentation. Several
              O'Reilly books have been written in DocBook including
              <bibl><author>Norm Walsh</author>'s <title>DocBook: The
              Definitive Guide</title></bibl>. Much of the <abbr
              expan='Linux Documentation Project'>LDP</abbr>
              (<hi>http://www.linuxdoc.org/</hi>) corpus is written in
              DocBook.
            </p>
          </div2>

        </div1>

        <div1 type="chapter">
          <head>XML on the Web</head>
          <p></p>
        </div1>

      </body>

      <back>
        <div1 type="index">
          <list>
            <head>INDEX</head>
            <item>SGML, 8, 89</item>
            <item>DocBook, 95-98</item>
            <item>TEI (Text Encoding Initiative), 92-95</item>
            <item>Text Encoding Initiative, See TEI</item>
          </list>
        </div1>
      </back>

    </text>
  </TEI.2>
```

The root element of this and all TEI documents is TEI.2. This root element is always divided into two parts: a header represented by a teiHeader element and the main content of the document represented by a text element. The header contains information about the source document (for instance, exactly which medieval manuscript the text was copied from), the encoding of the document, some keywords describing the document, and so forth.

The text element is itself divided into three parts:

Front matter in the front *element*
> The preface, table of contents, dedication page, pictures of the cover, and so forth. Each of these is represented by a div element with a type attribute whose value identifies the division as a table of contents, preface, title page, and so forth. Each of these divisions contains other elements laying out the content of that division.

The body of the work in the body *element*
> The individual chapters, acts, and so forth that make up the document. Each of these is represented by a div1 element with a type attribute that identifies this particular division as a volume, book, part, chapter, poem, act, and so forth. Each div1 element has a header child giving the title of the volume, book, part, chapter, etc.

Back matter in the back *element*
> The index, glossary, etc.

The divisions may be further subdivided; div1s can contain div2s, div2s can contain div3s, div3s can contain div4s, and so on up to div7. However, for any given work, there is a smallest division. This division contains paragraphs represented by p elements for prose or stanzas represented by lg elements for poetry. Stanzas are further broken up into individual lines represented by l elements.

Both lines and paragraphs contain mixed content; that is, they contain plain text. However, parts of this text may be marked up further by elements indicating that particular words or characters are peoples' names (name), corrections (corr), illegible (unclear), misspellings (sic), and so on.

This structure fairly closely reflects the structure of the actual documents that are being encoded in TEI. This is true of most narrative-oriented XML applications that need to handle fairly generic documents. TEI is a very representative example of typical XML document structure.

DocBook

DocBook (*http://www.docbook.org/*) is an SGML application designed for new documents, not old ones. It's especially common in computer documentation. Several O'Reilly books have been written in DocBook, including Norm Walsh and Leonard Muellner's *DocBook: The Definitive Guide*. No special tools are required to author it. Much of the Linux Documentation Project (LDP, *http://www.linuxdoc.org/*) corpus is written in DocBook. The current version of DocBook, 4.3, is available as both an SGML and an XML application. Example 6-2 shows a simple DocBook XML document based on the book you're reading now. Needless to say, the full version of this document would be much longer.

Example 6-2. A DocBook document

```
<?xml version="1.0" encoding="UTF-8" standalone="no"?>
<!DOCTYPE book PUBLIC "-//OASIS//DTD DocBook XML V4.3//EN"
                "docbook/docbookx.dtd">
```

Example 6-2. A DocBook document (continued)

```
<book>
  <title>XML in a Nutshell</title>
  <bookinfo>
    <author>
      <firstname>Elliotte Rusty</firstname>
      <surname>Harold</surname>
    </author>
    <author>
      <firstname>W. Scott</firstname>
      <surname>Means</surname>
    </author>
  </bookinfo>

  <toc>
    <tocchap><tocentry>Introducing XML</tocentry></tocchap>
    <tocchap><tocentry>XML as a Document Format</tocentry></tocchap>
    <tocchap><tocentry>XML as a "better" HTML</tocentry></tocchap>
  </toc>

  <chapter>
    <title>Introducing XML</title>
    <para></para>
  </chapter>

  <chapter>
    <title>XML as a Document Format</title>

    <para>
      XML is first and foremost a document format. It was always intended
      for web pages, books, scholarly articles, poems, short stories,
      reference manuals, tutorials, texts, legal pleadings, contracts,
      instruction sheets, and other documents that human beings would
      read. Its use as a syntax for computer data in applications like
      syndication, order processing, object serialization, database
      exchange and backup, electronic data interchange, and so forth is
      mostly a happy accident.
    </para>

    <sect1>
      <title>SGML's Legacy</title>
      <para></para>
    </sect1>
    <sect1>
      <title>TEI</title>
      <para></para>
    </sect1>

    <sect1>
      <title>DocBook</title>
      <para>
        <ulink url="http://www.docbook.org/">DocBook</ulink>
        is an SGML application designed for new documents, not old ones.
```

Example 6-2. A DocBook document (continued)

```
        It's especially common in computer documentation. Several
        O'Reilly books have been written in DocBook including
        <citation>Norm Walsh and Leonard Muellner's
        <citetitle>DocBook: The Definitive
        Guide</citetitle></citation>. Much of the <ulink
        url="http://www.linuxdoc.org/">Linux Documentation Project
        (LDP)</ulink> corpus is written in DocBook. </para>
    </sect1>

  </chapter>

  <chapter>
    <title>XML on the Web</title>
    <para></para>
  </chapter>

  <index>
    <indexentry>
      <primaryie>SGML, 8,  89</primaryie>
    </indexentry>
    <indexentry>
      <primaryie>DocBook, 95-98</primaryie>
    </indexentry>
    <indexentry>
      <primaryie>TEI (Text Encoding Initiative), 92-95</primaryie>
    </indexentry>
    <indexentry>
      <primaryie>Text Encoding Initiative</primaryie>
      <seeie>TEI</seeie>
    </indexentry>
  </index>

</book>
```

DocBook offers many advantages to technical authors. First and foremost, it's open, nonproprietary, and can be created with any text editor. It would feel a little silly to write open source documentation for open source software with closed and proprietary tools like Microsoft Word (which is not to say this hasn't been done). If your documents are written in DocBook, they aren't tied to any one platform, vendor, or application software. They're portable across essentially any plausible environment you can imagine.

Not only is DocBook theoretically editable with basic text editors, it's simple enough that such editing is practical as well. One of us (Harold) wrote an entire 1,200 page book in DocBook by hand in jEdit (*Processing XML with Java*, Addison Wesley, 2002). Of course, if you'd like a little help, there are a number of free tools available, including an Emacs major mode (*http://www.nwalsh.com/ emacs/docbookide/index.html*). Furthermore, like many good XML applications, DocBook is modular. You can use the pieces you need and ignore the rest. If you need tables, there's a very complete tables module. If you don't need tables, you don't need to know about or use this module. Other modules cover various entity sets and equations.

DocBook is an authoring format, not a format for finished presentation. Before a DocBook document is read by a person, it is converted to any of several formats, including the following:

- HTML
- XSL Formatting Objects
- Rich Text Format (RTF)
- T$_E$X

For example, if you want high-quality printed documentation for a program, you can convert a DocBook document to T$_E$X, then use the standard T$_E$X tools to convert the resulting T$_E$X file to a DVI and/or PostScript file and print that. If you just want to read it on your computer, then you'd probably convert it to HTML and load it into your web browser. For other purposes, you'd pick something else. With DocBook, all these formats come essentially for free. It's very easy to produce multiple output documents in different formats from a single DocBook source document. Indeed, this benefit isn't just limited to DocBook. Most well-thought-out XML input formats are just as easy to publish in other formats.

OpenOffice

While you can write markup by hand in a text editor, many non-programmers prefer a friendlier, more WYSIWYG approach. There's no reason a standard word processor can't save its data in XML, and indeed several now do, including Microsoft Word 2003 and OpenOffice.org Writer. Harold also wrote a much smaller book in XML using OpenOffice.org Writer (*Effective XML*, Addison Wesley).

For what it's worth, in hindsight I regret that decision. If I were doing it again, I would write the XML by hand in DocBook as I did with *Processing XML with Java*, rather than using OpenOffice. As much as good GUI tools can improve productivity, bad GUI tools can hinder it. A poorly designed GUI is no guarantee of ease of use.

Scott and I wrote this book in Microsoft Word, but mostly because the early editions predated the availability of high-quality XML publishing tools. That decision is hurting us now. For instance, the complicated tables in Chapter 27 are well beyond what Word can comfortably handle. In DocBook, they'd be a no-brainer. If we were starting from scratch, we'd write in DocBook.

Example 6-3 shows a fairly simple OpenOffice document. Again, the content comes from the book you're reading now. This differs from TEI and DocBook in several ways—for instance, it uses namespaces. TEI and DocBook don't. The title of the book and the names of the authors are not included because they'd normally be stored in a separate XML document containing only the metadata. Indexes and tables of contents are generated from the internal structure, content, and markup rather than being added explicitly. Perhaps the most unusual distinction is the lack of section elements of any kind. Instead, different chapters, sections, and subsections are identified by text:h elements with different levels. The contents of the section are everything that follows the text:h element until the next text:h element. Less obvious is that this format is more general because it's designed to handle several other OpenOffice document formats, including charts and spreadsheets, besides simple narrative content.

Example 6-3. An OpenOffice document

```
<?xml version="1.0" encoding="UTF-8"?>
<!DOCTYPE office:document-content
    PUBLIC "-//OpenOffice.org//DTD OfficeDocument 1.0//EN" "office.dtd">
<office:document-content
  xmlns:office="http://openoffice.org/2000/office"
  xmlns:style="http://openoffice.org/2000/style"
  xmlns:text="http://openoffice.org/2000/text"
  xmlns:fo="http://www.w3.org/1999/XSL/Format"
  office:class="text"
  office:version="1.0">

<office:script/>
<office:font-decls>
  <style:font-decl style:name="Courier" fo:font-family="Courier"
      style:font-pitch="variable"/>
  <style:font-decl style:name="Times" fo:font-family="Times"
      style:font-pitch="variable"/>
  <style:font-decl style:name="Helvetica"
      fo:font-family="Helvetica" style:font-family-generic="swiss"
      style:font-pitch="variable"/>
</office:font-decls>
<office:automatic-styles>
  <style:style style:name="P1" style:family="paragraph"
      style:parent-style-name="ChapterLabel"
      style:master-page-name="First Page">
   <style:properties style:page-number="0"/>
   </style:style>
   <style:style style:name="T1" style:family="text"
      style:parent-style-name="WW-Comment Reference">
    <style:properties fo:color="#000000"/>
   </style:style>
   <style:style style:name="T2" style:family="text"
      style:parent-style-name="emphasis">
   <style:properties fo:language="none" fo:country="none"/>
   </style:style>
   <style:style style:name="T3" style:family="text">
    <style:properties fo:language="none" fo:country="none"/>
   </style:style>
</office:automatic-styles>
<office:body>
<text:sequence-decls>
  <text:sequence-decl text:display-outline-level="0"
                      text:name="Illustration"/>
  <text:sequence-decl text:display-outline-level="0" text:name="Table"/>
  <text:sequence-decl text:display-outline-level="0" text:name="Text"/>
```

Example 6-3. An OpenOffice document (continued)

```
  <text:sequence-decl text:display-outline-level="0"
                       text:name="Drawing"/>
</text:sequence-decls>

<text:p text:style-name="ChapterTitle">Introducing XML</text:p>
<text:p text:style-name="Standard"></text:p>

<text:p text:style-name="ChapterTitle">XML as a Document Format</text:p>
<text:p text:style-name="Standard">XML is first and foremost a document format.
It was always intended for web pages, books, scholarly articles, poems, short
stories, reference manuals, tutorials, textbooks, legal pleadings, contracts,
instruction sheets, and other documents that human beings would read. Its use as
a syntax for computer data in applications such as order processing, object
serialization, database exchange and backup, and electronic data interchange is
mostly a happy accident.</text:p>

<text:h text:style-name="Heading 1" text:level="1">SGML's Legacy</text:h>
<text:p text:style-name="Standard"></text:p>

<text:h text:style-name="Heading 1" text:level="1">TEI</text:h>
<text:p text:style-name="Standard"></text:p>

<text:h text:style-name="Heading 1" text:level="1">DocBook</text:h>
<text:p text:style-name="Standard">DocBook
(<text:span text:style-name="online item">http://www.docbook.org/</text:span>)
<text:alphabetical-index-mark text:string-value="DocBook"
text:key1="narrative-oriented XML documents"/><text:s/>
<text:alphabetical-index-mark text:string-value="DocBook"/>is an SGML
application designed for new documents, not old ones. It's especially common in
computer documentation. Several O'Reilly books have been written in DocBook,
including
<text:alphabetical-index-mark text:string-value="Walsh, Norman"/>Norm
Walsh and Leonard <text:alphabetical-index-mark text:string-value="Muellner,
Leonard"/>Muellner's
<text:span text:style-name="emphasis">DocBook: The Definitive Guide</text:span>.
No special tools are required to author it. Much of the Linux Documentation
Project (LDP, <text:span text:style-name="online item">http://www.linuxdoc.org/</
text:span>) corpus is written in DocBook. </text:p>

<text:p text:style-name="ChapterTitle">XML on the Web</text:p>
<text:p text:style-name="Standard"></text:p>

</office:body>
</office:document-content>
```

This is actually only one piece of what OpenOffice saves (and it's been cleaned up some for display in this book). OpenOffice bundles up several related XML documents into a zip file and saves that. Before you can work with the raw XML, you'll need to unzip it. Once it is unzipped, the document like the one shown here is found in the file named *content.xml*. Other XML documents are used to hold styles, metadata, and settings. These can all be bundled into a single office:document element, but this is normally not done. The separation of content from presentation is a very useful feature of this application.

Despite that, overall, OpenOffice is a much more presentationally oriented format than either DocBook or TEI. This makes it more suitable as the file format for a WYSIWYG word processor, but less suitable for manipulation with XML tools such as SAX, DOM, and XSLT. Certainly, you can process an OpenOffice document with these tools; it's just that the markup has less semantics to lever off of. All a document really is a heading, paragraphs, lists, and tables (the latter two are not seen in this example). The basic semantics are impoverished compared to either DocBook or TEI. Much of the useful information in an OpenOffice document is tied up in style names rather than element names. If the authors did not use named styles, but simply formatted their document with italics, bold, Helvetica, and the like, then the semantics may well be irretrievable.

WordprocessingML

Beginning with Microsoft Office 2003 for Windows (but not Office 2004 for the Mac), Microsoft gave Word and the other Office components the ability to save all documents in XML, although by default it still picks a binary format. The XML application saved by Microsoft Word is named WordprocessingML. Unlike DocBook, TEI, and OpenOffice, all of which were designed from scratch without any legacy issues, WordprocessingML was designed more as an XML representation of an existing binary file format. This makes it a rather unusual example of a narrative document format. We would not recommend that you emulate its design in your own applications. Nonetheless, it can be educational to compare it to the other three formats.

Example 6-4 shows the same document as in the previous three examples, this time encoded in WordprocessingML. The WordprocessingML version seems the most opaque and cryptic of the four formats discussed in this chapter. This example makes it pretty obvious that XML is not magic pixie dust you can sprinkle on an existing format to create clean, legible, maintainable data.

The root element of a WordprocessingML document is w:wordDocument. Here, the w prefix is mapped to the namespace URI http://schemas.microsoft.com/office/word/2003/wordml. Several other namespaces are declared for different content that can be embedded in a Word file.

This root element can contain several different chunks of metadata. Here I've used three: o:DocumentProperties for basic metadata like author and title, a w:fonts element that lists the fonts used in the document and their metrics, and a w:styles element that lists the styles referenced in the document. All of these are optional. However, a document saved by Microsoft Word itself would include all of these and several more.

The actual content of the document is stored in a w:body element. The body is divided into sections (wx:sect elements), which can be further divided into subsections (wx:subsection elements). Unusually, these are completely optional; removing them would have no effect. They're mainly present for the convenience of humans. The real structure of the document is inferred not from the sections and subsections but from paragraphs with outline levels.

There are three basic text elements in WordprocessingML that you'll find inside the body: w:t, w:r, and w:p. w:t is for text; w:r is for a run of text, like a span in HTML; and w:p is for a paragraph. A w:p contains w:r elements, each of which contains one w:t element. Neither a w:r nor a w:p can contain text directly. Whitespace is significant within w:t elements, although not within most other elements. However, line breaks are treated the same as spaces. The actual line breaks are indicated by the paragraph boundaries. This matches the typical word-wrapping behavior of Word and most other word processors.

Beyond these and a few other elements, there are almost no semantics in Word-processingML markup. Instead, many characters are expended on precisely reproducing the appearance of the page, including fonts, font metrics, styles, line breaks, and so forth. In a document that's saved from Word (as opposed to being written by hand as this one was), the style information can easily occupy several dozen times the amount of space the content itself does. Headings are identified not by a separate heading element of some kind, but by setting the outline level property using a preceding sibling w:pPr element with a w:outlineLvl child. The use of sibling elements to set properties (instead of attributes or parent elements) is a very unusual pattern, one that's not well-supported by most XML processing tools.

Example 6-4. A WordprocessingML document

```
<?xml version="1.0" encoding="UTF-8"?>
<w:wordDocument
  xmlns:w="http://schemas.microsoft.com/office/word/2003/wordml"
  xmlns:wx="http://schemas.microsoft.com/office/word/2003/auxHint"
  xmlns:o="urn:schemas-microsoft-com:office:office"
  xml:space="preserve">
  <o:DocumentProperties>
    <o:Title>XML in a Nutshell</o:Title>
    <o:Author>W. Scott Means</o:Author>
    <o:LastAuthor>Elliotte Rusty Harold</o:LastAuthor>
    <o:Revision>2</o:Revision>
    <o:TotalTime>0</o:TotalTime>
    <o:LastPrinted>1601-01-01T04:00:00Z</o:LastPrinted>
    <o:Created>2004-05-25T00:40:00Z</o:Created>
    <o:LastSaved>2004-05-25T00:40:00Z</o:LastSaved>
    <o:Pages>1</o:Pages>
    <o:Words>162</o:Words>
    <o:Characters>925</o:Characters>
    <o:Company>Cafe au Lait</o:Company>
    <o:Lines>7</o:Lines>
    <o:Paragraphs>2</o:Paragraphs>
    <o:CharactersWithSpaces>1085</o:CharactersWithSpaces>
    <o:Version>11.4920</o:Version>
  </o:DocumentProperties>
  <w:fonts>
    <w:defaultFonts w:ascii="Times New Roman"
                    w:fareast="Times New Roman"
                    w:h-ansi="Times New Roman" w:cs="Times New Roman"/>
    <w:font w:name="Helvetica"><w:panose-1 w:val="020B0604020202030204"/>
```

Example 6-4. A WordprocessingML document (continued)

```
      <w:charset w:val="00"/>
      <w:family w:val="Swiss"/>
      <w:pitch w:val="variable"/>
      <w:sig w:usb-0="20003A87" w:usb-1="00000000" w:usb-2="00000000"
            w:usb-3="00000000" w:csb-0="000001FF" w:csb-1="00000000"/>
    </w:font>
  </w:fonts>
  <w:styles>
    <w:style w:type="character"  w:styleId="emphasis"  w:default="off"/>
  </w:styles>
  <w:body>
  <wx:sect>
    <w:p>
      <w:pPr>
         <w:outlineLvl w:val="0" />
      </w:pPr>
      <w:r>
        <w:t>Introducing XML</w:t>
      </w:r>
    </w:p>
    <w:p></w:p>
  </wx:sect>

  <wx:sect>
    <w:p>
      <w:pPr>
         <w:outlineLvl w:val="0" />
      </w:pPr>
      <w:r>
        <w:t>XML as a Document Format</w:t>
      </w:r>
    </w:p>

  <w:p>
    <w:r>
       <w:t>XML is first and foremost a document format. It was always intended
for web pages, books, scholarly articles, poems, short stories,
reference manuals, tutorials, texts, legal pleadings, contracts,
instruction sheets, and other documents that human beings would
read. Its use as a syntax for computer data in applications like
syndication, order processing, object serialization, database
exchange and backup, electronic data interchange, and so forth is
mostly a happy accident.</w:t>
    </w:r>
  </w:p>

  <wx:subsection>
    <w:p>
      <w:pPr>
         <w:outlineLvl w:val="1" />
      </w:pPr>
```

Example 6-4. A WordprocessingML document (continued)

```
      <w:r>
        <w:t>SGML's Legacy</w:t>
      </w:r>
    </w:p>
    <w:p></w:p>
  </wx:subsection>
  <wx:subsection>
    <w:p>
      <w:pPr>
        <w:outlineLvl w:val="1" />
      </w:pPr>
      <w:r>
        <w:t>TEI</w:t>
      </w:r>
    </w:p>
    <w:p></w:p>
  </wx:subsection>

  <wx:subsection>
    <w:p>
      <w:pPr>
        <w:outlineLvl w:val="1" />
      </w:pPr>
      <w:r>
        <w:t>DocBook</w:t>
      </w:r>
    </w:p>
    <w:p>
      <w:hlink w:bookmark="http://www.docbook.org/">
        <w:r>
          <w:rPr>
            <w:rStyle w:val="Hyperlink" />
          </w:rPr>
          <w:t>DocBook</w:t>
        </w:r>
      </w:hlink>
      <w:r>
      <w:t>
is an SGML application designed for new documents, not old ones.
It's especially common in computer documentation. Several
O'Reilly books have been written in DocBook including </w:t>
      </w:r>
      <w:r>
        <w:rPr>
          <w:rStyle w:val="emphasis"/>
        </w:rPr>
        <w:t>Norm Walsh and Leonard Muellner's DocBook: The
Definitive Guide</w:t>
      </w:r>
      <w:r>
        <w:t>. Much of the </w:t>
      </w:r>
```

Example 6-4. A WordprocessingML document (continued)

```
        <w:hlink w:bookmark="http://www.linuxdoc.org/">
          <w:r>
            <w:rPr>
              <w:rStyle w:val="Hyperlink" />
            </w:rPr>
            <w:t>Linux Documentation Project (LDP)</w:t>
          </w:r>
          </w:hlink>
          <w:r>
          <w:t> corpus is written in DocBook. </w:t>
          </w:r>
      </w:p>
    </wx:subsection>

  </wx:sect>

  <wx:sect>
    <w:p>
      <w:pPr>
        <w:outlineLvl w:val="0" />
      </w:pPr>
      <w:r>
        <w:t>XML on the Web</w:t>
      </w:r>
    </w:p>
    <w:p></w:p>
  </wx:sect>
  </w:body>
</w:wordDocument>
```

Two things strike me about this format. The first is the cryptic nature of the short tag names such as t, r, p, and the positively verbose rPr. The second is the large number of tags needed to mark up this fairly simple document. The problem seems to be that Word bundles all style definitions into the document, and then repeats styles for each paragraph, even if they're reused across the entire document. XML doesn't have to be verbose, but this example certainly is; and it is far less verbose than what I actually saw saved by Word 2003. DocBook and TEI are human legible, even in plain text form. OpenOffice.org and WordprocessingML really aren't, especially in their natural states.

Document Permanence

XML documents that are intended for computers to read are often transitory. For instance, a SOAP document that represents a request to a Windows server running .NET exists for just as long as it takes the client to send it to the server and for the server to parse it into its internal data structures. After that's done, the document will be discarded. It probably won't be around for two minutes, much less two years. It's an ephemeral communication between two systems, with no more permanence than any of billions of other messages that computers exchange on a daily basis, most of which are never even written to disk, much less archived for posterity.

Some applications do store more permanent computer-oriented data in XML. For instance, XML is the native file format of the Gnumeric spreadsheet. On the other hand, this format is really only understood by Gnumeric and perhaps the other Gnome applications. It's designed to meet the specific needs of that one program. Exchanging data with other applications, including ones that haven't even been invented yet, is a secondary concern.

XML documents meant for humans tend to be more permanent and less software bound, however. If you encode the Declaration of Independence in XML, you want people to be able to read it in 2, 200, or 2,000 years. You also want them to be able to read it with any convenient tool, including ones not invented yet. These requirements have some important implications for both the XML applications you design to hold the data and the tools you use to read and write them.

The first rule is that the format should be very well documented. There should be a schema, and that schema should be very well commented. Furthermore, there should be a significant amount of prose documentation as well. Prose documentation can't substitute for the formal documentation of a schema, but it's an invaluable asset in understanding the schema.

Standard formats like DocBook and TEI should be preferred to custom, one-off XML applications. Avoid proprietary schemas that are owned by any one person or company and whose future may depend on the fortunes of that company or individual. Even schemas that come from nonprofit consortia, like OASIS or TEI, should be licensed sufficiently liberally so that intellectual property restrictions won't let anyone throw road blocks in your path. At least one XML purveyor has gone so far as to file for patents on its DTDs. These applications should be avoided like the plague. Stick to schemas that may be freely copied and shared and that can be retrieved from many different locations.

Once you've settled on a standard application, try to avoid modifying it if you can. If you must modify it, then document your changes in excruciating, redundant detail. Include comments in both the schemas and documents, explaining what you've done. Use the parameter entities built into the DTDs to add new element types or subtract old ones, rather than modifying the DTD files themselves.

Conversely, the format shouldn't be too hard to reverse engineer if the documentation and schemas are lost. Make sure full names are used throughout for element and attribute names. DocBook's para element is superior to TEI's p element. Paragraph would be better still.

All of the inherent structure of the document should be indicated by markup and markup alone. It should not be left for the user to infer, nor should it be encoded using whitespace or other separators. For instance, here's an example of what not to do from SVG:

```
<polygon style="fill: blue; stroke: green; stroke-width: 12"
         points="350,75  379,161 469,161 397,215 423,301 350,250
                 277,301 303,215 231,161 321,161" />
```

The style attribute contains three separate and barely related items. Understanding this element requires parsing the non-XML CSS format. The points attribute is even worse. It's a long list of numbers, but there's no information about what each number is. You can't, for instance, see which are the x and which are the y coordinates. An approach like this is preferable:

```
<polygon fill="blue" stroke="green" stroke-width="12">
  <point x="350" y="75"/>
  <point x="379" y="161"/>
  <point x="469" y="161"/>
  <point x="397" y="215"/>
  <point x="423" y="301"/>
  <point x="350" y="250"/>
  <point x="277" y="301"/>
  <point x="303" y="215"/>
  <point x="231" y="161"/>
  <point x="321" y="161"/>
</polygon>
```

The attribute-based style syntax is actually allowed in SVG. However, the debate over which form to use for coordinates was quite heated in the W3C SVG working group. In the end, the working group decided (wrongly, in our opinion) that the more verbose form would never be adopted because of its size, even though most members felt it was more in keeping with the spirit of XML. We think the working group overemphasized the importance of document size in an era of exponentially growing hard disks and network bandwidth, not to mention ignoring the ease with which the second format could be compressed for transport or storage.

Stylesheets are important. We're all familiar with the injunction to separate presentation from content. You've heard enough warnings about not including mere style information like italics and font choices in your XML documents. However, be careful not to go the other way and include content in your stylesheets either. Author names, titles, copyrights and other such information that changes from document to document belongs in the document, not the stylesheet, even if it's metainformation about the document rather than the actual content of the document.

Always keep in mind that you're not just writing for the next couple months or years, but possibly for the next couple thousand of years. Have pity on the poor historians who are going to have to decipher your markup with limited tools to help them.

Transformation and Presentation

The markup in a typical XML document describes the document's structure, but it tends not to describe the document's presentation. That is, it says how the document is organized but not how it looks. Although XML documents are text, and a person could read them in native form if they really wanted to, much more commonly an XML document is rendered into some other format before being presented to a human audience. One of the key ideas of markup languages in general and XML in particular is that the input format need not be the same as the output format. To put it another way, what you see is not what you get, nor is it what you want to get. The input markup language is designed for the convenience of the writer. The output language is designed for the convenience of the reader.

Of course this requires a means of transforming the input format into the output format. Most XML documents undergo some kind of transformation before being presented to the reader. The transformation may be to a different XML vocabulary like XHTML or XSL-FO, or it may be to a non-XML format like PostScript or RTF.

XML's semiofficial transformation language is Extensible Stylesheet Language Transformations (XSLT). An XSLT document contains a list of template rules. Each template rule has a pattern noting which elements and other nodes it matches. An XSLT processor reads the input document. When it sees something in the input document that matches a template rule in the stylesheet, it outputs the template rule's template. The template can tell the processor which content from the input to include in the output. This allows, for example, the text of the output document to be the same while all the markup is changed. For instance, you could write a stylesheet that would transform DocBook documents into TEI documents. XSLT will be discussed in much more detail in Chapter 8.

However, XSLT is not the only transformation language you can use with your XML documents. Other stylesheet languages such as the Document Style Sheet and Semantics Language (DSSSL, *http://www.jclark.com/dsssl/*) are also available. So are a variety of proprietary tools like OmniMark (*http://developers.omnimark. com/*). Most of these have particular strengths and weaknesses for particular kinds of documents. Custom programs written in a variety of programming languages— such as Java, C++, Perl, and Python—can use a plethora of APIs, such as SAX, StAX, DOM, JDOM, and XOM, to transform documents. This is sometimes useful when you need something more than a mere transformation—for instance, interpreting certain elements as database queries and actually inserting the results of those queries into the output document, or asking the user to answer questions in the middle of the transformation. However, the biggest single factor when choosing which tool to use is simply which language and syntax you're most comfortable with. *De linguis non disputandum est.*

There are many different choices for the output format from a transformation. A PostScript file can be printed on paper, overhead transparencies, slides, or even T-shirts. A PDF document can be viewed in all these ways and shown on the screen as well. However, for screen display, PDF is vastly inferior to simple HTML, which has the advantages of being very broadly accessible across platforms and being very easy to generate via XSLT from source XML documents. Generating a PDF or a PostScript file normally requires an additional conversion step in which special software converts some custom XML output format like XSL-FO to what you actually want.

An alternative to a transformation-based presentation is to provide a descriptive stylesheet that simply states how each element in the original document should be formatted. This is the realm of Cascading Style Sheets (CSS). This works particularly well for narrative documents where all that's needed is a list of the fonts, styles, sizes, and so on to apply to the content of each element. The key is that when all markup is stripped from the document, what remains is more or less a plain text version of what you want to see. No reordering or rearrangement is necessary. This approach works less well for record-like documents where the raw content may be nothing more than an undifferentiated mass of numbers, dates, or other information that's hard to understand without the context and annotations provided by the markup. However, in this case, a combination of the two approaches works well. First, a transformation can produce a new document containing rearranged and annotated information. Then a CSS stylesheet can apply style rules to the elements in this transformed document.

Document
Format

7

XML on the Web

XML began as an effort to bring the full power and structure of SGML to the Web in a form that was simple enough for nonexperts to use. Like most great inventions, XML turned out to have uses far beyond what its creators originally envisioned. Indeed, there's a lot more XML off the Web than on it. Nonetheless, XML is still a very attractive language in which to write and serve web pages. Since XML documents must be well-formed and parsers must reject malformed documents, XML pages are less likely to have annoying cross-browser incompatibilities. Since XML documents are highly structured, they're much easier for robots to parse. Since XML element and attribute names reflect the nature of the content they hold, search-engine robots can more easily determine the true meaning of a page.

XML on the Web comes in three flavors. The first is XHTML, an XMLized variant of HTML 4.0 that tightens up HTML to match XML's syntax. For instance, XHTML requires that all start-tags correspond to a matching end-tag and that all attribute values be quoted. XHTML also adds a few bits of syntax to HTML, such as the XML declaration and empty-element tags that end with />. Most of XHTML can be displayed quite well in legacy browsers, with a few notable exceptions.

The second flavor of XML on the Web is direct display of XML documents that use arbitrary vocabularies in web browsers. Generally, the formatting of the document is supplied either by a CSS stylesheet or by an XSLT stylesheet that transforms the document into HTML (perhaps XHTML). This flavor requires an XML-aware browser and is not supported by older web browsers such as Netscape 4.0.

A third option is to mix raw XML vocabularies, such as MathML and SVG, with XHTML using Modular XHTML. Modular XHTML lets you embed RDF cataloging information, MathML equations, SVG pictures, and more inside your XHTML documents. Namespaces sort out which elements belong to which applications.

XHTML

XHTML is an official W3C recommendation. It defines an XML-compatible version of HTML, or rather it redefines HTML as an XML application instead of as an SGML application. Just looking at an XHTML document, you might not even realize that there's anything different about it. It still uses the same <p>, <li>, <table>, <h1>, and other tags you're familiar with. Elements and attributes have the same, familiar names they have in HTML. The syntax is still basically the same.

The difference is not so much what's allowed but what's not allowed. <p> is a valid XHTML tag, but <P> is not. <table border="0" width="515"> is legal XHTML; <table border=0 width=515> is not. A paragraph prefixed with a <p> and suffixed with a </p> is legal XHTML, but a paragraph that omits the closing </p> tag is not. Most existing HTML documents require substantial editing before they become well-formed and valid XHTML documents. However, once they are valid XHTML documents, they are automatically valid XML documents that can be manipulated with the same editors, parsers, and other tools you use to work with any XML document.

Moving from HTML to XHTML

Most of the changes required to turn an existing HTML document into an XHTML document involve making the document well-formed. For instance, given a legacy HTML document, you'll probably have to make at least some of these changes to turn it into XHTML:

- Add missing end-tags like </p> and </li>.
- Rewrite elements so that they nest rather than overlap. For example, change `<p><em>an emphasized paragraph</p></em>` to `<p><em>an emphasized paragraph</em></p>`.
- Put double or single quotes around attribute values. For example, change `<p align=center>` to `<p align="center">`.
- Add values (which are the same as the name) to all minimized Boolean attributes. For example, change `<input type="checkbox" checked>` to `<input type="checkbox" checked="checked">`.
- Replace any occurrences of & or < in character data or attribute values with `&amp;` and `&lt;`. For instance, change A&P to A**&**P and `<a href="http://www.google.com/search?client=googlet&q=Java%20XML">` to `<a href="http://www.google.com/search?client=googlet&amp;q=Java%20XML">`.
- Make sure the document has a single root html element.
- Change empty elements like `<hr>` to `<hr />` or `<hr></hr>`.
- Add hyphens to comments so that `<! this is a comment>` becomes `<!-- this is a comment -->`.
- Encode the document in UTF-8 or UTF-16, or add an XML declaration that specifies in which character set it is encoded.

XHTML doesn't merely require well-formedness; it also requires validity. In order to create a valid XHTML document, you'll need to make these changes as well:

- Add a DOCTYPE declaration to the document pointing to one of the three XHTML DTDs.
- Make all element and attribute names lowercase.
- Adjust the markup so that the document validates against the DTD—for example, eliminating nonstandard elements like marquee, adding required attributes like the alt attribute of img, or moving child elements out from inside elements where they're not allowed, such as a blockquote inside a p.

In addition, the XHTML specification imposes a couple of requirements that, strictly speaking, are not required for either well-formedness or validity. However, they do make parsing XHTML documents a little easier. These requirements are:

- The root element of the document must be html.
- There must be a DOCTYPE declaration that uses a PUBLIC ID to identify one of the three XHTML DTDs.

Finally, if you wish, you may—but do not have to—add an XML declaration or an xml-stylesheet processing instruction to the prolog of your document.

Example 7-1 shows an HTML document from the O'Reilly web site that exhibits many of the validity problems you'll find on the Web today. In fact, this is a much neater page than most. Nonetheless, not all attribute values are quoted. The noshade attribute of the HR element doesn't even have a value. There's no document type declaration. Tags are a mix of upper- and lowercase, mostly uppercase. The DD elements are missing end-tags, and there's some character data inside the second definition that's not part of a DT or a DD.

Example 7-1. A typical HTML document

```
<HTML><HEAD>
  <TITLE>O'Reilly Shipping Information</TITLE>
</HEAD>
<BODY BGCOLOR="#ffffff" VLINK="#0000CC" LINK="#990000" TEXT="#000000">
<table border=0 width=515>
<tr>
<td>
<IMG SRC="/www/graphics_new/generic_ora_header_wide.gif" BORDER=0>
<H2>U.S. Shipping Information </H2>
<HR size="1" align=left noshade>
<DL>
<DT> <B>UPS Ground Service (Continental US only -- 5-7 business
days):</B></DT>
<DD>
<PRE>
$   5.95 - $ 49.99 ......................... $ 4.50
$  50.00 - $ 99.99 ......................... $ 6.50
$100.00 - $149.99 ......................... $ 8.50
$150.00 - $199.99 ......................... $10.50
$200.00 - $249.99 ......................... $12.50
$250.00 - $299.99 ......................... $14.50
</PRE>
```

Example 7-1. A typical HTML document (continued)

```
<DT> <B>Federal Express:</B></DT>
(Shipping within 24 hours of receipt of order by O'Reilly)
<DD>
<PRE>
<EM>1 or 2 books</EM>:
Economy 2-day ........................... $ 8.75
Overnight Standard (Afternoon Delivery) ... $12.75
Overnight Priority (Morning Delivery) ..... $16.50
</PRE>
</DL>
<b>Alaska and Hawaii:</b> add $10 to Federal Express rates.
<P>
<A HREF="int-ship.html"><b>International Shipping Information</b></A>
<P>
<CENTER>
<HR SIZE="1" NOSHADE>
<FONT SIZE="1" FACE="Verdana, Arial, Helvetica">
<A HREF="http://www.oreilly.com/">
<B>O'Reilly Home</B></A> <B> | </B>
<A HREF="http://www.oreilly.com/sales/bookstores">
<B>O'Reilly Bookstores</B></A> <B> | </B>
<A HREF="http://www.oreilly.com/order_new/">
<B>How to Order</B></A> <B> | </B>
<A HREF="http://www.oreilly.com/oreilly/contact.html">
<B>O'Reilly Contacts<BR></B></A>
<A HREF="http://www.oreilly.com/international/">
<B>International</B></A> <B> | </B>
<A HREF="http://www.oreilly.com/oreilly/about.html">
<B>About O'Reilly</B></A> <B> | </B>
<A HREF="http://www.oreilly.com/affiliates.html">
<B>Affiliated Companies</B></A><p>
<EM>&copy; 2000, O'Reilly Media, Inc.</EM>
</FONT>
</CENTER>
</td>
</tr>
</table>

</BODY>
</HTML>
```

Example 7-2 shows this document after it's been converted to XHTML. All the previously noted problems, and a few more besides, have been fixed. A number of deprecated presentational attributes, such as the size and noshade attributes of hr, had to be replaced with CSS styles. We've also added the necessary document type and namespace declarations. This document can now be read by both HTML and XML browsers and parsers.

Example 7-2. A valid XHTML document

```
<!DOCTYPE html PUBLIC "-//W3C//DTD XHTML 1.0 Strict//EN"
    "http://www.w3.org/TR/xhtml1/DTD/xhtml1-strict.dtd">
<html xmlns="http://www.w3.org/1999/xhtml">
```

Example 7-2. A valid XHTML document (continued)

```
<head>
<meta name="generator" content="HTML Tidy, see www.w3.org" />
<style type="text/css">
  body      {backgroundColor: #FFFFFF; color: #000000}
  a:visited {color: #0000CC}
  a:link    {color: #990000}
</style>
<title>O'Reilly Shipping Information</title>
</head>
<body>
<table border="0" width="515">
<tr>
<td><img src="/www/graphics_new/generic_ora_header_wide.gif"
style="border-width: 0" alt="O'Reilly"/>
<h2>U.S. Shipping Information</h2>

<hr style="height: 1; text-align: left"/>
<dl>
<dt><b>UPS Ground Service (Continental US only -- 5-7 business
days):</b></dt>

<dd>
<pre>
$   5.95 - $ 49.99 ......................... $ 4.50
$ 50.00 - $ 99.99 ......................... $ 6.50
$100.00 - $149.99 ......................... $ 8.50
$150.00 - $199.99 ......................... $10.50
$200.00 - $249.99 ......................... $12.50
$250.00 - $299.99 ......................... $14.50
</pre>
</dd>

<dt><b>Federal Express:</b></dt>

<dd>(Shipping within 24 hours of receipt of order by O'Reilly)</dd>

<dd>
<pre>
<em>1 or 2 books</em>:
Economy 2-day ............................ $ 8.75
Overnight Standard (Afternoon Delivery) ... $12.75
Overnight Priority (Morning Delivery) ..... $16.50

</pre>
</dd>
</dl>

<b>Alaska and Hawaii:</b> add $10 to Federal Express rates.

<p><a href="int-ship.html"><b>International Shipping
Information</b></a></p>
```

Example 7-2. A valid XHTML document (continued)

```
<div style="font-size: xx-small; font-face: Verdana, Arial, Helvetica;
        text-align: center">
<hr style="height: 1"/>
<a
href="http://www.oreilly.com/"><b>O'Reilly Home</b></a> <b>|</b> <a
href="http://www.oreilly.com/sales/bookstores"><b>O'Reilly
Bookstores</b></a> <b>|</b> <a
href="http://www.oreilly.com/order_new/"><b>How to Order</b></a>
<b>|</b> <a href="http://www.oreilly.com/oreilly/contact.html"><b>
O'Reilly Contacts<br />
</b></a> <a href="http://www.oreilly.com/international/"><b>
International</b></a> <b>|</b> <a
href="http://www.oreilly.com/oreilly/about.html"><b>About
O'Reilly</b></a> <b>|</b> <a
href="http://www.oreilly.com/affiliates.html"><b>Affiliated
Companies</b></a></div>

<p style="font-size: xx-small;
        font-family: Verdana, Arial, Helvetica"><em>&copy; 2000,
O'Reilly Media, Inc.</em></p>
</td>
</tr>
</table>
</body>
</html>
```

Making all these changes can be quite tedious for large documents or collections of many documents. Fortunately, there's an open source tool that can do most of the work for you. Dave Ragget's Tidy, *http://tidy.sourceforge.net*, is a C program that has been ported to most major operating systems and can convert some pretty nasty HTML into valid XHTML. For example, to convert the file *bad.html* to *good.xml*, you would type:

> % `tidy --output-xhtml yes bad.html good.xml`

Tidy fixes as much as it can and warns you about what it can't fix so you can fix it manually—for instance, telling you that a required alt attribute is missing from an img element.

Three DTDs for XHTML

XHTML comes in three flavors, depending on which DTD you choose:

Strict

This is the W3C's recommended form of XHTML. This includes all the basic elements and attributes such as p and class. However, it does not include deprecated elements and attributes such as applet and center. It also forbids the use of presentational attributes such as the body element's bgcolor, vlink, link, and text. These capabilities are provided by CSS instead. Strict XHTML is identified with this DOCTYPE declaration:

```
<!DOCTYPE html PUBLIC "-//W3C//DTD XHTML 1.0 Strict//EN"
                      "DTD/xhtml1-strict.dtd" >
```

Example 7-2 uses this DTD.

Transitional

This is a looser form of XHTML for when you can't easily do without deprecated elements and attributes, such as applet and bgcolor. It is identified with
this DOCTYPE declaration:

```
<!DOCTYPE html PUBLIC "-//W3C//DTD XHTML 1.0 Transitional//EN"
                      "DTD/xhtml1-transitional.dtd" >
```

Frameset

This is the same as the transitional DTD except that it also allows frame-
related elements, such as frameset and iframe. It is identified with this
DOCTYPE declaration:

```
<!DOCTYPE html PUBLIC "-//W3C//DTD XHTML 1.0 Frameset//EN"
                      "DTD/xhtml1-frameset.dtd" >
```

All three DTDs use the same *http://www.w3.org/1999/xhtml* namespace. You
should choose the strict DTD unless you've got a specific reason to use another one.

Browser Support for XHTML

Many web browsers, especially Internet Explorer 5.0 and earlier and Netscape 4.79
and earlier, deal inconsistently with XHTML. Certainly they don't require it,
accepting as they do such a wide variety of malformed, invalid, and out-and-out
mistaken HTML. However, beyond that they do have some problems when they
encounter certain common XHTML constructs.

The XML declaration and processing instructions

Some browsers display processing instructions and the XML declaration inline.
These should be omitted if possible.

Few, if any, browsers recognize or respect the encoding declaration in the XML
declaration. Furthermore, many browsers won't automatically recognize UTF-8 or
UCS-2 Unicode text. If you use a non-ASCII character set, you should also include
a meta element in the header identifying the character set. For example:

```
<meta http-equiv="Content-type"
      content='text/html; charset=UTF-8'></meta>
```

Empty elements

Browsers deal inconsistently with both forms of empty element syntax. That is,
some browsers understand <hr/> but not <hr></hr> (typically rendering it as two
horizontal lines rather than one), while others recognize <hr></hr> but not <hr/>
(typically omitting the horizontal line completely). The most consistent rendering
seems to be achieved by using an empty-element tag with an optional attribute
such as class or id—for example, <hr class="empty" />. There's no real reason
for the class attribute here, except that its presence keeps browsers from choking
on the />. Any other attribute the DTD allows would serve equally well.

On the other hand, if a particular instance of an element happens to be empty, but not all instances of the element have to be empty—for instance, a p that doesn't contain any text—you should use two tags like <p></p> rather than one empty-element tag <p/>.

Entity references

Embedded scripts often contain reserved characters like & or < so the document that contains them is not well-formed. However, most JavaScript and VBScript interpreters won't recognize & or < in place of the operators they represent. If the script can't be rewritten without these operators (for instance, by changing a less-than comparison to a greater-than-or-equal-to comparison with the arguments flipped), then you should move to external scripts instead of embedded ones.

Furthermore, most non-XML-aware browsers don't recognize the ' predefined entity reference. You should avoid this if possible and just use the literal ' character instead. The only place this might be a problem is inside attribute values that are enclosed in single quotes because they contain double quotes. However, most browsers do recognize the " entity reference for the " character so you can enclose the attribute value in double quotes and escape the double quotes that are part of the attribute value as ".

Other unsupported features

There are a few other subtle differences between how browsers handle XHTML and how XHTML expects to be handled. For instance, XHTML allows character references and CDATA sections although almost no current browsers understand these constructs. However, you're unlikely to encounter these when converting from HTML to XHTML, and you can generally do without them if you're writing XHTML from scratch.

Mozilla, Opera 5.0 and later, and Netscape 6.0 and later can parse and display valid XHTML without any difficulties and without requiring page authors to jump through these hoops. Safari and Internet Explorer 5.5 and later can mostly display it as long as the pages are mislabeled as text/html. However, both get confused if the pages are labeled with the correct MIME type application/xhtml+xml. Regardless, since many users have not upgraded their browsers to the level XHTML requires, user-friendly web designers will be jumping through these hoops for some time to come.

Direct Display of XML in Browsers

Ultimately, one hopes that browsers will be able to display not just XHTML documents but any XML document as well. Since it's too much to ask that browsers provide semantics for all XML applications both current and yet-to-be-invented, stylesheets will be attached to each document to provide instructions about how each element will be rendered.

The current major stylesheet languages are:

- Cascading Style Sheets Level 1 (CSS1)
- Cascading Style Sheets Level 2 (CSS2)
- XSL Transformations 1.0

Eventually, there will be more versions of these, including at least CSS 2.1, CSS Level 3, and XSLT 2.0. However, let's begin by looking at how and how well existing style languages are supported by existing browsers.

The xml-stylesheet Processing Instruction

The stylesheet associated with a document is indicated by an xml-stylesheet processing instruction in the document's prolog, which comes after the XML declaration but before the root element start-tag. This processing instruction uses pseudo-attributes to describe the stylesheet (that is, they look like attributes but are not attributes because xml-stylesheet is a processing instruction and not an element).

The required href and type pseudo-attributes

There are two required pseudo-attributes for xml-stylesheet processing instructions. The value of the href pseudo-attribute gives the URL, possibly relative, where the stylesheet can be found. The type pseudo-attribute value specifies the MIME media type of the stylesheet, text/css for cascading stylesheets, application/xml for XSLT stylesheets. In Example 7-3, the xml-stylesheet processing instruction tells browsers to apply the CSS stylesheet *person.css* to this document before showing it to the reader.

Example 7-3. An XML document associated with a stylesheet

```
<?xml version="1.0"?>
<?xml-stylesheet href="person.css" type="text/css"?>
<person>
  Alan Turing
</person>
```

 Microsoft Internet Explorer uses type="text/xsl" for XSLT stylesheets. However, the text/xsl MIME media type has not been and will not be registered with the IANA. It is a figment of Microsoft's imagination. In the future, application/xslt+xml will be registered to identify XSLT stylesheets specifically.

In addition to these two required pseudo-attributes, there are four optional pseudo-attributes:

- media
- charset
- alternate
- title

The media pseudo-attribute

The media pseudo-attribute contains a short string identifying the medium this stylesheet should be used for—for example, paper, onscreen display, television, and so forth. It can specify either a single medium or a comma-separated list of media. The recognized values include:

screen
> Computer monitors

tty
> Teletypes, terminals, xterms, and other monospaced, text-only devices

tv
> Televisions, WebTVs, video game consoles, and the like

projection
> Slides, transparencies, and direct-from-laptop presentations that will be shown to an audience on a large screen

handheld
> PDAs, cell phones, GameBoys, and the like

print
> Paper

braille
> Tactile feedback devices for the sight-impaired

aural
> Screen readers and speech synthesizers

all
> All of the previously mentioned plus any that haven't been invented yet

For example, this xml-stylesheet processing instruction says that the CSS stylesheet at *http://www.cafeconleche.org/style/titus.css* should be used for television, projection, and print:

```
<?xml-stylesheet href="http://www.cafeconleche.org/style/titus.css"
                 type="text/css" media="tv, projection, print"?>
```

The charset pseudo-attribute

The charset pseudo-attribute specifies in which character set the stylesheet is written, using the same values as the encoding declaration. For example, to say that the CSS stylesheet *koran.css* is written in the ISO-8859-6 character set, you'd use this processing instruction:

```
<?xml-stylesheet href="koran.css" type="text/css" charset="ISO-8859-6"?>
```

The alternate and title pseudo-attributes

The alternate pseudo-attribute specifies whether this is the primary stylesheet for its media type or an alternate one for special cases. The default value is no, which indicates that it is the primary stylesheet. If alternate has the value yes, then the browser may (but does not have to) present the user a choice from among the alternate stylesheets. If it does offer a choice, then it uses the value of the title pseudo-attribute to tell the user how the stylesheets differ. For example, these three xml-stylesheet processing instructions offer the user a choice between large, small, and medium text:

```
<?xml-stylesheet href="big.css" type="text/css"
                 alternate="yes" title="Large fonts"?>
<?xml-stylesheet href="small.css" type="text/css"
                 alternate="yes" title="Small fonts"?>
<?xml-stylesheet href="medium.css" type="text/css" title="Normal fonts"?>
```

Browsers that aren't able to ask the user to choose a stylesheet will simply pick the first nonalternate sheet that most closely matches its media type (screen for a typical web browser).

Internet Explorer

Microsoft Internet Explorer 4.0 (IE4) and later includes an XML parser that can be accessed from VBScript or JavaScript. This is used internally to support channels and the Active Desktop. Your own JavaScript and VBScript programs can use this parser to read XML data and insert it into the web page. However, anything more straightforward, like simply displaying a page of XML from a specified URL, is beyond IE4's capabilities. Furthermore, IE4 doesn't understand any stylesheet language when applied to XML.

Internet Explorer 5 (IE5) and 5.5 (IE 5.5) do understand XML, although their parser is more than a little buggy; it rejects a number of documents it shouldn't reject, most embarrassingly the XML 1.0 specification itself. Internet Explorer 6 (IE6) has improved XML support somewhat, but it is still not completely conformant.

IE5 and later can directly display XML files, with or without an associated stylesheet. If no stylesheet is provided, then IE5 uses a default, built-in XSLT stylesheet that displays the tree structure of the XML document along with a little DHTML to allow the user to collapse and expand nodes in the tree. Figure 7-1 shows IE5 displaying Example 6-1 from the last chapter.

IE5 also supports parts of CSS Level 1 and a little of CSS Level 2. However, the support is spotty and inconsistent. Even some aspects of CSS that work for HTML documents fail when applied to XML documents. IE 5.5 and IE6 slightly improve coverage of CSS but don't support all CSS properties and selectors. In fact, many CSS features that work in IE6 for HTML still don't work when applied to XML documents.

IE5 and IE 5.5 support their own custom version of XSLT, based on a very early working draft of the XSLT specification. They do *not* support XSLT 1.0. You can tell the difference by looking at the namespace of the stylesheet. A stylesheet written for IE5 uses the *http://www.w3.org/TR/WD-xsl* namespace, whereas a stylesheet designed for standard-compliant XSLT processors uses the *http://www. w3.org/1999/XSL/Transform* namespace. Despite superficial similarities, these two languages are not compatible. A stylesheet written for IE5 will not work with any other XSLT processor, and a stylesheet written using standard XSLT 1.0 will not work in IE5. IE6 supports both real XSLT and Microsoft's nonstandard dialect.

```
<?xml version="1.0" encoding="UTF-8" standalone="no" ?>
<!DOCTYPE TEI.2 (View Source for full doctype...)>
- <TEI.2 TEIform="TEI.2">
  - <teiHeader type="text" status="new" TEIform="teiHeader">
    - <fileDesc TEIform="fileDesc">
      - <titleStmt TEIform="titleStmt">
          <title TEIform="title">XML in a Nutshell</title>
          <author TEIform="author">Harold, Elliotte Rusty</author>
          <author TEIform="author">Means,W. Scott</author>
        </titleStmt>
      - <publicationStmt TEIform="publicationStmt">
          <p TEIform="p" />
        </publicationStmt>
      - <sourceDesc default="NO" TEIform="sourceDesc">
          <p TEIform="p">Early manuscript draft</p>
        </sourceDesc>
      </fileDesc>
    </teiHeader>
  - <text id="HarXMLi" TEIform="text">
    - <front TEIform="front">
      - <div1 type="toc" org="uniform" sample="complete" part="N" TEIform="div1">
          <head TEIform="head">Table Of Contents</head>
        - <list type="simple" TEIform="list">
            <item TEIform="item">Introducing XML</item>
            <item TEIform="item">XML as a Document Format</item>
            <item TEIform="item">XML on the Web</item>
          </list>
        </div1>
```

Figure 7-1. A document that uses IE5's built-in stylesheet

Netscape and Mozilla

Netscape 4.x and earlier do not provide any significant support for displaying XML in the browser. Netscape 4.0.6 and later do use XML internally for some features such as "What's Related." However, the parser used isn't accessible to the page author, even through JavaScript.

Mozilla 1.0 and Netscape 6.0 and later do fully support display of XML in the browser. CSS Level 2 is almost completely supported, and XSLT support is pretty good too. Mozilla can read an XML web page, download the associated CSS or XSLT stylesheet, apply it to the document, and display the result to the end user, all completely automatically and more or less exactly as XML on the Web was always meant to work. Mozilla also partially supports MathML and SVG. The SVG support is not switched on by default as of Mozilla 1.7, and the MathML support requires some extra fonts with more mathematical symbols; neither of these is hard to add.

Alternative Approaches

Authoring your web pages in XML does not necessarily require serving them in XML. Fourth-generation and earlier browsers that don't support XML in any significant way will be with us for some time to come. Servicing users with these browsers requires standard, ordinary HTML that works in any browser back to Mosaic 1.0.

One popular option is to write the pages in XML but serve them in HTML. When the server receives a request for an XML document, it automatically converts the document to HTML and sends the converted document instead. More sophisticated servers can cache the converted documents. They can also recognize browsers that support XML and send them the raw XML instead.

The preferred way to perform the conversion is with an XSLT stylesheet and a Java servlet. Indeed, most XSLT engines, such as Xalan-J and SAXON, include servlets that do exactly this. However, other schemes are possible, for instance, using PHP or CGI instead of a servlet. The key is to make sure that browsers only receive what they know how to read and display. We'll talk more about XSLT in the next chapter.

Authoring Compound Documents with Modular XHTML

XHTML 1.1 divides the three XHTML DTDs into individual modules. Parameter entities connect the modules by including or leaving out particular modules. Modules include:

Structure module, %xhtml-struct.module;
> The absolute bare minimum of elements needed for an HTML document: html, head, title, and body

Text module, %xhtml-text.module;
> The basic elements that contain text and other inline elements: abbr, acronym, address, blockquote, br, cite, code, dfn, div, em, h1, h2, h3, h4, h5, h6, kbd, p, pre, q, samp, span, strong, and var

Hypertext module, %xhtml-hypertext.module;
> Elements used for linking, that is, the a element

List module, %xhtml-list.module;
> Elements used for the three kinds of lists: dl, dt, dd, ul, ol, and li

Applet module, %xhtml-applet.module;
> Elements needed for Java applets: applet and param

Presentation module, %xhtml-pres.module;
> Presentation oriented markup, that is, the b, big, hr, i, small, sub, sup, and tt elements

Edit module, %xhtml-edit.module;
> Elements for revision tracking: del and ins

Bi-Directional Text module, %xhtml-bdo.module;
> An indication of directionality when text in left-to-right languages, like English and French, is mixed with text in right-to-left languages, like Hebrew and Arabic

Basic Forms module, %xhtml-basic-form.module;
> Forms as defined in HTML 3.2 using the form, input, select, option, and textarea elements

Forms module, %xhtml-form.module;
> Forms as defined in HTML 4.0 using the form, input, select, option, textarea, button, fieldset, label, legend, and optgroup elements

Basic Tables module, %xhtml-basic-table.module;
> Minimal table support including only the table, caption, th, tr, and td elements

Tables module, %xhtml-table.module;
> More complete table support including not only the table, caption, th, tr, and td elements, but also the col, colgroup, tbody, thead, and tfoot elements

Image module, %xhtml-image.module;
> The img element

Client-Side Image Map module, %xhtml-csismap.module;
> The map and area elements, as well as extra attributes for several other elements needed to support client-side image maps

Server-Side Image Map module, %xhtml-ssismap.module;
> Doesn't provide any new elements, but adds the ismap attribute to the img element

Object module, %xhtml-object.module;
> The object element used to embed executable content like Java applets and ActiveX controls in web pages

Param module, %xhtml-param.module;
> The param element used to pass parameters from web pages to their embedded executable content, such as Java applets and ActiveX controls

Frames module, %xhtml-frames.module;
> The elements needed to implement frames including frame, frameset, and noframes

Iframe module, %xhtml-iframe.mod;
> The iframe element used for inline frames

Intrinsic Events module, %xhtml-events.module;
> Attributes to support scripting like onsubmit and onfocus that are attached to elements declared in other modules

Metainformation module, %xhtml-meta.module;
> The meta element used in headers

Scripting module, %xhtml-script.module;
> Elements that support JavaScript and VBScript: script and noscript

Stylesheet module, %xhtml-style.module;
> The `style` element used to define Cascading Style Sheets

Link module, %xhtml-link.module;
> The `link` element that specifies relationships to various external documents, such as translations, glossaries, and previous and next pages

Base module, %xhtml-base.module;
> The `base` element that specifies a URL against which relative URLs are resolved

Target module, %xhtml-target.module;
> The `target` attribute that specifies the destination frame or window of a link

Style Attribute module, %xhtml-inlstyle.module;
> The `style` attribute that applies CSS styles to individual elements in the document

Name Identification module, %xhtml-nameident.module;
> The `name` attribute, a deprecated earlier version of the `id` attribute

Legacy module, %xhtml-legacy.module;
> Deprecated elements and attributes including the `basefont`, `center`, `font`, `s`, `strike`, and `u` elements

Ruby module, %xhtml11-ruby.module;
> The `ruby`, `rbc`, `rtc`, `rb`, `rt`, and `rp` elements used in East Asian text to place small amounts of text next to body text, generally indicating pronunciation

Mixing XHTML into Your Applications

The advantage to dividing HTML into all these different modules is that you can pick and choose the pieces you want. If your documents use tables, include the Tables module. If your documents don't use tables, then leave it out. You get only the functionality you actually need.

For example, let's suppose you're designing a DTD for a catalog. Each item in the catalog is a `catalog_entry` element. Each `catalog_entry` contains a name, price, `item_number`, color, size, and various other common elements you're likely to find in catalogs. Furthermore, each `catalog_entry` contains a description of the item. The description contains formatted narrative text. In other words, it looks something like this:

```
<catalog_entry>
  <name>Aluminum Duck Drainer</name>
  <price>34.99</price>
  <item_number>54X8</item_number>
  <color>silver</color>
  <size>XL</size>
  <description>
    <p>
      This sturdy <strong>silver</strong> colored
      sink stopper dignifies the <em>finest
      kitchens</em>. It makes a great gift for
    </p>
```

```
<ul>
  <li>Christmas</li>
  <li>Birthdays</li>
  <li>Mother's Day</li>
</ul>
<p>and all other occasions!</p>
</description>
</catalog_entry>
```

It's easy enough to write this markup. The tricky part is validating it. Rather than reinventing a complete DTD to describe all the formatting that's needed in straightforward narrative descriptions, you can reuse XHTML. The XHTML 1.1 DTD makes heavy use of parameter entity references to define content specifications and attribute lists for the different elements. Three entity references are of particular note:

%Inline.mix;

A choice containing all the elements that don't generally require a line break, such as em, a, and q. That is, it resolves to:

```
br | span | em | strong | dfn | code | samp | kbd | var | cite | abbr |
acronym | q | tt | i | b | big | small | sub | sup | bdo | a | img | map
| applet | ruby | input | select | textarea | label | button | ins | del
| script | noscript
```

%Block.mix;

A choice containing all the elements that generally require a line break, like p, blockquote, and ul. That is, it resolves to:

```
h1 | h2 | h3| h4 | h5 | h6| ul| ol| dl| p | div | pre| blockquote
| address | hr | table | form | fieldset | ins | del | script | noscript
```

%Flow.mix;

A choice containing both of the previous; that is, it resolves to:

```
h1 | h2 | h3 | h4 | h5 | h6 | ul | ol | dl | p | div | pre | blockquote
| address | hr | table | form | fieldset | br | span | em | strong | dfn
| code | samp | kbd | var | cite | abbr | acronym | q | tt | i | b | big
| small | sub | sup | bdo | a | img | map | applet | ruby | input |
select | textarea | label | button | ins | del | script | noscript
```

You can declare that the description element contains essentially any legal XHTML fragment, like this:

```
<!ENTITY % xhtml PUBLIC "-//W3C//DTD XHTML 1.1//EN" "xhtml11.dtd">
%xhtml;
<!ELEMENT description (#PCDATA | %Flow.mix;)*>
```

If you wanted to require description to contain only block elements at the top level, you'd instead declare it like this:

```
<!ENTITY % xhtml PUBLIC "-//W3C//DTD XHTML 1.1//EN" "xhtml11.dtd">
%xhtml;
<!ELEMENT description ((%Block.mix;)*)>
```

The first two lines import the XHTML driver DTD from a relative URL. You can get this DTD and the other local files it depends on from the zip archive at *http://www.w3.org/TR/xhtml11/xhtml11.zip*. The second line uses an entity reference defined in that DTD to set the content specification for the description element.

The XHTML 1.1 driver DTD imports modules from two other W3C specifications, Modularization of XHTML (*http://www.w3.org/TR/ xhtml-modularization*) and Ruby Annotation (*http://www.w3.org/ TR/ruby*), using absolute URLs that point to the W3C's web site. If you're not reliably connected to the Internet at high speed, you might want to use the flat version of this DTD, *xhtml11-flat.dtd*, instead. This bundles all the different modules in a single file.

Unfortunately, this goes a little too far. It includes not only the pieces of HTML you want, such as p, em, and ul, but also a lot of elements you don't want in a printed catalog, such as a, applet, map, and a lot more. However, you can omit these. The main XHTML DTD imports each module inside an INCLUDE/IGNORE block, such as this one for the hypertext module:

```
<!-- Hypertext Module (required) ................................ -->
<!ENTITY % xhtml-hypertext.module "INCLUDE" >
<![%xhtml-hypertext.module;[
<!ENTITY % xhtml-hypertext.mod
 PUBLIC "-//W3C//ELEMENTS XHTML Hypertext 1.0//EN"
    "http://www.w3.org/TR/xhtml-modularization/DTD/xhtml-hypertext-1.mod" >
%xhtml-hypertext.mod;]]>
```

If the %xhtml-hypertext.module; parameter entity reference has previously been defined as IGNORE instead of INCLUDE, that declaration takes precedence; all the elements and attributes defined in the Hypertext module (specifically, the a element) are left out of the resulting DTD.

Let's say you just want the Structure, Basic Text, and List modules. Then you use a driver DTD that redefines the parameter entity references for the other modules as IGNORE. Example 7-4 demonstrates.

Example 7-4. A catalog DTD that uses basic XHTML but omits a lot of elements

```
<!ELEMENT catalog (catalog_entry*)>
<!ELEMENT catalog_entry (name, price, item_number, color, size, description)>
<!ELEMENT name (#PCDATA)>
<!ELEMENT size (#PCDATA)>
<!ELEMENT price (#PCDATA)>
<!ELEMENT item_number (#PCDATA)>
<!ELEMENT color (#PCDATA)>

<!-- throw away the modules we don't need -->
<!ENTITY % xhtml-hypertext.module "IGNORE" >
<!ENTITY % xhtml-ruby.module     "IGNORE" >
<!ENTITY % xhtml-edit.module     "IGNORE" >
<!ENTITY % xhtml-pres.module     "IGNORE" >
<!ENTITY % xhtml-applet.module   "IGNORE" >
<!ENTITY % xhtml-param.module    "IGNORE" >
<!ENTITY % xhtml-bidi.module     "IGNORE" >
<!ENTITY % xhtml-form.module     "IGNORE" >
<!ENTITY % xhtml-table.module    "IGNORE" >
<!ENTITY % xhtml-image.module    "IGNORE" >
<!ENTITY % xhtml-csismap.module  "IGNORE" >
```

```
<!ENTITY % xhtml-ssismap.module    "IGNORE" >
<!ENTITY % xhtml-meta.module       "IGNORE" >
<!ENTITY % xhtml-script.module     "IGNORE" >
<!ENTITY % xhtml-style.module      "IGNORE" >
<!ENTITY % xhtml-link.module       "IGNORE" >
<!ENTITY % xhtml-base.module       "IGNORE" >

<!-- import the XHTML DTD, at least those parts we aren't ignoring.
     You will probably need to change the system ID to point to
     whatever directory you've stored the DTD in.
-->
<!ENTITY % xhtml11.mod PUBLIC "-//W3C//DTD XHTML 1.1//EN"
                             "xhtml11/DTD/xhtml11.dtd">
%xhtml11.mod;

<!ELEMENT description ( %Block.mix; )+>
```

Mixing Your Applications into XHTML

An even more important feature of Modular XHTML is the option to add new elements that HTML doesn't support. For instance, to include SVG pictures in your documents, you just have to import the SVG DTD and redefine the Misc. extra parameter entity to allow the SVG root element svg. (This only lets you validate XHTML documents that contain SVG markup. It doesn't magically give the browser the ability to render these pictures.) You accomplish this by redefining any of these three parameter entity references:

%Inline.extra;
> Place the root elements of your application here if you want them to be added to the content specifications of inline elements, such as span, em, code, and textarea.

%Block.extra;
> Place the root elements of your application here if you want them to be added to the content specifications of block elements, such as div, h1, p, and pre.

%Misc.extra;
> Place the root elements of your application here if you want them to be added to the content specifications of both block and inline elements.

The definition of each of these parameter entities should be a list of the elements you want to add to the content specification separated by vertical bars and beginning with a vertical bar. For instance, to include MathML equations as both inline and block elements, you'd import the MathML DTD and redefine the Misc.extra parameter entity to include the MathML root element math like this:

```
<!ENTITY % Misc.extra "| math">
```

If you wanted to allow block-level MathML equations and SVG pictures, you'd import their respective DTDs and redefine the Block.extra parameter entity like this:

```
<!ENTITY % Block.extra "| math | svg">
```

XML on the Web

Order is important here. The MathML DTD and the `Block.extra` declaration both have to be parsed before the XHTML DTD is parsed. Example 7-5 demonstrates with a DTD that mixes MathML 1.0 and XHTML, throwing in a namespace declaration for good measure.

Example 7-5. A DTD that mixes MathML into XHTML and MathML

```
<!ENTITY % mathml SYSTEM "mathml/mathml.dtd">
%mathml;

<!ATTLIST math xmlns CDATA #FIXED "http://www.w3.org/1998/Math/MathML">

<!ENTITY % Misc.extra "| math">

<!ENTITY % xhtml PUBLIC "-//W3C//DTD XHTML 1.1//EN" "xhtml11/DTD/xhtml11.dtd">
%xhtml;
```

You can also mix new elements like `math` into individual elements like `p` without changing all the other block elements. The content specification for each XHTML element is defined by a parameter entity named *Element*.content, for example, `%p.content;`, `%em.content;`, `%td.content;` and so forth. The standard definition of `p.content` looks like this:

```
<!ENTITY % p.content
    "( #PCDATA | %Inline.mix; )*" >
```

To allow the `math` element to be a child of `p` elements, but not of every other block element, you would redefine `p.content` like this:

```
<!ENTITY % p.content "( #PCDATA | %Inline.mix; | math )*" >
```

The XHTML 1.1 DTD is quite sophisticated. There are a lot more tricks you can play by mixing and matching different parts of the DTD, mostly by defining and redefining different parameter entity references. The easiest way to learn about these is by reading the raw DTDs. In many cases, the comments in the DTD are more descriptive and accurate than the prose specification.

Mixing Your Own XHTML

The XHTML 1.1 DTD does not include all of the modules that are available. For instance, frames and the legacy presentational elements are deliberately omitted and cannot easily be turned on. This is the W3C's not-so-subtle way of telling you that you shouldn't be using these elements in the first place. If you do want to use them, you'll need to create your own complete DTD using the individual modules you require.

To do this, you must first define the namespace URI and prefixed names for your elements and attributes. The W3C provides a template you can adapt for this purpose at *http://www.w3.org/TR/xhtml-modularization/DTD/templates/template-qname-1.mod*. Example 7-6 demonstrates with a DTD fragment that defines the names for the `today` and `quoteoftheday` elements that one of the authors (Harold) uses on his web sites. The module is based on the W3C-provided template.

Example 7-6. A DTD module to define the today and quoteoftheday elements' names and namespaces

```
<!-- .......................................................... -->
<!-- CafeML Qualified Names Module ............................ -->
<!-- file: cafe-qname-1.mod

     This is an extension of XHTML, a reformulation of HTML as
     a modular XML application.

     This DTD module is identified by the PUBLIC and SYSTEM identifiers:

PUBLIC "-//Elliotte Rusty Harold//ELEMENTS CafeML Qualified Names 1.0//EN"
       "cafe-qname-1.mod"

     .......................................................... -->

<!-- NOTES:  Using the CafeML Qualified Names Extension

     This is a module for a markup language 'CafeML',
     which currently declares two extension elements, quoteoftheday
     and today. The parameter entity naming convention uses uppercase
     for the entity name and lowercase for namespace prefixes, hence
     this example uses 'CAFEML' and 'cafeml' respectively.

     Please note the three case variants:

         'CafeML'    the human-readable markup language name
         'CAFEML'    used as a parameter entity name prefix
         'cafeml'    used as the default namespace prefix

     The %NS.prefixed; conditional section keyword must be declared
     as "INCLUDE" in order to allow prefixing to be used.
-->

<!-- :::::::::::::::::::::::::::::::::::::::::::::::::::::::::::: -->

<!-- CafeML Qualified Names

     This module is contained in two parts, labeled Section 'A' and 'B':

         Section A declares parameter entities to support namespace-
         qualified names, namespace declarations, and name prefixing
         for CafeML.

         Section B declares parameter entities used to provide
         namespace-qualified names for all CafeML element types.

     The recommended step-by-step program for creating conforming
     modules is enumerated below, and spans both the CafeML Qualified
     Names Template and CafeML Extension Template modules.
-->
<!-- Section A: CafeML XML Namespace Framework ::::::::::::::::::: -->
```

Example 7-6. A DTD module to define the today and quoteoftheday elements' names and namespaces (continued)

```
<!-- 1. Declare a %CAFEML.prefixed; conditional section keyword, used
        to activate namespace prefixing. The default value should
        inherit '%NS.prefixed;' from the DTD driver, so that unless
        overridden, the default behavior follows the overall DTD
        prefixing scheme.
-->
<!ENTITY % NS.prefixed "IGNORE" >
<!ENTITY % CAFEML.prefixed "%NS.prefixed;" >


<!-- 2. Declare a parameter entity (e.g., %CAFEML.xmlns;) containing
        the URI reference used to identify the Module namespace:
-->
<!ENTITY % CAFEML.xmlns  "http://www.cafeconleche.org/xmlns/cafeml" >


<!-- 3. Declare parameter entities (e.g., %CAFEML.prefix;) containing
        the default namespace prefix string(s) to use when prefixing
        is enabled. These may be overridden in the DTD driver or the
        internal subset of a document instance. If no default prefix
        is desired, this may be declared as an empty string.

     NOTE: As specified in [XMLNAMES], the namespace prefix serves
     as a proxy for the URI reference and is not in itself significant.
-->
<!ENTITY % CAFEML.prefix  "cafeml" >


<!-- 4. Declare parameter entities (e.g., %CAFEML.pfx;) containing the
        colonized prefix(es) (e.g., '%CAFEML.prefix;:') used when
        prefixing is active, an empty string when it is not.
-->
<![%CAFEML.prefixed;[
<!ENTITY % CAFEML.pfx  "%CAFEML.prefix;:" >
]]>
<!ENTITY % CAFEML.pfx  "" >


<!-- 5. The parameter entity %CAFEML.xmlns.extra.attrib; may be
        redeclared to contain any non-CafeML namespace declaration
        attributes for namespaces embedded in CafeML. When prefixing
        is active it contains the prefixed xmlns attribute and any
        namespace declarations embedded in CafeML, otherwise an empty
        string.
-->
<![%CAFEML.prefixed;[
<!ENTITY % CAFEML.xmlns.extra.attrib
     "xmlns:%CAFEML.prefix; %URI.datatype;   #FIXED '%CAFEML.xmlns;'" >
]]>
<!ENTITY % CAFEML.xmlns.extra.attrib "" >

<!ENTITY % XHTML.xmlns.extra.attrib
     "%CAFEML.xmlns.extra.attrib;"
>
```

Example 7-6. A DTD module to define the today and quoteoftheday elements' names and namespaces (continued)

```
<!-- Section B: CafeML Qualified Names ::::::::::::::::::::::::::::::::: -->

<!-- This section declares parameter entities used to provide
     namespace-qualified names for all CafeML element types.
-->
<!-- module:  cafe-1.mod -->
<!ENTITY % CAFEML.quoteoftheday.qname   "%CAFEML.pfx;quoteoftheday" >
<!ENTITY % CAFEML.today.qname      "%CAFEML.pfx;today" >

<!-- end of cafe-qname-1.mod -->
```

Next you have to define the elements and attributes with these names in a module of your own creation. The W3C provides a template, which you can adapt for this purpose, at *http://www.w3.org/TR/xhtml-modularization/DTD/templates/template-1.mod.* This template uses the same techniques and follows the same patterns as XHTML's built-in modules, for example, parameter entity references that resolve to INCLUDE or IGNORE.

Example 7-7 demonstrates with a DTD fragment that defines the today and quoteoftheday elements. The today element can contain any block-level content through the Block.mix parameter entity and has a required date attribute. The quoteoftheday element always contains exactly one blockquote element followed by exactly one p element with no attributes.

Example 7-7. A DTD module to define the today and quoteoftheday elements

```
<!-- .......................................................... -->
<!-- CAFEML Extension Template Module ......................... -->
<!-- file: CafeML-1.mod

     This is an extension of XHTML, a reformulation of HTML as
     a modular XML application.

     This DTD module is identified by the PUBLIC and SYSTEM identifiers:

       PUBLIC "Elliotte Rusty Harold//ELEMENTS CafeML Qualified Names 1.0//EN"
       SYSTEM "CafeML-1.mod"

     Revisions:
     (none)
     .......................................................... -->

<!-- Extension Template

     This sample template module declares two extension elements,
     today and quoteoftheday. The parameter entity naming
     convention uses uppercase for the entity name and lowercase
     for namespace prefixes. Hence this example uses 'CAFEML' and
     'cafe' respectively.
```

XML on the Web

This module declares parameter entities used to provide
namespace-qualified names for all CAFEML element types,
as well as an extensible framework for attribute-based
namespace declarations on all element types.

The %NS.prefixed; conditional section keyword must be
declared as "INCLUDE" in order to allow prefixing to be used.
By default, foreign (i.e., non-XHTML) namespace modules should
inherit %NS.prefixed; from XHTML, but this can be overridden
when prefixing of only the non-XHTML markup is desired.

XHTML's default value for the 'namespace prefix' is an empty
string. The Prefix value can be redeclared either in a DTD
driver or in a document's internal subset as appropriate.

NOTE: As specified in [XMLNAMES], the namespace prefix serves as
a proxy for the URI reference and is not in itself significant.
-->

```
<!-- ............................................................ -->

<!-- 1. Declare the xmlns attributes used by CAFEML dependent on whether
        CAFEML's prefixing is active. This should be used on all CAFEML
        element types as part of CAFEML's common attributes.

        If the entire DTD is namespace-prefixed, CAFEML should inherit
        %NS.decl.attrib;. Otherwise it should declare %NS.decl.attrib;
        plus a default xmlns attribute on its own element types.
-->
<![%CAFEML.prefixed;[
<!ENTITY % CAFEML.xmlns.attrib
    "%NS.decl.attrib;"
>
]]>
<!ENTITY % CAFEML.xmlns.attrib
    "xmlns       %URI.datatype;          #FIXED '%CAFEML.xmlns;'"
>

<!-- now include the module's various markup declarations ........ -->

<!ENTITY % CAFEML.Common.attrib
    "%CAFEML.xmlns.attrib;
     id          ID                      #IMPLIED"
>

<!-- 2. In the attribute list for each element, declare the XML Namespace
        declarations that are legal in the document instance by including
        the %NamespaceDecl.attrib; parameter entity in the ATTLIST of
        each element type.
-->
```

Example 7-7. A DTD module to define the today and quoteoftheday elements (continued)

```
<!ENTITY % CAFEML.today.qname  "today" >
<!ELEMENT %CAFEML.today.qname; ( %Flow.mix; )* >
<!ATTLIST %CAFEML.today.qname;
     %CAFEML.Common.attrib;
     date CDATA #REQUIRED
>


<!ENTITY % CAFEML.quoteoftheday.qname  "quoteoftheday" >
<!ELEMENT %CAFEML.quoteoftheday.qname; ( %blockquote.qname;,
                                         %p.qname; ) >
<!ATTLIST %CAFEML.quoteoftheday.qname;
     %CAFEML.Common.attrib;
>


<!-- 3. If the module adds attributes to elements defined in modules that
        do not share the namespace of this module, declare those
        attributes so that they use the %CAFEML.pfx; prefix. For example:

<!ENTITY % CAFEML.img.myattr.qname "%CAFEML.pfx;myattr" >
<!ATTLIST %img.qname;
     %CAFEML.img.myattr.qname;  CDATA      #IMPLIED
>

 This would add a myattr attribute to the img element of the Image Module,
 but the attribute's name will be the qualified name, including prefix,
 when prefixes are selected for a document instance.

 We do not need to do this for this module.

-->


<!-- end of CafeML-1.mod -->
```

Next you need to write a document model module that defines the parameter entities used for content specifications in the various modules—not only the CafeML modules, but the XHTML modules as well. (This is how your elements become part of the various XHTML elements.) The W3C does not provide a template for this purpose. However, it's normally easy to adapt the document model module from either XHTML 1.1 or XHTML Basic to include your new elements. Example 7-8 is a document model module based on the XHTML 1.1 document model module.

Example 7-8. A document model module for CafeML

```
<!-- ................................................ -->
<!-- CafeML Model Module  ........................... -->
<!-- file: CafeML-model-1.mod

  PUBLIC "-//Elliotte Rusty Harold//ELEMENTS XHTML CafeML Model 1.0//EN"
  SYSTEM "CafeML-model-1.mod"
```

Example 7-8. A document model module for CafeML (continued)

```
    xmlns:cafeml="http://www.cafeconleche.org/xmlns/cafeml"
....................................................... -->

<!-- Define the content model for Misc.extra -->
<!ENTITY % Misc.extra
    "| %CAFEML.today.qname; | %CAFEML.quoteoftheday.qname; ">

<!-- ..................  Inline Elements  ..................... -->

<!ENTITY % HeadOpts.mix
    "( %meta.qname; )*" >

<!ENTITY % I18n.class "" >

<!ENTITY % InlStruct.class "%br.qname; | %span.qname;" >

<!ENTITY % InlPhras.class
    "| %em.qname; | %strong.qname; | %dfn.qname; | %code.qname;
    | %samp.qname; | %kbd.qname; | %var.qname; | %cite.qname;
    | %abbr.qname; | %acronym.qname; | %q.qname;" >

<!ENTITY % InlPres.class "" >

<!ENTITY % Anchor.class "| %a.qname;" >

<!ENTITY % InlSpecial.class "| %img.qname; " >

<!ENTITY % Inline.extra "" >

<!-- %Inline.class; includes all inline elements,
    used as a component in mixes
-->
<!ENTITY % Inline.class
    "%InlStruct.class;
    %InlPhras.class;
    %InlPres.class;
    %Anchor.class;
    %InlSpecial.class;"
>

<!-- %InlNoAnchor.class; includes all non-anchor inlines,
    used as a component in mixes
-->

<!ENTITY % InlNoAnchor.class
    "%InlStruct.class;
    %InlPhras.class;
    %InlPres.class;
    %InlSpecial.class;"
>
```

Example 7-8. A document model module for CafeML (continued)

```
<!-- %InlNoAnchor.mix; includes all non-anchor inlines
-->
<!ENTITY % InlNoAnchor.mix
    "%InlNoAnchor.class;
     %Misc.class;"
>

<!-- %Inline.mix; includes all inline elements, including %Misc.class;
-->
<!ENTITY % Inline.mix
    "%Inline.class;
     %Misc.class;"
>

<!-- .................... Block Elements ..................... -->
<!ENTITY % Heading.class
    "%h1.qname; | %h2.qname; | %h3.qname;
     | %h4.qname; | %h5.qname; | %h6.qname;" >

<!ENTITY % List.class "%ul.qname; | %ol.qname; | %dl.qname;" >

<!ENTITY % BlkStruct.class "%p.qname; | %div.qname;" >

<!ENTITY % BlkPhras.class
    "| %pre.qname; | %blockquote.qname; | %address.qname;" >

<!ENTITY % BlkPres.class "| %hr.qname;" >

<!ENTITY % Block.extra "" >

<!ENTITY % Table.class "| %table.qname;" >

<!ENTITY % BlkSpecial.class
    "%Table.class;"
>

<!-- %Block.class; includes all block elements,
     used as an component in mixes
-->
<!ENTITY % Block.class
    "%BlkStruct.class;
     %BlkPhras.class;
     %BlkPres.class;
     %BlkSpecial.class;
     %Block.extra;"
>

<!-- %Block.mix; includes all block elements plus %Misc.class;
-->
<!ENTITY % Block.mix
    "%Heading.class;
     | %List.class;
```

XML on the Web

Example 7-8. A document model module for CafeML (continued)

```
    | %Block.class;
    %Misc.class;"
>


<!-- ............... All Content Elements ................. -->

<!-- %Flow.mix; includes all text content, block and inline
-->
<!ENTITY % Flow.mix
    "%Heading.class;
    | %List.class;
    | %Block.class;
    | %Inline.class;
    %Misc.class;"
>

<!-- special content model for pre element -->
<!ENTITY % pre.content
    "( #PCDATA
    | %Inline.class; )*"
>

<!-- end of CafeML-model-1.mod -->
```

Finally, replace the standard XHTML DTD, which only imports the normal
XHTML modules, with a new one that imports the standard modules you want as
well as any new modules you've defined. Again, the W3C offers a template for
this purpose, which you can download from *http://www.w3.org/TR/xhtml-
modularization/DTD/templates/template.dtd.* This template is a minimal DTD that
makes the necessary imports and declares the necessary parameter entity references upon which all the other modules depend. Example 7-9 is a DTD based on
this template. It merges in the element module defined in Example 7-7, as well as
the standard XHTML tables, images, meta, and block presentation modules.

Example 7-9. An XHTML DTD that mixes in the Cafe DTD

```
<!-- ................................................................ -->
<!-- XHTML + CafeML DTD .......................................... -->
<!-- file: CafeML.dtd -->

<!-- CafeML DTD -->
<!-- Please use this formal public identifier to identify it:
        "-//Elliotte Rusty Harold//DTD XHTML CafeDTD//EN"
-->
<!ENTITY % XHTML.version  "-//W3C//DTD XHTML CafeDTD//EN" >

<!-- Bring in any qualified name modules outside of XHTML -->
<!ENTITY % CAFEML-qname.mod SYSTEM "cafe-qname-1.mod">
%CAFEML-qname.mod;

<!-- Define any extra prefixed namespaces that this DTD relies upon -->
<!ENTITY NS.prefixed.extras.attrib "" >
```

Example 7-9. An XHTML DTD that mixes in the Cafe DTD (continued)

```
<!-- Define the Content Model file for the framework to use -->
<!ENTITY % xhtml-model.mod SYSTEM "CafeML-model-1.mod" >

<!-- reserved for future use with document profiles -->
<!ENTITY % XHTML.profile  "" >

<!-- Bi-directional text support
     This feature-test entity is used to declare elements
     and attributes used for internationalization support.
     Set it to INCLUDE or IGNORE as appropriate for your markup language.
-->
<!ENTITY % XHTML.bidi            "IGNORE" >

<!-- :::::::::::::::::::::::::::::::::::::::::::::::::::::::::::::::::: -->
<!-- Pre-Framework Redeclaration placeholder  .................... -->
<!-- This serves as a location to insert markup declarations
     into the DTD prior to the framework declarations.
-->
<!ENTITY % xhtml-prefw-redecl.module "IGNORE" >
<![%xhtml-prefw-redecl.module;[
%xhtml-prefw-redecl.mod;
<!-- end of xhtml-prefw-redecl.module -->]]>

<!-- The events module should be included here if you need it. In this
     skeleton it is IGNOREd.
-->
<!ENTITY % xhtml-events.module "IGNORE" >

<!-- Modular Framework Module .................................. -->
<!ENTITY % xhtml-framework.module "INCLUDE" >
<![%xhtml-framework.module;[
<!ENTITY % xhtml-framework.mod
     PUBLIC "-//W3C//ENTITIES XHTML 1.1 Modular Framework 1.0//EN"
            "xhtml-framework-1.mod" >
%xhtml-framework.mod;]]>

<!-- Post-Framework Redeclaration placeholder .................. -->
<!-- This serves as a location to insert markup declarations
     into the DTD following the framework declarations.
-->
<!ENTITY % xhtml-postfw-redecl.module "IGNORE" >
<![%xhtml-postfw-redecl.module;[
%xhtml-postfw-redecl.mod;
<!-- end of xhtml-postfw-redecl.module -->]]>

<!-- Text Module (required) ............................. -->
<!ENTITY % xhtml-text.module "INCLUDE" >
<![%xhtml-text.module;[
<!ENTITY % xhtml-text.mod
     PUBLIC "-//W3C//ELEMENTS XHTML 1.1 Text 1.0//EN"
            "xhtml-text-1.mod" >
%xhtml-text.mod;]]>
```

XML on the
Web

Example 7-9. An XHTML DTD that mixes in the Cafe DTD (continued)

```
<!-- Hypertext Module (required) ................................ -->
<!ENTITY % xhtml-hypertext.module "INCLUDE" >
<![%xhtml-hypertext.module;[
<!ENTITY % xhtml-hypertext.mod
     PUBLIC "-//W3C//ELEMENTS XHTML 1.1 Hypertext 1.0//EN"
            "xhtml-hypertext-1.mod" >
%xhtml-hypertext.mod;]]>


<!-- Lists Module (required) .................................... -->
<!ENTITY % xhtml-list.module "INCLUDE" >
<![%xhtml-list.module;[
<!ENTITY % xhtml-list.mod
     PUBLIC "-//W3C//ELEMENTS XHTML 1.1 Lists 1.0//EN"
            "xhtml-list-1.mod" >
%xhtml-list.mod;]]>


<!-- Your modules can be included here.  Use the basic form defined above,
     and be sure to include the public FPI definition in your catalog file
     for each module that you define. You may also include W3C-defined
     modules at this point.
-->
<!-- CafeML Module (custom module)  ...................... -->
<!ENTITY % cafeml.module "INCLUDE" >
<![%cafeml.module;[
<!ENTITY % cafeml.mod
     PUBLIC "-//Cafe con Leche//XHTML Extensions today 1.0//EN"
            "CafeML-1.mod" >
%cafeml.mod;]]>


<!-- Tables Module (optional)  ...................... -->
<!ENTITY % xhtml-table.module "INCLUDE" >
<![%xhtml-table.module;[
<!ENTITY % xhtml-table.mod
     PUBLIC "-//W3C//ELEMENTS XHTML Tables 1.0//EN"
            "xhtml-table-1.mod" >
%xhtml-table.mod;]]>


<!-- Meta Module (optional)  ...................... -->
<!ENTITY % xhtml-meta.module "INCLUDE" >
<![%xhtml-meta.module;[
<!ENTITY % xhtml-meta.mod
    PUBLIC "-//W3C//ELEMENTS XHTML Meta 1.0//EN"
            "xhtml-meta-1.mod" >
%xhtml-meta.mod;]]>


<!-- Image Module (optional)  ...................... -->
<!ENTITY % xhtml-image.module "INCLUDE" >
<![%xhtml-image.module;[
<!ENTITY % xhtml-image.mod
     PUBLIC "-//W3C//ELEMENTS XHTML Images 1.0//EN"
            "xhtml-image-1.mod" >
%xhtml-image.mod;]]>
```

Example 7-9. An XHTML DTD that mixes in the Cafe DTD (continued)

```
<!-- Block Presentation Module (optional)  ...................... -->
<!ENTITY % xhtml-blkpres.module "INCLUDE" >
<![%xhtml-blkpres.module;[
<!ENTITY % xhtml-blkpres.mod
      PUBLIC "-//W3C//ELEMENTS XHTML Block Presentation 1.0//EN"
            "xhtml-blkpres-1.mod" >
%xhtml-blkpres.mod;]]>


<!-- Document Structure Module (required)  ...................... -->
<!ENTITY % xhtml-struct.module "INCLUDE" >
<![%xhtml-struct.module;[
<!ENTITY % xhtml-struct.mod
      PUBLIC "-//W3C//ELEMENTS XHTML 1.1 Document Structure 1.0//EN"
            "xhtml-struct-1.mod" >
%xhtml-struct.mod;]]>


<!-- end of CAFEML DTD ............................................. -->
<!-- ............................................................... -->
```

Prospects for Improved Web Search Methods

Part of the hype of XML has been that web search engines will finally understand what a document means by looking at its markup. For instance, you can search for the movie *Sneakers* and just get back hits about the movie without having to sort through "Internet Wide Area 'Tiger Teamers' mailing list," "Children's Side Zip Sneakers Recalled by Reebok," "Infant's 'Little Air Jordan' Sneakers Recalled by Nike," "Sneakers.com—Athletic shoes from Nike, Reebok, Adidas, Fila, New," and the 32,395 other results that Google pulled up on this search that had nothing to do with the movie.[*]

In practice, this is still vapor, mostly because few web pages are available on the frontend in XML, even though more and more backends are XML. The search-engine robots only see the frontend HTML. As this slowly changes, and as the search engines get smarter, we should see more and more useful results. Meanwhile, it's possible to add some XML hints to your HTML pages that knowledgeable search engines can take advantage of using the Resource Description Framework (RDF), the Dublin Core, and the robots processing instruction.

RDF

The Resource Description Framework (RDF, *http://www.w3.org/RDF/*) can be understood as an XML encoding for a particularly simple data model. An RDF document describes resources using triples. Each triple says that a *resource* has a *property* with a *value*. Resources are identified by URIs. Properties can be identified by URIs or by element-qualified names. The value can be a string of plain text, a chunk of XML, or another resource identified by a URI.

XML on the
Web

---

[*] In fairness to Google, four of the first ten hits it returned were about the movie.

The root element of an RDF document is an RDF element. Each resource the RDF element describes is represented as a Description element whose about attribute contains a URI pointing to the resource described. Each child element of the Description element represents a property of the resource. The contents of that child element are the value of that property. All RDF elements like RDF and Description are placed in the http://www.w3.org/1999/02/22-rdf-syntax-ns# namespace. Property values generally come from other namespaces.

For example, suppose we want to say that the book *XML in a Nutshell* has the authors W. Scott Means and Elliotte Rusty Harold. In other words, we want to say that the resource identified by the URI urn:isbn:0596002920 has one author property with the value "W. Scott Means" and another author property with the value "Elliotte Rusty Harold." Example 7-10 does this.

Example 7-10. A simple RDF document saying that W. Scott Means and Elliotte Rusty Harold are the authors of XML in a Nutshell

```
<rdf:RDF xmlns:rdf="http://www.w3.org/1999/02/22-rdf-syntax-ns#">

  <rdf:Description about="urn:isbn:0596002920">
    <author>Elliotte Rusty Harold</author>
    <author>W. Scott Means</author>
  </rdf:Description>

</rdf:RDF>
```

In this simple example, the values of the author properties are merely text. However, they could be XML as well. Indeed, they could be other RDF elements.

There's more to RDF, including containers, schemas, and nested properties. However, this will be sufficient description for web metadata.

Dublin Core

The Dublin Core, *http://purl.org/dc/*, is a standard set of 15 information items with specified semantics that reflect the sort of data you'd be likely to find in a card catalog or annotated bibliography. These are:

Title
    Fairly self-explanatory; this is the name by which the resource is known. For instance, the title of this book is *XML in a Nutshell*.

Creator
    The person or organization who created the resource, e.g., a painter, author, illustrator, composer, and so on. For instance, the creators of this book are W. Scott Means and Elliotte Rusty Harold.

Subject
    A list of keywords, very likely from some other vocabulary such as the Dewey Decimal System or Yahoo categories, identifying the topics of the resource. For instance, using the Library of Congress Subject Headings vocabulary, the subject of this book is "XML (Document markup language)."

Description

Typically, a brief amount of text describing the content of the resource in prose, but it may also include a picture, a table of contents, or any other description of the resource. For instance, a description of this book might be "A brief tutorial on and quick reference to XML and related technologies and specifications."

Publisher

The name of the person, company, or organization who makes the resource available. For instance, the publisher of this book is "O'Reilly Media, Inc."

Contributor

A person or organization who made some contribution to the resource but is not the primary creator of the resource. For example, the editors of this book, Laurie Petrycki, Simon St.Laurent, and Jeni Tennison, might be identified as contributors, as would Susan Hart, the artist who drew the picture on the cover.

Date

The date when the book was created or published, normally given in the form *YYYY-MM-DD*. For instance, this book's date might be 2004-09-23.

Type

The abstract kind of resource such as image, text, sound, or software. For instance, a description of this book would have the type "text."

Format

For hard objects like books, the physical dimensions of the resource. For instance, the paper version of *XML in a Nutshell* has the dimensions 6" × 9". For digital objects like web pages, this is possibly the MIME media type. For instance, an online version of this book would have the format text/html.

Identifier

A formal identifier for the resource, such as an ISBN number, a URI, or a Social Security number. This book's identifier is "0596007647."

Source

The resource from which the present resource was derived. For instance, the French translation of this book might reference the original English edition as its source.

Language

The language in which this resource is written, typically an ISO-639 language code, optionally suffixed with a hyphen and an ISO-3166 country code. For instance, the language for this book is "en-US." The language for the French translation of this book might be "fr-FR."

Relation

A reference to a resource that is in some way related to the current one, generally using a formal identifier, such as a URI or an ISBN number. For instance, this might refer to the web page for this book.

Coverage

The location, time, or jurisdiction the resource covers. For instance, the coverage of this book might be the U.S., Canada, Australia, the U.K., and Ireland. The coverage of the French translation of this book might be France, Canada, Haiti, Belgium, and Switzerland. Generally these will be listed in some formal syntax such as country codes.

Rights

Information about copyright, patent, trademark and other restrictions on the content of the resource. For instance, a rights statement about this book may say "Copyright 2004 O'Reilly Media, Inc."

Dublin Core can be encoded in a variety of forms including HTML meta tags and RDF. Here we concentrate on its encoding in RDF. Typically, each resource is described with an rdf:Description element. This element contains child elements for as many of the Dublin Core information items as are known about the resource. The name of each of these elements matches the name of one of the 14 Dublin Core properties. These are placed in the http://purl.org/dc/elements/1.1/ namespace. Example 7-11 shows an RDF-encoded Dublin Core description of this book.

Example 7-11. An RDF-encoded Dublin Core description for XML in a Nutshell

```
<?xml version="1.0" encoding="UTF-8" standalone="yes"?>
<rdf:RDF xmlns:rdf="http://www.w3.org/1999/02/22-rdf-syntax-ns#"
         xmlns:dc="http://purl.org/dc/elements/1.1/">

  <rdf:Description about="urn:isbn:0596002920">
    <dc:Title>XML in a Nutshell</dc:Title>
    <dc:Creator>W. Scott Means</dc:Creator>
    <dc:Creator>Elliotte Rusty Harold</dc:Creator>
    <dc:Subject>XML (Document markup language)</dc:Subject>.
    <dc:Description>
      A brief tutorial on and quick reference to XML and
      related technologies and specifications
    </dc:Description>
    <dc:Publisher>O'Reilly Media, Inc.</dc:Publisher>
    <dc:Contributor>Laurie Petrycki</dc:Contributor>
    <dc:Contributor>Simon St. Laurent</dc:Contributor>
    <dc:Contributor>Jeni Tennison</dc:Contributor>
    <dc:Contributor>Susan Hart</dc:Contributor>
    <dc:Date>2004-08-23</dc:Date>
    <dc:Type>text</dc:Type>
    <dc:Format>6" x 9"</dc:Format>
    <dc:Identifier>0596007647</dc:Identifier>
    <dc:Language>en-US</dc:Language>
    <dc:Relation>http://www.oreilly.com/catalog/xmlnut/</dc:Relation>
    <dc:Coverage>US UK ZA CA AU NZ</dc:Coverage>
    <dc:Rights>Copyright 2004 O'Reilly Media, Inc.</dc:Rights>
  </rdf:Description>

</rdf:RDF>
```

There is as yet no standard for how an RDF document should be associated with the XML document it describes. One possibility is for the rdf:RDF element to be embedded in the document it describes, for instance, as a child of the BookInfo element of the DocBook source for this book. Another possibility is that servers provide this meta information through an extra-document channel. For instance, a standard protocol could be defined that would allow search engines to request this information for any page on the site. A convention could be adopted so that for any URL *xyz* on a given web site, the URL *xyz/meta.rdf* would contain the RDF-encoded Dublin Core metadata for that URL.

Robots

In HTML, the robots meta tag tells search engines and other robots whether they're allowed to index a page. Walter Underwood has proposed the following processing instruction as an equivalent for XML documents:

```
<?robots index="yes" follow="no"?>
```

Robots will look for this in the prolog of any XML document they encounter. The syntax of this particular processing instruction is two pseudo-attributes, one named index and one named follow, whose values are either yes or no. If the index attribute has the value yes, then this page will be indexed by a search-engine robot. If index has the value no, then it won't be. Similarly, if follow has the value yes, then links from this document will be followed. If follow has the value no, then they won't be.

8

XSL Transformations (XSLT)

The Extensible Stylesheet Language (XSL) is divided into two parts: XSL Transformations (XSLT) and XSL Formatting Objects (XSL-FO). This chapter describes XSLT. Chapter 14 covers XSL-FO.

XSLT is an XML application for specifying rules by which one XML document is transformed into another XML document. An XSLT document—that is, an XSLT stylesheet—contains template rules. Each template rule has a pattern and a template. An XSLT processor compares the elements and other nodes in an input XML document to the template-rule patterns in a stylesheet. When one matches, it writes the template from that rule into the output tree. When it's done, it may further serialize the output tree into an XML document or some other format like plain text or HTML.

This chapter describes the template rules and a few other elements that appear in an XSLT stylesheet. XSLT uses the XPath syntax to identify matching nodes. We'll introduce a few pieces of XPath here, but most of it will be covered in Chapter 9.

An Example Input Document

To demonstrate XSL Transformations, we first need a document to transform. Example 8-1 shows the document used in this chapter. The root element is people, which contains two person elements. The person elements have roughly the same structure (a name followed by professions and hobbies) with some differences. For instance, Alan Turing has three professions, but Richard Feynman only has one. Feynman has a middle_initial and a hobby, but Turing doesn't. Still, these are clearly variations on the same basic structure. A DTD that permitted both of these would be easy to write.

Example 8-1. An XML document describing two people

```
<?xml version="1.0"?>
<people>
  <person born="1912" died="1954">
    <name>
      <first_name>Alan</first_name>
      <last_name>Turing</last_name>
    </name>
    <profession>computer scientist</profession>
    <profession>mathematician</profession>
    <profession>cryptographer</profession>
  </person>
  <person born="1918" died="1988">
    <name>
      <first_name>Richard</first_name>
      <middle_initial>P</middle_initial>
      <last_name>Feynman</last_name>
    </name>
    <profession>physicist</profession>
    <hobby>Playing the bongoes</hobby>
  </person>
</people>
```

Example 8-1 is an XML document. For purposes of this example, it will be stored in a file called *people.xml*. It doesn't have a DTD; however, this is tangential. XSLT works equally well with valid and invalid (but well-formed) documents. This document doesn't use namespaces either, although it could. XSLT works just fine with namespaces. Unlike DTDs, XSLT does pay attention to the namespace URIs instead of the prefixes. Thus, it's possible to use one prefix for an element in the input document and different prefixes for the same namespace in the stylesheet and output documents.

xsl:stylesheet and xsl:transform

An XSLT stylesheet is an XML document. It can and generally should have an XML declaration. It can have a document type declaration, although most stylesheets do not. The root element of this document is either stylesheet or transform; these are synonyms for each other, and you can use either. They both have the same possible children and attributes. They both mean the same thing to an XSLT processor.

The stylesheet and transform elements, like all other XSLT elements, are in the http://www.w3.org/1999/XSL/Transform namespace. This namespace is customarily mapped to the xsl prefix so that you write xsl:transform or xsl:stylesheet rather than simply transform or stylesheet.

XSLT

This namespace URI must be exactly correct. If even so much as a single character is wrong, the stylesheet processor will output the stylesheet itself instead of either the input document or the transformed input document. There's a reason for this (see Section 2.3 of the XSLT 1.0 specification, *Literal Result Element as Stylesheet*, if you really want to know), but the bottom line is that this weird behavior looks very much like a bug in the XSLT processor if you're not expecting it. If you ever do see your stylesheet processor spitting your stylesheet back out at you, the problem is almost certainly an incorrect namespace URI.

In addition to the xmlns:xsl attribute declaring this prefix mapping, the root element must have a version attribute with the value 1.0. Thus, a minimal XSLT stylesheet, with only the root element and nothing else, is as shown in Example 8-2.

Example 8-2. A minimal XSLT stylesheet

```
<?xml version="1.0"?>
<xsl:stylesheet version="1.0"
                xmlns:xsl="http://www.w3.org/1999/XSL/Transform">

</xsl:stylesheet>
```

Perhaps a little surprisingly, this is a complete XSLT stylesheet; an XSLT processor can apply it to an XML document to produce an output document. Example 8-3 shows the effect of applying this stylesheet to Example 8-1.

Example 8-3. people.xml transformed by the minimal XSLT stylesheet

```
<?xml version="1.0" encoding="utf-8"?>

    Alan
    Turing

computer scientist
mathematician
cryptographer

    Richard
    P
    Feynman

physicist
Playing the bongoes
```

You can see that the output consists of a text declaration plus the text of the input document. In this case, the output is a well-formed external parsed entity, but it is not itself a complete XML document.

Markup from the input document has been stripped. The net effect of applying an empty stylesheet, like Example 8-2, to any XML document is to reproduce the content but not the markup of the input document. To change that, we'll need to add template rules to the stylesheet telling the XSLT processor how to handle the specific elements in the input document. In the absence of explicit template rules, an XSLT processor falls back on built-in rules that have the effect shown here.

Stylesheet Processors

An XSLT processor is a piece of software that reads an XSLT stylesheet, reads an XML document, and builds an output document by applying the instructions in the stylesheet to the information in the input document. An XSLT processor can be built into a web browser, just as MSXML is in Internet Explorer 6. It can be built into a web or application server, as in the Apache XML Project's Cocoon (*http://xml.apache.org/cocoon*). Or it can be a standalone program run from the command line like Michael Kay's SAXON (*http://saxon.sourceforge.net*) or the Apache XML Project's Xalan (*http://xml.apache.org/xalan-j*).

Internet Explorer 5.0 and 5.5 partially support a very old and out-of-date working draft of XSLT, as well as various Microsoft extensions to this old working draft. They do not support XSLT 1.0, and indeed no XSLT stylesheets in this book work in IE5. Stylesheets that are meant for Microsoft XSLT can be identified by their use of the `http://www.w3.org/TR/WD-xsl` namespace. IE6 supports both `http://www.w3.org/1999/XSL/Transform` and `http://www.w3.org/TR/WD-xsl`. Good XSLT developers don't use `http://www.w3.org/TR/WD-xsl` and don't associate with developers who do.

Command-Line Processors

The exact details of how to install, configure, and run the XSLT processor naturally vary from processor to processor. Generally, you have to install the processor in your path, or add its *jar* file to your class path if it's written in Java. Then you pass in the names of the input file, stylesheet file, and output file on the command line. For example, using Xalan, Example 8-3 is created in this fashion:

```
% java org.apache.xalan.xslt.Process -IN people.xml -XSL minimal.xsl
  -OUT 8-3.txt
========= Parsing file:D:/books/xian/examples/08/minimal.xsl =========
=
Parse of file:D:/books/xian/examples/08/minimal.xsl took 771 milliseconds
========= Parsing people.xml ==========
Parse of people.xml took 90 milliseconds
=============================
Transforming...
transform took 20 milliseconds
XSLProcessor: done
```

For exact details, you'll need to consult the documentation that comes with your XSLT processor.

XSLT

The xml-stylesheet Processing Instruction

XML documents that will be served directly to web browsers can have an xml-stylesheet processing instruction in their prolog telling the browser where to find the associated stylesheet for the document, as discussed in the last chapter. If this stylesheet is an XSLT stylesheet, then the type pseudo-attribute should have the value application/xml. For example, this xml-stylesheet processing instruction says that browsers should apply the stylesheet found at the absolute URL *http:// www.oreilly.com/styles/people.xsl*. Relative URLs can also be used.

```
<?xml version="1.0"?>
<?xml-stylesheet type="application/xml"
                 href="http://www.oreilly.com/styles/people.xsl"?>
<people>
   ...
```

 Microsoft Internet Explorer uses type="text/xsl" for XSLT stylesheets. However, the text/xsl MIME media type has not been and will not be registered with the IANA. It is a figment of Microsoft's imagination. In the future, application/xslt+xml will be registered to identify XSLT stylesheets specifically.

Templates and Template Rules

To control what output is created from what input, you add template rules to the XSLT stylesheet. Each template rule is represented by an xsl:template element. This element has a match attribute that contains a pattern identifying the input it matches; it also contains a template that is instantiated and output when the pattern is matched. The terminology is a little tricky here: the xsl:template element is a template rule that contains a template. An xsl:template element is not itself the template.

The simplest match pattern is an element name. Thus, this template rule says that every time a person element is seen, the stylesheet processor should emit the text "A Person":

```
<xsl:template match="person">A Person</xsl:template>
```

Example 8-4 is a complete stylesheet that uses this template rule.

Example 8-4. An XSLT stylesheet with a match pattern

```
<?xml version="1.0"?>
<xsl:stylesheet version="1.0"
                xmlns:xsl="http://www.w3.org/1999/XSL/Transform">

  <xsl:template match="person">A Person</xsl:template>

</xsl:stylesheet>
```

Applying this stylesheet to the document in Example 8-1 produces this output:

```
<?xml version="1.0" encoding="utf-8"?>

  A Person

  A Person
```

There were two person elements in the input document. Each time the processor saw one, it emitted the text "A Person". The whitespace outside the person elements was preserved, but everything inside the person elements was replaced by the contents of the template rule, which is called the *template*.

The text "A Person" is called literal data characters, which is a fancy way of saying plain text that is copied from the stylesheet into the output document. A template may also contain literal result elements, i.e., markup that is copied from the stylesheet to the output document. For instance, Example 8-5 wraps the text "A Person" in between <p> and </p> tags.

Example 8-5. A simple XSLT stylesheet with literal result elements

```
<?xml version="1.0"?>
<xsl:stylesheet version="1.0"
                xmlns:xsl="http://www.w3.org/1999/XSL/Transform">

  <xsl:template match="person">
    <p>A Person</p>
  </xsl:template>

</xsl:stylesheet>
```

The output from this stylesheet is:

```
<?xml version="1.0" encoding="utf-8"?>

  <p>A Person</p>

  <p>A Person</p>
```

The <p> and </p> tags were copied from the input to the output. The only major restriction on the markup you may output is that it must be well-formed XML because the stylesheet must be well-formed XML. For instance, you cannot write a template rule like this:

```
<xsl:template match="person">
  A Person<p>
</xsl:template>
```

Here the <p> start-tag has no matching end-tag; therefore, the stylesheet is malformed. Any other markup in the XSLT stylesheet must be similarly well-formed. Empty-element tags must end with />, attribute values must be quoted, less-than signs must be escaped as <, all entity references must be declared in a DTD except for the five predefined ones, and so forth. XSLT has no exceptions to the rules of well-formedness.

XSLT

Calculating the Value of an Element with xsl:value-of

Most of the time, the text that is output is more closely related to the text that is input than it was in the last couple of examples. Other XSLT elements can select particular content from the input document and insert it into the output document.

One of the most generally useful elements of this kind is xsl:value-of. This element calculates the string value of an XPath expression and inserts it into the output. The value of an element is the text content of the element after all the tags have been removed and entity and character references have been resolved. The element whose value is taken is identified by a select attribute containing an XPath expression.

For example, suppose you just want to extract the names of all the people in the input document. Then you might use a stylesheet like Example 8-6. Here the person template outputs only the value of the name child element of the matched person in between <p> and </p> tags.

Example 8-6. A simple XSLT stylesheet that uses xsl:value-of

```
<?xml version="1.0"?>
<xsl:stylesheet version="1.0"
                xmlns:xsl="http://www.w3.org/1999/XSL/Transform">

  <xsl:template match="person">
    <p>
      <xsl:value-of select="name"/>
    </p>
  </xsl:template>

</xsl:stylesheet>
```

When an XSLT processor applies this stylesheet to Example 8-1, it outputs this text:

```
<?xml version="1.0" encoding="utf-8"?>

<p>
    Alan
    Turing
</p>

<p>
    Richard
    P
    Feynman
</p>
```

Applying Templates with xsl:apply-templates

By default, an XSLT processor reads the input XML document from top to bottom, starting at the root of the document and working its way down using preorder traversal. Template rules are activated in the order in which they match elements encountered during this traversal. This means a template rule for a parent will be activated before template rules matching the parent's children.

However, one of the things a template can do is change the order of traversal. That is, it can specify which element(s) should be processed next. It can specify that an element(s) should be processed in the middle of processing another element. It can even prevent particular elements from being processed. In fact, Examples 8-4 through 8-6 all implicitly prevent the child elements of each person element from being processed. Instead, they provided their own instructions about what the XSLT processor was and was not to do with those children.

The xsl:apply-templates element makes the processing order explicit. Its select attribute contains an XPath expression telling the XSLT processor which nodes to process at that point in the output tree.

For example, suppose you wanted to list the names of the people in the input document; however, you want to put the last names first, regardless of the order in which they occur in the input document, and you don't want to output the professions or hobbies. First you need a name template that looks like this:

```
<xsl:template match="name">
  <xsl:value-of select="last_name"/>,
  <xsl:value-of select="first_name"/>
</xsl:template>
```

However, this alone isn't enough; if this were all there was in the stylesheet, not only would the output include the names, it would also include the professions and hobbies. You also need a person template rule that says to apply templates to name children only, but not to any other child elements like profession or hobby. This template rule does that:

```
<xsl:template match="person">
  <xsl:apply-templates select="name"/>
</xsl:template>
```

Example 8-7 shows the complete stylesheet.

Example 8-7. A simple XSLT stylesheet that uses xsl:apply-templates

```
<?xml version="1.0"?>
<xsl:stylesheet version="1.0"
            xmlns:xsl="http://www.w3.org/1999/XSL/Transform">

  <xsl:template match="name">
    <xsl:value-of select="last_name"/>,
    <xsl:value-of select="first_name"/>
  </xsl:template>
```

```
<xsl:template match="person">
  <xsl:apply-templates select="name"/>
</xsl:template>

</xsl:stylesheet>
```

When an XSLT processor applies this stylesheet to Example 8-1, this is output:

```
<?xml version="1.0" encoding="utf-8"?>

Turing,
  Alan

Feynman,
  Richard
```

The order of the template rules in the stylesheet doesn't matter. It's only the order of the elements in the input document that matters.

Applying templates is also important when the child elements have templates of their own, even if you don't need to reorder the elements. For example, let's suppose you want a template rule for the root people element that wraps the entire document in an HTML header and body. Its template will need to use xsl:apply-templates to indicate where it wants the children of the root element to be placed. That template rule might look like this:

```
<xsl:template match="people">
  <html>
    <head><title>Famous Scientists</title></head>
    <body>
      <xsl:apply-templates select="person"/>
    </body>
  </html>
</xsl:template>
```

This template tells the XSLT processor to replace every people element in the input document (of which there is only one in Example 8-1) with an html element. This html element contains some literal character data and several literal result elements of which one is a body element. The body element contains an xsl:apply-templates element telling the XSLT processor to process all the person children of the current people element and insert the output of any matched templates into the body element of the output document.

If you'd rather apply templates to all types of children of the people element, rather than just person children, you can omit the select attribute as demonstrated in Example 8-8. You can also use more complex XPath expressions (discussed in the next chapter) to be more precise about which elements you want to apply templates to.

Example 8-8. An XSLT stylesheet that generates a complete HTML document

```
<?xml version="1.0"?>
<xsl:stylesheet version="1.0"
                xmlns:xsl="http://www.w3.org/1999/XSL/Transform">
```

Example 8-8. An XSLT stylesheet that generates a complete HTML document (continued)

```
<xsl:template match="people">
  <html>
    <head><title>Famous Scientists</title></head>
    <body>
      <xsl:apply-templates/>
    </body>
  </html>
</xsl:template>

<xsl:template match="name">
  <p><xsl:value-of select="last_name"/>,
  <xsl:value-of select="first_name"/></p>
</xsl:template>

<xsl:template match="person">
  <xsl:apply-templates select="name"/>
</xsl:template>

</xsl:stylesheet>
```

When an XSLT processor applies this stylesheet to Example 8-1, it outputs the well-formed HTML document shown in Example 8-9. Look closely at this example, and you may spot an important change that was not explicitly caused by the instructions in the stylesheet.

Example 8-9. The HTML document produced by applying Example 8-8 to Example 8-1

```
<html>
<head>
<title>Famous Scientists</title>
</head>
<body>
  <p>Turing,
    Alan</p>
  <p>Feynman,
    Richard</p>
</body>
</html>
```

The difference between Example 8-9 and all the previous output examples is that the text declaration has disappeared! Although there is an XSLT element you can use to specify whether you want a text declaration preceding your output (xsl:output), we haven't used that here. Instead, the XSLT processor noted that the root output element was html, and it adjusted itself accordingly. Since HTML output is such a common case, XSLT has special rules just to handle it. In addition to omitting the text declaration, the processor will use HTML empty-element syntax like <br>, instead of XML empty-element syntax like <br/>, in the output document. (The input document and stylesheet must still be well-formed XML.) There are about half a dozen other changes the XSLT processor may make when it knows it's outputting HTML, all designed to make the output more acceptable to existing web browsers than is well-formed XML.

The Built-in Template Rules

There are seven kinds of nodes in an XML document: the root node, element nodes, attribute nodes, text nodes, comment nodes, processing instruction nodes, and namespace nodes. XSLT provides a default built-in template rule for each of these seven kinds of nodes that says what to do with that node if the stylesheet author has not provided more specific instructions. These rules use special wild-card patterns to match all nodes of a given type. Together these template rules have major effects on which nodes are activated when.

The Default Template Rule for Text and Attribute Nodes

The most basic built-in template rule copies the value of text and attribute nodes into the output document. It looks like this:

```
<xsl:template match="text()|@*">
  <xsl:value-of select="."/>
</xsl:template>
```

The text( ) node test is a pattern matching all text nodes, just as first_name is a pattern matching all first_name element nodes. @* is a pattern matching all attribute nodes. The vertical bar combines these two patterns so that the template rule matches both text and attribute nodes. The rule's template says that whenever a text or attribute node is matched, the processor should output the value of that node. For a text node, this value is simply the text in the node. For an attribute, this value is the attribute value but not the name.

Example 8-10 is an XSLT stylesheet that pulls the birth and death dates out of the born and died attributes in Example 8-1. The default template rule for attributes takes the value of the attributes, but an explicit rule selects those values. The @ sign in @born and @died indicates that these are attributes of the matched element rather than child elements.

Example 8-10. An XSLT stylesheet that reads born and died attributes

```
<?xml version="1.0"?>
<xsl:stylesheet version="1.0"
                xmlns:xsl="http://www.w3.org/1999/XSL/Transform">

  <xsl:template match="people">
    <html>
      <head><title>Famous Scientists</title></head>
      <body>
        <dl>
          <xsl:apply-templates/>
        </dl>
      </body>
    </html>
  </xsl:template>

  <xsl:template match="person">
    <dt><xsl:apply-templates select="name"/></dt>
    <dd><ul>
```

```
      <li>Born: <xsl:apply-templates select="@born"/></li>
      <li>Died: <xsl:apply-templates select="@died"/></li>
    </ul></dd>
  </xsl:template>

</xsl:stylesheet>
```

When an XSLT processor applies this stylesheet to Example 8-1, it outputs the HTML document shown in Example 8-11.

Example 8-11. The HTML produced by applying Example 8-10 to Example 8-1

```
<html>
    <head>
        <title>Famous Scientists</title>
    </head>
    <body>
        <dl>

            <dt>
               Alan
               Turing
            </dt>

            <dd>
               <ul>
                  <li>Born: 1912</li>
                  <li>Died: 1954</li>
               </ul>
            </dd>

            <dt>
               Richard
               P
               Feynman
            </dt>
            <dd>
               <ul>
                  <li>Born: 1918</li>
                  <li>Died: 1988</li>
               </ul>
            </dd>

        </dl>
    </body>
</html>
```

It's important to note that although this template rule says what should happen when an attribute node is reached, by default, the XSLT processor never reaches attribute nodes and, therefore, never outputs the value of an attribute. Attribute values are output according to this template only if a specific rule applies templates to them, and none of the default rules do this because attributes are not considered to be children of their parents. In other words, if element E has an attribute A, then E is the parent of A, but A is not the child of E. (The biological metaphor breaks down here.) Applying templates to the children of an element with `<xsl:apply-templates/>` does not apply templates to attributes of the element. To do that, the `xsl:apply-templates` element must have a match pattern specifically selecting attributes.

The Default Template Rule for Element and Root Nodes

The most important template rule is the one that guarantees that children are processed. Here is that rule:

```
<xsl:template match="*|/">
  <xsl:apply-templates/>
</xsl:template>
```

The asterisk * is an XPath wildcard that matches all element nodes, regardless of what name they have or what namespace they're in. The forward slash / is an XPath expression that matches the root node. This is the first node the processor selects for processing, and, therefore, this is the first template rule the processor executes (unless a nondefault template rule also matches the root node). Again, the vertical bar combines these two expressions so that the rule matches both the root node and element nodes. In isolation, this rule means that the XSLT processor eventually finds and applies templates to all nodes except attribute and namespace nodes because every nonattribute, non-namespace node is either the root node, a child of the root node, or a child of an element. Only attribute and namespace nodes are not children of their parents. (You can think of them as disinherited nodes.)

Of course, templates may override the default behavior. For example, when you include a template rule matching person elements in your stylesheet, then children of the matched person elements are not necessarily processed, unless one of your own template rules says to process them.

The Default Template Rule for Comment and Processing Instruction Nodes

This is the default template rule for comments and processing instructions:

```
<xsl:template match="processing-instruction()|comment()"/>
```

It matches all comments and processing instructions. However, it does not output anything into the result tree. That is, unless a stylesheet provides specific rules matching comments or processing instructions, no part of these items will be copied from the input document to the output document.

The Default Template Rule for Namespace Nodes

A similar template rule matches namespace nodes and instructs the processor not to copy any part of the namespace node to the output. This is truly a built-in rule that must be implemented in the XSLT processor's source code; it can't even be written down in an XSLT stylesheet because there's no such thing as an XPath pattern matching a namespace node. That is, there's no namespace( ) node test in XPath. The XSLT processor inserts any necessary namespace declarations in the output document automatically, without any special assistance from namespace templates.

Modes

Sometimes the same input content needs to appear multiple times in the output document, formatted according to a different template each time. For instance, the titles of the chapters in a book would be formatted one way in the chapters themselves and a different way in the table of contents. Both xsl:apply-templates and xsl:template elements can have optional mode attributes that connect different template rules to different positions. A mode attribute on an xsl:template element identifies in which mode that template rule should be activated. An xsl:apply-templates element with a mode attribute only activates template rules with matching mode attributes. Example 8-12 demonstrates with a stylesheet that begins the output document with a list of people's names. This is accomplished in the toc mode. Then a separate template rule, as well as a separate xsl:apply-templates element in the default mode (really no mode at all), outputs the complete contents of all person elements.

Example 8-12. A stylesheet that uses modes

```
<?xml version="1.0"?>
<xsl:stylesheet version="1.0"
                xmlns:xsl="http://www.w3.org/1999/XSL/Transform">

  <xsl:template match="people">
    <html>
      <head><title>Famous Scientists</title></head>
      <body>
        <ul><xsl:apply-templates select="person" mode="toc"/></ul>
        <xsl:apply-templates select="person"/>
      </body>
    </html>
  </xsl:template>

  <!-- Table of Contents Mode Templates -->
  <xsl:template match="person" mode="toc">
    <xsl:apply-templates select="name" mode="toc"/>
  </xsl:template>

  <xsl:template match="name" mode="toc">
    <li><xsl:value-of select="last_name"/>,
    <xsl:value-of select="first_name"/></li>
  </xsl:template>

  <!-- Normal Mode Templates -->
  <xsl:template match="person">
    <p><xsl:apply-templates/></p>
  </xsl:template>

</xsl:stylesheet>
```

Example 8-13 shows the output when this stylesheet is applied to *people.xml*. The people template in Example 8-12 applies templates to its person children twice. The first time it does so in the toc mode. This selects the first person template rule in the stylesheet that outputs each person in the form <li>Turing, Alan</li>. The second time, it doesn't specify any mode. This selects the second person template rule in the stylesheet, which outputs all the character data of the person wrapped in a p element.

Example 8-13. Output from a stylesheet that uses modes to process each person twice with different templates

```
<html>
<head>
<title>Famous Scientists</title>
</head>
<body>
<ul>
<li>Turing,
    Alan</li>
<li>Feynman,
    Richard</li>
</ul>
<p>

      Alan
      Turing

    computer scientist
    mathematician
    cryptographer
  </p>
<p>

      Richard
      P
      Feynman

    physicist
    Playing the bongoes
  </p>
</body>
</html>
```

For every mode in the stylesheet, the XSLT processor adds one default template rule to its set of built-in rules. This applies to all element and root nodes in the specified mode and applies templates to their children in the same mode (since the usual built-in template rule for element and root nodes doesn't have a mode). For instance, the extra default rule for Example 8-10 looks like this:

```
<xsl:template match="*|/" mode="toc">
  <xsl:apply-templates mode="toc"/>
</xsl:template>
```

Attribute Value Templates

It's easy to include known attribute values in the output document as the literal content of a literal result element. For example, this template rule wraps each input person element in an HTML span element that has a class attribute with the value person:

```
<xsl:template match="person">
  <span class="person"><xsl:apply-templates/></span>
</xsl:template>
```

However, it's trickier if the value of the attribute is not known when the stylesheet is written, but instead must be read from the input document. The solution is to use an *attribute value template*. An attribute value template is an XPath expression enclosed in curly braces that's placed in the attribute value in the stylesheet. When the processor outputs that attribute, it replaces the attribute value template with its value. For example, suppose you want to write a name template that changes the input name elements to empty elements with first, initial, and last attributes like this:

```
<name first="Richard" initial="P" last="Feynman"/>
```

This template accomplishes that task:

```
<xsl:template match="name">
  <name first="{first_name}"
        initial="{middle_initial}"
        last="{last_name}" />
</xsl:template>
```

The value of the first attribute in the stylesheet is replaced by the value of the first_name element from the input document. The value of the initial attribute is replaced by the value of the middle_initial element from the input document, the value of the last attribute is replaced by the value of the last_name element from the input document.

XSLT and Namespaces

Match patterns, as well as select expressions, identify elements based on their local part and namespace URI. They do not consider the namespace prefix. Most commonly, the same namespace prefix is mapped to the same URI in both the input XML document and the stylesheet. However, this is not required. For instance, consider Example 8-14. This is exactly the same as Example 8-1, except that now all the elements have been placed in the namespace http://www.cafeconleche.org/namespaces/people.

Example 8-14. An XML document that uses a default namespace

```
<?xml version="1.0"?>
<people xmlns="http://www.cafeconleche.org/namespaces/people">

  <person born="1912" died="1954">
    <name>
```

Example 8-14. An XML document that uses a default namespace (continued)

```
    <first_name>Alan</first_name>
    <last_name>Turing</last_name>
  </name>
  <profession>computer scientist</profession>
  <profession>mathematician</profession>
  <profession>cryptographer</profession>
</person>

<person born="1918" died="1988">
  <name>
    <first_name>Richard</first_name>
    <middle_initial>P</middle_initial>
    <last_name>Feynman</last_name>
  </name>
  <profession>physicist</profession>
  <hobby>Playing the bongoes</hobby>
</person>

</people>
```

Except for the built-in template rules, none of the rules in this chapter so far will work on this document! For instance, consider this template rule from Example 8-8:

```
<xsl:template match="name">
  <p><xsl:value-of select="last_name"/>,
  <xsl:value-of select="first_name"/></p>
</xsl:template>
```

It's trying to match a name element in no namespace, but the name elements in Example 8-14 aren't in no namespace. They're in the http://www.cafeconleche.org/ namespaces/people namespace. This template rule no longer applies. To make it fit, we map the prefix pe to the namespace URI http://www.cafeconleche.org/ namespaces/people. Then instead of matching name, we match pe:name. That the input document doesn't use the prefix pe is irrelevant as long as the namespace URIs match up. Example 8-15 demonstrates by rewriting Example 8-8 to work with Example 8-14 instead.

Example 8-15. An XSLT stylesheet for input documents using the http://www.cafeconleche. org/namespaces/people

```
<?xml version="1.0"?>
<xsl:stylesheet version="1.0"
           xmlns:xsl="http://www.w3.org/1999/XSL/Transform"
           xmlns:pe="http://www.cafeconleche.org/namespaces/people">

  <xsl:template match="pe:people">
    <html>
      <head><title>Famous Scientists</title></head>
      <body>
        <xsl:apply-templates/>
      </body>
    </html>
```

```
  </xsl:template>

  <xsl:template match="pe:name">
    <p><xsl:value-of select="pe:last_name"/>,
    <xsl:value-of select="pe:first_name"/></p>
  </xsl:template>

  <xsl:template match="pe:person">
    <xsl:apply-templates select="pe:name"/>
  </xsl:template>

</xsl:stylesheet>
```

The output is essentially the same output you get by applying Example 8-8 to Example 8-1 except that it will have an extra xmlns:pe attribute on the root element.

Other XSLT Elements

This is hardly everything there is to say about XSLT. Indeed, XSLT does a lot more than the little we've covered in this introductory chapter. Other features yet to be discussed include:

- Named templates
- Numbering and sorting output elements
- Conditional processing
- Iteration
- Extension elements and functions
- Importing other stylesheets

These and more will all be covered in Chapter 24. Since XSLT is itself Turing complete and since it can invoke extension functions written in other languages like Java, chances are very good you can use XSLT to make whatever transformations you need to make.

Furthermore, besides these additional elements, you can do a lot more simply by expanding the XPath expressions and patterns used in the select and match attributes of the elements with which you're already familiar. These techniques will be explored in Chapter 9.

However, the techniques outlined in this chapter do lay the foundation for all subsequent, more advanced work with XSLT. The key to transforming XML documents with XSLT is to match templates to elements in the input document. Those templates contain both literal result data and XSLT elements that instruct the processor where to get more data. Everything you do with XSLT is based on this one simple idea.

XSLT

9

XPath

XPath is a non-XML language for identifying particular parts of XML documents. XPath lets you write expressions that refer to, for example, the first person element in a document, the seventh child element of the third person element, the ID attribute of the first person element whose contents are the string "Fred Jones", all xml-stylesheet processing instructions in the document's prolog, and so forth. XPath indicates nodes by position, relative position, type, content, and several other criteria. XSLT uses XPath expressions to match and select particular elements in the input document for copying into the output document or further processing. XPointer uses XPath expressions to identify the particular point in or part of an XML document to which an XLink links. The W3C XML Schema Language uses XPath expressions to define uniqueness and identity constraints. XForms relies on XPath to bind form controls to instance data, express constraints on user-entered values, and calculate values that depend on other values.

XPath expressions can also represent numbers, strings, or Booleans. This lets XSLT stylesheets carry out simple arithmetic for purposes such as numbering and cross-referencing figures, tables, and equations. String manipulation in XPath lets XSLT perform tasks such as making the title of a chapter uppercase in a headline or extracting the last two digits from a year.

The Tree Structure of an XML Document

An XML document is a tree made up of nodes. Some nodes contain one or more other nodes. There is exactly one root node, which ultimately contains all other nodes. XPath is a language for picking nodes and sets of nodes out of this tree. From the perspective of XPath, there are seven kinds of nodes:

- The root node
- Element nodes

- Text nodes
- Attribute nodes
- Comment nodes
- Processing-instruction nodes
- Namespace nodes

One thing to note are the constructs not included in this list: CDATA sections, entity references, and document type declarations. XPath operates on an XML document after all these items have been merged into the document. For instance, XPath cannot identify the first CDATA section in a document or tell whether a particular attribute value was directly included in the source element start-tag or merely defaulted from the declaration of the element in a DTD.

Consider the document in Example 9-1. This exhibits all seven kinds of nodes. Figure 9-1 is a diagram of the tree structure of this document.

Example 9-1. The example XML document used in this chapter

```
<?xml version="1.0"?>
<?xml-stylesheet type="application/xml" href="people.xsl"?>
<!DOCTYPE people [
 <!ATTLIST homepage xlink:type CDATA #FIXED "simple"
                    xmlns:xlink CDATA #FIXED "http://www.w3.org/1999/xlink">
 <!ATTLIST person id ID #IMPLIED>
]>
<people>

  <person born="1912" died="1954" id="p342">
    <name>
      <first_name>Alan</first_name>
      <last_name>Turing</last_name>
    </name>
    <!-- Did the word computer scientist exist in Turing's day? -->
    <profession>computer scientist</profession>
    <profession>mathematician</profession>
    <profession>cryptographer</profession>
    <homepage xlink:href="http://www.turing.org.uk/"/>
  </person>

  <person born="1918" died="1988" id="p4567">
    <name>
      <first_name>Richard</first_name>
      <middle_initial>&#x50;</middle_initial>
      <last_name>Feynman</last_name>
    </name>
    <profession>physicist</profession>
    <hobby>Playing the bongoes</hobby>
  </person>

</people>
```

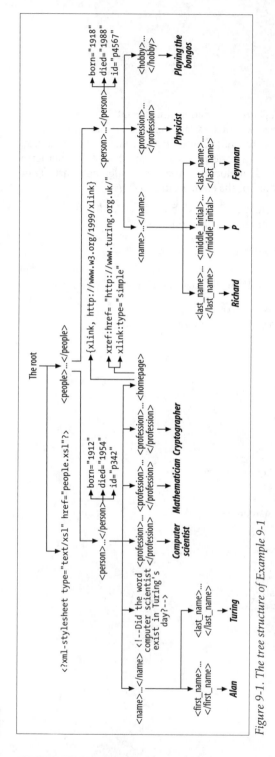

Figure 9-1. The tree structure of Example 9-1

The XPath data model has several nonobvious features. First of all, the root node of the tree is *not* the same as the root element. The root node of the tree contains the entire document including the root element, as well as any comments and processing instructions that occur before the root element start-tag or after the root element end-tag. In Example 9-1, this means the root node contains the xml-stylesheet processing instruction, as well as the root element people.

However, the XPath data model does not include everything in the document. In particular, the XML declaration, the DOCTYPE declaration, and the various parts of the DTD are *not* addressable via XPath, although if the DTD provides default values for any attributes, then those attributes are noted by XPath. The homepage element has an xlink:type attribute that was supplied by the DTD. Similarly, any references to parsed entities are resolved. Entity references, character references, and CDATA sections are not individually identifiable, although any data they contain is addressable. For example, XSLT cannot make all the text in CDATA sections bold because XPath doesn't know which text is and isn't part of a CDATA section.

Finally, xmlns and xmlns:*prefix* attributes are not considered attribute nodes. However, namespace nodes are attached to every element node for which a declaration is in scope. They are not attached to just the single element where the namespace is declared.

Location Paths

The most useful XPath expression is a *location path*. A location path identifies a set of nodes in a document. This set may be empty, may contain a single node, or may contain several nodes. These can be element nodes, attribute nodes, namespace nodes, text nodes, comment nodes, processing-instruction nodes, root nodes, or any combination of these. A location path is built out of successive *location steps*. Each location step is evaluated relative to a particular node in the document called the *context node*.

The Root Location Path

The simplest location path is the one that selects the root node of the document. This is simply the forward slash /. (You'll notice that a lot of XPath syntax is deliberately similar to the syntax used by the Unix shell. Here / is the root node of a Unix filesystem, and / is the root node of an XML document.) For example, this XSLT template rule uses the XPath pattern / to match the entire input document tree and wrap it in an html element:

```
<xsl:template match="/">
  <html><xsl:apply-templates/></html>
</xsl:template>
```

/ is an absolute location path because no matter what the context node is—that is, no matter where the processor was in the input document when this template rule was applied—it always means the same thing: the root node of the document. It is relative to which document you're processing, but not to anything within that document.

Child Element Location Steps

The second simplest location path is a single element name. This path selects all child elements of the context node with the specified name. For example, the XPath profession refers to all profession child elements of the context node. Exactly which elements these are depends on what the context node is, so this is a relative XPath. For example, if the context node is the Alan Turing person element in Example 9-1, then the location path profession refers to these three profession child elements of that element:

```
<profession>computer scientist</profession>
<profession>mathematician</profession>
<profession>cryptographer</profession>
```

However, if the context node is the Richard Feynman person element in Example 9-1, then the XPath profession refers to its single profession child element:

```
<profession>physicist</profession>
```

If the context node is the name child element of Richard Feynman or Alan Turing's person element, then this XPath doesn't refer to anything at all because neither of those has any profession child elements.

In XSLT, the context node for an XPath expression used in the select attribute of xsl:apply-templates and similar elements is the node that is currently matched. For example, consider the simple stylesheet in Example 9-2. In particular, look at the template rule for the person element. The XSLT processor will activate this rule twice, once for each person node in the document. The first time the context node is set to Alan Turing's person element. The second time the context node is set to Richard Feynman's person element. When the same template is instantiated with a different context node, the XPath expression in <xsl:value-of select="name"/> refers to a different element, and the output produced is therefore different.

Example 9-2. A very simple stylesheet for Example 9-1

```
<?xml version="1.0"?>
<xsl:stylesheet version="1.0"
            xmlns:xsl="http://www.w3.org/1999/XSL/Transform">

  <xsl:template match="people">
    <xsl:apply-templates select="person"/>
  </xsl:template>

  <xsl:template match="person">
    <xsl:value-of select="name"/>
  </xsl:template>

</xsl:stylesheet>
```

When XPath is used in other systems, such as XPointer or XForms, other means are provided for determining what the context node is.

Attribute Location Steps

Attributes are also addressable by XPath. To select a particular attribute of an element, use an @ sign followed by the name of the attribute you want. For example, the XPath expression @born selects the born attribute of the context node. Example 9-3 is a simple XSLT stylesheet that generates an HTML table of names and birth and death dates from documents like Example 9-1.

Example 9-3. An XSLT stylesheet that uses root element, child element, and attribute location steps

```
<?xml version="1.0"?>
<xsl:stylesheet version="1.0"
                xmlns:xsl="http://www.w3.org/1999/XSL/Transform">

  <xsl:template match="/">
    <html>
      <xsl:apply-templates select="people"/>
    </html>
  </xsl:template>

  <xsl:template match="people">
    <table>
      <xsl:apply-templates select="person"/>
    </table>
  </xsl:template>

  <xsl:template match="person">
    <tr>
      <td><xsl:value-of select="name"/></td>
      <td><xsl:value-of select="@born"/></td>
      <td><xsl:value-of select="@died"/></td>
    </tr>
  </xsl:template>

</xsl:stylesheet>
```

The stylesheet in Example 9-3 has three template rules. The first template rule has a match pattern that matches the root node, /. The XSLT processor activates this template rule and sets the context node to the root node. Then it outputs the start-tag <html>. This is followed by an xsl:apply-templates element that selects nodes matching the XPath expression people. If the input document is Example 9-1, then there is exactly one such node, the root element. This is selected and its template rule, the one with the match pattern of people, is applied. The XSLT processor sets the context node to the root people element and then begins processing the people template. It outputs a <table> start-tag and then encounters an xsl:apply-templates element that selects nodes matching the XPath expression person. Two child elements of this context node match the XPath expression person, so they're each processed in turn using the person template rule. When the XSLT processor begins processing each person element, it sets the context node to that element. It outputs that element's name child element value and born and died attribute values wrapped in a table row and three table cells. The net result is:

```
<html>
    <table>
        <tr>
            <td>
                Alan
                Turing

            </td>
            <td>1912</td>
            <td>1954</td>
        </tr>
        <tr>
            <td>
                Richard
                P
                Feynman

            </td>
            <td>1918</td>
            <td>1988</td>
        </tr>
    </table>
</html>
```

The comment( ), text( ), and processing-instruction( ) Location Steps

Although element, attribute, and root nodes account for 90% or more of what you need to do with XML documents, this still leaves four kinds of nodes that need to be addressed: namespace nodes, text nodes, processing-instruction nodes, and comment nodes. Namespace nodes are rarely handled explicitly. The other three node types have special node tests to match them. These are as follows:

- comment( )
- text( )
- processing-instruction( )

Since comments and text nodes don't have names, the comment( ) and text( ) location steps match any comment or text node child of the context node. Each comment is a separate comment node. Each text node contains the maximum possible contiguous run of text not interrupted by any tag. Entity references and CDATA sections are resolved into text and markup and do not interrupt text nodes.

By default, XSLT stylesheets do process text nodes but do not process comment nodes. You can add a comment template rule to an XSLT stylesheet so it will process comments too. For example, this template rule replaces each comment with the text "Comment Deleted" in italic:

```
<xsl:template match="comment()">
    <i>Comment Deleted</i>
</xsl:template>
```

With no arguments, the processing-instruction( ) location step selects all processing-instruction children of the context node. If it has an argument, then it only selects the processing-instruction children with the specified target. For example, the XPath expression processing-instruction('xml-stylesheet') selects all processing-instruction children of the context node whose target is xml-stylesheet.

Wildcards

Wildcards match different element and node types at the same time. There are three wildcards: *, node( ), and @*.

The asterisk (*) matches any element node regardless of name. For example, this XSLT template rule says that all elements should have their child elements processed but should not result in any output in and of themselves:

```
<xsl:template match="*"><xsl:apply-templates select="*"/></xsl:template>
```

The * does not match attributes, text nodes, comments, or processing-instruction nodes. Thus, in the previous example, output will only come from child elements that have their own template rules that override this one.

You can put a namespace prefix in front of the asterisk. In this case, only elements in the same namespace are matched. For example, svg:* matches all elements with the same namespace URI as the svg prefix is mapped to. As usual, it's the URI that matters, not the prefix. The prefix can be different in the stylesheet and the source document as long as the namespace URI is the same.

The node( ) wildcard matches not only all element types but also the root node, text nodes, processing-instruction nodes, namespace nodes, attribute nodes, and comment nodes.

The @* wildcard matches all attribute nodes. For example, this XSLT template rule copies the values of all attributes of a person element in the document into the content of an attributes element in the output:

```
<xsl:template match="person">
  <attributes><xsl:apply-templates select="@*"/></attributes>
</xsl:template>
```

As with elements, you can attach a namespace prefix to the wildcard to match attributes in a specific namespace. For instance, @xlink:* matches all XLink attributes provided that the prefix xlink is mapped to the http://www.w3.org/1999/xlink URI. Again, it's the URI that matters, not the actual prefix.

Multiple Matches with |

You often want to match more than one type of element or attribute but not all types. For example, you may want an XSLT template that applies to the profession and hobby elements but not to the name, person, or people elements. You can combine location paths and steps with the vertical bar (|) to indicate that you want to match any of the named elements. For instance, profession|hobby matches profession and hobby elements. first_name|middle_initial|last_name matches first_name, middle_initial, and last_name elements. @id|@xlink:type matches id and xlink:type attributes. *|@* matches elements and attributes but does not match text nodes, comment nodes, or processing-instruction nodes. For example, this XSLT template rule applies to all the nonempty leaf elements (elements that don't contain any other elements) of Example 9-1:

```
<xsl:template match="first_name|last_name|profession|hobby">
  <xsl:value-of select="text( )"/>
</xsl:template>
```

Compound Location Paths

The XPath expressions you've seen so far—element names, @ plus an attribute name, /, comment( ), text( ), and processing-instruction( )—are all single location steps. You can combine these with the forward slash to move around the hierarchy from the matched node to other nodes. Furthermore, you can use a period to refer to the context node, a double period to refer to the parent node, and a double forward slash to refer to descendants of the context node. With the exception of //, these are all similar to Unix shell syntax for navigating a hierarchical filesystem.

Building Compound Location Paths from Location Steps with /

Location steps can be combined with a forward slash (/) to make a compound location path. Each step in the path is relative to the one that preceded it. If the path begins with /, then the first step in the path is relative to the root node. Otherwise, it's relative to the context node. For example, consider the XPath expression /people/person/name/first_name. This begins at the root node, then selects all people element children of the root node, then all person element children of those nodes, then all name children of those nodes, and finally all first_name children of those nodes. Applied to Example 9-1, it indicates these two elements:

```
<first_name>Alan</first_name>
<first_name>Richard</first_name>
```

To indicate only the textual content of those two nodes, we have to go one step further. The XPath expression /people/person/name/first_name/text( ) selects the strings "Alan" and "Richard" from Example 9-1.

These two XPath expressions both began with /, so they're absolute location paths that start at the root. Relative location paths can also count down from the context node. For example, the XPath expression person/@id selects the id attributes of the person child elements of the context node.

Selecting from Descendants with //

A double forward slash (//) selects from all descendants of the context node, as well as the context node itself. At the beginning of an XPath expression, it selects from all of the nodes in the document. For example, the XPath expression //name selects all name elements in the document. The expression //@id selects all the id

---

attributes of any element in the document. The expression person//@id selects all the id attributes of any element contained in the person child elements of the context node, as well as the id attributes of the person elements themselves.

Selecting the Parent Element with ..

A double period (..) indicates the parent of the current node. For example, the XPath expression //@id identifies all id attributes in the document. Therefore, //@id/.. identifies all elements in the document that have id attributes. The XPath expression //middle_initial/../first_name identifies all first_name elements that are siblings of middle_initial elements in the document. Applied to Example 9-1, this selects <first_name>Richard</first_name> but not <first_name>Alan</first_name>.

Selecting the Context Node with .

Finally, the single period (.) indicates the context node. In XSLT this is most commonly used when you need to take the value of the currently matched node. For example, this template rule copies the content of each comment in the input document to a span element in the output document:

```
<xsl:template match="comment()">
  <span class="comment"><xsl:value-of select="."></span>
</xsl:template>
```

The . given as the value of the select attribute of xsl:value-of stands for the matched node. This works equally well for element nodes, attribute nodes, and all the other kinds of nodes. For example, this template rule matches name elements from the input document and copies their value into strongly emphasized text in the output document:

```
<xsl:template match="name">
  <strong><xsl:value-of select="."></strong>
</xsl:template>
```

Predicates

In general, an XPath expression may refer to more than one node. Sometimes this is what you want, but sometimes you want to further winnow the node-set. You want to select only some of the nodes the expression returns. Each step in a location path may (but does not have to) have a predicate that selects from the node-set current at that step in the expression. The predicate contains a Boolean expression, which is tested for each node in the context node list. If the expression is false, then that node is deleted from the list. Otherwise, it's retained.

For example, suppose you want to find all profession elements whose value is "physicist". The XPath expression //profession[. = "physicist"] does this. You can use single quotes around the string instead of double quotes, which is often useful when the XPath expression appears inside a double-quoted attribute value, for example, <xsl:apply-templates select="//profession[.= 'physicist']" />.

If you want to ask for all person elements that have a profession child element with the value "physicist", you'd use the XPath expression //person [profession="physicist"]. If you want to find the person element with id p4567, put an @ in front of the name of the attribute, as in //person[@id="p4567"].

In addition to the equals sign, XPath supports a full complement of relational operators, including <, >, >=, <=, and !=. For instance, the expression //person [@born<=1976] locates all person elements in the document with a born attribute whose numeric value is less than or equal to 1976. Note that if this expression is used inside an XML document, you still have to escape the less-than sign as <, for example, <xsl:apply-templates select="//person[@born <= 1976]"/>. XPath doesn't get any special exemptions from the normal well-formedness rules of XML. However, if the XPath expression appears outside of an XML document, as it may in some uses of XPointer, you may not need to escape the less-than sign.

XPath also provides Boolean and and or operators to combine expressions logically. For example, the XPath expression //person[@born<=1920 and @born>=1910] selects all person elements with born attribute values between 1910 and 1920, inclusive. //name[first_name="Richard" or first_name="Dick"] selects all name elements that have a first_name child with the value of either Richard or Dick.

In some cases, the predicate may not be a Boolean, but it can be converted to one in a straightforward fashion. Predicates that evaluate to numbers are true if they're equal to the position of the context node; otherwise, they're false. For instance, //name[2] selects the second name element in the document. (XPath indices begin at 1 as in Fortran, not 0 as in Java and C.) Predicates that indicate node-sets are true if the node-set is nonempty and false if it's empty. For example, suppose you want to select only those name elements in the document that have a middle_initial child element. The XPath expression //name selects all name elements. The XPath expression //name[middle_initial] selects all name elements and then checks each one to see if it has a middle_initial child element. Only those that do are retained. When applied to Example 9-1, this expression indicates Richard P. Feynman's name element but not Alan Turing's. String values are true if the string isn't the empty string, false if it is.

Any or all of the location steps in a location path can have predicates. For example, the XPath expression /people/person[@born < 1950]/name[first_name = "Alan"] first selects all people child elements of the root element (of which there's exactly one in Example 9-1). Then from those it chooses all person elements whose born attribute has a value numerically less than 1950. Finally, from that group of elements, it selects all name child elements that have a first_name child element with the value "Alan".

Unabbreviated Location Paths

Up until this point, we've been using what are called *abbreviated location paths*. These are easy to type, not usually verbose, and very familiar to most people. They're also the kind of XPath expression that works best for XSLT match patterns. However, XPath also offers an unabbreviated syntax for location paths, which is more verbose but perhaps less cryptic and definitely more flexible than abbreviated location paths.

Every location step in a location path has two required parts, an axis and a node test, and one optional part, the predicates. The axis tells you which direction to travel from the context node to look for the next nodes. The node test tells you which nodes to include along that axis, and the predicates further reduce the nodes according to some expression.

In an abbreviated location path, the axis and the node test are combined, while in an unabbreviated location path, they're separated by a double colon (::). For example, the abbreviated location path `people/person/@id` is composed of three location steps. The first step selects `people` element nodes along the child axis. The second step selects `person` element nodes along the child axis. The third step selects `id` attribute nodes along the attribute axis. When rewritten using the unabbreviated syntax, the same location path is `child::people/child::person/attribute::id`.

These full, unabbreviated location paths may be absolute if they start from the root node, just as abbreviated paths can be. The full form `/child::people/child::person`, for example, is equivalent to the abbreviated form `/people/person`.

Unabbreviated location paths may be used in predicates as well. For example, the abbreviated path `/people/person[@born<1950]/name[first_name="Alan"]` becomes `/child::people/child::person[ attribute::born < 1950 ] /child::name[ child::first_name = "Alan" ]` in the full form.

Overall, the unabbreviated form is quite verbose and not used much in practice. However, it does offer one crucial ability that makes it essential to know: it is the only way to access most of the axes from which XPath expressions can choose nodes. The abbreviated syntax lets you walk along the child, parent, self, attribute, and descendant-or-self axes. The unabbreviated syntax adds eight more axes:

ancestor
> All element nodes that contain the context node, that is, the parent node, the parent's parent, the parent's parent's parent, and so on up through the root node in reverse document order.

following-sibling
> All nodes that follow the context node and are children of the same parent node in document order. Attribute and namespace nodes do not have any siblings.

preceding-sibling
> All nodes that precede the context node and are children of the same parent node in reverse document order.

following
> All nodes that follow the end of the context node in document order except for descendant, attribute, and namespace nodes.

preceding
> All nodes that precede the start of the context node in reverse document order except for ancestor, attribute, and namespace nodes.

namespace

> If the context node is an element, all namespaces in scope on the context node, whether declared on the context node or one of its ancestors. If the context node is not an element, then the empty set.

descendant

> All descendants of the context node but not the context node itself.

ancestor-or-self

> All ancestors of the context node and the context node itself.

Example 9-4 demonstrates several of these axes using the full unabbreviated syntax. The goal is to produce a list of person elements that look more or less like this (after accounting for whitespace):

```
<dt>Richard P Feynman</dt>
<dd>
  <ul>
    <li>physicist</li>
    <li>Playing the bongoes</li>
  </ul>
</dd>
```

Example 9-4. An XSLT stylesheet that uses unabbreviated XPath syntax

```
<?xml version="1.0"?>
<xsl:stylesheet version="1.0"
                xmlns:xsl="http://www.w3.org/1999/XSL/Transform">

  <xsl:template match="/">
    <dl>
      <xsl:apply-templates select="descendant::person"/>
    </dl>
  </xsl:template>

  <xsl:template match="person">
    <dt><xsl:value-of select="child::name"/></dt>
    <dd>
      <ul>
        <xsl:apply-templates select="child::name/following-sibling::*"/>
      </ul>
    </dd>
  </xsl:template>

  <xsl:template match="*">
    <li><xsl:value-of select="self::*"/></li>
  </xsl:template>

  <xsl:template match="homepage"
                xmlns:xlink="http://www.w3.org/1999/xlink">
    <li><xsl:value-of select="attribute::xlink:href"/></li>
  </xsl:template>

</xsl:stylesheet>
```

The first template rule matches the root node. It applies templates to all descendants of the root node that happen to be person elements. That is, it moves from the root node along the descendant axis with a node test of person. This XPath expression could have been rewritten in the abbreviated syntax as //person.

The second template rule matches person elements. It places the value of the name child of each person element in a dt element. The location path used here, child::name, could have been rewritten in the abbreviated syntax as the single word name. Then it applies templates to all elements that follow the name element at the same level of the hierarchy. It begins at the context node person element, then moves along the child axis to find the name element. From there it moves along the following-sibling axis looking for elements with any name (*) after the name element that are also children of the same person element. There is no abbreviated equivalent for the following-sibling axis, so this really is the simplest way to make this statement.

The third template rule matches any element not matched by another template rule. It simply wraps that element in an li element. The XPath expression self::* selects the value of the currently matched element, that is, the context node. This expression could have been abbreviated as a single period.

The fourth and final template rule matches homepage elements. In this case we need to select the value of xlink:href attributes, so we move from the context homepage node along the attribute axis. The node test is looking for the xlink:href attributes. (More properly, it's looking for an attribute with the local name href whose prefix is mapped to the http://www.w3.org/1999/xlink namespace URI.)

General XPath Expressions

So far we've focused on the very useful subset of XPath expressions called location paths. Location paths identify a set of nodes in an XML document and are used in XSLT match patterns and select expressions. However, location paths are not the only possible type of XPath expression. XPath expressions can also return numbers, Booleans, and strings. For instance, these are all legal XPath expressions:

- 3.141529
- 2+2
- 'Rosalind Franklin'
- true( )
- 32.5 < 76.2
- position( )=last( )

XPath expressions that aren't node-sets can't be used in the match attribute of an xsl:template element. However, they can be used as values for the select attribute of xsl:value-of elements, as well as in the location path predicates.

Numbers

There are no pure integers in XPath. All numbers are 8-byte, IEEE 754 floating-point doubles, even if they don't have an explicit decimal point. This format is identical to Java's double primitive type. In addition to representing floating-point numbers ranging from 4.94065645841246544e-324 to 1.79769313486231570e+308 (positive or negative) and 0, this type includes special representations of positive and negative infinity and a special not a number (NaN) value used as the result of operations like dividing zero by zero.

XPath provides the five basic arithmetic operators that will be familiar to any programmer:

+   Addition

-   Subtraction

*   Multiplication

div Division

mod Taking the remainder

The more common forward slash couldn't be used for division because it's already used to separate location steps in a location path. Consequently, a new operator had to be chosen, div. The word mod was chosen instead of the more common % operator to calculate the remainder. Aside from these minor differences in syntax, all five operators behave exactly as they do in Java. For instance, 2+2 is 4, 6.5 div 1.5 is 4.33333333, 6.5 mod 1.5 is 0.5, and so on. The element `<xsl:value-of select="6*7"/>` inserts the string 42 into the output tree when the template is instantiated. More often, a stylesheet performs some simple arithmetic on numbers read from the input document. For instance, this template rule calculates the century in which a person was born:

```
<xsl:template match="person">
  <century>
    <xsl:value-of select="((@born - (@born mod 100)) div 100) + 1)"/>th
  </century>
</xsl:template>
```

Strings

XPath strings are ordered sequences of Unicode characters such as "Fred", "Ethel", "الـ بـ ل", or "Ξηνος". String literals may be enclosed in either single or double quotes as convenient. The quotes are not themselves part of the string. The only restriction XPath places on a string literal is that it must not contain the kind of quote that delimits it. That is, if the string contains single quotes, it has to be enclosed in double quotes and vice versa. String literals may contain whitespace including tabs, carriage returns, and line feeds, as well as backslashes and other characters that would be illegal in many programming languages. However, if the XPath expression is part of an XML document, some characters may need to be escaped to satisfy XML's well-formedness rules.

You can use the = and != comparison operators to check whether two strings are the same. You can also use the relational <, >, <=, and >= operators to compare strings, but unless both strings clearly represent numbers (e.g., "-7.5" or '54.2'), the results are unlikely to make sense. In general, you can't define any real notion of string order in Unicode without detailed knowledge of the language in which the string is written.

Other operations on strings are provided by XPath functions and will be discussed shortly.

Booleans

A Boolean is a value that has exactly two states, true or false. Every Boolean must have one of these binary values. XPath does not provide any Boolean literals. If you use `<xsl:value-of select="true"/>` in an XSLT stylesheet, then the XSLT processor looks for a child element of the context node named true. However, the XPath functions true( ) and false( ) can substitute for the missing literals quite easily.

Most of the time, however, Booleans are created by comparisons between other objects, most commonly numbers. XPath provides all the usual relational operators including =, !=, <, >, >=, and <=. In addition, the and and or operators can combine Boolean expressions according to the usual rules of logic.

Booleans are most commonly used in predicates of location paths. For example, in the location step person[profession="physicist"], profession="physicist" is a Boolean. It is either true or false; there is no other possibility. Booleans are also commonly used in the test attribute of xsl:if and xsl:when elements. For example, this XSLT template rule includes the profession element in the output only if its contents are "physicist" or "computer scientist":

```
<xsl:template match="profession">
  <xsl:if test=".='computer scientist' or .='physicist'">
    <xsl:value-of select="."/>
  </xsl:if>
</xsl:template>
```

This XSLT template rule italicizes the profession element if and only if its content is the string "computer scientist":

```
<xsl:template match="profession">
  <xsl:choose>
    <xsl:when test=".='computer scientist'">
      <i><xsl:value-of select="."/></i>
    </xsl:when>
    <xsl:otherwise>
      <xsl:value-of select="."/>
    </xsl:otherwise>
  </xsl:choose>
</xsl:template>
```

Finally, there's a not( ) function that reverses the sense of its Boolean argument. For example, if .='computer scientist' is true, then not(.='computer scientist') is false and vice versa.

XPath

XPath Functions

XPath provides many functions that you may find useful in predicates or raw expressions. All of these are discussed in Chapter 23. For example, the position( ) function returns the position of the current node in the context node list as a number. This XSLT template rule uses the position( ) function to calculate the number of the person being processed, relative to other nodes in the context node list:

```
<xsl:template match="person">
  Person <xsl:value-of select="position( )"/>,
    <xsl:value-of select="name"/>
</xsl:template>
```

Each XPath function returns one of these four types:

- Boolean
- Number
- Node-set
- String

There are no void functions in XPath; it is not nearly as strongly typed as languages like Java or even C. You can often use any of these types as a function argument regardless of which type the function expects, and the processor will convert it as best it can. For example, if you insert a Boolean where a string is expected, then the processor will substitute one of the two strings "true" or "false" for the Boolean. The one exception is functions that expect to receive node-sets as arguments. XPath cannot convert strings, Booleans, or numbers to node-sets.

Functions are identified by the parentheses at the end of the function name. Sometimes functions take arguments between the parentheses. For instance, the round( ) function takes a single number as an argument. It returns the number rounded to the nearest integer. For example, <xsl:value-of select="round(3.14)"/> inserts 3 into the output tree.

Other functions take more than one argument. For instance, the starts-with( ) function takes two arguments, both strings. It returns true if the first string starts with the second string. For example, this XSLT apply-templates element selects all name elements whose last name begins with the letter T:

```
<xsl:apply-templates select="name[starts-with(last_name, 'T')]"/>
```

In this example the first argument to the starts-with( ) function is actually a node-set, not a string. The XPath processor converts that node-set to its string value (the text content of the first element in that node-set) before checking to see whether it starts with T.

Some XSLT functions have variable-length argument lists. For instance, the concat( ) function takes as arguments any number of strings and returns one string formed by concatenating all those strings together in order. For example, concat("a", "b", "c", "d") returns "abcd".

In addition to the functions defined in XPath and discussed in this chapter, most uses of XPath, such as XSLT and XPointer, define many more functions that are useful in their particular context. You use these extra functions just like the built-in functions when you're using those applications. XSLT even lets you write extension functions in Java and other languages that can do almost anything, for example, making SQL queries against a remote database server and returning the result of the query as a node-set.

Node-Set Functions

The node-set functions operate on or return information about node-sets; that is, collections of XPath nodes. You've already encountered the position( ) function. Two related functions are last( ) and count( ). The last( ) function returns the number of nodes in the context node list, which also happens to be the same as the position of the last node in the list. The count( ) function is similar except that it returns the number of nodes in its node-set argument rather than in the context node list. For example, count(//name) returns the number of name elements in the document. Example 9-5 uses the position( ) and count( ) functions to list the people in the document in the form "Person 1 of 10, Person 2 of 10, Person 3 of 10...". In the second template, the position( ) function determines which person element is currently being processed, and the count( ) function determines how many total person elements there are in the document.

Example 9-5. An XSLT stylesheet that uses the position( ) and count( ) functions

```
<?xml version="1.0"?>
<xsl:stylesheet version="1.0"
                xmlns:xsl="http://www.w3.org/1999/XSL/Transform">

  <xsl:template match="people">
    <xsl:apply-templates select="person"/>
  </xsl:template>

  <xsl:template match="person">
    Person <xsl:value-of select="position( )"/>
    of <xsl:value-of select="count(//person)"/>:
    <xsl:value-of select="name"/>
  </xsl:template>

</xsl:stylesheet>
```

The id( ) function takes as an argument a string containing one or more IDs separated by whitespace and returns a node-set containing all the nodes in the document that have those IDs. These are attributes declared to have type ID in the DTD, not necessarily attributes named ID or id. (A DTD must be present in order for the id( ) function to work.) Thus, in Example 9-1, id('p342') indicates Alan Turing's person element; id('p342 p4567') indicates both Alan Turing and Richard Feynman's person elements.

The `id( )` allows you to form absolute location paths that don't start from the root. For example, `id('p342')/name` refers to Alan Turing's name element, regardless of where Alan Turing's person element is in the document, as long as it hasn't changed ID. This function is especially useful for XPointers, where it takes the place of HTML's named anchors.

Finally, there are three node-set functions related to namespaces. The `local-name( )` function accepts a node-set as an argument and returns the local part of the first node in that set. The `namespace-uri( )` function takes a node-set as an argument and returns the namespace URI of the first node in the set. Finally, the `name( )` function takes a node-set as an argument and returns the qualified name of the first node in that set. In all three functions, the argument may be omitted, in which case the context node's namespace is evaluated. For instance, when applied to Example 9-1, the XPath expression `local-name(//homepage/@xlink:href)` is `href`; `namespace-uri(//homepage/@xlink:href)` is `http://www.w3.org/1999/xlink`; and `name(//homepage/@xlink:href)` is `xlink:href`.

String Functions

XPath includes functions for basic string operations such as finding the length of a string or changing letters from upper- to lowercase. It doesn't have the full power of the string libraries in Python or Perl—for instance, there's no regular expression support—but it's sufficient for many simple manipulations you need for XSLT or XPointer.

The `string( )` function converts an argument of any type to a string in a reasonable fashion. Booleans are converted to the string "true" or the string "false." Node-sets are converted to the string value of the first node in the set. This is the same value calculated by the `xsl:value-of` element. That is, the string value of the element is the complete text of the element after all entity references are resolved and tags, comments, and processing instructions have been stripped out. Numbers are converted to strings in the format used by most programming languages, such as "1987," "299792500," or "2.71828."

 In XSLT, the `xsl:decimal-format` element and `format-number( )` function provide more precise control over formatting so you can insert separators between groups, change the decimal separator, use non-European digits, and make similar adjustments.

The normal use of most of the rest of the string functions is to manipulate or address the text content of XML elements or attributes. For instance, if date attributes were given in the format MM/DD/YYYY, then the string functions would allow you to target the month, day, and year separately.

The `starts-with( )` function takes two string arguments. It returns true if the first argument starts with the second argument. For example, `starts-with('Richard', 'Ric')` is true, but `starts-with('Richard', 'Rick')` is false. There is no corresponding `ends-with( )` function.

The contains( ) function also takes two string arguments. However, it returns true if the first argument contains the second argument—that is, if the second argument is a substring of the first argument—regardless of position. For example, contains('Richard', 'ar') is true, but contains('Richard', 'art') is false.

The substring-before( ) function takes two string arguments and returns the substring of the first argument that precedes the initial appearance of the second argument. If the second string doesn't appear in the first string, then substring-before( ) returns the empty string. For example, substring-before('MM/DD/YYYY', '/') is MM. The substring-after( ) function also takes two string arguments but returns the substring of the first argument that follows the initial appearance of the second argument. If the second string doesn't appear in the first string, then substring-after( ) returns the empty string. For example, substring-after ('MM/DD/YYYY', '/') is 'DD/YYYY'. substring-before(substring-after('MM/DD/YYYY', '/')', '/') is DD. substring-after(substring-after('MM/DD/YYYY', '/')', '/') is YYYY.

If you know the position of the substring you want, you can use the substring( ) method instead. This takes three arguments: the string from which the substring will be copied, the position in the string from which to start extracting, and the number of characters to copy to the substring. The third argument may be omitted, in which case the substring contains all characters from the specified start position to the end of the string. For example, substring('MM/DD/YYYY', 1, 2) is MM; substring('MM/DD/YYYY', 4, 2) is DD; and substring('MM/DD/YYYY', 7) is YYYY.

The string-length( ) function returns a number giving the length of its argument's string value or the context node if no argument is included. In Example 9-1, string-length(//name[position( )=1]) is 29. If that seems long to you, remember that all whitespace characters are included in the count. If it seems short to you, remember that markup characters are not included in the count.

Theoretically, you could use these functions to trim and normalize whitespace in element content. However, since this would be relatively complex and is such a common need, XPath provides the normalize-space( ) function to do this. For instance, in Example 9-1, the value of string(//name[position( )=1]) is:

```
Alan
Turing
```

This contains a lot of extra whitespace that was inserted purely to make the XML document neater. However, normalize-space(string(//name[position( )=1])) is much more reasonable:

```
Alan Turing
```

Although a more powerful string-manipulation library would be useful, XSLT is really designed for transforming the element structure of an XML document. It's not meant to have the more general power of a language like Perl, which can handle arbitrarily complicated and varying string formats.

Boolean Functions

The Boolean functions are few in number and quite straightforward. They all return a Boolean that has the value true or false. The true( ) function always returns true. The false( ) function always returns false. These substitute for Boolean literals in XPath.

The not( ) function reverses the sense of its Boolean argument. For example, not(@val>400) is almost always equivalent to (@val<=400). (NaN is a special case.)

The boolean( ) function converts its single argument to a Boolean and returns the result. If the argument is omitted, then it converts the context node. Numbers are converted to false if they're zero or NaN. All other numbers are true. Node-sets are false if they're empty and true if they contain at least one node. Strings are false if they have zero length, otherwise they're true. Note that according to this rule, the string "false" is in fact true.

Number Functions

XPath includes a few simple numeric functions for summing groups of numbers and finding the nearest integer to a number. It doesn't have the full power of the math libraries in Java or Fortran—for instance, there's no square root or exponentiation function—but it's got enough to do most of the basic math you need for XSLT or the even simpler requirements of XPointer.

The number( ) function can take any type as an argument and convert it to a number. If the argument is omitted, then it converts the context node. Booleans are converted to 1 if true and 0 if false. Strings are converted in a plausible fashion. For instance the string "7.5" will be converted to the number 7.5. The string "Fred" will be converted to NaN. Node-sets are converted to numbers by first converting them to their string value and then converting the resulting string to a number. The detailed rules are a little more complex, but as long as the object you're converting can reasonably be interpreted as a single number, chances are the number( ) function will do what you expect. If the object you're converting can't be reasonably interpreted as a single number, then the number( ) function will return NaN.

The round( ), floor( ), and ceiling( ) functions all take a single number as an argument. The floor( ) function returns the greatest integer less than or equal to its argument. The ceiling( ) function returns the smallest integer greater than or equal to its argument. The round( ) function returns its argument rounded to the nearest integer. When rounding numbers like 1.5 and -3.5 that are equally close to two integers, round( ) returns the greater of the two possibilities. (This means that -1.5 rounds to -1, but 1.5 rounds to 2.)

The sum( ) function takes a node-set as an argument. It converts each node in the set to its string value, then converts each of those strings to a number. It then adds up the numbers and returns the result.

10

XLinks

XLinks are an attribute-based syntax for attaching links to XML documents. XLinks can be simple Point A-to-Point B links, like the links you're accustomed to from HTML's A element. XLinks can also be bidirectional, linking two documents in both directions so you can go from A to B or B to A. XLinks can even be multidirectional, presenting many different paths between any number of XML documents. The documents don't have to be XML documents—XLinks can be placed in an XML document that lists connections between other documents that may or may not be XML documents themselves. Web graffiti artists take note: these third-party links let you attach links to pages you don't even control, like the home page of the *New York Times* or the C.I.A. At its core, XLink is nothing more and nothing less than an XML syntax for describing directed graphs, in which the vertices are documents at particular URIs and the edges are the links between the documents. What you put in that graph is up to you.

Current web browsers at most support simple XLinks that do little more than duplicate the functionality of HTML's A element. Many browsers, including Internet Explorer, don't support XLinks at all. However, custom applications may do a lot more. Since XLinks are so powerful, it shouldn't come as a surprise that they can do more than make blue underlined links on web pages. XLinks can describe tables of contents or indexes. They can connect textual emendations to the text they describe. They can indicate possible paths through online courses or virtual worlds. Different applications will interpret different sets of XLinks differently. Just as no one browser really understands the semantics of all the various XML applications, so too no one program can process all collections of XLinks.

Simple Links

A simple link defines a one-way connection between two resources. The source or *starting resource* of the connection is the link element itself. The target or *ending resource* of the connection is identified by a Uniform Resource Identifier (URI).

The link goes from the starting resource to the ending resource. The starting resource is always an XML element. The ending resource may be an XML document, a particular element in an XML document, a group of elements in an XML document, a span of text in an XML document, or something that isn't a part of an XML document, such as an MPEG movie or a PDF file. The URI may be something other than a URL, perhaps a book ISBN number like urn:isbn:1565922247.

A simple XLink is encoded in an XML document as an element of arbitrary type that has an xlink:type attribute with the value simple and an xlink:href attribute whose value is the URI of the link target. The xlink prefix must be mapped to the http://www.w3.org/1999/xlink namespace URI. As usual, the prefix can change as long as the URI stays the same. For example, suppose this novel element appears in a list of children's literature and we want to link it to the actual text of the novel available from the URL *ftp://archive.org/pub/etext/etext93/wizoz10.txt*:

```
<novel>
    <title>The Wonderful Wizard of Oz</title>
    <author>L. Frank Baum</author>
    <year>1900</year>
</novel>
```

We give the novel element an xlink:type attribute with the value simple, an xlink:href attribute that contains the URL to which we're linking, and an xmlns:xlink attribute that associates the prefix xlink with the namespace URI http://www.w3.org/1999/xlink like so:

```
<novel xmlns:xlink= "http://www.w3.org/1999/xlink"
       xlink:type = "simple"
       xlink:href = "ftp://archive.org/pub/etext/etext93/wizoz10.txt">
    <title>The Wonderful Wizard of Oz</title>
    <author>L. Frank Baum</author>
    <year>1900</year>
</novel>
```

This establishes a simple link from this novel element to the plain text file found at *ftp://archive.org/pub/etext/etext93/wizoz10.txt*. Browsers are free to interpret this link as they like. However, the most natural interpretation, and the one implemented by the few browsers that do support simple XLinks, is to make this a blue underlined phrase the user can click on to replace the current page with the file being linked to. Other schemes are possible, however.

XLinks are fully namespace aware. The xlink prefix is customary, although it can be changed. However, it must be mapped to the URI http://www.w3.org/1999/xlink. This can be done on the XLink element itself, as in this novel example, or it can be done on any ancestor of that element up to and including the root element of the document. Future examples in this chapter and the next use the xlink prefix exclusively and assume that this prefix has been properly declared on some ancestor element.

Every XLink element must have an xlink:type attribute indicating the kind of link (or part of a link) it is. This attribute has six possible values:

- simple
- extended

- locator
- arc
- title
- resource

Simple XLinks are the only ones that are really similar to HTML links. The remaining five kinds of XLink elements will be discussed in later sections.

The xlink:href attribute identifies the resource being linked to. It always contains a URI. Both relative and absolute URLs can be used, as they are in HTML links. However, the URI need not be a URL. For example, this link identifies, but does not locate, the print edition of *The Wonderful Wizard of Oz* with the ISBN number 0688069444:

```
<novel xmlns:xlink= "http://www.w3.org/1999/xlink"
       xlink:type = "simple"
       xlink:href = "urn:isbn:0688069444">
   <title>The Wonderful Wizard of Oz</title>
   <author>L. Frank Baum</author>
   <year>1900</year>
</novel>
```

Link Behavior

So far, we've been careful to talk in the abstract. We've said that an XLink describes a connection between two resources, but we haven't said much about how that connection is presented to the end user or what it makes software reading the document do. That's because there isn't one answer to these questions. For instance, when the browser encounters a novel element that uses an *http* URL, clicking the link should probably load the text of the novel from the URL into the current window, thereby replacing the document that contained the link. Then again, maybe it should open a new window and show the user the new document in that window. The proper behavior for a browser encountering the novel element that uses an *isbn* URN is even less clear. Perhaps it should reserve the book with the specified ISBN at the local library for the user to walk in and pick up. Or perhaps it should order the book from an online bookstore. In other cases something else entirely may be called for. For instance, the content of some links are embedded directly in the linking document, as in this image element:

```
<image width="248" height="173" xlink:type="simple"
       xlink:href="http://www.turing.org.uk/turing/pi1/sark.jpg" />
```

Here, the author most likely intends the browser to download and display the image as soon as it finds the link. And rather than opening a new window for the image or replacing the current document with the image, the image should be embedded into the current document.

Just as XML is more flexible than HTML in the documents it describes, so too is XLink more flexible in the links it describes. An XLink indicates that there's a connection between two documents, but it's up to the application reading the XLink to decide what that connection means. It's not necessarily a blue, underlined phrase the user clicks in a browser to jump from the source document to the target. It may indeed be that, just as an XML document may be a web page, but it may be something else, too.

Page authors can offer suggestions to browsers about how links should be handled by using the xlink:show and xlink:actuate attributes. The xlink:show attribute tells a browser or other application what to do when the link is activated—for example, whether to show the linked content in the same window or to open a new window to display it. The xlink:actuate attribute tells the browser when to show the content—for example, whether it should follow the link as soon as it sees it or whether it should wait for an explicit user request.

xlink:show

The optional xlink:show attribute has five possible values that suggest in what context the application loading an XLinked resource should display that resource:

new
> Open a new window and show the content of the link's URI (the ending resource) in that window.

replace
> Show the ending resource in the current window, replacing the current document.

embed
> Embed a picture of the ending resource in the current document at the location of the link element.

other
> Exhibit some behavior other than opening a new window, replacing the document in the existing window, or graphically embedding the resource in the existing document. Exactly what that behavior is may be specified by other, nonstandard markup that a particular application understands.

none
> Specify no behavior.

All five of these are only suggestions that browsers or other applications following XLinks are free to ignore. For example, a web spider would not open a window for any link and might ignore embedded links and treat the other four types identically. Mozilla might open a new tab in an existing window for xlink:show="new" rather than creating a completely new window. This is all allowed as long as it makes sense in the context of the application.

xlink:actuate

The optional xlink:actuate attribute has four possible values, which suggest when an application that encounters an XLink should follow it:

onLoad
> The link should be followed as soon as the application sees it.

onRequest
> The link should be followed when the user asks to follow it.

other

    When to follow the link is determined by other markup in the document not specified by XLink.

    No details are available about when or whether to follow this link. Indeed, following the link may not have any plausible meaning, as in the previous example where the link pointed to a book's ISBN number rather than a URL where the book could be found.

All four of these are only suggestions, which browsers or other applications following XLinks are free to ignore. For example, a web spider would use its own algorithms to decide when to follow and not follow a link. Differing behavior when faced with the same attributes is allowed as long as it makes sense for the application reading the document.

For example, a traditional link, such as is provided by HTML's A element and indicated by the first novel example, would be encoded like this:

```
<novel xlink:type="simple"
       xlink:href="ftp://archive.org/pub/etext/etext93/wizoz10.txt"
       xlink:actuate="onRequest" xlink:show="replace">
  <title>The Wonderful Wizard of Oz</title>
  <author>L. Frank Baum</author>
  <year>1900</year>
</novel>
```

This says to wait for an explicit user request to follow the link (e.g., by clicking on the content of the link) and then to replace the existing document with the document found at *ftp://archive.org/pub/etext/etext93/wizoz10.txt*. On the other hand, if you were using XLinks to embed images in documents, you'd want them traversed immediately and then embedded in the originating document. The following syntax would be appropriate:

```
<image xlink:type="simple"
       xlink:actuate="onLoad" xlink:show="embed"
       xlink:href="http://www.turing.org.uk/turing/pi1/bus.jpg"
       width="152" height="345" />
```

Both xlink:show and xlink:actuate are optional. An application should be prepared to do something reasonable if they're missing.

Link Semantics

A link describes a connection between two resources. These resources may or may not be XML documents; but even if they are XML documents, the relationships they have with each other can be quite varied. For example, links can indicate parent–child relationships, previous–next relationships, employer–employee relationships, customer–supplier relationships, and many more. XLink elements can have xlink:title and xlink:role attributes to specify the meaning of the connection between the resources. The xlink:title attribute contains a small amount of plain text describing the remote resource such as might be shown in a tool tip when the user moves the cursor over the link. The xlink:role attribute contains a

URI that somehow indicates the meaning of the link. For instance, the URI http://
www.isi.edu/in-notes/iana/assignments/media-types/text/css might be understood to mean that the link points to a CSS stylesheet for the document in which
the link is found. However, there are no standards for the meanings of role URIs.
Applications are free to assign their own meaning to their own URIs.

For example, this book element is a simple XLink that points to Scott's author
page at O'Reilly. The xlink:title attribute contains his name, while the
xlink:role attribute points contains the URI for the Dublin Core creator property, thereby indicating he's an author of this book.

```
<book xlink:type="simple"
 xlink:href="http://www.oreillynet.com/cs/catalog/view/au/751"
 xlink:title="W. Scott Means"
 xlink:role="http://purl.org/dc/elements/1.1/creator" >
  XML in a Nutshell
</book>
```

As with almost everything else related to XLink, exactly what browsers or other
applications will do with this information or how they'll present it to readers
remains to be determined.

Extended Links

Whereas a simple link describes a single unidirectional connection between one
XML element and one remote resource, an extended link describes a collection of
resources and a collection of paths between those resources. Each path connects
exactly two resources. Any individual resource may be connected to one of the
other resources, two of the other resources, zero of the other resources, all of the
other resources, or any subset of the other resources in the collection. It may even
be connected back to itself. In computer science terms, an extended link is a
directed, labeled graph in which the paths are arcs, the documents are vertices,
and the URIs are labels.

Simple links are very easy to understand by analogy with HTML links. However,
there's no obvious analogy for extended links. What they look like, how applications treat them, what user interfaces present them to people, is all up in the air.
No simple visual metaphors like "click on the blue underlined text to jump to a
new page" have been invented for extended links, and no browsers support them.
How they'll be used and what user interfaces will be designed for them remains to
be seen.

In XML, an extended link is represented by an extended link element; that is, an
element of arbitrary type that has an xlink:type attribute with the value extended.
For example, this is an extended link element that refers to the novel *The
Wonderful Wizard of Oz*:

```
<novel xlink:type="extended">
  <title>The Wonderful Wizard of Oz</title>
  <author>L. Frank Baum</author>
  <year>1900</year>
</novel>
```

Although this extended link is quite spartan, most extended links contain local resources, remote resources, and arcs between those resources. A remote resource is represented by a locator element, which is an element of any type that has an xlink:type attribute with the value locator. A local resource is represented by a resource element, which is an element of any type that has an xlink:type attribute with the value resource. And an arc between two resources, whether local or remote, is represented by an arc element—that is, an element of any type that has an xlink:type attribute with the value arc.

Locators

Each locator element has an xlink:type attribute with the value locator and an xlink:href attribute containing a URI for the resource it locates. For example, this novel element for *The Wonderful Wizard of Oz* contains three locator elements that identify particular editions of the book:

```
<novel xlink:type = "extended">
  <title>The Wonderful Wizard of Oz</title>
  <author>L. Frank Baum</author>
  <year>1900</year>
  <edition xlink:type="locator" xlink:href="urn:isbn:0688069444" />
  <edition xlink:type="locator" xlink:href="urn:isbn:0192839306" />
  <edition xlink:type="locator" xlink:href="urn:isbn:0700609857" />
</novel>
```

Most of the time each locator element also has an xlink:label attribute that serves as a name for the element. The value of this attribute can be any XML name that does not contain a colon (i.e., that does not have a namespace prefix). For instance, in the previous example, we could add labels based on the ISBN number, like this:

```
<novel xlink:type = "extended">
  <title>The Wonderful Wizard of Oz</title>
  <author>L. Frank Baum</author>
  <year>1900</year>
  <edition xlink:type="locator" xlink:href="urn:isbn:0688069444"
                                xlink:label="ISBN0688069444"/>
  <edition xlink:type="locator" xlink:href="urn:isbn:0192839306"
                                xlink:label="ISBN0192839306"/>
  <edition xlink:type="locator" xlink:href="urn:isbn:0700609857"
                                xlink:label="ISBN0700609857"/>
</novel>
```

The number alone cannot be used because XML names cannot start with digits. In this and most cases, the labels are unique within the extended link, but they don't absolutely have to be.

Locators may also have the optional semantic attributes xlink:title and xlink:role to provide more information about the remote resource and the link to it. These attributes have the same meanings they have for simple XLinks. The xlink:title attribute contains a small amount of text describing the remote resource, and the xlink:role attribute contains an absolute URI that somehow indicates the nature of the link. For instance, the edition elements could provide the publisher's name in the title and use a Dublin Core URI to indicate that the link is a formal identifier not meant to be traversed like this:

```
<novel xlink:type = "extended">
  <title>The Wonderful Wizard of Oz</title>
  <author>L. Frank Baum</author>
  <year>1900</year>
  <edition xlink:type="locator" xlink:href="urn:isbn:0688069444"
           xlink:title="William Morrow"
           xlink:role="http://purl.org/dc/elements/1.1/publisher"
           xlink:label="ISBN0688069444"/>
  <edition xlink:type="locator" xlink:href="urn:isbn:0192839306"
           xlink:title="Oxford University Press"
           xlink:role="http://purl.org/dc/elements/1.1/publisher"
           xlink:label="ISBN0192839306"/>
  <edition xlink:type="locator" xlink:href="urn:isbn:0700609857"
           xlink:title="University Press of Kansas"
           xlink:role="http://purl.org/dc/elements/1.1/publisher"
           xlink:label="ISBN0700609857"/>
</novel>
```

Arcs

Paths between resources are called *arcs*, and they are represented by arc elements; that is, elements of arbitrary type that have an xlink:type attribute with the value arc. Each arc element should have an xlink:from attribute and an xlink:to attribute. The xlink:from attribute identifies the source of the link. The xlink:to attribute identifies the target of the link. These attributes do not contain URIs as you might expect. Rather they contain a name matching the value of the xlink:label attribute of one of the locator elements in the extended link.

Example 10-1 shows an extended link that contains the first three novels in the Wizard of Oz series: *The Wonderful Wizard of Oz*, *The Marvelous Land of Oz*, and *Ozma of Oz*. Arcs connect the first book in the series to the second and the second to the third, and then back again. In this example, the root series element is the extended link element, each novel element is a locator element, and the next and previous elements are arc elements.

Example 10-1. An extended link with three locators and four arcs

```
<series xlink:type="extended" xmlns:xlink="http://www.w3.org/1999/xlink">

  <author>L. Frank Baum</author>
  <!-- locator elements -->
  <novel xlink:type="locator" xlink:label="oz1"
         xlink:href="ftp://archive.org/pub/etext/etext93/wizoz10.txt">
    <title>The Wonderful Wizard of Oz</title>
    <year>1900</year>
  </novel>
  <novel xlink:type="locator" xlink:label="oz2"
         xlink:href="ftp://archive.org/pub/etext/etext93/ozland10.txt">
    <title>The Marvelous Land of Oz</title>
    <year>1904</year>
  </novel>
```

Example 10-1. An extended link with three locators and four arcs (continued)

```
<novel xlink:type="locator" xlink:label="oz3"
      xlink:href="ftp://archive.org/pub/etext/etext93/wizoz10.txt">
  <title>Ozma of Oz</title>
  <year>1907</year>
</novel>

<!-- arcs -->
<next     xlink:type="arc" xlink:from="oz1" xlink:to="oz2" />
<next     xlink:type="arc" xlink:from="oz2" xlink:to="oz3" />
<previous xlink:type="arc" xlink:from="oz2" xlink:to="oz1" />
<previous xlink:type="arc" xlink:from="oz3" xlink:to="oz2" />
</series>
```

Figure 10-1 diagrams this extended link. Resources are represented by books. Arcs are represented by arrows. However, although we can understand this link in this sort of abstract sense, it doesn't really tell us anything about how a browser might present the link to a user and how users might choose which links to follow. For instance, this extended link might be interpreted as nothing more than a list of the order in which to print these documents. All details of interpretation are left up to the application.

Figure 10-1. An extended link with three resources and four arcs between them

Multiple arcs from one arc element

On occasion, a single arc element defines multiple arcs. If multiple elements share the same label, then an arc element that uses that label in either its xlink:to or xlink:from attribute defines arcs between all resources that share that label. Example 10-2 shows an extended link containing locator elements for three different online bookstores and one edition of *The Wonderful Wizard of Oz*. Each bookstore element has the label buy, and a single purchase arc element connects all of these. Figure 10-2 shows the graph structure of this extended link.

Example 10-2. An extended link with one arc element but three arcs

```
<book xlink:type="extended" xmlns:xlink="http://www.w3.org/1999/xlink">

  <author>L. Frank Baum</author>
  <title>The Wonderful Wizard of Oz</title>

  <!-- locator elements -->
  <edition xlink:type="locator" xlink:href="urn:isbn:0192839306"
          xlink:title="Oxford University Press"
          xlink:role="http://www.oup-usa.org/"
          xlink:label="ISBN0192839306"/>

  <store xlink:type="locator"
        xlink:href="http://www.amazon.com/exec/obidos/ASIN/0192839306"
        xlink:label="buy">Amazon</store>

  <store xlink:type="locator" xlink:href=
    "http://www.powells.com/cgi-bin/biblio?isbn=0192839306"
    xlink:label="buy">Powell's</store>

  <store xlink:type="locator" xlink:href=
"http://shop.bn.com/booksearch/isbninquiry.asp?isbn=0192839306"
    xlink:label="buy">Barnes &amp; Noble</store>

  <!-- arcs -->
  <purchase xlink:type="arc" xlink:from="ISBN0192839306" xlink:to="buy" />

</book>
```

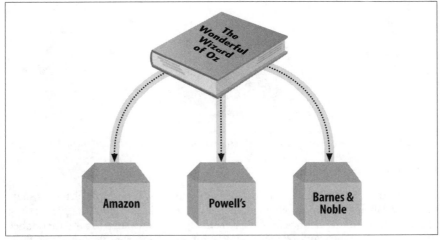

Figure 10-2. One arc element can generate several arcs

If an arc element does not have an xlink:to attribute, then it uses all the resources in the extended link as targets. If an arc element does not have an xlink:from attribute, then it uses all the resources in the extended link as sources.

However, it is an error for more than one arc element to define an arc between the same two resources, whether implicitly or explicitly. For example, if an extended link contains N resources and an arc element, such as `<edition xlink:type="arc"/>`, with neither an `xlink:to` or `xlink:from` attribute, then it cannot contain any other arc elements because this one arc element defines all N^2 possible arcs between the resources in the extended link.

Arc titles

Each arc element may optionally have an `xlink:title` attribute, just like all other XLink elements. This contains a small amount of text describing the arc, intended for humans to read. For instance, in Example 10-1, we might give these titles to the arcs:

```
<next     xlink:type="arc" xlink:from="oz1" xlink:to="oz2"
          xlink:title="Next" />
<next     xlink:type="arc" xlink:from="oz2" xlink:to="oz3"
          xlink:title="Next" />
<previous xlink:type="arc" xlink:from="oz2" xlink:to="oz1"
          xlink:title="Previous" />
<previous xlink:type="arc" xlink:from="oz3" xlink:to="oz2"
          xlink:title="Previous" />
```

When processing an extended link, a browser might show the title to the user as the contents of a link so they could choose which arc they wanted to follow from their current position, or they might appear in a pop-up menu when the user was on one of the referenced pages. XLink does not require or suggest any specific user interface for arcs or arc titles.

Arc roles

Arc elements cannot have `xlink:role` attributes. However, an arc element can have an `xlink:arcrole` attribute that contains an absolute URI identifying the nature of the arc. More specifically, this URI should point to a resource that indicates which relationship the arc describes (e.g., parent–child, employer–employee). However, there's really no way to validate this at all beyond checking to see that `xlink:arcrole` does contain a legal URI (and even that is not strictly required). For instance, in Example 10-2 we might add an `xlink:arcrole` attribute to the purchase arc that pointed to http://www.example.com/purchase_details.txt.

```
<purchase xlink:type="arc" xlink:from="ISBN0192839306" xlink:to="buy"
          xlink:arcrole="http://www.example.com/purchase_details.txt" />
```

The file *purchase_details.txt* might then contain the text "will be bought from." This would indicate that the source of the link is bought from the target of the link; that is, "*The Wonderful Wizard of Oz* will be bought from Amazon," or "*The Wonderful Wizard of Oz* will be bought from Powell's." However, although this usage is possible, XLink processors do not require it, and indeed there's really no way they could be asked to do this since that would require that they actually understand what they read. The `xlink:arcrole` attribute is optional. You don't have to include it on your arcs, and XLink processors don't have to do anything with it even if you do.

Local Resources

Locators represent remote resources; that is, resources that are not part of the document that contains the extended link. Extended links can also contain local resources in which the data is contained inside the extended link element. Each such resource is represented by a *resource element*, which is an element of arbitrary type that has an xlink:type attribute with the value resource. For instance, in Example 10-1, the series extended link element contains an author child element. This can be made a local resource simply by giving it an xlink:type="resource" attribute:

```
<author xlink:type="resource">L. Frank Baum</author>
```

A resource element can and generally does have the same attributes as a locator element; that is, xlink:label , xlink:role, and xlink:title. These all have the same semantics as they do for locator elements. For instance, the label is a name that arcs use to connect resources. An arc can connect a resource to a resource, a resource to a locator, a locator to a resource, or a locator to a locator. Arcs really don't care whether resources are local or remote. To link to or from this resource, an arc needs an xlink:label attribute, like this:

```
<author xlink:type="resource" xlink:label="baum">L. Frank Baum</author>
```

To establish links from this local resource to all the books, we'd simply add these three arc elements:

```
<book xlink:type="arc" xlink:from="baum" xlink:to="oz1" />
<book xlink:type="arc" xlink:from="baum" xlink:to="oz2" />
<book xlink:type="arc" xlink:from="baum" xlink:to="oz3" />
```

To move in the other direction, you'd simply reverse the values of the xlink:from and xlink:to attributes.

Title Elements

As you've seen, extended link elements, locator elements, arc elements, and resource elements can all have xlink:title attributes that provide a short blurb of text identifying the link. However, this isn't always enough. For instance, in a document that was a rather large extended link, you might want to mark up the titles using XHTML or some other vocabulary. To this end, a title can instead (or in addition) be provided as a title type child element, that is, an element whose xlink:type attribute has the value title.

For example, suppose you wanted to provide a more complete description of each edition of *The Wonderful Wizard of Oz* than simply who published it. Then you would give the edition element a title type element containing any convenient markup, like this:

```
<edition xlink:type="locator" xlink:href="urn:isbn:0700609857"
         xlink:title="University Press of Kansas"
         xlink:role="http://purl.org/dc/elements/1.1/identifier"
         xlink:label="ISBN0700609857">
  <publisher_info xlink:type="title">
    <ul>
```

```
        <li>The Kansas Centennial Edition</li>
        <li>Illustrated by Michael McCurdy</li>
        <li>Foreword by Ray Bradbury</li>
        <li>1999</li>
        <li>216 pages</li>
        <li>SRP: $24.95</li>
      </ul>
    </publisher_info>
  </edition>
```

What markup you use inside the title element is up to you as long as it's well-formed XML. XLink doesn't constrain it in any way; how the application interprets that markup is its own business. Here we've used basic HTML that a browser might perhaps be able to render. Once again, however, this is far enough past the bleeding edge that exact browser behavior, even when browsers do support extended XLinks, is hard to predict.

Linkbases

One of the most revolutionary features of XLinks is the ability to define links between documents you don't control. For instance, Example 10-1 is an extended link that describes and links three documents that neither of the authors of this book has anything to do with. Links between purely remote resources are called *third-party links*. A third-party link is created when an arc's xlink:from and xlink:to attributes both contain labels for locator elements. Links from a remote resource to a local resource are called *inbound links*. An inbound link is created when an arc's xlink:from attribute contains the label of a locator element and its xlink:to attribute contains the label of a resource element. Links from a local resource to a remote resource are called *outbound links*. An outbound link is established when an arc's xlink:from attribute contains the label of a resource element and its xlink:to attribute contains the label of a locator element. Simple links are also outbound links.

An XML document that contains any inbound or third-party links is called a *link-base*. A linkbase establishes links from documents other than the linkbase itself, perhaps documents that the author of the linkbase does not own and cannot control. Exactly how a browser or other application will load a linkbase and discover the links there is still an open question. It will probably involve visiting a web site that provides the linkbase. When the browser sees the extended link that attempts to establish links from a third web site, it should ask the user whether he wishes to accept the suggested links. It might even use the xlink:role and xlink:title attributes to help the user make this decision, although if past experience with cookies, Java applets, and ActiveX controls is any guide, the initial user interfaces are likely to be quite poor and the choices offered quite limited.

Once a browser has loaded a linkbase and arrived at a page that's referenced as the starting resource of one or more of the links in the linkbase, it should make this fact known to the user somehow and give them a means to traverse the link. Once again, the user interface for this activity remains to be designed. Perhaps it will be a pop-up window showing the third-party links associated with a page. Or perhaps it will simply embed the links in the page but use a different color underlining. The user could still activate them in exactly the same way they activate a normal HTML link.

If this is the scheme that's adopted, then it would be useful if the starting resource of the link didn't have to be an entire document, but could rather be just one part of it, such as a specific paragraph, personal name, or book title. Indeed, you can attach an XPointer to the URI identifying the starting resource of the link that chooses a particular part of or point in the starting document. This will be the subject of Chapter 11.

DTDs for XLinks

For a document that contains XLinks to be valid, all the XLink attributes that the document uses have to be declared in a DTD just like any other attributes. In most cases some of the attributes can be declared #FIXED. For example, this DTD fragment describes the novel element seen earlier:

```
<!ELEMENT novel   (title, author, year)>
<!ATTLIST novel   xmlns:xlink CDATA    #FIXED 'http://www.w3.org/1999/xlink'
                  xlink:type (simple) #FIXED 'simple'
                  xlink:href  CDATA    #REQUIRED>
<!ELEMENT title  (#PCDATA)>
<!ELEMENT author (#PCDATA)>
<!ELEMENT year   (#PCDATA)>
```

Given this DTD to fill in the fixed attributes xmlns:xlink and xlink:type, a novel element only needs an xlink:href attribute to be a complete simple XLink:

```
<novel xlink:href = "urn:isbn:0688069444">
  <title>The Wonderful Wizard of Oz</title>
  <author>L. Frank Baum</author>
  <year>1900</year>
</novel>
```

Documents that contain many XLink elements often use parameter entity references to define the common attributes. For example, suppose novel, anthology, and nonfiction are all simple XLink elements. Their XLink attributes could be declared in a DTD like this:

```
<!ENTITY % simplelink
  "xlink:type (simple) #FIXED 'simple'
  xlink:href  CDATA    #REQUIRED
  xmlns:xlink CDATA    #FIXED 'http://www.w3.org/1999/xlink'
  xlink:role  CDATA    #IMPLIED
  xlink:title CDATA    #IMPLIED
  xlink:actuate (onRequest | onLoad | other | none) 'onRequest'
  xlink:show (new | replace | embed | other | none) 'new'"
>
<!ATTLIST anthology   %simplelink;>
<!ATTLIST novel       %simplelink;>
<!ATTLIST nonfiction  %simplelink;>
```

Similar techniques can be applied to declarations of attributes for extended XLinks.

Base URIs

Relative URL references such as *sark.jpg*, *../pi1/sark.jpg*, and *turing/pi1/sark.jpg* must be resolved relative to an absolute base URI before being retrieved. When relative URLs are found in XLinks, xml-stylesheet processing instructions, system identifiers, and other locations in XML documents, they are normally resolved relative to the absolute base URL of the document or entity that contains them. For instance, if you find the element <image xlink:type="simple" xlink:href="pi1/sark.jpg" /> in a document at the URL *http://www.turing.org.uk/ turing/index.html*, you would expect to find the file *sark.jpg* at the URL *http:// www.turing.org.uk/turing/p1/sark.jpg*. This isn't a surprise. It's pretty much how links have worked in HTML for over a decade.

However, XML does add a couple of new wrinkles to this procedure. First, an XML document may be composed of multiple entities loaded from multiple different URLs, even on different servers. If this is the case, then a relative URL is resolved relative to the base URL of the specific entity in which it appears, not the base URL of the entire document.

Secondly, the base URL may be reset or changed from within the document by using xml:base attributes. Such an attribute may appear on the XLink element itself or on any ancestor element in the same entity. For example, this XLink points to *ftp://ftp.knowtion.net/pub/mirrors/gutenberg/etext93/wizoz10.txt*:

```
<novel xmlns:xlink = "http://www.w3.org/1999/xlink"
       xml:base="ftp://ftp.knowtion.net/pub/mirrors/gutenberg/etext93/"
       xlink:type = "simple"
       xlink:href = "wizoz10.txt">
  <title>The Wonderful Wizard of Oz</title>
  <author>L. Frank Baum</author>
  <year>1900</year>
</novel>
```

So does this one:

```
<novel xmlns:xlink = "http://www.w3.org/1999/xlink"
       xml:base="ftp://ftp.knowtion.net/"
       xlink:type = "simple"
       xlink:href = "/pub/mirrors/gutenberg/etext93/wizoz10.txt">
  <title>The Wonderful Wizard of Oz</title>
  <author>L. Frank Baum</author>
  <year>1900</year>
</novel>
```

And this one does too:

```
<series xml:base="ftp://ftp.knowtion.net/">
  <title>Oz Books</title>
  <author>L. Frank Baum</author>
  <novel xmlns:xlink = "http://www.w3.org/1999/xlink"
         xlink:type = "simple"
         xlink:href = "/pub/mirrors/gutenberg/etext93/">
    <title>The Wonderful Wizard of Oz</title>
    <year>1900</year>
```

```
    </novel>
    ...
  </series>
```

All of these link to the URL *ftp://ftp.knowtion.net/pub/mirrors/gutenberg/etext93/wizoz10.txt* regardless of where the document containing the XLink actually came from. The base URL is taken from the nearest xml:base attribute in the same entity, in preference to the base URL of the entity that contains the element.

xml:base attributes can themselves contain relative URLs. In this case, the base URL is formed by resolving this relative URL against the base URL specified by xml:base attributes higher up in the tree and/or the base URL of the entity that contains the element. For example, resolving the URLs in the xlink:href attributes in this authors element requires applying the URLs in three separate ancestor elements:

```
<authors xml:base="http://www.literature.org/authors/"
         xmlns:xlink = "http://www.w3.org/1999/xlink">
  <author xml:base="baum-l-frank/">
    <name>L. Frank Baum</name>
    <novel  xml:base = "the-wonderful-wizard-of-oz/">
      <title>The Wonderful Wizard of Oz</title>
      <year>1900</year>
      <chapter xlink:type="simple"
               xlink:href="introduction.html">Introduction</chapter>
      <chapter xlink:type="simple"
               xlink:href="chapter-01.html">The Cyclone</chapter>
      <chapter xlink:type="simple"
               xlink:href="chapter-02.html">The Council with the
                                            Munchkins</chapter>
      ...
    </novel>
  </author>
</authors>
```

What if the top element has a relative base URL or no xml:base attribute? Then you apply the absolute base URL of the entity that contains the root element. In theory, this entity should always have an absolute base URL against which relative URLs can be resolved as a last resort. After all the entity had to come from somewhere, right? Unfortunately, there are some corner cases where this isn't true. In particular many APIs lose track of the base URLs or create documents in memory without any base URLs, so full resolution isn't always possible. The relevant specifications are not perfectly clear on what happens here, though one possible interpretation is to simply declare that the base URI is the empty string. The URI specification defines this to mean the URI of the current document, whatever it is. However, in the common case where a document is read from an actual file or URL, it should always be possible to calculate an absolute base URL for every element.

There's one point we've made a couple of times, but it's worth calling out because it's not obvious and quite tricky. All base URL resolutions are performed within the scope of a single entity, not a single document. If a document is built from multiple entities, then it's the base URI of the entity that matters, not the base

URI of the document. Furthermore, xml:base attributes only have scope within the entity from which they come. They do not apply in any other entities. That is, if entity A includes entity B, no xml:base attributes in entity A will be used to resolve relative URLs in entity B. If the base URL cannot be fully resolved using xml:base attributes from entity B, then the final absolute URL is the URL from which entity B was loaded. xml:base attributes in ancestor elements from different entities are not considered.

Although we've emphasized the application of xml:base attributes to xlink:href attributes in this section, they also apply in many other contexts. For instance, they're used in XInclude and XHTML 2.0. However, xml:base is a relative latecomer to the XML table, so it's not universally applicable. For instance, XHTML 1.0 and 1.1 do not consider xml:base attributes when resolving relative URLs in a and img elements. Instead they use the traditional base element in the document's head.

11

XPointers

XPointers are a non-XML syntax for identifying locations inside XML documents. An XPointer is attached to the end of the URI as its fragment identifier to indicate a particular part of an XML document rather than the entire document. XPointer syntax builds on the XPath syntax used by XSLT and covered in Chapter 9. To the four fundamental XPath data types—Boolean, node-set, number, and string—XPointer adds points and ranges, as well as the functions needed to work with these types. It also adds some shorthand syntax for particularly useful and common forms of XPath expressions.

XPointers on URLs

A URL that identifies a document looks something like *http://java.sun.com:80/products/jndi/index.html*. In this example, the scheme *http* tells you what protocol the application should use to retrieve the document. The authority, *java.sun.com:80* in this example, tells you from which host the application should retrieve the document. The authority may also contain the port to connect to that host and the username and password to use. The path, */products/jndi/index.html* in this example, tells you which file in which directory to ask the server for. This may not always be a real file in a real filesystem, but it should be a complete document that the server knows how to generate and return. You're already familiar with all of this, and XPointer doesn't change any of it.

You probably also know that some URLs contain fragment identifiers that point to a particular named anchor inside the document the URL locates. This is separated from the path by the octothorpe, #. For example, if we added the fragment *download* to the previous URL, it would become *http://java.sun.com:80/products/jndi/index.html#download*. When a web browser follows a link to this URL, it looks for a named anchor in the document at *http://java.sun.com:80/products/jndi/index.html* with the name *download*, such as this one:

```
<a name="download"></a>
```

It would then scroll the browser window to the position in the document where the anchor with that name is found. This is a simple and straightforward system, and it works well for HTML's simple needs. However, it has one major drawback: to link to a particular point of a particular document, you must be able to modify the document to which you're linking in order to insert a named anchor at the point to which you want to link. XPointer endeavors to eliminate this restriction by allowing authors to specify where they want to link to using full XPath expressions as fragment identifiers. Furthermore, XPointer expands on XPath by providing operations to select particular points in or ranges of an XML document that do not necessarily coincide with any one node or set of nodes. For instance, an XPointer can describe the range of text currently selected by the mouse.

The most basic form of XPointer is simply an XPath expression—often, although not necessarily, a location path—enclosed in the parentheses of xpointer( ). For example, these are all acceptable XPointers:

```
xpointer(/)
xpointer(//first_name)
xpointer(id('sec-intro'))
xpointer(/people/person/name/first_name/text( ))
xpointer(//middle_initial[position( )=1]/../first_name)
xpointer(//profession[.="physicist"])
xpointer(/child::people/child::person[@index<4000])
xpointer(/child::people/child::person/attribute::id)
```

Not all of these XPointers necessarily refer to a single element. Depending on which document the XPointer is evaluated relative to, an XPointer may identify zero, one, or more than one node. Most commonly the nodes identified are elements, but they can also be attribute nodes or text nodes, as well as points or ranges.

If you're uncertain whether a given XPointer will locate something, you can back it up with an alternative XPointer. For example, this XPointer looks first for first_name elements. However, if it doesn't find any, it looks for last_name elements instead:

```
xpointer(//first_name)xpointer(//last_name)
```

The last_name elements will be found only if there are no first_name elements. You can string as many of these XPointer parts together as you like. For example, this XPointer looks first for first_name elements. If it doesn't find any, it then seeks out last_name elements. If it doesn't find any of those, it looks for middle_initial elements. If it doesn't find any of those, it returns an empty node-set:

```
xpointer(//first_name)xpointer(//last_name)xpointer(//middle_initial)
```

No special separator character or whitespace is required between the individual xpointer( ) parts, although whitespace is allowed. This XPointer means the same thing:

```
xpointer(//first_name) xpointer(//last_name) xpointer(//middle_initial)
```

XPointers in Links

Obviously, what an XPointer points to depends on which document it's applied to. This document is specified by the URL that the XPointer is attached to. For example, if you wanted a URL that pointed to the first name element in the document at *http://example.org/people.xml*, you would type:

```
http://example.org/people.xml#xpointer(//name[position( )=1])
```

If the XPointer uses any characters that are not allowed in URIs—for instance, the less than sign <, the double quotation mark ", or non-ASCII letters like é—then these must be hexadecimally escaped as specified by the URI specification before the XPointer is attached to the URI. That is, each such character is replaced by a percent sign followed by the hexadecimal value of each byte in the character in the UTF-8 encoding of Unicode. Thus, < would be written as %3C, " would be written as %22, and é would be written as %C3%A9.

In HTML, the URLs used in a elements can contain an XPointer fragment identifier. For example:

```
<a href = "http://www.example.org/people.xml#xpointer(//name[1])">
  The name of a person
</a>
```

If a browser followed this link, it would likely load the entire document at *http://www.example.org/people.xml* and then scroll the window to the beginning of the first name element in the document. However, no browsers yet support the XPointer xpointer scheme, so the exact behavior is open for debate. In some situations it might make sense for the browser to show only the specific element node(s) the XPointer referred to rather than the entire document.

Mozilla 1.4 and later supports the xpath1( ) XPointer scheme proposed by Simon St.Laurent. xpath1( ) is essentially the same as the xpointer( ) scheme discussed here. However, xpath1( ) does not include the XPath extensions for points and ranges that the xpointer( ) scheme does. It only supports pure XPath 1.0 expressions, simplifying implementation.

Since XPath can only locate nodes in a well-formed XML document, XPointers can only point into XML documents. You can't use them to link into non-well-formed HTML, plain text files, or other non-XML documents. However, linking from HTML documents is perfectly fine, as is printing XPointers in books, painting them on the sides of buildings, or communicating them by any means by which text can be communicated.

XPointers are more frequently used in XLinks. For example, this simple link points to the first book child of the bookcoll child of the testament root element in the document at the relative URL *ot.xml*:

```
<In_the_beginning xlink:type="simple"
    xlink:href="ot.xml#xpointer(/testament/bookcoll/book[position( )=1])">
  Genesis
</In_the_beginning>
```

In extended links, an XPointer can help identify both the starting and ending resources of an arc. For example, this extended XLink establishes an arc between the last v element in the document at the relative URL *ot.xml* and the first v element of the document at the relative URL *nt.xml*. Then it establishes a link from the first v element of *nt.xml* to the last v element of *ot.xml*:

```
<Bible xlink:type="extended" xmlns:xlink="http://www.w3.org/1999/xlink">

  <testament xlink:type="locator" xlink:label="ot"
            xlink:href="ot.xml#xpointer(//v[position( )=last( )])"/>
  <testament xlink:type="locator" xlink:label="nt"
            xlink:href="nt.xml#xpointer(//v[position( )=1])" />

  <next     xlink:from="ot" xlink:to="nt"/>
  <previous xlink:from="nt" xlink:to="ot"/>

</Bible>
```

Links can even be purely internal; that is, they can link from one place in the document to another place in the same document. The slide element shown in this example contains simple XLinks that point to the first and last slide elements in the document:

```
<slide xmlns:xlink="http://www.w3.org/1999/xlink">

  <point>Acme Wonder Goo is a delicious dessert topping!</point>
  <point>Acme Wonder Goo is a powerful floor cleaner!</point>
  <point>It's two products in one!</point>

  <first xlink:type="simple"
        xlink:href="#xpointer(//slide[position( )=1])">
    Start
  </first>
  <last  xlink:type="simple"
        xlink:href="#xpointer(//slide[position( )=last( )]))">
    End
  </last>
</slide>
```

When the XPath expressions used in an XPointer are themselves relative, the context node is the root node of the entity that contains the XPointer.

Shorthand Pointers

XPointers provide a number of convenient extensions to XPath. One of the simplest is the *shorthand pointer*. A shorthand pointer is similar to an HTML named anchor; that is, a shorthand pointer identifies the element it's pointing to by that element's ID. The ID is supplied by an ID type attribute of the element being pointed at rather than by a special a element with a name attribute. To link to an element with a shorthand pointer, append the usual fragment separator # to the URL followed by the ID of the element to which you're linking. For example, *http://www.w3.org/TR/1999/REC-xpath-19991116.xml#NT-AbsoluteLocationPath*

links to the element in the XPath 1.0 specification that has an ID type attribute with the value *NT-AbsoluteLocationPath.*

The ID attribute is an attribute declared to have an ID type in the document's DTD. It does not have to be named ID or id. Shorthand pointers cannot be used to link to elements in documents that don't have DTDs because such a document cannot have any ID type attributes.

 The inability to use IDs in documents without DTDs is a major shortcoming of XML. Work is ongoing to attempt to remedy this, perhaps by defining a generic ID attribute such as xml:id or by defining a namespace that identifies ID type attributes.

For example, suppose you wanted to link to the Motivation and Summary section of the *Namespaces in XML* recommendation at *http://www.w3.org/TR/1999/REC-xml-names-19990114/xml-names.xml.* A quick peek at the source code of this document reveals that it has an id attribute with the value sec-intro and that indeed this attribute is declared to have an ID type in the associated DTD. Its start-tag looks like this:

```
<div1 id='sec-intro'>
```

Thus, *http://www.w3.org/TR/1999/REC-xml-names-19990114/xml-names.xml#sec-intro* is a URL that points to this section. The name does not need to be (and indeed should not be) enclosed in xpointer( ) to make this work. Just the ID value is sufficient. This is basically just a convenient shorthand for an XPointer built around an XPath expression using the id( ) function. The same URL could have been written as *http://www.w3.org/TR/1999/REC-xml-names-19990114/xml-names.xml#xpointer(id(sec-intro)).*

Child Sequences

Another very common form of XPointer is one that descends exclusively along the child axis, selecting elements by their positions relative to their siblings. For example, xpointer(/child::*[position( ) = 1]/child::*[position( ) = 2]/child::*[position( ) = 3]) selects the third child element of the second child element of the root element of the document. The element( ) scheme allows you to abbreviate this syntax by providing only the numbers of the child elements separated by forward slashes. This is called a *child sequence.* For example, the previous XPointer could be rewritten using the element scheme in the much more compact form element(/1/2/3).

For example, the aforementioned Motivation and Summary section of the "Namespaces in XML" recommendation at *http://www.w3.org/TR/1999/REC-xml-names-19990114/xml-names.xml* is given as a div element. It so happens that this div element is the first child element of the second child element of the root element. Therefore, *http://www.w3.org/TR/1999/REC-xml-names-19990114/xml-names.xml#element(/1/2/1)* points to this section.

Namespaces

Since XPointers may appear in places that are not XML documents (HTML documents, database fields, magazine pages, etc.), they require their own mechanism for binding namespace prefixes to namespace URIs. This is done by placing one or more xmlns parts before the xpointer part. The syntax is xmlns(*prefix=URI*). For example, this XPointer maps the svg prefix to the http://www.w3.org/2000/svg namespace and then searches out all rect elements in that namespace:

    xmlns(svg=http://www.w3.org/2000/svg) xpointer(//svg:rect)

As with most other uses of namespaces, only the URI matters in an XPointer, not the prefix. The previous XPointer finds all rect elements in the namespace http://www.w3.org/2000/svg, regardless of what prefix they use or whether they're in the default namespace.

There is no way to define a default, unprefixed namespace for an XPointer. However, prefixed names in an XPointer can refer to unprefixed but namespace-qualified elements in the targeted document. For example, this XPointer finds the third div element in an XHTML document:

    xmlns(html=http://www.w3.org/1999/xhtml) xpointer(//html:div[3])

It uses the prefix html to identify the XHTML namespace, even though XHTML documents never use prefixes themselves.

More than one namespace prefix can be used simply by adding extra xmlns parts. For example, this XPointer seeks out svg elements in XHTML documents by declaring one prefix each for the SVG and XHTML namespaces:

    xmlns(svg=http://www.w3.org/2000/svg)
    xmlns(h=http://www.w3.org/1999/xhtml) xpointer(/h:html//svg:svg)

If an XPointer is included in an XML document, the namespace bindings established by that document do not apply to the XPointer. Only the bindings established by the xmlns parts apply to the XPointer. If the xpointer parts contain XPath expressions that refer to elements or attributes in a namespace, they must be preceded by xmlns parts declaring the namespaces.

Points

XPaths, shorthand pointers, and child sequences can only point to entire nodes or sets of nodes. However, sometimes you want to point to something that isn't a node, such as the third word of the second paragraph or the year in a date attribute that looks like date="01/03/1950". XPointer adds points and ranges to the XPath data model to make this possible. A *point* is the position preceding or following any tag, comment, processing instruction, or character in the #PCDATA. Points can also be positions inside comments, processing instructions, or attribute values. Points cannot be located inside an entity reference, although they can be located inside the entity's replacement text. A *range* is the span of parsed character data between two points. Nodes, points, and ranges are collectively called *locations*; a set that may contain nodes, points, and ranges is called a *location set*. In other words, a location is a generalization of the XPath node that includes points and ranges, as well as elements, attributes, namespaces, text nodes, comments, processing instructions, and the root node.

A point is identified by its *container node* and a non-negative index into that node. If the node contains child nodes—that is, if it's a document or element node—then there are points before and after each of its children (except at the ends, where the point after one child node will also be the point before the next child node). If the node does not contain child nodes—that is, if it's a comment, processing instruction, attribute, namespace, or text node—then there's a point before and after each character in the string value of the node, and again the point after one character will be the same as the point before the next character.

Consider the document in Example 11-1. It contains a novel element that has seven child nodes, three of which are element nodes and four of which are text nodes containing only whitespace.

Example 11-1. A novel document

```
<?xml version="1.0"?>
<?xml-stylesheet type="text/css" value="novel.css"?>
<!-- You may recognize this from the last chapter -->
<novel copyright="public domain">
  <title>The Wonderful Wizard of Oz</title>
  <author>L. Frank Baum</author>
  <year>1900</year>
</novel>
```

There are eight points directly inside the novel element numbered from 0 to 7, one immediately after and one immediately before each tag. Figure 11-1 identifies these points.

```
                  <novel copyright="public domain">*◄───────────Point 0
  Point 1 ──►*<title>The Wonderful Wizard of Oz</title>*◄──Point 2
  Point 3 ──►*<author>L. Frank Baum</author>*◄─────────────Point 4
  Point 5 ──►*<year>1900</year>*◄──────────────────────────Point 6
  Point 7 ─►*</novel>
```

Figure 11-1. The points inside the novel element

Inside the text node child of the year element, there are five points:

- Point 0 between <year> and 1
- Point 1 between 1 and 9
- Point 2 between 9 and 0
- Point 3 between 0 and 0
- Point 4 between 0 and </year>

Notice that the points occur between the characters of the text rather than on the characters themselves. Points are zero-dimensional. They identify a location, but they have no extension, not even a single character. To indicate one or more characters, you need to specify a range between two points.

XPointer adds two functions to XPath that make it very easy to select the first and last points inside a node: start-point( ) and end-point( ). For example, this XPointer identifies the first point inside the title element—that is, the point between the title node and its text node child:

```
xpointer(start-point(//title))
```

This XPointer indicates the point immediately before the </author> tag:

```
xpointer(end-point(//author))
```

If there were multiple title and author elements in the document, then these functions would select multiple points.

This XPointer points to the point immediately before the letter T in "The Wonderful Wizard of Oz":

```
xpointer(start-point(//title/text( )))
```

This point falls immediately after the point indicated by xpointer(start-point(//title)). These are two different points, even though they fall between the same two characters (> and T) in the text.

To select points other than the start-point or end-point of a node, you first need to form a range that begins or ends with the point of interest, using string-range( ), and then use the start-point or end-point function on that range. We take this up in the next section.

Ranges

A *range* is the span of parsed character data between two points. It may or may not represent a well-formed chunk of XML. For example, a range can include an element's start-tag but not its end-tag. This makes ranges suitable for uses such as representing the text a user selected with the mouse. Ranges are created with four functions XPointer adds to XPath:

- range( )
- range-to( )
- range-inside( )
- string-range( )

The range( ) Function

The range( ) function takes as an argument an XPath expression that returns a location set. For each location in this set, the range( ) function returns a range exactly covering that location; that is, the start-point of the range is the point immediately before the location, and the end-point of the range is the point immediately after the location. If the location is an element node, then the range begins right before the element's start-tag and finishes right after the element's end-tag. For example, consider this XPointer:

```
xpointer(range(//title))
```

When applied to Example 11-1, it selects a range exactly covering the single title element. If there were more than one title element in the document, it would return one range for each such title element. If there were no title elements in the document, then it wouldn't return any ranges.

Now consider this XPointer:

```
xpointer(range(/novel/*))
```

If applied to Example 11-1, it returns three ranges, one covering each of the three child elements of the novel root element.

The range-inside( ) Function

The range-inside( ) function takes as an argument an XPath expression that returns a location set. For each location in this set, it returns a range exactly covering the contents of that location. This will be the same as the range returned by range( ) for anything except an element node. For an element node, this range includes everything inside the element, but not the element's start-tag or end-tag. For example, when applied to Example 11-1, xpointer(range-inside(//title)) returns a range covering The Wonderful Wizard of Oz but not <title>The Wonderful Wizard of Oz</title>. For a comment, processing instruction, attribute, text, or namespace node, this range covers the string value of that node. For a range, this range is the range itself. For a point, this range begins and ends with that point.

The range-to( ) Function

The range-to( ) function is evaluated with respect to a context node. It takes a location set as an argument that should return exactly one location. The start-points of the context nodes are the start-points of the ranges it returns. The end-point of the argument is the end-point of the ranges. If the context node set contains multiple nodes, then the range-to( ) function returns multiple ranges.

 This function is underspecified in the XPointer specification. In particular, it is not clear what should happen if the argument contains more or less than one location.

For instance, suppose you want to produce a single range that covers everything between <title> and </year> in Example 11-1. XPointer does this by starting with the start-point of the title element and continuing to the end-point of the year element:

```
xpointer(//title/range-to(year))
```

Ranges do not necessarily have to cover well-formed fragments of XML. For instance, the start-tag of an element can be included but the end-tag left out. This XPointer selects <title>The Wonderful Wizard of Oz:

```
xpointer(//title/range-to(text( )))
```

It starts at the start-point of the title element, but it finishes at the end-point of the title element's text node child, thereby omitting the end-tag.

The string-range( ) Function

The string-range( ) function is unusual. Rather than operating on a location set—including various tags, comments, processing instructions, and so forth—it operates on the text of a document after all markup has been stripped from it. Tags are more or less ignored.

The string-range( ) function takes as arguments an XPath expression identifying locations and a substring to try to match against the XPath string value of each of those locations. It returns one range for each non-overlapping match, exactly covering the matched string. Matches are case sensitive. For example, this XPointer produces ranges for all occurrences of the word "Wizard" in title elements in the document:

```
xpointer(string-range(//title, "Wizard"))
```

If there are multiple matches, then multiple ranges are returned. For example, this XPointer returns two ranges when applied to Example 11-1, one covering the W in "Wonderful" and one covering the W in "Wizard":

```
xpointer(string-range(//title, "W"))
```

You can also specify an offset and a length to the function so that strings start a certain number of characters from the beginning of the match and continue for a specified number of characters. The point before the first character in the string to search is 1. For example, this XPointer selects the first four characters after the word "Wizard" in title elements:

```
xpointer(string-range(//title, "Wizard", 7, 4))
```

Nonpositive indices work backward in the document before the beginning of the match. For example, this XPointer selects the first four characters before the word "Wizard" in title elements:

```
xpointer(string-range(//title, "Wizard", -3, 4))
```

If the offset or length causes the range to fall outside the document, then no range is returned.

Since string ranges can begin and end at pretty much any character in the text content of a document, they're the way to indicate points that don't fall on node boundaries. Simply create a string range that either begins or ends at the position you want to point to, and then use start-point( ) or end-point( ) on that range. For example, this XPointer returns the point immediately before the word "Wizard" in the title element:

```
xpointer(start-point(string-range(//title, "Wizard")))
```

Relative XPointers

Normally, an XPointer is a fragment identifier attached to a URL. The root node of the document the URL points to is the context location for the XPointer. However, XPointers can also be used by themselves without explicit URLs in XML documents. By default, the context node for such an XPointer is the root node of the document where the XPointer appears. However, either the here( ) or the origin( ) function can change the context node for the XPointer's XPath expression.

here( )

The here( ) function is only used inside XML documents. It refers to the node that contains the XPointer or, if the node that contains the XPointer is a text node, the element node that contains that text node. here( ) is useful in relative links. For example, these navigation elements link to the page elements preceding and following the pages in which they're contained:

```
<page>
  content of the page...
  <navigation xlink:type="simple"
    xlink:href="#xpointer(here( )/../../preceding-sibling::page[1])">
    Previous
  </navigation>
  <navigation xlink:type="simple"
    xlink:href="#xpointer(here( )/../../following-sibling::page[1])">
    Next
  </navigation>
</page>
```

In these elements, the here( ) function refers to the xlink:href attribute nodes that contain the XPointer. The first .. selects the navigation parent element. The second .. selects its parent page element, and the final location step selects the previous or next page element.

origin( )

The origin( ) function is useful when the document has been loaded from an out-of-line link. It refers to the node from which the user is initiating traversal, even if that is not the node that defines the link. For example, consider an extended link like this one. It has many novel elements, each of which is a locator that shares the same label:

```
<series xlink:type="extended" xmlns:xlink="http://www.w3.org/1999/xlink">

  <!-- locator elements -->
  <novel xlink:type="locator" xlink:label="oz"
        xlink:href="ftp://archive.org/pub/etext/etext93/wizoz10.txt">
    <title>The Wonderful Wizard of Oz</title>
    <year>1900</year>
  </novel>
  <novel xlink:type="locator" xlink:label="oz"
        xlink:href="ftp://archive.org/pub/etext/etext93/ozland10.txt">
    <title>The Marvelous Land of Oz</title>
    <year>1904</year>
  </novel>
  <novel xlink:type="locator" xlink:label="oz"
        xlink:href="ftp://archive.org/pub/etext/etext93/wizoz10.txt">
    <title>Ozma of Oz</title>
    <year>1907</year>
  </novel>
  <!-- many more novel elements... -->
```

```
<sequel xlink:type="locator" xlink:label="next"
      xlink:href="#xpointer(origin( )/following-sibling::novel[1])" />
<next xlink:type="arc" xlink:from="oz" xlink:to="next" />

</series>
```

The sequel element uses an XPointer and the origin( ) function to define a
locator that points to the following novel in the series. If the user is reading *The
Wonderful Wizard of Oz*, then the sequel element locates *The Marvelous Land of
Oz*. If the user is reading *The Marvelous Land of Oz*, then that same sequel
element locates *Ozma of Oz*, and so on. The next element defines links from each
novel (since they all share the label oz) to its sequel. The ending resource changes
from one novel to the next.

12

XInclude

XInclude is a new technology developed at the W3C for combining multiple well-formed and optionally valid documents and fragments thereof into a single document. It's similar in effect to using external entity references to assemble a document from several component pieces. However, XInclude can assemble a document from resources that are themselves fully well-formed documents that include XML declarations and even document type declarations. It can also use XPointers to extract only a piece of an external document, rather than including the entire thing.

XInclude defines two elements, xi:include and xi:fallback, both in the http://www.w3.org/2001/XInclude namespace. An xi:include element has an href attribute that points to a document. An XInclude processor replaces all the xi:include elements in a master document with the documents they point to. These documents can be other XML documents or plain text documents like Java source code. If the xi:include element has an xpointer attribute, then the xi:include element is replaced by only those parts of the remote document that the XPointer indicates. If the processor cannot find the external document the href attribute points to, then it replaces the xi:include element with the contents of the element's xi:fallback child element instead.

 This chapter is based on the April 13, 2004 2nd Candidate Recommendation of XInclude. We think this draft is pretty stable, but it's possible some of the details described here may change before the final release. The most current version of the XInclude specification can be found at *http://www.w3.org/TR/xinclude/*.

The include Element

The key component of XInclude is the include element. This must be in the http://www.w3.org/2001/XInclude namespace. The xi or xinclude prefixes are customary, although, as always, the prefix can change as long as the URI remains the same. This element has an `href` attribute that contains a URL pointing to the document to include. For example, this element includes the document found at the relative URL *AlanTuring.xml*:

```
<xi:include xmlns:xi="http://www.w3.org/2001/XInclude"
            href="AlanTuring.xml"/>
```

Of course, you can use absolute URLs as well:

```
<xi:include xmlns:xi="http://www.w3.org/2001/XInclude"
   href="http://cafeconleche.org/books/xian3/examples/12/AlanTuring.xml"
   />
```

 Technically, the `href` attribute contains an IRI rather than a URI or URL. An IRI is like a URI except that it can contain non-ASCII characters such as é and Δ. These characters are normally encoded in UTF-8, and then each byte of the UTF-8 sequence is percent escaped to convert the IRI to a URI before resolving it. If you're working in English, and you're not writing an XInclude processor, you can pretty much ignore this. All standard URLs are legal IRIs. If you are working with non-English, non-ASCII IRIs, this just means you can use them exactly as you'd expect without having to manually hex-encode the non-ASCII characters yourself.

Normally, the namespace declaration is placed on the root element of the including document, and not repeated on each individual `xi:include` element. Henceforth in this chapter, we will assume that the namespace prefix `xi` is bound to the correct namespace URI.

Example 12-1 shows a document similar to Example 8-1 that contains two `xi:include` elements. The first one loads the document found at the relative URL *AlanTuring.xml*. The second loads the document found at the relative URL *RichardPFeynman.xml*.

Example 12-1. A document that uses XInclude to load two other documents

```
<?xml version="1.0"?>
<people xmlns:xi="http://www.w3.org/2001/XInclude" >
  <xi:include href="AlanTuring.xml"/>
  <xi:include href="RichardPFeynman.xml"/>
</people>
```

When an XInclude processor reads this document, it will parse the XML documents found at the two URLs and insert their contents (except for the XML and document type declarations, if any) into the finished document at the positions indicated by the `xi:include` elements. The `xi:include` elements are removed. XInclusion is not done by default, and many XML parsers do not understand or support XInclude. You either need to use a filter that resolves the `xi:include` elements before processing the documents further, or tell the parser that you want it to perform XInclusion. The exact details vary from one processor to the next. For example, using *xmllint* from *libxml*, the `--xinclude` option tells it to resolve XIncludes:

```
$ xmllint --xinclude http://cafeconleche.org/books/xian3/examples/12/12-1.xml
<?xml version="1.0"?>
<people xmlns:xi="http://www.w3.org/2001/XInclude">
  <person born="1912" died="1954"
   xml:base=
      "http://cafeconleche.org/books/xian3/examples/12/AlanTuring.xml">
      <name>
        <first_name>Alan</first_name>
        <last_name>Turing</last_name>
      </name>
      <profession>computer scientist</profession>
      <profession>mathematician</profession>
      <profession>cryptographer</profession>
    </person>
    <person born="1918" died="1988"
   xml:base=
      "http://cafeconleche.org/books/xian3/examples/12/RichardPFeynman.xml">
      <name>
        <first_name>Richard</first_name>
        <middle_initial>P</middle_initial>
        <last_name>Feynman</last_name>
      </name>
      <profession>physicist</profession>
      <hobby>Playing the bongoes</hobby>
    </person>
  </people>
```

You'll notice that the processor has added xml:base attributes to attempt to preserve the base URIs of the included elements. This is not so important here, where both the including document and the two included documents all live in the same directory. However, when assembling a document from different sources on different servers and different directories, this helps make sure the relative URLs in the included text are properly resolved.

It's also important to note that the inclusion is based on the parsed documents. It's not done as if by copying and pasting the raw text. XML declarations are not copied. Insignificant white space inside tags may not be quite the same after inclusion as it was before. Whitespace in the prolog and epilog is not copied at all. Document type declarations are not copied, but any default attribute values they defined are copied.

libxml includes fairly complete support for XInclude. Xerces-J 2.7 includes incomplete support for XInclude. Other parsers typically have none at all and will require the use of third-party libraries that do support XInclude, such as XOM's nu.xom.xinclude package. This is still fairly bleeding edge technology.

Including Text Files

By default, the XInclude processor assumes the document pointed to by an href attribute is a well-formed XML document. This document is parsed, and the content of the included document replaces the xi:include element in the including document. However, it is also nice to be able to include unparsed text when assembling a larger document. For instance, the program and XML examples in this book could be included directly from their source form. If you add a parse attribute to an xi:include element with the value text, then the document will be loaded as plain text and not parsed. For example, this element includes Example 12-1 as plain text, without parsing it:

```
<xi:include
  href="http://cafeconleche.org/books/xian3/examples/12/12-1.xml"
  parse="text"
/>
```

When parse="text", it is no longer necessary for the referenced document to be well-formed. Indeed, it need not be an XML document at all. It can be C source code, an email message, a classic HTML document, or almost anything else. The only restriction is that the included document must not contain any completely illegal characters, such as an ASCII NUL, or an unmatched half of a surrogate pair.

XInclude processors make use of any protocol metadata such as HTTP headers to determine the encoding of a referenced document so they can transcode it into Unicode before including it. If external metadata is not available, but the MIME media type is text/xml, application/xml, or some type that ends in +xml, then the processor will look inside the document for common signatures like byte-order marks or XML declarations that help it guess the encoding. If these standard mechanisms won't suffice, the document author can add an encoding attribute to the xi:include element, indicating the expected encoding of the document. For example, this element tries to load Example 12-1 using the Latin-1 encoding:

```
<xi:include
  href="http://cafeconleche.org/books/xian3/examples/12/12-1.xml"
  encoding="ISO-8859-1" parse="text"
/>
```

Finally, if all of those fail, the processor assumes the document is encoded in UTF-8. Any byte sequences that are undefined in the document's encoding (or what the XInclude processor thinks is the document's encoding) are a fatal error.

The parse attribute can also have the value xml to indicate that the referenced document should be parsed. However, this is the default so most authors don't bother to write parse="xml". Any other value is a fatal error.

Content Negotiation

HTTP clients and servers support a variety of accept headers that indicate which kinds of content the client is prepared to receive. For example, this browser request indicates that the client prefers French but is willing to read English; can handle HTML, plain text, and JPEG images; knows how to decode gzipped data; and recognizes the ASCII, Latin-1, and UTF-8 character sets:

```
GET /index.html HTTP/1.1
User-Agent: Mozilla/4.6 [en] (WinNT; I)
Host: www.cafeaulait.org
Accept: text/html, text/plain, image/jpeg
```

```
Accept-Encoding: gzip
Accept-Language: fr, en
Accept-Charset: us-ascii, iso-8859-1,utf-8
Connection: close
If-Modified-Since: Sun, 31 Oct 1999 19:22:07 GMT
```

The server that receives this request uses these headers to decide which version of a resource to send to the client. The same URL can return different content depending on how these headers are set. In browsers, this is normally controlled through preferences, but XInclude allows documents to control two of these headers, Accept and Accept-language, by attributes. Each xi:include element can have an accept and/or accept-language attribute. The values of these attributes should be legal values for the corresponding HTTP header fields. If one or both of these attributes is present, then the XInclude processor will add the relevant accept headers to the HTTP request it sends to the server. For example, this xi:include element indicates you want to include the French HTML version of Google's home page:

```
<xi:include  href="http://www.google.com" parse="text"
   accept-language="fr"  accept="text/html"
/>
```

This xi:include element indicates you want to include the English XML version of Google:

```
<xi:include  href="http://www.google.com"
   accept-language="en"  accept="application/xml"
/>
```

Both accept and accept-language can be used with parse="xml" and parse="text".

It's not necessarily true, of course, that any given URL will have a version with the language and content type you request. Most servers simply return the same page in the same language regardless of the accept headers. However, for those servers that do provide different translations and formats of the same resource, these two attributes enable you to specify which is preferred.

Fallbacks

Documents that reference resources on other sites are subject to all the usual problems of the Web: documents are deleted, documents move, servers crash, DNS records aren't updated fast enough, and more. The examples so far all fail completely if the resource at the end of an href attribute can't be found. However, XInclude offers authors a means to provide alternate content in the face of a missing document. Each XInclude element can contain a single xi:fallback child element. If the remote document can't be loaded, the contents of the xi:fallback element replace the xi:include element instead of the contents of the remote resource. For example:

```
<xi:include href="AlanTuring.xml">
  <xi:fallback>
    Oops! Could not find Alan Turing!
  </xi:fallback>
</xi:include>
```

There's no limit to what an xi:fallback element can contain. It can hold plain text, a child element, mixed content, or even another xi:include element to be resolved if the top one can't be. For example, this xi:include element tries to load the same document from three different sites:

```
<xi:include href="http://www.example.us/data.xml">
  <xi:fallback>
      <xi:include href="http://www.example.fr/data.xml">
        <xi:fallback>
          <xi:include href="http://www.example.cn/data.xml">
            <xi:fallback>
               Could not find the document in the U.S., France, or China.
            </xi:fallback>
          </xi:include>
        </xi:fallback>
      </xi:include>
  </xi:fallback>
</xi:include>
```

An xi:include element may not contain more than one xi:fallback child, and may not contain any xi:include or other child elements from the XInclude namespace. Otherwise, any children of the xi:include element not in the XInclude namespace are ignored, and do not appear in the result document after inclusion. The xi:fallback element is ignored if the resource specified by the parent xi:include element's href attribute is successfully loaded. An xi:fallback element may only appear as the child of an xi:include element. It is a fatal error for it to have any other parent.

Fallbacks are only processed for resource errors, mostly I/O errors that occur when loading the remote resource. Other problems—the remote document is malformed when parse="xml", an included text document contains characters that are illegal in XML, there is a syntax error in the xi:include element—are fatal errors. If any of these things happen, the processor simply gives up and reports the error.

XPointers

For various obscure architectural reasons, the URLs used in XPointer href attributes must not have fragment identifiers. Indeed, it is a fatal error if one does, in which case the XInclude processor will simply throw up its hands and give up. Instead, each xi:include element may have an xpointer attribute. This attribute contains an XPointer indicating what part of the document referenced by the href attribute should be included. For example, this xi:include element loads today's news from Cafe con Leche (which is delimited by a today element in the http://www.w3.org/1999/xhtml namespace), but not the rest of the page:

```
<xi:include href="http://www.cafeconleche.org/"
     xpointer="xmlns(pre=http://www.w3.org/1999/xhtml)
     xpointer(//pre:today)"/>
```

You could also use the element( ) scheme:

```
<xi:include href="http://www.cafeconleche.org/"
          xpointer="element(/1/2/4/1/1/4)"/>
```

If the href attribute is absent, then the XPointer refers to the current document.

XInclude processors are not required to support all XPointer schemes. In particular, they are not required to support the xpointer() or xmlns() schemes, although some processors, notably *libxml2*, do support it. All processors are required to support the element() scheme as well as bare-name XPointers, although in practice some implementations, especially those based on streaming APIs like SAX, do not support XPointers at all.

A syntax error in the XPointer is a resource error, which will cause the xi:fallback child element to be processed if present. It is not necessarily a fatal error.

Since XPointers only apply to XML documents, they may only be used when parse="xml". It is a fatal error if an xi:include element has an xpointer attribute and parse="text".

13

Cascading Style Sheets (CSS)

The names of most elements describe the semantic meaning of the content they contain. Often, however, this content needs to be formatted and displayed to users. For this to occur, there must be a step where formatting information is applied to the XML document, and the semantic markup is transformed into presentational markup. There is a variety of choices for the syntax of this presentation layer. However, two are particularly noteworthy:

- Cascading Style Sheets (CSS)
- XSL Formatting Objects (XSL-FO)

CSS is a non-XML syntax for describing the appearance of particular elements in a document. CSS is a very straightforward language; no transformation is performed. The parsed character data of the document is presented more or less exactly as it appears in the XML document, although, of course, you can always transform the document with XSLT and then apply a CSS stylesheet to it if you need to rearrange the content of a document before showing it to the user. A CSS stylesheet does not change the markup of an XML document at all; it merely applies styles to the content that already exists.

By way of contrast, XSL-FO is a complete XML application for describing the layout of text on a page. It has elements that represent pages, blocks of text on the pages, graphics, horizontal rules, and more. You do not normally work with this application directly. Instead, you write an XSLT stylesheet that transforms your document's native markup into XSL-FO. The application rendering the document reads the XSL-FO and displays it to the user.

In this chapter and the next, we'll demonstrate the features of the two major stylesheet languages by applying them to the simple well-formed XML document shown in Example 13-1. This document does not have a document type declaration and is not valid, although a DTD or schema could be added easily enough. In general, DTDs and schemas don't have any impact on stylesheets, except insofar as they change the document content through entity declarations, default attribute values, and the like.

Example 13-1. Marjorie Anderson's recipe for Southern Corn Bread

```
<?xml version="1.0" encoding="UTF-8" standalone="yes"?>
<?xml-stylesheet type="text/css" href="recipe.css"?>
<recipe source="Marjorie Anderson">
  <dish>Southern Corn Bread</dish>
  <ingredients>
    <ingredient>
      <quantity>1 cup</quantity>
      <component>flour</component>
    </ingredient>
    <ingredient>
      <quantity>4 tablespoons</quantity>
      <component>Royal Baking Powder</component>
    </ingredient>
    <ingredient>
      <quantity>1/2 teaspoon</quantity>
      <component>salt</component>
    </ingredient>
    <ingredient>
      <quantity>1 cup</quantity>
      <component>corn meal</component>
    </ingredient>
    <ingredient>
      <quantity>11/2 cups</quantity>
      <component>whole milk</component>
    </ingredient>
    <ingredient>
      <quantity>4 tablespoons</quantity>
      <component>melted butter</component>
    </ingredient>
  </ingredients>

  <directions>
    <step>Sift flour, baking powder, sugar &amp; salt together.</step>
    <step>Add 1 cup corn meal.</step>
    <step>
      Beat egg in cup and add beaten egg and 11/2 cups whole
      milk to make a batter. Stir well.
    </step>
    <step>
      Add melted shortening and beat until light and thoroughly mixed.
    </step>
    <step>
      Pour into greased shallow pan or greased muffin rings.
    </step>
    <step>
      Bake in hot oven at <temperature>425° F</temperature> for
      <duration>25 minutes</duration>.
    </step>
    <step optional="yes">
      Cut into squares if cooked in shallow pan.
    </step>
  </directions>
```

```
<story>
  After my mother-in-law <person>Marjorie Anderson</person> died,
  Beth and I found this recipe written on the "extra recipes"
  page in a local cookbook in her cupboard.
  This was published by The Episcopal Churchwomen,
  Church of Ascension, <city>Mt. Sterling</city>,
  <state>Kentucky</state>.
</story>

</recipe>
```

The Levels of CSS

At the time of this writing, there are several versions of CSS. CSS Level 1 was an early W3C Recommendation from 1996 for HTML only, although the extension to XML was obvious. The CSS Level 1 specification was incomplete and led to inconsistent browser implementations.

The next version, CSS Level 2, added many additional style properties. It also placed XML on an equal footing with HTML. Indeed, CSS Level 2 often works better with XML than with HTML because CSS styles don't have to interact with any predefined rendering semantics. For the most part, CSS Level 2 is a superset of CSS Level 1. That is, all CSS Level 1 stylesheets are also CSS Level 2 stylesheets that mean pretty much the same thing.

The current version is CSS 2.1. CSS 2.1 adds a few minor values to existing properties—for instance, orange is now recognized as a color—but mostly it removes those features of CSS Level 2 that have not been implemented by browsers. It also corrects a few bugs in the CSS2 specification.

The W3C is now working on CSS Level 3. When complete, it will modularize the CSS specification so software can implement particular subsets of CSS functionality without having to implement everything. For instance, an audio browser could implement audio stylesheets but ignore the visual formatting model. Furthermore, CSS Level 3 adds a number of features to CSS, including multi-column layouts, better support for non-Western languages—such as Arabic and Chinese—XML namespace support, more powerful selectors, paged media, and more. However, CSS Level 3 is not yet implemented by any browsers.

CSS Syntax

CSS syntax isn't XML syntax, but the syntax is so trivial this hardly matters. A CSS stylesheet is simply a list of the elements you want to apply the styles to, normally one to a line. If the element is in a namespace, then the qualified name like recipe:dish must be used. The prefix must be the same in the stylesheet as in the XML document. Each element name is followed by the list of styles you want to apply to that element. Comments can be inserted using the /*...*/ format familiar to C programmers. Whitespace isn't particularly significant, so it can be used to format the stylesheet. Example 13-2 is a simple CSS stylesheet for the recipe document in Example 13-1. Figure 13-1 shows the recipe document as rendered and displayed by the Opera 4.01 browser with this stylesheet.

Example 13-2. A CSS stylesheet for recipes

```
/* Defaults for the entire document */
recipe  {font-family: "New York", "Times New Roman", serif;
         font-size: 12pt }

/* Make the dish look like a headline */
dish    {
  display: block;
  font-family: Helvetica, Arial, sans-serif;
  font-size: 20pt;
  font-weight: bold;
  text-align: center
}

/* A bulleted list */
ingredient  {display: list-item; list-style-position: inside }

/* Format these two items as paragraphs */
directions, story {
  display: block;
  margin-top: 12pt;
  margin-left: 4pt
}
```

This stylesheet has four style rules. Each rule names the element(s) it formats and follows that with a pair of curly braces containing the style properties to apply to those elements. Each property has a name, such as font-family, and a value, such as "New York", "Times New Roman", serif. Properties are separated from each other by semicolons. Neither the names nor the values are case-sensitive. That is, font-family is the same as FONT-FAMILY or Font-Family. CSS 2.1 defines over 100 different style properties. However, you don't need to know all of these. Reasonable default values are provided for all the properties you don't set.

For example, the first rule applies to the recipe element and says that it should be formatted using the New York font at a 12-point size. If New York isn't available, then Times New Roman will be chosen instead; if that isn't available, then any convenient serif font will suffice. These styles also apply to all descendants of the recipe element; that is, child elements inherit the styles of their parents unless they specifically override them with different values for the same properties. Since recipe is the root element, this sets the default font for the entire document.

The second rule makes the dish element look like a heading, as you can see in Figure 13-1. It's set to a much larger sans-serif font and is made bold and centered. Furthermore, its display style is set to block. This means there'll be a line break between the dish and its next and previous sibling elements. The third rule formats the ingredients as a bulleted list, while the fourth rule formats both the directions and story elements as more-or-less straightforward paragraphs with a little extra whitespace around their top and lefthand sides.

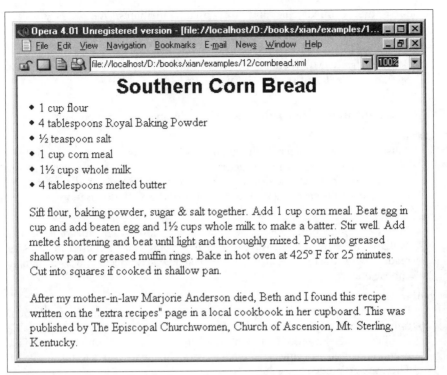

Figure 13-1. A semantically tagged XML document after a CSS stylesheet is applied

Not all the elements in the document have style rules and not all need them. For example, the step element is not specifically styled. Rather, it simply inherits a variety of styles from its ancestor elements directions and recipe, and uses some defaults. A different stylesheet could add a rule for the step element that overrides the styles it inherits. For example, this rule would set its font to 10-point Palatino:

```
step  {font-family: Palatino, serif; font-size: 10pt }
```

Associating Stylesheets with XML Documents

CSS stylesheets are primarily intended for use in web pages. Web browsers find the stylesheet for a document by looking for xml-stylesheet processing instructions in the prolog of the XML document. This processing instruction should have a type pseudo-attribute with the value text/css and an href pseudo-attribute whose value is an absolute or relative URL locating the stylesheet document. For example, this is the processing instruction that attaches the stylesheet in Example 13-2 (*recipe.css*) to the file in Example 13-1 (*cornbread.xml*), if both are found in the same directory:

```
<?xml-stylesheet type="text/css" href="recipe.css"?>
```

Including the required `type` and `href` pseudo-attributes, the `xml-stylesheet` processing instruction can have up to six pseudo-attributes:

`type`

> This is the MIME media type of the stylesheet; `text/css` for CSS and `application/xml` (not `text/xsl`!) for XSLT.

`href`

> This is the absolute or relative URL where the stylesheet can be found.

`charset`

> This names the character set in which the stylesheet is written, such as UTF-8 or ISO-8859-7. There's no particular reason this has to be the same as the character set in which the document is written. The names used are the same ones used for the `encoding` pseudo-attribute of the XML declaration.

`title`

> This pseudo-attribute names the stylesheet. If more than one stylesheet is available for a document, the browser may (but is not required to) present readers with a list of the titles of the available stylesheets and ask them to choose one.

`media`

> Printed pages, television screens, and computer displays are all fundamentally different media that require different styles. For example, comfortable reading on screen requires much larger fonts than on a printed page. This pseudo-attribute specifies the media types this stylesheet should apply to. There are 10 predefined values:

> - screen
> - tty
> - tv
> - projection
> - handheld

> - print
> - braille
> - embossed
> - speech
> - all

> By including several `xml-stylesheet` processing instructions, each pointing to a different stylesheet and each using a different media type, you can make a single document attractive in many different environments.

`alternate`

> This pseudo-attribute must be assigned one of the two values yes or no. yes means this is an alternate stylesheet, not normally used. no means this is the stylesheet that will be chosen unless the user indicates that she wants a different one. The default is no.

For example, this group of `xml-stylesheet` processing instructions could be placed in the prolog of the recipe document to make it more accessible on a broader range of devices:

```
<?xml-stylesheet type="text/css" href="recipe.css" media="screen"
        alternate="no"  title="For Web Browsers" charset="US-ASCII"?>
<?xml-stylesheet type="text/css" href="printable_recipe.css" media="print"
        alternate="no" title="For Printing" charset="ISO-8859-1"?>
```

```
<?xml-stylesheet type="text/css" href="big_recipe.css" media="projection"
        alternate="no" title="For presentations" charset="UTF-8"?>
<?xml-stylesheet type="text/css" href="tty_recipe.css" media="tty"
        alternate="no" title="For Lynx" charset="US-ASCII"?>
<?xml-stylesheet type="text/css" href="small_recipe.css" media="handheld"
        alternate="no" title="For Palm Pilots" charset="US-ASCII"?>
```

Selectors

CSS provides limited abilities to select the elements to which a given rule applies. Many stylesheets only use element names and lists of element names separated by commas, as shown in Example 13-2. However, CSS provides some other basic selectors you can use, although they're by no means as powerful as the XPath syntax of XSLT.

The Universal Selector

The asterisk matches any element at all; that is, it applies the rule to everything in the document that does not have a more specific, conflicting rule. For example, this rule says that all elements in the document should use a large font:

```
* {font-size: large}
```

Matching Descendants, Children, and Siblings

An element name A followed by another element name B matches all B elements that are descendants of A elements. For example, this rule matches quantity elements that are descendants of ingredients elements, but not other ones that appear elsewhere in the document:

```
ingredients quantity {font-size: medium}
```

If the two element names are separated by a greater-than sign (>), then the second element must be an immediate child of the first in order for the rule to apply. For example, this rule gives quantity children of ingredient elements the same font-size as the ingredient element:

```
ingredient > quantity {font-size: inherit}
```

If the two element names are separated by a plus sign (+), then the second element must be the next sibling element immediately after the first element. For example, this style rule sets the border-top-style property for only the first story element following a directions element:

```
directions + story {border-top-style: solid}
```

Attribute Selectors

Square brackets allow you to select elements with particular attributes or attribute values. For example, this rule hides all step elements that have an optional attribute:

```
step[optional] {display: none}
```

This rule hides all elements that have an optional attribute regardless of the element's name:

```
*[optional] {display: none}
```

An equals sign selects an element by a given attribute's value. For example, this rule hides all step elements that have an optional attribute with the value yes:

```
step[optional="yes"] {display: none}
```

The ~= operator selects elements that contain a given word as part of the value of a specified attribute. The word must be complete and separated from other words in the attribute value by whitespace, as in a NMTOKENS attribute. That is, this is not a substring match. For example, this rule makes bold all recipe elements whose source attribute contains the word "Anderson":

```
recipe[source~="Anderson"] {font-weight: bold}
```

Finally, the |= operator matches against the first word in a hyphen-separated attribute value, such as Anderson-Harold or fr-CA.

CSS also provides a special syntax for selecting elements with a given ID value, even when you don't know exactly the name of the ID type attribute. Simply separate the ID from the element name with a sharp sign (#). For example, this rule applies to the single step element whose ID type attribute has the value P833:

```
step#P833 { font-weight: 800 }
```

Pseudo-Class Selectors

Pseudo-class selectors match elements according to a condition not involving their name. There are seven of these separated from the element name by a colon.

first-child
> This pseudo-class matches the first child element of the named element. When applied to Example 13-1, this rule italicizes the first, and only the first, step element:
>
> ```
> step:first-child {font-style: italic}
> ```

link
> This pseudo-class matches the named element if and only if that element is the source of an as yet unvisited link. For example, this rule makes all links in the document blue and underlined:
>
> ```
> *:link {color: blue; text-decoration: underline}
> ```

visited
> This pseudo-class applies to all visited links of the specified type. For example, this rule marks all visited links as purple and underlined:
>
> ```
> *:visited {color: purple; text-decoration: underline}
> ```

active
> This pseudo-class applies to all elements that the user is currently activating (for example, by clicking the mouse on). Exactly what it means to activate an element depends on the context, and indeed not all applications can activate elements. For example, this rule marks all active elements as red:
>
> ```
> *:active {color: red}
> ```

linking

These pseudo-classes are not yet well-supported for XML documents because most browsers don't recognize XLinks. So far, only Mozilla and Netscape 6/7 recognize XLinks, and they are the only browsers that will apply these pseudo-classes to XML.

hover

This pseudo-class applies to elements on which the cursor is currently positioned but has not yet activated. For example, this rule marks all these elements as green and underlined:

```
*:hover {color: green; text-decoration: underline}
```

focus

This pseudo-class applies to the element that currently has the focus. For example, this rule draws a one-pixel red border around the element with the focus, assuming there is such an element:

```
*:focus {border: 1px solid red }
```

lang

This pseudo-class matches all elements in the specified language as determined by the xml:lang attribute. For example, this rule uses the David New Hebrew font for all elements written in Hebrew (more properly, all elements whose xml:lang attribute has the value he or any subtype thereof):

```
*:lang(he) {font-family: "David New Hebrew"}
```

Pseudo-Element Selectors

Pseudo-element selectors match things that aren't actually elements. Like pseudo-class selectors, they're attached to an element selector by a colon. There are four of these:

- first-letter
- first-line
- before
- after

The first-letter pseudo-element selects the first letter of an element. For example, this rule makes the first letter of the story element a drop cap:

```
story:first-letter {
  font-size: 200%;
  font-weight: bold;
  float: left;
  padding-right: 3pt
}
```

The first-line pseudo-element applies formatting to all characters in the first line of a block-level element. If the browser window is resized so that characters move into or out of the first line, then the formatting changes to match. For example, this rule formats the first line of the story element in small capitals instead of lowercase letters:

```
story:first-line {font-variant: small-caps}
```

The before and after pseudo-elements select the points immediately before and after the specified element. You can't really apply font or text styles to a zero-width point, but you can insert text at that point using the content property. For example, this rule inserts the string "Ingredients!" before the ingredients element:

```
ingredients:before {content: "Ingredients! "}
```

This rule places the number of the step in front of each step element in the form 1., 2., 3., and so on:

```
step:before {
  content: counter(step) ". ";
  counter-increment: step;
}
```

The Display Property

Display is one of the most important CSS properties. This property determines how the element will be positioned on the page. There are 18 legal values for this property. However, the two primary values are inline and block. The display property can also be used to create lists and tables, as well as to hide elements completely.

Inline Elements

Setting the display to inline, the default value, places the element in the next available position from left to right, much as each word in this paragraph is positioned. (The exact direction can change for right-to-left languages like Hebrew or top-to-bottom languages like traditional Chinese.) The text may be wrapped from one line to the next if necessary, but there won't be any hard line breaks between each inline element. In Examples 13-1 and 13-2, the quantity, step, person, city, and state elements were all formatted as inline. This didn't need to be specified explicitly because it's the default.

Block Elements

In contrast to inline elements, an element set to display:block is separated from its siblings, generally by a line break. For example, in HTML, paragraphs and headings are block elements. In Examples 13-1 and 13-2, the dish, directions, and story elements were all formatted with display:block.

CSS 2.1 adds an inline-block value that formats the element's contents as if it were a block-level element, but formats the element itself as if it were an inline element. This normally just means there's extra margins and padding around the element's content, but no line breaks before or after it.

List Elements

An element whose display property is set to list-item is also formatted as a block-level element. However, a bullet is inserted at the beginning of the block. The list-style-type, list-style-image, and list-style-position properties control which character or image is used for a bullet and exactly how the list is indented. For example, this rule would format the steps as a numbered list rather than rendering them as a single paragraph:

```
step {
  display: list-item;
  list-style-type: decimal;
  list-style-position: inside
}
```

Hidden Elements

An element whose display property is set to none is not included in the rendered document the reader sees. It is invisible and does not occupy any space or affect the placement of other elements. For example, this style rule hides the story element completely:

```
story {display: none}
```

Table Elements

There are 10 display values that identify elements as parts of a table. These are:

- table
- inline-table
- table-row-group
- table-header-group
- table-footer-group
- table-row
- table-column-group
- table-column
- table-cell
- table-caption

These display values have the obvious meanings by analogy with HTML 4.0 table tags. Their use should be consistent with each other and with other elements in the document. For instance, an element formatted as a table-row element should have a parent element formatted as a table and child elements formatted as table cells. For example, these three rules format the ingredients as a simple table:

```
ingredients       { display: table     }
ingredient        { display: table-row  }
quantity, component { display: table-cell }
```

Pixels, Points, Picas, and Other Units of Length

Many CSS properties represent lengths. Some of the most important (though far from all) of these include:

- border-width
- font-size
- line-height
- margin-left
- margin-top
- margin-right
- margin-bottom
- left
- top
- height
- width

CSS provides many different units to specify length. They fall into two groups:

- Absolute units of length, such as inches, centimeters, millimeters, points, and picas
- Relative units, such as ems, exes, pixels, and percentages

Absolute units of length are appropriate for printed media (that is, paper), but they should be avoided in other media. Relative units should be used for all other media, except for pixels, which probably shouldn't be used at all. For example, this style rule sets the dish element to be exactly 0.5 centimeters high:

```
dish { height: 0.5cm }
```

However, documents intended for display on screen media like television sets and computer monitors should not be set to fixed sizes. For one thing, the size of an inch or other absolute unit can vary depending on the resolution of the monitor. For another, not all users like the same defaults, and what looks good on one monitor may be illegible on another. Instead, you should use units that are relative to something, such as an em, which is relative to the width of the uppercase letter M, in the current font, or ex, which is relative to the height of the lowercase letter x in the current font. For example, this rule sets the line-height property of the story element to 1.5 times the height of the letter x:

```
story { line-height: 1.5ex}
```

Pixel is also a relative unit, although what it's relative to is the size of a pixel on the current display. This is generally somewhere in the vicinity of a point, but it can vary from system to system. In general, we don't recommend using pixels unless you need to line something up with a bitmapped graphic displayed at exactly a 1:1 ratio. Web pages formatted with pixel lengths invariably look too small or too large on most users' monitors.

One very useful technique is to specify lengths as percentages of some other length, which varies from property to property. For instance, if the line-height is given as a percentage, then it's calculated with respect to the font-height of the same element. These two rules set the font-height of the dish element to 0.5 centimeters and the line-height of the dish element to 0.75 centimeters:

```
dish { font-height: 0.5cm }
dish { line-height: 150% }
```

Font Properties

Fonts are one of the most basic things designers want to set with CSS. Is the text italic? Is it bold? What typeface and size are used? CSS provides properties to set all these basic characteristics of text. In particular, you can set these properties:

font-family
> This is a list of font names, separated by commas, in order of preference. The last name in the list should always be one of the generic names: serif, sans-serif, monospace, cursive, or fantasy. Multiword names like "Times New Roman" should be enclosed in quotes.

font-style

The value italic indicates that an italic version of the font should be used if one is available. The value oblique suggests that the text should be algorithmically slanted, as opposed to using a specially designed italic font. The default is normal (no italicizing or slanting). An element can also be set to inherit the font-style of the parent element.

font-size

This is the size of the font. This should be specified as one of the values xx-small, x-small, small, medium, large, x-large, or xx-large. Alternately, it can be given as a percentage of the font-size of the parent element. It can also be specified as a length like 0.2cm or 12pt, but this should only be done for print media.

font-variant

If this property is set to small-caps, then lowercase text is rendered in smaller capitals LIKE THIS instead of normal lowercase letters.

font-weight

This property determines how bold or light the text is. It's generally specified as one of the keywords normal (the default), bold, bolder, or lighter. It can also be set to any multiple of 100 from 100 (lightest) to 900 (darkest). However, not all browsers provide nine different levels of boldness.

font-stretch

This property adjusts the space between letters to make the text more or less compact. Legal values include normal (the default), wider, narrower, ultra-condensed, extra-condensed, condensed, semi-condensed, semi-expanded, expanded, extra-expanded, and ultra-expanded.

For example, this style rule uses all of the previous properties to make the dish element a suitably impressive headline:

```
dish {
    font-family: Helvetica, Arial, sans-serif;
    font-size: x-large;
    font-style: italic;
    font-variant: small-caps;
    font-weight: 900;
    font-stretch: semi-expanded
}
```

Text Properties

Text properties cover those aspects of text formatting other than what can be adjusted merely by changing the font. These include how far the text is indented, how the paragraph is aligned, and so forth. The most common of these properties include:

text-indent

The text-indent property specifies how far in to indent the first line of the block. (Indents of all lines are generally applied via margin properties.) Hanging indents can be specified by making text-indent negative. This property only applies to block-level elements. For example, this style rule indents the first line of the story element by 0.5 inches from the left side:

```
story { text-indent: 0.5in }
```

text-align

The text-align property can be set to left, right, center, or justify to align the text with the left edge of the block or the right edge of the block, to center the text in the block, or to spread the text out across the block. This property only applies to block-level elements.

text-decoration

The text-decoration property can be set to underline, overline, line-through, or blink to produce the obvious effects. Note, however, that the CSS specification specifically allows browsers to ignore the request to make elements blink. This is a good thing.

text-transform

The text-transform property has three main values: capitalize, uppercase, and lowercase. Uppercase changes all the text to capital letters LIKE THIS. Lowercase changes all the text to lowercase letters like this. Capitalize simply uppercases the first letter of each word Like This, but leaves the other letters alone. The default value of this property is none, which performs no transformation. It can also be set to inherit to indicate that the same transform as used on the parent element should be used.

 Changing the case in English is fairly straightforward, but this isn't true of all languages. In particular, software written by native English speakers tends to do a very poor job of algorithmically changing the case in ligature-heavy European languages, like Maltese, or context-sensitive languages, like Arabic. Outside of English text, it's best to make the transformations directly in the source document rather than relying on the stylesheet engine to make the correct decisions about which letters to capitalize.

white-space

The white-space property determines whether text is wrapped. It has four legal values in CSS2: normal, pre, nowrap, and inherit. CSS 2.1 adds pre-wrap and pre-line. normal is, of course, the default and simply means to wrap the text wherever convenient, much as is done in this paragraph. pre means to preserve all line breaks and whitespace in the document, as does the pre element in HTML. nowrap means that runs of whitespace can be condensed, but that line breaks will not be inserted. pre-wrap means that the text can be wrapped but runs of whitespace will not be compressed to a single space. Furthermore, all line breaks in the source will still be line breaks in the formatted document. Pre-line means runs of whitespace will be compressed, but line breaks will not be changed to spaces. In other words, all line breaks are preserved and others may be added as necessary. Finally, inherit simply takes on the same behavior as the parent element.

Colors

CSS has several properties for changing the color of various items:

`color`
> The color of the text itself (black on this page)

`background-color`
> The color of the background behind the text (white on this page)

`border-color`
> The color of a visible box surrounding the text

CSS uses a 24-bit color space to specify colors, much as HTML does. Always keep in mind, however, that just because you can specify a color doesn't mean any given device can render it. A black-and-white printer isn't going to print red no matter how you identify it; it might give you some nice shades of gray though. Like many other properties, color depends on the medium in which the document is presented.

The simplest way to choose a color is through one of these 16 named constants: `aqua`, `black`, `blue`, `fuchsia`, `gray`, `green`, `lime`, `maroon`, `navy`, `olive`, `purple`, `red`, `silver`, `teal`, `white`, and `yellow`. CSS 2.1 adds `orange` to this list. There are also a number of colors that are defined to be the same as some part of the user interface. For instance, `WindowText` is the same color as text in windows on the local system.

Beyond this small list, you can specify the color of an item by specifying the three components—red, green, and blue—of each color, much as you do for background colors on HTML pages. Each component is given as a number between 0 and 255, with 255 being the maximum amount of the color. Numbers can be given in decimal or hexadecimal. For example, these rules use hexadecimal syntax to color the `dish` element pure red, the `story` element pure green, and the `directions` element pure blue:

```
dish       { color: #FF0000 }
story      { color: #00FF00 }
directions { color: #0000FF }
```

If you prefer, you can specify the color as decimals separated by commas inside an `rgb( )` function. For example, white is `rgb(255,255,255)`; black is `rgb(0,0,0)`. Colors in which each component is equal form various shades of gray. These rules use decimal syntax to color the `ingredient` element a light shade of gray but its `quantity` child element a darker shade of gray:

```
ingredient { color: rgb(43,43,43) }
quantity   { color: rgb(21,21,21) }
```

You can also specify the color as percentages of each primary color from 0 to 100%. For example, the previous rules can be rewritten like this:

```
ingredient { color: rgb(16.9%,16.9%,16.9%) }
quantity   { color: rgb(8.2%,8.2%,8.2%) }
```

14

XSL Formatting Objects (XSL-FO)

The previous chapter covered CSS; this chapter discusses XSL-FO. In distinct contrast to CSS, XSL-FO is a complete XML application for describing the precise layout of text on a page. It has elements that represent sequences of pages, blocks of text on the pages, graphics, horizontal rules, and more. Most of the time, however, you don't write XSL-FO directly. Instead, you write an XSLT stylesheet that transforms your document's native markup into XSL-FO. The application rendering the document reads the XSL-FO and displays it to the user. Since no major browsers currently support direct rendering of XSL-FO documents, there's normally a third step in which another processor transforms the XSL-FO into a readable format, such as PDF or TEX.

Once again, we demonstrate the features of XSL-FO by applying it to the simple well-formed XML document shown in Example 13-1 (in the last chapter) and repeated here in Example 14-1 for convenience.

Example 14-1. Marjorie Anderson's recipe for Southern Corn Bread

```
<?xml version="1.0" encoding="UTF-8" standalone="yes"?>
<recipe source="Marjorie Anderson">
  <dish>Southern Corn Bread</dish>
  <ingredients>
    <ingredient>
      <quantity>1 cup</quantity>
      <component>flour</component>
    </ingredient>
    <ingredient>
      <quantity>4 tablespoons</quantity>
      <component>Royal Baking Powder</component>
    </ingredient>
    <ingredient>
      <quantity>1/2 teaspoon</quantity>
      <component>salt</component>
    </ingredient>
```

```
   <ingredient>
     <quantity>1 cup</quantity>
     <component>corn meal</component>
   </ingredient>
   <ingredient>
     <quantity>1¹/2 cups</quantity>
     <component>whole milk</component>
   </ingredient>
   <ingredient>
     <quantity>4 tablespoons</quantity>
     <component>melted butter</component>
   </ingredient>
 </ingredients>

 <directions>
   <step>Sift flour, baking powder, sugar &amp; salt together.</step>
   <step>Add 1 cup corn meal.</step>
   <step>
     Beat egg in cup and add beaten egg and 1¹/2 cups whole
     milk to make a batter. Stir well.
   </step>
   <step>
     Add melted shortening and beat until light and thoroughly mixed.
   </step>
   <step>
     Pour into greased shallow pan or greased muffin rings.
   </step>
   <step>
     Bake in hot oven at <temperature>425° F</temperature> for
     <duration>25 minutes</duration>.
   </step>
   <step optional="yes">
     Cut into squares if cooked in shallow pan.
   </step>
 </directions>

 <story>
   After my mother-in-law <person>Marjorie Anderson</person> died,
   Beth and I found this recipe written on the "extra recipes"
   page in a local cookbook in her cupboard.
   This was published by the The Episcopal Churchwomen,
   Church of Ascension, <city>Mt. Sterling</city>,
   <state>Kentucky</state>.
 </story>
</recipe>
```

XSL Formatting Objects

An XSL-FO document describes the layout of a series of nested rectangular areas (boxes, for short) that are placed on one or more pages. These boxes contain text or occasionally other items, such as an external image or a horizontal rule. There are four kinds of areas:

- Block areas
- Inline areas
- Line areas
- Glyph areas

Block and inline areas are created by particular elements in the formatting objects document. Line and glyph areas are created by the formatter as necessary. For the most part, the rendering engine decides exactly where to place the areas and how big to make them based on their contents. However, you can specify properties for these areas that adjust both their relative and absolute position, spacing, and size on a page. Most of the time, the individual areas don't overlap. However, they can be forced to do so by setting the properties absolute-position, left, bottom, right, and top.

Considered by itself, each box has a content area in which its content, generally text but possibly an image or a rule, is placed. This content area is surrounded by a padding area of blank space. An optional border can surround the padding. The size of the area is the combined size of the border, padding, and content. The box may also have a margin that adds blank space outside the box's area, as diagramed in Figure 14-1.

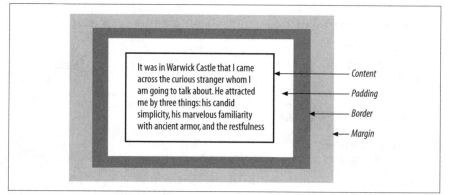

Figure 14-1. Content, padding, border, and margin of an XSL-FO area

Text properties—such as font-family, font-size, alignment, and font-weight—can be applied by attaching the appropriate properties to one of the boxes that contains the text. Text takes on the properties specified on the nearest enclosing box. Properties are set by attaching attributes to the elements that generate the boxes. With the exception of a few XSL-FO extensions, these properties have the same semantics as the CSS properties of the same name. Only the syntax for applying the properties to particular ranges of text is different.

The elements in the XSL-FO document do not map in a one-to-one fashion to the areas on the page. Instead, the XSL-FO document contains a slightly more abstract representation of the document. The formatting software uses the XSL-FO elements to decide which areas to create and where to place them. In the process, it will split the large blocks into smaller line and glyph areas. It may also split single block areas that the XSL-FO document describes into multiple block areas if a page break is required in the middle of a large block, although XSL-FO does let you prevent these breaks if necessary. The formatter also generates the correct number of pages for the content that's found. In short, the XSL-FO document contains hints and instructions that the formatter uses to decide where to place items on which pages, but you do not need to specify the exact position of each and every box.

The Structure of an XSL-FO Document

The root element of all XSL-FO documents is fo:root. This element normally declares the fo prefix mapped to the http://www.w3.org/1999/XSL/Format namespace URI. As always, the prefix can change as long as the URI stays the same. In this chapter, we assume that the prefix fo has been associated with http://www.w3.org/1999/XSL/Format. Thus, a typical FO document looks like this:

```
<?xml version="1.0" encoding="UTF-8"?>
<fo:root xmlns:fo="http://www.w3.org/1999/XSL/Format">
  <!-- Formatting object elements -->
</fo:root>
```

Of course, normally this isn't written as directly as it is here. Instead, it's formed by an XSLT template like this one:

```
<xsl:template match="/">
  <fo:root>
    <xsl:apply-templates/>
  </fo:root>
</xsl:template>
```

The fo:root element must contain two things: a fo:layout-master-set and one or more fo:page-sequences. The fo:layout-master-set contains elements describing the overall layout of the pages themselves; that is, how large the pages are, whether they're in landscape or portrait mode, how wide the margins are, and so forth. The fo:page-sequence contains the actual text that will be placed on the pages, along with the instructions for formatting that text as italic, 20 points high, justified, and so forth. It has a master-reference attribute identifying the particular page master that will be used to layout this content. Adding these elements, a formatting objects document looks like this:

```
<?xml version="1.0" encoding="UTF-8"?>
<fo:root xmlns:fo="http://www.w3.org/1999/XSL/Format">
  <fo:layout-master-set>
    <!-- page masters -->
  </fo:layout-master-set>
  <fo:page-sequence master-reference="first">
    <!-- data to place on the page -->
  </fo:page-sequence>
</fo:root>
```

The formatting engine uses the layout master set to create a page. Then it adds content to the page from the fo:page-sequence until the page is full. Then it creates the next page in the sequence and places the next batch of content on that page. This process continues until all the content has been positioned.

XSL-FO

Laying Out the Master Pages

XSL-FO 1.0 only defines one kind of master page, the `fo:simple-page-master`. This represents a standard rectangular page with margins on all four sides. This page master also has a unique name given by a `master-name` attribute. For example, this element describes a page master named `first` that represents an 8.5 × 11-inch page with 1-inch margins on all four sides:

```
<fo:simple-page-master margin-right="1in"  margin-left="1in"
                       margin-bottom="1in" margin-top="1in"
                       page-width="8.5in"  page-height="11in"
                       master-name="first">
   <!-- Separate parts of the page go here -->
</fo:simple-page-master>
```

The part of the page inside the margins is divided into five regions: the start region, the end region, the before region, the after region, and the body region. Where these fall on a page depends on the writing direction. In left-to-right, top-to-bottom languages like English, start is on the lefthand side, end is on the right-hand side, before is on top, and after is on bottom, as diagramed in Figure 14-2. However, if the text were Hebrew, then the start region would be on the right-hand side of the page, and the end region would be on the lefthand side of the page. If the text were traditional Chinese, then the start would be on top, the end on bottom, the before on the righthand side, and the after on the lefthand side. Other combinations are possible.

These regions are represented by `fo:region-start`, `fo:region-end`, `fo:region-before`, `fo:region-after`, and `fo:region-body` child elements of the `fo:simple-page-master` element. You can place different content into each of the five regions. For instance, the after region often contains a page number, and the before region may contain the title of the book or chapter.

The body region and the corresponding `fo:region-body` element are required. The other four are optional. By default, the body region takes up the entire page, and the other four regions have zero area. To specify this simplest page, you add an empty `fo:region-body` child element to the `fo:simple-page-master` element like this:

```
<fo:simple-page-master margin-right="1in"  margin-left="1in"
                       margin-bottom="1in" margin-top="1in"
                       page-width="8.5in"  page-height="11in"
                       master-name="first">
   <fo:region-body/>
</fo:simple-page-master>
```

However, you can add extent attributes to the four nonbody regions to specify the height of the before and after regions and the width of the start and end regions. Then the region body should have margin properties that are at least as large as the extent of each region to push it out of the way of each nonbody region. Other-wise, content placed in the body will be drawn on top of content placed in the other four regions. For example, this `fo:simple-page-master` element has 0.5-inch margins on each side, representing the unprintable area on many common printers. The start and end regions are 0.5 inches wide. The before and after regions are 1 inch wide. The body has margins that match the region sizes.

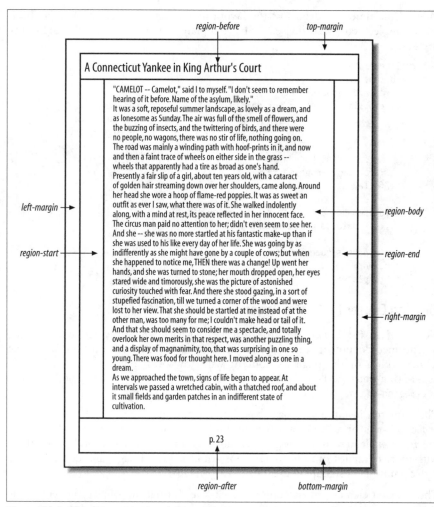

Figure 14-2. *The five regions in a left-to-right, top-to-bottom writing system*

```
<fo:simple-page-master margin-right="0.5in"  margin-left="0.5in"
                       margin-bottom="0.5in" margin-top="0.5in"
                       page-width="8.5in"    page-height="11in"
                       master-name="first">
    <fo:region-before extent="0.5in"/>
    <fo:region-after  extent="0.5in"/>
    <fo:region-start  extent="0.5in"/>
    <fo:region-end    extent="0.5in"/>
    <fo:region-body   margin-top="1.0in"  margin-bottom="1.0in"
                      margin-left="0.5in" margin-right="0.5in"/>
</fo:simple-page-master>
```

Most of the time, the details of the layout-master set are fixed in the stylesheet. For example, here's the revised XSLT template that includes a full fo:layout-master-set:

```
<xsl:template match="/">
  <fo:root>
    <fo:layout-master-set>
      <fo:simple-page-master margin-right="1in"  margin-left="1in"
                             margin-bottom="1in" margin-top="1in"
                             page-width="8.5in"  page-height="11in"
                             master-name="first">
        <fo:region-body/>
      </fo:simple-page-master>
    </fo:layout-master-set>

    <fo:page-sequence master-reference="first">
      <!-- data to place on the page -->

    </fo:page-sequence>
  </fo:root>
</xsl:template>
```

Flowing Content into the Pages

Next, add an fo:flow child to the fo:page-sequence where the actual text of the transformed document appears. This element has a flow-name attribute specifying which region of the page its content will flow into. Possible values include xsl-region-body, xsl-region-start, xsl-region-end, xsl-region-before, and xsl-region-after.

The formatter instantiates a page based on the page master named by the fo:page-sequence's master-reference attribute, fills one of its regions with content from the fo:flow element until the page is full, then instantiates a second page, fills it with more content from the fo:flow, instantiates a third page, and continues this process until it's used up all the data in the fo:flow.

The fo:flow element must contain block-level formatting object elements. The most basic of these is fo:block. Others include fo:block-container, fo:list-block, fo:table, and fo:table-and-caption. We'll begin with the most basic, fo:block. A fo:block can contain a combination of raw text and formatting objects, such as fo:external-graphic, fo:inline, fo:page-number, fo:footnote, and even other fo:block elements. For the moment, we'll restrict ourselves to simple text. For example, here's a basic fo:flow for the recipe:

```
<fo:flow flow-name="xsl-region-body">
  <fo:block>Southern Corn Bread</fo:block>

  <fo:block>1 cup flour</fo:block>
  <fo:block>4 tablespoons Royal Baking Powder</fo:block>
  <fo:block>1/2 teaspoon salt</fo:block>
  <fo:block>1 cup corn meal</fo:block>
  <fo:block>11/2 cups whole milk</fo:block>
  <fo:block>4 tablespoons melted butter</fo:block>
```

```
<fo:block>Sift flour, baking powder, sugar &amp; salt together.
  Add 1 cup corn meal.
  Beat egg in cup and add beaten egg and 1¹/2 cups whole
  milk to make a batter. Stir well.
  Add melted shortening and beat until light and thoroughly mixed.
  Pour into greased shallow pan or greased muffin rings.
  Bake in hot oven at 425° F for 25 minutes.
  Cut into squares if cooked in shallow pan.</fo:block>

<fo:block>After my mother-in-law Marjorie Anderson died,
  Beth and I found this recipe written on the "extra recipes"
  page in a local cookbook in her cupboard.
  This was published by the The Episcopal Churchwomen,
  Church of Ascension, Mt. Sterling, Kentucky.</fo:block>

</fo:flow>
```

Here's an XSLT template that produces the content of this fo:flow element (modulo insignificant whitespace) from Example 14-1 through judicious use of the default template rules:

```
<xsl:template match="dish|ingredient|directions|story">
  <fo:block><xsl:apply-templates/></fo:block>
</xsl:template>
```

Generating the Finished Document

We now have the minimum set of pieces needed to put together a full XSL-FO document. Example 14-2 is an XSLT stylesheet that transforms documents like Example 14-1 into XSL Formatting Objects documents.

Example 14-2. An XSLT to XSL-FO transform

```
<?xml version="1.0"?>
<xsl:stylesheet version="1.0"
                xmlns:xsl="http://www.w3.org/1999/XSL/Transform"
                xmlns:fo="http://www.w3.org/1999/XSL/Format">

  <xsl:template match="/">
    <fo:root>
      <fo:layout-master-set>
        <fo:simple-page-master margin-right="1in"  margin-left="1in"
                               margin-bottom="1in" margin-top="1in"
                               page-width="8.5in"  page-height="11in"
                               master-name="first">
          <fo:region-body/>
        </fo:simple-page-master>
      </fo:layout-master-set>

      <fo:page-sequence master-reference="first">

        <fo:flow flow-name="xsl-region-body">
          <xsl:apply-templates/>
        </fo:flow>
```

Example 14-2. An XSLT to XSL-FO transform (continued)

```
    </fo:page-sequence>

  </fo:root>
 </xsl:template>

 <xsl:template match="dish|ingredient|directions|story">
   <fo:block><xsl:apply-templates/></fo:block>
 </xsl:template>

</xsl:stylesheet>
```

Example 14-3 shows the complete XSL-FO document produced by running the cornbread recipe through an XSLT engine, such as Xalan, with this stylesheet. The whitespace is a little off because of the way XSLT treats whitespace in the transform document. However, this won't be significant when the document is rendered.

Example 14-3. An XSL-FO document describing a recipe for cornbread

```
<?xml version="1.0" encoding="utf-8"?>
<fo:root xmlns:fo="http://www.w3.org/1999/XSL/Format">
<fo:layout-master-set>
<fo:simple-page-master margin-right="1in" margin-left="1in"
margin-bottom="1in" margin-top="1in" page-width="8.5in" page-height="11in"
master-name="first"><fo:region-body/></fo:simple-page-master>
</fo:layout-master-set><fo:page-sequence master-reference="first">
<fo:flow flow-name="xsl-region-body">
  <fo:block>Southern Corn Bread</fo:block>

    <fo:block>
      1 cup
      flour
    </fo:block>
    <fo:block>
      4 tablespoons
      Royal Baking Powder
    </fo:block>
    <fo:block>
      1/2 teaspoon
      salt
    </fo:block>
    <fo:block>
      1 cup
      corn meal
    </fo:block>
    <fo:block>
      11/2 cups
      whole milk
    </fo:block>
    <fo:block>
      4 tablespoons
      melted butter
    </fo:block>
```

```
<fo:block>
 Sift flour, baking powder, sugar &amp; salt together.
 Add 1 cup corn meal.

   Beat egg in cup and add beaten egg and 1¹/2 cups whole
    milk to make a batter. Stir well.

   Add melted shortening and beat until light and thoroughly mixed.

   Pour into greased shallow pan or greased muffin rings.

   Bake in hot oven at 425° F for
   25 minutes.

   Cut into squares if cooked in shallow pan.
</fo:block>
<fo:block>
 After my mother-in-law Marjorie Anderson died,
 Beth and I found this recipe written on the "extra recipes"
 page in a local cookbook in her cupboard.
 This was published by the The Episcopal Churchwomen,
 Church of Ascension, Mt. Sterling,
 Kentucky.
</fo:block>
```

```
</fo:flow></fo:page-sequence></fo:root>
```

The final step in this process is to convert the formatting objects document into some other format that can be viewed on screen or on paper. This requires running a formatting program such as the Apache XML Project's open source FOP (*http://xml.apache.org/fop/*). FOP is a Java program. At the time of this writing, it has some significant holes in its coverage, but it is making progress. It includes shell scripts for DOS and Windows that set up the classpath and launch the Java program. For example, on Windows, this command line transforms the file *cornbread.fo* into a PDF document:

```
C:\> fop -fo cornbread.fo -pdf cornbread.pdf
```

FOP can also transform XSL-FO documents into plain text, raw PostScript, a PCL file, SVG slides, or display it on the screen using the Java 2D API. This command produces the window shown in Figure 14-3.

There are several other programs for working with XSL-FO documents:

- RenderX's XEP (*http://xep.xattic.com*) is a payware Java XSL-FO-to-PDF converter program much like FOP.

- Sebastian Rahtz's PassiveTEX (*http://www.hcu.ox.ac.uk/TEI/Software/passivetex/*) is an open source collection of T$_E$X macros for converting XSL-FO documents to T$_E$X. A reasonably modern T$_E$X distribution is required.

- The Antenna House XSL Formatter (*http://www.antennahouse.com*) is a payware Windows program that can print and display XSL-FO documents using the Windows GDI.

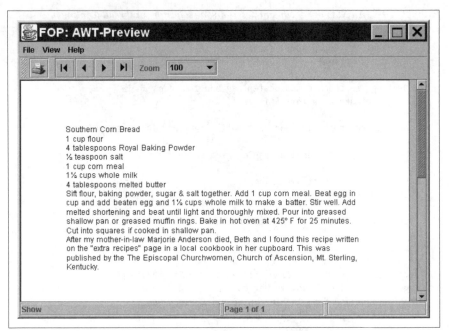

Figure 14-3. The XSL-FO recipe document in FOP's AWT preview

- IBM's XSL Formatting Objects Composer (*http://www.alphaworks.ibm.com/ tech/xfc*) is a free-as-in-beer Java program that implements a "substantial portion" of XSL Formatting Objects 1.0. It can display XSL-FO documents on the screen or convert them to PDF.

XSL-FO Properties

The finished document shown in Figure 14-3 is quite spartan. It simply breaks the original XML document into a few separate paragraphs. After quite a lot of work, it still hasn't reached the polish that was achieved much more simply with CSS (back in the last chapter in Example 13-2 and Figure 13-1). Adding the sparkle of different fonts, bold headlines, bulleted lists, and other desirable features requires setting the relevant properties on the individual formatting objects. These are set through optional attributes of the formatting object elements like fo:block. The good news is that most of the property names and semantics are exactly the same as they are for CSS. For example, to make the text in an fo:block element bold, add a font-weight attribute with the value bold, like this:

```
<fo:block font-weight="bold">Southern Corn Bread</fo:block>
```

The similarity with the equivalent CSS rule is obvious:

```
dish { font-weight: bold }
```

The property name is the same. The property value is the same. The meaning of the property is the same. Similarly, you can use all the font-weight keywords and values that you learned for CSS, like lighter and 100, 200, 300, 400, etc. Only the syntactic details of how the value bold is assigned to the property font-weight and how that property is then attached to the dish element has changed. When XSL-FO and CSS converge, they do so closely.

Many other properties come across from CSS by straight extrapolation. For instance, in Example 13-2 the dish element was formatted with this rule:

```
dish    {
  display: block;
  font-family: Helvetica, Arial, sans-serif;
  font-size: 20pt;
  font-weight: bold;
  text-align: center
}
```

In XSL-FO, it will be formatted with this XSLT template:

```
<xsl:template match="dish">
  <fo:block font-family="Helvetica, Arial, sans-serif" font-size="20pt"
          font-weight="bold" text-align="center">
    <xsl:apply-templates/>
  </fo:block>
</xsl:template>
```

Similarly, the margin properties set the margins on the various elements:

```
<xsl:template match="directions|story">
  <fo:block margin-top="12pt" margin-left="4pt">
    <xsl:apply-templates/>
  </fo:block>
</xsl:template>
```

In a few cases, CSS properties become XSL-FO elements rather than attributes. For instance, to format the ingredients as a bulleted list, we have to use the fo:list-block, fo:list-item, fo:list-item-label, and fo:list-item-body elements. This XSLT template does that:

```
<xsl:template match="ingredient">
  <fo:list-item>
            <!-- Unicode Bullet Character -->
    <fo:list-item-label>&#x2022;</fo:list-item-label>
    <fo:list-item-body><xsl:apply-templates/></fo:list-item-body>
  </fo:list-item>
</xsl:template>
```

We now have the pieces needed to put together a more attractive XSL-FO document. Example 14-4 is an XSLT stylesheet that transforms documents like Example 14-1 into XSL-FO documents.

Example 14-4. An XSLT-to-XSL-FO transform

```
<?xml version="1.0" encoding="UTF-8"?>
<xsl:stylesheet version="1.0"
            xmlns:xsl="http://www.w3.org/1999/XSL/Transform"
            xmlns:fo="http://www.w3.org/1999/XSL/Format">
```

Example 14-4. An XSLT-to-XSL-FO transform (continued)

```
<xsl:template match="/">
  <fo:root>
    <fo:layout-master-set>
      <fo:simple-page-master margin-right="1in"   margin-left="1in"
                             margin-bottom="1in" margin-top="1in"
                             page-width="8.5in"  page-height="11in"
                             master-name="first">
        <fo:region-body/>
      </fo:simple-page-master>
    </fo:layout-master-set>

    <fo:page-sequence master-reference="first">

      <fo:flow flow-name="xsl-region-body">
        <xsl:apply-templates/>

      </fo:flow>

    </fo:page-sequence>

  </fo:root>
</xsl:template>

<xsl:template match="recipe">
  <fo:block font-family="Times, 'Times New Roman', serif"
            font-size="12pt">
    <xsl:apply-templates/>
  </fo:block>
</xsl:template>
<xsl:template match="dish">
  <fo:block font-family="Helvetica, Arial, sans-serif" font-size="20pt"
            font-weight="bold" text-align="center">
    <xsl:apply-templates/>
  </fo:block>

</xsl:template>
<xsl:template match="directions|story">
  <fo:block margin-top="12pt" margin-left="4pt">
    <xsl:apply-templates/>
  </fo:block>
</xsl:template>

<xsl:template match="ingredients">
  <fo:list-block><xsl:apply-templates/></fo:list-block>
</xsl:template>

<xsl:template match="ingredient">
  <fo:list-item>
              <!-- Unicode Bullet Character -->
    <fo:list-item-label>
      <fo:block>&#x2022;</fo:block>
    </fo:list-item-label>
```

Example 14-4. An XSLT-to-XSL-FO transform (continued)

```
      <fo:list-item-body>
        <fo:block><xsl:apply-templates/></fo:block>
      </fo:list-item-body>
    </fo:list-item>
  </xsl:template>

</xsl:stylesheet>
```

Example 14-5 shows the XSL-FO document produced by applying the previous transform to the cornbread recipe in Example 14-1. The whitespace has been cleaned up a little by hand, although that won't affect the final rendered result.

Example 14-5. An XSL-FO document describing a recipe for cornbread

```
<?xml version="1.0" encoding="utf-8"?>
<fo:root xmlns:fo="http://www.w3.org/1999/XSL/Format">
  <fo:layout-master-set>
    <fo:simple-page-master margin-right="1in" margin-left="1in"
      margin-bottom="1in" margin-top="1in" page-width="8.5in"
      page-height="11in" master-name="first">
        <fo:region-body/>
    </fo:simple-page-master>
  </fo:layout-master-set>
  <fo:page-sequence master-reference="first">
    <fo:flow flow-name="xsl-region-body">
      <fo:block font-family="Times, 'Times New Roman', serif"
                font-size="12pt">
        <fo:block font-family="Helvetica, Arial, sans-serif"
          font-size="20pt" font-weight="bold"
          text-align="center">Southern Corn Bread</fo:block>
<fo:list-block>
  <fo:list-item><fo:list-item-label><fo:block>•</fo:block>
  </fo:list-item-label><fo:list-item-body><fo:block>
    1 cup
    flour
  </fo:block></fo:list-item-body></fo:list-item>
  <fo:list-item><fo:list-item-label><fo:block>•</fo:block>
  </fo:list-item-label><fo:list-item-body><fo:block>
    4 tablespoons
    Royal Baking Powder
  </fo:block></fo:list-item-body></fo:list-item>
  <fo:list-item><fo:list-item-label><fo:block>•</fo:block>
  </fo:list-item-label><fo:list-item-body><fo:block>
    1/2 teaspoon
    salt
  </fo:block></fo:list-item-body></fo:list-item>
  <fo:list-item><fo:list-item-label><fo:block>•</fo:block>
  </fo:list-item-label><fo:list-item-body><fo:block>
    1 cup
    corn meal
  </fo:block></fo:list-item-body></fo:list-item>
```

```
    <fo:list-item><fo:list-item-label><fo:block>•</fo:block>
    </fo:list-item-label><fo:list-item-body><fo:block>
      1¹/2 cups
      whole milk
    </fo:block></fo:list-item-body></fo:list-item>
    <fo:list-item><fo:list-item-label><fo:block>•</fo:block>
    </fo:list-item-label><fo:list-item-body><fo:block>
      4 tablespoons
      melted butter
    </fo:block></fo:list-item-body></fo:list-item>
  </fo:list-block>

  <fo:block margin-top="12pt" margin-left="4pt">
    Sift flour, baking powder, sugar &amp; salt together.
    Add 1 cup corn meal.

      Beat egg in cup and add beaten egg and 1¹/2 cups whole
       milk to make a batter. Stir well.

      Add melted shortening and beat until light and thoroughly mixed.

      Pour into greased shallow pan or greased muffin rings.

      Bake in hot oven at 425° F for
      25 minutes.

      Cut into squares if cooked in shallow pan.

  </fo:block>

  <fo:block margin-top="12pt" margin-left="4pt">
    After my mother-in-law Marjorie Anderson died,
    Beth and I found this recipe written on the "extra recipes"
    page in a local cookbook in her cupboard.
    This was published by the The Episcopal Churchwomen,
    Church of Ascension, Mt. Sterling,
    Kentucky.
  </fo:block>
```

```
</fo:block></fo:flow></fo:page-sequence></fo:root>
```

This document can be run through a formatter to produce a PDF file for viewing. Figure 14-4 shows the final result of this process.

XSL-FO does add a number of properties that CSS 2.1 doesn't provide. To name just a few, XSL-FO has properties to control hyphenation, insert leaders, specify the number of columns on a page, and determine where page breaks occur and which paragraphs must be kept together. CSS has none of these. For the most part, XSL-FO's properties are a superset of CSS's properties.

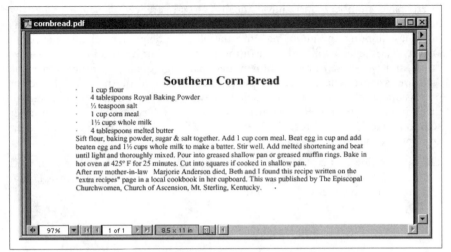

Figure 14-4. The recipe document after conversion from XSL-FO to PDF

Choosing Between CSS and XSL-FO

CSS is a very straightforward, easy-to-learn, easy-to-use language for formatting web pages. To the extent that CSS has gotten a reputation as buggy and difficult to use, that's mostly because of inconsistent, nonstandard browser implementations. Opera 4.0 and later, Netscape 6.0 and later, Mozilla, and Safari provide extensive support for most features of CSS Level 2, with only a few minor bugs. Internet Explorer's support is much weaker, but it borders on usable.

It's hard to imagine any text-based web site you can't produce by using XSLT to transform a document into HTML and then applying a CSS stylesheet. Alternately, you can transform the XML document into another XML document and apply the CSS stylesheet to that. If the element content in the original XML document is exactly what you want to display in the output document, in the correct order, you can even omit the XSLT transformation step, as we did in Examples 13-1 and 13-2 in the previous chapter.

Perhaps most importantly, CSS is already well-understood by web designers and well-supported by current browsers. XSL-FO is not directly supported by any browsers. To view an XSL-FO document, you must first convert it into the inconvenient PDF format. PDF does not adjust as well as HTML to the wide variety of monitors and screen sizes in use today. Viewing it inside a web browser requires a special plug-in. The limited open source tools that support XSL-FO are beta quality at best. Personally, we see little reason to use anything other than CSS on the Web.

On the other hand, XSL-FO does go beyond CSS in some respects that are important for high-quality printing. For example, XSL-FO offers multiple column layouts; CSS doesn't. XSL-FO can condition formatting on what's actually in the document; CSS can't. XSL-FO allows you to place footnotes, running headers, and other information in the margins of a page; CSS doesn't. XSL-FO lets you

XSL-FO

insert page numbers and automatically cross-reference particular pages by number; CSS doesn't. And for printing, the requirement to render into PDF is much less limiting and annoying since the ultimate delivery mechanism is paper anyway. CSS Level 3 will add some of these features, but it will still focus on ease-of-use and web-based presentation rather than high-quality printing. Once the software is more reliable and complete, XSL-FO should be the clear choice for professionally typeset books, magazines, newspapers, and other printed matter that's rendered from XML documents. It should be very competitive with other solutions like Quark XPress, TₑX, troff, and FrameMaker. CSS does not even attempt to compete in this area.

The bottom line is this: CSS is right for web pages; XSL-FO is right for printed matter. XSLT is a crucial step in getting an input document ready for eventual presentation with either CSS or XSL-FO.

15

Resource Directory Description Language (RDDL)

RDDL, the Resource Directory Description Language, is an XML application invented by Jonathan Borden, Tim Bray, and various other members of the *xml-dev* mailing list to describe XML applications identified by namespace URLs. A RDDL document lives at the namespace URL for the application it describes. RDDL is a hybrid of XHTML Basic and one custom element, `rddl:resource`. A `rddl:resource` element is a simple XLink that points to a resource related to the application the RDDL document describes. Humans with browsers can read the XHTML parts to learn about the application. Software can read the `rddl:resource` elements.

What's at the End of a Namespace URL?

The people who wrote the namespaces specification couldn't agree on what should be put at the end of a namespace URL. Should it be a DTD, a schema, a specification document, a stylesheet, software for processing the application, or something else? All of these are possible, but none of them are required for any particular XML application. Some applications have DTDs; some don't. Some applications have schemas; some don't. Some applications have stylesheets; some don't. Thus, for the most part, namespaces have been purely formal identifiers. They do not actually locate or identify anything.

"Namespaces in XML" specifically states that "The namespace name, to serve its intended purpose, should have the characteristics of uniqueness and persistence. It is not a goal that it be directly usable for retrieval of a schema (if any exists)." That is, it is not required that there be anything in particular, such as a DTD or a schema, at the end of the namespace URL. Indeed, it's not even required that the namespace name be potentially resolvable. It might be an irresolvable URN such as `urn:isbn:1565922247`. On the other hand, this doesn't say that there can't be anything at the end of a namespace URL, just that there doesn't have to be.

Nonetheless, this hasn't stopped numerous developers from typing namespace URLs into their web browser location bars and filling the error logs at the W3C and elsewhere with 404 Not Found errors. It hasn't stopped weekly questions on the *xml-dev* mailing list about whether it's possible to parse an XML document on a system that's disconnected from the Net. Eventually, the membership of the *xml-dev* mailing list reached consensus that it was time to put something at the end of namespace URLs, even if they didn't have to.

However, the question still remained, what to put there? All the reasons for not choosing any one thing to put at the end of a namespace URL still applied. Rick Jelliffe suggested fixing the problem by introducing an additional layer of indirection, and Tim Bray proposed doing it with XHTML and XLinks. Instead of putting just one of these at the end of the namespace URL, an XML document containing a list of all the things related to the XML application identified by that particular URL could be put at the end of the namespace URL.

Experience had proven that when presented with a string beginning with http, developers would type it into a browser location bar.* Therefore, the basic syntax of RDDL had to be something that looked reasonable when loaded into a browser: preferably, HTML. Furthermore, to make machine processing simple, it also had to be well-formed, perhaps valid, XML. Naturally, XHTML came to mind, and modular XHTML provided just enough extensibility to permit the extra syntax RDDL needed.

RDDL Syntax

A RDDL document is an XHTML Basic document, plus one new element: rddl:resource. XHTML Basic is a subset of XHTML that includes the Structure, Text, Hypertext, List, Basic Forms, Basic Tables, Image, Object, Metainformation, Link, and Base modules. There are no frames or deprecated presentational elements like font and bold. However, this is enough to write pretty much anything you'd reasonably want to write about an XML application.

In addition, a RDDL document contains one new element, resource, which is placed in the http://www.rddl.org/ namespace. This URL is normally mapped to the rddl prefix. The prefix can change as long as the URL remains the same. However, the RDDL DTD declares the resource element with the name rddl:resource, so a RDDL document will be valid only if it uses the prefix rddl.

A rddl:resource element is a simple XLink whose xlink:href attribute points to the related resource and whose xlink:role and xlink:arcrole attributes identify the nature and purpose of that related resource. The rddl:resource element can appear anywhere a p element can appear and contain anything a div element can contain. Web browsers generally ignore the rddl:resource start- and end-tags, but will display their content. Automated software searching for related resources

---

* In the immortal words of Claude L. Bullard, "All the handwaving about URN/URI/URL doesn't avoid the simple fact that if one puts http:// anywhere in browser display space, the system colors it blue and puts up a finger. The monkey expects a resource and when it doesn't get one, it shocks the monkey. Monkeys don't read specs to find out why they should be shocked. They turn red and put up a finger."

only pays attention to the `rddl:resource` elements and their attributes, while ignoring all the XHTML.

Recall the person vocabulary used several times in this book. When last seen in Chapter 8, it looked as shown in Example 15-1. All elements in this document are in the default namespace `http://www.cafeconleche.org/namespaces/people`.

Example 15-1. An XML document describing two people that uses a default namespace

```
<?xml version="1.0"?>
<people xmlns="http://www.cafeconleche.org/namespaces/people">

  <person born="1912" died="1954">
    <name>
      <first_name>Alan</first_name>
      <last_name>Turing</last_name>
    </name>
    <profession>computer scientist</profession>
    <profession>mathematician</profession>
    <profession>cryptographer</profession>
  </person>

  <person born="1918" died="1988">
    <name>
      <first_name>Richard</first_name>
      <middle_initial>P</middle_initial>
      <last_name>Feynman</last_name>
    </name>
    <profession>physicist</profession>
    <hobby>Playing the bongoes</hobby>
  </person>

</people>
```

Various chapters have developed stylesheets, DTDs, and (still-to-come) schemas for this application. Example 15-2 is a very simple RDDL document that brings these all together. This document should be placed at the namespace for that application, `http://www.cafeconleche.org/namespaces/people`. The DOCTYPE declaration loads the RDDL DTD rather than the XHTML Basic DTD, but the difference is only in the addition of the single `rddl:resource` element. This document is both valid and well-formed. Figure 15-1 shows this document in Mozilla, where it looks like any other HTML document.

Example 15-2. A RDDL document

```
<!DOCTYPE html PUBLIC "-//XML-DEV//DTD XHTML RDDL 1.0//EN"
                  "http://www.rddl.org/rddl-xhtml.dtd">
<html xmlns="http://www.w3.org/1999/xhtml"
      xmlns:xlink="http://www.w3.org/1999/xlink"
      xmlns:rddl="http://www.rddl.org/">
<head>
  <title>An XML Application Describing People</title>

</head>
```

Example 15-2. A RDDL document (continued)

```
<body>
<h1>An XML Application Describing People</h1>
<rddl:resource xlink:type="simple"
  xlink:href="urn:isbn:0596007647"
  xlink:role="http://dublincore.org/documents/dcmi-type-vocabulary/#text"
  xlink:arcrole="http://www.rddl.org/purposes#normative-reference">
  <p>
    http://www.cafeconleche.org/namespaces/people is the namespace URL
    for an XML application describing people in a record-like
    fashion used as an example in <cite>XML in a Nutshell</cite>, third
    edition by Elliotte Rusty Harold and W. Scott Means (O'Reilly Media,
    2004).
  </p>
</rddl:resource>

<h2>Related Resources</h2>
<p>
Several examples in this book address this application in one way or
another. These include:
</p>

<ul>
<li>
 <rddl:resource xlink:type="simple"
  xlink:href="http://www.cafeconleche.org/books/xian3/examples/03/3-5.dtd"
  xlink:role="http://www.isi.edu/in-notes/iana/assignments/media-types/
application/xml-dtd"
  xlink:arcrole="http://www.rddl.org/purposes#validation">
    <a href="http://www.cafeconleche.org/books/xian3/examples/03/3-5.dtd">
      Example 3-1</a>: A data oriented DTD describing people
  </rddl:resource>
</li>
<li>
<rddl:resource xlink:type="simple"
 xlink:href="http://www.cafeconleche.org/books/xian3/examples/08/8-15.xsl"
 xlink:role="http://www.w3.org/1999/XSL/Transform"
 xlink:arcrole="http://www.isi.edu/in-notes/iana/assignments/media-types/text/
html">
  <a href="http://www.cafeconleche.org/books/xian3/examples/08/8-15.xsl">
    Example 8-15</a>: An XSLT stylesheet for people documents
 </rddl:resource>
</li>
</ul>

<p>
  This document itself is
  <a href="http://www.cafeconleche.org/books/xian3/examples/15/15-2.html">
   Example 15-2</a> from the RDDL chapter.
</p>

</body>
</html>
```

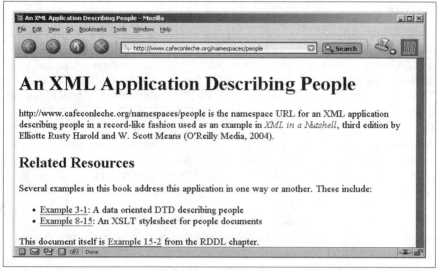

Figure 15-1. To a web browser, a RDDL document is just another HTML document

This document contains three `rddl:resource` elements indicating related resources. Two of them are inside list items, and one of them contains a paragraph at the top of the page. The first one links to the unofficial specification for the people application, this book itself. The `xlink:href` attribute uses an `isbn` URI to identify the book. The `xlink:role` contains a URL from the Dublin Core that indicates that the nature of this resource is text. The `xlink:arcrole` attribute contains a well-known URL defined in the RDDL specification to indicate that the purpose of this resource is normative reference.

The second `rddl:resource` element points to the DTD first defined in Chapter 3. Its nature is indicated by a MIME media type URL, and its purpose is validation. The `xlink:href` attribute links to the actual location of the DTD. However, a typical browser won't recognize this, so the `rddl:resource` element contains an ordinary HTML `a` link that the browser will color blue and the user can click on. It's not uncommon to duplicate markup in a RDDL document—one set of tags for the machines and another set of tags for the humans—each of which say pretty much the same thing.

The final `rddl:resource` element points to the XSLT stylesheet defined in Chapter 8. Here the `xlink:role` attribute contains the namespace URI for XSLT, indicating that this resource is an XSLT stylesheet. The `xlink:arcrole` attribute contains the MIME media type URL for HTML, indicating that this stylesheet will transform documents into HTML.

This is a very simple example. A real-world RDDL document would contain a lot more HTML to tell people reading it in a browser just what the application was about. Machines will ignore the HTML and look at the `xlink:role` and `xlink:arcrole` attributes to figure out exactly what they can do with each related resource.

Natures

The *nature* of a related resource says what the resource is. For example, the nature of a web page might be HTML, and the nature of an image might be JPEG. The nature is indicated by a URL. Normally, this nature URL is a namespace URL for XML applications and a MIME media type URL for everything else. For instance, the XSLT nature is written as *http://www.w3.org/1999/XSL/Transform*. The JPEG nature is written as *http://www.isi.edu/in-notes/iana/assignments/media-types/image/jpeg*.

The RDDL specification specifies 24 natures that can be used in xlink:role attributes. In addition, you are welcome to define your own, but, when possible, you should use the standard natures so that automated software can understand your documents and locate the necessary related resources. These are the standard natures and their URLs:

CSS stylesheet	*http://www.isi.edu/in-notes/iana/assignments/media-types/text/css*
DTD	*http://www.isi.edu/in-notes/iana/assignments/media-types/application/xml-dtd*
A mailbox	*http://www.rddl.org/natures#mailbox*
Generic HTML	*http://www.isi.edu/in-notes/iana/assignments/media-types/text/html*
HTML 4.0	*http://www.w3.org/TR/html4/*
HTML 4 Strict	*http://www.w3.org/TR/html4/strict*
HTML 4 Transitional	*http://www.w3.org/TR/html4/transitional*
HTML 4 Frameset	*http://www.w3.org/TR/html4/frameset*
XHTML	*http://www.w3.org/1999/xhtml*
XHTML 1.0 Strict	*http://www.w3.org/TR/xhtml1/DTD/xhtml1-strict*
XHTML 1.0 Transitional	*http://www.w3.org/TR/xhtml/1/DTD/xhtml/1-transitional*
RDF schema	*http://www.w3.org/2000/01/rdf-schema#*
RELAX core grammar	*http://www.xml.gr.jp/xmlns/relaxCore*
RELAX namespace grammar	*http://www.xml.gr.jp/xmlns/relaxNamespace*
Schematron schema	*http://www.ascc.net/xml/schematron*
OASIS Open Catalog	*http://www.rddl.org/natures#SOCAT*
W3C XML Schema Language schema	*http://www.w3.org/2001/XMLSchema*
XML character data	*http://www.w3.org/TR/REC-xml.html#dt-chardata*
XML escaped text	*http://www.w3.org/TR/REC-xml.html#dt-escape*
XML unparsed entity	*http://www.w3.org/TR/REC-xml.html#dt-unparsed*
IETF RFC	*http://www.ietf.org/rfc/rfc2026.txt*
ISO standard	*http://www.iso.ch/*
Python software	*http://www.rddl.org/natures/software#python*
Java software	*http://www.rddl.org/natures/software#java*

Many other natures can be reasonably derived by following these examples. For instance, a PNG image could be given the nature *http://www.isi.edu/in-notes/iana/assignments/media-types/image/png* because PNG documents have the MIME media type image/png. Software written in Ruby could be given the nature *http://www.rddl.org/natures/software#ruby*. An RDF document can have the nature *http://www.w3.org/1999/02/22-rdf-syntax-ns#* taken from its namespace, and so forth.

Purposes

The *purpose* of a related resource indicates what the resource will be used for. Purposes distinguish between resources with the same natures used for different things. For example, DocBook has multiple XSLT stylesheets for transforming DocBook documents into HTML, XHTML, chunked HTML, and XSL-FO. These are all related resources with the same nature but different purposes. Unlike natures, purposes are optional. You don't have to use them if you don't need to distinguish between resources with the same nature, but you can if you'd like.

Purpose names are URLs. These URLs are placed in xlink:arcrole attributes of a rddl:resource element. The RDDL specification defines 21 different well-known purpose URLs, mostly in the form *http://www.rddl.org/purposes#purpose*. In addition, you are welcome to define your own, but you should use the standard URLs for the standard purposes so that automated software can understand your documents and locate the necessary related resources. These are the well-known purposes:

Validation	*http://www.rddl.org/purposes#validation*
Schema-validation	*http://www.rddl.org/purposes#schema-validation*
DTD module	*http://www.rddl.org/purposes#module*
Schema module	*http://www.rddl.org/purposes#schema-module*
DTD notations module	*http://www.rddl.org/purposes#notations*
DTD entities module	*http://www.rddl.org/purposes#entities*
Software module	*http://www.rddl.org/purposes#software-module*
Software package	*http://www.rddl.org/purposes#software-package*
Software project	*http://www.rddl.org/purposes#software-project*
JAR	*http://www.rddl.org/purposes#JAR*
XSLT extension	*http://www.rddl.org/purposes/software#xslt-extension*
Reference	*http://www.rddl.org/purposes#reference*
Normative reference	*http://www.rddl.org/purposes#normative-reference*
Non-normative reference	*http://www.rddl.org/purposes#non-normative-reference*
Prior-version	*http://www.rddl.org/purposes#prior-version*
Definition	*http://www.rddl.org/purposes#definition*
Icon	*http://www.rddl.org/purposes#icon*
Alternate	*http://www.rddl.org/purposes#alternate*
Canonicalization	*http://www.rddl.org/purposes#canonicalization*
RDDL Directory	*http://www.rddl.org/purposes#directory*
RDDL Target	*http://www.rddl.org/purposes#target*

Furthermore, the purpose of an XSLT stylesheet is often the URI for the nature of the resource that is produced by the transformation. For instance, the purpose of a stylesheet that converted documents into strict XHTML would probably be *http://www.w3.org/TR/xhtml1/DTD/xhtml1-strict*.

RDDL

III

Record-Like Documents

16

XML as a Data Format

Despite the intentions of XML's inventors, who mostly envisioned XML as a format for web pages and other narrative documents to be read by people, the most common applications of XML today involve the storage and transmission of information for use by different software applications and systems. New technologies and frameworks (such as Web Services) depend heavily on XML content to communicate and negotiate between dissimilar applications. The structures appropriate for such applications differ from those used for the more traditional narrative documents in XML. They are more rigid in some ways: for instance, they tend to favor strongly typed element content and rarely allow mixed content; while being less rigid in others: the order of child elements rarely matters, for example. Thus, in many applications, the elements tend to look more like database records and less like web pages or books.

The appropriate techniques used to design, build, and maintain a record-like XML application vary greatly, depending on the required functionality and intended audience. This chapter discusses a variety of concerns, techniques, and technologies that should be considered when designing a new record-like XML application.

Why Use XML for Data?

Before XML, individual programmers had to invent a new data format every time they needed to save a file or send a message. In most cases, the data was never intended for use outside the original program, so programmers would store it in the most convenient format they could devise, which was often very tightly coupled to the program's internal data structures. Indeed, the earliest versions of Microsoft Word wrote at least part of their files by dumping memory straight to disk, and then opened those files by reading the data back into memory. This made understanding the data format and loading it into any other program extremely difficult. A few de facto file formats evolved over the years (RTF, CSV, ASN.1, and the ubiquitous Windows *.ini* file format), but in too many cases, the data written by one program could usually be read only by that same program. In fact, it was often possible for only that specific *version* of the same program to read the data.

In recent years, however, XML has begun to solve this problem and make data a lot more portable. The rapid proliferation of free XML tools throughout the programming community has made XML the obvious choice when the time comes to select a data-storage or transmission format for their application. For all but the most trivial applications, the benefits of using XML to store and retrieve data far outweigh the additional overhead of including an XML parser in your application. The unique strengths of using XML as a software data format include:

Simple syntax
 Easy to generate and parse.

Support for nesting
 Nested elements allow programs to represent complex structures easily.

Easy to debug
 Human-readable data format is easy to explore and create with a basic text editor.

Language- and platform-independent
 XML and Unicode guarantee that your data files will be portable across virtually every popular computer architecture and language combination in use today.

Building on these basic strengths, XML makes possible new types of applications that would have been previously impossible (or very costly) to implement.

Mixed Environments

Modern enterprise applications often involve software running on different computer platforms with a variety of operating systems. Choosing a communication protocol involves finding the lowest common denominator available on each system. Thanks to the enormous number of XML parsers that can be freely integrated with applications in a wide variety of environments, XML has become a popular format for data sharing.

Imagine an application server that needs to display data from a mainframe to users connected to a corporate web site. In this case, XML acts as the "glue" to connect the web server with a legacy application on a mainframe. The web server can send an XML request to the application server. The application server converts the request to what the legacy server expects and calls the legacy application. In the reverse direction, the application server converts the legacy server's response to XML before passing it back to the web server. Using a technology like XSLT, the web server can then transform the XML into a number of acceptable web formats for distribution to clients. By adopting XML as the common language of your enterprise, it becomes easier to reuse existing data in new ways.

Even on smaller systems, XML can be useful for sharing information between applications written in different languages or running in different environments. If a Perl program and a Java program need to communicate, generating and processing XML can be simpler than creating a custom format for the conversation. The XML documents exchanged can also serve as a record of the communications. Most importantly, the XML format provides a gateway to additional systems or programs that need to join the conversation. Each new system only needs to understand how to read and write the common XML format, rather than understanding every different format used by other participants.

Communications Protocols

Building flexible communications protocols that link disparate systems has always been a difficult area in computing. With the proliferation of computer networking and the Internet, building distributed systems has become even more important.

While XML itself is only a data format, not a protocol, XML's flexibility and platform agnosticism has inspired some new developments on the protocol front. XML messaging started even before the XML specification was finished and has continued to evolve since then.

XML as a part of the Web: REST

One of the earliest approaches, and still one of the best, is transmitting XML over HTTP. The server assembles an XML document and sends it to a client just like it sends an HTML file or a GIF image. For example, suppose a developer is building a service that takes a U.S. Zip Code and returns current weather information such as temperature and barometric pressure. The browser or other client application can encode the Zip Code as a query, producing a URL like *http://example.com/weatherNow.cgi?zip=95472*.

It then sends a normal HTTP GET request to the server *example.com* requesting a representation of the resource */weatherNow.cgi?zip=95472*. The server constructs an XML document representing the current weather for the Zip Code 95472, which might look something like Example 16-1.

Example 16-1. An XML document containing the weather in Sebastopol

```
<?xml version="1.0" encoding="UTF-8"?>
<weatherNow xmlns="http://example.com/weatherNow/" >
  <temperature>57</temperature>
  <pressure>29.97</pressure>
  <pressureChange>rising</pressureChange>
</weatherNow>
```

This simple web-based approach has been gathering supporters under the banner of Representational State Transfer (REST, *http://rest.blueoxen.net/cgi-bin/wiki.pl*). In the REST model, XML exchanges are treated in a very web-like way, using HTTP methods (GET, PUT, POST, DELETE) as verbs, XML documents as messages, and URIs to identify the services. REST doesn't have all the APIs, $200 an hour consultants, and six-figure middleware products that more complex web

Data Format

service–based approaches like SOAP support. But that's because it really doesn't need them. REST is simple, straightforward, and gets the job done with minimal effort.

XML for procedure calls over HTTP: XML-RPC

Other developers have chosen to use XML with more traditional programming approaches, like remote procedure calls (RPC). XML-RPC (*http://www.xmlrpc.com*) is a very simple protocol that encodes the method name and arguments as an XML document and transmits it using HTTP POST. The remote server responds with another XML document encoding the method's return value or an error message. The XML-RPC vocabulary defines elements representing six primitive data types (plus arrays and structs) common in pre-object-oriented languages.

If our hypothetical weather service was implemented using XML-RPC, a client request might look like Example 16-2.

Example 16-2. An XML-RPC request for the weather in Sebastopol

```
POST /weatherNow HTTP 1.0
User-Agent: myXMLRPCClient/1.0
Host: example.com
Content-Type: application/xml
Content-Length: 170

<?xml version="1.0"?>
<methodCall>
  <methodName>weatherNow</methodName>
  <params>
    <param>
      <value><string>95472</string></value>
    </param>
  </params>
</methodCall>
```

Note that this example includes both an HTTP header and the XML document payload.

The XML is designed to represent a method call of the form weatherNow("95472"). XML-RPC supports a variety of parameter types, but in this case, the method only requires one parameter, the Zip Code. Parameter order matters as it does in programming languages, although it's also possible (with a struct parameter) to send name–value pairs to the method. The reply from a service providing the weatherNow method might look like Example 16-3.

Example 16-3. An XML-RPC response containing the weather in Sebastopol

```
HTTP/1.0 200 OK
Date: Sat, 06 Oct 2001 23:20:04 GMT
Server: Apache.1.3.31 (Unix)
Connection: close
Content-Type: application/xml
Content-Length: 519
```

Example 16-3. An XML-RPC response containing the weather in Sebastopol (continued)

```xml
<?xml version="1.0"?>
<methodResponse>
  <params>
    <param>
      <value>
        <struct>
          <member>
            <name>temperature</name>
            <value><int>57</int></value>
          </member>
          <member>
            <name>pressure</name>
            <value><double>29.96</double></value>
          </member>
          <member>
            <name>pressureChange</name>
            <value><boolean>1</boolean></value>
          </member>
        </struct>
      </value>
    </param>
  </params>
</methodResponse>
```

This response provides the temperature, pressure, and pressure change as a struct, a set of name–value pairs. The values are of different types—an int for the temperature, a double for the pressure, and a boolean to indicate whether the pressure is rising or falling. Responses are only allowed to include one param element (despite its enclosing params element), so a struct or an array will be necessary if a method needs to return more than a single value.

XML-RPC is limited by its strict adherence to the procedure call metaphor and its non-extensible vocabulary, but the simplicity of that approach has meant that a lot of different implementations are available for a wide array of environments. Developers using XML-RPC will rarely, if ever, see the actual XML underlying their procedure calls.

XML envelopes and messages: SOAP

SOAP offers much more flexibility than XML-RPC, but it is much more complex as well. SOAP (formerly the Simple Object Access Protocol, but now an acronym without meaning) uses XML to encapsulate information being sent between programs. Like XML-RPC, SOAP started out using HTTP POST requests, and this is still the most common way to use SOAP, although other transport protocols are allowed.

> This discussion focuses on SOAP 1.1. A later specification, SOAP 1.2, is now a W3C recommendation, but SOAP 1.1 still dominates in common use. You may also want to explore the WS-I Basic Profile at *http://ws-i.org/Profiles/BasicProfile-1.0-2004-04-16.html*, built on SOAP 1.1, for suggestions for maximizing SOAP interoperability.

SOAP provides three features that differentiate it from plain XML messaging. The first is a structure for messages containing a SOAP-ENV:Envelope, an optional SOAP-ENV:Header for metadata, and a SOAP-ENV:Body. The second, now largely deprecated, is "SOAP Encoding" (or "Section 5 Encoding") for RPC messages. It provides structure much like the XML-RPC format, though it leaves open the choice of element names. The last feature is an explicit vocabulary for error messages, which are called faults. A simple SOAP request for the Zip Code weather server might look like Example 16-4.

Example 16-4. A SOAP request for the weather in Sebastopol

```
<?xml version="1.0" ?>
<SOAP-ENV:Envelope
    xmlns:SOAP-ENV="http://schemas.xmlsoap.org/soap/envelope/"
    xmlns:xsi="http://http://www.w3.org/2001/XMLSchema-instance"
    xmlns:xsd="http://http://www.w3.org/2001/XMLSchema">
  <SOAP-ENV:Body xmlns="http://example.com/weatherNow/">
    <weatherForZip xsi:type="xsd:string">95472</weatherForZip>
  </SOAP-ENV:Body>
</SOAP-ENV:Envelope>
```

The response to this request could be encoded as in Example 16-5.

Example 16-5. A SOAP response containing the weather in Sebastopol

```
<?xml version="1.0" ?>
<SOAP-ENV:Envelope
    xmlns:env="http://www.w3.org/2003/05/soap-envelope">
  <SOAP-ENV:Body xmlns="http://example.com/weatherNow/">
    <weatherStatus>
      <temperature xsi:type="xsd:int">57</temperature>
      <pressure xsi:type="xsd:double">29.97</pressure>
      <pressureChange xsi:type="xsd:boolean">1</pressureChange>
    </weatherStatus>
  </SOAP-ENV:Body>
</SOAP-ENV:Envelope>
```

Most of what's gained in SOAP beyond ordinary XML is a wrapper structure that lets developers add their own details to the messages. The SOAP-ENV:Header element, which can appear as the first child element of SOAP-ENV:Envelope, may be used to add extra information to a request, appearing before the body. Headers are used for a variety of tasks, from routing messages to the proper recipient to ensuring that a recipient understands a particular request before attempting to process the message.

When used in an HTTP environment, the request would typically be sent as a POST request from the client, generating the response from the server. SOAP can be used over a variety of other protocols, provided that all the senders and receivers understand both the protocol being used and as much of the SOAP messages as they need to process the request.

SOAP is built on XML and uses XML technologies like XML Schema, but in practice, very few developers actually work with the XML directly. Toolkits analyze existing objects or accept XML Schemas describing formats and then generate the markup automatically.

The Web Services Description Language (WSDL) can somewhat automate this process. A WSDL document is itself an XML document that describes a SOAP service. In many cases, it is easier to focus on the WSDL document and related XML Schemas for a service than to work with the SOAP messages themselves. A third vocabulary—Universal Description, Discovery, and Integration (UDDI)—helps programs locate WSDL-described SOAP web services, although UDDI hasn't achieved such a broad adoption as SOAP and WSDL.

A number of organizations are working on Web Service-based technologies, including the W3C (*http://www.w3.org/2002/ws/*), OASIS (*http://oasis-open.org*), and the Web Services Interoperability Organization (*http://ws-i.org/*). The field is developing rapidly, with vendors offering a wide variety of sometimes conflicting proposals.

Other options: BEEP and XMPP

Two other protocols, both from the Internet Engineering Task Force (IETF), may also be worth considering. The Blocks Extensible Exchange Protocol, or BEEP (*http://www.beepcore.org*), solves a different problem than SOAP, XML-RPC, and REST. Rather than building documents that travel over existing protocols, BEEP uses XML as a foundation for protocols built on TCP sockets. BEEP supports HTTP-style message-and-reply, as well as more complex synchronous and asychronous modes of communication. SOAP messages can be transmitted over BEEP, and so can a wide variety of other XML and binary information.

The IETF is also home to the Extensible Messaging and Presence Protocol (XMPP), the protocol used by the Jabber instant messaging software. Jabber (*http://jabber.org*) has grown from its chat roots to a toolkit frequently used by developers to allow computers, rather than people, to talk to each other.

Object Serialization

Like the issue of communications, the question of where and how to store the state of persistent objects has been answered in various ways over the years. In many popular object-oriented languages, such as C++ and Java, the runtime environment frequently handles object-serialization mechanics. Unfortunately, most of these technologies predate XML.

Most existing serialization methods are highly language- and architecture-specific. The serialized object is most often stored in a binary format that is not human readable. These files break easily if corrupted, and maintaining compatibility as the object's structure changes frequently requires custom work on the part of the programmer.

The features that make XML popular as a communications protocol also make it popular as a format for serializing objects. Viewing the object's contents, making manual modifications, and even repairing damaged files is easy. XML's flexible nature allows the file format to expand ad infinitum while maintaining backward compatibility with older file versions. XML's labeled hierarchies are a clean fit for nested object structures, and conversions from objects to XML and back can be reasonably transparent. Mapping arbitrary XML to object structures is a harder problem, but hardly an insurmountable one.

A number of tools serialize objects written in various environments as XML documents and can recreate the objects from the XML. Java 1.4, for example, adds an API for Long-Term Persistence (*http://java.sun.com/j2se/1.4/docs/guide/beans/ changes14.html#ltp*) to the java.beans package, giving developers an alternative to its existing (and still supported) opaque binary serialization format. Example 16-6 shows a simple applet persisted as XML.

Example 16-6. A Java frame serialized in XML

```xml
<?xml version="1.0" encoding="UTF-8"?>
<java version="1.4.2_03" class="java.beans.XMLDecoder">
 <object class="SwingCubScout">
  <void property="contentPane">
   <void method="add">
    <object class="javax.swing.JLabel">
     <void property="background">
      <object class="java.awt.Color">
       <int>255</int>
       <int>255</int>
       <int>0</int>
       <int>255</int>
      </object>
     </void>
     <void property="foreground">
      <object class="java.awt.Color">
       <int>0</int>
       <int>0</int>
       <int>255</int>
       <int>255</int>
      </object>
     </void>
     <void property="font">
      <object class="java.awt.Font">
       <string>Sans</string>
       <int>1</int>
       <int>24</int>
      </object>
     </void>
     <void property="text">
      <string>Cub Scouts!</string>
     </void>
    </object>
   </void>
  </void>
  <void property="name">
   <string>panel0</string>
  </void>
 </object>
</java>
```

This XML vocabulary looks a lot like Java and is clearly designed for use within a Java framework, although other environments may import and export the serialization. Microsoft's .NET Framework includes similar capabilities but uses an XML Schema-based approach. There is an incredible number of options for this kind of serialization process, available from many different vendors. Some depend on XML Schema, while others have their own models or work directly from existing object structures.

File Formats

Many single-user desktop applications open and save files. Games store the current state of the game. Word processors store text. Spreadsheets store numbers. Personal finance programs store monetary transactions. What unites these applications is that the data is read and written only at well-defined times, generally when the user selects Save or Open from the File menu. The formats designed for such storage are rarely a simple dump of the objects in-memory. What's sensible for storage on disk is rarely what makes sense for in-memory manipulation. Instead, special code is written to load and save a custom format that represents the information to be saved.

Most such file formats should be based on XML. It is much easier to invent, define, and use an XML format for such files than to devise some custom binary format. The first advantage is simply the wide availability of tools to parse and write XML. Unlike a custom format, basing your own format on XML means you don't have to test and debug parsers and serializers. Just use one of the well-tested, well-established, and debugged standard tools like Xerces or MSXML. You write less code, which translates into fewer bugs and faster time to market.

A second advantage to choosing XML for the format is that the files will be more accessible to other tools and developers. They too can use standard parsers to read the files. It may not be immediately obvious to such third parties what all the elements and attributes mean, but it's a lot easier for them to reverse engineer XML than some undocumented, proprietary binary file format. If you include a schema or DTD for the format, then it's even easier for third parties to understand the format and write their own programs that can work with it. XML formats lead much more interoperable software and expand the universe of tools that can work with your formats. They make interoperability of independent software much easier to achieve.

 The developers of OpenOffice.org have created a format that combines several different standards for interoperability. They use ZIP files as containers for XML and graphics files, making it easy to share compound documents as compact files.

Databases

XML can play a role in the communications between databases and other software, providing information in an easily reusable form. On the client side, XML data files can be used to offload some nontransactional data search and retrieval applications from busy web servers down to the desktop web browser. On the server side, XML can be used as an alternate delivery mechanism for query results.

XML is also finding use as a supplement to information stored in relational databases, and more and more relational databases include native support for XML, both as a data-retrieval format and a data type. Native XML databases, which store XML documents and provide querying and retrieval tools, are also becoming more widely available. These tools provide a more structured way of storing XML information than collecting documents in a filesystem.

 For more information on the wide variety of XML and data-management tools available and ways to use XML with databases, see *http://www.rpbourret.com/xml/XMLDatabaseProds.htm*.

RDF

In certain cases, especially where the data contained in the documents is metadata describing other documents, you may want to look at the Resource Description Framework (RDF). RDF can be written in an XML syntax, but its data model is built around more generic graphs instead of XML's strictly hierarchical trees. When you process an XML document using XML tools, you get a tree—a collection of nested containers holding information. When you process an RDF document using RDF tools—even if the RDF is encoded as XML—you get a collection of "triples." In English, a triple takes the rather stilted form "*Subject* has a *Property* whose value is *Object*." For example, "W. Scott Means has an email address whose value is *smeans@ewm.biz*." However, to make the identification of subjects, properties, and objects less ambiguous, these are all named with URIs, so we'd actually write "*http://www.oreillynet.com/cs/catalog/view/au/751?x-t=book. view&CMP=IL7015* has the property *http://www.w3.org/2000/10/swap/pim/ contact#mailbox*, whose value is *mailto:smeans@ewm.biz*." In XML, this would be written as shown in Example 16-7.

Example 16-7. An RDF statement encoded in XML

```
<?xml version="1.0"?>
<rdf:RDF xmlns:rdf="http://www.w3.org/1999/02/22-rdf-syntax-ns#"
          xmlns:contact="http://www.w3.org/2000/10/swap/pim/contact#">

  <contact:Person rdf:about=
"http://www.oreillynet.com/cs/catalog/view/au/751?x-t=book.view&amp;CMP=IL7015">
    <contact:mailbox rdf:resource="mailto:smeans@ewm.biz"/>

</rdf:RDF>
```

The advantage to this rather opaque approach is that, like XML itself, RDF is much easier for computers to process than natural language. In particular, as long as all statements are written in this restricted Subject-Property-Object triple form, computers can reason about statements and infer new truths based on existing triples. For instance, by knowing that the book *XML in a Nutshell* has an author property with the value W. Scott Means, and that W. Scott Means has an email property with the value *smeans@ewm.biz*, an RDF inferencing engine can deduce that the email address of an author of this book is *smeans@ewm.biz*. When many such triples are available from many different sources with standardized URIs,

RDF software should demonstrate knowledge (if not exactly intelligence) that is greater than the sum of its parts. At least that's the theory. Honestly, we're a little skeptical. RDF's approach does put an additional layer of abstraction between the serialization of the data and the internal structure of the data, and that layer is useful if you have data that is heavily self-referential or doesn't neatly fit into a nested container structure.

It's possible to create formats that can be processed either as XML or as RDF, giving consumers of the document flexibility about how they would prefer to process it. RSS 1.0 is such a format (although it does seem to be the least successful of several RSS variants). For a look at what is involved in mixing RDF into an XML environment, see *http://www.xml.com/pub/a/2002/10/30/rdf-friendly.html*.

Developing Record-Like XML Formats

Despite the mature status of most of XML's core technologies, XML application development is only now being recognized as a distinct discipline. Many architects and XML developers are attempting to apply existing design methodologies (like UML) and design patterns to the problem of constructing markup languages, but a widely accepted design process for creating XML applications still does not exist.

 The term "XML application" is often used in XML contexts to describe an XML vocabulary for a particular domain rather than the software used to process it. This may seem a little strange to developers who are used to creating software applications, but it makes sense if you think about integrating a software application with an XML application, for instance.

XML applications can range in scope from a proprietary vocabulary used to store a single computer program's configuration settings to an industry-wide standard for storing consumer loan applications. Although the specifics and sometimes the sequence will vary, the basic steps involved in creating a new XML application are as follows:

1. Determine the requirements of the application.
2. Look for existing applications that might meet those requirements.
3. Choose a validation model.
4. Decide on a namespace structure.
5. Plan for expansion.
6. Consider the impact of the design on application developers.
7. Determine how old and new versions of the application will coexist.

The following sections explore each of these steps in greater depth.

Data Format

Basic Application Requirements

The first step in designing a new XML application is like the first step in many design methodologies. Before the application can be designed, it is important to determine exactly what needs the application will fulfill. Some basic questions must be answered before proceeding.

Where and how will new documents be created?

Documents that will be created automatically by a software application or database server can be structured differently than those that need to be created by humans using an editor. While software wouldn't have a problem generating 100 elements with attributes that indicate cross-references, a human being probably would find those expectations frustrating.

If you have an application or a legacy format to which you're adding XML, you may already have data structures you need to map to the XML. Depending on the other requirements for the application, you may be able to base your XML format on the existing structures. If you're starting from scratch or need to share the information with other programs that don't share those structures, you probably need to look at the data itself and build the application creating the XML around the information.

How complex will the document be?

Obviously, the complexity of the data that will be modeled by the XML document has some impact on how the application will be designed. A document containing a few simple element types is much easier to describe than one that contains dozens of different elements with complex data type requirements. The complexity of an application will affect what type of validation should be used and how documents will be created and processed.

How will documents be consumed?

If the XML documents using this vocabulary will only pass between similar programs, it may make sense to model the XML documents directly on the internal structures of the programs without much concern for how easy or difficult that makes using the document for other programs or for humans. If there's a substantial chance that this information needs to be reused by other applications, read by humans (for debugging purposes or for direct access to information), or will be stored for unknown future use, it probably makes sense to ensure that the document is easy to read and process even if that makes creating the document a slightly more difficult task.

How widely will the resulting documents be distributed?

Generally, the audience for a new XML application is known in advance. Some documents are created and read by the same application without ever leaving a single system. Other documents will be used to transmit important business information between the IT systems of different organizations. Some documents are created for publication on the Web to be viewed by hundreds or even thousands of people around the world. XML formats that will be shared widely typically need comprehensive documentation readily available to potential users. Formal validation models may also be more important for documents that are shared outside of a small community of trusted participants.

Will others need to incorporate this document structure into their own applications?

Some XML applications are never intended to be shared and are only useful when incorporated into other XML applications. Others are useful standards on their own but are also suitable for inclusion in other applications. Here are a few different methods that might be used to incorporate markup from one application into another:

Simple inclusion
> Markup from one application is included within a container element of another application. Embedding XHTML content in another document is a common example of this.

Mixed element inclusion
> Markup from one application is mixed inline with content from another application. This can complicate validation and makes the including application sensitive to changes in the included application. The Global Document Annotation (GDA, *http://www.oasis-open.org/cover/gda.html*) Initiative provides an example of this type of application.

Mixed attribute inclusion
> Some XML applications are comprised of attributes that may be attached to elements from the host application. XLink is a prime example of this type of application, defining only attributes that may be used in other vocabularies.

Answering these questions will provide a basic set of requirements to keep in mind when deciding whether to build a new application, acquire an existing application, or some combination of the two.

Investigating Available Options

Before committing to designing and implementing a new XML application, it is a good idea to take a few minutes to search the Internet for prior art. Since the first version of the XML Recommendation was released in 1998, thousands of new XML applications have been developed and released around the world. Although the quality and completeness of these applications vary greatly, it is often more efficient to start with an existing DTD or schema (however imperfect) than to start from scratch. In some cases, supporting software is already available, potentially saving software development work as well.

XML vocabulary development

It is also possible that the work your application needs to do may fit into an existing generic framework, such as XML-RPC or SOAP. If this is the case, you may or may not need to create your own XML vocabulary. XML-RPC only uses its own vocabulary, while different styles of SOAP may reduce the amount of work your vocabulary needs to perform.

Data Format

Beyond the average search engine, XML Cover Pages (*http://xml.coverpages.org*) provides information about a wide variety of XML-related vocabularies, software, and projects. The search for existing applications may also find potential collaborators, which is helpful if the XML format is intended for use across multiple organizations.

Planning for Growth

Some applications may not need to evolve over time, but some thought should be given to how users of the application will be able to extend it to meet their own needs. In DTD-based applications, this is done by providing parameter entity "hooks" into the document type definition, which could either be referenced or redefined by an instance document. Take the simple DTD shown in Example 16-8.

Example 16-8. extensible.dtd

```
<!ENTITY % varContent "(EMPTY)">
<!ELEMENT variable %varContent;>
```

This fragment is not a very interesting application by itself, but since it provides the capability for extension, the document author can make it more useful by providing an alternative entity declaration for the content of the variable element, as shown in Example 16-9.

Example 16-9. Document extending extensible.dtd

```
<?xml version="1.0"?>
<!DOCTYPE variable SYSTEM "extensible.dtd"
[
<!ENTITY % varContent "(#PCDATA)">
]>
<variable>Useful content.</variable>
```

The W3C XML Schema language provides more comprehensive and controlled support for extending markup using the extension, include, redefine, and import elements. These mechanisms can be used in conjunction to create very powerful, customizable application frameworks.

Choosing a Validation Method

The first major implementation decision when designing a new XML application is what type of validation (if any) will be performed on instance documents. In many cases, prototyping a set of instance documents is the best way to determine what level of validation must be performed.

If your application is simply saving some internal program state between invocations (such as window positions or menu configurations within a GUI application), the structure is fixed by the program logic itself. Even though these configuration documents will always be written and read by the same program, writing a schema and validating documents on input can detect file corruption, not to mention bugs in the software itself. All too often we've watched our computers crash because various software (most often Microsoft Word) went down in flames when it encountered content in a document it had assumed could not possibly be present (most recently while working on Chapter 27 of this book). Validation may be a key defense against such attacks, intentional or otherwise.

Validation is even more important when XML documents are exchanged between different related systems that are not maintained by the same development organization. In this case, a DTD or schema can serve as a definitive blueprint to ensure that all systems are sending and receiving information in the expected formats. If something does go wrong and one process begins rejecting the other processes' inputs, validation can help assign the blame and the concomitant responsibility for fixing the problem.

The most rigorous type of validation is required when developing a new XML standard that will be implemented independently by many different vendors without any explicit control or restrictions. For example, the XHTML 1.1 standard is enforced by a very explicit and well-documented DTD that is hosted by the W3C. This well-known public DTD allows tool and application vendors to ensure that their systems will interoperate as long as instance documents conform to the standard.

After determining the level of validation for a particular application, it must be decided what validation language will be used. DTDs are still the most widely supported standard, although they lack the expressive power that is required by many record-like applications. The W3C XML Schema language provides very rich type and content model expression, but brings with it a commensurate level of complexity.

Developers can also provide both DTDs and XML Schemas for a given vocabulary, or even combine them with other vocabularies for describing XML structures, notably RELAX NG (*http://www.oasis-open.org/committees/relax-ng/*) and Schematron (*http://www.ascc.net/xml/resource/schematron/schematron.html*). Some organizations, particularly the W3C, are using RELAX NG as a base and generating DTDs and XML Schemas from the RELAX NG schemas. RDDL, described in Chapter 15, provides a set of tools for supporting and explaining such combinations for formats that use namespaces.

Namespace Support

Virtually every XML application that will be shared with the public should include at least a basic level of namespace support. Even if there are no current plans to publish documents in a particular vocabulary to the outside world, it is much simpler to implement namespaces from the ground up than it is to retrofit an existing application with a namespace.

Namespaces affect everything from how the document is validated to how it is transformed (using a stylesheet language such as XSLT). Here are a few namespace issues to consider before selecting a URI and starting work.

Data Format

Will instance documents need to be validated using a DTD?

If so, some planning of how namespace prefixes will be assigned and incorporated into the DTD is necessary. DTDs are not namespace aware, so strategic use of parameter entities can make modification of prefixes much simpler down the road.

Will markup from this application need to be embedded in other applications?

If so, some thought needs to be given to potential name collisions. The safest approach is to force every element and possibly every attribute from your application to be explicitly qualified with a namespace. This can be done within an XML Schema by setting the `elementFormDefault` and `attributeFormDefault` attributes of the `schema` element to `qualified`. If you expect to be mixing the vocabulary only at the element level, you should probably leave your attributes unqualified.

Are there legacy XML document formats to support?

If an application will include existing XML documents, some thought should be given to the effort involved in migrating them. In many cases, where the document didn't use namespaces at all, simply adding a default namespace declaration will be sufficient to make the documents work with applications that depend on namespaces to distinguish among vocabularies. Once documents and document formats are out "in the wild," it's difficult to get people to change. It may be necessary to keep programs around that handle both the original format and the new format or to create transformations from the older format to the new format. These multiple levels of processing or transformation are maintenance problems over time, so it's generally worth encouraging users to switch to the new format, possibly turning off the old one at some point.

Maintaining Compatibility

Maintaining backward compatibility with existing documents and processing software is a primary concern for XML applications that are widely used by diverse audiences. Standards organizations face formidable difficulties when updating a popular application (such as HTML). While few applications will become as widespread as HTML, some thought should be given in advance to how new versions of a schema or DTD will interact with existing documents.

One possible, although problematic, approach to maintaining backward compatibility is to create a new, distinct namespace that will be used to mark new element declarations or perhaps to change the namespace of the entire document to reflect a substantially changed version. This has substantial costs, however, and generally makes sense only when the new functionality is itself a separate vocabulary. Working with documents that have parts written in different namespace-indicated versions is a tough problem for developers.

A better strategy is only to *extend* existing applications without removing prior functionality. In this case, it is a good idea to ensure that each instance document for an application has some readily identifiable marker that associates it with a particular version of a DTD or schema. The good news is that the highly transformable nature of XML makes it very easy to migrate old documents to new document formats.

Removing functionality is possible, but frequently difficult, once a format is widely used. Deprecating functionality—marking it as a likely target for removal a version or several before it is actually removed—is one approach. While deprecated features often linger in implementations long after they've been targeted for removal, they change the expectations of developers building new applications and make it possible, if slow, to remove functionality.

Sharing Your XML Format

Creating a data format is often only the first step in making it useful. If an XML vocabulary is used only for a particular process inside a software application, there may not be much reason to publish information about how it works, except for future developers who may work on that application. If, on the other hand, the data format is intended for widespread use by people or organizations who may not normally interact with each other beyond the exchange of messages, then it probably makes sense to provide much more support for the format.

There is a variety of different kinds of information about a data format that are frequently worth sharing:

- Human-readable documentation, perhaps even in a variety of languages
- Schemas and DTDs formally defining the structures and content
- Stylesheets and transformations for presenting the data or converting it from one format to another
- Code for processing the data, perhaps even in a variety of languages or environments

The first two approaches—human-readable documentation and schemas—are typically the foundations. Formal definitions and rough understandings of what goes where often work for formats that are used by individual programmers or small groups, but sharing formats widely often requires further explanation. Stylesheets and code are additional options that may simplify adoption for developers.

The appropriate level of publicity for an XML vocabulary can vary widely, from no publicity at all to publishing a RDDL document or a support site to registering the format in one of the XML application registries, or to creating a working group at some kind of standards body or consortium.

17

XML Schemas

Although document type definitions can enforce basic structural rules on documents, many applications need a more powerful and expressive validation method. The W3C developed the XML Schema Recommendation to address these needs. Schemas can describe complex restrictions on elements and attributes. Multiple schemas can be combined to validate documents that use multiple XML vocabularies. This chapter provides a rapid introduction to key W3C XML Schema concepts and usage, starting with the fundamental structures that are common to all schemas. We begin with a very simple schema and proceed to add more functionality to it until every major feature of XML Schemas has been introduced.

Overview

An XML Schema is an XML document containing a formal description of what comprises a valid XML document. A W3C XML Schema Language schema is an XML Schema written in the particular syntax recommended by the W3C.

In this chapter, when we use the word "schema" without further qualification, we are referring specifically to a schema written in the W3C XML Schema language. However, there are numerous other XML Schema languages, including RELAX NG and Schematron, each with their own strengths and weaknesses.

An XML document described by a schema is called an *instance document*. If a document satisfies all the constraints specified by the schema, it is considered to be *schema-valid*. The schema document is associated with an instance document through one of the following methods:

- An `xsi:schemaLocation` attribute on an element contains a list of namespaces used within that element and the URLs of the schemas with which to validate elements and attributes in those namespaces.

- An `xsi:noNamespaceSchemaLocation` attribute contains a URL for the schema used to validate elements that are not in any namespace.
- A validating parser may be instructed to validate a given document against an explicitly provided schema, ignoring any hints that might be provided within the document itself.

Schemas Versus DTDs

DTDs provide the capability to do basic validation of the following items in XML documents:

- Element nesting
- Element occurrence constraints
- Permitted attributes
- Attribute types and default values

However, DTDs do not provide fine control over the format and data types of element and attribute values. Other than the various special attribute types (`ID`, `IDREF`, `ENTITY`, `NMTOKEN`, and so forth), once an element or attribute has been declared to contain character data, no limits may be placed on the length, type, or format of that content. For narrative documents (such as web pages, book chapters, newsletters, etc.), this level of control is probably good enough.

But as XML makes inroads into more record-like applications, such as remote procedure calls and object serialization, more precise control over the text content of elements and attributes becomes important. The W3C XML Schema standard includes the following features:

- Simple and complex data types
- Type derivation and inheritance
- Element occurrence constraints
- Namespace-aware element and attribute declarations

The most important of these features is the addition of simple data types for parsed character data and attribute values. Schemas can enforce much more specific rules about the contents of elements and attributes than DTDs can. In addition to a wide range of built-in simple types (such as `string`, `integer`, `decimal`, and `dateTime`), the schema language provides a framework for declaring new data types, deriving new types from old types, and reusing types from other schemas.

Besides simple data types, schemas can place more explicit restrictions on the number and sequence of child elements that can appear in a given location. This is even true when elements are mixed with character data, unlike the mixed content supported by DTDs.

 There are a few things that DTDs do that XML Schema can't do, such as defining general entities. XML Inclusions (XInclude) may be able to replace some uses of general entities, but DTDs remain extremely convenient for short entities.

Namespace Issues

As XML documents are exchanged between different people and organizations around the world, proper use of namespaces becomes critical to prevent misunderstandings. Depending on what type of document is being viewed, a simple element like `<fullName>Zoe</fullName>` could have widely different meanings. It could be a person's name, a pet's name, or the name of a ship that recently docked. By associating every element with a namespace URI, it is possible to distinguish between two elements with the same local name.

Because the "Namespaces in XML" recommendation was released after the XML 1.0 recommendation, DTDs do not provide explicit support for namespaces. Unlike DTDs (where element and attribute declarations must include a namespace prefix), schemas validate against the combination of the namespace URI and local name, rather than the prefixed name.

XML Schema uses namespaces internally for several purposes. The XML Schema vocabulary is in its own namespace, the vocabulary being defined is in its namespace, and components used within the schema (groups, attribute groups, and types) may also have namespaces. XML Schema processing also uses namespaces within instance documents to include directives to the schema processor. For example, the special attributes used to associate an element with a schema (`schemaLocation` and `noNamespaceSchemaLocation`) must be associated with the official XML Schema instance namespace URI (`http://www.w3.org/2001/XMLSchema-instance`) in order for the schema processor to recognize it as an instruction to itself.

Schema Basics

This section will construct, step-by-step, a simple schema document representing a typical address book entry, introducing different features of the XML Schema language as needed. Example 17-1 shows a very simple, well-formed XML document.

Example 17-1. addressdoc.xml

```
<?xml version="1.0"?>
<fullName>Scott Means</fullName>
```

Assuming that the `fullName` element can only contain a simple string value, the schema for this document would look like Example 17-2.

Example 17-2. address-schema.xsd

```
<?xml version="1.0"?>
<xs:schema xmlns:xs="http://www.w3.org/2001/XMLSchema">
 <xs:element name="fullName" type="xs:string"/>
</xs:schema>
```

It is also common to associate the sample instance document explicitly with the schema document. Since the `fullName` element is not in any namespace, the `xsi:noNamespaceSchemaLocation` attribute is used, as shown in Example 17-3.

Example 17-3. addressdoc.xml with schema reference

```
<?xml version="1.0"?>
<fullName xmlns:xsi="http://www.w3.org/2001/XMLSchema-instance"
  xsi:noNamespaceSchemaLocation="address-schema.xsd">Scott Means</fullName>
```

Validating the simple document against its schema requires a validating XML parser that supports schemas such as the open source Xerces parser from the Apache XML Project (*http://xml.apache.org/xerces2-j/*). This is written in Java and includes a command-line program called dom.Writer that can be used to validate *addressdoc.xml*, like this:

```
% java dom.Writer -V -S addressdoc.xml
```

Since the document is valid, dom.Writer will simply echo the input document to standard output. An invalid document will cause the parser to generate an error message. For instance, adding b elements to the contents of the fullName element violates the schema rules:

```
<?xml version="1.0"?>
<fullName xmlns:xsi="http://www.w3.org/2001/XMLSchema-instance"
  xsi:noNamespaceSchemaLocation="address-schema.xsd">Scott <b>Means</b>
</fullName>
```

If this document were validated with dom.Writer, the following validity errors would be detected by Xerces:

```
[Error] addressdoc.xml:4:13: Element type "b" must be declared.
[Error] addressdoc.xml:4:31: Datatype error: In element 'fullName' : Can not
have element children within a simple type content.
```

Document Organization

Now that there is a basic schema and a valid document from which to work, it is time to examine the structure of a schema document and its contents. Every schema document consists of a single root xs:schema element. This element contains declarations for all elements and attributes that may appear in a valid instance document.

> The XML elements that make up an XML Schema must belong to the XML Schema namespace (http://www.w3.org/2001/XMLSchema), which is frequently associated with the xs: prefix. For the remainder of this chapter, all schema elements will be written using the xs: prefix to indicate that they belong to the Schema namespace.

Instance elements declared using top-level xs:element elements in the schema (immediate child elements of the xs:schema element) are considered global elements. For example, the simple schema in Example 17-2 globally declares one element: fullName. According to the rules of schema construction, any element that is declared globally may appear as the root element of an instance document.

In this case, since only one element has been declared, that shouldn't be a problem. But when building more complex schemas, this side effect must be taken into consideration. If more than one element is declared globally, a schema-valid document may not contain the root element you expect.

Naming conflicts are another potential problem with multiple global declarations. When writing schema declarations, it is an error to declare two things of the same type at the same scope. For instance, trying to declare two global elements called fullName would generate an error. But declaring an element and an attribute with the same name would not create a conflict because the two names are not used in the same way.

Annotations

Now that there is a working schema, it's good practice to include some documentary material about who authored it, what it was for, any copyright restrictions, etc. Since an XML Schema document is an XML document in its own right, one simple option would be to use XML comments to include documentary information.

The major drawback to using XML comments is that parsers are not obliged to keep comments intact when parsing XML documents, and applications have to do a lot of work to negotiate their internal structures. This increases the likelihood that, at some point, important documentation will be lost during an otherwise harmless transformation or edit. Encoding documentation as markup inline with the element and type declarations they refer to opens up endless possibilities for automatic documentation generation.

To accommodate this extra information, most schema elements may contain an optional xs:annotation element as their first child element. The annotation element may then, in turn, contain any combination of xs:documentation and xs:appinfo elements, which are provided to contain extra human-readable and machine-readable information, respectively.

The xs:documentation element

As a concrete example, let's add some authorship and copyright information to the simple schema document, as shown in Example 17-4.

Example 17-4. address-schema.xsd with annotation

```
<xs:schema xmlns:xs="http://www.w3.org/2001/XMLSchema">

  <xs:annotation>
   <xs:documentation xml:lang="en-US">
     Simple schema example from O'Reilly's
     <a href="http://www.oreilly.com/catalog/xmlnut">XML in a Nutshell.</a>
     Copyright 2004 O'Reilly Media, Inc.
   </xs:documentation>
  </xs:annotation>

  <xs:element name="fullName" type="xs:string"/>

</xs:schema>
```

The `xs:documentation` element permits an `xml:lang` attribute to identify the language of the brief message. This attribute can also be applied to the `xs:schema` element to set the default language for the entire document. For more information about using the `xml:lang` attribute, see Chapters 5 and 21.

Also, notice that the documentation element contains additional markup: an a element (à la HTML). The `xs:documentation` element is allowed to contain any well-formed XML, not just schema elements.

The xs:appinfo element

In reality, there is little difference between the `xs:documentation` element and the `xs:appinfo` element. Either one can contain any combination of character data or markup the schema author wants to include. But the developers of the schema specification intended the `xs:documentation` element to contain human-readable content, while the `xs:appinfo` element would contain application-specific extension information related to a particular schema element.

For example, let's say that it is necessary to encode context-sensitive help text with each of the elements declared in a schema. This text might be used to generate tool-tips in a GUI or system prompts in a voicemail system. Either way, it would be very convenient to associate this information directly with the particular element in question using the `xs:appinfo` element, like this:

```
. . .
<xs:element name="fullName" type="xs:string">
  <xs:annotation>
    <xs:appinfo>
      <help-text>Enter the person's full name.</help-text>
    </xs:appinfo>
  </xs:annotation>
</xs:element>
. . .
```

Although schemas allow very sophisticated and powerful rules to be expressed, they cannot possibly encompass every conceivable need that a developer might face. That is why it is important to remember that there is a facility that can be used to include your own application-specific information directly within the actual schema declarations.

 Schematron is especially well-suited to use in annotations and is capable of checking a wide variety of conditions well beyond the bounds of XML Schema. For more information about Schematron, see *http://www.ascc.net/xml/resource/schematron/schematron.html*.

Element Declarations

XML documents are composed primarily of nested elements, and `xs:element` is one of the most often used declarations in a typical schema. This simple example schema already includes a single global element declaration that tells the schema processor that instance documents must consist of a single element, `fullName`:

```
<xs:element name="fullName" type="xs:string">
```

This declaration uses two attributes to describe the element that can appear in the instance document: name and type. The name attribute is self-explanatory, but the type attribute requires some additional explanation.

Simple types

Schemas support two different types of content: simple and complex. Simple content consists of pure text that does not contain nested elements.

In the previous example, the type="xs:string" attribute tells the schema processor that this element can only contain simple content of the built-in type xs:string. Table 17-1 lists a representative sample of the built-in simple types that are defined by the schema specification. See Chapter 22 for a complete listing.

Table 17-1. Built-in simple schema types

Type	Description
anyURI	A Uniform Resource Identifier
base64Binary	Base64-encoded binary data
boolean	May contain either true or false, 0 or 1
byte	A signed byte quantity >= -128 and <= 127
dateTime	An absolute date and time
duration	A length of time, expressed in units of years, months, days, hours, etc.
ID, IDREF, IDREFS, ENTITY, ENTITIES, NOTATION, NMTOKEN, NMTOKENS	Same values as defined in the attribute declaration section of the XML 1.0 Recommendation
integer	Any positive or negative integer
language	May contain same values as xml:lang attribute from the XML 1.0 Recommendation
Name	An XML name
string	Unicode string

Since attribute values cannot contain elements, attributes must always be declared with simple types. Also, an element that is declared to have a simple type cannot have any attributes. This means that if an attribute must be added to the fullName element, some fairly significant changes to the element declaration are required.

Attribute Declarations

To make the fullName element more informative, it would be nice to add a language attribute to provide a hint as to how it should be pronounced. Although adding an attribute to an element sounds like a fairly simple task, it is complicated by the fact that elements with simple types (like xs:string) cannot have attribute values.

Attributes are declared using the xs:attribute element. Attributes may be declared globally by top-level xs:attribute elements (which may be referenced from anywhere within the schema) or locally as part of a complex type definition that is associated with a particular element.

To incorporate a language attribute into the fullName element declaration, a new complex type based on the built-in xs:string type must be created. To do this, three new schema elements must be used: xs:complexType, xs:simpleContent, and xs:extension:

```
<xs:element name="fullName">

  <xs:complexType>
    <xs:simpleContent>
      <xs:extension base="xs:string">
        <xs:attribute name="language" type="xs:language"/>
      </xs:extension>
    </xs:simpleContent>
  </xs:complexType>

</xs:element>
```

This declaration no longer has a type attribute. Instead, it has an xs:complexType child element. This element tells the schema processor that the fullName element may have attributes, but the xs:simpleContent element tells the processor that the content of the element is a simple type. To specify what type of simple content, it uses the base attribute of the xs:extension element to *derive* a new type from the built-in xs:string type. The xs:attribute element within the xs:extension element indicates that this derived type may have an attribute called language that contains values conforming to the built-in simple type xs:language (mentioned in Table 17-1). Type derivation is an important part of schema creation and will be covered in more detail later in this chapter.

Attribute groups

In DTDs, parameter entities are used to encapsulate repeated groups of attribute declarations that are shared between different element types. Schemas provide the same functionality in a more formal fashion using the xs:attributeGroup element.

An attribute group is simply a named group of xs:attribute declarations (or references to other attribute groups) that can be referenced from within a complex type definition. The attribute group must be declared as a global xs:attributeGroup element with a unique name attribute. The group is referenced within a complex type definition by including another xs:attributeGroup element with a ref attribute that matches the desired top-level attribute group name.

Within the fullName schema, an attribute group could be used to create a package of attributes related to a person's nationality. This package of attributes could be used on several elements, including the fullName element, without repeating the same attribute declarations. Then, if it were later necessary to extend this collection of attributes, it could be done in a single location:

```
<xs:element name="fullName">
  . . .
      <xs:extension base="xs:string">
        <xs:attributeGroup ref="nationality"/>
      </xs:extension>
  . . .
</xs:element>
```

XML Schemas

```
<xs:attributeGroup name="nationality">
  <xs:attribute name="language" type="xs:language"/>
</xs:attributeGroup>
```

Working with Namespaces

So far, namespaces have only been dealt with as they relate to the schema processor and schema language itself. But the schema specification was written with the intention that schemas could support and describe XML namespaces.

Target Namespaces

Associating a schema with a particular XML namespace is extremely simple: add a targetNamespace attribute to the root xs:schema element, like so:

```
<xs:schema xmlns:xs="http://www.w3.org/2001/XMLSchema"
  targetNamespace="http://namespaces.oreilly.com/xmlnut/address">
```

> It is important to remember that many XML 1.0 documents are not associated with namespaces at all. To validate these documents, it is necessary to use a schema that doesn't have a targetNamespace attribute. When developing schemas that are not associated with a target namespace, you should always explicitly qualify schema elements (like xs:element) to keep them from being confused with global declarations for your application.

However, making that simple change impacts numerous other parts of the example application. Trying to validate the *addressdoc.xml* document as it stands (with the xsi:noNamespaceSchemaLocation attribute) causes the Xerces schema processor to report this validity error:

```
General Schema Error: Schema in address-schema.xsd has a different target
namespace from the one specified in the instance document :.
```

To rectify this, it is necessary to change the instance document to reference the new, namespace-enabled schema properly. This is done using the xsi:schemaLocation attribute, like so:

```
<fullName xmlns:xsi="http://www.w3.org/2001/XMLSchema-instance"
  xsi:schemaLocation="http://namespaces.oreilly.com/xmlnut/address
    address-schema.xsd"
  language="en">Scott Means</fullName>
```

Notice that the schemaLocation attribute value contains two tokens. The first is the target namespace URI that matches the target namespace of the schema document. The second is the physical location of the actual schema document.

Unfortunately, there are still problems. If this document is validated, the validator will report errors like these two:

```
Element type "fullName" must be declared.
Attribute "language" must be declared for element type "fullName".
```

This is because, even though a schema location has been declared, the element still doesn't actually belong to a namespace. Either a default namespace must be declared or a namespace prefix that matches the target namespace of the schema must be used. The following document uses a default namespace:

```
<fullName xmlns:xsi="http://www.w3.org/2001/XMLSchema-instance"
    xsi:schemaLocation="http://namespaces.oreilly.com/xmlnut/address
        address-schema.xsd"
    xmlns="http://namespaces.oreilly.com/xmlnut/address"
    language="en">Scott Means</fullName>
```

But before this document can be successfully validated, it is necessary to fix one other problem that was introduced when a target namespace was added to the schema. Within the element declaration for the fullName element, there is a reference to the nationality attribute group. By associating the schema with a target namespace, every global declaration has been implicitly associated with that namespace. This means that the ref attribute of the attribute group element in the element declaration must be updated to point to an attribute group that belongs to the new target namespace.

The clearest way to do this is to declare a new namespace prefix in the schema that maps to the target namespace, and use it to prefix any references to global declarations:

```
<xs:schema xmlns:xs="http://www.w3.org/2001/XMLSchema"
    targetNamespace="http://namespaces.oreilly.com/xmlnut/address"
    xmlns:addr="http://namespaces.oreilly.com/xmlnut/address">
    . . .
        <xs:attributeGroup ref="addr:nationality"/>
    . . .
```

Now, having made these three simple changes, the document will once again validate cleanly against the schema.

> The obvious lesson from this is that namespaces should be incorporated into your schema design as early as possible. If not, there will likely be a large amount of cleanup involved as various assumptions that used to be true are no longer valid.

Controlling Qualification

One of the major headaches with DTDs is that they have no explicit support for namespace prefixes since they predate the "Namespaces in XML" recommendation. Although "Namespaces in XML" went to great pains to explain that prefixes were only placeholders and only the namespace URIs really matter, it was painful and awkward to design a DTD that could support arbitrary prefixes. Schemas correct this by validating against namespace URIs and local names rather than prefixed names.

The elementFormDefault and attributeFormDefault attributes of the xs:schema element control whether locally declared elements and attributes must be namespace-qualified within instance documents. Suppose the attribute attributeFormDefault is set to qualified in the schema, like this:

XML Schemas

```
<xs:schema xmlns:xsi="http://www.w3.org/2001/XMLSchema"
    targetNamespace="http://namespaces.oreilly.com/xmlnut/address"
    xmlns:addr="http://namespaces.oreilly.com/xmlnut/address"
    attributeFormDefault="qualified">
```

Now, if *addressdoc.xml* is validated against the schema, the validator reports the
following error:

```
Attribute "language" must be declared for element type "fullName".
```

Since the default attribute form has been set to qualified, the schema processor
doesn't recognize the unqualified language attribute as belonging to the same
schema as the fullName element. This is because attributes, unlike elements, don't
inherit the default namespace from the xmlns="..." attribute. They must always
be explicitly prefixed if they need to belong to a particular namespace.

The easiest way to fix the instance document is to declare an explicit namespace
prefix and use it to qualify the element and attribute, as shown in Example 17-5.

Example 17-5. addressdoc.xml with explicit namespace prefix

```
<?xml version="1.0"?>
<addr:fullName xmlns:xsi="http://www.w3.org/2001/XMLSchema-instance"
  xsi:schemaLocation="http://namespaces.oreilly.com/xmlnut/address
    address-schema.xsd"
  xmlns:addr="http://namespaces.oreilly.com/xmlnut/address"
  addr:language="en">Scott Means</addr:fullName>
```

The elementFormDefault attribute serves the same function in regards to
namespace qualification of nested elements. If it is set to qualified, which is
normal practice, nested elements must belong to the target namespace of the
schema (either through a default namespace declaration or an explicit prefix).

Complex Types

A schema assigns a type to each element and attribute it declares. In
Example 17-5, the fullName element has a *complex type*. Elements with complex
types may contain nested elements and have attributes. Only elements can
contain complex types. Attributes always have simple types.

Since the type is declared using an xs:complexType element embedded directly in
the element declaration, it is also an anonymous type, rather than a named type.

New types are defined using xs:complexType or xs:simpleType elements. If a new
type is declared globally with a top-level element, it needs to be given a name so
that it can be referenced from element and attribute declarations within the
schema. If a type is defined inline (inside an element or attribute declaration), it
does not need to be named. But since it has no name, it cannot be referenced by
other element or attribute declarations. When building large and complex
schemas, data types will need to be shared among multiple different elements. To
facilitate this reuse, it is necessary to create named types.

To show how named types and complex content interact, let's expand the
example schema. A new address element will contain the fullName element, and

the person's name will be divided into a first- and last-name component. A typical instance document would look like Example 17-6.

Example 17-6. addressdoc.xml after adding address, first, and last elements

```
<?xml version="1.0"?>
<addr:address xmlns:xsi="http://www.w3.org/2001/XMLSchema-instance"
    xsi:schemaLocation="http://namespaces.oreilly.com/xmlnut/address
      address-schema.xsd"
    xmlns:addr="http://namespaces.oreilly.com/xmlnut/address"
    addr:language="en">
  <addr:fullName>
    <addr:first>Scott</addr:first>
    <addr:last>Means</addr:last>
  </addr:fullName>
</addr:address>
```

To accommodate this new format, fairly substantial structural changes to the schema are required, as shown in Example 17-7.

Example 17-7. address-schema.xsd to support address element

```
<xs:schema xmlns:xs="http://www.w3.org/2001/XMLSchema"
  targetNamespace="http://namespaces.oreilly.com/xmlnut/address"
  xmlns:addr="http://namespaces.oreilly.com/xmlnut/address"
  elementFormDefault="qualified">
<xs:element name="address">
  <xs:complexType>
    <xs:sequence>
      <xs:element name="fullName">
        <xs:complexType>
          <xs:sequence>
            <xs:element name="first" type="addr:nameComponent"/>
            <xs:element name="last" type="addr:nameComponent"/>
          </xs:sequence>
        </xs:complexType>
      </xs:element>
    </xs:sequence>
  </xs:complexType>
</xs:element>

<xs:complexType name="nameComponent">
  <xs:simpleContent>
    <xs:extension base="xs:string"/>
  </xs:simpleContent>
</xs:complexType>
</xs:schema>
```

The first major difference between this schema and the previous version is that the root element name has been changed from fullName to address. The same result could have been accomplished by creating a new top-level element declaration for the new address element, but that would have opened a loophole allowing a valid instance document to contain only a fullName element and nothing else.

The address element declaration defines a new anonymous complex type. Unlike the old definition, this complex type is defined to contain complex content using the xs:sequence element. The sequence element tells the schema processor that the contained list of elements must appear in the target document in the exact order they are given. In this case, the sequence contains only one element declaration.

The nested element declaration is for the fullName element, which then repeats the xs:complexType and xs:sequence definition process. Within this nested sequence, two element declarations appear for the first and last elements.

These two element declarations, unlike all prior element declarations, explicitly reference a new complex type that's declared in the schema: the addr:nameComponent type. It is fully qualified to differentiate it from possible conflicts with built-in schema data types.

The nameComponent type is declared by the xs:complexType element immediately following the address element declaration. It is identified as a named type by the presence of the name attribute, but in every other way it is constructed the same way it would have been as an anonymous type.

Occurrence Constraints

One feature of schemas that should be welcome to DTD developers is the ability to explicitly set the minimum and maximum number of times an element may occur at a particular point in a document using minOccurs and maxOccurs attributes of the xs:element element. For example, this declaration adds an optional middle name to the fullName element:

```
<xs:element name="fullName">
  <xs:complexType>
    <xs:sequence>
      <xs:element name="first" type="addr:nameComponent"/>
      <xs:element name="middle" type="addr:nameComponent"
          minOccurs="0"/>
      <xs:element name="last" type="addr:nameComponent"/>
    </xs:sequence>
  </xs:complexType>
</xs:element>
```

Notice that the element declaration for the middle element has a minOccurs value of 0. The default value for both minOccurs and maxOccurs is 1, if they are not provided explicitly. Therefore, setting minOccurs to 0 means that the middle element may appear 0 to 1 times. This is equivalent to using the ? operator in a DTD declaration. Another possible value for the maxOccurs attribute is unbounded, which indicates that the element in question may appear an unlimited number of times. This value is used to produce the same effect as the * and + operators in a DTD declaration. The advantage over DTDs comes when you use values other than 0, 1, or unbounded, letting you specify things like "this element must appear at least twice but no more than four times."

Types of Element Content

So far you have seen elements that only contain character data and elements that only contain other elements. The next several sections cover each of the possible types of element content individually, from most restrictive to least restrictive:

- Empty
- Simple content
- Mixed content
- Any type

Empty Elements

In many cases, it is useful to declare an element that cannot contain anything. Most of these elements convey all of their information via attributes or simply by their position in relation to other elements (e.g., the br element from XHTML). Let's add a contact-information element to the address element that will be used to contain a list of ways to contact a person. Example 17-8 shows the sample instance document after adding the new contacts element and a sample phone entry.

Example 17-8. addressdoc.xml with contact element

```
<?xml version="1.0"?>
<addr:address xmlns:xsi="http://www.w3.org/2001/XMLSchema-instance"
    xsi:schemaLocation="http://namespaces.oreilly.com/xmlnut/address
      address-schema.xsd"
    xmlns:addr="http://namespaces.oreilly.com/xmlnut/address"
    addr:language="en">
  <addr:fullName>
    <addr:first>William</addr:first>
    <addr:middle>Scott</addr:middle>
    <addr:last>Means</addr:last>
  </addr:fullName>
  <addr:contacts>
    <addr:phone addr:number="888.737.1752"/>
  </addr:contacts>
</addr:address>
```

Supporting this new content requires further modifications to the schema document. Although it would be possible to declare the new element inline within the existing address-element declaration, for clarity it makes sense to create a new global type and reference it by name:

```
<xs:element name="address">
  <xs:complexType>
    <xs:sequence>
      <xs:element name="fullName">
. . .
      </xs:element>
      <xs:element name="contacts" type="addr:contactsType" minOccurs="0"/>
    </xs:sequence>
```

```
    <xs:attributeGroup ref="addr:nationality"/>
  </xs:complexType>
</xs:element>
```

The declaration for the new contactsType complex type looks like this:

```
<xs:complexType name="contactsType">
  <xs:sequence>
    <xs:element name="phone" minOccurs="0" maxOccurs="unbounded">
      <xs:complexType>
        <xs:attribute name="number" type="xs:string"/>
      </xs:complexType>
    </xs:element>
  </xs:sequence>
</xs:complexType>
```

The syntax used to declare an empty element is actually very simple. Notice that the xs:element declaration for the previous phone element contains a complex type definition that only includes a single attribute declaration. This tells the schema processor that the phone element may only contain complex content (elements), and since no additional nested element declarations are provided, it must remain empty.

The complexContent Element

The preceding example actually took a shortcut with the schema language. One of the early fullName element declarations used the xs:simpleContent element to indicate that the element could only contain simple content (no nested elements). There is a corresponding content-declaration element that specifies that a complex type can only contain complex content (elements). This is the xs:complexContent element.

When the phone element was declared using an xs:complexType element with no nested element declarations, the schema processor automatically inferred that it should contain only complex content. The phone element declaration could be rewritten like so, using the xs:complexContent element:

```
<xs:element name="phone" minOccurs="0">
  <xs:complexType>
    <xs:complexContent>
      <xs:restriction base="xs:anyType">
        <xs:attribute name="number" type="xs:string"/>
      </xs:restriction>
    </xs:complexContent>
  </xs:complexType>
</xs:element>
```

The most common reason to use the xs:complexContent element is to derive a complex type from an existing type. This example derives a new type by restriction from the built-in xs:anyType type. xs:anyType is the root of all of the built-in schema types and represents an unrestricted sequence of characters and markup. Since the xs:complexType indicates that the element can only contain element content, the effect of this restriction is to prevent the element from containing either character data or markup.

Simple Content

Earlier, the xs:simpleContent element was used to declare an element that could only contain simple content:

```
<xs:element name="fullName">
  <xs:complexType>
    <xs:simpleContent>
      <xs:extension base="xs:string">
        <xs:attribute name="language" type="xs:language"/>
      </xs:extension>
    </xs:simpleContent>
  </xs:complexType>
</xs:element>
```

The base type for the extension in this case was the built-in xs:string data type. But simple types are not limited to the predefined types. The xs:simpleType element can define new simple data types, which can be referenced by element and attribute declarations within the schema.

Defining New Simple Types

To show how new simple types can be defined, let's extend the phone element from the example application to support a new attribute called location. This attribute will be used to differentiate between work and home phone numbers. This attribute will have a new simple type called locationType, which will be referenced from the contactsType definition:

```
<xs:complexType name="contactsType">
  <xs:sequence>
    <xs:element name="phone" minOccurs="0">
      <xs:complexType>
        <xs:attribute name="number" type="xs:string"/>
        <xs:attribute name="location" type="addr:locationType"/>
      </xs:complexType>
    </xs:element>
  </xs:sequence>
</xs:complexType>

<xs:simpleType name="locationType">
  <xs:restriction base="xs:string"/>
</xs:simpleType>
```

Of course, a location type that just maps to the built-in xs:string type isn't particularly useful. Fortunately, schemas can strictly control the possible values of simple types through a mechanism called *facets*.

Facets

In schema-speak, a facet is an aspect of a possible value for a simple data type. Depending on the base type, some facets make more sense than others. For example, a numeric data type can be restricted by the minimum and maximum possible values it could contain. But these types of restrictions wouldn't make

XML Schemas

sense for a boolean value. The following list covers the different facet types that are supported by a schema processor:

- length (or minLength and maxLength)
- pattern
- enumeration
- whiteSpace
- maxInclusive and maxExclusive
- minInclusive and minExclusive
- totalDigits
- fractionDigits

Facets are applied to simple types using the xs:restriction element. Each facet is expressed as a distinct element within the restriction block, and multiple facets can be combined to further restrict potential values of the simple type.

Handling whitespace

The whiteSpace facet controls how the schema processor will deal with any whitespace within the target data. Whitespace normalization takes place before any of the other facets are processed. There are three possible values for the whiteSpace facet:

preserve
> Keep all whitespace exactly as it was in the source document (basic XML 1.0 whitespace handling for content within elements).

replace
> Replace occurrences of #x9 (tab), #xA (line feed), and #xD (carriage return) characters with #x20 (space) characters.

collapse
> Perform the replace step first, then collapse multiple-space characters into a single space.

Restricting length

The length-restriction facets are fairly easy to understand. The length facet forces a value to be *exactly* the length given. The minLength and maxLength facets can set a definite range for the lengths of values of the type given. For example, take the nameComponent type from the schema. What if a name component could not exceed 50 characters (because of a database limitation, for instance)? This rule can be enforced by using the maxLength facet. Incorporating this facet requires a new simple type to reference from within the nameComponent complex type definition:

```
<xs:complexType name="nameComponent">
  <xs:simpleContent>
    <xs:extension base="addr:nameString"/>
  </xs:simpleContent>
</xs:complexType>
```

```
<xs:simpleType name="nameString">
  <xs:restriction base="xs:string">
    <xs:maxLength value="50"/>
  </xs:restriction>
</xs:simpleType>
```

The new nameString simple type is derived from the built-in xs:string type, but it can contain no more than 50 characters (the default is unlimited). The same approach can be used with the length and minLength facets.

Enumerations

One of the more useful types of restriction is the simple enumeration. In many cases, it is sufficient to restrict possible values for an element or attribute to a member of a predefined list. For example, values of the new locationType simple type defined earlier could be restricted to a list of valid options, like so:

```
<xs:simpleType name="locationType">
  <xs:restriction base="xs:string">
    <xs:enumeration value="work"/>
    <xs:enumeration value="home"/>
    <xs:enumeration value="mobile"/>
  </xs:restriction>
</xs:simpleType>
```

Then, if the location attribute in any instance document contained a value not found in the list of enumeration values, the schema processor would generate a validity error.

Numeric facets

Almost half of the of built-in data types defined by the schema specification represent numeric data of one type or another. The following two sections cover all of the numeric facets available, but see Chapter 22 for a comprehensive list of which of these facets are applicable to which data types.

Minimum and maximum values. Four facets control the minimum and maximum values of items:

- minInclusive
- minExclusive
- maxInclusive
- maxExclusive

The primary difference between the inclusive and exclusive flavors of the min and max facets is whether the value given is considered part of the set of allowable values. For example, the following two facet declarations are equivalent when restricting xs:integer:

```
<xs:maxInclusive value="0"/>
<xs:maxExclusive value="1"/>
```

The difference between inclusive and exclusive becomes more significant when dealing with decimal or floating-point values. For example, if minExclusive were set to 5.0, the equivalent minInclusive value would require an infinite number of nines to the right of the decimal point (4.99999). These facets can also be applied to date and time values.

Length and precision. There are two facets that control the length and precision of decimal numeric values: totalDigits and fractionDigits. The totalDigits facet determines the total number of digits (only digits are counted, not signs or decimal points) that are allowed in a complete number. fractionDigits determines the number of those digits that must appear to the right of the decimal point in the number.

Enforcing format

The xs:pattern facet can place very sophisticated restrictions on the format of string values. The pattern facet compares the value in question against a regular expression, and if the value doesn't conform to the expression, it generates a validation error. For example, this xs:simpleType element declares a Social Security number simple type using the pattern facet:

```
<xs:simpleType name="ssn">
  <xs:restriction base="xs:string">
    <xs:pattern value="\d\d\d-\d\d-\d\d\d\d"/>
  </xs:restriction>
</xs:simpleType>
```

This new simple type enforces the rule that a Social Security number consists of three digits, a dash followed by two digits, another dash, and finally four more digits. The actual regular expression language is very similar to that of the Perl programming language. See Chapter 22 for more information on the full pattern-matching language.

Lists

XML 1.0 provided a few very simple list types that could be declared as possible attribute values: IDREFS, ENTITIES, and NMTOKENS. Schemas have generalized the concept of lists and provide the ability to declare lists of arbitrary types.

These list types are themselves simple types and may be used in the same places other simple types are used. For example, if the fullName element were expanded to accommodate multiple middle names, one approach would be to declare the middle element to contain a list of nameString values:

```
<xs:element name="middle" type="addr:nameList" minOccurs="0"/>
. . .
<xs:complexType name="nameList">
  <xs:simpleContent>
    <xs:extension base="addr:nameListType"/>
  </xs:simpleContent>
</xs:complexType>

<xs:simpleType name="nameListType">
  <xs:list itemType="addr:nameString"/>
</xs:simpleType>
```

After this change has been made, the middle element of an instance document can contain an unlimited list of names, each of which can contain up to 50 characters separated by whitespace. The use of xs:complexType here will greatly simplify adding attributes later.

Unions

In some cases, it is useful to allow potential values for elements and attributes to have any of several types. The xs:union element allows a type to be declared that can draw from multiple type spaces. For example, it might be useful to allow users to enter their own one-word descriptions into the location attribute of the phone element, as well as to choose from a list. The location attribute declaration could be modified to include a union that incorporated the locationType type and the xs:NMTOKEN types:

```
<xs:attribute name="location">
 <xs:simpleType>
  <xs:union memberTypes="addr:locationType xs:NMTOKEN"/>
 </xs:simpleType>
</xs:attribute>
```

Now the location attribute can contain either addr:locationType or xs:NMTOKEN content.

Mixed Content

XML 1.0 provided the ability to declare an element that could contain parsed character data (#PCDATA) and unlimited occurrences of elements drawn from a provided list. Schemas provide the same functionality plus the ability to control the number and sequence in which elements appear within character data.

Allowing Mixed Content

The mixed attribute of the complexType element controls whether character data may appear within the body of the element with which it is associated. To illustrate this concept, Example 17-9 gives us a new schema that will be used to validate form-letter documents.

Example 17-9. formletter.xsd

```
<xs:schema xmlns:xs="http://www.w3.org/2001/XMLSchema">
  <xs:element name="letter">
    <xs:complexType mixed="true"/>
  </xs:element>
</xs:schema>
```

This schema seems to declare a single element called letter that may contain character data and nothing else. But attempting to validate the following document produces an error, as shown in Example 17-10.

Example 17-10. formletterdoc.xml

```
<letter xmlns:xsi="http://www.w3.org/2001/XMLSchema-instance"
  xsi:noNamespaceSchemaLocation="formletter.xsd">Hello!</letter>
```

The following error is generated:

```
The content of element type "letter" must match "EMPTY".
```

This is because there's no complex content for the letter element. Setting mixed to true is not the same as declaring an element that may contain a string. The character data may only appear in relation to other complex content, which leads to the subject of relative element positioning.

Controlling Element Placement

You have already seen the xs:sequence element, which dictates that the elements it contains must appear in exactly the same order in which they appear within the sequence element. In addition to xs:sequence, schemas also provide the xs:choice and xs:all elements to control the order in which elements may appear. These elements may be nested to create sophisticated element structures.

Expanding the form-letter example, a sequence adds support for various letter components to the formletter.xsd schema:

```
<xs:element name="letter">
  <xs:complexType mixed="true">
    <xs:sequence>
      <xs:element name="greeting"/>
      <xs:element name="body"/>
      <xs:element name="closing"/>
    </xs:sequence>
  </xs:complexType>
</xs:element>
```

Now, thanks to the xs:sequence element, a letter must include a greeting element, a body element, and a closing element, in that order. But, in some cases, what is desired is that one and only one element appear from a collection of possibilities. The xs:choice element supports this. For example, if the greeting element needed to be restricted to contain only one salutation out of a permissible list, it could be declared to do so using xs:choice:

```
<xs:element name="greeting">
  <xs:complexType mixed="true">
    <xs:choice>
      <xs:element name="hello"/>
      <xs:element name="hi"/>
      <xs:element name="dear"/>
    </xs:choice>
  </xs:complexType>
</xs:element>
```

Now one of the permitted salutations must appear in the greeting element for the letter to be considered valid.

The remaining element-order enforcement construct is the xs:all element. Unlike the xs:sequence and xs:choice elements, the xs:all element must appear at the top of the content model and can only contain elements that are optional or appear only once. The xs:all construct tells the schema processor that each of the contained elements must appear once in the target document, but can appear in any order. This could be applied in the form letter example. If the form letter had certain elements that had to appear in the body element, but not in any particular order, xs:all could be used to control their appearance:

```
<xs:element name="body">
  <xs:complexType mixed="true">
    <xs:all>
      <xs:element name="item"/>
      <xs:element name="price"/>
      <xs:element name="arrivalDate"/>
    </xs:all>
  </xs:complexType>
</xs:element>
```

This would allow the letter author to mix these elements into the narrative without being restricted to any particular order. Also, it would prevent the author from inserting multiple references to the same value by accident. A valid document instance, including the new body content, might look like Example 17-11.

Example 17-11. formletterdoc.xml

```
<letter xmlns:xsi="http://www.w3.org/2001/XMLSchema-instance"
  xsi:noNamespaceSchemaLocation="formletter.xsd">
  <greeting><hello/> Bob!</greeting>
  <body>
    Thank you for ordering the <item/> ($<price/>). It should arrive
    by <arrivalDate/>.
  </body>
  <closing/>
</letter>
```

 The element order constructs are not just limited to complex types with mixed content. If the mixed attribute is not present, the declared sequence of child elements is still enforced, but no character data is permitted between them.

Using Groups

Just as the xs:attributeGroup element allows commonly used attributes to be grouped together and referenced as a unit, the xs:group element allows sequences, choices, and model groups of individual element declarations to be grouped together and given a unique name. These groups can then be included in another element-content model using an xs:group element with the ref attribute set to the same value as the name attribute of the source group. When you do this, any occurrence constraints have to be specified on the reference to the group rather than on the definition of the group.

Allowing Any Content

It is often necessary to allow users to include any type of markup content they see fit. Also, it is useful to tell the schema processor to validate the content of a particular element against another application's schema. Incorporating XHTML content into another document is an example of this usage.

These applications are supported by the xs:any element. This element accepts attributes that indicate what level of validation should be performed on the included content, if any. Also, it accepts a target namespace that can be used to limit the vocabulary of included content. For instance, going back to the address-book example, to associate a rich-text notes element with an address entry, you could add the following element declaration to the address element declaration:

```
<xs:element name="notes" minOccurs="0">
  <xs:complexType>
    <xs:sequence>
      <xs:any namespace="http://www.w3.org/1999/xhtml"
              minOccurs="0" maxOccurs="unbounded"
              processContents="skip"/>
    </xs:sequence>
  </xs:complexType>
</xs:element>
```

The attributes of the xs:any element tell the schema processor that zero or more elements belonging to the XHTML namespace (http://www.w3.org/1999/xhtml) may occur at this location. Notice that this is done by setting minOccurs to 0 and maxOccurs to unbounded. It also states that these elements should be skipped. This means that no validation will be performed against the actual XHTML namespace by the parser. Other possible values for the processContents attribute are lax and strict. When set to lax, the processor will attempt to validate any element it can find a declaration for and silently ignore any unrecognized elements. The strict option requires every element to be declared and valid per the schema associated with the namespace given.

There is also support in schemas to declare that any attribute may appear within a given element. The xs:anyAttribute element may include the namespace and processContents attributes, which perform the same function as they do in the xs:any element. For example, adding the following markup to the address element would allow any XLink attributes to appear in an instance document:

```
<xs:element name="address">
  <xs:complexType>
    . . .
    <xs:attributeGroup ref="addr:nationality"/>
    <xs:attribute name="ssn" type="addr:ssn"/>
    <xs:anyAttribute namespace="http://www.w3.org/1999/xlink"
        processContents="skip"/>
  </xs:complexType>
</xs:element>
```

This style of vocabulary mixing may seem strange given the effort that normally goes into creating constraints with schemas, but it fits well with the architecture of XLink.

Using Multiple Documents

As an application grows and becomes more complex, it is important to take steps to maintain readability and extensibility. Things like separating a large schema into multiple documents, importing declarations from external schemas, and deriving new types from existing types are all typical tasks that will face designers of real-world schemas.

Just as large computer programs are separated into multiple physical source files, large schemas can be separated into smaller, self-contained schema documents. Although a single large schema could be arbitrarily separated into multiple smaller documents, taking the time to group related declarations into reusable modules can simplify future schema development.

There are three mechanisms that include declarations from external schemas for use within a given schema: xs:include, xs:redefine, and xs:import. The next three sections will discuss the differences between these methods and when and where they should be used.

Including external declarations

The xs:include element is the most straightforward way to bring content from an external schema into your own schema. To demonstrate how xs:include might be used, Example 17-12 shows a new schema document called *physical-address.xsd* that contains a declaration for a new complex type called physicalAddressType.

Example 17-12. physical-address.xsd

```
<xs:schema xmlns:xs="http://www.w3.org/2001/XMLSchema"
  targetNamespace="http://namespaces.oreilly.com/xmlnut/address"
  xmlns:addr="http://namespaces.oreilly.com/xmlnut/address"
  attributeFormDefault="qualified" elementFormDefault="qualified">

  <xs:annotation>
    <xs:documentation xml:lang="en-us">
      Simple schema example from O'Reilly's
      <a href="http://www.oreilly.com/catalog/xmlnut">XML in a
        Nutshell.</a>
      Copyright 2004 O'Reilly Media, Inc.
    </xs:documentation>
  </xs:annotation>

  <xs:complexType name="physicalAddressType">
    <xs:sequence>
      <xs:element name="street" type="xs:string" maxOccurs="3"/>
      <xs:element name="city" type="xs:string"/>
      <xs:element name="state" type="xs:string"/>
    </xs:sequence>
  </xs:complexType>

</xs:schema>
```

The *address-book.xsd* schema document can include and reference this declaration:

```
<xs:schema xmlns:xs="http://www.w3.org/2001/XMLSchema"
  targetNamespace="http://namespaces.oreilly.com/xmlnut/address"
  xmlns:addr="http://namespaces.oreilly.com/xmlnut/address"
  attributeFormDefault="qualified" elementFormDefault="qualified">
. . .

  <xs:include schemaLocation="physical-address.xsd"/>

  <xs:element name="address">
   <xs:complexType>
    <xs:sequence>
. . .
      <xs:element name="physicalAddress"
        type="addr:physicalAddressType"/>
. . .
    </xs:sequence>
. . .
   </xs:complexType>
  </xs:element>
```

Content that has been included using the xs:include element is treated as though it were actually a part of the including schema document. But unlike external entities, the included document must be a valid schema in its own right. That means that it must be a well-formed XML document and have an xs:schema element as its root element. Also, the target namespace of the included schema must match that of the including document. (It can include references to content defined in the including schema, however.)

Modifying external declarations

The xs:include element allows external declarations to be included and used as-is by another schema document. But, sometimes, it is useful to extend and modify types and declarations from another schema, which is where the xs:redefine element comes in.

Functionally, the xs:redefine elements works very much like the xs:include element. The major difference is that within the scope of the xs:redefine element, types from the included schema may be redefined without generating an error from the schema processor. For example, the xs:redefine element could extend the physicalAddressType type to include longitude and latitude attributes without modifying the original declaration in *physical-address.xsd*:

```
<xs:schema xmlns:xs="http://www.w3.org/2001/XMLSchema"
  targetNamespace="http://namespaces.oreilly.com/xmlnut/address"
  xmlns:addr="http://namespaces.oreilly.com/xmlnut/address"
  attributeFormDefault="qualified" elementFormDefault="qualified">
. . .
<xs:redefine schemaLocation="physical-address.xsd">
  <xs:complexType name="physicalAddressType">
    <xs:complexContent>
      <xs:extension base="addr:physicalAddressType">
```

```
          <xs:attribute name="latitude" type="xs:decimal"/>
          <xs:attribute name="longitude" type="xs:decimal"/>
        </xs:extension>
      </xs:complexContent>
    </xs:complexType>
  </xs:redefine>
  . . .
</xs:schema>
```

Importing schemas for other namespaces

The xs:include and xs:redefine elements are useful when the declarations are all part of the same application. But as more public schemas become available, incorporating declarations from external sources into custom applications will be important. The xs:import element is provided for this purpose.

Using xs:import, it is possible to make the global types and elements that are declared by a schema belonging to another namespace accessible from within an arbitrary schema. The W3C has used this functionality to create *type libraries*. A sample type library was developed by the schema working group and can be viewed on the W3C web site at *http://www.w3.org/2001/03/XMLSchema/TypeLibrary.xsd*. The library includes schema type declarations for representing text, arrays, lists, mathematics, measured quantities, and binary data.

To use some of the types from this library in a schema, include the following xs:import element as a child of the root schema element:

```
<xs:import namespace="http://www.w3.org/2001/03/XMLSchema/TypeLibrary"
    schemaLocation="http://www.w3.org/2001/03/XMLSchema/TypeLibrary.xsd"/>
```

Derived Complex Types

We have been using the xs:extension and xs:restriction elements without going too deeply into how or why they work. The schema language provides functionality for extending existing types, which is conceptually similar to that of inheritance in object-oriented programming. The extension and restriction elements allow new types to be defined either by expanding or limiting the potential values of existing types.

Deriving by extension

When deriving a new type from an existing type, the resulting type is equivalent to appending the contents of the new declaration to the contents of the base declaration. For instance, the following example declares a new type called mailingAddressType that extends the physicalAddressType type to include a Zip Code:

```
<xs:complexType name="mailingAddressType">
  <xs:complexContent>
    <xs:extension base="addr:physicalAddressType">
      <xs:sequence>
        <xs:element name="zipCode" type="xs:string"/>
```

XML Schemas

```
      </xs:sequence>
    </xs:extension>
  </xs:complexContent>
</xs:complexType>
```

This declaration appends a required element, zipCode, to the existing physicalAddressType type. The biggest benefit of this approach is that as new declarations are added to the underlying type, the derived type will automatically inherit them.

Deriving by restriction

When a new type is a logical subset of an existing type, the xs:restriction element allows this relationship to be expressed directly. Like the xs:extension type, it allows a new type to be created based on an existing type. In the case of simple types, this restriction is a straightforward application of additional constraints on the value of that simple value.

In the case of complex types, it is not quite so straightforward. Unlike the extension process, it is necessary to completely reproduce the parent type definition as part of the restriction definition. By omitting parts of the parent definition, the restriction element creates a new, constrained type. As an example, this xs:complexType element derives a new type from the physicalAddressType that only allows a single street element to contain the street address. The original physicalAddressType looks like:

```
<xs:complexType name="physicalAddressType">
  <xs:sequence>
    <xs:element name="street" type="xs:string" maxOccurs="3"/>
    <xs:element name="city" type="xs:string"/>
    <xs:element name="state" type="xs:string"/>
  </xs:sequence>
</xs:complexType>
```

The restricted version looks like:

```
<xs:complexType name="simplePhysicalAddressType">
  <xs:complexContent>
    <xs:restriction base="addr:physicalAddressType">
      <xs:sequence>
        <xs:element name="street" type="xs:string"/>
        <xs:element name="city" type="xs:string"/>
        <xs:element name="state" type="xs:string"/>
      </xs:sequence>
    </xs:restriction>
  </xs:complexContent>
</xs:complexType>
```

Notice that this type very closely resembles the physicalAddressType, except the maxOccurs="3" attribute has been removed from the street element declaration.

Using derived types

One of the chief benefits of creating derived types is that the derived type may appear in place of the parent type within an instance document. (Applications

---

that read the schema, like data binding applications, can use its type hierarchy for processing the document as well.) The xsi:type attribute tells the schema processor that the element on which it appears conforms to a type that is derived from the normal type expected. For example, take the instance document in Example 17-13, which conforms to the address schema.

Example 17-13. addressdoc.xml using a derived type

```
<?xml version="1.0"?>
<addr:address xmlns:xsi="http://www.w3.org/2001/XMLSchema-instance"
    xsi:schemaLocation="http://namespaces.oreilly.com/xmlnut/address
      address-schema.xsd"
    xmlns:addr="http://namespaces.oreilly.com/xmlnut/address"
    addr:language="en"
    addr:ssn="123-45-6789">
. . .
  <physicalAddress addr:latitude="34.003855" addr:longitude="-81.034808"
    xsi:type="addr:simplePhysicalAddressType">
    <street>1400 Main St.</street>
    <city>Columbia</city>
    <state>SC</state>
  </physicalAddress>
. . .
</addr:address>
```

Notice that the physicalAddress element has an xsi:type attribute that informs the validator that the current element conforms to the simplePhysicalAddressType, rather than the physicalAddressType that would normally be expected. This feature is particularly useful when developing internationalized applications, as distinct address types could be derived for each country and then flagged in the instance document for proper validation.

Substitution Groups

A feature that is closely related to derived types is the *substitution group*. A substitution group is a collection of elements that are all interchangeable with a particular element, called the *head element*, within an instance document. To create a substitution group, all that is required is that an element declaration include a substitutionGroup attribute that names the head element for that group. Then, anywhere that the head element's declaration is referenced in the schema, any member of the substitution group may also appear. Unlike derived types, it isn't necessary to use the xsi:type attribute in an instance document to identify the type of the substituted element.

 The primary restriction on substitution groups is that every element in the group must be either of the same type as or derived from the head element's type. Declaring a numeric element and trying to add it to a substitution group based on a string element would generate an error from the schema processor. The elements must also be declared globally and in the target namespace of the schema.

Controlling Type Derivation

Just as some object-oriented programming languages allow the creator of an object to dictate the limits on how an object can be extended, the schema language allows schema authors to place restrictions on type extension and restriction.

Abstract Elements and Types

The abstract attribute applies to type and element declarations. When it is set to true, that element or type cannot appear directly in an instance document. If an element is declared as abstract, a member of a substitution group based on that element must appear. If a type is declared as abstract, no element declared with that type may appear in an instance document.

The Final Attribute

Until now, the schema has placed no restrictions on how other types or elements could be derived from its elements and types. The final attribute can be added to a complex type definition and set to either #all, extension, or restriction. On a simple type definition, it can be set to #all or to a list containing any combination of the values list, union, and/or restriction, in any order. When a type is derived from another type that has the final attribute set, the schema processor verifies that the desired derivation is legal. For example, a final attribute could prevent the physicalAddressType type from being extended:

```
<xs:complexType name="physicalAddressType" final="extension">
```

Since the main schema in *address-schema.xsd* attempts to redefine the physicalAddressType in an xs:redefine block, the schema processor generates the following errors when it attempts to validate the instance document:

```
ComplexType 'physicalAddressType': cos-ct-extends.1.1: Derivation by
extension is forbidden by either the base type physicalAddressType_redefined
or the schema.
Attribute "addr:latitude" must be declared for element type
"physicalAddress".
Attribute "addr:longitude" must be declared for element type
"physicalAddress".
```

The first error is a result of trying to extend a type that has been marked to prevent extension. The next two errors occur because the new, extended type was not parsed and applied to the content in the document. Now that you've seen how this works, removing this particular "feature" from the physicalAddressType definition gets the schema working again.

Setting fixed Facets

Similar to the final attribute, the fixed attribute is provided to mark certain facets of simple types as immutable. Facets that have been marked as fixed="true" cannot be overridden in derived types.

Uniqueness and Keys

Perhaps one of the most welcome features of schemas is the ability to express more sophisticated relationships between values in elements and attributes of a document. The limitations of the primitive index capability provided by the XML 1.0 ID and IDREF attributes became readily apparent as documents began to include multiple distinct types of element data with complex data keys. The two facilities for enforcing element uniqueness in schemas are the xs:unique and xs:key elements.

Forcing uniqueness

The xs:unique element enforces element and attribute value uniqueness for a specified set of elements in a schema document. This uniqueness constraint is constructed in two phases. First, the set of all of the elements to be evaluated is defined using a restricted XPath expression. Next, the precise element and attribute values that must be unique are defined.

To illustrate, let's add logic to the address schema to prevent the same phone number from appearing multiple times within a given contacts element. To add this restriction, the element declaration for contacts includes a uniqueness constraint:

```
<xs:element name="contacts" type="addr:contactsType" minOccurs="0">
  <xs:unique name="phoneNums">
    <xs:selector xpath="addr:phone"/>
    <xs:field xpath="@addr:number"/>
  </xs:unique>
</xs:element>
```

Now, if a given contacts element contains two phone elements with the same value for their number attributes, the schema processor will generate an error.

This is the basic algorithm that the schema processor follows to enforce these restrictions:

1. Use the xpath attribute of the single xs:selector element to build a set of all of the elements to which the restriction will apply.

2. Logically combine the values referenced by each xs:field element for each selected element. Compare the combinations of values that you get for each of the elements.

3. Report any conflicts as a validity error.

 The very perceptive among you are right: the contactsType type definition only permits a single phone child element. So this particular restriction would not be very useful. Modifying the contactsType definition to permit multiple child elements is not difficult.

Keys and references

The xs:key element is closely related to the xs:unique element. Logically, the xs:key element functions exactly the same way the xs:unique element does. It uses the xs:selector element to define a set of elements it applies to, then one or more xs:field elements are used to define which values make up this particular key. The difference between these elements is that xs:key says that every selected element *must* have a value for each of the fields specified, whereas with xs:unique, it doesn't matter if some of the selected elements don't have values for the fields. Having created a fairly full-featured address element, creating a collection of these elements called addressBook would be an excellent way to show this feature in operation.

First, the new addressBook element is declared, including a key based on the ssn attribute of each address entry:

```
<xs:element name="addressBook">
  <xs:complexType>
    <xs:sequence maxOccurs="unbounded">
      <xs:element ref="addr:address"/>
    </xs:sequence>
  </xs:complexType>
  <xs:key name="ssnKey">
    <xs:selector xpath="addr:address"/>
    <xs:field xpath="@addr:ssn"/>
  </xs:key>
</xs:element>
```

(If the ssn attribute was optional, you'd need to use xs:unique rather than xs:key in this example.)

Now that the key is defined, you can add a new element to the address element declaration that connects a particular address record with another record. For example, to list references to the children of a particular person in the address book, add the following declaration for a kids element:

```
<xs:element name="address">
  <xs:complexType>
    <xs:sequence>
      <xs:element name="fullName">
. . .
      </xs:element>
      <xs:element name="kids" minOccurs="0">
        <xs:complexType>
          <xs:sequence maxOccurs="unbounded">
            <xs:element name="kid">
              <xs:complexType>
                <xs:attribute name="ssn" type="addr:ssn"/>
              </xs:complexType>
            </xs:element>
          </xs:sequence>
        </xs:complexType>
      </xs:element>
. . .
    </xs:sequence>
    <xs:attributeGroup ref="addr:nationality"/>
    <xs:attribute name="ssn" type="addr:ssn"/>
    <xs:anyAttribute namespace="http://www.w3.org/1999/xlink"
        processContents="skip"/>
  </xs:complexType>
</xs:element>
```

Now, an xs:keyref element in the addressBook element declaration enforces the constraint that the ssn attribute of a particular kid element must match an ssn attribute on an address element in the current document:

```
<xs:element name="addressBook">
  . . .
  <xs:key name="ssnKey">
    <xs:selector xpath="addr:address"/>
    <xs:field xpath="@addr:ssn"/>
  </xs:key>
  <xs:keyref name="kidSSN" refer="addr:ssnKey">
    <xs:selector xpath="addr:address/addr:kids/addr:kid"/>
    <xs:field xpath="@addr:ssn"/>
  </xs:keyref>
</xs:element>
```

Now, if any kid element in an instance document refers to a nonexistent address record, the schema validator will report an error.

XML Schemas

18

Programming Models

This chapter briefly explains the most popular programming techniques for parsing, manipulating, and generating XML data. XML support is available for virtually every programming platform in use today, from supercomputer to cell phone. If you can't find XML support built into your programming environment, a quick Google search will likely locate a library.

Common XML Processing Models

XML's structured and tagged text can be processed by developers in several ways. Programs can look at XML as plain text, as a stream of events, as a tree, or as a serialization of some other structure. Tools supporting all of these options are widely available.

Text-Based XML Processing

At their foundation, XML documents are text. The content and markup are both represented as text, and text-editing tools can be extremely useful for XML document inspection, creation, and modification. XML's textual foundations make it possible for developers to work with XML directly, using XML-specific tools only when they choose to.

One of the original design goals of XML was for documents to be easy to parse. For very simple documents that do not depend on features such as attribute defaulting and validation, it is possible to parse tags, attributes, and text data using standard programming tools such as regular expressions and tokenizers, but the complexity of processing grows rapidly as documents use more features. Unless the application can completely control the content of incoming documents, it is almost always preferable to use one of the many high-quality XML parsers that are freely available for most programming languages.

Textual tools are a key part of the XML toolset, however. Many developers use text editors such as *vi*, Emacs, NotePad, WordPad, BBEdit, and UltraEdit to create or modify XML documents. Regular expressions—in environments such as sed, grep, Perl, and Python—can be used for search and replace or for tweaking documents prior to XML parsing or XSLT processing. Various standards are beginning to take advantage of regular expression matching after a particular document has been parsed. The W3C's XML Schema recommendation, for instance, includes regular-expression matching as one mechanism for validating data types, as discussed in Chapter 17.

Text-based processing can be performed in conjunction with other XML processing. Parsing and then serializing XML documents after other processing has taken place doesn't always produce the desired results. XSLT, for instance, will remove entity references and replace them with entity content. Preserving entities requires replacing them in the original document with unique place-holders, and then replacing the placeholder as it appears in the result. With regular expressions, this is quite easy to do.

 XML's dependence on Unicode means that developers need to be careful about the text-processing tools they choose. Many development environments have been upgraded to support Unicode, but there are still tools available that don't. Before using text-processing tools on the results of an XML parse, make sure they support Unicode. Text-processing tools being applied to raw XML documents must support the character encoding used for the document. Most modern languages (including Java, C#, Perl 5.6, and Python 2.2) and tools support Unicode. The difficult cases tend to arise in C and C++ where you have to worry about using wchar versus char and understand what a wchar actually is on a particular platform.

Event-Driven XML Processing

As an XML parser reads a document, it moves from the beginning of the document to the end. It may pause to retrieve external resources—for a DTD or an external entity, for instance—but it builds an understanding of the document as it moves along. Tree-based XML technologies (such as the DOM) combine these incremental parsing events into a monolithic image of an XML document once parsing has been completed successfully.

Event-based parsers, on the other hand, report these interim events to their client applications as they happen. Some common parsing events are element start-tag read, element content read, and element end-tag read. For example, consider the document in Example 18-1.

Example 18-1. Simple XML document

```
<name><given>Keith</given><family>Johnson</family></name>
```

An event-based parser might report events such as this:

```
startElement:name
startElement:given
content: Keith
endElement:given
startElement:family
content:Johnson
endElement:family
endElement:name
```

The list and structure of events can become much more complex as features such as namespaces, attributes, whitespace between elements, comments, processing instructions, and entities are added, but the basic mechanism is quite simple and generally very efficient.

Event-based applications are generally more complex than tree-based applications. Processing events typically means the creation of a state machine, code that understands the current context and can route the information in the events to the proper consumer. Because events occur as the document is read, applications must be prepared to discard results should a fatal error occur partway through the document. Also, accessing a wide variety of data scattered throughout a document is much more involved than it would be if the entire document were parsed into a tree structure.

The upside to an event-based API is speed and efficiency. Because event-based APIs stream the document to the client application, your program can begin working with the data from the beginning of the document before the end of the document is seen. It doesn't have to wait for the entire document to be read before commencing. For instance, a brokerage program receiving a long list of requests to buy individual stocks could execute the first trade before the parser reads the second trade, execute the second trade before the parser reads the third trade, and so forth. This could save crucial seconds on the initial trades if the document includes many separate orders.

Even more important than speed is size. XML documents can be quite large, sometimes ranging into the gigabytes. An event-based API does not need to store all this data in memory at one time. It can process the document in small, easily handled chunks, then reclaim that storage. In practice, even on the largest, beefiest servers with gigabytes of RAM, XML documents larger than a couple of hundred megabytes can't be processed with a tree-based API. In an embedded environment (like a cell phone), memory limitations mandate streaming APIs.

Event-based parsers also more naturally fit certain tasks, such as content filtering. Filters can process and modify events before passing them to another processor, efficiently performing a wide range of transformations. Filters can be chained, providing a relatively simple means of building XML processing pipelines, where the information from one processor flows directly into another. Applications that want to feed information directly from XML documents into their own internal structures may find events to be the most efficient means of doing that. Even parsers that report XML documents as complete trees, as described in the next section, typically build those trees from a stream of events.

The Simple API for XML (SAX), described in Chapters 20 and 26, is the most commonly used event-based API. SAX2, the current version, is hosted at *http://sax.sourceforge.net/*. Expat, a widely used XML parser written in C, also uses an event-based API. For information on the expat parser and its API, see *http://expat.sourceforge.net*.

Tree-based XML Processing

XML documents, because of the requirements for well-formedness, can be readily described using tree structures. Elements are inherently hierarchical, as they may contain other elements, text content, comments, and so forth.

There is a wide variety of tree models for XML documents. XPath (described in Chapter 9), used in XSLT transformations, has a slightly different set of expectations than does the Document Object Model (DOM) API, which is also different from the XML Information Set (Infoset), another W3C project. XML Schema (described in Chapter 17 and 22) defines a Post-Schema Validation Infoset (PSVI), which has more information in it (derived from the XML Schema) than any of the others.

Developers who want to manipulate documents from their programs typically use APIs that provide access to an object model representing the XML document. Tree-based APIs typically present a model of an entire document to an application once parsing has successfully concluded. Applications don't have to worry about manually maintaining parsing context or partial processing when a parse error is encountered, as the tree-based parser generally handles errors on its own. Rather than following a stream of events, an application can just navigate through the tree to find the desired pieces of a document.

Working with a tree model has substantial advantages. The entire document is always available, and moving well-balanced portions of a document from one place to another or modifying them is fairly easy. The complete context for any given part of the document is always available. When using APIs that support it, developers can use XPath expressions to locate content and make decisions based on content anywhere in the document. (DOM Level 3 adds formal support for XPath, and various implementations already provide their own nonstandard support.)

Tree models of documents have a few drawbacks. They can take up large amounts of memory, typically three to ten times the original document's file size. Navigating documents can require additional processing after the parse, as developers have more options available to them. (Tree models don't impose the same kinds of discipline as event-based processing.) These issues can make it difficult to scale and share applications that rely on tree models, although they may still be appropriate where small numbers of documents or small documents are being used.

The Document Object Model (DOM), described in Chapters 19 and 25, is the most common tree-based API. JDOM (*http://jdom.org/*), DOM4J (*http://dom4j.org/*), and XOM (*http://www.cafeconleche.org/ XOM*) are Java-only alternatives. (XOM is an object model promoted by Elliotte Rusty Harold, one of the authors.)

Pull-Based XML Processing

The most recent entrant into the XML processing arena is the so-called *pull* processing model. One of the most widely used pull processors is the Microsoft .NET XMLReader class. The pull model is most similar to the event-based model in that it makes the contents of the XML document available progressively as the document is parsed.

Unlike the event model, the pull approach relies on the client application to request content from the parser at its own pace. For example, a pull client might include the following code to parse the simple document shown in Example 18-1:

```
reader.ReadStartElement("name")
reader.ReadStartElement("given")
givenName = reader.ReadString( )
reader.ReadEndElement( )
reader.ReadStartElement("family")
familyName = reader.ReadString( )
reader.ReadEndElement( )
reader.ReadEndElement( )
```

The pull client requests the XML content it expects to see from the pull parser. In practice, this makes pull client code easier to read and understand than the corresponding event-based code would be. It also tends to reduce the need to create stacks and structures to contain document information, as the code itself can be written to mirror recursive descent parsing.

In the Java world, BEA, Sun, and several individual developers have collaborated to create the Streaming API for XML (StAX). StAX and other pull parsers share the advantages of streaming with SAX such as speed, parallelism, and memory efficiency while offering an API that is more comfortable to many developers. In essence, SAX and other push parsers are based on the Observer design pattern. StAX, XMLReader, and other pull parsers are based on the Iterator design pattern.

Transformations

Another facility available to the XML programmer is document transformation. The Extensible Stylesheet Language Transformation (XSLT) language, covered in Chapter 8, is the most popular tool currently available for transforming XML to HTML, XML, or any other regular language that can be expressed in XSLT. In some cases, using a transformation to perform pre- or post-processing on XML data can reduce the complexity of a DOM or SAX application. For instance, XSLT could be used as a preprocessor for a screen-scraping application that starts from XHTML documents. The complex XHTML document could be transformed into a smaller, more accessible application-specific XML format that could then be read by a script.

Transformations may be used by themselves, in browsers, or at the command line, but many XSLT implementations and other transformation tools offer SAX or DOM interfaces, simplifying the task of using them to build document processing pipelines.

Abstracting XML Away

Developers who want to take advantage of XML's cross-platform benefits but have no patience for the details of markup can use various tools that rely on XML but don't require direct exposure to XML's structures. Web Services, mentioned in Chapter 16, can be seen as a move in this direction. You can still touch the XML directly if you need to, but toolkits make it easier to avoid doing so.

These kinds of applications are generally built as a layer on top of event- or tree-based processing, presenting their own API to the underlying information. We feel that in most cases, the underlying XML data is as clear and accessible as it can be. Additional layers of abstraction above the XML simply add to the overall complexity and rigidity of the application.

Standards and Extensions

The SAX and DOM specifications, along with the various core XML specifications, provide a foundation for XML processing. Implementations of these standards, especially implementations of the DOM, sometimes vary from the specification. Some extensions are formally specified—Scalable Vector Graphics (SVG), for instance, specifies extensions to the DOM that are specific to working with SVG. Others are just kind of tacked on, adding functionality that a programmer or vendor felt was important but wasn't in the original specification. The multiple levels and modules of the DOM have also led to developers claiming support for the DOM but actually supporting particular subsets (or extensions) of the available specifications.

Porting standards also leads to variations. SAX was developed for Java, and the core SAX project only defines a Java API. The DOM uses Interface Definition Language (IDL) to define its API, but various implementations have interpreted the IDL slightly differently. SAX2 and the DOM are somewhat portable, but moving between environments may require some unlearning and relearning.

Some environments also offer libraries well outside the SAX and DOM interfaces. Perl and Python both offer libraries that combine event and tree processing—for instance, permitting applications to work on partial trees rather than SAX events or full DOM trees. These nonstandard approaches do not make moving between environments easy, but they can be very useful.

Combining Approaches

While text, events, trees, and transformations may seem very different, it isn't unusual to combine them. Most parsers that produce DOM trees also offer the option of SAX events, and there are a number of tools that can create DOM trees from SAX events or vice versa. Some tools that accept and generate SAX events actually build internal trees—many XSLT processors operate this way, using optimized internal models for their trees rather than the generic DOM. XSLT processors themselves often accept either SAX events or DOM trees as input and can produce these models (or text) for their output.

Most programmers who want direct access to XML documents start with DOM trees, which are easier to figure out initially. If they have problems that are better solved in event-based environments, they can either rewrite their code for events—it's a big change—or mix and match event processing with tree processing.

Common XML Processing Issues

As with any technology, there are several ways to accomplish most design goals when developing a new XML application, as well as a few potential problems worth knowing about ahead of time. An understanding of the intended uses for these features can help ensure that new applications will be compatible not only with their intended target audience, but also with other XML processing systems that may not even exist yet.

What You Get Is Not What You Saw

The XML specification provides several loopholes that permit XML parsers to play fast and loose with your document's literal contents, while retaining the semantic meaning. Comments can be omitted and entity references silently replaced by the parser without any warning to the client application. Non-validating parsers aren't required to retrieve external DTDs or entities, although the parser should at least warn applications that this is happening. While reconstructing an XML document with exactly the same logical structure and content is possible, guaranteeing that it will match the original in a byte-by-byte comparison generally is not.

> XML Canonicalization defines a more consistent form of XML and a process for producing it that permits a much higher degree of predictability in reconstructing a document from its logical model. For details, see *http://www.w3.org/TR/xml-c14n*.

Authors of simple XML processing tools that act on data without storing or modifying it might not consider these constraints particularly restrictive. The ability to reconstruct an XML document precisely from in-memory data structures, however, becomes more critical for authors of XML editing tools and content-management solutions. While no parser is required to make all comments, whitespace, and entity references available from the parse stream, many do or can be made to do so with the proper configuration options.

The only real option to ensure that a parser reports documents as you want, and not just the minimum required by the XML specification, is to check its documentation and configure (or choose) the parser accordingly.

To Read the DTD or Not To Read the DTD?

DTDs come in two forms: internal and external and sometimes both. The XML specification requires all parsers to read the internal DTD subset. Validation requires reading the external DTD subset (if any); but if you don't validate, this is optional. Reading the external DTD subset takes extra time, especially if the DTD is large and/or stored on a remote network host, so you may not want to load it if you're not validating. Most parsers provide options to specify whether the external DTD subset and other external entities should be resolved. If validation were all a DTD did, then the decision of whether to load the DTD would be easy. Unfortunately, DTDs also augment a document's infoset with several important properties, including:

- Entity definitions
- Default attribute values
- Whether boundary whitespace is ignorable

At the extreme, since a document with a malformed DTD is itself malformed, a DTD can make a document readable or unreadable. This means whether a parser reads the external DTD subset or not can have a significant impact on what the parser reports. For maximum interoperability documents should be served without external DTD subsets. In this case parser behavior is deterministic and reproducible, regardless of configuration. On the flip side a consumer of XML documents should attempt to read any external DTD subset the document references if they want to be sure of receiving what the sender intended. Be conservative in what you send (don't use external DTD subsets) and liberal in what you accept (do read any external DTD subsets for documents you receive).

Whitespace

How parsers treat whitespace is one of the most commonly misunderstood areas of XML processing. There are four basic rules you need to remember:

1. All whitespace in element content is always reported.
2. Whitespace in attribute values is *normalized*.
3. Whitespace in the prolog and epilog and within tags but outside attribute values is not reported.
4. All non-escaped line breaks (carriage returns, line feeds, carriage return-line feed pairs, and, in XML 1.1, NEL and line separator) are converted to line feeds.

Consider Example 18-2.

Example 18-2. Various kinds of whitespace

```
<?xml version="1.0"?>

<!DOCTYPE person  SYSTEM "person.dtd ">

<person  source="Alan Turing: the Enigma,
                 Andrew Hodges, 1983">
  <name>
    <first>Alan</first>
    <last>Turing</last>
  </name>
  <profession  id="p1"
               value="computer  scientist "
               source="" />
```

Example 18-2. Various kinds of whitespace (continued)

```
<profession  id="p2"
             value="mathematician"/>
<profession  id="p3"
             value="cryptographer"/>
</person>
```

When a parser reads this document, it will report all the whitespace in the element content to the client application. This includes boundary whitespace like that between the <name> and <first> start-tags and the </last> and </name> end-tags. If the DTD says that the name element cannot contain mixed content, the whitespace is considered to be *whitespace in element content*, also called *ignorable whitespace*. However, the parser still reports it. The client application receiving the content from the parser may choose to ignore boundary whitespace, whether it's ignorable or not, interpreting it as purely for the purpose of pretty printing; but that's up to the client application. The parser always reports it all.

The parser does *not* report the line breaks and other whitespace in the prolog and epilog. Nor does it report the line breaks and whitespace in the tags such as that between the id and value attributes in the profession elements. Nothing in your program should depend on this.

The parser will normalize all the whitespace in attribute values. At a minimum, this means it will turn line breaks like those in the source attribute into spaces. If the DTD says the attribute has type CDATA or does not declare it, or if the DTD has not been read or does not exist, then that's all. However, if the attribute has any other type such as ID, NMTOKENS, or an enumeration, then the parser will strip all leading and trailing whitespace from the attribute and compress all remaining runs of whitespace to a single space each. However, normalization is only performed on literal whitespace. Spaces, tabs, line feeds, and carriage returns embedded with character or entity references are converted to their replacement text and then retained. They are not normalized like literal whitespace.

Entity References

There are three kinds of references in XML instance documents (plus another couple in the DTD we can ignore for the moment):

1. Numeric character references, such as   and

2. The five predefined entity references, &, >, ", ', and <

3. General entity references defined by the DTD, such as &chapter1; and

The first two kinds are easy to handle. The parser always resolves them and never tells you anything about them. As a parser client, you can simply ignore these and the right thing will happen. The parser will report the replacement text in the same way it reports regular text. It won't ever tell you that these entity references were used. On rare occasion you may be able to set a special property on the parser to have it tell you about these things, but you almost never want to do that. The only case where that might make sense is if you're writing an XML editor that tries to round-trip the source form of a document.

The third case is trickier. These entity references may refer to external files on remote sites you don't necessarily want to connect to for reasons of performance, availability, or security. Even if they're internal entities, they may be defined in the external DTD subset in a remote document. Parsers vary in whether they load such entities by default. Most parsers and APIs do provide a means of specifying whether external entities should or should not be loaded, although this is not universal. For instance, XOM always resolves external entities, while the XML parser in Mozilla never resolves them. Parsers that do not resolve an external entity should nevertheless notify the client application that the entity was not loaded—for instance, calling `skippedEntity()` in SAX or inserting an `EntityReference` object into the tree in DOM. How the program responds to such notifications is a question that must be answered in the context of each application. Sometimes it's a fatal problem. Other times it's something you can work around or even ignore, but do be aware that you need to consider this possibility unless the parser is configured to always resolve external entities.

Recently, a few parser vendors have become concerned about the so-called billion laugh attacks. In brief, it works by defining entity references that progressively double in size, especially in the internal DTD subset where the entities must be resolved:

```
<!ENTITY ha1 "Ha! ">
<!ENTITY ha2 "&ha1; &ha1;">
<!ENTITY ha3 "&ha2; &ha2;">
<!ENTITY ha4 "&ha3; &ha3;">
<!ENTITY ha5 "&ha4; &ha4;">
<!ENTITY ha6 "&ha5; &ha5;">
...
<!ENTITY ha31 "&ha30; &ha30;">
<!ENTITY ha32 "&ha31; &ha31;">
...
<root>&ha32;</root>
```

So far this attack is purely theoretical. Nonetheless, some parser vendors have started adding options to their parsers not to resolve entities defined in the internal DTD subset either (which is nonconformant to the XML Recommendation). Other palliatives include setting maximum limits on entity size or recursion depth in entity reference. In general these options are not turned on by default, because they are nonconformant.

CDATA Sections

The golden rule of handling CDATA sections is this: ignore them. When writing code to process XML, pretend CDATA sections do not exist, and everything will work just fine. The content of a CDATA section is plain text. It will be reported to your application as plain text, just like any other text, whether enclosed in a CDATA section, escaped with character references, or typed out literally when escaping is not necessary. For example, these two example elements are exactly the same as far as anything in your code should know or care:

```
<example><![CDATA[<?xml version="1.0"?>
<root>
```

```
   Hello!
</root>]]></example>
<example>&lt;?xml version="1.0"?>
&lt;root>
   Hello!
&lt;/root></example>
```

Do not write programs or XML documents that depend on knowing the difference between the two. Parsers rarely (and never reliably) inform you of the
difference. Furthermore, passing such documents through a processing chain
often removes the CDATA sections completely, leaving only the content intact but
represented differently—for instance, with numeric character references representing the unserializable characters. CDATA sections are a minor convenience for
human authors, nothing more. Do not treat them as markup.

This also means you should not attempt to nest one XML (or HTML) document
inside another using CDATA sections. XML documents are not designed to nest
inside one another. The correct solution to this problem is to use namespaces to
sort out which markup is which, rather than trying to treat a document as an
envelope for other documents. Similarly do not use CDATA sections to escape
malformed markup such as is found in many HTML systems. Instead, use a tool
such as Tidy to correct the malformed HTML before embedding it in an XML
document.

Comments

Despite a long history in HTML of using comments for tasks like Server-Side
Includes (SSI) and for hiding JavaScript code and Cascading Style Sheets, using
comments for anything other than human-readable notes is generally a bad idea in
XML. XML parsers may (and frequently do) discard comments entirely, keeping
them from reaching an application at all. Transformations generally discard
comments as well.

Processing Instructions

XML parsers are required to provide client applications access to XML processing
instructions. Processing instructions provide a mechanism for document authors
to communicate with XML-aware applications behind the scenes in a way that
doesn't interfere with the content of the document. DTD and schema validation
both ignore processing instructions, making it possible to use them anywhere in a
document structure without changing the DTD or schema. The processing
instruction's most widely recognized application is its ability to embed stylesheet
references inside XML documents. The following XML fragment shows a
stylesheet reference:

```
<?xml-stylesheet type="text/css" href="test.css"?>
```

An XML-aware application, such as Internet Explorer 6.0, would be capable of
recognizing the XML author's intention to display the document using the *test.css*
stylesheet. This processing instruction can also be used to link to XSLT stylesheets
or other kinds of stylesheets not yet developed, although the client application
needs to understand how to process them to make this work. Applications that do

not understand the processing instructions can still parse and use the information in the XML document while ignoring the unfamiliar processing instruction.

The furniture example from Chapter 21 (see Figure 21-1) gives a hypothetical application of processing instructions. A processing instruction in the *bookcase.xml* file signals the furniture example's processor to verify the parts list from the document against the true list of parts required to build the furniture item:

```
<parts_list>
    <part_name id="A" count="1">END PANEL</part_name>
    <part_name id="B" count="2">SIDE PANEL</part_name>
    <part_name id="C" count="1">BACK PANEL</part_name>
    <part_name id="D" count="4">SHELF</part_name>
    <part_name id="E" count="8">HIDDEN CONNECTORS</part_name>
    <part_name id="F" count="8">CONNECTOR SCREWS</part_name>
    <part_name id="G" count="22">7/16" TACKS</part_name>
    <part_name id="H" count="16">SHELF PEGS</part_name>
</parts_list>

<?furniture_app    verify_parts_list?>
```

This processing instruction is meaningless unless the parsing application understands the given type of processing instruction.

The XML specification also permits the association of the processing instruction's target—the XML name immediately after the <? with a notation, as described in the next section—but this is not required and is rarely used in XML.

Notations

The notation syntax of XML provides a way for the document author to specify an external unparsed entity's type within the XML document's framework. If an application requires access to external data that cannot be represented in XML, consider declaring a notation name and using it where appropriate when declaring external unparsed entities. For example, if an XML application were an annotated Java source-code format, the compiled bytecode could then be referenced as an external unparsed entity.

Notations effectively provide metadata, identifiers that applications may apply to information. Using notations requires making declarations in the DTD, as described in Chapter 3. One use of notations is with NOTATION-type attributes. For example, if a document contained various scripts designed for different environments, it might declare some notations and then use an attribute on a containing element to identify what kind of script it contained:

```
<!NOTATION DOS PUBLIC "-//MS/DOS Batch File/">
<!NOTATION BASH PUBLIC "-//UNIX/BASH Shell Script/">
<!ELEMENT batch_code (#PCDATA)*>
<!ATTLIST batch_code
    lang NOTATION (DOS | BASH)>
. . .
<batch_code lang="DOS">
  echo Hello, world!
</batch_code>
```

Applications that read this document and recognized the public identifier could interpret the foreign element data correctly, based on its type. (Notations can also have system identifiers, and applications can use either approach.)

Categorizing processing instructions is the other use of notations. For instance, the previous furniture_app processing-instruction example could have been declared as a notation in the DTD:

```
<!NOTATION furniture_app SYSTEM "http://namespaces.example.com/furniture">
```

Then the furniture-document processing application could verify that the processing instruction was actually intended for itself and not for another application that used a processing instruction with the same name.

Unparsed Entities

Unparsed entities combine attribute and notation declarations to define references to content that will require further (unspecified) processing by the application. Unparsed entities are described in more detail in Chapter 3, but although they are a feature available to applications, they are also rarely used.

Generating XML Documents

One area of XML development that isn't often addressed is that of generating XML documents for consumption by other applications. Although there are several approaches for processing XML documents, there are relatively few techniques currently used to create new documents.

One of the simplest (and most common) approaches is to use the string and/or file processing facilities of your target development environment to construct the XML document directly. This approach has the benefit of being easy to understand, efficient, and readily accessible to every programmer. This Java statement emits a simple XML document to a file output stream:

```
FileWriter out = new FileWriter("message.xml");
out.write("<message>Hello, world!</message>");
```

It's not hard to see how this approach would be implemented in any other programming language. For example, in C++, the following statement creates the desired result:

```
ofstream fout;
fout.open("message.xml", ios::app);
fout << "<message>Hello, world!</message>";
```

This is a completely valid approach, and it should be considered when the XML document is not overly complex and the structure of the document will not change substantially over the lifetime of the application. The disadvantage of this approach is that it is much easier to generate a document that is not well-formed or is invalid, since no validation or verification of the structure of the document occurs as it is generated. When using this technique, you of course have to make sure that both your code and the data coming in will produce well-formed XML.

If all of that data validation sounds like a hassle, you may want to explore Genx (*http://www.tbray.org/ongoing/genx/docs/Guide.html*), a C library created by Tim Bray, one of the editors of the XML specification, that generates Canonical XML.

Another common approach involves using a tree-based API, such as the DOM, to create an XML document tree dynamically. The benefit of this approach is that the library enforces well-formedness constraints, and in the case of DOM Level 3, it can be configured to enforce validity constraints as well.

The disadvantage of the library approach is that it is frequently more complex and less efficient than the simple string-processing approach. This code fragment creates the same document as before but with DOM:

```
DOMImplementation di;
...
di.createDocument(null, null, null);
Document doc;
Element elMsg = doc.createElement("message");
elMsg.appendChild(doc.createTextNode("Hello, world!"));
doc.appendChild(elMsg);
LSSerializer lss;
. . .
FileWriter out = new FileWriter("message.xml");
out.write(lss.writeToString(doc));
```

This is quite a bit more complex than the simple string-based approach shown previously.

Programming
Models

19

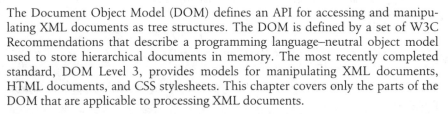

Document Object Model (DOM)

The Document Object Model (DOM) defines an API for accessing and manipulating XML documents as tree structures. The DOM is defined by a set of W3C Recommendations that describe a programming language–neutral object model used to store hierarchical documents in memory. The most recently completed standard, DOM Level 3, provides models for manipulating XML documents, HTML documents, and CSS stylesheets. This chapter covers only the parts of the DOM that are applicable to processing XML documents.

This chapter is based on the DOM Level 3 Core Recommendation, which was released on April 7, 2004. This version of the recommendation, along with any errata that have been reported, is available on the W3C web site (*http://www.w3.org/TR/DOM-Level-3-Core/*). Level 3 introduces several key features that were lacking from earlier DOM Levels, including:

- Validation—it is now possible to enforce validity constraints during programmatic manipulation of the DOM tree.

- Type information—post-validation element and attribute type information is now available through standard DOM interfaces.

- Support for XML 1.1—allows the developer to select which version of the XML recommendation a given DOM document will conform to.

DOM Foundations

At its heart, the DOM is a set of abstract interfaces. Various DOM implementations use their own objects to support the interfaces defined in the DOM specification. The DOM interfaces themselves are specified in modules, making it possible for implementations to support parts of the DOM without having to support all of it. XML parsers, for instance, aren't required to provide support for the HTML-specific parts of the DOM, and modularization has provided a simple mechanism that allows software developers to identify which parts of the DOM are supported or not supported by a particular implementation.

Successive versions of the DOM are defined as *levels*. The Level 1 DOM was the W3C's first release, and it focused on working with HTML and XML in a browser context. Effectively, it supported dynamic HTML and provided a base for XML document processing. Because it expected documents to exist already in a browser context, Level 1 only described an object structure and how to manipulate it, not how to load a document into that structure or reserialize a document from that structure.

Subsequent levels have added functionality. DOM Level 2, which was published as a set of specifications, one per module, includes updates for the Core and HTML modules of Level 1, as well as new modules for Views, Events, Style, Traversal, and Range. DOM Level 3 added Abstract Schemas, Load, Save, XPath, and updates to the Core and Events modules.

Other W3C specifications have defined extensions to the DOM particular to their own needs. Mathematical Markup Language (MathML), Scalable Vector Graphics (SVG), Synchronized Multimedia Integration Language (SMIL), and SMIL Animation have all defined DOMs that provide access to details of their own vocabularies.

For a complete picture of the requirements these modules are supposed to address, see *http://www.w3.org/TR/DOM-Requirements*. For a listing of all of the DOM specifications, including those still under development, see *http://www.w3.org/DOM/DOMTR*. The DOM has also been included by reference in a variety of other specifications, notably the Java API for XML Processing (JAXP).

Developers using the DOM for XML processing typically rely on the Core module as the foundation for their work.

DOM Notation

The Document Object Model is intended to be operating system- and language-neutral; therefore, all DOM interfaces are specified using the Interface Description Language (IDL) notation defined by the Object Management Group. To conform to the language of the specification, this chapter and Chapter 25 will use IDL terminology when discussing interface specifics. For example, the word "attribute" in IDL-speak refers to what would be a member variable in C++. This should not be confused with the XML term "attribute," which is a name-value pair that appears within an element's start-tag.

The language-independent IDL interface must then be translated (according to the rules set down by the OMG) into a specific language binding. Take the following interface, for example:

```
interface NodeList {
    Node                    item(in unsigned long index);
    readonly attribute unsigned long    length;
};
```

This interface would be expressed as a Java interface like this:

```
package org.w3c.dom;

public interface NodeList {
    public Node item(int index);

    public int getLength( );

}
```

The same interface would be described for ECMAScript this way:

```
Object NodeList
    The NodeList object has the following properties:
      length
        This read-only property is of type Number.
    The NodeList object has the following methods:
      item(index)
        This method returns a Node object.
        The index parameter is of type Number.
        Note: This object can also be dereferenced using square
        bracket notation (e.g. obj[1]). Dereferencing with an
        integer index is equivalent to invoking the item method
        with that index.
```

The tables in this chapter represent the information DOM presents as IDL, conveying both the available features and when they became available. DOM implementations vary in their interpretations of these features—be sure to check the documentation of the implementation you choose for details on how it maps the standard DOM interfaces to your particular language.

DOM Strengths and Weaknesses

Like all programming tools, the DOM is better for addressing some classes of problems than others. Since the DOM object hierarchy stores references between the various nodes in a document, the entire document must be read and parsed before it is available to a DOM application. This step also demands that the entire document be stored in memory, often with a significant amount of overhead. Some early DOM implementations required many times the original document's size when stored in memory. This memory usage model makes DOM unsuitable for applications that deal with very large documents or have a need to perform some intermediate processing on a document before it has been completely parsed.

However, for applications that require random access to different portions of a document at different times, or applications that need to modify the structure of an XML document on the fly, DOM is one of the most mature and best-supported technologies available.

Structure of the DOM Core

The DOM Core interfaces provide generic access to all supported document content types. The DOM also defines a set of HTML-specific interfaces that expose specific document structures, such as tables, paragraphs, and img elements, directly. Besides using these specialized interfaces, you can access the same information using the generic interfaces defined in the core.

Since XML is designed as a venue for creating new, unique, structured markup languages, standards bodies cannot define application-specific interfaces in advance. Instead, the DOM Core interfaces are provided to manipulate document elements in a completely application-independent manner.

The DOM Core is further segregated into the Fundamental and Extended Interfaces. The Fundamental Interfaces are relevant to both XML and HTML documents, whereas the Extended Interfaces deal with XML-only document structures, such as entity declarations and processing instructions. All DOM Core interfaces are derived from the Node interface, which provides a generic set of methods for accessing a document or document fragment's tree structure and content.

Generic Versus Specific DOM Interfaces

To simplify different types of document processing and enable efficient implementation of DOM by some programming languages, there are actually two distinct methods for accessing a document tree from within the DOM Core: through the generic Node interface and through specific interfaces for each node type. Although there are several distinct types of markup that may appear within an XML document (elements, attributes, processing instructions, and so on), the relationships between these different document features can be expressed as a typical hierarchical tree structure. Elements are linked to both their predecessors and successors, as well as their parent and child nodes. Although there are many different types of nodes, the basic parent, child, and sibling relationships are common to everything in an XML document.

The generic Node interface captures the minimal set of attributes and methods that are required to express this tree structure. A given Node contains all of the tree pointers required to locate its parent node, child nodes, and siblings. The next section describes the Node interface in detail.

In addition to the generic Node interface, the DOM also defines a set of XML-specific interfaces that represent distinct document features, such as elements, attributes, processing instructions, and so on. All of the specific interfaces are derived from the generic Node interface, which means that a particular application can switch methods for accessing data within a DOM tree at will by casting between the generic Node interface and the actual specific object type it represents. "Specific Node-Type Interfaces" later in this chapter discusses the specific interfaces and their relationship to the generic Node interface.

Node and Other Generic Interfaces

The Node interface is the DOM Core class hierarchy's root. Though never instantiated directly, it is the root interface of all specific interfaces, and you can use it to extract information from any object within a DOM document tree without knowing its actual type. It is possible to access a document's complete structure and content using only the methods and properties exposed by the Node interface. As shown in Table 19-1, this interface contains information about the type, location, name, and value of the corresponding underlying document data.

Table 19-1. The Node interface

Name	Type	Read-only	2.0	3.0
Attributes				
attributes	NamedNodeMap	×		
baseURI	DOMString	×		×
childNodes	NodeList	×		
firstChild	Node	×		
lastChild	Node	×		
localName	DOMString	×	×	
namespaceURI	DOMString	×	×	
nextSibling	Node	×		
nodeName	DOMString	×		
nodeType	unsigned short	×		
nodeValue	DOMString			
ownerDocument	Document	×	×	
parentNode	Node	×		
prefix	DOMString		×	
previousSibling	Node	×		
textContent	DOMString			×
Methods				
appendChild	Node			
cloneNode	Node			
compareDocumentPosition	unsigned short			×
getFeature	DOMObject			×
getUserData	DOMUserData			×
hasAttributes	boolean		×	
hasChildNodes	boolean			
insertBefore	Node			
isDefaultNamespace	boolean			×
isEqualNode	boolean			×
isSameNode	boolean			×
isSupported	boolean		×	
lookupNamespaceURI	DOMString			×

Table 19-1. The Node interface (continued)

Name	Type	Read-only	2.0	3.0
lookupPrefix	DOMString			×
normalize	void		×	
removeChild	Node			
replaceChild	Node			
setUserData	DOMUserData			×

Since the Node interface is never instantiated directly, the nodeType attribute contains a value that indicates the given instance's specific object type. Based on the nodeType, it is possible to cast a generic Node reference safely to a specific interface for further processing. Table 19-2 shows the node type values and their corresponding DOM interfaces, and Table 19-3 shows the values they provide for nodeName, nodeValue, and attributes attributes.

Table 19-2. The DOM node types and interfaces

Node type	DOM interface
ATTRIBUTE_NODE	Attr
CDATA_SECTION_NODE	CDATASection
COMMENT_NODE	Comment
DOCUMENT_FRAGMENT_NODE	DocumentFragment
DOCUMENT_NODE	Document
DOCUMENT_TYPE_NODE	DocumentType
ELEMENT_NODE	Element
ENTITY_NODE	Entity
ENTITY_REFERENCE_NODE	EntityReference
NOTATION_NODE	Notation
PROCESSING_INSTRUCTION_NODE	ProcessingInstruction
TEXT_NODE	Text

Table 19-3. The DOM node types and method results

Node type	nodeName	nodeValue	Attributes
ATTRIBUTE_NODE	att name	att value	null
CDATA_SECTION_NODE	#cdata-section	content	null
COMMENT_NODE	#comment	content	null
DOCUMENT_FRAGMENT_NODE	#document-fragment	null	null
DOCUMENT_NODE	#document	null	null
DOCUMENT_TYPE_NODE	document type name	null	null
ELEMENT_NODE	tag name	null	NamedNodeMap
ENTITY_NODE	entity name	null	null
ENTITY_REFERENCE_NODE	name of entity referenced	null	null

Table 19-3. The DOM node types and method results (continued)

Node type	nodeName	nodeValue	Attributes
NOTATION_NODE	notation name	null	null
PROCESSING_INSTRUCTION_NODE	target	content excluding the target	null
TEXT_NODE	#text	content	null

Note that the nodeValue attribute returns the contents of simple text and comment nodes but returns nothing for elements. Prior to DOM Level 3, retrieving the text content of an element required locating any child Text nodes it might contain, but DOM Level 3 introduced the getTextContent( ) and setTextContent( ) convenience methods.

The NodeList Interface

The NodeList interface provides access to the ordered content of a node. Most frequently, it is used to retrieve text nodes and child elements of element nodes. See Table 19-4 for a summary of the NodeList interface.

Table 19-4. The NodeList interface

Name	Type	Read-only	2.0	3.0
Attribute				
length	Long	×		
Method				
item	Node			

The NodeList interface is extremely basic and is generally combined with a loop to iterate through the children of a node, as in the following example:

```
NodeList nl = nd.getChildNodes( );
for (int i = 0; i < nl.getLength( ); i++) {
  Node ndChild = nl.item(i);
  if (ndChild.getNodeType( ) == Node.COMMENT_NODE) {
    System.out.println("found comment: " + ndChild.getNodeValue( ));
  }
}
```

The NamedNodeMap Interface

The NamedNodeMap interface is used for unordered collections whose contents are identified by name. In practice, this interface is used to access attributes of elements. See Table 19-5 for a summary of the NamedNodeMap interface.

Table 19-5. The NamedNodeMap interface

Name	Type	Read-only	2.0	3.0
Attribute				
length	Long	×		
Methods				
getNamedItem	Node			
getNamedItemNS	Node		×	
removeNamedItem	Node			
removeNamedItemNS	Node			
setNamedItem	Node			
setNamedItemNS	Node		×	

Relating Document Structure to Nodes

Although the DOM doesn't specify an interface to cause a document to be parsed, it does specify how the document's syntax structures are encoded as DOM objects. A document is stored as a hierarchical tree structure, with each item in the tree linked to its parent, children, and siblings:

```
<sample bogus="value"><text_node>Test data.</text_node></sample>
```

Figure 19-1 shows how the preceding short sample document would be stored by a DOM parser.

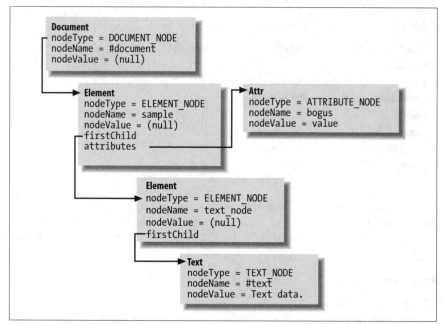

Figure 19-1. Document storage and linkages

Each Node-derived object in a parsed DOM document contains references to its parent, child, and sibling nodes. These references make it possible for applications to enumerate document data using any number of standard tree-traversal algorithms. "Walking the tree" is a common approach to finding information stored in a DOM and is demonstrated in Example 19-1 at the end of this chapter.

Specific Node-Type Interfaces

Although it is possible to access the data from the original XML document using only the Node interface, the DOM Core provides a number of specific node-type interfaces that simplify common programming tasks. These specific node types can be divided into two broad types: structural nodes and content nodes.

Structural Nodes

Within an XML document, a number of syntax structures exist that are not formally part of the content. The following interfaces provide access to the portions of the document that are not related to element data.

DocumentType

The DocumentType interface provides access to the XML document type definition's notations, entities, internal subset, public ID, and system ID. Since a document can have only one DOCTYPE declaration, only one DocumentType node can exist for a given document. It is accessed via the doctype attribute of the Document interface. The definition of the DocumentType interface is shown in Table 19-6.

Table 19-6. The DocumentType interface, derived from Node

Name	Type	Read-only
Attributes		
entities	NamedNodeMap	×
internalSubset	DOMString	×
name	DOMString	×
notations	NamedNodeMap	×
publicId	DOMString	×
systemId	DOMString	×

Using additional fields available since DOM Level 2, it is now possible to fully reconstruct a parsed document using only the information provided within the DOM framework. No programmatic way to modify DocumentType node contents currently exists.

ProcessingInstruction

The ProcessingInstruction node type provides direct access to a processing instruction's contents. Though processing instructions appear in the document's text, they may also appear before or after the root element, as well as in DTDs. Table 19-7 describes the ProcessingInstruction node's attributes.

Table 19-7. The ProcessingInstruction interface, derived from Node

Name	Type	Read-only
Attributes		
data	DOMString	
target	DOMString	×

Remember that the only syntactically defined part is the target name, which is an XML name token. The remaining data (up to the terminating >) is free-form. See Chapter 18 for more information about uses (and potential misuses) of XML processing instructions.

Notation

XML notations formally declare the format for external unparsed entities and processing instruction targets. The list of all available notations is stored in a NamedNodeMap within the document's DOCTYPE node, which is accessed from the Document interface. The definition of the Notation interface is shown in Table 19-8.

Table 19-8. The Notation interface, derived from Node

Name	Type	Read-only
Attributes		
publicId	DOMString	×
systemId	DOMString	×

Entity

The name of the Entity interface is somewhat ambiguous, but its meaning becomes clear when it is connected with the EntityReference interface, which is also part of the DOM Core. The Entity interface provides access to the entity declaration's notation name, public ID, and system ID. Parsed entity nodes have childNodes, while unparsed entities have a notationName. The definition of this interface is shown in Table 19-9.

Table 19-9. The Entity interface, derived from Node

Name	Type	Read-only	2.0	3.0
Attributes				
inputEncoding	DOMString	×		×
notationName	DOMString	×		
publicId	DOMString	×		
systemId	DOMString	×		
xmlEncoding	DOMString	×		×
xmlVersion	DOMString	×		×

DOM Level 3 introduces three new attributes that apply to external parsed entities: inputEncoding, xmlEncoding, and xmlVersion. This additional information makes it possible to properly enforce XML well-formedness constraints for external parsed entities based on the value of the xmlVersion attribute. The two encoding related attributes make it possible to precisely reconstruct external parsed entity files from their DOM tree representation.

All members of this interface are read-only and cannot be modified at runtime.

Content Nodes

The actual data conveyed by an XML document is contained completely within the document element. The following node types map directly to the XML document's nonstructural parts, such as character data, elements, and attribute values.

Document

Each parsed document causes the creation of a single Document node in memory. (Empty Document nodes can be created through the DOMImplementation interface.) This interface provides access to the document type information and the single, top-level Element node that contains the entire body of the parsed document (the documentElement). It also provides access to the class factory methods that allow an application to create new content nodes that were not created by parsing a document. Table 19-10 shows all attributes and methods of the Document interface.

Table 19-10. The Document interface, derived from Node

Name	Type	Read-only	2.0	3.0
Attributes				
doctype	DocumentType	×		
documentElement	Element	×		
documentURI	DOMString			×
domConfig	DOMConfiguration	×		×
implementation	DOMImplementation	×		
inputEncoding	DOMString	×		×
strictErrorChecking	boolean			×
xmlEncoding	DOMString	×		×
xmlStandalone	boolean	×		×
xmlVersion	DOMString			×
Methods				
adoptNode	Node			×
createAttribute	Attr			
createAttributeNS	Attr		×	
createCDATASection	CDATASection			
createComment	Comment			
createDocumentFragment	DocumentFragment			

Table 19-10. The Document interface, derived from Node (continued)

Name	Type	Read-only	2.0	3.0
createElement	Element			
createElementNS	Element		×	
createEntityReference	EntityReference			
createProcessingInstruction	ProcessingInstruction			
createTextNode	Text			
getElementById	Element		×	
getElementsByTagName	NodeList			
getElementsByTagNameNS	NodeList		×	
importNode	Node		×	
normalizeDocument	void			×
renameNode	Node			×

The various create...() methods are important for applications that wish to modify the structure of a document that was previously parsed. Note that nodes created using one Document instance may only be inserted into the document tree belonging to the Document that created them. DOM Level 2 provided a new importNode() method that allows a node, and possibly its children, to be essentially copied from one document to another. DOM Level 3 introduced the adoptNode() method that actually moves an entire node subtree from one document to another.

Besides the various node-creation methods, some methods can locate specific XML elements or lists of elements. The methods getElementsByTagName() and getElementsByTagNameNS() return a list of all XML elements with the name, and possibly namespace, specified. The getElementById() method returns the single element with the given ID attribute.

DOM Level 3 also introduced several attributes that are useful when an application wishes to reconstruct an XML document to its original, pre-parsing format. The inputEncoding, xmlEncoding, and xmlStandalone attributes preserve information about the values of the XML declaration from the original document as well as the character encoding of the document before it was parsed (and converted to Unicode).

One of the major additions to DOM in Level 3 was the inclusion of document validation support within the DOM tree itself. The normalizeDocument() method provides the developer with a mechanism for essentially "re-parsing" the XML document from the DOM tree in memory. Various parameters available through the domConfig attribute control how this normalization will occur. It is also possible to change the target version of XML by modifying the xmlVersion attribute before normalization. This will cause the DOM to enforce the XML name construction rules associated with the selected XML version. See Chapter 21 for more information about the differences between XML Versions 1.0 and 1.1.

DocumentFragment

Applications that allow real-time editing of XML documents sometimes need to temporarily park document nodes outside the hierarchy of the parsed document. A visual editor that wants to provide clipboard functionality is one example. When the time comes to implement the cut function, it is possible to move the cut nodes temporarily to a DocumentFragment node without deleting them, rather than having to leave them in place within the live document. Then, when they need to be pasted back into the document, they can be reinserted using a method such as Node.appendChild(). The DocumentFragment interface, derived from Node, has no interface-specific attributes or methods.

Element

Element nodes are the most frequently encountered node type in a typical XML document. These nodes are parents for the Text, Comment, EntityReference, ProcessingInstruction, CDATASection, and child Element nodes that comprise the document's body. They also allow access to the Attr objects that contain the element's attributes. Table 19-11 shows all attributes and methods supported by the Element interface.

Table 19-11. The Element interface, derived from Node

Name	Type	Read-only	2.0	3.0
Attributes				
schemaTypeInfo	TypeInfo	×		×
tagName	DOMString	×		
Methods				
getAttribute	DOMString			
getAttributeNode	Attr			
getAttributeNodeNS	Attr		×	
getAttributeNS	DOMString	×		
getElementsByTagName	NodeList			
getElementsByTagNameNS	NodeList		×	
hasAttribute	boolean	×		
hasAttributeNS	boolean		×	
removeAttribute	void			
removeAttributeNode	Attr			
removeAttributeNS	Attr		×	
setAttribute	void			
setAttributeNode	Attr			
setAttributeNodeNS	Attr			
setAttributeNS	Attr	×		
setIdAttribute	void	×		×
setIdAttributeNode	void	×		×
setIdAttributeNS	void	×		×

Attr

Since XML attributes may contain either text values or entity references, the DOM stores element attribute values as Node subtrees. The following XML fragment shows an element with two attributes:

```
<!ENTITY bookcase_pic SYSTEM "bookcase.gif" NDATA gif>
<!ELEMENT picture EMPTY>
<!ATTLIST picture
    src ENTITY #REQUIRED
    alt CDATA #IMPLIED>
. . .
<picture src="bookcase_pic" alt="3/4 view of bookcase"/>
```

The first attribute contains a reference to an unparsed entity; the second contains a simple string. Since the DOM framework stores element attributes as instances of the Attr interface, a few parsers make the contents of attributes available as actual subtrees of Node objects. In this example, the src attribute would contain an EntityReference object instance. Note that the nodeValue of the Attr node gives the flattened text value from the Attr node's children. Table 19-12 shows the attributes and methods supported by the Attr interface.

Table 19-12. The Attr interface, derived from Node

Name	Type	Read-only	2.0	3.0
Attributes				
specified	boolean	×		
isId	boolean	×		×
name	DOMString	×		
value	DOMString			
ownerElement	Element	×	×	
schemaTypeInfo	TypeInfo	×		×

Besides the attribute name and value, the Attr interface exposes the specified flag that indicates whether this particular attribute instance was included explicitly in the XML document or inherited from the !ATTLIST declaration of the DTD. There is also a back pointer to the Element node that owns this attribute object.

CharacterData

Several types of data within a DOM node tree represent blocks of character data that do not include markup. CharacterData is an abstract interface that supports common text-manipulation methods, which are used by the concrete interfaces Comment, Text, and CDATASection. Table 19-13 shows the attributes and methods supported by the CharacterData interface.

Table 19-13. The CharacterData interface, derived from Node

Name	Type	Read-only	DOM 2.0
Attributes			
data	DOMString		
length	unsigned long	×	
Methods			
appendData	void		
deleteData	void		
insertData	void		
replaceData	void		

Comment

DOM parsers are not required to make the contents of XML comments available after parsing, and relying on comment data in your application is poor programming practice at best. If your application requires access to metadata that should not be part of the basic XML document, consider using processing instructions instead. The Comment interface, derived from CharacterData, has no interface-specific attributes or methods, only those it inherits from its superinterfaces.

EntityReference

If an XML document contains references to general entities within the body of its elements, the DOM-compliant parser may pass these references along as EntityReference nodes. This behavior is not guaranteed because the parser is free to expand any entity or character reference included with the actual Unicode character sequence it represents. The EntityReference interface, derived from Node, has no interface-specific attributes or methods.

Text

The character data of an XML document is stored within Text nodes. Text nodes are children of either Element or Attr nodes. After parsing, every contiguous block of character data from the original XML document is translated directly into a single Text node. Once the document has been parsed, however, it is possible that the client application may insert, delete, and split Text nodes so that Text nodes may be side by side within the document tree. Table 19-14 describes the Text interface.

Table 19-14. The Text interface, derived from CharacterData

Name	Type	Read-only	2.0	3.0
Attributes				
isElementContentWhitespace	boolean	×		
wholeText	DOMString	×		×

Table 19-14. The Text interface, derived from CharacterData (continued)

Name	Type	Read-only	2.0	3.0
Methods				
replaceWholeText	Text			×
splitText	Text			

The splitText method provides a way to split a single Text node into two nodes at a given point. This split would be useful if an editing application wished to insert additional markup nodes into an existing island of character data. After the split, it is possible to insert additional nodes into the resulting gap.

Another useful addition (introduced in Level 3) is the wholeText attribute. This attribute returns all of the text contained in the selected Text node, as well as any adjacent Text nodes, in document order. Prior to Level 3, it was necessary to enumerate all children of a given node and concatenate them manually to get the entire text contained within a node.

CDATASection

CDATA sections provide a simplified way to include characters that would normally be considered markup in an XML document. These sections are stored within a DOM document tree as CDATASection nodes. The CDATASection interface, derived from Text, has no interface-specific attributes or methods.

The DOMImplementation Interface

The DOMImplementation interface could be considered the highest level interface in the DOM. It exposes the hasFeature() method, which allows a programmer using a given DOM implementation to detect if specific features are available. In DOM Level 2, it introduced facilities for creating new DocumentType nodes, which can then be used to create new Document instances.

The only method added to the DOMImplementation interface for Level 3 was the getFeature() method. This method allows DOM implementers to provide access to extended functionality, which is not part of the DOM specification itself, through the use of extension objects. These objects implement the DOMObject interface, which generally maps to the generic object (e.g., the Java Object) type in the underlying programming language (if the language is object-oriented). Table 19-15 describes the DomImplementation interface.

Table 19-15. The DOMImplementation interface

Name	Type	2.0	3.0
Methods			
createDocument	Document	×	
createDocumentType	DocumentType	×	
getFeature	DOMObject		×
hasFeature	boolean		

DOM Level 3 Interfaces

DOM Level 3 includes several new interfaces that support features, such as:

- XML Version 1.1
- Dynamic DOM implementation selection
- Generic post-validation document type information
- Dynamic error handling

The following sections describe the new interfaces that were introduced in DOM Level 3.

DOMStringList

The DOMStringList interface models a simple utility class that contains an ordered list of DOMString objects. Table 19-16 describes the DOMStringList interface.

Table 19-16. The DOMStringList interface

Name	Type	Read-only
Attribute		
length	unsigned long	×
Methods		
contains	boolean	
item	DOMString	

NameList

The NameList interface models an ordered collection of names and corresponding namespace URIs. One use of this interface is in modeling the linkage between namespace prefixes and namespace URIs. Table 19-17 describes the NameList interface.

Table 19-17. The NameList interface

Name	Type	Read-only
Attribute		
length	unsigned long	×
Methods		
contains	boolean	
containsNS	boolean	
getName	DOMString	
getNamespaceURI	DOMString	

DOMImplementationList

The DOMImplementationList interface models a list of DOMImplementation objects, as shown in Table 19-18.

Table 19-18. The DOMImplementationList interface

Name	Type	Read-only
Attribute		
length	unsigned long	×
Method		
item	DOMImplementation	

DOMImplementationSource

The DOMImplementationSource interface, shown in Table 19-19, allows a DOM client to dynamically select a particular DOM implementation from a list of available implementations based on a requested feature set. It also allows the client to retrieve a complete list of all DOMImplementation objects that are available at runtime.

Table 19-19. The DOMImplementationSource interface

Name	Type	Read-only
Methods		
getDOMImplementation	DOMImplementation	
getDOMImplementationList	DOMImplementationList	

TypeInfo

One of the major enhancements provided by DOM Level 3 is the presence of type information within the DOM tree after a document has been parsed and validated. The TypeInfo interface, described in Table 19-20, provides a very simple interface that allows a DOM implementation to provide schema-independent type information for elements and attributes within the DOM tree.

Table 19-20. The TypeInfo interface

Name	Type	Read-only
Attributes		
typeName	DOMString	×
typeNamespace	DOMString	×
Method		
isDerivedFrom	boolean	

UserDataHandler

DOM Level 3 provides the ability for developers to attach their own user-defined data to any Node within a live DOM tree. The UserDataHandler interface is a callback interface that may be implemented by the developer when he wishes to receive notifications regarding operations that might be performed on various nodes (i.e., nodes are cloned, deleted, moved, and so forth). Its method is listed in Table 19-21.

Table 19-21. The UserDataHandler interface

Name	Type	Read-only
Method		
handle	void	

DOMError

Prior to Level 3, all error handling within the DOM was done through the DOMException mechanism. Level 3 provides a new error handling facility that allows the developer to register a callback object (which implements the DOMErrorHandler interface) that will be notified when an error occurs during DOM operations. The DOMError interface describes an object that contains the details of such an error. The DOMError interface is described in Table 19-22.

Table 19-22. The DOMError interface

Name	Type	Read-only
Attributes		
location	DOMLocator	×
message	DOMString	×
relatedData	DOMObject	×
relatedException	DOMObject	×
severity	unsigned short	×
type	DOMString	×

DOMErrorHandler

Unlike earlier DOM Levels, Level 3 allows a DOM developer to create a callback object that may receive notifications when errors occur during DOM processing. This is done by developing an object that implements the DOMErrorHandler interface. Then, when an error occurs during a DOM operation (such as a validity error during a node insert), the handleError( ) method will be called with detailed error information. Its method is listed in Table 19-23.

Table 19-23. The DOMErrorHandler interface

Name	Type	Read-only
Method		
handleError	boolean	

DOMLocator

The DOMLocator interface, shown in Table 19-24, describes a location within a DOM document. It is primarily used by the new DOMError interface to provide detailed information about where a particular error has occurred.

Table 19-24. The DOMLocator interface

Name	Type	Read-only
Attributes		
byteOffset	long	×
columnNumber	long	×
lineNumber	long	×
relatedNode	Node	×
utf16Offset	long	×
uri	DOMString	×

DOMConfiguration

The `DOMConfiguration` interface, shown in Table 19-25, provides a generic container for configuring various parameters that influence the processing of XML documents when they are first parsed or when they are reprocessed using the `Document.normalizeDocument( )` method. For a complete list of parameters that are recognized by DOM Level 3 implementations, see the `DOMConfiguration` reference section in Chapter 25.

Table 19-25. The DOMConfiguration interface

Name	Type	Read-only
Attribute		
parameterNames	DOMStringList	×
Methods		
canSetParameter	boolean	
getParameter	DOMUserData	
setParameter	void	

Parsing a Document with DOM

Although DOM Level 2 doesn't specify an actual interface for parsing a document, most implementations provide a simple parsing interface that accepts a reference to an XML document file, stream, or URI. After this interface successfully parses and validates the document (if it is a validating parser), it generally provides a mechanism for getting a reference to the `Document` interface's instance for the parsed document. The following code fragment shows how to parse a document using the Apache Xerces XML DOM parser:

```
// create a new parser
DOMParser dp = new DOMParser( );

// parse the document and get the DOM Document interface
dp.parse("http://www.w3.org/TR/2000/REC-xml-20001006.xml");
Document doc = dp.getDocument( );
```

DOM Level 3 adds standard mechanisms for loading XML documents and reserializing (saving) DOM trees as XML. JAXP also provides standardized approaches for these processes in Java, although JAXP and DOM Level 3 offer different approaches.

A Simple DOM Application

Example 19-1 illustrates how you might use the interfaces discussed in this chapter in a typical programming situation. This application takes a document that uses the *furniture.dtd* sample DTD from Chapter 21 and validates that the parts list included in the document matches the actual parts used within the document.

Example 19-1. Parts checker application

```
/**
 * PartsCheck.java
 *
 * DOM Usage example from the O'Reilly _XML in a Nutshell_ book.
 *
 */

// we'll use the Apache Software Foundation's Xerces parser.
import org.apache.xerces.parsers.*;
import org.apache.xerces.framework.*;

// import the DOM and SAX interfaces
import org.w3c.dom.*;
import org.xml.sax.*;

// get the necessary Java support classes
import java.io.*;
import java.util.*;

/**
 * This class is designed to check the parts list of an XML document that
 * represents a piece of furniture for validity.  It uses the DOM to
 * analyze the actual furniture description and then check it against the
 * parts list that is embedded in the document.
 */
public class PartsCheck {
  // static constants
  public static final String FURNITURE_NS =
      "http://namespaces.oreilly.com/furniture/";
  // contains the true part count, keyed by part number
  HashMap m_hmTruePartsList = new HashMap( );

  /**
   * The main function that allows this class to be invoked from the command
   * line.  Check each document provided on the command line for validity.
   */
```

Example 19-1. Parts checker application (continued)

```java
public static void main(String[] args) {
    PartsCheck pc = new PartsCheck( );

    try {
        for (int i = 0; i < args.length; i++) {
            pc.validatePartsList(args[i]);
        }
    } catch (Exception e) {
        System.err.println(e);
    }
}

/**
 * Given a system identifier for an XML document, this function compares
 * the actual parts used to the declared parts list within the document.  It
 * prints warnings to standard error if the lists don't agree.
 */
public void validatePartsList(String strXMLSysID) throws IOException,
        SAXException
{
    // create a new parser
    DOMParser dp = new DOMParser( );

    // parse the document and get the DOM Document interface
    dp.parse(strXMLSysID);
    Document doc = dp.getDocument( );

    // get an accurate parts list count
    countParts(doc.getDocumentElement( ), 1);

    // compare it to the parts list in the document
    reconcilePartsList(doc);
}

/**
 * Updates the true parts list by adding the count to the current count
 * for the part number given.
 */
private void recordPart(String strPartNum, int cCount)
{
    if (!m_hmTruePartsList.containsKey(strPartNum)) {
        // this part isn't listed yet
        m_hmTruePartsList.put(strPartNum, new Integer(cCount));
    } else {
        // update the count
        Integer cUpdate = (Integer)m_hmTruePartsList.get(strPartNum);
        m_hmTruePartsList.put(strPartNum, new Integer(cUpdate.intValue( ) +
cCount));
    }
}
```

Example 19-1. Parts checker application (continued)

```java
/**
 * Counts the parts referenced by and below the given node.
 */
private void countParts(Node nd, int cRepeat)
{
  // start the local repeat count at 1
  int cLocalRepeat = 1;

  // make sure we should process this element
  if (FURNITURE_NS.equals(nd.getNamespaceURI( ))) {
    Node ndTemp;

    if ((ndTemp = nd.getAttributes( ).getNamedItem("repeat")) != null) {
      // this node specifies a repeat count for its children
      cLocalRepeat = Integer.parseInt(ndTemp.getNodeValue( ));
    }

    if ((ndTemp = nd.getAttributes( ).getNamedItem("part_num")) != null) {
      // start the count at 1
      int cCount = 1;
      String strPartNum = ndTemp.getNodeValue( );

      if ((ndTemp = nd.getAttributes( ).getNamedItem("count")) != null) {
        // more than one part needed by this node
        cCount = Integer.parseInt(ndTemp.getNodeValue( ));
      }

      // multiply the local count by the repeat passed in from the parent
      cCount *= cRepeat;

      // add the new parts count to the total
      recordPart(strPartNum, cCount);
    }
  }

  // now process the children
  NodeList nl = nd.getChildNodes( );
  Node ndCur;

  for (int i = 0; i < nl.getLength( ); i++) {
    ndCur = nl.item(i);

    if (ndCur.getNodeType( ) == Node.ELEMENT_NODE) {
      // recursively count the parts for the child, using the local repeat
      countParts(ndCur, cLocalRepeat);
    }
  }
}

/**
 * This method reconciles the true parts list against the list in the document.
 */
```

Example 19-1. Parts checker application (continued)

```
private void reconcilePartsList(Document doc)
{
  Iterator iReal = m_hmTruePartsList.keySet( ).iterator( );

  String strPartNum;
  int cReal;
  Node ndCheck;

  // loop through all of the parts in the true parts list
  while (iReal.hasNext( )) {
    strPartNum = (String)iReal.next( );
    cReal = ((Integer)m_hmTruePartsList.get(strPartNum)).intValue( );

    // find the part list element in the document
    ndCheck = doc.getElementById(strPartNum);

    if (ndCheck == null) {
      // this part isn't even listed!
      System.err.println("missing <part_name> element for part #" +
          strPartNum + " (count " + cReal + ")");
    } else {
      Node ndTemp;

      if ((ndTemp = ndCheck.getAttributes( ).getNamedItem("count")) != null) {
        int cCheck = Integer.parseInt(ndTemp.getNodeValue( ));

        if (cCheck != cReal) {
          // counts don't agree
          System.err.println("<part_name> element for part #" +
              strPartNum + " is incorrect:  true part count = " + cReal +
              " (count in document is " + cCheck + ")");
        }
      } else {
        // they didn't provide a count for this part!
        System.err.println("missing count attribute for part #" +
            strPartNum + " (count " + cReal + ")");
      }
    }
  }
}
```

When this application is run over the *bookcase.xml* sample document from Chapter 21, it generates the following output:

```
missing count attribute for part #HC (count 8)

<part_name> element for part #A is incorrect:  true part count = 2 (count in
document is 1)
```

To compile and use this sample application, download and install the Xerces Java Parser from the Apache-XML project (*http://xml.apache.org/xerces-j*). The code was originally compiled and tested with Sun's JDK Version 1.3.1.

20

Simple API for XML (SAX)

The Simple API for XML (SAX) is an event-based API for reading XML documents. Many different XML parsers implement the SAX API, including Xerces, Crimson, the Oracle XML Parser for Java, and Ælfred. SAX was originally defined as a Java API and is primarily intended for parsers written in Java. Therefore, this chapter focuses on the Java version of the API. However, SAX has been ported to most other major object-oriented languages, including C++, Python, Perl, and Eiffel. The translation from Java is usually fairly obvious.

The SAX API is unusual among XML APIs because it's an event-based push model rather than a tree-based pull model. As the XML parser reads an XML document, it sends the program information from the document in real time. Each time the parser sees a start-tag, an end-tag, character data, or a processing instruction, it tells your program. The document is presented to your program one piece at a time from beginning to end. You can either save the pieces you're interested in until the entire document has been read, or process the information as soon as you receive it. You do not have to wait for the entire document to be read before acting on the data at the beginning of the document. Most importantly, the entire document does not have to reside in memory. This feature makes SAX the API of choice for very large documents that do not fit into available memory.

This chapter covers SAX2 exclusively. In 2004, all major parsers that support SAX also support SAX2. The major change in SAX2 from SAX1 is the addition of namespace support, which necessitated changing the names and signatures of almost every method and class in SAX. The old SAX1 methods and classes are still available, but they're now deprecated, and you shouldn't use them.

SAX is primarily a collection of interfaces in the org.xml.sax package. One such interface is XMLReader. This interface represents the XML parser. It declares methods to parse a document and configure the parsing process, for instance, by turning validation on or off. To parse a document with SAX, first create an instance of XMLReader with the XMLReaderFactory class in the org.xml.sax.helpers package. This class has a static createXMLReader( ) factory method that produces the parser-specific implementation of the XMLReader interface. The Java system property org.xml.sax.driver specifies the concrete class to instantiate:

```
try {
  XMLReader parser = XMLReaderFactory.createXMLReader( );
  // parse the document...
}
catch (SAXException ex) {
  // couldn't create the XMLReader
}
```

The call to XMLReaderFactory.createXMLReader( ) is wrapped in a try-catch block that catches SAXException. This is the generic checked exception superclass for almost anything that can go wrong while parsing an XML document. In this case, it means either that the org.xml.sax.driver system property wasn't set, or that it was set to the name of a class that Java couldn't find in the class path.

 Do not use the SAXParserFactory and SAXParser classes included with JAXP. These classes were designed by Sun to fill a gap in SAX1. They are unnecessary and indeed actively harmful in SAX2. For instance, they are not namespace aware by default. SAX2 applications should use XMLReaderFactory and XMLReader instead.

You can choose which concrete class to instantiate by passing its name as a string to the createXMLReader( ) method. This code fragment instantiates the Xerces parser by name:

```
try {
  XMLReader parser = XMLReaderFactory.createXMLReader(
    "org.apache.xerces.parsers.SAXParser");
  // parse the document...
}
catch (SAXException ex) {
  // couldn't create the XMLReader
}
```

Now that you've created a parser, you're ready to parse some documents with it. Pass the system ID of the document you want to read to the parse( ) method. The system ID is either an absolute or a relative URL encoded in a string. For example, this code fragment parses the document at *http://www.slashdot.org/slashdot.xml*:

```
try {
  XMLReader parser = XMLReaderFactory.createXMLReader( );
  parser.parse("http://www.slashdot.org/slashdot.xml");
}
catch (SAXParseException ex) {
  // Well-formedness error
}
catch (SAXException ex) {
  // Could not find an XMLReader implementation class
}
```

```
catch (IOException ex) {
    // Some sort of I/O error prevented the document from being completely
    // downloaded from the server
}
```

The parse( ) method throws a SAXParseException if the document is malformed, an IOException if an I/O error such as a broken socket occurs while the document is being read, and a SAXException if anything else goes wrong. Otherwise, it returns void. To receive information from the parser as it reads the document, you must configure it with a ContentHandler.

The ContentHandler Interface

ContentHandler, shown in stripped-down form in Example 20-1, is an interface in the org.xml.sax package. You implement this interface in a class of your own devising. Next, you configure an XMLReader with an instance of your implementation. As the XMLReader reads the document, it invokes the methods in this object to tell your program what's in the XML document. You can respond to these method invocations in any way you see fit.

 The ContentHandler class has no relation to the moribund java.net. ContentHandler class. However, you may encounter a name conflict if you import both java.net.* and org.xml.sax.* in the same class. It's better to import just the java.net classes you actually need, rather than the entire package.

Example 20-1. The org.xml.sax.ContentHandler interface

```
package org.xml.sax;

public interface ContentHandler {
    public void setDocumentLocator(Locator locator);
    public void startDocument( ) throws SAXException;
    public void endDocument( ) throws SAXException;
    public void startPrefixMapping(String prefix, String uri)
      throws SAXException;
    public void endPrefixMapping(String prefix) throws SAXException;
    public void startElement(String namespaceURI, String localName,
      String qualifiedName, Attributes atts) throws SAXException;
    public void endElement(String namespaceURI, String localName,
      String qualifiedName) throws SAXException;
    public void characters(char[ ] text, int start, int length)
      throws SAXException;
    public void ignorableWhitespace(char[ ] text, int start, int length)
      throws SAXException;
    public void processingInstruction(String target, String data)
      throws SAXException;
    public void skippedEntity(String name) throws SAXException;

}
```

Every time the XMLReader reads a piece of the document, it calls a method in its ContentHandler. Suppose a parser reads the simple document shown in Example 20-2.

Example 20-2. A simple XML document

```
<?xml version="1.0" encoding="ISO-8859-1"?>
<?xml-stylesheet type='text/css' href='person.css'?>
<!DOCTYPE person SYSTEM "person.dtd">
<person xmlns="http://xml.oreilly.com/person">
  <name:name xmlns:name="http://xml.oreilly.com/name">
    <name:first>Sydney</name:first>
    <name:last>Lee</name:last>
  </name:name>
  <assignment project_id="p2"/>
</person>
```

The parser will call these methods in its ContentHandler with these arguments in this order. The values of the arguments passed to each method are given after each method name:

1.

    setDocumentLocator(Locator locator)
        locator: org.apache.xerces.readers.DefaultEntityHandler@1f953d

2.

    startDocument( )

3.

    processingInstruction(String target, String data)
        target: "xml-stylesheet"
        data: "type='text/css' href='person.css'"

4.

    startPrefixMapping(String prefix, String namespaceURI)
        prefix: ""
        namespaceURI: "http://xml.oreilly.com/person"

5.

    startElement(String namespaceURI, String localName, String qualifiedName,
    Attributes atts)
        namespaceURI: "http://xml.oreilly.com/person"
        localName: "person"
        qualifiedName: "person"
        atts: {} (no attributes, an empty list)

6.

    ignorableWhitespace(char[] text, int start, int length)
        text: <?xml version="1.0" encoding="ISO-8859-1"?>
        <?xml-stylesheet type='text/css' href='person.css'?>
        <!DOCTYPE person SYSTEM "person.dtd">
        <person xmlns="http://xml.oreilly.com/person">
          <name:name xmlns:name="http://xml.oreilly.com/name">
            <name:first>Sydney</name:first>
            <name:last>Lee</name:last>

```
        </name:name>
        <assignment project_id="p2"/>
      </person>
   start: 181
   length: 3
```

7.
```
   startPrefixMapping(String prefix, String uri)
       prefix: "name"
       uri: "http://xml.oreilly.com/name")
```

8.
```
   startElement(String namespaceURI, String localName, String qualifiedName,
   Attributes atts)
       namespaceURI: "http://xml.oreilly.com/name"
       localName: "name"
       qualifiedName: "name:name"
       atts: {} (no attributes, an empty list)
```

9.
```
   ignorableWhitespace(char[] text, int start, int length)
       text: <?xml version="1.0" encoding="ISO-8859-1"?>
       <?xml-stylesheet type='text/css' href='person.css'?>
       <!DOCTYPE person SYSTEM "person.dtd">
       <person xmlns="http://xml.oreilly.com/person">
         <name:name xmlns:name="http://xml.oreilly.com/name">
           <name:first>Sydney</name:first>
           <name:last>Lee</name:last>
         </name:name>
         <assignment project_id="p2"/>
       </person>
   start: 236
   length: 5
```

10.
```
   startElement(String namespaceURI, String localName, String qualifiedName,
   Attributes atts)
       namespaceURI: "http://xml.oreilly.com/name"
       localName: "first"
       qualifiedName: "name:first"
       atts: {} (no attributes, an empty list)
```

11.
```
   characters(char[] text, int start, int length)
       text: <?xml version="1.0" encoding="ISO-8859-1"?>
       <?xml-stylesheet type='text/css' href='person.css'?>
       <!DOCTYPE person SYSTEM "person.dtd">
       <person xmlns="http://xml.oreilly.com/person">
         <name:name xmlns:name="http://xml.oreilly.com/name">
           <name:first>Sydney</name:first>
           <name:last>Lee</name:last>
         </name:name>
         <assignment project_id="p2"/>
       </person>
   start: 253
   length: 6
```

12.

```
endElement(String namespaceURI, String localName, String qualifiedName)
    namespaceURI: "http://xml.oreilly.com/name"
    localName: "first"
    qualifiedName: "name:first"
```

13.

```
ignorableWhitespace(char[] text, int start, int length)
    text: <?xml version="1.0" encoding="ISO-8859-1"?>
    <?xml-stylesheet type='text/css' href='person.css'?>
    <!DOCTYPE person SYSTEM "person.dtd">
    <person xmlns="http://xml.oreilly.com/person">
      <name:name xmlns:name="http://xml.oreilly.com/name">
        <name:first>Sydney</name:first>
        <name:last>Lee</name:last>
      </name:name>
      <assignment project_id="p2"/>
    </person>
    start: 272
    length: 5
```

14.

```
startElement(String namespaceURI, String localName, String qualifiedName,
Attributes atts)
    namespaceURI: "http://xml.oreilly.com/name"
    localName: "last"
    qualifiedName: "name:last"
    atts: {} (no attributes, an empty list)
```

15.

```
characters(char[] text, int start, int length)
    text: <?xml version="1.0" encoding="ISO-8859-1"?>
    <?xml-stylesheet type='text/css' href='person.css'?>
    <!DOCTYPE person SYSTEM "person.dtd">
    <person xmlns="http://xml.oreilly.com/person">
      <name:name xmlns:name="http://xml.oreilly.com/name">
        <name:first>Sydney</name:first>
        <name:last>Lee</name:last>
      </name:name>
      <assignment project_id="p2"/>
    </person>
    start: 288
    length: 3
```

16.

```
endElement(String namespaceURI, String localName, String qualifiedName)
    namespaceURI: "http://xml.oreilly.com/name"
    localName: "last"
    qualifiedName: "name:last"
```

17.

```
ignorableWhitespace(char[] text, int start, int length)
    text: <?xml version="1.0" encoding="ISO-8859-1"?>
    <?xml-stylesheet type='text/css' href='person.css'?>
    <!DOCTYPE person SYSTEM "person.dtd">
```

```
    <person xmlns="http://xml.oreilly.com/person">
      <name:name xmlns:name="http://xml.oreilly.com/name">
        <name:first>Sydney</name:first>
        <name:last>Lee</name:last>
      </name:name>
      <assignment project_id="p2"/>
    </person>
start: 303
length: 3
```

18.

```
endElement(String namespaceURI, String localName, String qualifiedName)
    namespaceURI: "http://xml.oreilly.com/name"
    localName: "name"
    qualifiedName: "name:name"
```

19.

```
endPrefixMapping(String prefix)
    prefix: "name"
```

20.

```
ignorableWhitespace(char[] text, int start, int length)
    text: <?xml version="1.0" encoding="ISO-8859-1"?>
    <?xml-stylesheet type='text/css' href='person.css'?>
    <!DOCTYPE person SYSTEM "person.dtd">
    <person xmlns="http://xml.oreilly.com/person">
      <name:name xmlns:name="http://xml.oreilly.com/name">
        <name:first>Sydney</name:first>
        <name:last>Lee</name:last>
      </name:name>
      <assignment project_id="p2"/>
    </person>
start: 318
length: 3
```

21.

```
startElement(String namespaceURI, String localName, String qualifiedName,
Attributes atts)
    namespaceURI: "http://xml.oreilly.com/person"
    localName: "assignment"
    qualifiedName: "assignment
    atts: {project_id="p2"}
```

22.

```
endElement(String namespaceURI, String localName, String qualifiedName)
    namespaceURI: "http://xml.oreilly.com/person"
    localName: "assignment"
    qualifiedName: "assignment"
```

23.

```
ignorableWhitespace(char[] text, int start, int length)
    text: <?xml version="1.0" encoding="ISO-8859-1"?>
    <?xml-stylesheet type='text/css' href='person.css'?>
    <!DOCTYPE person SYSTEM "person.dtd">
    <person xmlns="http://xml.oreilly.com/person">
```

```
        <name:name xmlns:name="http://xml.oreilly.com/name">
          <name:first>Sydney</name:first>
          <name:last>Lee</name:last>
        </name:name>
        <assignment project_id="p2"/>
      </person>
    start: 350
    length: 1
```

24.

```
    endElement(String namespaceURI, String localName, String qualifiedName)
        namespaceURI: "http://xml.oreilly.com/person"
        localName: "person"
        qualifiedName: "person"
```

25.

```
    endPrefixMapping(String prefix)
        prefix: ""
```

26.

```
    endDocument()
```

Some pieces of this are not deterministic. Note that the char array passed to each call to characters() and ignorableWhitespace() actually contains the entire document! The specific text block that the parser really returns is indicated by the second two arguments. This is an optimization that Xerces-J performs. Other parsers are free to pass different char arrays as long as they set the start and length arguments to match. Indeed, the parser is also free to split a long run of plain text across multiple calls to characters() or ignorableWhitespace(), so you cannot assume that these methods necessarily return the longest possible contiguous run of plain text. Other details that may change from parser to parser include attribute order within a tag and whether a Locator object is provided by calling setDocumentLocator().

Suppose you want to count the number of elements, attributes, processing instructions, and characters of plain text that exist in a given XML document. To do so, first write a class that implements the ContentHandler interface. The current count of each of the four items of interest is stored in a field. The field values are initialized to zero in the startDocument() method, which is called exactly once for each document parsed. Each callback method in the class increments the relevant field. The endDocument() method reports the total for that document. Example 20-3 is such a class.

Example 20-3. The XMLCounter ContentHandler

```
import org.xml.sax.*;

public class XMLCounter implements ContentHandler {

  private int numberOfElements;
  private int numberOfAttributes;
  private int numberOfProcessingInstructions;
  private int numberOfCharacters;
```

Example 20-3. The XMLCounter ContentHandler (continued)

```java
public void startDocument( ) {
  numberOfElements = 0;
  numberOfAttributes = 0;
  numberOfProcessingInstructions = 0;
  numberOfCharacters = 0;
}

// We should count either the start-tag of the element or the end-tag,
// but not both. Empty elements are reported by each of these methods.
public void startElement(String namespaceURI, String localName,
 String qualifiedName, Attributes atts)  {
  numberOfElements++;
  numberOfAttributes += atts.getLength( );
}

public void endElement(String namespaceURI, String localName,
 String qualifiedName)  { }

public void characters(char[ ] text, int start, int length) {
  numberOfCharacters += length;
}

public void ignorableWhitespace(char[ ] text, int start, int length) {
  numberOfCharacters += length;
}

public void processingInstruction(String target, String data)
 throws SAXException {
  numberOfProcessingInstructions++;
}

// Now that the document is done, we can print out the final results
public void endDocument( ) {
  System.out.println("Number of elements: " + numberOfElements);
  System.out.println("Number of attributes: " + numberOfAttributes);
  System.out.println("Number of processing instructions: "
   + numberOfProcessingInstructions);
  System.out.println("Number of characters of plain text: "
   + numberOfCharacters);
}

// Do-nothing methods we have to implement only to fulfill
// the interface requirements:
public void setDocumentLocator(Locator locator) { }
public void startPrefixMapping(String prefix, String uri) { }
public void endPrefixMapping(String prefix)  { }
public void skippedEntity(String name)  { }

}
```

This class needs to override most methods in the ContentHandler interface. However, if you really want to provide only one or two ContentHandler methods, you may want to subclass the DefaultHandler class instead. This adapter class implements all methods in the ContentHandler interface with do-nothing methods, so you only have to override methods you're genuinely interested in.

Next, build an XMLReader, and configure it with an instance of this class. Finally, parse the documents you want to count, as in Example 20-4.

Example 20-4. The DocumentStatistics driver class

```java
import org.xml.sax.*;
import org.xml.sax.helpers.*;
import java.io.IOException;

public class DocumentStatistics {

  public static void main(String[] args) {

    XMLReader parser;
    try {
     parser = XMLReaderFactory.createXMLReader();
    }
    catch (SAXException e) {
      // fall back on Xerces parser by name
      try {
        parser = XMLReaderFactory.createXMLReader(
          "org.apache.xerces.parsers.SAXParser");
      }
      catch (SAXException eex) {
        System.err.println("Couldn't locate a SAX parser");
        return;
      }
    }

    if (args.length == 0) {
      System.out.println(
        "Usage: java DocumentStatistics URL1 URL2...");
    }

    // Install the Content Handler
    parser.setContentHandler(new XMLCounter());

    // start parsing...
    for (int i = 0; i < args.length; i++) {

      // command line should offer URIs or file names
      try {
        parser.parse(args[i]);
      }
```

Example 20-4. The DocumentStatistics driver class (continued)

```
    catch (SAXParseException ex) { // well-formedness error
      System.out.println(args[i] + " is not well formed.");
      System.out.println(ex.getMessage()
        + " at line " + ex.getLineNumber()
        + ", column " + ex.getColumnNumber());
    }
    catch (SAXException ex) { // some other kind of error
      System.out.println(ex.getMessage());
    }
    catch (IOException ex) {
      System.out.println("Could not report on " + args[i]
        + " because of the IOException " + ex);
    }

  }

 }

}
```

Running the program in Example 20-4 across the document in Example 20-2 results in the following output:

```
D:\books\xian\examples\18>java DocumentStatistics 20-2.xml
Number of elements: 5
Number of attributes: 1
Number of processing instructions: 1
Number of characters of plain text: 29
```

This generic program of Example 20-4 works on any well-formed XML document. Most SAX programs are more specific and only work with certain XML applications. They look for particular elements or attributes in particular places and respond to them accordingly. They may rely on patterns that are enforced by a validating parser. Still, this behavior comprises the fundamentals of SAX.

The complicated part of most SAX programs is the data structure you build to store information returned by the parser until you're ready to use it. Sometimes, this information can be as complicated as the XML document itself, in which case you may be better off using DOM, which at least provides a ready-made data structure for an XML document. You usually want only some information, though, and the data structure you construct should be less complex than the document itself.

Features and Properties

SAX uses properties and features to control parser behavior. Each feature and property has a name that's an absolute URI. Like namespace URIs, absolute URIs are only used to name things and do not necessarily point to a real page you can load into a web browser. Features are either true or false; that is, they're Booleans. Properties have values of an appropriate Object type. Different parsers support different groups of features and properties, although there are a few standard ones most parsers support.

The *http://xml.org/sax/features/validation* feature controls whether a parser validates. If this feature is true, then the parser will report validity errors in the document to the registered ErrorHandler; otherwise, it won't. This feature is turned off by default. To turn a feature on, pass the feature's name and value to the XMLReader's setFeature( ) method:

```
try {
  parser.setFeature("http://xml.org/sax/features/validation", true);
}
catch (SAXNotSupportedException ex) {
  System.out.println("Cannot turn on validation right now.");
}
catch (SAXNotRecognizedException ex) {
  System.out.println("This is not a validating parser.");
}
```

Not all parsers can validate. If you try to turn on validation in a parser that doesn't validate or set any other feature the parser doesn't provide, setFeature( ) throws a SAXNotRecognizedException. If you try to set a feature the parser does recognize but cannot change at the current time—e.g., you try to turn on validation when the parser has already read half of the document—setFeature( ) throws a SAXNotSupportedException. Both are subclasses of SAXException.

You can check a feature's current value using XMLReader's getFeature( ) method. This method returns a boolean and throws the same exceptions for the same reasons as setFeature( ). If you want to know whether the parser validates, you can ask in the following manner:

```
try {
  boolean isValidating =
    parser.getFeature("http://xml.org/sax/features/validation");
}
catch (SAXException ex) {
  System.out.println("This is not a validating parser");
}
```

Properties are similar to features, but they allow a broader choice than a simple Boolean on/off, true/false dichotomy. Each property value is an object of unspecified type. For example, to determine the version of XML (1.0 or 1.1) used by the document, read the http://xml.org/sax/properties/document-xml-version property with the getProperty( ) method:

```
try {
  String version = (String) parser.getProperty(
   "http://xml.org/sax/properties/document-xml-version");
  if ("1.0".equals(version) {
    System.out.println("A good conservative document");
  }
  else if ("1.1".equals(version) {
    System.out.println("A dangerously radical document");
  }
  else {
    System.out.println("A  very strange document: " + version);
  }
}
```

```
    catch (SAXNotSupportedException ex) {
      System.out.println(
        "Cannot provide the version of XML used by the document right now.");
    }
    catch (SAXNotRecognizedException ex) {
      System.out.println("Parser does not recognize the " +
        "http://xml.org/sax/properties/document-xml-version property");
    }
```

You can change a property value by invoking the setProperty( ) method with two arguments. The first is the URI of the property to set. The second is the object specifying the value for the property. For example, this code fragment attempts to set the http://xml.org/sax/properties/LexicalHandler property to a new instance of the MyLexicalHandlerClass. The parser reports lexical events (comments, CDATA sections, and entity references) to the org.xml.sax.ext.LexicalHandler implementation object named by this property:

```
    try {
      parser.setProperty(
        "http://xml.org/sax/properties/LexicalHandler",
        new MyLexicalHandlerClass( )
      );
    }
    catch (SAXException ex) {
      System.out.println("This parser does not provide lexical events.");
    }
```

If you pass in the wrong kind of object for a property (e.g., an object that does not implement the LexicalHandler interface for the http://xml.org/sax/properties/ LexicalHandler property), then setProperty( ) throws a SAXNotSupportedException.

Not all features and properties can be set. Some features such as http://xml.org/ sax/properties/document-xml-version are read-only. Others can be set at some times but not others. For example, you cannot turn on validation when the parser is already halfway through a document. An attempt to do so will fail and throw a SAXNotSupportedException. However, you can change a parser's features after parsing one document, but before parsing the next. You can read most feature and property values at any time, although a few (such as http://xml.org/sax/ properties/document-xml-version) can only be read when the parser is reading a document.

Filters

A SAX filter sits between the parser and the client application and intercepts the messages that these two objects pass to each other. It can pass these messages unchanged or modify, replace, or block them. To a client application, the filter looks like a parser, that is, an XMLReader. To the parser, the filter looks like a client application, that is, a ContentHandler.

SAX filters are implemented by subclassing the org.xml.sax.helpers.
XMLFilterImpl class.* This class implements all the required interfaces of SAX for
both parsers and client applications. That is, its signature is as follows:

```
public class XMLFilterImpl implements XMLFilter, XMLReader,
    ContentHandler, DTDHandler, ErrorHandler
```

Your own filters will extend this class and override those methods that correspond to the messages you want to filter. For example, if you wanted to filter out
all processing instructions, you would write a filter that would override the
processingInstruction( ) method to do nothing, as shown in Example 20-5.

Example 20-5. A SAX filter that removes processing instructions

```
import org.xml.sax.helpers.XMLFilterImpl;

public class ProcessingInstructionStripper extends XMLFilterImpl {

  public void processingInstruction(String target, String data) {
    // Because this does nothing, processing instructions read in the
    // document are *not* passed to client application
  }

}
```

If instead you wanted to replace a processing instruction with an element whose
name was the same as the processing instruction's target and whose text content
was the processing instruction's data, you'd call the startElement( ), characters( ),
and endElement( ) methods from inside the processingInstruction( ) method after
filling in the arguments with the relevant data from the processing instruction, as
shown in Example 20-6.

Example 20-6. A SAX filter that converts processing instructions to elements

```
import org.xml.sax.*;
import org.xml.sax.helpers.*;

public class ProcessingInstructionConverter extends XMLFilterImpl {

  public void processingInstruction(String target, String data)
    throws SAXException {

    // AttributesImpl is an adapter class in the org.xml.sax.ext package
    // for precisely this case. We don't really want to add any attributes
    // here, but we need to pass something as the fourth argument to
    // startElement( ).
    Attributes emptyAttributes = new AttributesImpl( );
```

---

* There's also an org.xml.sax.XMLFilter interface. However, this interface is arranged exactly backward for most use cases. It filters messages from the client application to the parser, but not the
  much more important messages from the parser to the client application. Furthermore, implementing the XMLFilter interface directly requires a lot more work than subclassing XMLFilterImpl.
  Experienced SAX programmers almost never implement XMLFilter directly rather than subclassing XMLFilterImpl.

Example 20-6. A SAX filter that converts processing instructions to elements (continued)

```
    // We won't use any namespace for the element
    startElement("", target, target, emptyAttributes);
    // converts String data to char array
    char[] text = data.toCharArray();
    characters(text, 0, text.length);

    endElement("", target, target);

  }

}
```

We used this filter before passing Example 20-2 into a program that echoes an XML document onto System.out and were a little surprised to see this come out:

```
<xml-stylesheet>type="text/css" href="person.css"</xml-stylesheet>
<person xmlns="http://xml.oreilly.com/person">
  <name:name xmlns:name="http://xml.oreilly.com/name">
    <name:first>Sydney</name:first>
    <name:last>Lee</name:last>
  </name:name>
  <assignment project_id="p2"></assignment>
</person>
```

This document is not well-formed! The specific problem is that there are two independent root elements. However, on further consideration, that's really not too surprising. Well-formedness checking is normally done by the underlying parser when it reads the text form of an XML document. SAX filters should, but are not absolutely required to, provide well-formed XML data to client applications. Indeed, they can produce substantially more malformed data than this by including start-tags that are not matched by end-tags; text that contains illegal characters, such as the formfeed or the vertical tab; and XML names that contain non-name characters, such as * and §. You need to be very careful before assuming data you receive from a filter is valid or well-formed.

If you want to invoke a method without filtering it, or you want to invoke the same method in the underlying handler, you can prefix a call to it with the super keyword. This invokes the variant of the method from the superclass. By default, each method in XMLFilterImpl just passes the same arguments to the equivalent method in the parent handler. Example 20-7 demonstrates with a filter that changes all character data to uppercase by overriding the characters( ) method.

Example 20-7. A SAX filter that converts text to uppercase

```
import org.xml.sax.*;
import org.xml.sax.helpers.*;

public class UpperCaseFilter extends XMLFilterImpl {

  public void characters(char[] text, int start, int length)
    throws SAXException {
```

Example 20-7. A SAX filter that converts text to uppercase (continued)

```
    String temp = new String(text, start, length);
    temp = temp.toUpperCase( );
    text = temp.toCharArray( );
    super.characters(text, 0, text.length);

  }

}
```

Using a filter involves these steps:

1. Create a filter object, normally by invoking its own constructor.

2. Create the XMLReader that will actually parse the document, normally by calling XMLReaderFactory.createXMLReader( ).

3. Attach the filter to the parser using the filter's setParent( ) method.

4. Install a ContentHandler in the filter.

5. Parse the document by calling the filter's parse( ) method.

Details can vary a little from application to application. For instance, you might install other handlers besides the ContentHandler or change the parent between documents. However, once the filter has been attached to the underlying XMLReader, you should not directly invoke any methods on this underlying parser; you should only talk to it through the filter. For example, this is how you'd use the filter in Example 20-7 to parse a document:

```
    XMLFilter filter = new UpperCaseFilter( );
    filter.setParent(XMLReaderFactory.createXMLReader( ));
    filter.setContentHandler(yourContentHandlerObject);
    filter.parse(document);
```

Notice specifically that you invoke the filter's parse( ) method, not the underlying parser's parse( ) method.

IV

Reference

21

XML Reference

This chapter is intended to serve as a comprehensive reference to the Extensible Markup Language (XML) W3C recommendations for both XML 1.0 and 1.1. We have made every effort to cover the contents of the official W3C document exhaustively. However, if you are implementing an XML parser, editor, or other tool, you should also review the latest revision of these recommendations on the Web at *http://www.w3.org/TR/REC-xml* and *http://www.w3.org/TR/xml11/*. This book refers to the XML 1.0 Third Edition dated 04 February 2004 and the XML 1.1 Recommendation dated 04 February 2004, which was edited in place 15 April 2004.

The endorsement of the Extensible Markup Language (XML) 1.1 Recommendation in February of 2004 has introduced some challenges within the XML community. The markup language described by 1.1 is not precisely a superset of the language described by Version 1.0, which means that some documents that are well-formed under 1.0 rules will not be well-formed under 1.1 rules. The main narrative of this chapter adheres to the rules laid out by the 1.0 Recommendation. Notes such as this one will appear when necessary to outline the differences between XML 1.0 and XML 1.1.

When deciding which version of XML is appropriate for your application, consider that unless you specifically need to use markup names that contain characters not available in Unicode 2.0, XML 1.0 will most likely be the correct choice.

How to Use This Reference

This chapter consists of examples of XML documents and DTDs, followed by detailed reference sections that describe every feature of the XML specification and a listing of possible well-formedness and validity errors. The syntax items of

XML are introduced in the rough order in which they appear in an XML document. Each entry explains the syntactic structure, where it can be used, and the applicable validity and well-formedness constraints. Each reference section contains a description of the XML language structure, an informal syntax, and an example of the syntax's usage where appropriate.

Annotated Sample Documents

These examples are intended as a mnemonic aid for XML syntax and as a quick map from a specific instance of an XML language construct to its corresponding XML syntax reference section. The sample document and DTD incorporate features defined in the XML 1.0 and Namespaces in XML recommendations.

The sample XML application describes the construction of a piece of furniture. Within the figures, each distinct language construct is enclosed in a box, with the relevant reference section name provided as a callout. By locating a construct in the sample, then locating the associated reference section, you can quickly recognize and learn about unfamiliar XML syntax. Four files make up this sample application:

bookcase.xml
> The document shown in Figure 21-1 uses *furniture.dtd* to describe a simple bookcase.

furniture.dtd
> The XML document type definition shown in Figure 21-2 provides a simple grammar for describing components and assembly details for a piece of furniture.

bookcase_ex.ent
> The external entity file shown in Figure 21-3 contains additional bookcase-specific elements for the *bookcase.xml* document.

parts_list.ent
> Figure 21-4 contains an external parsed general entity example that contains the parts list for the bookcase example document.

The following annotations label parts of the XML document:

- **XML Declaration**
- **Version Information**
- **Encoding Declaration**
- **Standalone Declaration**

```xml
<?xml version="1.0" encoding="UTF-8" standalone="no"?>
<!--
    Bookcase.xml

    Sample file using the furniture.dtd element declarations.
-->
<?xml-stylesheet href="furniture.css" type="text/css"?>
<!DOCTYPE furniture_item SYSTEM "furniture.dtd"
[
<!ENTITY % bookcase_ex SYSTEM "Bookcase_ex.ent">
%bookcase_ex;
<!ENTITY bookcase_pic SYSTEM "bookcase.gif" NDATA gif>
<!ENTITY parts_list SYSTEM "parts_list.ent">
]>
<furniture_item xmlns="http://namespaces.oreilly.com/furniture/">
    <desc><![CDATA[<p>Four Shelf Bookcase</p>]]>&cright_notice;</desc>
    <model_num>XIAN-BC/1</model_num>
    <picture src="bookcase_pic" type="gif"/>
    <diagram>
        <svg:svg width="396" height="538"
            xmlns:svg="http://www.w3.org/2000/svg-20000303-stylable">
            <svg:desc>Bookcase Diagram</svg:desc>
            <svg:rect transform="matrix(1 0 0 -1 -50 639)" x="59.861" y="207.628"
                width="286.326" height="421.953"/>
            <svg:rect transform="matrix(1 0 0 -1 40.42 729.4)"
                x="59.861" y="207.628" width="286.326" height="421.953"/>
            <svg:path d="M9.861 11.93 192.93 92.93"/>
            <svg:path d="M292.419 430.116 192.93 92.93"/>
            <svg:path d="M13.628 435.139 192.93 92.93"/>
            <svg:path d="M292.419 10.674 192.93 92.93"/>
        </svg:svg>
    </diagram>
    &parts_list;
    <?furniture_app verify_parts_list?>
    <assembly id="HC" repeat="8">
        <part part_num="E"/>
        <part part_num="F"/>
    </assembly>

    <assembly repeat="4">
        <fastener part_num="H" count="4"/>
        <part part_num="D"/>
        <assembly>
            <fastener part_num="G" count="22"/>
            <assembly repeat="2">
                <fastener part_num="HC" count="4"/>
                <part part_num="A"/>
                <part part_num="B"/>
            </assembly>
            <part part_num="C"/>
        </assembly>
    </assembly>
</furniture_item>
```

Annotations (labels pointing to the code):
- Comments
- External Subset
- Names
- Whitespace
- Parameter Entity Declarations
- Parameter Entity References
- Parameter Entities
- Unparsed Entities
- External General Entities
- Internal DTD Subset
- DOCTYPE Declaration
- Root Element
- CDATA Section
- General Entity References
- Empty Element Tags
- Start-tag
- Attributes
- End-tag
- Processing Instructions

Figure 21-1. bookcase.xml

```
<!--
    furniture.dtd

    A vocabulary for describing furniture.
-->

<!ELEMENT furniture_item (desc, %extra_tags; user_tags?, parts_list,
assembly+)>
```
— Element Type Declaration

```
<!ATTLIST furniture_item
    xmlns CDATA #FIXED "http://namespaces.oreilly.com/furniture/"
>

<!ELEMENT p (#PCDATA)>

<!ELEMENT desc (#PCDATA | p)* >
```
— Mixed Element Type
```
<!ATTLIST desc
    xml:lang NMTOKEN 'en'
```
— xml:lang
```
    xml:space (default|preserve) 'preserve'
```
— xml:space
```
>
```
— Enumeration Type
```
<!ELEMENT user_tags ANY>
```
— Any Element Type
```
<!ELEMENT parts_list (part_name+)>
<!ELEMENT part_name (#PCDATA)>
<!ATTLIST part_name
    id ID #REQUIRED
    count CDATA "1"
>
```
Constrained Child Nodes
```
<!ELEMENT assembly (fastener*, (assembly | part), (assembly | part)+) >
<!ATTLIST assembly
    id ID #IMPLIED
>
```
— Attribute List Declaration
```
<!ELEMENT fastener EMPTY >
<!ATTLIST fastener
```
— Empty Element Type
```
    part_num IDREF #REQUIRED
    count CDATA "1"
>
```
— Default Values
```
<!ELEMENT part EMPTY>
<!ATTLIST part
    part_num IDREF #REQUIRED
    count CDATA "1"
>
<!ENTITY % private 'IGNORE'>
<!ENTITY % public 'INCLUDE'>
<![ %private; [
```
Character References
```
    <!ENTITY cright_notice "&#xa9; 2000 Furniture Makers. DO NOT
DISTRIBUTE">
```
— General Entity Declarations
— Internal General Entities
```
]]>
<![ %public; [
    <!ENTITY cright_notice "&#xa9; 2000 Furniture Makers.">
]]>
```
— Conditional Sections

Figure 21-2. furniture.dtd

```
<!ENTITY % extra_tags "model_num, picture, diagram,">
<!ELEMENT model_num (#PCDATA)>
<!ELEMENT picture EMPTY>
<!ATTLIST picture
    src ENTITY #REQUIRED
>

<!NOTATION dos SYSTEM "dos_batch">
<!NOTATION perl SYSTEM "perl">

<!ELEMENT batch_script (#PCDATA)>

<!ATTLIST batch_script
    lang NOTATION (dos | perl) #IMPLIED          ──Notation Attribute Type
>

<!ELEMENT diagram ANY>

<!ELEMENT svg:svg (svg:desc, (svg:rect | svg:path)+)>
<!ATTLIST svg:svg
    width CDATA "1"
    height CDATA "1"
    xmlns:svg CDATA #FIXED "http://www.w3.org/2000/svg"
>

<!ELEMENT svg:desc (#PCDATA)>

<!ELEMENT svg:rect EMPTY>
<!ATTLIST svg:rect
    transform CDATA "1"
    x CDATA "1"
    y CDATA "1"
    width CDATA "1"
    height CDATA "1"
>

<!ELEMENT svg:path EMPTY>
<!ATTLIST svg:path
    d CDATA "1"
>

<!NOTATION gif SYSTEM "images/gif">          ──Notation Declaration
```

Figure 21-3. bookcase_ex.ent

```
<parts_list>
    <part_name id="A" count="1">END PANEL</part_name>
    <part_name id="B" count="2">SIDE PANEL</part_name>
    <part_name id="C" count="1">BACK PANEL</part_name>
    <part_name id="D" count="4">SHELF</part_name>
    <part_name id="E" count="8">HIDDEN CONNECTORS</part_name>
    <part_name id="F" count="8">CONNECTOR SCREWS</part_name>

    <part_name id="G" count="22">7/16&quot; TACKS</part_name>

    <part_name id="H" count="16">SHELF PEGS</part_name>
</parts_list>
                                            Predefined Entity Reference
```

Figure 21-4. parts_list.ent

XML Syntax

For each section of this reference that maps directly to an XML language structure, an informal syntax reference describes that structure's form. The following conventions are used with these syntax blocks:

Format	Meaning
DOCTYPE	Bold text indicates literal characters that must appear as written within the document (e.g., **DOCTYPE**).
encoding-name	Italicized text indicates that the user must replace the text with real data. The item indicates what type of data should be inserted (e.g., *encoding-name* = en-us).
|	The vertical bar indicates that only one out of a list of possible values can be selected.
[]	Square brackets indicate that a particular portion of the syntax is optional.

Global Syntax Structures

Every XML document is broken into two primary sections: the prolog and the document element. A few documents may also have comments or processing instructions that follow the root element in a sort of *epilog* (an unofficial term). The prolog contains structural information about the particular type of XML document you are writing, including the XML declaration and document type declaration. The prolog is optional, and if a document does not need to be validated against a DTD, it can be omitted completely. The only required structure in a well-formed XML document is the top-level document element itself.

The following syntax structures are common to the entire XML document. Unless otherwise noted within a subsequent reference item, the following structures can appear anywhere within an XML document.

Characters

XML documents are inherently text documents, which are composed of characters. To ensure that documents are portable across disparate computer systems and can contain content in as many written human languages as possible, XML parsers are required to implement the Unicode standard. This does not mean that all XML documents must be saved and edited in Unicode, but it does mean that the XML parser must be able to convert your document from its native character encoding to Unicode. All XML parsers are required to support (as a minimum) either UTF-8 or UTF-16 as input encoding formats. For more information on encoding formats and Unicode, see Chapter 27.

 One of the primary differences between XML 1.0 and XML 1.1 is the definition of which Unicode characters are valid within an XML document. In XML 1.0, many of the ASCII control characters (such as BEL and NAK) were explicitly disallowed within XML documents. XML 1.1 permits any Unicode character these 60 control characters (except for null, x0000) as long as they're escaped with numeric character references. XML 1.1 also requires that the C1 controls between 0x0080 and 0x009F be escaped with numeric character references, which XML 1.0 does not require.

Whitespace

XML 1.0 defines whitespace as a space, tab, carriage return, or line feed. XML 1.1 also includes the newline character NEL (#x85) and Unicode line separator (#x2028) in whitespace. Whitespace serves the same purpose in XML as it does in most programming and natural languages: to separate tokens and language elements from one another. To an XML parser, all whitespace in element content is significant and will be passed to the client application. Whitespace within tags—for instance, between attributes—is not significant. Consider the following example:

```
<p>  This sentence has extraneous
    line breaks.</p>
```

After parsing, the character data from this example element is passed to the underlying application as:

```
    This sentence has extraneous
line breaks.
```

Although XML specifies that all whitespace in element content be preserved for use by the client application, an additional facility is available to the XML author to further hint that an element's character data's space and formatting should be preserved. For more information, see the discussion of the xml:space attribute in "Special Attributes" later in this chapter.

To simplify the lives of software developers, parsers are expected to normalize all occurrences of the carriage return (#xD) character to a single line feed (#xA) character. When the carriage return character appears directly before a line feed, it is simply removed. This results in a document that contains only single line feed characters to mark line ends. In XML 1.1, this normalization to a line feed character also occurs for the Unicode characters #x85 (NEXT LINE, NEL) and #x2028 (LINE SEPARATOR).

Names

XML 1.0 names must adhere to the following lexical conventions:

- Begin with a letter, ideograph, _, or : character.
- After the first character, be composed only of letters, digits, ., -, _, and : characters.

In this context, a letter is any Unicode character that matches the Letter production from the XML 1.0 EBNF grammar at the end of this chapter.

 See the XML 1.1 EBNF grammar production for Name to see which characters are permitted within XML 1.1 names.

According to the XML 1.0 specification, the : character may be used freely within names, although the character is now officially reserved as part of the "Namespaces in XML" recommendation. Even if a document does not use namespaces, the colon should still not be used within identifiers to maintain compatibility with namespace-aware parsers. See the "Namespaces" section in this chapter for more information about how namespace-aware identifiers are formed.

Names should also avoid starting with the three-letter sequence X, M, L (in any case combination), unless specifically sanctioned by an XML specification.

Character References

&#decimal-number;
&#xhexadecimal-number;

All XML parsers are based on the Unicode character set, no matter what the external encoding of the XML file is. It is theoretically possible to author documents directly in Unicode, but many text-editing, storage, and delivery systems do not fully support the Unicode character set. To allow XML authors to include Unicode characters in their documents' content without forcing them to abandon their existing editing tools, XML provides the *character reference* mechanism.

A character reference allows an author to insert a Unicode character by number (either decimal or hexadecimal) into the output stream produced by the parser to an XML application. Consider an XML document that includes the following character data:

    © 2002 O'Reilly & Associates

In this example, the parser would replace the character reference with the actual Unicode character and pass it to the client application:

    © 2002 O'Reilly & Associates

Character references may not be used in element or attribute names, although they may be used in attribute values. Note that hexadecimal character references are case-insensitive (i.e., &xa9; is equivalent to &xA9;).

Predefined Entities

Besides user-defined entity references, XML includes the five named entity references shown in Table 21-1 that can be used without being declared. These references are a subset of those available in HTML documents.

Table 21-1. Predefined entities

Entity	Character	XML declaration
<	<	<!ENTITY lt "&#60;">
>	>	<!ENTITY gt ">">
&	&	<!ENTITY amp "&#38;">
'	'	<!ENTITY apos "'">
"	"	<!ENTITY quot """>

The < and & entities must be used wherever < or & appear in element content or attribute values. The > entity is frequently used wherever > appears in document content, but it is only mandatory to avoid putting the sequence]]> into content. ' and " are generally used only within attribute values to avoid conflicts between the value and the quotes used to contain the value.

Although the parser must recognize these entities regardless of whether they have been declared, you can declare them in your DTD without generating errors.

The presence of these "special" predefined entities creates a conundrum within an XML document. Because it is possible to use these references without declaring them, it is possible to have a valid XML document that includes references to entities that were never declared. The XML specification actually encourages document authors to declare these entities to support older SGML parsers that don't predefine these entities. In practical terms, declaring these entities only adds unnecessary complexity to your document.

CDATA (Character Data) Sections

<!CDATA[*unescaped character & markup data*]]>

XML documents consist of markup and character data. The < or & characters cannot be included inside normal character data without using a character or entity reference, such as & or &. By using a reference, the resulting < and & characters are not recognized as markup by the parser, but they will become part of the data stream to the parser's client application.

For large blocks of character data—particularly if the data contains markup, such as an HTML or XML fragment—the CDATA section can be used. Within a CDATA block, every character between the opening and closing strings is treated as character data. Thus, special characters can be included in a CDATA section with impunity, except for the CDATA closing sequence,]]>.

CDATA sections are very useful for tasks such as enclosing XML or HTML documents inside of tutorials explaining how to use markup, but it is difficult to process the contents of CDATA sections using XSLT, the DOM, or SAX as anything other than text.

 CDATA sections cannot be nested. The character sequence]]> cannot appear within data that is being escaped, or the CDATA block will be closed prematurely. This situation should not be a problem ordinarily, but if an application includes XML documents as unparsed character data, it is important to be aware of this constraint. If it is necessary to include the CDATA closing sequence in the data, close the open CDATA section, include the closing characters using character references to escape them, then reopen the CDATA section to contain the rest of the character data.

Entities

An XML entity can best be understood as a macro replacement facility, in which the replacement can be either parsed (the text becomes part of the XML document) or unparsed. If unparsed, the entity declaration points to external binary data that cannot be parsed. Additionally, the replacement text for parsed entities can come from a string or the contents of an external file. During parsing, a parsed entity reference is replaced by the substitution text that is specified in the entity declaration. The replacement text is then reparsed until no more entity or character references remain.

To simplify document parsing, two distinct types of entities are used in different situations: general and parameter. The basic syntax for referencing both entity types is almost identical, but specific rules apply to where each type can be used.

Parameter Entity References

%name;

When an XML parser encounters a parameter entity reference within a document's DTD, it replaces the reference with the entity's text. Whether the replacement text is included as a literal or included from an external entity, the parser continues parsing the replacement text as if it had always been a part of the document. This parsing has interesting implications for nested entity references:

```
<!ENTITY % YEAR "2001">
<!ENTITY COPYRIGHT "&#xa9; %YEAR;">

. . .

<copyright_notice>&COPYRIGHT;</copyright_notice>
```

After the necessary entity replacements are made, the previous example would yield the following canonical element:

```
<copyright_notice>© 2001</copyright_notice>
```

 XML treats parameter entity references differently depending on where they appear within the DTD. References within the literal value of an entity declaration (such as Copyright © %YEAR;) are valid only as part of the external subset. Within the internal subset, parameter entity references may occur only where a complete markup declaration could exist. In other words, within the internal subset, parameter references can be used only to include complete markup declarations.

Parameter entity references are recognized only within the DTD; therefore, the % character has no significance within character data and does not need to be escaped.

General Entity References

&name;

General entity references are recognized only within the parsed character data in the body of an XML document. They may appear within the parsed character data contained between element start- and end-tags, or within the value of an attribute. They are not recognized within a document's DTD (except inside default values for attributes) or within CDATA sections.

 The sequence of operations that occurs when a parsed general entity is included by the XML parser can lead to interesting side effects. An entity's replacement text is, in turn, read by the parser. If character or general entity replacements exist in the entity replacement text, they are also parsed and included as parsing continues.

Comments

```
<!-- comment text -->
```

Comments can appear anywhere in a document or DTD, outside of other markup tags. XML parsers are not required to preserve contents of comment blocks, so they should be used only to store information that is not a part of your application. In reality, most information you might consider storing in a comment block probably should be made an official part of your XML application. Rather than storing data that will be read and acted on by an application in a comment, as is frequently done in HTML documents, you should store it within the element structure of the actual XML document. Enhancing the readability of a complex DTD or temporarily disabling blocks of markup are effective uses of comments.

The character sequence -- cannot be included within a comment block, except as part of the tag closing text. Because comments cannot be nested, commenting out a comment block is impossible.

Processing Instructions

```
<?target processing-instruction data?>
```

Processing instructions provide an escape mechanism that allows an XML application to include instructions to an XML processor that are not validated. The processing instruction target can be any legal XML name, except xml in any combination of upper- and lowercase (see Chapter 2). Linking to a stylesheet to provide formatting instructions for a document is a common use of this mechanism. According to the principles of XML, formatting instructions should remain separate from the actual content of a document, but some mechanism must associate the two. Processing instructions are significant only to applications that recognize them.

The notation facility can indicate exactly what type of processing instruction is included, and each individual XML application must decide what to do with the additional data. No action is required by an XML parser when it recognizes that a particular processing instruction matches a declared notation. When this facility is used, applications that do not recognize the public or system identifiers of a given processing instruction target should realize that they could not properly interpret its data portion.

XML Declaration

```
<?xml version="version_number" [encoding="encoding-name"][standalone="yes|no"]?>
```

The XML declaration serves several purposes. It tells the parser what version of the specification was used, how the document is encoded, and whether the document is completely self-contained or not.

If you need to create an XML document that takes advantage of XML 1.1 features, you need to set the version pseudo-attribute to 1.1:

```
<?xml version="1.1"?>
```

Character Encoding Autodetection

The XML declaration (possibly preceded by a Unicode byte-order mark) must be the very first item in a document so that the XML parser can determine which character encoding was used to store the document. A chicken-and-egg problem exists, involving the XML declaration's encoding="..." clause: the parser can't parse the clause if it doesn't know what character encoding the document uses. However, since the first five characters of the document must be the string <?xml (if it includes an XML declaration), the parser can read the first few bytes of a document and, in most cases, determine the character encoding before it has read the encoding declaration.

The XML declaration, if included, must be the first thing that appears in an XML document. Nothing, except possibly a Unicode byte-order mark, may appear before this structure's initial < character. If no XML declaration is present, the document is assumed to conform to the XML 1.0 Recommendation.

Version Information

... **version**="*version_number*" ...

The version information attribute denotes which version of the XML specification was used to create the current document. At this time, the only possible version numbers are 1.0 and 1.1.

Encoding Declaration

... **encoding**="*encoding-name*" ...

The encoding declaration, if present, indicates which character-encoding was used to store the document. Although all XML documents are ultimately handled as Unicode by the parser, the external storage scheme may be anything from an ASCII text file using the Latin-1 character set (ISO-8859-1) to a file with native Japanese characters.

XML parsers may also recognize other encodings, but the XML specification only requires that they recognize UTF-8 and UTF-16 encoded documents. Most parsers also support additional character encodings. For a thorough discussion of character-encoding schemes, see Chapter 27.

Standalone Declaration

... **standalone**="*yes|no*" ...

If a document is completely self contained (the DTD, if there is one, is contained completely within the original document), then the standalone="yes" declaration may be used. If this declaration is not given, the value no is assumed, and all external entities are read and parsed.

From the standpoint of an XML application developer, this flag has no effect on how a document is parsed. However, if it is given, it must be accurate. Setting standalone="yes" when a document does require DTD declarations that are not present in the main document file is a violation of XML validity rules.

DTD (Document Type Definition)

Chapter 2 explained the difference between well-formed and valid documents. Well-formed documents that include and conform to a given DTD are considered valid. Documents that include a DTD and violate the rules of that DTD are invalid. The DTD is comprised of both the *internal subset* (declarations contained directly within the document) and the *external subset* (declarations that are included from outside the main document).

Parameter Entities

The parameter entity mechanism is a simple macro replacement facility that is only valid within the context of the DTD. Parameter entities are declared and then referenced from within the DTD or possibly from within other entity declarations. The source of the entity replacement text can be either a literal string or the contents of an external file. Parameter entities simplify maintenance of large, complex documents by allowing authors to build libraries of commonly used entity declarations.

Parameter Entity Declarations

```
<!ENTITY % name "Replacement text.">
<!ENTITY % name SYSTEM "system-literal">
<!ENTITY % name PUBLIC "pubid-literal" "system-literal">
```

Parameter entities are declared within the document's DTD and must be declared before they are used. The declaration provides two key pieces of information:

- The name of the entity, which is used when it is referenced
- The replacement text, either directly or indirectly through a link to an external entity

Be aware that an XML parser performs some preprocessing on the replacement text before it is used in an entity reference. Most importantly, parameter entity references in the replacement text are recursively expanded before the final version of the replacement text is stored. Character references are also replaced immediately with the specified character. This replacement can lead to unexpected side effects, particularly when constructing parameter entities that declare other parameter entities. For full disclosure of how entity replacement is implemented by an XML parser and what kinds of unexpected side effects can occur, see Appendix D of the XML 1.0 specification. The specification is available on the World Wide Web Consortium web site (*http://www.w3.org/TR/REC-xml#sec-entexpand*).

Parsed General Entities

```
<!ENTITY name "Replacement text.">
<!ENTITY name SYSTEM "system-literal">
<!ENTITY name PUBLIC "pubid-literal" "system-literal">
```

Parsed general entities are declared within the document type definition and then referenced within the document's text and attribute content. When the document is parsed, the entity's replacement text is substituted for the entity reference. The parser then resumes parsing, starting with the text that was just replaced.

Parsed general entities are declared within the DTD using a superset of the syntax used to declare parameter entities.

Internal entities store the replacement text inline as a literal string. The replacement text within an internal entity is included completely in the entity declaration itself, obviating the need for an external file to contain the replacement text. This situation closely resembles the string replacement macro facilities found in many popular programming languages and environments:

```
<!ENTITY name "Replacement text">
```

When a parsed general entity is referenced, the contents of the external entity are included in the document, and the XML parser resumes parsing, starting with the newly included text.

 There are actually two types of general entities permitted by the XML Recommendation: parsed and unparsed. An unparsed entity is declared using the same syntax as a general parsed external entity, but with the addition of an XML notation name to the declaration:

```
<!ENTITY name SYSTEM "system-literal" notation-name>
<!ENTITY name PUBLIC "pubid-literal" "system-literal"
notation-name>
```

Unparsed general entities are not referenced using the &*name*; syntax. To reference unparsed external entities, it is necessary to declare an attribute using the attribute type ENTITY or ENTITIES.

Unparsed external general entities are one of the features of XML that is poorly understood, poorly supported, and not generally used in practice. It is our recommendation that alternative mechanisms be used to reference external non-XML data (such as XLinks or simple URI strings).

Text Declarations

```
<?xml[ version="version_number"] encoding="encoding-name"?>
```

Files that contain external parsed entities must include a text declaration if the entity file uses a character encoding other than UTF-8 or UTF-16, or if its contents conform to the XML 1.1 Recommendation. This declaration would be followed by the replacement text of the external parsed entity. Entities with no text declaration are assumed to conform to the XML 1.0 Recommendation.

External parsed entities may contain only document content or a completely well-formed subset of the DTD. This restriction is significant because it indicates that external parameter entities cannot be used to play token-pasting games by splitting XML syntax constructs into multiple files, then expecting the parser to reassemble them.

External Subset

The document type declaration can include part or all of the document type definition from an external file. This external portion of the DTD is referred to as the external DTD subset and may contain markup declarations, conditional sections, and parameter entity references. It must include a text declaration if the DTD requires features of XML 1.1 or if the character encoding is not UTF-8 or UTF-16:

```
<?xml[ version="version_number"] encoding="encoding-name"?>
```

This declaration (if present) would then be followed by a series of complete DTD markup statements, including ELEMENT, ATTLIST, ENTITY, and NOTATION declarations, as well as conditional sections, and processing instructions. For example:

```
<!ELEMENT furniture_item (desc, %extra_tags; user_tags?, parts_list,
    assembly+)>

<!ATTLIST furniture_item
    xmlns CDATA #FIXED "http://namespaces.oreilly.com/furniture/"
>
...
```

Internal DTD Subset

The internal DTD subset is the portion of the document type definition included directly within the document type declaration between the [and] characters. The internal DTD subset can contain markup declarations and parameter entity references, but not conditional sections. A single document may have both internal and external DTD subsets, which, when taken together, form the complete document type definition. The following example shows an internal subset, which appears between the [and] characters:

```
<!DOCTYPE furniture_item SYSTEM "furniture.dtd"
[
<!ENTITY % bookcase_ex SYSTEM "Bookcase_ex.ent">

%bookcase_ex;

<!ENTITY bookcase_pic SYSTEM "bookcase.gif" NDATA gif>
<!ENTITY parts_list SYSTEM "parts_list.ent">
]>
```

Element Type Declaration

Element type declarations provide a template for the actual element instances that appear within an XML document. The declaration determines what type of content, if any, can be contained within elements with the given name. The following sections describe the various element content options available.

 Since namespaces are not explicitly included in the XML 1.0 Recommendation, element and attribute declarations within a DTD must give the complete (qualified) name that will be used in the target document. This means that if namespace prefixes will be used in instance documents, the DTD must declare elements and attributes just as they will appear, prefixes and all. While parameter entities may allow instance documents to use different prefixes, this still makes complete and seamless integration of namespaces into a DTD-based application very awkward.

Empty Element Type

`<!ELEMENT` *name* `EMPTY>`

Elements that are declared empty cannot contain content or nested elements. Within the document, empty elements may use one of the following two syntax forms:

```
<name [attribute="value" ...]/>
<name [attribute="value" ...]></name>
```

Any Element Type

`<!ELEMENT` *name* `ANY>`

This content specifier acts as a wildcard, allowing elements of this type to contain character data or instances of any valid element types that are declared in the DTD.

Mixed Content Element Type

`<!ELEMENT` *name* `(#PCDATA [ |` *name* `]+)*>`
`<!ELEMENT` *name* `(#PCDATA)>`

Element declarations that include the #PCDATA token can include text content mixed with other nested elements that are declared in the optional portion of the element declaration. If the #PCDATA token is used, it is not possible to limit the number of times or sequence in which other nested elements are mixed with the parsed character data. If only text content is desired, the asterisk is optional.

Constrained Child Nodes

`<!ELEMENT name (child_node_regexp)[? | * | +]>`

XML provides a simple regular-expression syntax that can be used to limit the order and number of child elements within a parent element. This language includes the following operators:

Operator	Meaning
Name	Matches an element of the given name
( )	Groups expressions for processing as sets of sequences (using the comma as a separator) or choices (using | as a separator)
?	Indicates that the preceding name or expression can occur zero or one times at this point in the document
*	Indicates that the preceding name or expression can occur zero or more times at this point in the document
+	Indicates that the preceding name or expression must occur one or more times at this point in the document

Attribute List Declaration

`<!ATTLIST element_name [attribute_name attribute_type default_decl]*>`

In a valid XML document, it is necessary to declare the attribute names, types, and default values that are used with each element type.

The attribute name must obey the rules for XML names, and no duplicate attribute names may exist within a single declaration.

Attributes are declared as having a specific type. Depending on the declared type, a validating XML parser will constrain the values that appear in instances of those attributes within a document. The following table lists the various attribute types and their meanings:

Attribute type	Meaning
CDATA	Simple character data.
ID	A unique ID value within the current XML document. No two ID attribute values within a document can have the same value, and no element can have two attributes of type ID.
IDREF, IDREFS	A single reference to an element ID (IDREF) or a list of IDs (IDREFS), separated by spaces. Every ID token must refer to a valid ID located somewhere within the document that appears as the ID type attribute's value.
ENTITY, ENTITIES	A single reference to a declared unparsed external entity (ENTITY) or a list of references (ENTITIES), separated by whitespace.
NMTOKEN, NMTOKENS	A single name token value (NMTOKEN) or a list of name tokens (NMTOKENS), separated by spaces.

NOTATION Attribute Type

... NOTATION (*notation [| notation]**) ...

The NOTATION attribute mechanism lets XML document authors indicate that the character content of some elements obey the rules of some formal language other than XML. The following short sample document shows how notations might be used to specify the type of programming language stored in the code_fragment element:

```
<?xml version="1.0"?>
<!DOCTYPE code_fragment
[
<!NOTATION java_code PUBLIC "Java source code">
<!NOTATION c_code PUBLIC "C source code">
<!NOTATION perl_code PUBLIC "Perl source code">
<!ELEMENT code_fragment (#PCDATA)>
<!ATTLIST code_fragment
          code_lang NOTATION (java_code | c_code | perl_code) #REQUIRED>

]>
<code_fragment code_lang="c_code">
    main( ) { printf("Hello, world."); }
</code_fragment>
```

Enumeration Attribute Type

... (*name_token [| name_token]**) ...

This syntax limits the possible values of the given attribute to one of the name tokens from the provided list:

```
<!ELEMENT door EMPTY>
<!ATTLIST door
          state (open | closed | missing) "open">
. . .
<door state="closed"/>
```

Default Values

If an optional attribute is not present on a given element, a default value may be provided to be passed by the XML parser to the client application. The following table shows various forms of the attribute default value clause and their meanings:

Default value clause	Explanation
#REQUIRED	A value must be provided for this attribute.
#IMPLIED	A value may or may not be provided for this attribute.
[#FIXED] "*default value*"	If this attribute has no explicit value, the XML parser substitutes the given default value. If the #FIXED token is provided, this attribute's value must match the given default value. In either case, the parent element always has an attribute with this name.

The #FIXED modifier indicates that the attribute may contain only the value given in the attribute declaration. Although redundant, it is possible to provide an explicit attribute value on an element when the attribute was declared as #FIXED. The only restriction is that the attribute value must exactly match the value given in the #FIXED declaration.

Special Attributes

Some attributes are significant to XML:

xml:space

> The xml:space attribute tells an XML application whether the whitespace within the specified element is significant:
>
> ```
> <!ATTLIST element_name xml:space (default|preserve)
>     default_decl>
> <!ATTLIST element_name xml:space (default) #FIXED 'default' >
> <!ATTLIST element_name xml:space (preserve) #FIXED 'preserve' >
> ```

xml:lang

> The xml:lang attribute allows a document author to specify the human language for an element's character content. If used in a valid XML document, the document type definition must include an attribute type declaration with the xml:lang attribute name. See Chapter 5 for an explanation of language support in XML.

Notation Declaration

```
<!NOTATION notation_name SYSTEM "system-literal">
<!NOTATION notation_name PUBLIC "pubid-literal">
<!NOTATION notation_name PUBLIC "pubid-literal" "system-literal">
```

Notation declarations are used to provide information to an XML application about the format of the document's unparsed content. Notations are used by unparsed external entities, processing instructions, and some attribute values.

Notation information is not significant to the XML parser, but it is preserved for use by the client application. The public and system identifiers are made available to the client application so that it may correctly interpret non-XML data and processing instructions.

Conditional Sections

The conditional section markup provides support for conditionally including and excluding content at parse time within an XML document's external subset. Conditional sections are not allowed within a document's internal subset. The following example illustrates a likely application of conditional sections:

```
<!ENTITY % debug 'IGNORE' >
<!ENTITY % release 'INCLUDE' >

<!ELEMENT addend (#PCDATA)>
<!ELEMENT result (#PCDATA)>
```

```
<![%debug;[
<!ELEMENT sum (addend+, result)>
]]>
<![%release;[
<!ELEMENT sum (result)>
]]>
```

Document Body

Elements are an XML document's lifeblood. They provide the structure for character data and attribute values that make up a particular instance of an XML document type definition. The !ELEMENT and !ATTLIST declarations from the DTD restrict the possible contents of an element within a valid XML document. Combining elements and/or attributes that violate these restrictions generates an error in a validating parser.

Start-Tags and End-Tags

<element_name [attribute_name="attribute value"]*> ...</element_name>

Elements that have content (either character data, other elements, or both) must start with a start-tag and end with an element end-tag.

Empty-Element Tags

<element_name [attribute_name="attribute value"]*></element_name>
<element_name [attribute_name="attribute value"]* />

Empty elements have no content and are written using either the start- and end-tag syntax mentioned previously or the empty-element syntax. The two forms are functionally identical, but the empty-element syntax is more succinct and more frequently used.

Attributes

attribute_name="attribute value"
attribute_name='attribute value'

Elements may include attributes. The order of attributes within an element tag is not significant and is not guaranteed to be preserved by an XML parser. Attribute values must appear within either single or double quotations. Attribute values within a document must conform to the rules explained in the "Constraints" section of this chapter.

Note that whitespace may appear around the = character.

The value that appears in the quoted string is tested for validity, depending on the attribute type provided in the ATTLIST declaration for the element type. Attribute values can contain general entity references, but cannot contain references to external parsed entities. See the "Constraints" section of this chapter for more information about attribute-value restrictions.

Namespaces

Although namespace support was not part of the original XML 1.0 Recommendation, Namespaces in XML was approved less than a year later (January 14, 1999). Namespaces are used to uniquely identify the element and attribute names of a given XML application from those of other applications. See Chapter 4 for more detailed information.

The following sections describe how namespaces impact the formation and interpretation of element and attribute names within an XML document.

Unqualified Names

name

An unqualified name is an XML element or attribute name that is not associated with a namespace. This could be because it has no namespace prefix and no default namespace has been declared. All unprefixed attribute names are unqualified because they are never automatically associated with a default namespace. XML parsers that do not implement namespace support (of which there are very few) or parsers that have been configured to ignore namespaces will always return unqualified names to their client applications. Two unqualified names are considered to be the same if they are lexically identical.

Qualified Names

[*prefix:*]*local_part*

A qualified name is an element or attribute name that is associated with an XML namespace. There are three possible types of qualified names:

- Unprefixed element names that are contained within the scope of a default namespace declaration
- Prefixed element names
- Prefixed attribute names

Unlike unqualified names, qualified names are considered the same only if their namespace URIs (from their namespace declarations) and their local parts match.

Default Namespace Declaration

`xmlns="`*namespace_URI*`"`

When this attribute is included in an element start-tag, it and any unprefixed elements contained within it are automatically associated with the namespace URI given. If the `xmlns` attribute is set to the empty string, any effective default namespace is ignored, and unprefixed elements are not associated with any namespace.

An important caveat about default namespace declarations is that they do not affect unprefixed attributes. Unprefixed attributes are never explicitly named in any namespace, even if their containing element is.

Namespace Prefix Declaration

`xmlns:prefix="namespace_URI"`

This declaration associates the namespace URI given with the prefix name given. Once it has been declared, the prefix may qualify the current element name, attribute names, or any other element or attribute name within the scope of the element that declares it. Nested elements may redefine a given prefix, using a different namespace URI if desired, and XML 1.1 documents may undefine a namespace prefix by setting it to an empty string:

`xmlns:prefix=""`

Constraints

In addition to defining the basic structures used in documents and DTDs, XML 1.0 defines a list of rules regarding their usage. These constraints put limits on various aspects of XML usage, and documents cannot in fact be considered to be "XML" unless they meet all of the well-formedness constraints. Parsers are required to report violations of these constraints, although only well-formedness constraint violations require that processing of the document halt completely. Namespace constraints are defined in Namespaces in XML, not XML 1.0.

Well-Formedness Constraints

Well-formedness refers to an XML document's physical organization. Certain lexical rules must be obeyed before an XML parser can consider a document well-formed. These rules should not be confused with validity constraints, which determine whether a particular document is valid when parsed using the document structure rules contained in its DTD. The Backus-Naur Form (BNF) grammar rules must also be satisfied. The following sections contain all well-formedness constraints recognized by XML Version 1.0 parsers, including actual text from the 1.0 specification.

PEs in Internal Subset

Text from specification

In the internal DTD subset, parameter entity references can occur only where markup declarations can occur, not within markup declarations. (This does not apply to references that occur in external parameter entities or to the external subset.)

Explanation

It is only legal to use parameter entity references to build markup declarations within the external DTD subset. In other words, within the internal subset, parameter entities may only be used to include complete markup declarations.

External Subset

Text from specification

The external subset, if any, must match production for extSubset.

Explanation

The extSubset production constrains what type of declaration may be contained in the external subset. This constraint generally means that the external subset of the DTD must only include whole declarations or parameter entity references. See the extSubset production in the EBNF grammar at the end of this chapter for specific limitations.

PE Between Declarations

Text from specification

The replacement text of a parameter entity reference in a DeclSep must match the production extSubsetDecl.

Explanation

The replacement text of parameter entities may contain declarations that might not be allowed if the replacement text appeared directly. Parameter entity references in the internal subset cannot appear within declarations, but this rule does not apply to declarations that have been included via parameter entities.

Element Type Match

Text from specification

The Name in an element's end-tag must match the element type in the start-tag.

Explanation

Proper element nesting is strictly enforced, and every open tag must be matched by a corresponding close tag.

Unique Att Spec

Text from specification

No attribute name may appear more than once in the same start-tag or empty-element tag.

Explanation

Attribute names must be unique within a given element.

No External Entity References

Text from specification

Attribute values cannot contain direct or indirect entity references to external entities.

Explanation

XML parsers report an error when asked to replace references to external parsed entities within attribute values.

No < in Attribute Values

Text from specification

The replacement text of any entity referred to directly or indirectly in an attribute value (other than "<") must not contain a <.

Explanation

This restriction is meant to simplify the task of parsing XML data. Since attribute values can't even appear to contain element data, simple parsers need not track literal strings. Just by matching < and > characters, simple parsers can check for proper markup formation and nesting.

Legal Character

Text from specification

Characters referred to using character references must match the production for Char.

Explanation

Any characters that the XML parser generates must be real characters. A few character values in Unicode are not valid standalone characters.

Entity Declared

Text from specification

In a document without any DTD, a document with only an internal DTD subset that contains no parameter entity references, or a document with standalone='yes' for an entity reference that does not occur within the external subset or a parameter entity, the Name given in the entity reference must match that in an entity declaration that does not occur within the external subset or a parameter entity, except that well-formed documents need not declare any of the following entities: amp, lt, gt, apos, quot. The declaration of a parameter entity must precede any reference to it. Similarly, the declaration of a general entity must precede any reference to it, which appears in a default value in an attribute-list declaration. Note that if entities are declared in the external subset or in external parameter entities, a non-validating processor is not obligated to read and process their declarations; for such documents, the rule that an entity must be declared is a well-formedness constraint only if `standalone='yes'`.

Explanation

This long constraint lists the only situations in which an entity reference may appear without a corresponding entity declaration. Since a nonvalidating parser is not obliged to read and parse the external subset, the parser must give the document the benefit of the doubt, if an entity could possibly have been declared.

Parsed Entity

Text from specification

An entity reference must not contain the name of an unparsed entity. Unparsed entities may be referred to only in attribute values declared to be of type ENTITY or ENTITIES.

Explanation

Since unparsed entities can't be parsed, don't try to force the parser to parse them.

No Recursion

Text from specification

A parsed entity must not contain a recursive reference to itself, either directly or indirectly.

Explanation

Be careful how you structure your entities; make sure you don't inadvertently create a circular reference:

```
<!ENTITY a "&b;">
<!ENTITY b "&c;">
<!ENTITY c "&a;"> <!--wrong!-->
```

In DTD

Text from specification

Parameter entity references may only appear in the DTD.

Explanation

This constraint is self-evident because the % character has no significance outside of the DTD. Therefore, it is perfectly legal to have an element like this in your document:

```
<ok>%noproblem;</ok>
```

The text %noproblem; is passed on by the parser without generating an error.

Validity Constraints

The following sections contain all validity constraints that are enforced by a validating parser. Each includes actual text from the XML 1.0 specification and a short explanation of what the constraint actually means.

Root Element Type

Text from specification

The Name in the document type declaration must match the element type of the root element.

Explanation

The name provided in the DOCTYPE declaration identifies the root element's name and must match the name of the root element in the document.

Proper Declaration/PE Nesting

Text from specification

Parameter entity replacement text must be properly nested with markup declarations. That is to say, if either the first character or the last character of a markup declaration is contained in the replacement text for a parameter entity reference, both must be contained in the same replacement text.

Explanation

This constraint means you can't create a parameter entity that completes one DTD declaration and begins another; the following XML fragment would violate this constraint:

```
<!ENTITY % finish_it ">">
<!ENTITY % bad "won't work" %finish_it; <!--wrong!-->
```

Standalone Document Declaration

Text from specification

The standalone document declaration must have the value no if any external markup declarations contain declarations of: attributes with default values, if elements to which these attributes apply appear in the document without specifications of values for these attributes, or entities (other than amp, lt, gt, apos, quot), if references to those entities appear in the document, or attributes with values subject to normalization, where the attribute appears in the document with a value which will change as a result of normalization, or element types with element content, if whitespace occurs directly within any instance of those types.

Explanation

This laundry list of potential standalone flag violations can be read to mean, "If you have an external subset in your DTD, ensure that your document doesn't depend on anything in it if you say standalone='yes' in your XML declaration." A more succinct interpretation would be, "If your document has an external DTD subset, just set standalone to no."

Element Valid

Text from specification

An element is valid if there is a declaration matching elementdecl where the Name matches the element type and either the declaration matches EMPTY and the element has no content, or the declaration matches children and the sequence of child elements belongs to the language generated by the regular expression in the content model, with optional whitespace (characters matching the nonterminal S) between the start-tag and the first child element, between child elements, or between the last child element and the end-tag. Note that a CDATA section containing only whitespace does not match the nonterminal S, and hence cannot appear in these positions. The declaration matches Mixed and the content consists of character data and child elements whose types match names in the content model. The declaration matches ANY, and the types of any child elements have been declared.

Explanation

If a document includes a DTD with element declarations, make sure the actual elements in the document match the rules set down in the DTD.

Attribute Value Type

Text from specification

The attribute must have been declared; the value must be of the type declared for it.

Explanation

All attributes used on elements in valid XML documents must have been declared in the DTD, including the xml:space and xml:lang attributes. If you declare an attribute for an element, make sure that every instance of that attribute has a value conforming to the type specified. (For attribute types, see the "Attribute List Declaration" entry earlier in this chapter.)

Unique Element Type Declaration

Text from specification

No element type may be declared more than once.

Explanation

Unlike entity and attribute declarations, only one declaration may exist for a particular element type.

Proper Group/PE Nesting

Text from specification

Parameter entity replacement text must be properly nested with parenthesized groups. That is to say, if either of the opening or closing parentheses in a choice, seq, or Mixed construct is contained in the replacement text for a parameter entity, both must be contained in the same replacement text.

For interoperability, if a parameter entity reference appears in a choice, seq, or Mixed construct, its replacement text should contain at least one non-blank character, and neither the first nor last non-blank character of the replacement text should be a connector (| or ,).

Explanation

This constraint restricts the way parameter entities can be used to construct element declarations. It is similar to the "Proper Declaration/PE Nesting" constraint in that parameter entities may not be used to complete or open new parenthesized expressions. It prevents the XML author from hiding significant syntax elements inside parameter entities.

No Duplicate Types

Text from specification

The same name must not appear more than once in a single mixed-content declaration.

Explanation

Don't list the same element type name more than once in the same mixed-content declaration.

ID

Text from specification

Values of type ID must match the Name production. A name must not appear more than once in an XML document as a value of this type; i.e., ID values must uniquely identify the elements that bear them.

Explanation

No two attribute values for attributes declared as type ID can have the same value. This constraint is not restricted by element type, but it is global across the entire document.

One ID per Element Type

Text from specification

No element type may have more than one ID attribute specified.

Explanation

Each element can have at most one ID type attribute.

ID Attribute Default

Text from specification

An ID attribute must have a declared default of #IMPLIED or #REQUIRED.

Explanation

To avoid potential duplication, you can't declare an ID attribute to be #FIXED or provide a default value for it.

IDREF

Text from specification

Values of type IDREF must match the Name production, and values of type IDREFS must match Names; each Name must match the value of an ID attribute on some element in the XML document; i.e., IDREF values must match the value of some ID attribute.

Explanation

ID references must refer to actual ID attributes that exist within the document.

Entity Name

Text from specification

Values of type ENTITY must match the Name production, and values of type ENTITIES must match Names; each Name must match the name of an unparsed entity declared in the DTD.

Explanation

Attributes declared to contain entity references must contain references to unparsed entities declared in the DTD.

Name Token

Text from specification

Values of type NMTOKEN must match the Nmtoken production; values of type NMTOKENS must match Nmtokens.

Explanation

If an attribute is declared to contain a name or list of names, the values must be legal XML name tokens.

Notation Attributes

Text from specification

Values of this type must match one of the notation names included in the declaration; all notation names in the declaration must be declared.

Explanation

Attributes that must contain notation names must contain names that reference notations declared in the DTD.

One Notation per Element Type

Text from specification

No element type may have more than one NOTATION attribute specified.

Explanation

A given element can have only one attribute declared with the NOTATION attribute type. This constraint is provided for backward compatibility with SGML.

No Notation on Empty Element

Text from specification

For compatibility, an attribute of type NOTATION must not be declared on an element declared EMPTY.

Explanation

Empty elements cannot have NOTATION attributes in order to maintain compatibility with SGML.

Enumeration

Text from specification

Values of this type must match one of the Nmtoken tokens in the declaration.

Explanation

Assigning a value to an enumerated type attribute that isn't listed in the enumeration is illegal in the DTD.

Required Attribute

Text from specification

If the default declaration is the keyword #REQUIRED, then the attribute must be specified for all elements of the type in the attribute-list declaration.

Explanation

Required attributes must appear in the document and have a value assigned to them if they are declared as #REQUIRED in the DTD.

Attribute Default Legal

Text from specification

The declared default value must meet the lexical constraints of the declared attribute type.

Explanation

If you provide a default attribute value, it must obey the same rules that apply to a normal attribute value within the document.

Fixed Attribute Default

Text from specification

If an attribute has a default value declared with the #FIXED keyword, instances of that attribute must match the default value.

Explanation

If you choose to provide an explicit value for a #FIXED attribute in your document, it must match the default value given in the attribute declaration.

Proper Conditional Section/PE Nesting

Text from specification

If any of the "<![", "[", or "]]>" of a conditional section is contained in the replacement text for a parameter entity reference, all of them must be contained in the same replacement text.

Explanation

If you use a parameter entity to contain the beginning of a conditional section, the parameter entity must also contain the end of the section.

Entity Declared

Text from specification

In a document with an external subset or external parameter entities with standalone='no', the Name given in the entity reference must match that in an entity declaration. For interoperability, valid documents should declare the entities amp, lt, gt, apos, quot. The declaration of a parameter entity must precede any reference to it. Similarly, the declaration of a general entity must precede any attribute-list declaration containing a default value with a direct or indirect reference to that general entity.

Explanation

Parameter and general entity declarations must precede any references to these entities. All entity references must refer to previously declared entities. The specification also states that declaring the five predefined general entities (amp, lt, gt, apos, and quot) is a good idea. In reality, declaring the predefined general entities adds unnecessary complexity to most applications.

Notation Declared

Text from specification

The Name must match the declared name of a notation.

Explanation

External unparsed entities must use a notation that is declared in the document.

Unique Notation Name

Text from specification

Only one notation declaration can declare a given Name.

Explanation

Declaring two notations with the same name is illegal.

Namespace Constraints

The following list contains all constraints defined by the namespaces specification. Each includes actual text from the Namespaces in XML specification and a short explanation of what the constraint actually means.

Leading "XML"

Text from specification

Prefixes beginning with the three-letter sequence x, m, l, in any case combination, are reserved for use by XML and XML-related specifications.

Explanation

Just like most other names in XML, namespace prefixes names can't begin with xml unless they've been defined by the W3C.

Prefix Declared

Text from specification

The namespace prefix, unless it is xml or xmlns, must have been declared in a namespace declaration attribute in either the start-tag of the element where the prefix is used or in an ancestor element (i.e., an element in whose content the prefixed markup occurs). The prefix xml is by definition bound to the namespace name http://www.w3.org/XML/1998/namespace. The prefix xmlns is used only for namespace bindings and is not itself bound to any namespace name.

Explanation

You have to declare all namespaces before you can use them. The prefixes have no meaning without the declarations, so using a prefix without a declaration context is an error. The namespace with the prefix xml is permanently defined, so there is no need to redeclare it. The xmlns prefix used by namespace declarations is not considered a namespace prefix itself, and no declaration is needed for it.

XML 1.0 Document Grammar

The Extended Backus-Naur Form (EBNF) grammar, shown in the following section, was collected from the *XML 1.0 Recommendation*, Third Edition. It brings all XML language productions together in a single location and describes the syntax that is understood by XML 1.0–compliant parsers. Each production has been numbered and cross-referenced using superscripted numbers.

EBNF Grammar for XML 1.0 (Third Edition)

Document

[1] document ::= prolog[22] element[39] Misc[27]*

Character range

[2] Char ::= #x9 | #xA | #xD | [#x21-#xD7FF] | [#xE000-#xFFFD] | [#x10000-#x10FFFF] /* any Unicode character, excluding the surrogate blocks, FFFE, and FFFF. */

Whitespace

[3] S ::= (#x20 | #x9 | #xD | #xA)+

Names and tokens

[4] NameChar ::= Letter[84]| Digit[88] | '.' | '-' | '_' | ':' | CombiningChar[87] | Extender[89]

[5] Name ::= (Letter[84]| '_' | ':') (NameChar[4])*

[6] Names ::= Name[5](#x20 Name[5])*

[7] Nmtoken ::= (NameChar[4])+

[8] Nmtokens ::= Nmtoken[7](#x20 Nmtoken[7])*

Literals

[9] EntityValue ::= '"' ([^%&"] | PEReference[69] | Reference[67])* '"' | "'" ([^%&'] | PEReference[69] | Reference[67])* "'"

[10] AttValue ::= '"' ([^<&"] | Reference[67])* '"' | "'" ([^<&'] | Reference[67])* "'"

[11] SystemLiteral ::= ('"' [^"]* '"') | ("'" [^']* "'")

[12] PubidLiteral ::= '"' PubidChar[13]* '"' | "'" (PubidChar[13] - "'")* "'"

[13] PubidChar ::= #x20 | #xD | #xA | [a-zA-Z0-9] | [-'()+,./:=?;!*#@$_%]

Character data

[14] CharData ::= [^<&]* - ([^<&]* ']]>' [^<&]*)

Comments

[15] Comment ::= '<!--' ((Char[2] - '-') | ('-' (Char[2] - '-')))* '-->'

Processing instructions

[16] PI ::= '<?' PITarget[17](S(Char[2]* - (Char[2]* '?>' Char[2]*)))? '?>'

[17] PITarget ::= Name[5]- (('X' | 'x') ('M' | 'm') ('L' | 'l'))

CDATA sections

[18] CDSect ::= CDStart[19] CData[20] CDEnd[21]

[19] CDStart ::= '<![CDATA['

[20] CData ::= (Char[2]* - (Char[2]* ']]>' Char[2]*))

[21] CDEnd ::= ']]>'

Prolog

[22] prolog ::= XMLDecl[23]? Misc[27]* (doctypedecl[28] Misc[27]*)?

[23] XMLDecl ::= '<?xml' VersionInfo[24] EncodingDecl[80]? SDDecl[32]? S[3]? '?>'

[24] VersionInfo ::= S[3] 'version' Eq("'" VersionNum[26] "'" | '"' VersionNum[26] '"')

[25] Eq ::= S[3]? '=' S[3]?

[26] VersionNum ::= '1.0'

[27] Misc ::= Comment[15] | PI[16] | S[3]

Document type definition

[28] doctypedecl ::= '<!DOCTYPE' S[3] Name[5](S[3] ExternalID[75])? S[3]? ('[' intSubset[28b] ']' S[3]?)? '>'

[28a] DeclSep ::= PEReference[69] | S[3]

[28b] intSubset ::= (markupdecl[29] | DeclSep[28a])*

[29] markupdecl ::= elementdecl[45] | AttlistDecl[52] | EntityDecl[70] | NotationDecl[82] | PI[16] | Comment[15]

External subset

[30] extSubset ::= TextDecl[77]? extSubsetDecl[31]

[31] extSubsetDecl ::= (markupdecl[29] | conditionalSect[61] | DeclSep[28a])*

Standalone document declaration

[32] SDDecl ::= S[3] 'standalone' Eq(("'" ('yes' | 'no') "'") | ('"' ('yes' | 'no') '"'))

Element

[39] element ::= EmptyElemTag[44] | STag[40] content[43] ETag[42]

Start-tag

[40] STag ::= '<' Name[5] (S[3] Attribute[41])* S[3]? '>'

[41] Attribute ::= Name[5] Eq[25] AttValue[10]

End-tag

[42] ETag ::= '</' Name[5] S[3]? '>'

Content of elements

[43] content ::= CharData[14]? ((element[39] | Reference[69] | CDSect[18] | PI[16] | Comment[15]) CharData[14]?)*

Tags for empty elements

[44] EmptyElemTag ::= '<' Name[5](S[3] Attribute[41])* S[3]? '/>'

Element type declaration

[45] elementdecl ::= '<!ELEMENT' S[3] Name[5] S[3] contentspec[46] S[3]? '>'

[46] contentspec ::= 'EMPTY' | 'ANY' | Mixed[51] | children[47]

Element-content models

[47] children ::= (choice[49] | seq[50]) ('?' | '*' | '+')?

[48] cp ::= (Name[5] | choice[49] | seq[50]) ('?' | '*' | '+')?

[49] choice ::= '(' S[3]? cp[48] (S[3]? '|' S[3]? cp[48])+ S[3]? ')'

[50] seq ::= '(' S[3]? cp[48](S[3]? ',' S[3]? cp[48])* S[3]? ')'

Mixed-content declaration

[51] Mixed ::= '(' S^3? '#PCDATA' (S^3? '|' S^3? Name^5)* S^3? ')*' | '(' S^3? '#PCDATA' S^3? ')'

Attribute-list declaration

[52] AttlistDecl ::= '<!ATTLIST' S^3 Name^5 AttDef^{53}* S^3? '>'

[53] AttDef ::= S^3 Name^5 S^3 AttType^{54} S^3 DefaultDecl^{60}

Attribute types

[54] AttType ::= StringType^{55} | TokenizedType^{56} | EnumeratedType^{57}

[55] StringType ::= 'CDATA'

[56] TokenizedType ::= 'ID'

```
| 'IDREF'
| 'IDREFS'
| 'ENTITY'
| 'ENTITIES'
| 'NMTOKEN'
| 'NMTOKENS'
```

Enumerated attribute types

[57] EnumeratedType ::= NotationType^{58} | Enumeration^{59}

[58] NotationType ::= 'NOTATION' S^3'(' S^3? Name^5(S^3? '|' S^3? Name^5)* S^3? ')'

[59] Enumeration ::= '(' S^3? Nmtoken^7(S^3? '|' S^3? Nmtoken^7)* S^3? ')'

Attribute defaults

[60] DefaultDecl ::= '#REQUIRED' | '#IMPLIED' | (('#FIXED' S^3)? AttValue^{10})

Conditional section

[61] conditionalSect ::= includeSect^{62} | ignoreSect^{63}

[62] includeSect ::= '<![' S^3? 'INCLUDE' S^3? '[' extSubsetDecl^{31}']]>'

[63] ignoreSect ::= '<![' S^3? 'IGNORE' S^3? '[' ignoreSectContents^{64}* ']]>'

[64] ignoreSectContents ::= Ignore^{65}('<![' ignoreSectContents^{64}']]>' Ignore^{65})*

[65] Ignore ::= Char^2* - (Char^2* ('<![' | ']]>') Char^2*)

Character reference

[66] CharRef ::= '&#' [0-9]+ ';' | '&#x' [0-9a-fA-F]+ ';'

Entity reference

[67] Reference ::= EntityRef[68] | CharRef[66]

[68] EntityRef ::= '&' Name[5] ';'

[69] PEReference ::= '%' Name[5] ';'

Entity declaration

[70] EntityDecl ::= GEDecl[71] | PEDecl[72]

[71] GEDecl ::= '<!ENTITY' S[3] Name[5] S[3] EntityDef[73] S[3]? '>'

[72] PEDecl ::= '<!ENTITY' S[3]'%' S[3] Name[5] S[3] PEDef[74] S[3]? '>'

[73] EntityDef ::= EntityValue[9] | (ExternalID[75] NDataDecl[76]?)

[74] PEDef ::= EntityValue[9] | ExternalID[76]

External entity declaration

[75] ExternalID ::= 'SYSTEM' S[3] SystemLiteral[11] | 'PUBLIC' S[3] PubidLiteral[12] S[3] SystemLiteral[11]

[76] NDataDecl ::= S[3] 'NDATA' S[3] Name[5]

Text declaration

[77] TextDecl ::= '<?xml' VersionInfo[24]? EncodingDecl[80] S[3]? '?>'

Well-formed external parsed entity

[78] extParsedEnt ::= TextDecl[77]? content[43]

Encoding declaration

[80] EncodingDecl ::= S[3] 'encoding' Eq[25] ('"' EncName[81]'"' | "'" EncName[81]"'")

[81] EncName ::= [A-Za-z] ([A-Za-z0-9._] | '-')* /* Encoding name contains only Latin characters */

Notation declarations

[82] NotationDecl ::= '<!NOTATION' S[3] Name[5] S[3](ExternalID[75] | PublicID[83]) S[3]? '>'

[83] PublicID ::= 'PUBLIC' S[3] PubidLiteral[12]

Characters

[84] Letter ::= BaseChar[85] | Ideographic[86]

[85] BaseChar ::= [#x0041-#x005A] | [#x0061-#x007A] | [#x00C0-#x00D6] | [#x00D8-#x00F6] | [#x00F8-#x00FF] | [#x0100-#x0131] | [#x0134-#x013E] | [#x0141-#x0148] | [#x014A-#x017E] | [#x0180-#x01C3] | [#x01CD-#x01F0] |

[#x01F4-#x01F5] | [#x01FA-#x0217] | [#x0250-#x02A8] | [#x02BB-#x02C1] |
#x0386 | [#x0388-#x038A] | #x038C | [#x038E-#x03A1] | [#x03A3-#x03CE] |
[#x03D0-#x03D6] | #x03DA | #x03DC | #x03DE | #x03E0 | [#x03E2-#x03F3] |
[#x0401-#x040C] | [#x040E-#x044F] | [#x0451-#x045C] | [#x045E-#x0481] |
[#x0490-#x04C4] | [#x04C7-#x04C8] | [#x04CB-#x04CC] | [#x04D0-#x04EB] |
[#x04EE-#x04F5] | [#x04F8-#x04F9] | [#x0531-#x0556] | #x0559 | [#x0561-
#x0586] | [#x05D0-#x05EA] | [#x05F0-#x05F2] | [#x0621-#x063A] | [#x0641-
#x064A] | [#x0671-#x06B7] | [#x06BA-#x06BE] | [#x06C0-#x06CE] | [#x06D0-
#x06D3] | #x06D5 | [#x06E5-#x06E6] | [#x0905-#x0939] | #x093D | [#x0958-
#x0961] | [#x0985-#x098C] | [#x098F-#x0990] | [#x0993-#x09A8] | [#x09AA-
#x09B0] | #x09B2 | [#x09B6-#x09B9] | [#x09DC-#x09DD] | [#x09DF-#x09E1] |
[#x09F0-#x09F1] | [#x0A05-#x0A0A] | [#x0A0F-#x0A10] | [#x0A13-#x0A28] |
[#x0A2A-#x0A30] | [#x0A32-#x0A33] | [#x0A35-#x0A36] | [#x0A38-#x0A39] |
[#x0A59-#x0A5C] | #x0A5E | [#x0A72-#x0A74] | [#x0A85-#x0A8B] | #x0A8D |
[#x0A8F-#x0A91] | [#x0A93-#x0AA8] | [#x0AAA-#x0AB0] | [#x0AB2-#x0AB3] |
[#x0AB5-#x0AB9] | #x0ABD | #x0AE0 | [#x0B05-#x0B0C] | [#x0B0F-#x0B10] |
[#x0B13-#x0B28] | [#x0B2A-#x0B30] | [#x0B32-#x0B33] | [#x0B36-#x0B39] |
#x0B3D | [#x0B5C-#x0B5D] | [#x0B5F-#x0B61] | [#x0B85-#x0B8A] | [#x0B8E-
#x0B90] | [#x0B92-#x0B95] | [#x0B99-#x0B9A] | #x0B9C | [#x0B9E-#x0B9F] |
[#x0BA3-#x0BA4] | [#x0BA8-#x0BAA] | [#x0BAE-#x0BB5] | [#x0BB7-#x0BB9] |
[#x0C05-#x0C0C] | [#x0C0E-#x0C10] | [#x0C12-#x0C28] | [#x0C2A-#x0C33] |
[#x0C35-#x0C39] | [#x0C60-#x0C61] | [#x0C85-#x0C8C] | [#x0C8E-#x0C90] |
[#x0C92-#x0CA8] | [#x0CAA-#x0CB3] | [#x0CB5-#x0CB9] | #x0CDE | [#x0CE0-
#x0CE1] | [#x0D05-#x0D0C] | [#x0D0E-#x0D10] | [#x0D12-#x0D28] | [#x0D2A-
#x0D39] | [#x0D60-#x0D61] | [#x0E01-#x0E2E] | #x0E30 | [#x0E32-#x0E33] |
[#x0E40-#x0E45] | [#x0E81-#x0E82] | #x0E84 | [#x0E87-#x0E88] | #x0E8A |
#x0E8D | [#x0E94-#x0E97] | [#x0E99-#x0E9F] | [#x0EA1-#x0EA3] | #x0EA5 |
#x0EA7 | [#x0EAA-#x0EAB] | [#x0EAD-#x0EAE] | #x0EB0 | [#x0EB2-#x0EB3] |
#x0EBD | [#x0EC0-#x0EC4] | [#x0F40-#x0F47] | [#x0F49-#x0F69] | [#x10A0-
#x10C5] | [#x10D0-#x10F6] | #x1100 | [#x1102-#x1103] | [#x1105-#x1107] |
#x1109 | [#x110B-#x110C] | [#x110E-#x1112] | #x113C | #x113E | #x1140 |
#x114C | #x114E | #x1150 | [#x1154-#x1155] | #x1159 | [#x115F-#x1161] |
#x1163 | #x1165 | #x1167 | #x1169 | [#x116D-#x116E] | [#x1172-#x1173] |
#x1175 | #x119E | #x11A8 | #x11AB | [#x11AE-#x11AF] | [#x11B7-#x11B8] |
#x11BA | [#x11BC-#x11C2] | #x11EB | #x11F0 | #x11F9 | [#x1E00-#x1E9B] |
[#x1EA0-#x1EF9] | [#x1F00-#x1F15] | [#x1F18-#x1F1D] | [#x1F21-#x1F45] |
[#x1F48-#x1F4D] | [#x1F50-#x1F57] | #x1F59 | #x1F5B | #x1F5D | [#x1F5F-
#x1F7D] | [#x1F80-#x1FB4] | [#x1FB6-#x1FBC] | #x1FBE | [#x1FC2-#x1FC4] |
[#x1FC6-#x1FCC] | [#x1FD0-#x1FD3] | [#x1FD6-#x1FDB] | [#x1FE0-#x1FEC] |
[#x1FF2-#x1FF4] | [#x1FF6-#x1FFC] | #x2126 | [#x212A-#x212B] | #x212E |
[#x2180-#x2182] | [#x3041-#x3094] | [#x30A1-#x30FA] | [#x3105-#x312C] |
[#xAC00-#xD7A3]

[86] Ideographic ::= [#x4E00-#x9FA5] | #x3007 | [#x3021-#x3029]

[87] CombiningChar ::= [#x0300-#x0345] | [#x0360-#x0361] | [#x0483-#x0486]
| [#x0591-#x05A1] | [#x05A3-#x05B9] | [#x05BB-#x05BD] | #x05BF | [#x05C1-
#x05C2] | #x05C4 | [#x064B-#x0652] | #x0670 | [#x06D6-#x06DC] | [#x06DD-
#x06DF] | [#x06E0-#x06E4] | [#x06E7-#x06E8] | [#x06EA-#x06ED] | [#x0901-
#x0903] | #x093C | [#x093E-#x094C] | #x094D | [#x0951-#x0954] | [#x0962-

#x0963] | [#x0981-#x0983] | #x09BC | #x09BE | #x09BF | [#x09C0-#x09C4] |
[#x09C7-#x09C8] | [#x09CB-#x09CD] | #x09D7 | [#x09E2-#x09E3] | #x0A02 |
#x0A3C | #x0A3E | #x0A3F | [#x0A40-#x0A42] | [#x0A47-#x0A48] | [#x0A4B-
#x0A4D] | [#x0A70-#x0A71] | [#x0A81-#x0A83] | #x0ABC | [#x0ABE-#x0AC5] |
[#x0AC7-#x0AC9] | [#x0ACB-#x0ACD] | [#x0B01-#x0B03] | #x0B3C | [#x0B3E-
#x0B43] | [#x0B47-#x0B48] | [#x0B4B-#x0B4D] | [#x0B56-#x0B57] | [#x0B82-
#x0B83] | [#x0BBE-#x0BC2] | [#x0BC6-#x0BC8] | [#x0BCA-#x0BCD] | #x0BD7 |
[#x0C01-#x0C03] | [#x0C3E-#x0C44] | [#x0C46-#x0C48] | [#x0C4A-#x0C4D] |
[#x0C55-#x0C56] | [#x0C82-#x0C83] | [#x0CBE-#x0CC4] | [#x0CC6-#x0CC8] |
[#x0CCA-#x0CCD] | [#x0CD5-#x0CD6] | [#x0D02-#x0D03] | [#x0D3E-#x0D43] |
[#x0D46-#x0D48] | [#x0D4A-#x0D4D] | #x0D57 | #x0E31 | [#x0E34-#x0E3A] |
[#x0E47-#x0E4E] | #x0EB1 | [#x0EB4-#x0EB9] | [#x0EBB-#x0EBC] | [#x0EC8-
#x0ECD] | [#x0F18-#x0F19] | #x0F35 | #x0F37 | #x0F39 | #x0F3E | #x0F3F |
[#x0F71-#x0F84] | [#x0F86-#x0F8B] | [#x0F90-#x0F95] | #x0F97 | [#x0F99-
#x0FAD] | [#x0FB1-#x0FB7] | #x0FB9 | [#x20D0-#x20DC] | #x20E1 | [#x302A-
#x302F] | #x3099 | #x309A

[88] Digit ::= [#x0030-#x0039] | [#x0660-#x0669] | [#x06F0-#x06F9] |
[#x0966-#x096F] | [#x09E6-#x09EF] | [#x0A66-#x0A6F] | [#x0AE6-#x0AEF] |
[#x0B66-#x0B6F] | [#x0BE7-#x0BEF] | [#x0C66-#x0C6F] | [#x0CE6-#x0CEF] |
[#x0D66-#x0D6F] | [#x0E50-#x0E59] | [#x0ED0-#x0ED9] | [#x0F21-#x0F29]

[89] Extender ::= #x00B7 | #x02D0 | #x02D1 | #x0387 | #x0640 | #x0E46 |
#x0EC6 | #x3005 | [#x3031-#x3035] | [#x309D-#x309E] | [#x30FC-#x30FE]

XML 1.1 Document Grammar

The following grammar provides the EBNF productions for the XML 1.1 recommendation.

EBNF Grammar for XML 1.1

Document

[1] document ::= prolog[22] element[39] Misc[27]* - Char[2]* RestrictedChar[2a] Char[2]*

Character range

[2] Char ::= [#x1-#xD7FF] | [#xE000-#xFFFD] | [#x10000-#x10FFFF] /* any Unicode character, excluding the surrogate blocks, FFFE, and FFFF. */

[2a] RestrictedChar ::= [#x1-#x8] | [#xB-#xC] | [#xE-#x1F] | [#x7F-#x84] |
[#x86-#x9F]

Whitespace

[3] S ::= (#x20 | #x9 | #xD | #xA)+

Names and tokens

[4] NameStartChar ::= ":" | [A-Z] | "_" | [a-z] | [#xC0-#xD6] | [#xD8-#xF6]
| [#xF8-#x2FF] | [#x370-#x37D] | [#x37F-#x1FFF] | [#x200C-#x200D] |
[#x2070-#x218F] | [#x2C00-#x2FEF] | [#x3001-#xD7FF] | [#xF900-#xFDCF] |
[#xFDF0-#xFFFD] | [#x10000-#xEFFFF]

[4a] NameChar ::= NameStartChar[4] | "-" | "." | [0-9] | #xB7 | [#x0300-
#x036F] | [#x203F-#x2040]

[5] Name ::= NameStartChar[4] (NameChar[4a])*

[6] Names ::= Name[5] (#x20 Name[5])*

[7] Nmtoken ::= (NameChar[4a])+

[8] Nmtokens ::= Nmtoken[7](#x20 Nmtoken[7])*

Literals

[9] EntityValue ::= '"' ([^%&"] | PEReference[69] | Reference[67])* '"' | "'"
([^%&'] | PEReference[69] | Reference[67])* "'"

[10] AttValue ::= '"' ([^<&"] | Reference[67])* '"' | "'" ([^<&'] |
Reference[67])* "'"

[11] SystemLiteral ::= ('"' [^"]* '"') | ("'" [^']* "'")

[12] PubidLiteral ::= '"' PubidChar[13]* '"' | "'" (PubidChar[13] - "'")* "'"

[13] PubidChar ::= #x20 | #xD | #xA | [a-zA-Z0-9] | [-'()+,./:=?;!*#@$_%]

Character data

[14] CharData ::= [^<&]* - ([^<&]* ']]>' [^<&]*)

Comments

[15] Comment ::= '<!--' ((Char[2] - '-') | ('-' (Char[2] - '-')))* '-->'

Processing instructions

[16] PI ::= '<?' PITarget[17](S[3](Char[2]* - (Char[2]* '?>' Char[2]*)))? '?>'

[17] PITarget ::= Name[5] - (('X' | 'x') ('M' | 'm') ('L' | 'l'))

CDATA sections

[18] CDSect ::= CDStart[19] CData[20] CDEnd[21]

[19] CDStart ::= '<![CDATA['

[20] CData ::= (Char[2]* - (Char[2]* ']]>' Char[2]*))

[21] CDEnd ::= ']]>'

Prolog

[22] prolog ::= XMLDecl[23] Misc[27]* (doctypedecl[28] Misc[27]*)?

[23] XMLDecl ::= '<?xml' VersionInfo[24] EncodingDecl[80]? SDDecl[32]? S[3]?'?>'

[24] VersionInfo ::= S[3] 'version' Eq[25]("'" VersionNum[26] "'" | '"'
VersionNum[26] '"')

[25] Eq ::= S[3]? '=' S[3]?

[26] VersionNum ::= '1.1'

[27] Misc ::= Comment[15] | PI[16] | S[3]

Document type definition

[28] doctypedecl ::= '<!DOCTYPE' S[3] Name[5](S[3] ExternalID)? S[3]? ('['
intSubset[28b]']' S[3]?)? '>'

[28a] DeclSep ::= PEReference[69] | S[3]

[28b] intSubset ::= (markupdecl[29] | DeclSep[28a])*

[29] markupdecl ::= elementdecl[45] | AttlistDecl[52] | EntityDecl[70] |
NotationDecl[82] | PI[16] | Comment[15]

External subset

[30] extSubset ::= TextDecl[77]? extSubsetDecl[31]

[31] extSubsetDecl ::= (markupdecl[29] | conditionalSect[61] | DeclSep[28a])*

Standalone document declaration

[32] SDDecl ::= #x20+ 'standalone' Eq[25](("'" ('yes' | 'no') "'") | ('"'
('yes' | 'no') '"'))

Element

[39] element ::= EmptyElemTag[44] | STag[40] content[43] ETag[42]

Start-tag

[40] STag ::= '<' Name[5] (S[3] Attribute[41])* S[3]? '>'

[41] Attribute ::= Name Eq AttValue

End-tag

[42] ETag ::= '</' Name[5] S[3]? '>'

Content of elements

[43] content ::= CharData[14]? ((element[39] | Reference[67] | CDSect[18] | PI[16] |
Comment[15]) CharData[14]?)*

Tags for empty elements

[44] EmptyElemTag ::= '<' Name[5](S[3] Attribute[41])* S[3]? '/>'

Element type declaration

[45] elementdecl ::= '<!ELEMENT' S[3] Name[5] S[3] contentspec[46] S[3]? '>'

[46] contentspec ::= 'EMPTY' | 'ANY' | Mixed[51] | children[47]

Element-content models

[47] children ::= (choice[49] | seq[50]) ('?' | '*' | '+')?

[48] cp ::= (Name[5] | choice[49] | seq[50]) ('?' | '*' | '+')?

[49] choice ::= '(' S[3]? cp[48](S[3]? '|' S[3]? cp[48])+ S[3]? ')'

[50] seq ::= '(' S[3]? cp[48](S[3]? ',' S[3]? cp[48])* S[3]? ')'

Mixed-content declaration

[51] Mixed ::= '(' S[3]? '#PCDATA' (S[3]? '|' S[3]? Name[5])* S[3]? ')*' | '(' S[3]? '#PCDATA' S[3]? ')'

Attribute-list declaration

[52] AttlistDecl ::= '<!ATTLIST' S[3] Name[5] AttDef[53]* S[3]? '>'

[53] AttDef ::= S[3] Name[3] S[3] AttType[3] S[3] DefaultDecl[3]

Attribute types

[54] AttType ::= StringType[55] | TokenizedType[56] | EnumeratedType[57]

[55] StringType ::= 'CDATA'

[56] TokenizedType ::= 'ID'

```
    | 'IDREF'
    | 'IDREFS'
    | 'ENTITY'
    | 'ENTITIES'
    | 'NMTOKEN'
    | 'NMTOKENS'
```

Enumerated attribute types

[57] EnumeratedType ::= NotationType[58] | Enumeration[59]

[58] NotationType ::= 'NOTATION' S[3]'(' S[3]? Name[5](S[3]? '|' S[3]? Name[5])* S[3]? ')'

[59] Enumeration ::= '(' S[3]? Nmtoken[7](S[3]? '|' S[3]? Nmtoken[7])* S[3]? ')'

Attribute defaults

[60] DefaultDecl ::= '#REQUIRED' | '#IMPLIED' | (('#FIXED' S[3])? AttValue[10])

Conditional section

[61] conditionalSect ::= includeSect[62] | ignoreSect[63]

[62] includeSect ::= '<![' S[3]? 'INCLUDE' S[3]? '[' extSubsetDecl[31]']]>'

[63] ignoreSect ::= '<![' S[3]? 'IGNORE' S[3]? '[' ignoreSectContents[64]* ']]>'

[64] ignoreSectContents ::= Ignore[65]('<![' ignoreSectContents[64]']]>' Ignore[65])*

[65] Ignore ::= Char[2]* - (Char[2]* ('<![' | ']]>') Char[2]*)

Character reference

[66] CharRef ::= '&#' [0-9]+ ';' | '&#x' [0-9a-fA-F]+ ';'

Entity reference

[67] Reference ::= EntityRef[68] | CharRef[66]

[68] EntityRef ::= '&' Name[5]';'

[69] PEReference ::= '%' Name[5]';'

Entity declaration

[70] EntityDecl ::= GEDecl[71] | PEDecl[72]

[71] GEDecl ::= '<!ENTITY' S[3] Name[5] S[3] EntityDef[73] S[3]? '>'

[72] PEDecl ::= '<!ENTITY' S[3]'%' S[3] Name[5] S[3] PEDef[74] S[3]? '>'

[73] EntityDef ::= EntityValue[9] | (ExternalID[75] NDataDecl[76]?)

[74] PEDef ::= EntityValue[9] | ExternalID[75]

External entity declaration

[75] ExternalID ::= 'SYSTEM' S[3] SystemLiteral[11] | 'PUBLIC' S[3] PubidLiteral[12] S[3] SystemLiteral[11]

[76] NDataDecl ::= S[3] 'NDATA' S[3] Name[5]

Text declaration

[77] TextDecl ::= '<?xml' VersionInfo[24]? EncodingDecl[80] S[3]? '?>'

Well-formed external parsed entity

[78] extParsedEnt ::= TextDecl[77]? content[43] - Char[2]* RestrictedChar[2a] Char[2]*

Encoding declaration

[80] EncodingDecl ::= S[3] 'encoding' Eq[25] ('"' EncName[81]'"' | "'" EncName[81]"'")

[81] EncName ::= [A-Za-z] ([A-Za-z0-9._] | '-')* /* Encoding name contains only Latin characters */

Notation declarations

[82] NotationDecl ::= '<!NOTATION' S[3] Name[5] S[3](ExternalID[75] | PublicID[83]) S? '>'

[83] PublicID ::= 'PUBLIC' S[3] PubidLiteral[12]

22

Schemas Reference

The W3C XML Schema Language (schemas) is a declarative language used to describe the allowed contents of XML documents by assigning types to elements and attributes. The schema language includes several dozen standard types and allows you to define your own custom types. The combination of the information in an XML document instance and the types applied to that information by the schema is sometimes called the Post Schema Validation Infoset (PSVI).

A schema processor reads both an input XML document and a schema (which is itself an XML document because the W3C XML Schema Language is an XML application) and determines whether the document adheres to the constraints in the schema. A document that satisfies all the schema's constraints, and in which all the document's elements and attributes are declared, is said to be *schema-valid*, although in this chapter we will mostly just call such documents *valid*. A document that does not satisfy all of the constraints is said to be *invalid*.

The Schema Namespaces

All standard schema elements are in the `http://www.w3.org/2001/XMLSchema` namespace. In this chapter, we assume that this URI is mapped to the xs prefix using an appropriate `xmlns:xs` declaration. This declaration is almost always placed on the root element start-tag:

```
<xs:schema xmlns:xs="http://www.w3.org/2001/XMLSchema">
```

In addition, several attributes are used in instance documents to associate schema information with them, including `schemaLocation` and type. These attributes are in the `http://www.w3.org/2001/XMLSchema-instance` namespace. In this chapter, we assume that this URI is mapped to the xsi prefix with an appropriate `xmlns:xsi` declaration on either the element where this attribute appears or one of its ancestors.

In a few cases, schema elements may contain elements from other arbitrary namespaces or no namespace at all. This occurs primarily inside xs:appinfo and xs:documentation elements, which provide supplementary information about the schema itself, the documents the schema describes to systems that are not schema validators, or to people reading the schema.

Finally, most schema elements can have arbitrary attributes from other namespaces. For instance, this allows you to make an xs:attribute element a simple XLink by giving it xlink:type and xlink:href attributes or to identify the language of an xs:notation using an xml:lang attribute. However, this capability is not used much in practice.

Schema Elements

The W3C XML Schema Language defines 42 elements, which naturally divide into several categories:

One root element
    xs:schema

Three declaration elements
    xs:element, xs:attribute, and xs:notation

Eight elements for defining types
    xs:complexContent, xs:complexType, xs:extension, xs:list, xs:restriction, xs:simpleContent, xs:simpleType, and xs:union

Seven elements for defining content models
    xs:all, xs:any, xs:anyAttribute, xs:attributeGroup, xs:choice, xs:group, and xs:sequence

Five elements for specifying identity constraints
    xs:field, xs:key, xs:keyref, xs:selector, and xs:unique

Three elements for assembling schemas out of component parts
    xs:import, xs:include, and xs:redefine

Twelve facet elements for constraining simple types
    xs:enumeration, xs:fractionDigits, xs:length, xs:maxExclusive, xs:maxInclusive, xs:maxLength, xs:minExclusive, xs:minInclusive, xs:minLength, xs:pattern, xs:totalDigits, and xs:whiteSpace

Three elements for documenting schemas
    xs:appinfo, xs:annotation, and xs:documentation

Elements in this section are arranged alphabetically from xs:all to xs:whiteSpace. Each element begins with a sample implementation in the following form:

```
<xs:elementName
   attribute1 = "allowed attribute values"
   attribute2 = "allowed attribute values"
>
  <!-- Content model -->
</xs:elementName>
```

Most attribute values can be expressed as one of the 44 XML Schema built-in simple types, such as xs:string, xs:ID, or xs:integer. Values that should be replaced by an instance of the type are italicized. Values that take a literal form are listed in regular type. Some attribute values are specified as an enumeration of the legal values in the form (value1 | **value2** | value3 | etc.). In this case, the default value, if there is one, is given in boldface.

Element content models are given in a comment in the form they might appear in an ELEMENT declaration in a DTD. For example, an xs:all element may contain a single optional xs:annotation child element followed by zero or more xs:element elements. Thus, its content model is written like this:

```
<!-- ( xs:annotation?, xs:element* ) -->
```

xs:all

```
<xs:all
  id = "ID"
  maxOccurs = "1"
  minOccurs = "(0 | 1)">
  <!-- ( xs:annotation?, xs:element* ) -->
</xs:all>
```

The xs:all element indicates that every element represented by one of its child xs:element elements must appear. However, the order of the child elements in the instance element does not matter. For example, an xs:all element can require that each FullName element have exactly one FirstName child and exactly one LastName child, but that the order of the two child elements does not matter; the first name can come first or the last name can come first.

The xs:all element must be the top group in its content model (i.e., an xs:choice or xs:sequence cannot contain an xs:all element). The complete group represented by the xs:all element can occur either zero or one time as indicated by its minOccurs and maxOccurs attributes. By default, it must occur exactly once. Furthermore, the minOccurs and maxOccurs attributes of each of the individual xs:element elements inside the xs:all element must also be set to either 0 or 1. xs:all cannot indicate, for example, that a FullName element must contain between zero and five FirstNames and between one and three LastNames in any order.

xs:annotation

```
<xs:annotation
  id = "ID">
  <!-- ( xs:appinfo | xs:documentation )* -->
</xs:annotation>
```

The xs:annotation element is ignored by schema validators. Its purpose is to provide metainformation about the schema or schema element in which it appears. Information intended for human readers is placed in xs:documentation child elements. Information intended for software programs is placed in xs:appinfo child elements.

xs:any

```
<xs:any
   id = "ID"
   maxOccurs = "nonNegativeInteger | unbounded"
   minOccurs = "nonNegativeInteger"
   namespace = " ##any | ##other | anyURI* ##targetNamespace? ##local? "
   processContents = " lax | skip | strict ">
   <!-- xs:annotation? -->
</xs:any>
```

The wildcard element xs:any is useful when writing schemas for languages such as XSLT that routinely include markup from multiple vocabularies that are unknown when the schema is written. It indicates that between minOccurs and maxOccurs elements from one or more namespaces identified by the namespace attribute may appear at that position in a content model. As well as literal namespace URIs, the special value ##targetNamespace can be included in the list to indicate that any element from the schema's target namespace can be used. The special value ##local can be included in the list to indicate that elements not in any namespace can be used. Instead of the list of namespace URIs, you can use the special value ##any to indicate that all elements from any namespace or no namespace are allowed, or the special value ##other to indicate that elements from namespaces other than the schema's target namespace can be used.

The processContents attribute indicates whether the elements represented by xs:any have to be declared or whether they can be completely unfamiliar to the schema. It has one of these three values:

strict
: Elements represented by this xs:any element must be declared or have an xsi:type attribute. Furthermore, the element must be valid according to its declaration or type.

skip
: Elements represented by this xs:any element need not be declared in the schema and need not be valid even if they are declared.

lax
: Elements represented by this xs:any element must be validated if they are declared or if they have an xsi:type attribute, but must not be validated if they are neither declared nor have an xsi:type attribute.

The default value is strict.

xs:anyAttribute

```
<xs:anyAttribute
   id = "ID"
   namespace = "##any | ##other | anyURI* ##targetNamespace? ##local?"
   processContents = "(lax | skip | strict)" >
   <!-- (xs:annotation?) -->
</xs:anyAttribute>
```

The xs:anyAttribute element appears inside xs:complexType elements, where it indicates that elements of that type can have any attribute from one or more namespaces. It can also appear inside xs:attributeGroup elements, where it adds attributes from one or more namespaces as potential members of the group. The `namespace` attribute contains a whitespace-separated list of the namespace URIs that are allowed for this element's attributes. As well as literal namespace URIs, the special value `##targetNamespace` can be included in the list to indicate that any attribute from the schema's target namespace can be used. The special value `##local` can be included in the list, indicating that attributes not in any namespace (unprefixed attributes) may be used. Instead of the list of namespace URIs, you can use the special value `##any` to indicate that all attributes from any namespace are allowed or the special value `##other` to indicate that attributes from namespaces other than the schema's target namespace can be used.

The `processContents` attribute indicates whether the attributes themselves have to be declared, generally as top-level attributes. It has one of these three values:

strict
> Attributes represented by this `xs:anyAttribute` element must be declared, and the attribute must be valid according to its declaration. This is the default.

lax
> Attributes represented by this `xs:anyAttribute` element must be valid if they are declared but must not be validated if they are not declared.

skip
> Attributes represented by this `xs:anyAttribute` element need not be declared in the schema and need not be valid even if they are declared.

Schemas Reference

xs:appinfo

```
<xs:appinfo
  source = "anyURI">
  <!-- any well-formed XML markup -->
</xs:appinfo>
```

The `xs:appinfo` element appears exclusively inside `xs:annotation` elements, where it provides machine-readable information about the schema or schema element it's documenting. It has no effect on schema validation. It can contain absolutely any XML markup: an XSLT stylesheet for the schema, a schema for the schema, a schema in a different schema language such as Schematron, or anything else you can imagine. The only restriction is that the contents must be well-formed. Alternately, instead of or in addition to including this information directly, the `source` attribute can point to it using a URI.

xs:attribute

```
<xs:attribute
  default = "string"
  fixed = "string"
  form = "( qualified | unqualified )
  id = "ID"
  name = "NCName"
  ref = "QName"
  type = "QName"
  use = "( optional | prohibited | required )">
  <!-- ( xs:annotation?, xs:simpleType? ) -->
</xs:attribute>
```

The xs:attribute element declares an attribute. Inside an xs:complexType element it indicates that elements of that type can have an attribute with the specified name and type.

Attributes

default, *optional*
> The default value of the attribute reported for those elements in the instance document that do not contain an explicit specification of this attribute.

fixed, *optional*
> A default value for this attribute that may not be overridden in the instance document. An xs:attribute element cannot have both fixed and default attributes.

form, *optional*
> If this has the value qualified, then the attribute must be in the schema's target namespace. If this has the value unqualified, then the attribute must not be in any namespace. The default value for this is set by the attributeFormDefault attribute on the root xs:schema element.

id, *optional*
> An XML name unique among all of the ID-type attributes in this schema document.

name, *optional*
> The local name of the attribute.

ref, *optional*
> The qualified name of an attribute declared by a top-level xs:attribute element elsewhere in the schema. Either the name or ref attribute should be provided, but not both.

type, *optional*
> The qualified name of the type of the attribute, either a built-in simple type such as xs:integer or a user-defined simple type.

use, *optional*
> One of the three keywords—optional, prohibited, or required—which have the following meanings:
>
> optional
>> Authors of instance documents may or may not include this attribute as they choose. This is the default.
>
> prohibited
>> Authors of instance documents must not include this attribute. This is typically used to remove legal attribute values when defining a subtype that would otherwise inherit an attribute declaration from its base type.
>
> required
>> Authors of instance documents must include this attribute on all elements of the requisite type.

Contents

The xs:attribute element may contain a single xs:annotation element to describe itself. This has no effect on the attribute type.

In place of a type attribute, the xs:attribute element may contain a single xs:simpleType element that provides an anonymous type for the attribute derived from a base simple type.

---

xs:attributeGroup

```
<xs:attributeGroup
  id = "ID"
  name = "NCName"
  ref = "QName">
  <!--
    ( xs:annotation?, (xs:attribute | xs:attributeGroup)*,
      xs:anyAttribute? )
  -->
</xs:attributeGroup>
```

The xs:attributeGroup element is used in two ways. At the top level of the schema, it has a name attribute and defines a new attribute group. The attributes in the group are indicated by the child elements of the xs:attributeGroup element. Inside an xs:complexType element or another xs:attributeGroup, it has a ref attribute but no name and adds the attributes in the referenced group to the type or group's list of attributes.

xs:choice

Schemas
Reference

```
<xs:choice
  id = "ID"
  maxOccurs = "( nonNegativeInteger | unbounded )"
  minOccurs = "nonNegativeInteger">
  <!--
    ( xs:annotation?, (xs:element | xs:group | xs:choice
    | xs:sequence | xs:any)*)
  -->
</xs:choice>
```

The xs:choice element indicates that any element or group represented by one of its child elements may appear at that position in the instance document. At the least, minOccurs elements from the choice must appear. At most, maxOccurs elements from the choice must appear. The default for both minOccurs and maxOccurs is 1.

xs:complexContent

```
<xs:complexContent
  id = "ID"
  mixed = "( true | false )">
  <!-- ( xs:annotation?, (xs:restriction | xs:extension) ) -->
</xs:complexContent>
```

The xs:complexContent element is used inside xs:complexType elements to derive a new complex type from an existing complex type by restriction or extension. When deriving by extension, the mixed attribute must have the same value as the base type's mixed attribute. When deriving by restriction, the mixed attribute can have the value false to disallow mixed content that would be allowed in the base type. It can have the value true only if the base type allows mixed content. In other words, a derived type can disallow mixed content that's allowed in the base type, but cannot allow it if the base type doesn't already allow it.

xs:complexType

```
<xs:complexType
  abstract = "( true | false )"
  block = "( #all | extension | restriction )"
  final = "( #all | extension | restriction )"
  id = "ID"
  mixed = "( true | false )"
  name = "NCName"
  >
  <!-- ( xs:annotation?, (xs:simpleContent | xs:complexContent
       | ((xs:group | xs:all | xs:choice | xs:sequence)?,
          ((xs:attribute | xs:attributeGroup)*, xs:anyAttribute?)))) -->
</xs:complexType>
```

The xs:complexType element defines a new complex type, that is, an element type that can potentially contain child elements, attributes, or both. The valid child elements and attributes for elements of this type are specified by the contents of the xs:complexType element. The mixed attribute specifies whether the complex type is allowed to contain text interspersed with its child elements. If the xs:complexType element is a top-level element, then it has a name attribute and defines a named type. Otherwise, if the xs:complexType element appears inside an xs:element element, then it does not have a name attribute and defines an anonymous type for that element alone.

If the abstract attribute has the value true, then no elements of this type can be included in instance documents—only elements of subtypes derived from this type, which are marked as elements of the subtype by an xsi:type attribute, can be included. If the final attribute has the value restriction, then this type cannot be subtyped by restriction. If the final attribute has the value extension, then this type cannot be subtyped by extension. If the final attribute has the value #all, then this type cannot be subtyped by either restriction or extension. The default value of the final attribute is set by the finalDefault attribute on the root xs:schema element. If the block attribute has the value extension or restriction, then instances of this type cannot be replaced in instance documents by instances of subtypes derived from this type by extension or restriction, respectively, although such subtypes may still be defined and used for other elements. If the block attribute has the value #all, then this type cannot be replaced in instance documents by instances of any subtype. The default value of the block attribute is set by the blockDefault attribute on the root xs:schema element.

xs:documentation

```
<xs:documentation
  source = "anyURI"
  xml:lang = "language">
  <!-- any well-formed XML markup -->
</xs:documentation>
```

The xs:documentation element appears exclusively inside xs:annotation elements, where it provides human-readable information about the schema or schema element it's annotating. It has no effect on schema validation. It can contain absolutely any XML markup: XHTML, DocBook, or just plain text. The only restriction is that the contents must be well-formed. Alternately, instead of or in addition to including this information directly, the source attribute can point to it using a URI. The xml:lang attribute can indicate the language in which the description is written. You could even include multiple xs:documentation elements in different languages.

xs:element

```
<xs:element
  abstract = "( true | false )"
  block = "( #all | extension | restriction | substitution )"
  default = "string"
  final = "( #all | extension | restriction )"
  fixed = "string"
  form = "( qualified | unqualified )"
  id = "ID"
  maxOccurs = "( nonNegativeInteger | unbounded )"
  minOccurs = "nonNegativeInteger"
  name = "NCName"
  nillable = "( true | false )"
  ref = "QName"
  substitutionGroup = "QName"
  type = "QName">
  <!-- ( xs:annotation?,
       ((xs:simpleType | xs:complexType)?,
       (xs:unique | xs:key | xs:keyref)*) ) -->
</xs:element>
```

The xs:element element declares an element, including its name and type. Used at the top level of the schema, it indicates a potential root element. Used inside an xs:complexType element, it indicates a potential child element of another element. Alternately, instead of specifying a name and a type, it can have a ref attribute that points to a top-level element declaration elsewhere in the schema.

Attributes

abstract, *optional*

If the abstract attribute has the value true, then only elements from this element's substitution group are allowed in instance documents, not elements actually declared by this declaration.

default, *optional*

default is the default value of the element reported for empty elements matching this declaration in the instance document.

block, *optional*

If the block attribute contains the value extension or restriction, then this element cannot be replaced in instance documents by instances of subtypes derived from this element's type by extension or restriction, respectively. If the block attribute has the value substitution, then this element cannot be replaced in instance documents by members of this element's substitution group. If the block attribute has the value #all, then this element cannot be replaced in instance documents by subtype instances or substitution group members.

final, *optional*

> The final attribute controls which elements can refer to this element as the head of their substitution group. If the value contains the keyword restriction, then restrictions of this element's type cannot do so. If the value contains the keyword extension, then extensions of this element's type cannot do so. If the value is #all, then neither extensions nor restrictions of this type can do so.

form, *optional*

> If the form attribute has the value qualified, then the element is in the schema's target namespace. If it has the value unqualified, then the element is not in any namespace. The default value is set by the elementFormDefault attribute on the root xs:schema element. This attribute can only be used on locally declared elements. All globally declared elements are always in the schema's target namespace.

id, *optional*

> id is an XML name unique within ID-type attributes in this schema document.

maxOccurs, *optional*

> This signifies the maximum number of times this element may be repeated in valid instance documents.

minOccurs, *optional*

> This signifies the minimum number of times this element must be repeated in valid instance documents.

name, *optional*

> This contains the required name of the element. If this is omitted, the xs:element should be empty and must have a ref attribute that points to another element declaration.

nillable, *optional*

> If nillable has the value true, then this element can be specified as being "nil" using an xsi:nil="true" attribute in the instance document.

ref, *optional*

> The qualified name of an element declared by a top-level xs:element element.

substitutionGroup, *optional*

> This is the qualified name of a globally declared element for which this element may substitute in instance documents.

type, *optional*

> This is the qualified name of the type of the element, either a built-in simple type such as xs:integer, xs:anyType, or a user-defined type.

Contents

The xs:element element may contain an optional xs:annotation. If and only if the xs:element element does not have a type attribute, then it must have either an xs:simpleType child element or an xs:complexType child element that provides an anonymous type for this element. Finally, it may have any number of xs:key, xs:keyref, and xs:unique elements that set uniqueness and identity constraints.

xs:enumeration

```
<xs:enumeration
  id = "ID"
  value = "anySimpleType">
  <!-- (xs:annotation?) -->
</xs:enumeration>
```

The xs:enumeration facet element is used inside xs:restriction elements to derive new simple types by listing all valid values. The value attribute contains a single valid value of the type specified by the parent xs:restriction's base attribute. This xs:restriction element contains one xs:enumeration child element for each valid value.

xs:extension

```
<xs:extension
  base = "QName"
  id = "ID">
  <!-- (xs:annotation?,
        ((xs:group | xs:all | xs:choice | xs:sequence)?,
        ((xs:attribute | xs:attributeGroup)*, xs:anyAttribute?))) -->
</xs:extension>
```

The xs:extension element is used inside xs:simpleContent and xs:complexContent elements to derive a new complex type that adds attributes and/or child elements not present in the base type. The base type being extended is given by the value of the base attribute. The child elements and attributes added to the base type's content model are specified by the content of the xs:extension element. An instance of such an extended type must have all the child elements required by the base type followed by all the child elements required in the xs:extension.

xs:field

```
<xs:field
  id = "ID"
  xpath = "XPath expression">
  <!-- (xs:annotation?) -->
</xs:field>
```

One or more xs:field elements are placed inside each xs:unique, xs:key, and xs:keyref element to define a value calculated by the XPath expression in the xpath attribute. The context node for this expression is set in turn to each element in the node set selected by the xs:selector element.

Not all XPath expressions are allowed here. In particular, the XPath expression must limit itself to the child axis, except for the last step, which may use the attribute axis. The only node tests used are name tests (element and attribute names, the * wildcard, and the prefix:* wildcard). Abbreviated syntax must be used, and predicates are not allowed. Thus, person/name/first_name/@id is a legal XPath expression for this attribute, but person//name/@id is not. Several instances of this restricted form of XPath expression can be combined with the vertical bar so that person/name/first_name/@id | person/name/last_name/@id is also an acceptable XPath expression. Finally, the XPath expression may begin with .// so that .//name/@id is legal. However, this is the only place the descendant-or-self axis can be used. No other forms of XPath expression are allowed here.

xs:fractionDigits

```
<xs:fractionDigits
  fixed = "( true | false )"
  id = "ID"
  value = "nonNegativeInteger" >
  <!-- (xs:annotation?) -->
</xs:fractionDigits>
```

The xs:fractionDigits facet element is used when deriving from xs:decimal (and its subtypes) by restriction. It limits the number of non-zero digits allowed after the decimal point to, at most, the number specified by the value attribute. This sets only the maximum number of digits after the decimal point. If you want to set the minimum number of digits required, you'll have to use the xs:pattern element instead. If the fixed attribute has the value true, then types derived from this type are not allowed to override the value of fractionDigits given here.

xs:group

```
<xs:group
  name = "NCName"
  ref  = "NCName"
  minOccurs = "nonNegativeInteger"
  maxOccurs = "nonNegativeInteger | unbounded">
  <!-- ( xs:annotation?, (xs:all | xs:choice | xs:sequence) ) -->
</xs:group>
```

The xs:group element can be used in two ways. As a top-level element with a name attribute, it defines a model group that can be referenced from complex types elsewhere in the schema. The content model of the group is established by a child xs:all, xs:choice, or xs:sequence element.

The second use is inside an xs:complexType element. Here, the xs:group element indicates that the contents of the group should appear at this point in the instance document at least as many times as indicated by the minOccurs attribute and at most as many times as indicated by the maxOccurs attribute. The default for both of these is 1. The group to be included is indicated by the ref attribute that contains the name of a top-level xs:group element found elsewhere in the schema.

xs:import

```
<xs:import
  id = "ID"
  namespace = "anyURI"
  schemaLocation = "anyURI" >
  <!-- ( xs:annotation? ) -->
</xs:import>
```

Since each schema document has exactly one target namespace, the top-level xs:import element is needed to create schemas for documents that involve multiple namespaces. The namespace attribute contains the namespace URI for the application that the imported schema describes. If the imported schema describes elements and types in no namespace, then the namespace attribute is omitted. The optional schemaLocation attribute contains a relative or absolute URL pointing to the actual location of the schema document to import.

There is no limit to import depth. Schema A can import schema B, which itself imports schema C and schema D. In such a case, schema A can use definitions and declarations from all four schemas. Even recursion (schema A imports schema B, which imports schema A) is not prohibited. Since the imported schema must describe a different target namespace than the importing schema, conflicts between definitions in the multiple schemas are normally not a problem. However, if conflicts do arise, then the schema is in error and cannot be used. There are no precedence rules for choosing between multiple conflicting definitions or declarations.

xs:include

```
<xs:include
    id = "ID"
    schemaLocation = "anyURI">
    <!-- (annotation?) -->
</xs:include>
```

The top-level xs:include element is used to divide a schema into multiple separate documents. The schemaLocation attribute contains a relative or absolute URI pointing to the schema document to include. It differs from xs:import in that all included files describe the same target namespace.

There is no limit to inclusion depth. Schema A can include schema B, which itself includes schema C and schema D. In such a case, schema A can use definitions and declarations from all four documents. Even recursion (schema A includes schema B, which includes schema A) is not prohibited, although it is strongly discouraged. Instance documents would refer only to the top-level schema A in their xsi:schemaLocation or xsi:noNamespaceSchemaLocation attribute.

Validation is performed after all includes are resolved. If there are any conflicts between the including schema and an included schema—for instance, one schema declares that the FullName element has a simple type, and another declares that the FullName element has a complex type—then the schema is in error and cannot be used. Most of the time, schemas should be carefully managed so that each element and type is defined in exactly one schema document.

xs:key

```
<xs:key
    id = "ID"
    name = "NCName" >
    <!-- (xs:annotation?, (xs:selector, xs:field+) ) -->
</xs:key>
```

Keys establish uniqueness and co-occurrence constraints among various nodes in the document. For example, you can define a key for an Employee element based on its EmployeeNumber child element and then require that each Assignment element have a team attribute whose contents are a list of employee keys.

The xs:key element defines a new key. It appears only as a child of an xs:element element following the element's type. The name of the key is specified by the name attribute. The elements that have a value for this key are identified by the xs:selector child element. The value of the key for each of these nodes is given by the xs:field child element and must be unique within that set. If there is more than one xs:field child element, then the key is formed by concatenating the value of each field.

xs:keyref

```
<xs:keyref
  id = "ID"
  name = "NCName"
  refer = "QName" >
  <!-- (xs:annotation?, (xs:selector, xs:field+) ) -->
</xs:keyref>
```

The xs:keyref element is placed inside xs:element elements to require that the element selected by the xs:selector must match an xs:key or xs:unique with the name given by the refer attribute. The key that is referred to must be a child of one of the ancestors of this xs:keyref. The value that is matched against the specified key is determined by the concatenation of the values of the xs:field child elements.

xs:length

```
<xs:length
  fixed = "( true | false )"
  id = "ID"
  value = "nonNegativeInteger" >
  <!-- (xs:annotation?) -->
</xs:length>
```

The xs:length facet element specifies the exact number of characters in a type derived from xs:string, xs:QName, xs:anyURI, or xs:NOTATION. When applied to a list type, such as xs:ENTITIES, this facet specifies the number of items in the list. Finally, when applied to xs:hexBinary and xs:base64Binary, it specifies the number of *bytes* in the decoded data, rather than the number of *characters* in the encoded data. If the fixed attribute has the value true, then types derived from this type are not allowed to override the value of length given here.

xs:list

```
<xs:list
  id = "ID"
  itemType = "QName" >
  <!-- (xs:annotation?, (xs:simpleType?) ) -->
</xs:list>
```

The xs:list element is placed inside an xs:simpleType element to derive a new list simple type from a base atomic type or union type identified by the itemType attribute. Alternately, instead of referencing an existing simple type with itemType, a new anonymous atomic type for the list can be created by an xs:simpleType child element. In either case, the newly defined simple type is a whitespace-separated list of atomic values.

xs:maxExclusive

```
<xs:maxExclusive
  fixed = "( true | false )"
  id = "ID"
  value = "anySimpleType" >
  <!-- (xs:annotation?) -->
</xs:maxExclusive>
```

The xs:maxExclusive facet element applies to all ordered types, including xs:decimal, xs:float, xs:double, xs:date, xs:duration, xs:dateTime, xs:time, xs:gDay, xs:gMonthYear, xs:gMonth, xs:gYear, and their subtypes. The value attribute contains the maximum value in a form appropriate for the type. For example, the maximum for a type derived from xs:integer might be 75; the maximum for a type derived from xs:double might be 1.61803; and the maximum for a type derived from xs:date might be 2004-10-26. All instances of this type must be *strictly less-than* the maximum value. They may not be equal to the maximum. If the fixed attribute has the value true, then types derived from this type are not allowed to override the value of maxExclusive given here.

xs:maxInclusive

```
<xs:maxInclusive
  fixed = "( true | false )"
  id = "ID"
  value = "anySimpleType" >
  <!-- (xs:annotation?) -->
</xs:maxInclusive>
```

The xs:maxInclusive facet element applies to all ordered types, including xs:decimal, xs:float, xs:double, xs:date, xs:duration, xs:dateTime, xs:time, xs:gDay, xs:gMonthYear, xs:gMonth, xs:gYear, and their subtypes. The value attribute contains the maximum value in a form appropriate for the type. For example, the maximum for a type derived from xs:integer might be 75; the maximum for a type derived from xs:double might be 1.61803; and the maximum for a type derived from xs:date might be 2004-10-26. All instances of this type must be *less-than or equal to* the maximum value. If the fixed attribute has the value true, then types derived from this type are not allowed to override the value of maxInclusive given here.

xs:maxLength

```
<xs:maxLength
  fixed = "( true | false )"
  id = "ID"
  value = "nonNegativeInteger" >
  <!-- (xs:annotation?) -->
</xs:maxLength>
```

The xs:maxLength facet element specifies the maximum number of characters in a type derived from xs:string, xs:QName, xs:anyURI, or xs:NOTATION. It can also be used to restrict xs:hexBinary and xs:base64Binary. However, in this case, it refers to the maximum number of *bytes* in the decoded data rather than the maximum number of *characters* in the encoded data. Finally, when applied to a list type, such as xs:IDREFS, it describes the maximum number of items in the list. If the fixed attribute has the value true, then types derived from this type are not allowed to override the value of maxLength given here.

xs:minExclusive

```
<xs:minExclusive
   fixed = "( true | false )"
   id = "ID"
   value = "anySimpleType" >
   <!-- (xs:annotation?) -->
</xs:minExclusive>
```

The xs:minExclusive facet element applies to all ordered types, including xs:decimal, xs:float, xs:double, xs:date, xs:duration, xs:dateTime, xs:time, xs:gDay, xs:gMonthYear, xs:gMonth, xs:gYear, and their subtypes. The value attribute contains the minimum value in a form appropriate for the type. For example, the minimum for a type derived from xs:integer might be 75, the minimum for a type derived from xs:double might be 1.61803, and the minimum for a type derived from xs:date might be 2005-10-26. All instances of this type must be *strictly greater-than* the minimum value. They may not be equal to the minimum. If the fixed attribute has the value true, then types derived from this type are not allowed to override the value of minExclusive given here.

xs:minInclusive

```
<xs:minInclusive
   fixed = "( true | false )"
   id = "ID"
   value = "anySimpleType" >
   <!-- (xs:annotation?) -->
</xs:minInclusive>
```

The xs:minInclusive facet element applies to all ordered types, including xs:decimal, xs:float, xs:double, xs:date, xs:duration, xs:dateTime, xs:time, xs:gDay, xs:gMonthYear, xs:gMonth, xs:gYear, and their subtypes. The value attribute contains the minimum value in a form appropriate for the type. For example, the minimum for a type derived from xs:integer might be 75; the minimum for a type derived from xs:double might be 1.61803; and the minimum for a type derived from xs:date might be 2005-10-26. All instances of this type must be *greater-than or equal to* the minimum value. If the fixed attribute has the value true, then types derived from this type are not allowed to override the value of minInclusive given here.

xs:minLength

```
<xs:minLength
   fixed = "( true | false )"
   id = "ID"
   value = "nonNegativeInteger" >
   <!-- (xs:annotation?) -->
</xs:minLength>
```

The xs:minLength facet element specifies the minimum number of characters in a type derived from xs:string, xs:QName, xs:anyURI, or xs:NOTATION. It can also be used to restrict xs:hexBinary and xs:base64Binary. However, in this case, it refers to the minimum number of *bytes* in the decoded data, rather than the minimum number of *characters* in the encoded data. Finally, when applied to a list type, such as xs:IDREFS, it describes the minimum number of items in the list. If the fixed attribute has the value true, then types derived from this type are not allowed to override the value of minLength given here.

xs:notation

```
<xs:notation
  id = "ID"
  name = "NCName"
  public = "PUBLIC identifier"
  system = "anyURI" >
  <!-- (xs:annotation?) -->
</xs:notation>
```

The top-level xs:notation element defines a notation. It's the schema equivalent of a
<!NOTATION> declaration in a DTD. Each notation has a name, a public ID, and a
system ID identified by the relevant attribute on this element.

xs:pattern

```
<xs:pattern
  id = "ID"
  value = "regular expression" >
  <!-- (xs:annotation?) -->
</xs:pattern>
```

Schemas
Reference

The xs:pattern facet element is used to derive new simple types by specifying a regular
expression against which values of the type are compared. It applies to all simple
types. The schema regular-expression grammar is quite similar to that used in Perl 5.6
and later. (The big change from earlier versions of Perl is support for Unicode character class-based regular expressions.) Most strings and characters match themselves,
but a few characters have special meanings, as summarized in Table 22-1. In this table,
A and *B* are subexpressions; *n* and *m* are nonnegative integers; *a*, *b*, *c*, and *d* are all single
Unicode characters; and *X* is a name.

Table 22-1. XML Schema regular-expression syntax

Pattern	Matches
(A)	A string that matches A
A | B	A string that matches A or a string that matches B
AB	A string that matches A followed by a string that matches B
A?	Zero or one repetitions of a string that matches A
A*	Zero or more repetitions of a string that matches A
A+	One or more repetitions of a string that matches A
A{n,m}	A sequence of between n and m strings, each of which matches A
A{n}	A sequence of exactly n strings, each of which matches A
A{n,}	A sequence of at least n strings, each of which matches A
[abcd]	Exactly one of the characters listed inside the square brackets
[^abcd]	Exactly one character not listed inside the square brackets
[a-z]	Exactly one character with a Unicode value between a and z, inclusive
[a-z-[d-h]]	Exactly one character included in the outer range but not in the inner range
\n	The newline, &#xOA;
\r	The carriage return, &#xOD;
\t	The tab, 	

Table 22-1. XML Schema regular-expression syntax (continued)

Pattern	Matches
\\	The backslash, \
|	The vertical bar, |
\.	The period, .
\-	The hyphen, -
\^	The caret, ∧
\?	The question mark, ?
*	The asterisk, *
\+	The plus sign, +
\{	The left curly brace, {
\}	The right curly brace, }
\(	The left parenthesis, (
\)	The right parenthesis,)
\[	The left square bracket, [
\]	The right square bracket,]
.	Any single character except a carriage return or line feed
\s	A space, tab, carriage return, or line feed
\S	Any single character except a space, tab, carriage return, or line feed
\i	An XML name-start character
\c	An XML name character
\d	A decimal digit
\D	Any single character except a decimal digit
\w	A "word character," that is, any single character that is not a punctuation mark, a separator, or "other" (as defined by Unicode)
\W	Any single character that is a punctuation mark, a separator, or "other" (as defined by Unicode)
\p{X}	Any single character from the Unicode character class X; character class names are listed in Table 22-2
\P{X}	Any single character not in the Unicode character class X
\p{IsX}	Any single character from the Unicode character block X. Block names include BasicLatin, Latin-1Supplement, LatinExtended-A, LatinExtended-B, IPAExtensions, SpacingModifierLetters, CombiningDiacriticalMarks, Greek, Cyrillic, Armenian, Hebrew, Arabic, Syriac, Thaana, Devanagari, Bengali, Gurmukhi, Gujarati, Oriya, Tamil, Telugu, Kannada, Malayalam, Sinhala, Thai, Lao, Tibetan, Myanmar, Georgian, HangulJamo, Ethiopic, Cherokee, UnifiedCanadianAboriginalSyllabics, Ogham, Runic, Khmer, Mongolian, LatinExtendedAdditional, GreekExtended, GeneralPunctuation, SuperscriptsandSubscripts, CurrencySymbols, CombiningMarksforSymbols, LetterlikeSymbols, NumberForms, Arrows, MathematicalOperators, MiscellaneousTechnical, ControlPictures, OpticalCharacterRecognition, EnclosedAlphanumerics, BoxDrawing, BlockElements, GeometricShapes, MiscellaneousSymbols, Dingbats, BraillePatterns, CJKRadicalsSupplement, KangxiRadicals, IdeographicDescriptionCharacters, CJKSymbolsandPunctuation, Hiragana, Katakana, Bopomofo, HangulCompatibilityJamo, Kanbun, BopomofoExtended, EnclosedCJKLettersandMonths, CJKCompatibility, CJKUnifiedIdeographsExtensionA, CJKUnifiedIdeographs, YiSyllables, YiRadicals, HangulSyllables, HighSurrogates, HighPrivateUseSurrogates, LowSurrogates, PrivateUse, CJKCompatibilityIdeographs, AlphabeticPresentationForms, ArabicPresentationForms-A, CombiningHalfMarks, CJKCompatibilityForms, SmallFormVariants, ArabicPresentationForms-B, Specials, HalfwidthandFullwidthForms, Specials, OldItalic, Gothic, Deseret, ByzantineMusicalSymbols, MusicalSymbols, MathematicalAlphanumericSymbols, CJKUnifiedIdeographsExtensionB, CJKCompatibilityIdeographsSupplement, Tags, and PrivateUse. The characters from many of these blocks are shown in Chapter 27.
\P{IsX}	Any single character not in the Unicode character block X

You can also include or exclude classes of Unicode characters using the \p{X} or \P{X} pattern and the classes listed in Table 22-2.

Table 22-2. Unicode character classes

Unicode character class	Includes
L	Letters
Lu	Uppercase letters
Ll	Lowercase letters
Lt	Titlecase letters
Lm	Modifier letters
Lo	Other letters
M	All marks
Mn	Nonspacing marks
Mc	Spacing combining marks
Me	Enclosing marks
N	Numbers
Nd	Decimal digits
Nl	Number letters
No	Other numbers
P	Punctuation
Pc	Connector punctuation
Pd	Dashes
Ps	Opening punctuation
Pe	Closing punctuation
Pi	Initial quotes
Pf	Final quotes
Po	Other punctuation
Z	Separators
Zs	Spaces
Zl	Line breaks
Zp	Paragraph breaks
S	Symbols
Sm	Mathematical symbols
Sc	Currency symbols
Sk	Modifier symbols
So	Other symbols
C	Other characters (nonletters, nonsymbols, nonnumbers, nonseparators)
Cc	Control characters
Cf	Format characters
Co	Private use characters
Cn	Unassigned code points

xs:redefine

```
<xs:redefine
  id = "ID"
  schemaLocation = "anyURI" >
  <!-- (annotation | (simpleType | complexType | group | attributeGroup))*
  -->
</xs:redefine>
```

The xs:redefine element is used much like xs:include. That is, it inserts definitions and declarations for the same target namespace from a schema document found at a URL specified by the schemaLocation attribute. However, unlike xs:include, xs:redefine can override type, model group, and attribute group definitions from the included schema. The new type and group definitions are children of the xs:redefine element. They must extend or restrict the original definition of the redefined type or group. Note, however, that xs:redefine cannot override element and attribute declarations made in the included schema.

xs:restriction

```
<xs:restriction
  base = "QName"
  id = "ID">
  <!-- ( xs:annotation?, (
       (xs:simpleType?,
       ( xs:minExclusive | xs:minInclusive | xs:maxExclusive
       | xs:maxInclusive | xs:totalDigits | xs:fractionDigits
       | xs:length | xs:minLength | xs:maxLength | xs:enumeration
       | xs:whiteSpace | xs:pattern)*)
       | ( (xs:group | xs:all | xs:choice | xs:sequence)?,
         ((xs:attribute | xs:attributeGroup)*, xs:anyAttribute?) )
       ) -->
</xs:restriction>
```

The xs:restriction element derives a new type from an existing base type identified by either a base attribute or an xs:simpleType child element. When deriving by restriction, all valid values of the derived type must also be legal values of the base type. However, the reverse is not true. The valid values of the derived type are a subset of the valid values of the base type. For derived simple types, the allowed values are identified by the various facet child elements of the xs:restriction element. For derived complex types, the allowed values are identified by the same elements you'd find inside an xs:complexType element—that is, zero or one group elements such as xs:all, xs:choice, or xs:sequence followed by attribute representation elements such as xs:attribute, xs:attributeGroup, and xs:anyAttribute.

xs:schema

```
<xs:schema
  attributeFormDefault = "( qualified | unqualified )"
  elementFormDefault   = "( qualified | unqualified )"
  blockDefault = "( #all | extension | restriction | substitution )"
  finalDefault = "( #all | extension | restriction )"
```

```
      id = "ID"
      targetNamespace = "anyURI"
      version = "token"
      xml:lang = "language" >
      <!-- (
            (xs:include | xs:import | xs:redefine | xs:annotation)*,
            (((xs:simpleType | xs:complexType | xs:group
            | xs:attributeGroup) | xs:element | xs:attribute
            | xs:notation), xs:annotation*)*
      ) -->
   </xs:schema>
```

xs:schema is the root element of all schema documents. It contains all the top-level elements described elsewhere in this chapter. First come all the elements that somehow reference other schema documents, including xs:include, xs:import, and xs:redefine. These are followed by the various elements that define types and groups and declare elements and attributes. As usual, xs:annotation elements can be placed anywhere that is convenient.

Attributes

attributeFormDefault, *optional*

> This sets the default value for the form attribute of xs:attribute elements. This specifies whether locally declared attributes are namespace qualified by the target namespace. If this attribute is not used, locally declared attributes are unqualified unless the form attribute of the xs:attribute element has the value qualified.

elementFormDefault, *optional*

> This sets the default for the form attribute of xs:element elements. This specifies whether locally declared elements are namespace-qualified by the target namespace. By default, locally declared elements are unqualified unless the form attribute of the xs:element element has the value qualified.

blockDefault, *optional*

> The blockDefault attribute establishes the default value for the block attributes of xs:element and xs:complexType elements in this schema.

finalDefault, *optional*

> The finalDefault attribute establishes the default value for the final attributes of xs:element and xs:complexType elements in this schema.

id, *optional*

> id is an XML name unique within ID-type attributes in this schema document.

targetNamespace, *optional*

> The namespace URI for the XML application described by this schema. If not present, then this schema describes elements in no namespace. If the XML application uses multiple namespaces, then there must be a separate schema document for each different namespace. These schemas can be connected with xs:import elements.

version, *optional*

> You can use this attribute to specify the version of the schema, e.g., 1.0, 1.0.1, 1.1, 1.2, 1.3b1, 2.0, etc. This refers to the version of the specific schema, not the version of the W3C XML Schema Language used in this document.

xml:lang, *optional*

This is the human language in which this schema is primarily written, such as en or fr-CA.

 elementFormDefault is part of a misguided effort to make child elements and attributes equivalent. If you're using namespaces at all, just put all elements in the target namespace of the schema and set elementFormDefault to qualified.

xs:selector

```
<xs:selector
  id = "ID"
  xpath = "XPath expression" >
  <!-- (xs:annotation?) -->
</xs:selector>
```

A single xs:selector element is placed inside each xs:unique, xs:key, and xs:keyref element to specify the element nodes for which the key or key reference is defined. The node set is selected by an XPath expression contained in the value of the xpath attribute. The context node for this XPath expression is the element matched by the xs:element declaration in which the xs:unique, xs:key, or xs:keyref element appears.

Not all XPath expressions are allowed here. In particular, the XPath expression must be an abbreviated location path that limits itself to the child axis. The only node tests used are element name, the * wildcard, and the *prefix*:* wildcard. Abbreviated syntax must be used; predicates are not allowed. Thus, person/name/first_name is a legal XPath expression for this attribute, but person//name and name/first_name/@id are not. Several instances of this restricted form of XPath expression can be combined with the vertical bar so that person/name/first_name | person/name/last_name is also an acceptable XPath expression. Finally, the XPath expression may begin with .// so that .// name is valid. However, this is the only place the descendant-or-self axis can be used; no other forms of XPath expression are allowed here.

xs:sequence

```
<xs:sequence
  id = "ID"
  maxOccurs = "( nonNegativeInteger | unbounded)"
  minOccurs = "nonNegativeInteger" >
  <!-- ( xs:annotation?,
        ( xs:element | xs:group | xs:choice | xs:sequence | xs:any )*
      )
  -->
</xs:sequence>
```

The xs:sequence element indicates that the elements represented by its child elements should appear at that position in the instance document in the order they're listed here. The sequence must repeat at least minOccurs times and at most maxOccurs times. The default for both minOccurs and maxOccurs is 1. The maxOccurs attribute can be set to unbounded to indicate that the sequence may repeat indefinitely.

xs:simpleContent

```
<xs:simpleContent
  id = "ID" >
  <!-- (xs:annotation?, (xs:restriction | xs:extension)) -->
</xs:simpleContent>
```

The xs:simpleContent element is used inside xs:complexType elements whose content is a simple type, such as xs:string or xs:integer, rather than child elements or mixed content. This is customarily done when the only reason an element has a complex type instead of a simple type is because it can have attributes.

xs:simpleType

```
<xs:simpleType
  final = "( #all | list | union | restriction )"
  id = "ID"
  name = "NCName" >
  <!-- (xs:annotation?, (xs:restriction | xs:list | xs:union)) -->
</xs:simpleType>
```

The xs:simpleType element defines a new simple type for elements and attributes. A simple type is composed purely of text but no child elements—#PCDATA, in DTD parlance. A top-level xs:simpleType element has a name given in the name attribute by which it can be referred to from the type attribute of xs:element and xs:attribute elements. Alternately, an xs:element or xs:attribute element can have an xs:simpleType child without a name attribute that defines an *anonymous type* for that element or attribute.

New types are derived from existing types in one of three ways: by restricting the range of a base type using an xs:restriction child element, by combining multiple base types with an xs:union child element, or by allowing multiple values of a base type separated by whitespace with an xs:list child element.

The final attribute can be used to prevent a simple type from being subtyped. If final contains the value list, the type cannot be extended by listing. If final contains the value restriction, the type cannot be extended by restriction. If final contains the value union, the type cannot become a member of a union. These three values can be combined in a whitespace-separated list. For instance, final="list union" prevents derivation by list and union but not by restriction. If final has the value #all, the type cannot be used as a base type in any way.

xs:totalDigits

```
<xs:totalDigits
  fixed = "( true | false )"
  id = "ID"
  value = "positiveInteger" >
  <!-- (xs:annotation?) -->
</xs:totalDigits>
```

Schemas
Reference

The xs:totalDigits facet element is used when deriving from xs:decimal elements and its descendants (xs:integer, xs:long, xs:nonNegativeInteger, xs:unsignedLong, etc.) by restriction. It specifies the maximum number of non-zero digits allowed in the number, including both the integer and fractional parts, but not counting the decimal point or the sign. This only sets the maximum number of digits. If you want to specify a minimum number of digits, use the xs:pattern element instead. If the fixed attribute has the value true, then types derived from this type are not allowed to override the value of fractionDigits given here.

xs:union

```
<xs:union
  id = "ID"
  memberTypes = "List of QName" >
  <!-- (xs:annotation?, (xs:simpleType*)) -->
</xs:union>
```

The xs:union element is placed inside an xs:simpleType to indicate that an element or attribute can contain any one of multiple types. For example, it can say that an element can contain either an xs:integer or an xs:token. The names of the types that participate in the union are listed in the memberTypes attribute separated by whitespace. Furthermore, the types defined in the xs:simpleType children of the xs:union are also members of the union.

xs:unique

```
<xs:unique
  id = "ID"
  name = "NCName" >
  <!-- (xs:annotation?, xs:selector, xs:field+ ) -->
</xs:unique>
```

The xs:unique element requires that a specified subset of elements and/or attributes in the instance document have unique values calculated from each of those elements/attributes. This is similar to the constraint imposed by declaring an attribute to have type xs:ID, but it is much more flexible. The xs:selector child element uses XPath to specify the subset of nodes from the instance document over which uniqueness is calculated. The xs:field children use XPath expressions to specify what properties of those nodes must be unique within the subset.

xs:whiteSpace

```
<xs:whiteSpace
  fixed = "( true | false )"
  id = "ID"
  value = "(collapse | preserve | replace)" >
  <!-- (xs:annotation?) -->
</xs:whiteSpace>
```

The xs:whiteSpace facet element is unusual because it does not constrain values. Instead, it tells the validator how it should normalize whitespace before validating the value against other facets. The value attribute has one of three values:

preserve
> All whitespace is significant; this is conceptually similar to the pre element in HTML.

collapse
> Before the value is validated, tabs, carriage returns, and line feeds are replaced by spaces; leading and trailing whitespace is deleted; and runs of more than one consecutive space are condensed to a single space.

replace
> Tabs, carriage returns, and line feeds are replaced by spaces before the value is validated.

For schema purposes, whitespace consists of the characters defined as whitespace in XML 1.0: the space, carriage return, tab, and line feed. It does not include the two new whitespace characters added in XML 1.1: NEL (#x85) and the Unicode line separator (#x2028).

Built-in Types

The W3C XML Schema Language provides 44 built-in simple types for text strings. Each type has a value space and a lexical space. The value space is the set of unique meanings for the type, which may or may not be text. In some sense, the value space is composed of Platonic forms. The lexical space is the set of text strings that correspond to particular points in the value space. For example, the xs:boolean type has the value space true and false. However, its lexical space contains four strings: true, false, 0, and 1. true and 1 both map to the same value true, while false and 0 map to the single value false. In cases like this where multiple strings in the lexical space map to a single value, then one of those strings is selected as the canonical lexical representation. For instance, the canonical lexical representations of true and false are the strings true and false.

The primitive types are organized in a hierarchy. All simple types descend from an abstract ur-type called xs:anySimpleType, which is itself a descendant of an abstract ur-type called xs:anyType that includes both simple and complex types. Simple types are derived from other simple types by union, restriction, or listing. For example, the xs:nonNegativeInteger type is derived from the xs:integer type by setting its minInclusive facet to 0. The xs:integer type is derived from the xs:decimal type by setting its fractionDigits facet to 0. Figure 22-1 diagrams the complete hierarchy of built-in types. The xs:simpleType element allows you to apply facets to these types to create your own derived types that extend this hierarchy.

The types are organized alphabetically in the following section. For each type, the value and lexical spaces are described, and some examples of permissible instances are provided.

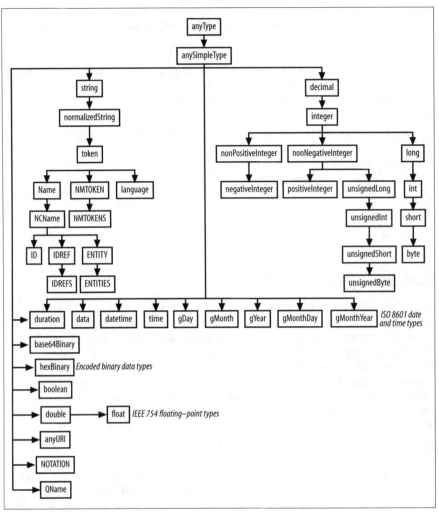

Figure 22-1. The simple type hierarchy

xs:anyURI

The xs:anyURI type indicates a Uniform Resource Identifier. This includes not only Uniform Resource Locators (URLs), but also Uniform Resource Names (URNs). Both relative and absolute URLs are allowed. Legal xs:anyURI values include the following:

- http://www.cafeaulait.org/
- http://[FEDC:BA98:7654:3210:FEDC:BA98:7654:3210]/
- http://www.w3.org/TR/xmlschema-2/#anyURI
- #xpointer(/book/chapter%5B20%5D/sect1%5B2%5D)
- gopher://spinaltap.micro.umn.edu/00/Weather/

- `mailto:elharo@metalab.unc.edu`
- `chapters/ch03.html`
- `http://ibiblio.org/nywc/compositions.phtml?category=Concertos`

More specifically, elements of this type must be composed exclusively of the ASCII letters A–Z and a–z and digits 0–9, as well as the ASCII punctuation marks -, _, ., !, ~, *, ', (, and). In addition, the ASCII punctuation marks ;, /, ?, :, @, &, =, +, $, %, [,], and , may be used for their intended purposes in URLs; e.g., the forward slash can be used as the path separator but not as part of a filename. All other characters must be escaped by encoding each byte of their UTF-8 representation as a percent sign followed by the hexadecimal value of the character. Although there are other restrictions on what does and does not make a legal URI, in practice, the only conditions that schema processors check are the limitations on the characters that may appear.

Constraining facets that apply to `xs:anyURI` are `length`, `minLength`, `maxLength`, `pattern`, `enumeration`, and `whiteSpace`.

xs:base64Binary

The `xs:base64Binary` type represents an arbitrary sequence of bytes that has been encoded in ASCII characters using the Base-64 algorithm defined in RFC 2045, *Multipurpose Internet Mail Extensions (MIME) Part One: Format of Internet Message Bodies*. The letters A–Z and a–z, the digits 0–9, and the punctuation marks + and / are used to encode data according to an algorithm that maps four of these characters to three arbitrary bytes. The equals sign is used to pad data at the end if necessary.

The constraining facets that apply to `xs:base64Binary` are `length`, `minLength`, `maxLength`, `pattern`, `enumeration`, and `whiteSpace`. Unlike string types, the values specified by the `length`, `minLength`, and `maxLength` facets refer to the number of bytes in the decoded data, not to the number of characters in the encoded data.

xs:boolean

The `xs:boolean` type represents a logical Boolean whose value is either true or false. There are exactly four legal values for elements and attributes whose type is Boolean:

- true
- false
- 0
- 1

0 is the same as false, and 1 is the same as true. Only two constraining facets apply to `xs:boolean`: `pattern` and `whiteSpace`.

xs:byte

The `xs:byte` type represents an integer with a value between -128 and 127. It is a subtype of the `xs:short` type. Legal values include any sequence of digits whose value is less than or equal to 127 and greater than or equal to -128. An optional leading plus or minus sign is allowed. For example, these are legal bytes:

- 127
- -128
- 0
- 52
- +52
- 0000052

Constraining facets that apply to xs:byte are length, minInclusive, maxInclusive, minExclusive, maxExclusive, pattern, enumeration, whiteSpace, and totalDigits.

xs:date

The xs:date type represents a specific day in history such as September 26, 2005. Dates are written in the form *CCYY-MM-DD*. For example, September 26, 2005 is written as 2005-09-26. Dates in the far future and distant past can be written with more than four digits in the year, but at least four digits are required. Dates before year 1 are written with a preceding minus sign. (There was no year 0.) An optional time zone indicator in the form ±*hh:mm* may be suffixed to provide a time zone as an offset from Coordinated Universal Time (Greenwich Mean Time, UTC). For example, 2005-09-26-05:00 is September 26, 2005 in the U.S. Eastern time zone. A Z can be used instead to indicate UTC. These are all valid values of type xs:date:

- 2001-01-01
- 1999-12-31Z
- 0482-11-24
- -0052-10-23
- 2002-12-23+12:00
- 87500-01-01

Constraining facets that apply to xs:date are minInclusive, maxInclusive, minExclusive, maxExclusive, pattern, enumeration, and whiteSpace. Note, however, that when the time zone is not specified, it's not always possible to determine unambiguously whether one date begins after another.

xs:dateTime

The xs:dateTime type represents a specific moment in history, such as 3:32 P.M., September 26, 2003. Date-times are written in the form *CCYY-MM-DDThh:mm:ss*. For example, 3:32 P.M., September 26, 2003 is written as 2003-09-26T15:32:00. Decimal fractions of a second can be indicated by appending a period and any number of digits after the seconds. Dates in the far future and distant past can be written with more than four digits in the year, but at least four digits are required. Dates before year 1 are written with a preceding minus sign. (There was no year 0.) An optional time zone indicator in the form ±*hh:mm* may be suffixed to provide a time zone as an offset from Coordinated Universal Time (Greenwich Mean Time, UTC). For example, 2003-09-26T15:32:00-05:00 is 3:32 P.M., September 26, 2003 in the U.S. Eastern time zone. A Z can be used instead to indicate UTC. These are all valid values of type xs:dateTime:

- 2001-01-01T03:32:00-05:00

- 1999-12-31T00:00:00Z

- 2002-12-23T17:08:30.121893632178

Constraining facets that apply to xs:dateTime are minInclusive, maxInclusive, minExclusive, maxExclusive, pattern, enumeration, and whiteSpace. Note, however, that when the time zone is not specified, it's not always possible to unambiguously determine whether one time falls after another.

xs:decimal

xs:decimal is the base type for all numeric built-in schema types, except xs:float and xs:double. It represents a base 10 number with any finite number of the digits 0–9 before and after the decimal point. It may be prefixed with either a plus sign or a minus sign. These are all valid values of type xs:decimal:

- 3.1415292

- 03.1415292

- 127

- +127

- -128

- 0.0

- 0.

- .0

This type is not conducive to localization. Only European digits can be used, and only a period can be used as a decimal point. Exponential and scientific notation are not supported.

Constraining facets that apply to xs:decimal are minInclusive, maxInclusive, minExclusive, maxExclusive, pattern, enumeration, whiteSpace, fractionDigits, and totalDigits.

xs:double

The xs:double type is designed to represent eight-byte, binary floating-point numbers in IEEE 754 format, such as is used by the double type in Java and many C compilers. This includes the special values INF for infinity and NaN for not a number, used for the results of unconventional operations like dividing by zero and taking the square root of a negative number. Because not all binary numbers can be precisely represented by decimal numbers, it is possible that two different decimal representations in the lexical space map to the same value (and vice versa). In this case, the closest approximation IEEE-754 value is chosen. These are all legal values of type xs:double:

- 3.1415292

- -03.1415292

- 6.022E23

- 127E-13

- +2.998E+10

- -128e12

- 0.0
- INF
- NaN
- -INF

Constraining facets that apply to xs:double are minInclusive, maxInclusive, minExclusive, maxExclusive, pattern, enumeration, and whiteSpace.

xs:duration

The xs:duration type represents a length of time such as 15 minutes; 2 hours; or 3 years, 7 months, 2 days, 8 hours, 32 minutes, and 12 seconds. It does not have a specific beginning or end, just a length. Durations are represented using the ISO-8601 standard format PnYnMnDTnHnMnS. nY gives the number of years, nM the number of months, nD the number of days, nH the number of hours, nM the number of minutes, and nS the number of seconds. The number of years, months, days, hours, minutes, and seconds are all given as nonnegative integers. The number of seconds is a decimal number with as many places after the decimal point as necessary. For example, in this format, 3 years, 7 months, 2 days, 8 hours, 32 minutes, and 12 seconds is written as P3Y7M2DT8H32M12S. Any values that are zero can be omitted. Thus, a duration of 2 years and 2 minutes can be written as P2YT2M. If there are no hours, minutes, or seconds, then the T is omitted. Thus, a duration of two years is written as P2Y. A leading minus sign before the P indicates a negative duration.

Constraining facets that apply to xs:duration are minInclusive, maxInclusive, minExclusive, maxExclusive, pattern, enumeration, and whiteSpace. However, because the number of days in a month varies from 28 to 31 and the number of days in a year varies from 365 to 366, durations are not always perfectly ordered. For instance, whether P1M is greater than, equal to, or less than P30D depends on which month it is.

xs:ENTITIES

The xs:ENTITIES type indicates that the value is a whitespace-separated list of XML 1.0 unparsed entity names declared in the instance document's DTD. This is the same as the DTD ENTITIES attribute type.

Constraining facets that apply to xs:ENTITIES are length, minLength, maxLength, enumeration, pattern, and whiteSpace. The length, minLength, and maxLength facets all refer to the number of entity names in the list.

xs:ENTITY

The xs:ENTITY type is a subtype of xs:NCNAME with the additional restriction that the value be declared as an unparsed entity in the document's DTD. The legal lexical values of type xs:ENTITY are exactly the same as for xs:NCNAME. Constraining facets that apply to xs:ENTITY are length, minLength, maxLength, pattern, enumeration, and whiteSpace.

 A schema cannot declare either parsed or unparsed entities. An XML document that uses any entities other than the five predefined ones must have a DOCTYPE declaration and a DTD.

xs:float

The xs:float type represents four-byte, binary floating-point numbers in IEEE-754 format, such as is the float type in Java and many C compilers. This includes the special values INF for infinity and NaN for not a number, used for the results of unconventional operations like dividing by zero and taking the square root of a negative number. Because not all binary numbers can be precisely represented by decimal numbers, it is possible that two different decimal representations in the lexical space map to the same value (and vice versa). In this case, the closest approximation of the IEEE-754 value is chosen. These are all legal values of type xs:float:

- 3.1415292
- -03.1415292
- 6.022E23
- 127E-13
- +2.998E+10
- -128e12
- 0.0
- INF
- NaN
- -INF

Constraining facets that apply to xs:float are minInclusive, maxInclusive, minExclusive, maxExclusive, pattern, enumeration, and whiteSpace.

xs:gDay

The xs:gDay type represents a certain day of the month such as the 14th or the 23rd in no particular month. The format used is ---DD plus an optional time zone suffix in the form ±hh:mm or Z to indicate Coordinated Universal Time (UTC). These are all valid xs:gDay values:

- ---01
- ---28
- ---29Z
- ---31+02:00
- ---15-11:00

The g indicates that the day is given in the Gregorian calendar. Schema date types are not localizable to non-Gregorian calendars. If you need a different calendar, you'll need to derive from xs:string using the pattern facet.

Constraining facets that apply to xs:gDay are minInclusive, maxInclusive, minExclusive, maxExclusive, pattern, enumeration, and whiteSpace. However, if the time zones are not specified, it may not be possible to conclusively determine whether one day is greater than or less than another. If time zones are specified, days are compared by when they start. Thus ---29-05:00 is greater than ---29Z, which is greater than ---29+02:00.

xs:gMonth

The xs:gMonth type represents a certain month of the year in the Gregorian calendar as an integer between --01 and --12. An optional time zone suffix in the form ±*hh:mm* or Z to indicate Coordinated Universal Time (UTC) can be added as well. These are all valid xs:gMonth values:

- --01
- --12
- --12Z
- --09+02:00
- --03-11:00

 The original release of XML Schema Part 2: Datatypes had a mistake here. It specified extra hyphens after the month part; for instance, --01-- and --12--. Some schema processors still allow or require this format.

The *g* indicates that the month is given using the Gregorian calendar. Schema date types are not localizable to non-Gregorian calendars. If you need a different calendar, you'll need to derive from xs:string using the pattern facet.

Constraining facets that apply to xs:gMonth are minInclusive, maxInclusive, minExclusive, maxExclusive, pattern, enumeration, and whiteSpace. However, if the time zones are not specified, it may not be possible to determine conclusively whether one month starts before another. If time zones are specified, months are compared by their first moment. Thus, --12-05:00 is greater than --12-Z, which is greater than --12+02:00.

xs:gMonthDay

The xs:gMonthDay type represents a certain day of a certain month in no particular year. It is written in the format --*MM-DD*, plus an optional time zone suffix in the form ±*hh:mm* or Z to indicate Coordinated Universal Time (UTC). These are all valid xs:gMonthDay values:

- --10-31
- --12-25Z
- --01-01+05:00
- --07-04-02:00

The *g* indicates that the month and day are specified in the Gregorian calendar. Schema date types are not localizable to non-Gregorian calendars. For a different calendar, you'll have to derive from xs:string using the pattern facet.

Constraining facets that apply to xs:gMonthDay are minInclusive, maxInclusive, minExclusive, maxExclusive, pattern, enumeration, and whiteSpace. However, if the time zones are not specified, it is not always possible to determine conclusively whether one day starts before another. If time zones are specified, days are compared by their first moment in the same year.

xs:gYear

The xs:gYear type represents a year in the Gregorian calendar. It is written in the format *CCYY*, plus an optional time zone suffix in the form *±hh:mm* or Z to indicate Coordinated Universal Time (UTC). Dates before year 1 can be indicated by a preceding minus sign. At least four digits are used, but additional digits can be added to indicate years after 9999 or before 9999 BCE. These are all valid xs:gYear values in their order of occurrence:

- -15000000000
- 0004
- 0600
- 1492
- 2002+10:00
- 2004Z
- 2004-04:30
- 100000
- 800000000

Constraining facets that apply to xs:gYear are minInclusive, maxInclusive, minExclusive, maxExclusive, pattern, enumeration, and whiteSpace. However, if the time zones are not specified, it may not be possible to determine conclusively whether one year starts before another. If time zones are specified, years are compared by their first moment.

xs:gYearMonth

The xs:gYearMonth type represents a month and year in the Gregorian calendar, such as March, 2005. It is written in the format *CCYY-MM*, plus an optional time zone suffix in the form ±ηη:μμ or Z to indicate Coordinated Universal Time (UTC). Dates before year 1 can be indicated by a minus sign. At least four digits are used, but additional digits can be added to indicate years after 9999 or before 9999 BCE. These are all valid xs:gYearMonth values in their order of occurrence:

- -15000000000-05
- 0004-04
- 0600-10
- 1492-11
- 2005-03+10:00
- 2005-03Z
- 2005-03-04:30
- 100000-07
- 100000-08

Constraining facets that apply to xs:gYearMonth are minInclusive, maxInclusive, minExclusive, maxExclusive, pattern, enumeration, and whiteSpace. However, if the time zones are not specified, it may not be possible to determine conclusively whether one month and year starts before another.

xs:hexBinary

The xs:hexBinary type represents an arbitrary sequence of bytes that has been encoded by replacing each byte of data with two hexadecimal digits from 0 through F (A is 10, B is 11, C is 12, etc.). Either upper- or lowercase letters may be used in whatever character set the document is written. In UTF-8 or ASCII, this has the effect of exactly doubling the space used for the data.

The constraining facets that apply to xs:hexBinary are length, minLength, maxLength, pattern, enumeration, and whiteSpace. Unlike string types, the values specified by the length, minLength, and maxLength facets refer to the number of bytes in the decoded data, not to the number of characters in the encoded data.

xs:ID

xs:ID is a subtype of xs:NCName with the additional restriction that the value is unique among other items of type xs:ID within the same document. The legal lexical values of type xs:ID are exactly the same as for xs:NCName. Constraining facets that apply to xs:ID are length, minLength, maxLength, pattern, enumeration, and whiteSpace.

xs:IDREF

xs:IDREF is a subtype of xs:NCName, with the additional restriction that the value is used elsewhere in the instance document on an item with type xs:ID. The legal lexical values of type xs:IDREF are exactly the same as for xs:NCName. Constraining facets that apply to xs:IDREF are length, minLength, maxLength, pattern, enumeration, and whiteSpace.

xs:IDREFS

The xs:IDREFS type indicates that the value is a whitespace-separated list of xs:ID type values used elsewhere in the instance document. This is similar to the DTD IDREFS attribute type.

Constraining facets that apply to xs:IDREFS are length, minLength, maxLength, enumeration, pattern, and whiteSpace. The length, minLength, and maxLength facets all refer to the number of IDREFs in the list.

xs:int

The xs:int type represents a signed integer small enough to be represented as a four-byte, two's complement number, such as Java's int primitive data type. It is derived from xs:long by setting the maxInclusive facet to 2147483647 and the minInclusive facet to -2147483648. These are all legal values of type xs:int:

- 200
- 200000
- -200000
- +2147483647

- -2147483648
- 0

Constraining facets that apply to xs:int are minInclusive, maxInclusive, minExclusive, maxExclusive, pattern, enumeration, whiteSpace, and totalDigits.

xs:integer

The xs:integer type represents a mathematical integer of arbitrary size. The type is derived from xs:double by fixing the fractionDigits facet at 0. It may be prefixed with either a plus sign or a minus sign. If no sign is present, a plus is assumed. These are all legal values of type xs:integer:

- 3
- 3000
- 3498473298479832619832649007326483264873246783463374
- +127
- -128
- 0
- +0
- -0

Constraining facets that apply to xs:integer are minInclusive, maxInclusive, minExclusive, maxExclusive, pattern, enumeration, whiteSpace, and totalDigits.

xs:language

Elements and attributes with type xs:language contain a language code as defined in RFC 1766, *Tags for the Identification of Languages*. These are essentially the acceptable values for the xml:lang attribute described in Chapter 5. If possible, this should be one of the two-letter language codes defined in ISO 639, possibly followed by a country code. For languages that aren't listed in ISO 639, you can use one of the i-codes registered with IANA. If the language you need isn't present in either of these sets, you can make up your own language tag beginning with the prefix "x-" or "X-". Thus, these are acceptable language values:

- en
- en-US
- en-GB
- fr-CA
- i-klingon
- x-quenya
- X-PigLatin

Constraining facets that apply to xs:language are length, minLength, maxLength, pattern, enumeration, and whiteSpace.

xs:long

The xs:long type represents a signed integer that can be represented as an eight-byte, two's complement number, such as Java's long primitive data type. It is derived from xs:integer by setting the maxInclusive facet to 9223372036854775807 and the minInclusive facet to -9223372036854775808. These are all legal values of type xs:long:

- 2
- 200
- +9223372036854775807
- -9223372036854775808
- 5000000000
- 0

Constraining facets that apply to xs:long are minInclusive, maxInclusive, minExclusive, maxExclusive, pattern, enumeration, whiteSpace, and totalDigits.

xs:Name

xs:Name is a subtype of xs:token that is restricted to legal XML 1.0 names. In other words, the value must consist exclusively of letters, digits, ideographs, and the underscore, hyphen, period, and colon. Digits, the hyphen, and the period may not be used to start a name, although they may be used inside the name. These are all legal values of type xs:Name:

- G127
- _128
- Limit
- xml-stylesheet
- svg:rect
- Υποτροφίες
- 京

Constraining facets that apply to xs:Name are length, minLength, maxLength, pattern, enumeration, and whiteSpace.

XML 1.1 names that are not legal XML 1.0 names are not allowed. At the time of this writing, the schema working group has not yet decided how or when to update the schema specification to account for the changes in name rules in XML 1.1. They may issue an erratum to the schemas specification, or they may wait until Version 1.1 of the W3C XML Schema specification is published.

xs:NCName

An xs:NCName is a noncolonized name as defined in "Namespaces in XML" 1.0. This is a legal XML name that does not contain a colon. The value must consist exclusively of letters, digits, ideographs, and the underscore, hyphen, and period. Digits, the hyphen, and the period may not be used to start a name, although they may be used inside the name. Name characters allowed in XML 1.1 but not in XML 1.0, such as the Ethiopic alphabet, are not allowed. These are all legal values of type xs:NCName:

- I-10
- _128
- Limit
- xml-stylesheet
- エリオツト

Constraining facets that apply to xs:NCName are length, minLength, maxLength, pattern, enumeration, and whiteSpace.

xs:negativeInteger

The xs:negativeInteger type represents a mathematical integer that is strictly less than zero. It is derived from xs:integer by setting the maxInclusive facet to -1. These are all legal values of type xs:negativeInteger:

- -2
- -200
- -9223372036854775809
- -922337203685477580892233720368547758089223372036854775808923372036854775808
- -34

Constraining facets that apply to xs:negativeInteger are minInclusive, maxInclusive, minExclusive, maxExclusive, pattern, enumeration, whiteSpace, and totalDigits.

xs:NMTOKEN

An xs:NMTOKEN is the schema equivalent of the DTD NMTOKEN attribute type. It is a subtype of xs:token that is restricted to legal XML 1.0 name tokens. These are the same as XML 1.0 names except that there are no restrictions on what characters may be used to start the name token. XML 1.1 names are only allowed if they are also XML 1.0 names. In other words, the value must consist of one or more letters, digits, ideographs, and the underscore, hyphen, period, and colon. These are all legal values of type xs:NMTOKEN:

- 127
- -128
- Limit
- integration
- svg:rect
- πυργοδαικτος
- 乱

Constraining facets that apply to xs:NMTOKEN are length, minLength, maxLength, pattern, enumeration, and whiteSpace.

xs:NMTOKENS

The xs:NMTOKENS type is the schema equivalent of the DTD NMTOKENS attribute type. xs:NMTOKENS is derived from xs:NMTOKEN by list. Thus, a value of type xs:NMTOKENS contains one or more whitespace-separated XML 1.0 name tokens. These are all legal values of type xs:NMTOKENS:

- 127 126 125 124 123 122 121 120 119 118
- -128
- Limit Integral Sum Sup Liminf Limsup
- Jan Feb Mar Apr May June July Sept Nov Dec
- svg:rect

Constraining facets that apply to xs:NMTOKENS are length, minLength, maxLength, enumeration, pattern, and whiteSpace. The length, minLength, and maxLength facets all refer to the number of name tokens in the list.

xs:nonNegativeInteger

The xs:nonNegativeInteger type represents a mathematical integer that is greater than or equal to zero. It is derived from xs:integer by setting the minInclusive facet to 0. These are all legal values of type xs:nonNegativeInteger:

- 2
- +200
- 9223372036854775809
- 922337203685477580892233720368547758089223372036854775808922337203685477580892233720368
- 0

Constraining facets that apply to xs:nonNegativeInteger are minInclusive, maxInclusive, minExclusive, maxExclusive, pattern, enumeration, whiteSpace, and totalDigits.

xs:nonPositiveInteger

The xs:nonPositiveInteger type represents a mathematical integer that is less than or equal to zero. It is derived from xs:integer by setting the maxInclusive facet to 0. These are all legal values of type xs:nonPositiveInteger:

- -2
- -200
- -9223372036854775809
- -922337203685477580892233720368547758089223372036854775808922337203685477580892233720368
- 0

Constraining facets that apply to xs:nonPositiveInteger are minInclusive, maxInclusive, minExclusive, maxExclusive, pattern, enumeration, whiteSpace, and totalDigits.

xs:normalizedString

xs:normalizedString is derived from xs:string by setting the whiteSpace facet to replace so that the carriage return (#xD) and tab (#x9) characters are replaced by spaces in the normalized value. (The new whitespace characters added in XML 1.1, NEL and line separator, are not affected.) A normalized string can contain any characters that are allowed in XML, although depending on context, special characters such as <, &, and " may have to be escaped with character or entity references in the usual way. All legal strings are also legal lexical representations of type xs:normalizedString. However, a schema-aware parser that presents the normalized value of an element, instead of the literal characters in the document, will replace all carriage returns and tabs with spaces before passing the string to the client application.

Constraining facets that apply to xs:normalizedString are length, minLength, maxLength, pattern, enumeration, and whiteSpace.

xs:NOTATION

The xs:NOTATION type restricts a value to those qualified names declared as notations using an xs:notation element in the schema. This is an abstract type. In other words, you cannot directly declare that an element or attribute has type xs:NOTATION. Instead, you must first derive a new type from xs:NOTATION, most commonly by enumeration, and then declare that your element or attribute possesses the subtype. Constraining facets that apply to xs:NOTATION are length, minLength, maxLength, pattern, enumeration, and whiteSpace.

xs:positiveInteger

The xs:positiveInteger type represents a mathematical integer that is strictly greater than zero. It is derived from xs:integer by setting the minInclusive facet to 1. These are all legal values of type xs:positiveInteger:

- 1
- +2
- 9223372036854775809
- 92233720368547758089223372036854775809892233720368
- 34

Constraining facets that apply to xs:positiveInteger are minInclusive, maxInclusive, minExclusive, maxExclusive, pattern, enumeration, whiteSpace, and totalDigits.

xs:QName

An xs:QName is a base type that is restricted to namespace-qualified names. The logical value of a qualified name is a namespace URI, local part pair. Lexically, qualified names are the same as XML 1.0 names except that they may not contain more than one colon and that colon may not be the first character in the name. A qualified name may or may not be prefixed. If it is prefixed, then the prefix must be properly mapped to a namespace URI. If it is not prefixed, then the name must occur in the scope of a default namespace. These are all legal values of type xs:QName, provided that this condition is met in context:

- xsl:apply-templates
- svg:rect
- limit
- xml:lang
- body
- xlink:href

Constraining facets that apply to xs:QName are length, minLength, maxLength, pattern, enumeration, and whiteSpace.

xs:short

The xs:short type indicates a signed integer small enough to be represented as a two-byte, two's complement number such as Java's short primitive data type. It is derived from xs:int by setting the maxInclusive facet to 32767 and the minInclusive facet to -32768. These are all legal values of type xs:int:

- 2000
- +2000
- -2000
- 32767
- -32768
- 0

Constraining facets that apply to xs:short are minInclusive, maxInclusive, minExclusive, maxExclusive, pattern, enumeration, whiteSpace, and totalDigits.

xs:string

This is the most general simple type. Elements and attributes with type xs:string can contain any sequence of characters allowed in XML, although depending on context, certain characters such as <, &, and " may have to be escaped with character or entity references in the usual way.

Constraining facets that apply to xs:string are length, minLength, maxLength, pattern, enumeration, and whiteSpace.

xs:time

The xs:time type represents a specific time of day on no particular day, such as 3:32 P.M. Times are written in the form ±hh:mm:ss.xxx using a 24-hour clock and as many fractions of a second as necessary. For example, 3:41 P.M. is written as 15:41:00. 3:41 A.M. and 0.5 seconds is written as 03:41:00.5. The Z suffix indicates Coordinated Universal Time (Greenwich Mean Time, UTC). Otherwise, the time zone can be indicated as an offset in hours and minutes from UTC. For example, 15:41:00-05:00 is 3:41 P.M., in the U.S. Eastern time zone. The time zone may be omitted, in which case the actual time is somewhat nondeterministic. These are all valid values of type xs:time:

- 03:32:00-05:00
- 00:00:00Z
- 08:30:34.121893632178
- 23:59:59

Constraining facets that apply to xs:time are minInclusive, maxInclusive, minExclusive, maxExclusive, pattern, enumeration, and whiteSpace. Note, however, that when the time zone is not specified, it's not always possible to determine unambiguously whether one time falls after another.

xs:token

xs:token is a subtype of xs:normalizedString whose normalized value does not contain any line feed (#xA) or tab (#x9) characters, does not have any leading or trailing whitespace (as whitespace is defined by XML 1.0, not XML 1.1), and has no sequence of two or more spaces. All legal strings are also legal lexical representations of type xs:token. However, a schema-aware parser that presents the normalized value of an element instead of the literal characters in the document will trim leading and trailing whitespace and compress all other runs of whitespace characters with a single space before passing the string to the client application.

Constraining facets that apply to xs:token are length, minLength, maxLength, pattern, enumeration, and whiteSpace.

xs:unsignedByte

The xs:unsignedByte type represents a nonnegative integer that can be stored in one byte, such as the unsigned char type used by some (but not all) C compilers. It is derived from xs:unsignedShort by setting the maxInclusive facet to 255 (2^8-1). These are all legal values of type xs:unsignedByte:

- 3
- 200
- +255
- 50
- 0

Constraining facets that apply to xs:unsignedByte are minInclusive, maxInclusive, minExclusive, maxExclusive, pattern, enumeration, whiteSpace, and totalDigits.

xs:unsignedInt

The xs:unsignedInt type represents a nonnegative integer that can be stored in four bytes, such as the unsigned int type used by some C compilers. It is derived from xs:unsignedLong by setting the maxInclusive facet to 4294967295 (2^{32}-1). These are all legal values of type xs:unsignedInt:

- 2
- 200
- +4294967295

- 100000

- 0

Constraining facets that apply to xs:unsignedInt are minInclusive, maxInclusive, minExclusive, maxExclusive, pattern, enumeration, whiteSpace, and totalDigits.

xs:unsignedLong

The xs:unsignedLong type represents a nonnegative integer that can be stored in eight bytes, such as the unsigned long type used by some C compilers. It is derived from xs:nonNegativeInteger by setting the maxInclusive facet to 18446744073709551615 (2^{64}-1). These are all legal values of type xs:unsignedLong:

- 2

- 200

- +9223372036854775807

- 18446744073709551615

- 5000000000

- 0

Constraining facets that apply to xs:unsignedLong are minInclusive, maxInclusive, minExclusive, maxExclusive, pattern, enumeration, whiteSpace, and totalDigits.

xs:unsignedShort

The xs:unsignedShort type represents a nonnegative integer that can be stored in two bytes, such as the unsigned short type used by some C compilers. It is derived from xs:unsignedInt by setting the maxInclusive facet to 65535 (2^{16}-1). These are all legal values of type xs:unsignedShort:

- 3

- 300

- +65535

- 50000

- 0

Constraining facets that apply to xs:unsignedShort are minInclusive, maxInclusive, minExclusive, maxExclusive, pattern, enumeration, whiteSpace, and totalDigits.

Instance Document Attributes

The W3C XML Schema Language defines four attributes in the http://www.w3.org/2001/XMLSchema-instance namespace (here mapped to the xsi prefix), which are attached to elements in the instance document rather than elements in the schema. These are as follows: xsi:nil, xsi:type, xsi:schemaLocation, and xsi:noNamespaceSchemaLocation. All four of these attributes are special because the schemas do not need to declare them.

xsi:nil

The xsi:nil attribute indicates that a certain element does not have a value or that the value is unknown. This is not the same as having a value that is zero or the empty string. Semantically, it is equivalent to SQL's null. For example, in this full_name element, the last_name child has a nil value:

```
<full_name xmlns:xsi="http://www.w3.org/2001/XMLSchema-instance">
  <first_name>Cher</first_name>
  <last_name xsi:nil="true"/>
</full_name>
```

It is not relevant whether an empty-element tag or a start-tag/end-tag pair is used to represent the nil element. However, a nil element may not have any content.

In order for this document to be valid, the element declaration for the name element must explicitly specify that nil values are allowed by setting the nillable attribute to true. For example:

```
<xs:element name="last_name" type="xs:string" nillable="true"/>
```

xsi:noNamespaceSchemaLocation

The xsi:noNamespaceSchemaLocation attribute locates the schema for elements that are not in any namespace. (Attributes that are not in any namespace are assumed to be declared in the same schema as their parent element.) Its value is a relative or absolute URL where the schema document can be found. It is most commonly attached to the root element but can appear further down the tree. For example, this person element claims that it should be validated against the schema found at *http://example.com/person.xsd*:

```
<person xsi:noNamespaceSchemaLocation="http://example.com/person.xsd">
  <name>
    <first_name>Alan</first_name>
    <last_name>Turing</last_name>
  </name>
  <profession>computer scientist</profession>
  <profession>mathematician</profession>
  <profession>cryptographer</profession>
</person>
```

These are only suggestions. Schema processors may use other means of locating the relevant schemas and ignore the hint provided by xsi:noNamespaceSchemaLocation.

xsi:schemaLocation

The xsi:schemaLocation attribute locates schemas for elements and attributes that are in a specified namespace. Its value is a namespace URI followed by a relative or absolute URL where the schema for that namespace can be found. It is most commonly attached to the root element but can appear further down the tree. For example, this person element in the http://www.cafeconleche.org/namespaces/person namespace claims that it should be validated against the schema found at *http://www.elharo.com/person.xsd*:

```
·<person xmlns="http://www.cafeconleche.org/namespaces/person"
  xmlns:xsi="http://www.w3.org/2001/XMLSchema-instance"
  xsi:schemaLocation="http://www.cafeconleche.org/namespaces/person
                      http://www.elharo.com/person.xsd">
  <name>
    <first_name>Alan</first_name>
    <last_name>Turing</last_name>
  </name>
  <profession>computer scientist</profession>
  <profession>mathematician</profession>
  <profession>cryptographer</profession>
</person>
```

If more than one namespace is used in a document, each namespace must have its own schema. The namespace URIs and schema URLs can be listed in sequence in the same xsi:schemaLocation attribute. For example, the xsi:schemaLocation attribute on this person element says that items from the http://www.cafeconleche.org/namespaces/person namespace should be validated against the schema found at *http://www.elharo.com/person.xsd*, while items from the http://www.cafeconleche.org/namespaces/names namespace should be validated against the schema found at the relative URL *names.xsd*:

```
<person xmlns="http://www.cafeconleche.org/namespaces/person"
  xmlns:xsi="http://www.w3.org/2001/XMLSchema-instance"
  xsi:schemaLocation="http://www.cafeconleche.org/namespaces/person
                      http://www.elharo.com/person.xsd
                      http://www.cafeconleche.org/namespaces/names
                      names.xsd">
  <name xmlns="http://www.cafeconleche.org/namespaces/names">
    <first_name>Alan</first_name>
    <last_name>Turing</last_name>
  </name>
  <profession>computer scientist</profession>
  <profession>mathematician</profession>
  <profession>cryptographer</profession>
</person>
```

These are only suggestions. Schema processors are allowed to use other means of locating the relevant schemas and to ignore the hints provided by xsi:schemaLocation.

xsi:type

The xsi:type attribute may be used in instance documents to indicate the type of an element, even when a full schema is not available. For example, this length element has type xs:decimal:

```
<length xsi:type="xs:decimal">23.5</length>
```

More importantly, the xsi:type attribute enables a limited form of polymorphism. That is, it allows you to make an element an instance of a derived type where an instance of the base type would normally be expected. The instance of the derived type must carry an xsi:type attribute identifying it as an instance of the derived type.

For example, suppose a schema says that a ticket element has type TicketType. If the schema also defines BusTicketType and AirplaneTicketType elements as subtypes of TicketType, then a ticket element could also use the BusTicketType and AirplaneTicketType content models provided it had an xsi:type="BusTicketType" or xsi:type="AirplaneTicketType" attribute.

23

XPath Reference

XPath is a non-XML syntax for expressions that identifies particular nodes and groups of nodes in an XML document. It is used by both XPointer and XSLT, as well as by some native XML databases and query languages.

The XPath Data Model

XPath views each XML document as a tree of nodes. Each node has one of seven types:

Root

Each document has exactly one root node, which is the root of the tree. This node contains one comment node child for each comment outside the document element, one processing-instruction node child for each processing instruction outside the root element, and exactly one element node child for the root element. It does not contain any representation of the XML declaration, the document type declaration, or any whitespace that occurs before or after the root element. The root node has no parent node. The root node's value is the value of the root element.

Element

An element node has a name, a namespace URI, a parent node, and a list of child nodes, which may include other element nodes, comment nodes, processing-instruction nodes, and text nodes. An element node also has a collection of attributes and a collection of in-scope namespaces, none of which are considered to be children of the element. The string-value of an element node is the complete, parsed text between the element's start- and end-tags that remains after all tags, comments, and processing instructions are removed and all entity and character references are resolved.

Attribute

An attribute node has a name, a namespace URI, a value, and a parent element. However, although elements are parents of attributes, attributes are not children of their parent elements. The biological metaphor breaks down here. `xmlns` and `xmlns:prefix` attributes are not represented as attribute nodes. An attribute node's value is the normalized attribute value.

Text

Each text node represents the maximum possible contiguous run of text between tags, processing instructions, and comments. A text node has a parent node but does not have children. A text node's value is the text of the node.

Namespace

A namespace node represents a namespace in scope on an element. In general, each namespace declaration by an `xmlns` or `xmlns:prefix` attribute produces a namespace node on that element and on all of its descendant elements (unless overridden by another namespace declaration). Like attribute nodes, each namespace node has a parent element but is not the child of that parent. The name of a namespace node is the prefix. The value of a namespace node is the namespace URI.

Processing instruction

A processing-instruction node has a target, data, a parent node, and no children. The name of a processing-instruction node is its target. The value of a processing-instruction node is the data of the processing instruction, not including any initial whitespace.

Comment

A comment node represents a comment. It has a parent node and no children. The value of a comment is the string content of the comment, not including the `<!--` and `-->`.

The XML declaration and the document type declaration are not included in XPath's view of an XML document. All entity references, character references, and `CDATA` sections are resolved before the XPath tree is built. The references themselves are not included as a separate part of the tree.

Data Types

Each XPath expression evaluates to one of four types:

Boolean

A binary value that is either true or false. In XPath, Booleans are most commonly produced by using the comparison operators =, !=, <, >, <=, and >=. Multiple conditions can be combined using the and and or operators, which have their usual meaning in logic (e.g., 3>2 or 2>1 is true). XPath does not offer Boolean literals. However, the `true()` and `false()` functions fill that need.

Number

All numbers in XPath are IEEE 754-compliant, 64-bit floating-point numbers. This is the same as the double type in Java. Numbers range from 4.94065645841246544e-324d to 1.79769313486231570e+308d, and are either positive or negative. Numbers also include the special values Inf (positive infinity), -Inf (negative infinity), and NaN (not a number), which is used for the results of illegal operations, such as dividing by zero. XPath provides all the customary operators for working with numbers, including:

+   Addition

-   Subtraction; however, this operator should always be surrounded by whitespace to avoid accidental misinterpretation as part of an XML name

*   Multiplication

div Division

mod Taking the remainder

String

Sequence of zero or more Unicode characters. String literals are enclosed in either single or double quotes, as convenient. Unlike Java, XPath does not allow strings to be concatenated with the plus sign. However, the concat( ) function serves this purpose.

Node-set

Collection of zero or more nodes from an XML document. Location paths produce most node-sets. A single node-set can contain multiple types of nodes: root, element, attribute, namespace, comment, processing instruction, and text.

Some standards that use XPath also define additional data types. For instance, XSLT defines a result tree fragment type that represents the result of processing an XSLT instruction or instantiating a template. XPointer defines a location set type that extends node-sets to include points and ranges.

Location Paths

Node-sets are returned by location-path expressions. Location paths consist of location steps. Each location step contains an axis and a node test separated by a double colon. That is, a location step looks like this:

```
axis::node test
```

The axis specifies in which direction from the context node the processor searches for nodes. The node test specifies which nodes along that axis are selected. These are some location steps with different axes and node tests:

```
child::set
descendant-or-self::node( )
ancestor-or-self::*
attribute::xlink:href
```

Each location step may be suffixed with predicates enclosed in square brackets that further winnow the node-set. For example:

```
child::set[position( )=2]
descendant-or-self::node( )[.='Eunice']
ancestor-or-self::*[position( )=2][.="Celeste"]
attribute::xlink:href[starts-with(., 'http')]
```

Each individual location step is itself a relative location path. The context node against which the relative location path is evaluated is established by some means external to XPath—for example, by the current matched node in an XSLT template.

Location steps can be combined by separating them with forward slashes. Each step in the resulting location path sets the context node (or nodes) for the next path in the step. For example:

```
ancestor-or-self::*/child::*[position( )=1]
child::document/child::set[position( )=2]/following-sibling::*
descendant::node( )[.='Eunice']/attribute::ID
```

An absolute location path is formed by prefixing a forward slash to a relative location path. This sets the context node for the first step in the location path to the root of the document. For example, these are all absolute location paths:

```
/descendant::ship/ancestor-or-self::*/child::*[position( )=1]
/child::document/child::set[position( )=2]/following-sibling::*
/descendant::node( )[.='Eunice']/attribute::ID
```

Multiple location paths can be combined with the union operator (|) to form an expression that selects a node-set containing all the nodes identified by any of the location paths. For example, this expression selects a node-set containing all the set children of the context node, all the vector descendants of the context node, all ancestor elements of the context node, and all attributes of the context node named href:

```
child::set | descendant::vector | ancestor::* | attribute::href
```

Abbreviated Syntax

An abbreviated syntax is available for particularly common location steps. In this syntax, five axes may use this shorthand:

.

> The context node

..

> The parent node

name

> The child element or elements with the specified name

//

> All descendants of the context node, and the context node itself

@name

> The attribute of the context node with the specified name

Using the abbreviated syntax, the previous examples can be rewritten in the following manner:

```
set
.//.
ancestor-or-self::*
@xlink:href
set[position( )=2]
.//.[.='Eunice']
ancestor-or-self::*[position( )=2][.="Celeste"]
@xlink:href[starts-with('http')]
ancestor-or-self::*/*[position( )=1]
document/set[position( )=2]/following-sibling::*
.//.[.='Eunice']/@ID
//ship/ancestor-or-self::*/*[position( )=1]
/document/set[position( )=2]/following-sibling::*
/descendant::node( )[.='Eunice']/@ID
set | ./*//vector | ancestor::* | @href
```

Not all location steps can be rewritten using the abbreviated syntax. In particular, only the `child`, `self`, `attribute`, `descendant-or-self`, and `parent` axes can be abbreviated. The remaining axes must be spelled out in full.

Axes

Each XPath location step moves along an axis from a context node. The context node is a particular root, element, attribute, comment, processing-instruction, namespace, or text node in the XML document. (In practice, it's almost always an element node or the root node.) The context node may be a node selected by the previous location step in the location path, or it may be determined by extra-XPath rules, such as which node is matched by an xsl:template element.

However the context node is determined, it has some relationship to every other node in the document. The various axes divide the document into different over-lapping sets, depending on their relationship to the context node. There are exactly 13 axes you can use in an XPath location step:

child
>   All children of the context node. Only root and element nodes have children. Attribute and namespace nodes are not children of any node, although they do have parent nodes.

descendant
>   All nodes contained inside the context node—that is, a child node, a child of a child node, a child of a child of a child node, and so on. Only root and element nodes have descendants. Like the child axis, the descendant axis never contains attribute or namespace nodes.

descendant-or-self
>   Any descendant of the context node or the context node itself. // is an abbreviation for /descendant-or-self::node( )/.

parent

> The element or root node that immediately contains the context node. Only the root node does not have a parent node. .. is an abbreviation for parent::node( ).

ancestor

> The root node and all element nodes that contain the context node. The root node itself has no ancestors.

ancestor-or-self

> All ancestors of the context node, as well as the node itself.

following-sibling

> All nodes that follow the end of the context node and have the same parent node. Attribute and namespace nodes do not have siblings.

preceding-sibling

> All nodes that precede the start of the context node and have the same parent node. Attribute and namespace nodes do not have siblings.

following

> All nodes that begin after the context node ends, except for attribute nodes and namespace nodes; that is, all nodes after the context node except descendants.

preceding

> All nodes that end before the context node begins, except for attribute nodes and namespace nodes; that is, all nodes before the context node except ancestors.

attribute

> All attributes of the context node; the axis is empty if the context node is not an element node. This axis does not contain xmlns and xmlns:*prefix* attributes. @*name* is an abbreviation for attribute::*name*.

namespace

> All namespaces in scope (not merely declared) on the context node; this axis is empty if the context node is not an element node.

self

> The context node itself. A single period (.) is an abbreviation for self::node( ).

Node Tests

Each location step has at least an axis and a node test. The node test further refines the nodes selected by the location step. In an unabbreviated location step, a double colon (::) separates the axis from the node test. There are seven kinds of node tests:

name

> An XML name matches all elements with the same name. However, along the attribute axis it matches all attributes with the same name instead; along the namespace axis it matches all namespaces with that prefix. As usual, if the element or attribute name is prefixed, only the URI to which the prefix is

mapped matters, not the prefix itself. Unprefixed names always match nodes in no namespace, never names in the default namespace.

prefix:*

Along most axes, this node test matches all element nodes whose namespace URIs are the same as the namespace URI to which this prefix is mapped, regardless of name. However, along the attribute axis, this node test matches all attribute nodes whose namespace URIs are the same as the namespace URI to which this prefix is mapped.

comment( )

This matches all comment nodes.

text( )

This matches all text nodes. Each text node is a maximum contiguous run of text between other types of nodes.

processing-instruction( )
processing-instruction('*target*')

With no arguments, this node test selects all processing instructions. With a single string argument, it selects all processing instructions that have the specified target.

node( )

This node test selects all nodes, regardless of type: attribute, namespace, element, text, comment, processing instruction, and root.

*

This test normally selects all element nodes, regardless of name. However, if the axis is the attribute axis, then it selects all attribute nodes. If the axis is the namespace axis, then it selects all namespace nodes.

Predicates

Each location step may have zero or more predicates. A *predicate* is an XPath expression enclosed in square brackets that follows the node test in the location step. This expression most commonly, but not necessarily, returns a Boolean value. In the following location path:

```
/person[1]/profession[.="physicist"][position( )<3]
```

[1], [.="physicist"], and [position( )<3] are predicates. An XPath processor works from left to right in an expression. After it has evaluated everything that precedes the predicate, it's left with a context node list that may contain no nodes, one node, or more than one node. For most axes, including child, following-sibling, following, and descendant, this list is in document order. For the ancestor, preceding, and preceding-sibling axes, this list is in reverse document order.

The predicate is evaluated against each node in the context node list. If the expression returns true, then that node is retained in the list. If the expression returns false, then the node is removed from the list. If the expression returns a number, then the node being evaluated is left in the list if and only if the number is the same as the position of that node in the context node list. If the expression returns a non-Boolean, nonnumber type, then that return value is converted to a Boolean using the `boolean()` function, described later, to determine whether it retains the node in the set.

XPath Functions

XPath 1.0 defines 27 built-in functions for use in XPath expressions. Various technologies that use XPath, such as XSLT and XPointer, also extend this list with functions they need. XSLT even allows user-defined extension functions.

Every function is evaluated in the context of a particular node, called the *context node*. The higher-level specification in which XPath is used, such as XSLT or XPointer, decides exactly how this context node is determined. In some cases, the function operates on the context node. In other cases, it operates on the argument, if present, and the context node, if no argument exists. The context node is ignored in other cases.

In the following sections, each function is described with at least one signature in this form:

> *return-type function-name(type argument, type argument, ...)*

Compared to languages like Java, XPath argument lists are quite loose. Some XPath functions take a variable number of arguments and fill in the arguments that are omitted with default values or the context node.

Furthermore, XPath is weakly typed. If you pass an argument of the wrong type to an XPath function, it generally converts that argument to the appropriate type using the `boolean()`, `string()`, or `number()` functions, described later. The exceptions to the weak-typing rule are the functions that take a node-set as an argument. Standard XPath 1.0 provides no means of converting anything that isn't a node-set into a node-set. In some cases, a function can operate equally well on multiple argument types. In this case, its type is given simply as `object`.

boolean( )

boolean `boolean(object o)`

The `boolean()` function converts its argument to a Boolean according to these rules:

- Zero and NaN are false. All other numbers are true.
- Empty node-sets are false. Nonempty node-sets are true.
- Empty strings are false. Nonempty strings are true.

ceiling( )

number `ceiling(number x)`

The `ceiling()` function returns the smallest integer greater-than or equal to x. For example, `ceiling(3.141592)` is 4. `ceiling(-3.141592)` is -3. Before the ceiling is calculated, nonnumber types are converted to numbers as if by the `number()` function.

concat( )

string concat(*string s1, string s2*)
string concat(*string s1, string s2, string s3*)
string concat(*string s1, string s2, string s3, string s4, ...*)

This function concatenates its arguments in order from left to right and returns the combined string. It may take two or more arguments. Nonstrings may be passed to this function as well, in which case they're converted to strings automatically as if by the string( ) function.

contains( )

boolean contains(*string s1, string s2*)

This function returns true if s2 is a substring of s1—that is, if s1 contains s2. Otherwise, it is false. For example, contains("A very Charming cat", "Charm") is true, but contains("A very Charming cat", "Marjorie") is false. The test is case-sensitive. For example, contains("A very charming cat", "Charm") is false. Nonstrings may also be passed to this function, in which case they're automatically converted to strings as if by the string( ) function.

count( )

number count(*node-set set*)

The count( ) function returns the number of nodes in the argument node-set, that is, the size of the set.

false( )

boolean false( )

The false( ) function always returns false. It makes up for the lack of Boolean literals in XPath.

floor( )

number floor(*number x*)

The floor( ) function returns the greatest integer less-than or equal to x. For example, floor(3.141592) is 3. floor(-3.141592)is -4. Before the floor of a non-number type is calculated, it is converted to a number as if by the number( ) function.

id( )

node-set id(*string IDs*)
node-set id(*node-set IDs*)

The id( ) function returns a node-set containing all elements in the document with any of the specified IDs. (More specifically, those elements that have an attribute declared to be type ID in the input document's DTD.) If the argument is a string, then this string is interpreted as a whitespace-separated list of IDs, and the function returns a node-set containing any elements that have an ID matching one of these IDs. If the argument is a node-set, then each node in the set is converted to a string, which is in turn treated as a whitespace-separated list of IDs. The returned node-set contains all the elements whose ID matches any ID in the string-value of any of these nodes. Finally, if the argument is any other type, then it's converted to a string, as by the string( ) function, and it returns the same result as passing that string-value to id( ) directly.

lang( )

boolean lang(*string languageCode*)

The lang( ) function returns true if the context node is written in the language specified by the languageCode argument; otherwise, it is false. The nearest xml:lang attribute on the context node or one of its ancestors determines the language of any given node. If no such xml:lang attribute exists, then lang( ) returns false.

The lang( ) function takes into account country and other subcodes before making its determination. For example, lang('fr') returns true for elements whose language code is fr-FR, fr-CA, or fr. However, lang('fr-FR') is not true for elements whose language code is fr-CA or fr.

last( )

number last( )

The last( ) function returns the size of (i.e., the number of nodes in) the context node-set.

local-name( )

string local-name( )
string local-name(*node-set nodes*)

With no arguments, this function returns the context node's local name, that is, the part of the name after the colon, or the entire name if it isn't prefixed. For a node-set argument, it returns the local name of the first node in the node-set. If the node-set is empty or the first node in the set does not have a name (e.g., it's a comment or root node), then it returns the empty string.

name( )

string name( )
string name(*node-set nodes*)

With no arguments, this function returns the qualified (prefixed) name of the context node or the empty string if the context node does not have a name (e.g., it's a comment or root node). With a node-set as an argument, it returns the qualified name of the first node in the node-set. If the node-set is empty or if the set's first node does not have a name, then it returns the empty string.

namespace-uri( )

string namespace-uri( )
string namespace-uri(*node-set nodes*)

With no arguments, this function returns the namespace URI of the context node. With a node-set as an argument, it returns the namespace URI of the first node in the node-set. If this node does not have a namespace URI (i.e., it's not an element or an attribute node; it is an element or attribute node, but is not in any namespace; or the node-set is empty), then it returns the empty string.

normalize-space( )

string normalize-space( )
string normalize-space(*string s*)

The normalize-space( ) function strips all leading and trailing whitespace from its argument and replaces each run of whitespace with a single space character. Among other effects, this removes all line breaks. If the argument is omitted, it normalizes the string-value of the context node. A nonstring may be passed to this function, in which case it's automatically converted to a string, as if by the string( ) function, and that string is normalized and returned.

not( )

boolean not(*boolean b*)

The not( ) function inverts its argument; that is, false becomes true and true becomes false. For example, not(3 > 2) is false, and not(2+2=5) is true. Non-Booleans are converted as by the boolean( ) function before being processed.

number( )

number number( )
number number(*object o*)

The number( ) function converts its argument to a number according to these rules:

- A string is converted by first stripping leading and trailing whitespace and then picking the IEEE 754 value that is closest (according to the IEEE 754 round-to-nearest rule) to the mathematical value represented by the string. If the string does not seem to represent a number, it is converted to NaN. Exponential notation (e.g., 75.2E-12) is not recognized.
- True Booleans are converted to 1; false Booleans are converted to 0.
- Node-sets are first converted to the string-value of the first node in the set. This string is then converted to a number.

If the argument is omitted, then it converts the context node.

position( )

number position( )

The position( ) function returns a number equal to the position of the current node in the context node-set. For most axes, it counts forward from the context node. However, if the axis in use is ancestor, ancestor-or-self, preceding, or preceding-sibling, then it counts backward from the context node instead.

round( )

number round(*number x*)

The round( ) function returns the integer closest to x. For example, round(3.141592) returns 3. round(-3.141592) returns -3. If two integers are equally close to x, then the one that is closer to positive infinity is returned. For example, round(3.5) returns 4, and round(-3.5) returns -3. Nonnumber types are converted to numbers as if by the number( ) function, before rounding.

starts-with( )

boolean starts-with(*string s1, string s2*)

The starts-with( ) function returns true if s1 starts with s2; otherwise, it is false. For example, starts-with("Charming cat", "Charm") is true, but starts-with ("Charming cat", "Marjorie") is false. The test is case-sensitive. For example, starts-with("Charming cat", "charm") is false. Nonstrings may be passed to this function as well, in which case they're automatically converted to strings, as if by the string( ) function, before the test is made.

string( )

string string( )
string string(*object o*)

The string( ) function converts an object to a string according to these rules:

- A node-set is converted to the string-value of the first node in the node-set. If the node-set is empty, it's converted to the empty string.
- A number is converted to a string as follows:

  —NaN is converted to the string NaN.

  —Positive Inf is converted to the string Infinity.

  —Negative Inf is converted to the string -Infinity.

- Integers are converted to their customary English form with no decimal point and no leading zeros. A minus sign is used if the number is negative, but no plus sign is used for positive numbers.
- Nonintegers (numbers with nonzero fractional parts) are converted to their customary English form with a decimal point, with at least one digit before the decimal point and at least one digit after the decimal point. A minus sign is used if the number is negative, but no plus sign is used for positive numbers.

- A Boolean with the value true is converted to the English word "true." A Boolean with the value false is converted to the English word "false." Lowercase is always used.

The object to be converted is normally passed as an argument, but if omitted, the context node is converted instead.

> The XPath specification specifically notes that the "string function is not intended for converting numbers into strings for presentation to users." The primary problem is that it's not localizable and not attractive for large numbers. If you intend to show a string to an end user, use the format-number( ) function and/or xsl:number element in XSLT instead.

string-length( )

number string-length(*string s*)
number string-length( )

The string-length( ) function returns the number of characters in its argument. For example, string-length("Charm") returns 5. If the argument is omitted, it returns the number of characters in the string-value of the context node. A nonstring may be passed to this function, in which case it's automatically converted to a string, as if by the string( ) function, and that string's length is returned.

substring( )

string substring(*string s, number index, number length*)
string substring(*string s, number index*)

The substring( ) function returns the substring of s starting at index and continuing for length characters. The first character in the string is at position 1 (not 0, as in Java and JavaScript). For example, substring('Charming cat', 1, 5) returns "Charm". If length is omitted, then the substring to the end of the string is returned. For example, substring('Charming cat', 10) returns "cat". As usual, any type of object may be passed to this function in place of the normal argument, in which case it is automatically converted to a string before extracting the substring.

substring-after( )

string substring-after(*string s1, string s2*)

The substring-after( ) function returns the substring of s1 that follows the first occurrence of s2 in s1, or it returns the empty string, if s1 does not contain s2. For example, substring-after('Charming cat', 'harm') returns "ing cat". The test is case-sensitive. As usual, nonstring objects may be passed to this function, in which case they're automatically converted to strings, as if by the string( ) function.

substring-before( )

string substring-before(*string s1, string s2*)

The substring-before( ) function returns the substring of s1 that precedes the first occurrence of the s2 in s1, or it returns the empty string if s1 does not contain s2. For example, substring-before('Charming cat', 'ing') returns "Charm". The test is case-sensitive. Nonstring objects may be passed to this function, in which case they're automatically converted to strings as if by the string( ) function.

sum( )

number sum(*node-set nodes*)

The sum( ) function converts each node in the node-set to a number, as if by the number( ) function; then it adds up those numbers and returns the sum.

translate( )

string translate(*string s1, string s2, string s3*)

The translate( ) function looks in s1 for any characters found in s2. It replaces each character with the corresponding character from s3. For example, translate("XML in a Nutshell", " ", "_") replaces the spaces with underscores and returns "XML_in_a_Nutshell". translate("XML in a Nutshell", "XMLN", "xmln") replaces the uppercase letters with lowercase letters and returns "xml in a nutshell". If s3 is shorter than s2, then characters in s1 and s2 with no corresponding character in s3 are simply deleted. For example, translate("XML in a Nutshell", " ", "") deletes the spaces and returns "XMLinaNutshell". Once again, nonstring objects may be passed to this function, in which case they're automatically converted to strings as if by the string( ) function.

true( )

boolean true( )

The true( ) function simply returns true. It makes up for the lack of Boolean literals in XPath.

24

XSLT Reference

Extensible Stylesheet Language Transformations (XSLT) is a functional programming language used to specify how an input XML document is converted into another text document—possibly, although not necessarily, another XML document. An XSLT processor reads both an input XML document and an XSLT stylesheet (which is itself an XML document because XSLT is an XML application) and produces a result tree as output. This result tree may then be serialized into a file or written onto a stream. Documents can be transformed using a standalone program or as part of a larger program that communicates with the XSLT processor through its API.

The XSLT Namespace

All standard XSLT elements are in the `http://www.w3.org/1999/XSL/Transform` namespace. In this chapter, we assume that this URI is mapped to the `xsl` prefix using an appropriate `xmlns:xsl` declaration somewhere in the stylesheet. This mapping is normally declared on the root element, like this:

```
<xsl:stylesheet version="1.0"
      xmlns:xsl="http://www.w3.org/1999/XSL/Transform">
  <!-- XSLT top-level elements go here -->
</xsl:stylesheet>
```

XSLT Elements

XSLT defines 36 elements, which break down into three overlapping categories:

* Two root elements:
    ```
    xsl:stylesheet
    xsl:transform
    ```

- Twelve top-level elements, which may appear as immediate children of the root and are the following:

xsl:attribute-set	xsl:decimal-format
xsl:import	xsl:include
xsl:key	xsl:namespace-alias
xsl:output	xsl:param
xsl:preserve-space	xsl:strip-space
xsl:template	xsl:variable

- Twenty-two instruction elements, which appear in the content of elements that contain templates. Here, we don't mean the xsl:template element. We mean the content of that and several other elements, such as xsl:for-each and xsl:message, which are composed of literal result elements, character data, and XSLT instructions that are processed to produce part of the result tree. These elements are as follows:

xsl:apply-imports	xsl:apply-templates
xsl:attribute	xsl:call-template
xsl:choose	xsl:comment
xsl:copy	xsl:copy-of
xsl:element	xsl:fallback
xsl:for-each	xsl:if
xsl:message	xsl:number
xsl:otherwise	xsl:processing-instruction
xsl:sort	xsl:text
xsl:value-of	xsl:variable
xsl:with-param	xsl:when

Most XSLT processors also provide various nonstandard extension elements and allow you to write your own extension elements in languages such as Java and JavaScript.

Elements in this section are arranged alphabetically from xsl:apply-imports to xsl:with-param. Each element begins with a synopsis in the following form:

```
<xsl:elementName
    attribute1 = "allowed attribute values"
    attribute2 = "allowed attribute values"
>
  <!-- Content model -->
</xsl:elementName>
```

Most attribute values are one of the following types:

expression

An XPath expression. In cases where the expression is expected to return a value of a particular type, such as node-set or number, it is prefixed with the type and a hyphen; for example, node-set-expression or number-expression. However, XPath is weakly typed, and, in most cases, any supplied type will be converted to the requested type. For instance, an attribute that should evaluate to a string might in fact contain a number or a node-set. The processor automatically converts this number or set to a string, according to the rules given in the last chapter for XPath's string( ) function. The only exception to this rule is node-set-expression. XSLT does not convert other types to node-sets automatically. If an attribute requires a `node-set-expression`, then it is an error to set its value to another type of expression such as a Boolean or string.

QualifiedName
> An XML name, such as `set` or `mathml:set`. If the name is in a nondefault namespace, then it has a prefix.

PrefixedName
> An XML name that must have a prefix such as `mathml:set` but not `set`.

pattern
> An XSLT match pattern; that is, a group of one or more XPath location-path expressions separated by |., in which each location step uses only the `child` or `attribute` axis. The initial step may be an `id( )` or `key( )` function call with a literal argument.

langcode
> An RFC 1766 language code, such as `en` or `fr-CA`.

string
> A literal string of text.

char
> A single Unicode character.

enumerated type
> One value in a finite list of values. The values shown here are separated by vertical bars, as in an enumerated content model in an `ATTLIST` declaration.

URI
> A relative or absolute URI. In practice, these are normally URLs. Relative URIs are relative to the location of the stylesheet itself.

Some attributes can contain attribute value templates. This is an XPath expression enclosed in curly braces, which is evaluated to provide the final value of the attribute. When this is the case, it is indicated in the description of each attribute.

Potentially, nonempty elements have content models given in a comment in the form they might appear in an `ELEMENT` declaration. If an element can contain a template, we use the word "template" to stand in for all the possible elements that may appear.

It's worth noting that XSLT is unusually forgiving compared to most other XML specifications. First of all, the stylesheet may contain top-level elements from any namespace except XSLT (although not from no namespace at all). Elements defined here may contain any attribute from any non-XSLT namespace. And even though many conditions are defined as errors, XSLT processors are always allowed to recover from them in a sensible way. For example, you're not allowed to put an `xsl:attribute` element inside an `xsl:comment` element, which would attempt to add an attribute to a comment. However, if you do that, the processor is allowed to simply ignore the offending `xsl:attribute` element when creating the comment.

xsl:apply-imports

```
<xsl:apply-imports />
```

The `xsl:apply-imports` instruction processes the current node using only templates that were imported into the stylesheet with `xsl:import`. A template rule that overrides a template rule in an imported stylesheet can invoke the overridden template rule with `xsl:apply-imports`.

xsl:apply-templates

```
<xsl:apply-templates select="node-set-expression" mode="QualifiedName">
    <! -- (xsl:sort | xsl:with-param)* -- >
</xsl:apply-templates>
```

The `xsl:apply-templates` instruction tells the processor to search for and apply the highest-priority template rule in the stylesheet that matches each node identified by the select attribute.

Attributes

select, *optional*

This is an XPath expression that returns a node-set. Each node in this set will be processed further. If the select attribute is omitted, then all child nodes of the context node should be processed.

mode, *optional*

If the mode attribute is present, then only templates that have a matching mode attribute will be applied. If the mode attribute is absent, then only templates without a mode attribute will be applied.

Contents

The `xsl:apply-templates` element may have `xsl:sort` child elements to specify the order in which the selected nodes will be processed. Without any `xsl:sort` children, the default is to process nodes in document order.

The `xsl:apply-templates` element may have `xsl:with-param` child elements to pass parameter values to the matched templates.

xsl:attribute

```
<xsl:attribute
    name      = "QualifiedName"
    namespace = "URI">
    <! -- template for the attribute value -- >
</xsl:attribute>
```

The `xsl:attribute` instruction adds an attribute to an element in the result tree. This element can be a child of an `xsl:attribute-set` element, an `xsl:element` instruction, or a literal result element. In each case, all `xsl:attribute` elements must precede all literal result elements and other instructions that insert content into the output element.

Attributes

name, *required, attribute value template*

The name of the attribute this instruction creates.

namespace, *optional, attribute value template*

The namespace URI of the attribute. If a nonempty namespace URI is specified, then the processor will pick an appropriate prefix for the attribute—probably, but not necessarily, the one used in the name attribute.

Contents

The contents of this element are a template whose instantiation only produces text nodes. The value of the attribute added to the result tree is determined by instantiating the template.

xsl:attribute-set

```
<xsl:attribute-set
 name = "QualifiedName"
 use-attribute-sets = "QualifiedName1 QualifiedName2...">
<! --  xsl:attribute*  -- >
</xsl:attribute-set>
```

The xsl:attribute-set top-level element defines a collection of attributes that can be applied to elements elsewhere in the stylesheet. For instance, you could define an attribute set that includes the necessary attributes to create a simple XLink, and then you could attach the set to each simple XLink element.

Attributes

name, *required*

The name attribute gives a name for the set, by which xsl:element and other xsl:attribute-set elements can load this attribute set.

use-attribute-sets, *optional*

The use-attribute-sets attribute adds attributes from a different attribute set into this attribute set. More than one attribute set can be loaded by separating multiple names with whitespace. The attributes defined in all loaded sets and all attributes defined by child xsl:attribute elements are merged so that no attribute appears in the set more than once. It is an error if an attribute set uses itself directly or indirectly.

Contents

This element contains zero or more xsl:attribute elements. Each such element adds one attribute to the set.

xsl:call-template

```
<xsl:call-template   name = "QualifiedName">
   <! --  xsl:with-param*  -- >
</xsl:call-template>
```

The xsl:call-template instruction invokes a template by name. The current node and context node list are the same for the called template as for the calling template. Templates may be called recursively; an xsl:template element may contain an xsl:call-template element that calls that very xsl:template element. This technique is useful for doing things you'd accomplish with loops in a traditional procedural programming language.

Attribute

name, *required*
> The name of the xsl:template element to call.

Contents

This element contains zero or more xsl:with-param elements that pass parameters to the named template.

xsl:choose

```
<xsl:choose>
  <! -- (xsl:when+, xsl:otherwise?) -- >
</xsl:choose>
```

The xsl:choose element selects one (or none) of a sequence of alternatives.

Contents

This element contains one or more xsl:when elements, each of which has a test condition. The contents of the first xsl:when child whose test condition is true are output.

The xsl:choose element may have an optional xsl:otherwise element whose contents are output only if none of the test conditions in any of the xsl:when elements is true.

If the xsl:choose does not have an xsl:otherwise child element, and none of the test conditions in any of the xsl:when child elements is true, then this element does not produce output.

xsl:comment

```
<xsl:comment>
  <! -- template -- >
</xsl:comment>
```

The xsl:comment instruction inserts a comment into the result tree.

Contents

The content of xsl:comment is a template that will be instantiated to form the text of the comment inserted into the result tree. The result of instantiating this template should only be text nodes that do not contain the double hyphen (--) or end with a hyphen.

xsl:copy

```
<xsl:copy
  use-attribute-sets = "QualifiedName1 QualifiedName2...">
  <! -- template -- >
</xsl:copy>
```

The xsl:copy element copies the current node from the source document into the output document. It copies the node itself and any namespace nodes the node possesses. However, it does not copy the node's children or attributes.

Attribute

use-attribute-sets, *optional*

> A whitespace-separated list of xsl:attribute-set names. These attribute sets are merged, and all attributes in the merged set are added to the copied element.

Contents

If the current node is an element node, attributes can be added via xsl:attribute children. If the current node is the root node or an element node (a node that can have children), then xsl:copy may contain a template that specifies the content of the element inserted into the result tree. All xsl:attribute elements must precede the output template.

xsl:copy-of

```
<xsl:copy-of
  select = "expression" />
```

The xsl:copy-of instruction inserts whatever is identified by the select attribute into the output document. This instruction copies the specific nodes identified by the expression, as well as all those nodes' children, attributes, namespaces, and descendants. This is how it differs from xsl:copy. If the expression selects something other than a node-set, such as a number, then the expression is converted to its string-value, and the string is output.

Attribute

select, *required*

> An XPath expression identifying the object to copy into the result tree.

xsl:decimal-format

```
<xsl:decimal-format
  name               = "QualifiedName"
  decimal-separator  = "char"
  grouping-separator = "char"
  infinity           = "string"
  minus-sign         = "char"
  NaN                = "string"
  percent            = "char"
  per-mille          = "char"
  zero-digit         = "char"
  digit              = "char"
  pattern-separator  = "char" />
```

The xsl:decimal-format top-level element defines a pattern by which the format-number( ) function can convert floating-point numbers into text strings. The defaults work well for English, but details may change for other languages and locales, such as French or Chinese.

Attributes

name, *optional*

> The string by which the format-number( ) function identifies the xsl:decimal-format element to use. If this attribute is omitted, then this element establishes the default decimal format used by the format-number( ) function.

decimal-separator, *optional*

The character that separates the integer part from the fractional point in a floating-point number. This character is a period (decimal point) in English and a comma in French. It may be something else in other languages. If not specified, the default is a period.

grouping-separator, *optional*

The character that separates groups of digits; for example, the comma that separates every three digits in English or the space in French. If this is not specified, the comma is the default.

infinity, *optional*

The string that represents IEEE 754 infinity; Infinity by default.

minus-sign, *optional*

The character prefixed to negative numbers; a hyphen by default.

NaN, *optional*

The string that represents IEEE 754 Not a Number; NaN by default.

percent, *optional*

The character that represents a percent; % by default.

per-mille, *optional*

The character that represents a per mille; ‰ by default.

zero-digit, *optional*

The character that represents zero; 0 by default. Digits 1 through 9 will be represented by the nine subsequent Unicode values after this one. For instance, setting zero-digit to A would set 1 to B, 2 to C, 3 to D, and so on. This is also the character used to represent 0 in format patterns.

digit, *optional*

The character that represents a digit in a format pattern; # by default.

pattern-separator, *optional*

The character that separates positive and negative subpatterns in a format pattern; ; by default.

xsl:element

```
<xsl:element
  name              = "QualifiedName"
  namespace         = "URI"
  use-attribute-sets = "QualifiedName1 QualifiedName2...">
  <! -- template -- >
</xsl:element>
```

The xsl:element instruction inserts an element into the result tree. The element's name is given by the name attribute. The element's namespace URI, if any, is given by the optional namespace attribute. Attributes can be added via xsl:attribute children or by referencing an xsl:attribute-set declared elsewhere in the stylesheet from the use-attribute-sets attribute. Finally, the element's contents are determined by instantiating the template contained in the xsl:element element's content.

Attributes

name, *required, attribute value template*

The name of the element this instruction creates.

namespace, *optional, attribute value template*
> The namespace URI of the element this instruction creates. If this attribute is omitted, then the namespace is determined by matching the name's prefix (or lack thereof) to the namespace declarations in scope at this point in the stylesheet.

use-attribute-sets, *optional*
> A whitespace-separated list of names of xsl:attribute-set elements declared as top-level elements elsewhere in the stylesheet. These attribute sets are merged, and all attributes in the merged set are added to the element.

Contents

The contents of this element are a template. Once instantiated, this template forms the content of the element inserted into the result tree.

---

xsl:fallback

```
<xsl:fallback>
  <! -- template -- >
</xsl:fallback>
```

The xsl:fallback instruction normally appears as a child of an extension element. If the processor does not recognize the extension element, then it instantiates the contents of all the element's xsl:fallback children in order. If the processor does recognize the element in which the xsl:fallback element appears, then the contents of the xsl:fallback element will not be output.

Contents

The contents of this element are a template that is instantiated and output if and only if the XSLT processor does not recognize the xsl:fallback element's parent element.

---

xsl:for-each

```
<xsl:for-each  select = "node-set-expression">
  <! -- (xsl:sort*, template) -- >
</xsl:for-each>
```

The xsl:for-each instruction iterates over the nodes identified by its select attribute and applies templates to each one.

Attribute

select, *required*
> An XPath node-set expression identifying which nodes to iterate over.

Contents

Normally, the selected nodes are processed in the order in which they appear in the document. However, nodes can be sorted using xsl:sort child elements. The first such element is the primary sort key, the second is the secondary sort key, and so on.

The xsl:for-each element must also contain a template that is instantiated once for each member of the node-set returned by the node-set expression in the select attribute.

xsl:if

```
<xsl:if test = "boolean-expression">
  <! -- template -- >
</xsl:if>
```

The xsl:if instruction contains a template that is instantiated if and only if the XPath expression contained in its test attribute is true. There is no xsl:else or xsl:else-if element. For these purposes, use xsl:choose instead.

Attribute

test, *required*

An XPath expression returning a Boolean. If this expression is true, the contents of the xsl:if element are instantiated. If it's false, they're not.

Contents

A template is instantiated if the test attribute evaluates to true.

xsl:import

```
<xsl:import href = "URI" />
```

The xsl:import top-level element imports the XSLT stylesheet found at the URI given by the href attribute. Source documents are processed using the combination of templates in the imported and importing stylesheets. In the event of a conflict between templates in the two stylesheets, the ones in the importing stylesheet take precedence. In the event of a conflict between imported stylesheets, the last one imported takes precedence.

All xsl:import elements must be immediate children of the root xsl:stylesheet element. Furthermore, they must appear before all other top-level elements.

An imported stylesheet may itself import another stylesheet. A stylesheet may not import a stylesheet that was already imported, directly or indirectly. That is, it's an error if A imports B, which imports A, thus creating a circular reference.

Attribute

href, *required*

The relative or absolute URI of the stylesheet to import. Relative URIs are resolved relative to the base URI of the importing stylesheet.

xsl:include

```
<xsl:include href = "URI" />
```

The xsl:include top-level element copies the contents of the xsl:stylesheet or xsl:transform element found at the URI given by the href attribute. Unlike xsl:import, whether a template or other element comes from the including or the included stylesheet has absolutely no effect on the precedence of the various rules.

An included stylesheet may include another stylesheet. A stylesheet may not include a stylesheet that was already included, directly or indirectly; it is an error if A includes B, which includes A.

Attribute

href, *required*
> The relative or absolute URI of the stylesheet to include. Relative URIs are resolved relative to the including stylesheet's base URI.

xsl:key

```
<xsl:key
  name  = "QualifiedName"
  match = "pattern"
  use   = "expression" />
```

The xsl:key top-level element defines one or more keys that can be referenced from elsewhere in the stylesheet using the key( ) function. Each key has a name, a string-value, and a node.

Attributes

name, *required*
> The key's name.

match, *required*
> An XSLT match pattern, like that used by xsl:template, specifying which nodes have this key. If this pattern matches more than one node in the source document, then a single xsl:key element may define many keys, all with the same name and possibly the same value, but with different nodes.

use, *required*
> An XPath expression that is converted to a string to give the value of keys defined by this element. The expression is evaluated with respect to each key's node. If match identifies multiple nodes, then use may produce different values for each key.

xsl:message

```
<xsl:message
  terminate = "yes" | "no">
  <! -- template  -- >
</xsl:message>
```

The xsl:message instruction sends a message to the XSLT processor. Which messages the processor understands and what it does with messages it understands is processor-dependent. Printing debugging information on stderr or stdout is one common use of xsl:message.

Attribute

terminate, *optional*
> If the attribute is present and has the value yes, then the XSLT processor should halt after the message is delivered and acted on.

Contents

An xsl:message element's content is a template instantiated to create an *XML fragment*. The result is then delivered to the XSLT processor as the message.

XSLT Reference

The XSLT specification does not define *XML fragment*, and various XSLT processors interpret it differently. It may be a result tree fragment or an XML fragment, as defined by the now moribund XML Fragment Interchange working draft. It may be something else. Clarification from the W3C is necessary but does not seem to be forthcoming.

xsl:namespace-alias

```
<xsl:namespace-alias
    stylesheet-prefix = "prefix"
    result-prefix     = "prefix" />
```

The top-level xsl:namespace-alias element declares that one namespace URI in the stylesheet should be replaced by a different namespace URI in the result tree. Aliasing is particularly useful when transforming XSLT into XSLT using XSLT; consequently, it is not obvious which names belong to the input, which belong to the output, and which belong to the stylesheet.

Attributes

stylesheet-prefix, *required*
> The prefix bound to the namespace used inside the stylesheet itself. May be set to #default to indicate that the nonprefixed default namespace should be used.

result-prefix, *required*
> The prefix bound to the namespace used in the result tree. May be set to #default to indicate that the nonprefixed default namespace should be used.

xsl:number

```
<xsl:number
    value = "number-expression"
    count = "pattern"
    from  = "pattern"
    level = "single" | "multiple" | "any"
    format = "letter or digit"
    lang   = "langcode"
    letter-value = "alphabetic" | "traditional"
    grouping-separator = "char"
    grouping-size = "number" />
```

The xsl:number instruction inserts a formatted integer into the result tree.

Attributes

value, *optional*
> This XPath expression returns the number to be formatted. If necessary, the result of the expression is rounded to the nearest integer. The value attribute is often omitted, in which case the number is calculated from the position of the current node in the source document. The position is calculated as specified by the level, count, and from attributes.

count, *optional*

> This attribute contains a pattern that specifies which nodes should be counted at those levels. The default is to count all nodes with the same node type (element, text, attribute, etc.) and name as the current node.

from, *optional*

> This attribute contains a pattern identifying the node from which counting starts; that is, it identifies a node that serves as a cutoff point. Any nodes that precede this node are not counted, even if they match the count pattern.

level, *optional*

> This attribute specifies which levels of the source tree should be considered in determining the position of the current node. It can be set to single to count the preceding siblings of the current node's ancestor that match the count pattern. It can be set to any to count all nodes in the document that match the count pattern and precede the current node. It can be set to multiple to produce hierarchical sequences of numbers such as 2.7.3, where each number in the sequence is calculated from the preceding sibling's ancestor node that matches the count pattern. The default is single.

format, *optional, attribute value template*

> This attribute determines how the list is numbered. Format tokens and sequences they produce include the following:

1	1, 2, 3, 4, 5, 6, . . .
01	01, 02, 03, 04, 05, 06, 07, 08, 09, 10, 11, 12, . . .
A	A, B, C, D, . . . , Z, AA, AB, AC, . . .
a	a, b, c, d, . . . , z, aa, ab, ac, . . .
i	i, ii, iii, iv, v, vi, vii, viii, ix, x, xi, . . .
I	I, II, III, IV, V, VI, VII, VIII, IX, X, XI, XII, . . .

lang, *optional, attribute value template*

> This is the RFC 1766 language code describing the language in which the number should be formatted (e.g., en or fr-CA).

letter-value, *optional, attribute value template*

> The default is traditional. However, you can set this attribute to alphabetic to indicate that a format of I should start the sequence I, J, K, L, M, N, . . . rather than I, II, III, IV, V, VI, . . .

grouping-separator, *optional, attribute value template*

> This is the character that separates groups of digits. For instance, in English, the comma customarily separates every three digits, as in 2,987,667,342. In French, a space is used instead, so this number would be formatted as 2 987 667 342.

grouping-size, *optional, attribute value template*

> This is the number of digits in each group. In most languages, including English, digits are divided into groups of three. However, a few languages use groups of four.

xsl:otherwise

```
<xsl:otherwise>
 <! -- template -- >
</xsl:otherwise>
```

The xsl:otherwise element only appears as the last child element of an xsl:choose element. It serves as the default result if no xsl:when element in the same xsl:choose element is instantiated.

Contents

The contents are a template that is instantiated if and only if none of the xsl:choose element's xsl:when sibling elements is true.

xsl:output

```
<xsl:output
    method                = "xml" | "html" | "text" | "PrefixedName"
    version               = "NMTOKEN"
    encoding              = "encoding_name"
    omit-xml-declaration  = "yes" | "no"
    standalone            = "yes" | "no"
    doctype-public        = "PUBLIC_ID"
    doctype-system        = "SYSTEM_ID"
    cdata-section-elements = "element_name_1 element_name_2..."
    indent                = "yes" | "no"
    media-type            = "string" />
```

The top-level xsl:output element helps determine the exact formatting of the XML document produced when the result tree is stored in a file, written onto a stream, or otherwise serialized into a sequence of bytes. It has no effect on the production of the result tree itself.

Attributes

method, *optional*

The default method is xml, which simply means that the serialized output document will be a well-formed external parsed entity or XML document. If method is set to html, or if the method attribute is not present and the root element of the output tree is html, in any combination of case, then the processor attempts to generate HTML that is more compatible with existing browsers. For example, empty-element tags like <br/> are converted to <br>. The text method outputs only the contents of the text nodes in the output tree. It strips all markup. XSLT processors may also recognize and support other values that are indicated by prefixed names, such as saxon:xhtml and jd:canonical-xml.

version, *optional*

A name token that identifies the output method's version. In practice, this has no effect on the output.

encoding, *optional*

The encoding the serializer should use, such as ISO-8859-1 or UTF-16.

omit-xml-declaration, *optional*

If this attribute has the value yes, then no XML declaration is included. If it has the value no or is not present, then an XML declaration is included.

standalone, *optional*

The value of the standalone attribute in the XML declaration. Like that attribute, it must have the value yes or no.

doctype-public, *optional*
> The public identifier used in the document type declaration.

doctype-system, *optional*
> The system identifier used in the document type declaration.

cdata-section-elements, *optional*
> A whitespace-separated list of qualified element names in the result tree whose contents should be emitted using CDATA sections.

indent, *optional*
> If this attribute has the value yes, then the processor is allowed (but not required) to insert extra whitespace to attempt to "pretty-print" the output tree. The default is no.

media-type, *optional*
> The output's MIME media type, such as text/html or application/xml.

xsl:param

```
<xsl:param
  name   = "QualifiedName"
  select = "expression">
<! -- template -- >
</xsl:param>
```

Inside an xsl:template element, an xsl:param element receives a named argument passed to the template by xsl:with-param. It also provides a default value that's used when the caller does not provide a value for the parameter. A top-level xsl:param element defines a global variable that can be set from the outside environment when invoking the stylesheet. If an xsl:apply-templates or xsl:call-template passes in a parameter value using xsl:with-param when the template is invoked, that value overrides any default value the xsl:param element may have. The parameter can be dereferenced using the form $*name* in expressions.

Attributes

name, *required*
> The parameter's name.

select, *optional*
> An XPath expression that is evaluated to produce the parameter's value. If xsl:param has a select attribute, then it must be an empty element. If a nonempty xsl:param element does not have a select attribute, then the value is the result of instantiating the template in the content. If an empty xsl:param element does not have a select attribute, then the value is the empty string.

Contents

An xsl:param element's content is a template that is instantiated to produce a result-tree fragment. This result-tree fragment then becomes the parameter's value. A nonempty xsl:param element must not have a select attribute.

XSLT Reference

xsl:preserve-space

```
<xsl:preserve-space
  elements="QualifiedName_1 QualifiedName_2..." />
```

The top-level xsl:preserve-space element specifies which elements in the source document will not have whitespace stripped from them before they are transformed. Whitespace stripping removes text nodes that contain only whitespace (the space character, the tab character, the carriage return, and the line feed). By default, whitespace is preserved in an element unless its name is listed in the elements attribute of an xsl:strip-space element. This element allows you to override the list given in xsl:strip-space; if an element is listed in both xsl:strip-space and xsl:preserve-space, then its whitespace is preserved.

Attribute

elements, *required*
> A whitespace-separated list of elements in which space should be preserved. Besides element names, the elements attribute can contain an asterisk to indicate that whitespace should be preserved in all elements. It can also contain a namespace prefix followed by a colon and an asterisk to indicate that whitespace should be preserved in all elements in the given namespace.

xsl:processing-instruction

```
<xsl:processing-instruction
  name = "target">
  <!-- template -- >
</xsl:processing-instruction>
```

The xsl:processing-instruction element inserts a processing instruction into the result tree.

Attribute

name, *required, attribute value template*
> The processing instruction's target.

Contents

The xsl:processing-instruction element's contents are a template that is instantiated to produce the processing-instruction data. This template may include XSLT instructions, provided that the result of instantiating this template is text that does not contain the two-character string ?>.

xsl:sort

```
<xsl:sort
  select     = "string-expression"
  data-type  = "text" | "number" | "PrefixedName"
  lang       = "langcode"
  order      = "ascending" | "descending"
  case-order = "upper-first" | "lower-first" />
```

The xsl:sort instruction appears as a child of either xsl:apply-templates or xsl:for-each. It changes the order in which templates are applied to the context node list from document order to another order, such as alphabetic. You can perform multiple key sorts (e.g., sort first by last name, then by first name, then by middle name) using multiple xsl:sort elements in descending order of the keys' importance.

Attributes

select, *optional*

> The key to sort by. If select is omitted, then the sort key is set to the value of the current node.

data-type, *optional, attribute value template*

> By default, sorting is purely alphabetic. However, alphabetic sorting leads to strange results with numbers. For instance, 10, 100, and 1,000 all sort before 2, 3, and 4. You can specify numeric sorting by setting data-type to number.

lang, *optional, attribute value template*

> Sorting is language dependent. Setting the lang attribute to an RFC 1766 language code changes the language. The default language is system dependent.

order, *optional, attribute value template*

> The order by which strings are sorted, either descending or ascending. The default is ascending order.

case-order, *optional, attribute value template*

> upper-first or lower-first to specify whether uppercase letters sort before lowercase letters or vice versa. The default depends on the language.

xsl:strip-space

```
<xsl:strip-space
    elements="QualifiedName_1 QualifiedName_2..." />
```

The top-level xsl:strip-space element specifies which elements in the source document have whitespace stripped from them before they are transformed. Whitespace stripping removes all text nodes that contain only whitespace (the space character, the tab character, the carriage return, and the line feed). By default, whitespace is not stripped from an element unless its name is listed in the elements attribute of an xsl:strip-space element.

This element does not trim leading or trailing whitespace, or otherwise normalize whitespace in elements that contain even a single nonwhitespace character.

Attribute

elements, *required*

> A whitespace-separated list of elements in which space should be stripped. Besides element names, the elements attribute can contain an asterisk to indicate that whitespace should be stripped in all elements or contain a namespace prefix followed by a colon and asterisk to indicate that whitespace should be stripped in all elements in the given namespace.

xsl:stylesheet

```
<xsl:stylesheet
  xmlns:xsl="http://www.w3.org/1999/XSL/Transform"
  id = "ID"
  extension-element-prefixes = "prefix1 prefix2..."
  exclude-result-prefixes = "prefix1 prefix2..."
  version = "1.0">
  <! -- (xsl:import*, top-level-elements)  -- >
</xsl:stylesheet>
```

The xsl:stylesheet element is the root element for XSLT documents.

Attributes

xmlns:xsl, *technically optional but de facto required*
> A standard namespace declaration that maps the prefix xsl to the namespace URI http://www.w3.org/1999/XSL/Transform. The prefix can be changed if necessary.

id, *optional*
> Any XML name that's unique within this document's ID type attributes.

extension-element-prefixes, *optional*
> A whitespace-separated list of namespace prefixes used by this document's extension elements.

exclude-result-prefixes, *optional*
> A whitespace-separated list of namespace prefixes whose declarations should not be copied into the output document.

version, *required*
> Currently, always the value 1.0. However, XSLT 2.0 may be released in the lifetime of this edition with a concurrent updating of this number.

Contents

Any xsl:import elements, followed by any other top-level elements in any order.

xsl:template

```
<xsl:template
  match    = "pattern"
  priority = "number"
  name     = "QualifiedName"
  mode     = "QualifiedName">
  <! -- (xsl:param*, template)  -- >
</xsl:template>
```

The xsl:template top-level element is the key to all of XSLT. Confusingly, the xsl:template element itself is not a template. Rather, it contains a template. The entire xsl:template element is called a *template rule*. The match attribute contains a pattern against which nodes are compared as they're processed. If the pattern matches a node, then the template (i.e., the contents of the template rule) is instantiated and inserted into the output tree.

Attributes

match, *optional*

> A pattern against which nodes can be compared. This pattern is a location path using only the child, attribute, and descendant-or-self axes or a combination of several such location paths.

priority, *optional*

> A number. If more than one template rule with the same import precedence matches a given node, the one with the highest priority is chosen. If this attribute is not present, then the template rule's priority is calculated in the following way:
>
> - Template rules with match patterns composed of just an element or attribute name (e.g., person or @profession) have priority 0.
>
> - Template rules with match patterns composed of just a processing-instruction('*target*') node test have priority 0.
>
> - Template rules with match patterns in the form *prefix*:* have priority -0.25.
>
> - Template rules with match patterns that just have a wildcard node test (*, @*, comment( ), node( ), text( ), and processing-instruction( )) have priority -0.5. (This means that built-in template rules have priority -0.5. However, they are also imported before all other template rules, and thus never override any explicit template rule, regardless of priority.)
>
> - Template rules with any other patterns (person[name='Feynman'], people/person/@profession, person/text( ), etc.) have priority 0.5.
>
> It is an error if two or more template rules match a node and have the same priority. However, in this case, most XSLT processors choose the last template rule occurring in the stylesheet, rather than signaling the error.

name, *optional*

> A name by which this template rule can be invoked from an xsl:call-template element, rather than by node matching.

mode, *optional*

> If the xsl:template element has a mode, then this template rule is matched only when the calling instruction's mode attribute matches this mode attribute's value.

Contents

The template that should be instantiated when this element is matched or called by name.

---

xsl:text

```
<xsl:text
   disable-output-escaping = "yes" | "no">
   <! -- #PCDATA -- >
</xsl:text>
```

The xsl:text instruction is used inside templates to indicate that its contents should be output as text. Its contents are pure text, not elements. If the contents are composed exclusively of whitespace, then that whitespace is copied literally into the output document, rather than being stripped as it would be, by default, in most other elements.

Attribute

`disable-output-escaping`, *optional*

Setting the `disable-output-escaping` attribute to yes indicates that characters such as < and &—which are normally replaced by entity or character references such as < or <—should instead be output as the literal characters themselves. Note that the `xsl:text` element's content in the stylesheet must still be well-formed, and any < or & characters must be written as <, &, or the equivalent character references. However, when the output document is serialized, these references are replaced by the actual represented characters rather than references that represent them.

xsl:transform

```
<xsl:transform
  xmlns:xsl="http://www.w3.org/1999/XSL/Transform"
  id = "ID"
  extension-element-prefixes = "prefix1 prefix2..."
  exclude-result-prefixes = "prefix1 prefix2..."
  version = "1.0">
  <! -- (xsl:import*, top-level-elements) -- >
</xsl:transform>
```

The `xsl:transform` element is a seldom-used synonym for the `xsl:stylesheet` root element. It has the same attributes and contents as `xsl:stylesheet` and is used in exactly the same way as `xsl:stylesheet`. See the description of the `xsl:stylesheet` element for the discussion of its attributes and content.

xsl:value-of

```
<xsl:value-of
   select = "expression"
   disable-output-escaping = "yes" | "no" />
```

The `xsl:value-of` element computes the string-value of an XPath expression and inserts it into the result tree. The string-values of the seven different kinds of nodes are as follows:

element
> The text content of the element after all entity references are resolved and all tags, comments, and processing instructions are stripped

text
> The text of the node

attribute
> The normalized value of the attribute

root
> The value of the root element

processing instruction
> The processing instruction data (<?, ?>, and the target are not included)

comment
> The text of the comment (<!-- and --> are not included)

namespace
> The namespace URI

You can compute values of things that aren't nodes. The value of a node-set is the value of the first node in the set. The value of a string expression is the string. The value of a number expression is the string form of the number. The value of a Boolean expression is the string true if the Boolean is true or the string false if the Boolean is false.

Attributes

select, *required*
> This is the XPath expression whose value is inserted into the result tree.

disable-output-escaping, *optional*
> If this attribute has the value yes, then when the output document is serialized, characters such as < and & in the value are not replaced with entity or character references. This may result in a malformed document.

xsl:variable

```
<xsl:variable
  name   = "QualifiedName"
  select = "expression">
  <! -- template -- >
</xsl:variable>
```

The xsl:variable element binds a name to a value of any type (string, number, node-set, etc.). This variable can then be dereferenced elsewhere using the form $name in an expression.

> The word "variable" is a little misleading. Once the value of an xsl:variable is set, it cannot be changed. An xsl:variable is more like a named constant than a traditional variable.

name, *required*
> The variable's name.

select, *optional*
> An XPath expression that sets the value of the variable. If xsl:variable has a select attribute, then it must be an empty element.

Contents

A template that is instantiated to produce the variable's value as a result-tree fragment. If an xsl:variable is not an empty element, it must not have a select attribute. If xsl:variable is empty and does not have a select attribute, then its value is the empty string.

xsl:when

```
<xsl:when
  test = "boolean-expression">
  <! -- template -- >
</xsl:when>
```

The xsl:when element only appears as a child of an xsl:choose element.

Attribute

test, *required*

> An XPath expression that evaluates to either true or false. The xsl:when contents are inserted into the result tree if and only if this is the first xsl:when element in the xsl:choose element whose test attribute evaluates to true.

Contents

The template to be instantiated and inserted into the result tree if the test attribute is true.

---

xsl:with-param

```
<xsl:with-param
  name   = "QualifiedName"
  select = "expression">
  <! -- template -- >
</xsl:with-param>
```

The xsl:with-param element passes a named parameter to a template that expects it. This can either be a child of xsl:apply-templates or xsl:call-template. An xsl:template element receives the parameter via an xsl:param element with the same name. If a template expects to receive a particular parameter and doesn't get it, then it can take the default from the xsl:param element instead.

Attributes

name, *required*

> The name of the parameter.

select, *optional*

> An XPath expression evaluated to form the value of the parameter. If xsl:with-param has a select attribute, then it must be an empty element. If xsl:with-param does not have a select attribute, then the value is taken from the element's contents.

Contents

A template that is instantiated and passed as the parameter's value. If xsl:with-param is not an empty element, it must not have a select attribute. If xsl:with-param is empty and does not have a select attribute, then its value is the empty string.

XSLT Functions

XSLT supports all functions defined in XPath. In addition, it defines 10 extra functions. Most XSLT processors also make several extension functions available and allow you to write your own extension functions in Java or other languages. The extension API is nonstandard and processor-dependent.

XPath and XSLT functions are weakly typed. Although one type or another is occasionally preferred, the processor normally converts any type you pass in to the type the function expects. Functions that only take node-sets as arguments are an exception to the weak-typing rule. Other data types, including strings, numbers, and Booleans, cannot be converted to node-sets automatically.

XPath and XSLT functions also use optional arguments, which are filled in with defaults if omitted. In the following sections, we list the most common and useful variations of each function.

current( )

node-set current( )

The current( ) function returns a node-set containing a single node, the current node. Outside of an XPath predicate, the current node and the context node (represented by a period in the abbreviated XPath syntax) are identical. However, in a location step predicate, the context node changes according to the location path, while the current node stays the same.

document( )

node-set document(*string uri*)
node-set document(*node-set uris*)
node-set document(*string uri, node-set base*)
node-set document(*node-set uris, node-set base*)

The document( ) function loads the XML document at the URI specified by the first argument and returns a node-set containing that document's root node. The URI is normally given as a string, but it may be given as another type that is converted to a string. If the URI is given as a node-set, then each node in the set is converted to a string, and the returned node-set includes root nodes of all documents referenced by the URI argument.

If the URI contains a fragment identifier, then the node-set returned may indicate something other than the root node and thus contain more than one node. If an error occurs while retrieving a document, most XSLT processors stop processing the stylesheet.

The document( ) function may also take a node-set as an optional second argument, in which case the base URI of the first node (in document order) in this set is used to resolve relative URIs given in the first argument. If the second argument is omitted, then base URIs are resolved relative to the stylesheet's location.

element-available( )

boolean element-available(*string qualifiedName*)

element-available( ) returns true if and only if the argument identifies an XSLT instruction element the processor recognizes. If the qualified name maps to a non-XSLT namespace URI, then it refers to an extension element. Assuming use of a fully conformant processor, you don't need to use this function to test for standard elements; just use it for extension elements.

format-number( )

string format-number(*number x, string pattern*)
string format-number(*number x, string pattern, string decimalFormat*)

The format-number( ) function converts the number x to a string using the pattern specified by the second argument, as well as the xsl:decimal-format element named by the third argument (or the default decimal format, if the third argument is omitted).

This function's behavior is modeled after the java.text.DecimalFormat class in Java 1.1 (not 1.2 or later). The pattern specifies whether leading and trailing zeros should be printed, whether the number's fractional part is printed, the number of digits in a group, and the leading and trailing suffixes for negative and positive numbers. The patterns are described using an almost Backus-Naur Form grammar, given here:

```
pattern     -> subpattern{;subpattern}
subpattern  -> {prefix}integer{.fraction}{suffix}
prefix      -> '\\u0000'..'\\uFFFD' - specialCharacters
suffix      -> '\\u0000'..'\\uFFFD' - specialCharacters
integer     -> '#'* '0'* '0'
fraction    -> '0'* '#'*
```

The first line is not pure BNF. The first subpattern is used for positive numbers. The second subpattern, which may not be present, is used for negative numbers. If it's not present, negative numbers use the positive format but are prefixed with a minus sign. Table 24-1 defines the symbols used in the grammar.

Table 24-1. Symbols used in the pattern grammar

Symbol	Meaning
0	A digit, including leading or trailing zeros; may be set to a different character using the zero-digit attribute of xsl:decimal-format.
#	A digit, except for leading or trailing zeros; may be set to a different character using the digit attribute of xsl:decimal-format.
.	A decimal separator; may be set to a different character using the decimal-separator attribute of xsl:decimal-format.
,	A grouping separator; may be set to a different character using xsl:decimal-format's grouping-separator attribute.
;	Separates the positive and negative format patterns in a format string; may be set to a different character using the pattern-separator attribute of xsl:decimal-format.
-	A default negative prefix; may be set to a different character using xsl:decimal-format's minus-sign attribute.
%	Multiplies by 100 and shows as percentage; may be set to a different character using xsl:decimal-format's percent attribute.
‰	Multiplies by 1,000 and shows as per mille; may be set to a different character using xsl:decimal-format's permille attribute.
X	Indicates that any other character can be used in the prefix or suffix.
'	Used to quote special characters in a prefix or suffix.

For instance, #,##0.### is a common decimal-format pattern. The # mark indicates any digit character except a leading or trailing zero. The comma is the grouping separator. The period is the decimal separator. The 0 is a digit that is printed even if it's an insignificant zero. This pattern is interpreted as follows:

1. The integer part contains as many digits as necessary.

2. The grouping separator separates every three digits.

3. If the integer part only contains zeros, a single zero is placed before the decimal separator.

4. Up to three digits are printed after the decimal point. However, any trailing zeros are not printed.

5. No separate pattern is included for negative numbers. Thus, negative numbers are printed the same as positive numbers, but they are prefixed with a minus sign.

function-available( )

boolean function-available(*string qualifiedName*)

function-available( ) returns true if the argument identifies a function in the processor's function library; false otherwise. If the qualified name maps to a non-null namespace URI, then it refers to an extension function. Otherwise, it refers to a built-in function from XPath or XSLT. Assuming you're using a fully conformant processor, however, you don't need to test for standard functions, only for extension functions.

generate-id( )

string generate-id(*node-set node*)
string generate-id( )

The generate-id( ) function returns a string that can be used as the value of an ID type attribute. This function always produces the same string for the same node and a different string for a different node. If the node-set contains more than one node, then only the first node in the set is considered. If the argument is omitted, then the node-set is set to the context node. If the node-set is empty, then the empty string is returned.

key( )

node-set key(*string keyName, string value*)
node-set key(*string keyName, node-set values*)

The key( ) function returns a node-set containing all nodes in the source document that have a key with the name given by the first argument and the value given by the second argument. If the second argument is a node-set, then the node-set returned contains all nodes that have a key with the specified name and a value that matches that of any node in the second argument. Otherwise, the returned node-set contains all nodes that have a key with the specified name and a value that matches the second argument's string-value. Key names and values are assigned to nodes using the xsl:key element.

system-property( )

object system-property(*string qualifiedPropertyName*)

The system-property( ) function returns the value of the named property. The type of the returned object is processor- and property-dependent. If the processor does not recognize the property name, then it returns an empty string.

XSLT processors are required to recognize and return values for these three properties:

xsl:version
> A number specifying the version of XSLT implemented by the processor; this is normally 1.0, but it may become 2.0 during this book's life span.

xsl:vendor
> A string identifying the XSLT processor's vendor; for instance, Apache Software Foundation for Xalan or SAXON 6.5.3 from Michael Kay for SAXON.

xsl:vendor-url
> A string containing a URL for the XSLT processor's vendor; for instance, http:// xml.apache.org/xalan for Xalan or http://saxon.sourceforge.net for SAXON.

Implementations may also recognize and return values for other processor-dependent properties.

unparsed-entity-uri( )

string unparsed-entity-uri(*string entityName*)

The unparsed-entity-uri( ) function returns the URI of the unparsed entity with the specified name declared in the source document's DTD or the empty string, if no unparsed entity with that name exists.

TrAX

Unfortunately, there is no standard API for XSLT that works across languages and engines: each vendor provides its own unique API. The closest thing to a standard XSLT API is the Transformations API for XML (TrAX), included in JAXP. However, this is limited to Java and is not even supported by all Java-based XSLT engines. Nonetheless, since it is the closest thing to a standard there is, we will discuss it here.

Code that transforms an XML document using an XSLT stylesheet through TrAX follows these six steps. All of the classes mentioned are in the javax.xml. transform package, a standard part of Java 1.4 and later and a separately install-able option in earlier versions.

1. Call the TransformerFactory.newInstance( ) factory method to create a new TransformerFactory object.
2. Construct a Source object from the XSLT stylesheet.

3. Pass this Source object to the TransformerFactory object's newTransform( ) method to create a Transform object.

4. Construct a Source object from the input XML document you wish to transform.

5. Construct a Result object into which the transformed XML document will be output.

6. Pass the Source and the Result to the Transform object's transform( ) method.

The source can be built from a DOM Document object, a SAX InputSource, or an InputStream—represented by the javax.xml.transform.dom.DOMSource, javax.xml. transform.sax.SAXSource, and javax.xml.transform.stream.StreamSource classes, respectively. The result of the transform can be a DOM Document object, a SAX ContentHandler, or an OutputStream. These are represented by the javax.xml. transform.dom.DOMResult, javax.xml.transform.sax.SAXResult, and javax.xml. transform.stream.StreamResult classes, respectively.

For example, this code fragment uses the XSLT stylesheet found at *http://www. cafeconleche.org/books/xian/examples/08/8-8.xsl* to transform the file *people.xml* in the current working directory onto System.out:

```
TransformerFactory factory = TransformerFactory.newInstance( );
URL u = new URL(
  "http://www.cafeconleche.org/books/xian/examples/08/8-8.xsl");
InputStream in    = u.openStream( );
Source stylesheet = new StreamSource(in);
Transformer xform = factory.newTransformer(stylesheet);
InputStream people = new FileInputStream("people.xml");
Source original   = new StreamSource(people);
Result transformed = new StreamResult(System.out);
xform.transform(original, transformed);
```

The procedure is much the same when the source or result is a DOM Document object or a SAX event stream. Just use the DOMSource, SAXSource, DOMResult, and/or SAXResult classes as appropriate. For example, this code fragment transforms the DOM Document object doc according to the stylesheet at *http://www.cafeconleche.org/ books/xian/examples/08/8-8.xsl* and passes the result through the SAX ContentHandler object named handler:

```
Document doc;
// Build the doc object in the usual way...
TransformerFactory factory = TransformerFactory.newInstance( );
URL u = new URL(
  "http://www.cafeconleche.org/books/xian/examples/08/8-8.xsl");
InputStream in    = u.openStream( );
Source stylesheet = new StreamSource(in);
Transformer xform = factory.newTransformer(stylesheet);
ContentHandler handler = new XMLCounter( ); // From Chapter 19
Source original   = new DOMSource(doc);
Result transformed = new SAXResult(handler);
xform.transform(original, transformed);
```

25

DOM Reference

This reference section documents the W3C Document Object Model (DOM) Level 3 Core Recommendation dated 07 April 2004. The latest version of this recommendation, along with any errata that have been reported, is available on the W3C DOM Activity's web site (*http://www.w3.org/DOM/DOMTR*). The symbols (2) and (3) will be used throughout this chapter to indicate in which DOM level a feature became available.

The Document Object Model (DOM) is a language- and platform-independent object framework for manipulating structured documents (see Chapter 19 for additional information). Just as XML is a generic specification for creating markup languages, the DOM Core defines a generic library for manipulating markup-based documents. The W3C DOM is actually a family of related recommendations that provide functionality for many types of document manipulation, including event handling, styling, traversing trees, manipulating HTML documents, and so forth. But most of these recommendations are built on the basic functionality provided by the Core DOM.

The DOM presents a programmer with a document stored as a hierarchy of Node objects. The Node interface is the base interface for every member of a DOM document tree. It exposes attributes common to every type of document object and provides a few simple methods to retrieve type-specific information without resorting to downcasting. This interface also exposes all methods used to query, insert, and remove objects from the document hierarchy. The Node interface makes it easier to build general-purpose tree-manipulation routines that are not dependent on specific document element types.

Object Hierarchy

The following table shows the DOM object hierarchy:

Object	Permitted child objects
Document	Element (one is the maximum) ProcessingInstruction Comment DocumentType (one is the maximum)
DocumentFragment	Element ProcessingInstruction Comment Text CDATASection EntityReference
DocumentType	None (leaf node)
EntityReference	Element ProcessingInstruction Comment Text CDATASection EntityReference
Element	Element Text Comment ProcessingInstruction CDATASection EntityReference
Attr	Text EntityReference
ProcessingInstruction	None (leaf node)
Comment	None (leaf node)
Text	None (leaf node)
CDATASection	None (leaf node)
Entity	Element ProcessingInstruction Comment Text CDATASection EntityReference
Notation	None (leaf node)

Object Reference

This section details the XML DOM Level 3 Core objects. The reference sections detail the descriptions, attributes, and methods of each object in the language-independent IDL specification. Java examples and bindings are presented to illustrate usage.

DOM
Reference

Attr

The Attr interface represents the value assigned to an attribute of an XML element. The parentNode, previousSibling, and nextSibling of an Attr are always null. Although the Attr interface inherits the Node base interface, many basic Node methods are not applicable.

An XML element can acquire an attribute in several ways. An element has an attribute value if:

- The XML document explicitly provides an attribute value.
- The document DTD specifies a default attribute value.
- An attribute is added programmatically using the setAttribute() or setAttributeNode() methods of the Element interface.

An Attr object can have EntityReference objects as children. The value attribute provides the expanded DOMString representation of this attribute.

```
//Get the element's size attribute as an Attr object
Attr attrName = elem.getAttributeNode("size");
```

Attributes

The following attributes are defined for the Attr object:

isId: boolean[3]

Returns true if this attribute contains a unique identifier for the parent element node. Attributes are tagged as identifiers by the DTD, the schema, or by using one of the setIdAttribute( ) methods of the Element interface. Read-only.

Java binding

```
public boolean isId( );
```

name: DOMString

The name of the attribute. Read-only.

Java binding

```
public String getName( );
```

Java example

```
// Dump element attribute names
Attr attr;

for (int i = 0; i < elem.getAttributes( ).getLength( ); i++) {
    // temporarily alias the attribute
    attr = (Attr)(elem.getAttributes( ).item(i));
    System.out.println(attr.getName( ));
    }
```

ownerElement: Element[2]

This property provides a link to the Element object that owns this attribute. If the attribute is currently unowned, it equals null. Read-only.

Java binding
```
public Element getOwnerElement( );
```

schemaTypeInfo: TypeInfo[3]

This property provides a link to any type information that may be available for this attribute, based the DTD or Schema associated with the parent document. May be unreliable if the node has been moved from one element to another. Read-only.

Java binding
```
public TypeInfo getSchemaTypeInfo( );
```

specified: boolean

This indicates whether this attribute was explicitly set in the XML source for the parent element or is a default value specified in the DTD or schema. Read-only.

Java binding
```
public boolean getSpecified( );
```

Java example
```
// Dump element attribute names
for (int i = 0; i < elem.getAttributes( ).getLength( ); i++) {
    // temporarily alias the attribute
    attr = (Attr)elem.getAttributes( ).item(i);
    // only show attributes that were explicitly included in the XML
    //source file
     // (i.e. ignore default attributes from the DTD.)
     if (attr.getSpecified( )) {
         System.out.println(attr.getName( ));
     }
}
```

value: DOMString

This attribute provides a simple way to set and retreive the Attr object's text value. When used to get the text value, the attribute includes the expanded value of any general entity references. When used to set the value, it creates a child Text node that contains the string value. Attempting to set the value on a read-only node raises the NO_MODIFICATION_ALLOWED_ERR DOM exception.

Java bindings
```
public String getValue( );
public void setValue(String value);
```

```
// Make all attribute values lowercase
Attr attr;

for (int i = 0; i < elem.getAttributes().getLength( ); i++) {
    attr = (Attr)(elem.getAttributes( ).item(i));
    attr.setValue(attr.getValue( ).toLowerCase( ));
}
```

Methods

The Attr object has no methods.

CDATASection

The CDATASection interface contains the unparsed, unescaped data contained within CDATA blocks in an XML document. Although this interface inherits the Text interface, adjacent CDATASection blocks are not merged by the normalize() method of the Element interface.

Java example

```
// Open an XML source file
try {
    FileInputStream fis = new FileInputStream("phone_list.xml");
    StringBuffer sb = new StringBuffer( );
    // read the XML source file into memory
    int ch;
    while ((ch = fis.read( )) != -1) {
        sb.append((char)ch);
    }

    // now, create a CDATASection object to contain it within
    // an element of our document using the CDATA facility
    CDATASection ndCDATA = doc.createCDATASection(sb.toString( ));
} catch (IOException e) {
    ...
```

CDATASection is a pure subclass of the Text interface and has no attributes or methods of its own. See the "Text" interface section of this chapter for a list of applicable methods for accessing character data in nodes of this type.

CharacterData

The CharacterData interface is completely abstract, extending the basic Node interface only to support manipulation of character data. Every DOM object type that deals with text data inherits, directly or indirectly, from this interface.

This interface's string-handling facilities are similar to those found in most modern programming languages. Like C/C++ string-processing routines, all CharacterData routines are zero-based.

Java example

```
// Create a new, unattached Text node
Text ndText = doc.createTextNode("The truth is out there.");
// cast it to the CharacterData interface
CharacterData ndCD = (CharacterData)ndText;
```

Attributes

The following attributes are defined for CharacterData:

data: DOMString

This attribute allows access to the "raw" data of the CharacterData node. Although a given DOM implementation cannot arbitrarily limit the amount of character data that can be stored in a CharacterData node, you may need to use the substringData method to retrieve the data in manageable sections because of implementation constraints.

Exceptions

NO_MODIFICATION_ALLOWED_ERR
  Raised on a write attempt when the data attribute is read-only for this DOM object type.

DOMSTRING_SIZE_ERR
  Raised if the read value that would be returned is too large to be contained by a DOMString type in the given implementation.

Java bindings

```
public String getData( ) throws DOMException;
public void setData(String data) throws DOMException;
```

Java example

```
// Quote the CharacterData node contents
CharacterData ndCD =
 doc.createTextNode("Unquoted text.");
...
ndCD.setData('\"' + ndCD.getData( ) + '\"');
```

length: unsigned long

The size of the DOMString stored in the data attribute. For all methods of this interface that take an index parameter, the valid range for the index is 0 <= index < length. This value can be 0 since it is possible to have an empty CharacterData node. Read-only.

Java binding

```
public long getLength( );
```

Java example

```
// Display the contents of a CharacterData node
CharacterData ndCD = (CharacterData)doc.createTextNode("This string has
 30 characters.");

System.out.println("The string \'" + ndCD.getData( ) + "\' has "
        + Long.toString(ndCD.getLength( )) + " characters.");
```

Methods

The following methods are defined for CharacterData:

---

appendData: arg

This method appends contents of the arg parameter to the current contents of the data attribute.

Argument

arg: DOMString
> The string to append.

Exception

NO_MODIFICATION_ALLOWED_ERR
> Raised if this node is read-only.

Java binding

```
public void appendData(String arg) throws DOMException;
```

Java example

```
// Append to an existing string
// Create a new Text object and reference the CharacterData interface

CharacterData ndCD = (CharacterData)doc.createTextNode("The truth is ");
// flip a coin

ndCD.appendData((Math.random( ) < 0.5) ? "out there." : "in here.");
System.out.println(ndCD.getData( ));
```

---

deleteData: offset, count

This truncates the DOMString in the data attribute. This method removes count characters, starting at the offset position.

Arguments

offset: unsigned long
> The position in the data attribute to remove count characters.

count: unsigned long
> The count of characters to remove. If the offset + count is >= the length attribute, the remainder—starting at position offset—is deleted.

Exceptions

INDEX_SIZE_ERR
> Raised if the offset parameter is not a valid zero-based index into the data DOMString.

NO_MODIFICATION_ALLOWED_ERR
> Raised if the node is read-only.

Java binding

```
public void deleteData(long offset, long count)
                throws DOMException;
```

```
// Create a new Text object and reference the CharacterData interface
CharacterData ndCD = doc.createTextNode("The truth is not out there.");

// change of heart
ndCD.deleteData(12, 4);

System.out.println(ndCD.getData( ));
```

insertData: offset, arg

This method takes a string, splits the data attribute's current contents at the given offset, then inserts the string from the arg parameter between the two substrings.

Arguments

offset: unsigned long
   The zero-based offset in the data attribute where the insertion is made.

arg: DOMString
   The string to be inserted.

Exceptions

INDEX_SIZE_ERR
   Raised if the offset parameter is not a valid, zero-based index into the data DOMString.

NO_MODIFICATION_ALLOWED_ERR
   Raised if the node is read-only.

Java binding

```
public void insertData(long offset, String arg) throws
   DOMException;
```

Java example

```
// Insert data into a string
boolean fCynical = true;

// create a new Text object, and reference the CharacterData interface
CharacterData ndCD = doc.createTextNode("The truth is out there.");

...

// check for cynicism
if (fCynical) {
    ndCD.insertData(12, " not");
}

System.out.println(ndCD.getData( ));
```

replaceData: offset, count, arg

This replaces a substring within the data attribute with another string value arg, using the specified offset and count parameters.

Arguments

offset: long

The offset of the beginning of the replacement region.

count: long

The number of characters to replace. If offset + count is >= the length attribute, everything beyond the offset character position is replaced.

arg: DOMString

The replacement string.

The replaceData operation is the equivalent of the following code fragment:

```
cdNode.deleteData(offset, count);
cdNode.insertData(offset, arg);
```

Exceptions

INDEX_SIZE_ERR

Raised if the offset parameter is not a valid, zero-based index into the data DOMString.

NO_MODIFICATION_ALLOWED_ERR

Raised if the node is read-only.

Java binding

```
public void replaceData(long offset, long count,
                        String arg) throws DOMException;
```

Java example

```
// Create a new Text object and reference the CharacterData interface
CharacterData ndCD = doc.createTextNode("The truth is not out there.");

// replace the truth
String strFind = "truth";
String strReplace = "dog";

ndCD.replaceData(ndCD.getData( ).indexOf(strFind), strFind.length( ),
                strReplace);

System.out.println(ndCD.getData( ));
```

---

substringData: offset, count

This returns a DOMString that contains a subset of the string stored in the data attribute. The offset and count arguments define the substring. Although the offset argument must represent a valid position within the node data, the endpoint of the substring could fall past the end of the data attribute. If this happens, the method returns everything between the offset position and the end of the data string.

Arguments

offset: unsigned long

Zero-based, starting offset of the substring to return. A valid offset must be > = 0 and < the length attribute of the node.

count: unsigned long

Count of characters to return.

Exceptions

INDEX_SIZE_ERR

Raised if the given offset is < 0, >= the length attribute, or if the count parameter is negative.

DOMSTRING_SIZE_ERR

Raised if the value that would be returned is too large to be contained by a DOMString type in the given implementation.

Java binding

```
public String substringData(unsigned long offset, unsigned long count)
                    throws DOMException;
```

Java example

```
// Get a reference to the CharacterData interface
CharacterData ndCD = doc.createTextNode("The truth is out there.");

// we only want the "truth"
String strTruth = ndCD.substringData(4, 5);

System.out.println("The substring is '" + strTruth + '\'');
```

Comment

This object contains the text of an XML comment (everything between the opening `<!--` and closing `-->`). It inherits from CharacterData.

 The DOM specification does not require XML parsers to preserve the original document comments after the document is parsed. Some implementations strip comments as part of the parsing process.

Java example

```
// Create a comment
Comment ndComment = doc.createComment("Document was parsed by DOM utility.");

// and add it to the document
doc.appendChild(ndComment);
```

Document

The Document interface represents an entire, well-formed XML document. Once the Document object is created via the DOMImplementation interface, you can access every aspect of the underlying XML document through the various tree-navigation methods exposed by the Node interface, the parent of the Document interface.

In DOM documents, document elements cannot exist outside of a parent document. For this reason, the Document interface exposes several factory methods used to create new document elements.

Attributes

The following attributes are defined for the Document object:

DOM
Reference

doctype: DocumentType

This attribute returns an instance of the DocumentType interface representing the document type declaration for this document. If no DOCTYPE declaration was in the document, this property is null. Prior to DOM Level 3, the DocumentType node associated with a document was immutable and could not be created directly. In Level 3 implementations, the doctype attribute is a shortcut to the DocumentType node that is currently linked into the document node hierarchy. Read-only.

Java binding

```
public DocumentType getDoctype( );
```

Java example

```
// Get the parsed DTD information for this document
DocumentType docType = docIn.getDoctype( );

if (docType == null) {
    System.out.println("warning: no DTD provided");
}
```

documentElement: Element

This attribute points to the single Element node that is the root of the XML document tree. Read-only.

Java binding

```
public Element getDocumentElement( );
```

Java example

```
// Identify the root element
Element elRoot = docIn.getDocumentElement( );
System.out.println("This is a '" + elRoot.getTagName( ) + "' document.");
```

documentURI: DOMString[3]

The location of the document, or null if the document was created using the createDocument( ) method of the DOMImplementation interface. No lexical checking of the URI itself is done during the set operation.

Java binding

```
public String getDocumentURI( );
public void setDocumentURI(string documentURI);
```

domConfig: DOMConfiguration[3]

Returns the DOMConfiguration object instance associated with this document. The DOMConfiguration controls the operation of the normalizeDocument( ) method. See the DOMConfiguration interface for a detailed list of parameters and their effects on the behavior of normalizeDocument( ). Read-only.

Java binding

```
public DOMConfiguration getDomConfig( );
```

implementation: DOMImplementation

This returns a reference to the DOMImplementation that is responsible for this document. It is conceivable (using Adobe's SVG plug-in within Microsoft's Internet Explorer, for example) that a single application might use DOM objects from multiple DOM implementations. Read-only.

Java binding

```
public DOMImplementation getImplementation( );
```

Java example

```
// Ensure the support of DOM Level 1 XML
DOMImplementation di = doc.getImplementation( );
if (!di.hasFeature("XML", "1.0")) {
    return false;
}
```

inputEncoding: DOMString[3]

Gives the character encoding detected when the document was parsed. See Chapter 5 for more information about character encodings. Is null when encoding is not known. Read-only.

Java binding

```
public String getInputEncoding( );
```

strictErrorChecking: boolean[3]

When set to false, DOM implementations are free to ignore error conditions (such as invalid characters in identifiers) that would ordinarily raise a DOMException. Although exceptions will not be raised, the behavior of the implementation after encountering an error is undefined. The default value of this attribute is true.

Java binding

```
public boolean getStrictErrorChecking( );
public void setStrictErrorChecking(boolean strictErrorChecking);
```

xmlEncoding: DOMString[3]

Returns the character encoding specified in the encoding pseudo-attribute of the XML declaration from the original document. See Chapter 5 for more information about character encodings. Is null when encoding is not known. Read-only.

Java binding

```
public String getXmlEncoding( );
```

xmlStandalone: boolean[3]

Returns the value of the standalone pseudo-attribute of the XML declaration from the original document. Returns false when not specified in the declaration. Note that this value returns the standalone value from the original declaration and may not be accurate.

Java binding

```
public boolean getXmlStandalone( );
public void setXmlStandalone(boolean xmlStandalone) throws DOMException;
```

xmlVersion: DOMString[3]

Returns the value of the version pseudo-attribute of the XML declaration of the document. For documents without an XML declaration, this value defaults to "1.0". Changing this value to "1.1" changes how methods that check for invalid characters in XML names (createElement( ), setAttribute( ), etc.) behave, per the XML 1.1 standard. For more information on the differences between XML 1.0 and 1.1, see Chapters 2 and 21.

Java binding

```
public String getXmlVersion( );
public void setXmlVersion(string xmlVersion) throws DOMException;
```

Methods

The following methods are defined for the Document object:

adoptNode: adoptNode, source[3]

Similar to importNode( ), this method is used to migrate a DOM Node from one Document instance to another. The source node is removed from the DOM tree of its parent document and prepared to be inserted into the adopting document, unlike the importNode( ) method which creates a copy of the source node and leaves the original in place. The following table explains the behavior of this method for the individual node types:

Node type	Result
ATTRIBUTE_NODE	Adopts the source attribute and all its children. The ownerElement attribute is set to null, and the specified flag is set to true.
DOCUMENT_FRAGMENT_NODE	Adopts the DocumentFragment node along with all of its child nodes.
DOCUMENT_NODE	Cannot be adopted.
DOCUMENT_TYPE_NODE	Cannot be adopted.
ELEMENT_NODE	Adopts the element as well as all child nodes. Adopts the attribute nodes that have their specified flag set, and may insert additional attributes based on the DTD or schema of the target document.
ENTITY_NODE	Cannot be adopted.
ENTITY_REFERENCE_NODE	Adopts only the EntityReference node. Its value, if any, is taken from the DTD of the document doing the import.
NOTATION_NODE	Cannot be adopted.
PROCESSING_INSTRUCTION_NODE, TEXT_NODE, CDATA_SECTION_NODE, COMMENT_NODE	All adopted without restrictions.

Since the newly adopted node was not created by the target document, it is possible that the names of elements, attributes, etc., may not conform to the XML version of the new document (see the xmlVersion attribute). Consider using the normalizeDocument( ) method to ensure that adopted nodes are well-formed.

Argument

source: Node
> The node to be adopted.

Exceptions

NOT_SUPPORTED_ERR
> Thrown if an attempt is made to import an unsupported Node type, such as a Document node.

NO_MODIFICATION_ALLOWED_ERR
> Thrown if the source node is read-only.

Java binding
```
public Node adoptNode(Node source) throws DOMException;
```

createAttribute: name

This function creates an Attr object with the given name. Attr nodes construct complex element attributes that can include EntityReference objects and text data.

Argument

name: DOMString
> The name of the XML attribute.

Return value

The new Attr object.

Exception

INVALID_CHARACTER_ERR
> Indicates that the name you passed to createAttribute() is not a valid XML name. See Chapter 2 for the XML restrictions on name construction.

Java binding
```
public Node adoptNode(Node source) throws DOMException;
```

createAttributeNS: namespaceURI, qualifiedName[2]

This method serves the same purpose as the createAttribute method, but is used when the attribute is in a namespace.

Arguments

namespaceURI: DOMString
> The URI associated with the namespace prefix in the qualifiedName parameter.

qualifiedName: DOMString
> The name of the attribute to instantiate; includes the namespace prefix associated with the namespace URI given in the namespaceURI parameter.

Return values

The new Attr object is returned with the following attribute values:

Attribute	Value
Node.nodeName	The complete, fully qualified name given in the qualifiedName parameter
Node.namespaceURI	The given namespace URI
Node.prefix	The namespace prefix, which is parsed from the qualifiedName parameter
Node.localName	The local part of the qualified name, located to the right of the : character
Attr.name	The qualifiedName

Exceptions

INVALID_CHARACTER_ERR

Indicates that the name passed to createAttributeNS() is not a valid XML name. See Chapter 2 for the XML restrictions on name construction.

NAMESPACE_ERR

Raised if the qualifiedName is malformed or has a prefix but no namespaceURI, or if the reserved xml namespace prefix was used incorrectly.

Java binding

```
public Attr createAttributeNS(String namespaceURI, String qualifiedName)
            throws DOMException;
```

---

createCDATASection: data

This creates a new CDATASection node that contains the data text.

Argument

data: DOMString

The text contained by the new CDATASection object.

Exception

NOT_SUPPORTED_ERR

Occurs if you try to call this method on an HTML document.

Java binding

```
public CDATASection createCDATASection(String data) throws DOMException;
```

Java example

```
// Use CDATASection to embed XML characters
CDATASection cds = doc.createCDATASection(
"<xml_example>This is sample text.</xml_example>");
```

---

createComment: data

This returns a new Comment node containing the specified string. See the "Comment" object reference earlier in this chapter for special restrictions that apply to the contents of Comment nodes.

Argument

data: DOMString

The comment text.

Comment text restriction

The XML specification indicates that the -- characters must not appear in the comment text for compatibility reasons. Despite this warning, some DOM implementations don't flag comments containing double hyphens as syntax errors.

Java binding

```
public Comment createComment(String data);
```

Java example

```
// Create a timestamp comment
StringBuffer sb = new StringBuffer( );
Date dtNow = new Date( );
sb.append("\tModified " + dtNow.toString( ) + '\n');
Comment cmt = doc.createComment(sb.toString( ));
```

---

createDocumentFragment( )

This returns an empty DocumentFragment object. See the "DocumentFragment" reference later in this chapter for a discussion of a document fragment's uses and limitations.

Java binding

```
public DocumentFragment createDocumentFragment( );
```

---

createElement: tagName

This creates a new, empty Element node for use within the parent document. The element name is given as an argument to the method. The resulting Element node belongs to the parent Document object, but is not part of the document element hierarchy. See the "NOT_SUPPORTED_ERR [unsigned short, value: 9]" reference later in this chapter for more information about how the document hierarchy manipulation methods are used.

Argument

tagName: DOMString
> The XML name used to create the new Element node. This name is assigned to the nodeName attribute of the resulting Element node.

Return value

The new Element object.

Exception

INVALID_CHARACTER_ERR
> Indicates that the name you passed to createElement() is not a legal XML name. See Chapter 2 for the XML restrictions on name construction.

Java binding

```
public Element createElement(String tagName) throws DOMException;
```

Java example

```
// Create the new my_tag Element
Element elOut = doc.createElement("my_tag");
```

createElementNS: namespaceURI, qualifiedName[(2)]

This method serves the same purpose as the createElement method but is used when the element is in a namespace.

Arguments

namespaceURI: DOMString
> The namespace URI.

qualifiedName: DOMString
> The name of the element to instantiate, including the namespace prefix associated with the namespace URI given in the namespaceURI parameter.

Return values

The new Element object is returned with the following attribute values:

Attribute	Value
Node.nodeName	The complete, fully qualified name given in the qualifiedName parameter
Node.namespaceURI	The given namespace URI
Node.prefix	The namespace prefix, which is parsed from the qualifiedName parameter
Node.localName	The local part of the qualified name, located to the right of the : character
Element.tagName	The full element tag name, which is the same as the qualifiedName

Exceptions

INVALID_CHARACTER_ERR
> Indicates that the name you passed to createElementNS( ) is not a legal XML name. See Chapter 2 for the XML restrictions on name construction.

NAMESPACE_ERR
> Raised if the qualifiedName is malformed, has a prefix but no namespaceURI, or if the reserved xml namespace prefix was used incorrectly.

Java binding

```
public Element createElementNS(String namespaceURI,
                               String qualifiedName)
                throws DOMException;
```

createEntityReference: name

This creates an EntityReference object.

Argument

name: DOMString
> The name of the XML entity to be referenced. The name must match an XML entity declaration that is valid in the current document.

Exceptions

INVALID_CHARACTER_ERR
> Indicates that the name you passed to createEntityReference( ) is not a legal valid XML name. See Chapter 2 for the XML restrictions on name construction.

NOT_SUPPORTED_ERR
> Generated if you attempted to create an entity reference using an HTML document.

Java binding
```
public EntityReference createEntityReference(String name)
                        throws DOMException;
```

Java example
```
// Create an entity reference
EntityReference er = doc.createEntityReference("name_entity");
```

---

createProcessingInstruction: target, data

This creates a new ProcessingInstruction node with the given target name and data values. The processing instruction target name "xml" (case-insensitive) is reserved and can't be used by an application.

Arguments
target: DOMString
> The target name of the processing instruction.

data: DOMString
> The application-specific data for the resulting ProcessingInstruction node.

Exceptions
INVALID_CHARACTER_ERR
> Indicates that the name you passed in to createProcessingInstruction is not a legal XML name. See Chapter 2 for the XML restrictions on name construction.

NOT_SUPPORTED_ERR
> Generated if you attempt to create a ProcessingInstruction using an HTML document.

Java binding
```
public ProcessingInstruction createProcessingInstruction(String target,
                             String data) throws DOMException;
```

Java example
```
// Add the application-specific processing instruction
ProcessingInstruction pi = doc.createProcessingInstruction("my_app",
        "action=\"save\"");
```

---

createTextNode: data

This creates a new Text node that contains the given data string.

Argument
data: DOMString
> The string that will be the contents of the new node.

Java binding
```
public Text createTextNode(String data);
```

Java example
```
// Create a new node that contains character data
Text txtDesc = doc.createTextNode(
"Character data contents for a new Element.");
```

getElementById: elementID[2]

This method returns the Element node with the given value for its ID attribute.

 It is important not to confuse attributes that have the name ID with ID attributes. *ID attributes* are attributes that were declared with the ID attribute type within the document type definition. See the "Attribute List Declaration" entry in Chapter 21 for more information about ID attributes.

Argument
elementID: DOMString
The unique ID value for the desired element.

Return value
A single Element object that has the requested ID attribute or null, if no match is found.

Java binding
```
public Element getElementById(String elementId);
```

getElementsByTagName: tagName

This function returns a list of Element nodes from the current document whose tagName attribute matches the given tagName parameter. The nodes are returned in the same order in which they appear in the source document.

Argument
tagName: DOMString
The name of the tag to use as a filter. The special name * matches any tag.

Java binding
```
public NodeList getElementsByTagName(String tagName);
```

Java example
```
// Get a list of all phone numbers in the document
NodeList nl = doc.getElementsByTagName("phone_number");
```

getElementsByTagNameNS: namespaceURI, localName[2]

Like the getElementsByTagName( ) method, this method returns a list of Element nodes (a NodeList object) that have the criteria given namespaceURI and localName. The resulting list contains all elements matching the namespace URI and local name restrictions, as they would be encountered in the original order of the document.

namespaceURI: DOMString
> The namespace URI of the elements to be matched. The special * value matches any namespace.

localName: DOMString
> The local name part of the elements to be matched. The special value * matches any local name.

Java binding
```
public NodeList getElementsByTagNameNS(String namespaceURI,
                                       String localName);
```

---

importNode: importedNode, deep[2]

This method's name is somewhat deceptive. It creates a copy of a Node object from another document that can be inserted within the current document's node hierarchy. Specifics of this copy operation vary, depending on the type of copied node, as described in this table:

Node type	Result	Effect of deep flag
ATTRIBUTE_NODE	Adopts the source attribute and all its children. The ownerElement attribute is set to null, and the specified flag is set to true.	None.
DOCUMENT_FRAGMENT_NODE	Creates an empty DocumentFragment node.	Fully copies the children of the source DocumentFragment node.
DOCUMENT_NODE	Cannot be imported.	N/A.
DOCUMENT_TYPE_NODE	Cannot be imported.	N/A.
ELEMENT_NODE	Adopts the attribute nodes with the specified flag set to the new element.	Recursively copies all the source element's children.
ENTITY_NODE	Adopts the publicId, systemId, and notationName attributes.	Recursively copies all of the Entity node's children.
ENTITY_REFERENCE_NODE	Adopts only the EntityReference node. Its value, if any, is taken from the DTD of the document doing the import.	None.
NOTATION_NODE	Imports the notation node, but since the DocumentType interface is read-only in Level 2, it cannot be included in the target document.	None.
PROCESSING_INSTRUCTION_NODE	Adopts the target and data values.	None.
TEXT_NODE, CDATA_SECTION_NODE, COMMENT_NODE	Adopts the data and length attributes.	None.

The new (copied) node object is returned based on the arguments.

Arguments

importedNode: Node
> The node duplicated for use in the current document hierarchy.

DOM Reference

deep: boolean
>   Whether to copy the single node given or the entire subtree of its children. For details, see the previous table.

Exception

NOT_SUPPORTED_ERR
>   Thrown if an attempt is made to import an unsupported Node type, such as a Document node.

Java binding
```
public Node importNode(Node importedNode, boolean deep)
    throws DOMException;
```

---

normalizeDocument( ) [3]

This method performs the equivalent of a load and save operation, returning the document to its "normal" form. This includes coalescing Text nodes, possibly expanding EntityReference nodes, etc. The types of operations that occur during the normalization process are controlled by the values of the parameters in the DOMConfiguration object (see the domConfig attribute). For a list of the standard configuration parameters available, see the DOMConfiguration interface.

Java binding
```
public void normalizeDocument( );
```

---

renameNode: n, namespaceURI, qualifiedName[3]

Allows Element and Attr type nodes to be renamed. Whenever possible, the nodeName attribute of the target Node is modified directly. If simply changing the name is not possible, a node is created with the new name and the child nodes of the old node are moved to the new node. If the node is an Element node, renaming it will cause it to lose the default attributes of the old node name and gain those corresponding to its new name.

Arguments

n: Node
>   The node to rename.

namespaceURI: DOMString
>   The namespace URI for the renamed node.

qualifiedName: DOMString
>   The new qualified name for the node.

Exceptions

NOT_SUPPORTED_ERR
>   Thrown if the target nodeType is not ELEMENT_NODE or ATTRIBUTE_NODE, or if the implementation does not support renaming the documentElement.

INVALID_CHARACTER_ERR
>   Thrown if the new qualified name is not a name according to the contents of the xmlVersion attribute.

WRONG_DOCUMENT_ERR
>   Thrown if an attempt is made to rename a node from a different document.

NAMESPACE_ERR

> Raised if the qualifiedName is malformed or has a prefix but no namespaceURI, or if the reserved xml namespace prefix was used incorrectly.

Java binding

```
public Node renameNode(Node n, String namespaceURI,
String qualifiedName) throws DOMException;
```

DocumentFragment

The DocumentFragment is a lightweight container used to store XML document fragments temporarily. Since it has no properties or methods of its own, it can only provide the same functionality exposed by the Node object. It is intended to serve as a container for at least one well-balanced XML subtree.

This object's most obvious application is in the case of clipboard or drag-and-drop operations in a visual editor. The user may elect to select several subtrees that appear at the same level of the tree to be copied:

```
<document>
    <parent>
        <child_1></child_1>
        <child_2></child_2>
    </parent>
    <parent>
    </parent>
</document>
```

If the user decides to copy the two child nodes to the clipboard, the DOM application would do the following:

- Create a DocumentFragment object.
- Attach copies of the child nodes to the new object using the cloneNode() and appendChild( ) methods.

Then, when the user decides to paste the copied nodes to a new location, the new DocumentFragment node is passed to this target node's appendChild() method. During the copy operation, the DocumentFragment node itself is ignored, and only the children are attached to the target node.

Java example

```
// Create a Document Fragment object
DocumentFragment dfNorm = doc.createDocumentFragment();
```

DocumentType

The Document interface includes a single attribute, docType, that points either to a description of the DTD for the current document or to null if none exists.

Java example

```
// get document type information
DocumentType dtDoc = doc.getDoctype();
```

DOM
Reference

Attributes

The DocumentType object contains the following attributes:

entities: NamedNodeMap

This attribute provides a list of all general entities declared in the document's DTD. If the same entity is declared more than once within a single document, only the first occurrence is preserved in this NamedNodeMap. Note that parameter entity declarations are not available through the DocumentType interface. Each member of this list implements the Entity interface. Read-only.

Java binding

```
public NamedNodeMap getEntities( );
```

Java example

```
// Dump the document entities
NamedNodeMap nnm = doc.getDoctype( ).getEntities( );

Entity ndEnt;
for (int i = 0; i < nnm.getLength( ); i++) {
    ndEnt = (Entity)(nnm.item(i));

    System.out.println(ndEnt.getNodeName( ));

    if (ndEnt.getPublicId( ) != null) {
        System.out.println("\tPublic Identifier: " +
                            ndEnt.getPublicId( ));
    }

    if (ndEnt.getSystemId( ) != null) {
        System.out.println("\tSystem Identifier: " +
                            ndEnt.getSystemId( ));
    }

    if (ndEnt.getNotationName( ) != null) {
        System.out.println("\tNotation Name: " +
                            ndEnt.getNotationName( ));
    }
}
```

internalSubset: DOMString

This attribute contains the document's internal subset as a string value. The content's actual format depends on the level of support provided by a particular XML parser. Read-only.

Java binding

```
public String getInternalSubset( );
```

name: DOMString

This is the name of the DTD, which is the XML name following the XML DOCTYPE keyword in the source document. Read-only.

Java binding
```
public String getName( );
```

Java example
```
// Display document type information
DocumentType dtDoc = doc.getDoctype( );

System.out.println("This is a " + dtDoc.getName( ) + " document.");
```

notations: NamedNodeMap

A NamedNodeMap contains a list of XML notation declarations for the current document. Each member of this list implements the Notation interface, and the list itself is read-only.

Java binding
```
public NamedNodeMap getNotations( );
```

Java example
```
// Dump the document notations
NamedNodeMap nnm = doc.getDoctype( ).getNotations( );
Notation ndNotation;
for (int i = 0; i < nnm.getLength( ); i++) {
    ndNotation = (Notation)nnm.item(i);

    System.out.println(ndNotation.getNodeName( ));
    if (ndNotation.getPublicId( ) != null) {
        System.out.println("\tPublic Identifier: " +
                            ndNotation.getPublicId( ));
    }
    if (ndNotation.getSystemId( ) != null) {
        System.out.println("\tSystem Identifier: " +
                            ndNotation.getSystemId( ));
    }
}
```

publicId: DOMString

This is the public identifier of the external subset. Read-only.

Java binding
```
public String getPublicId( );
```

DOM Reference

systemId: DOMString

The system identifier (URI) of this document's external subset. Read-only.

Java binding
```
public String getSystemId( );
```

Methods

The DocumentType object has no methods.

DOMConfiguration[(3)]

This interface is accessible through the domConfig attribute of a given DOM Document object. This object is essentially a list of configuration options that affect how documents are loaded, saved, and validated by the DOM implementation. By using the setParameter( ) method to modify these options, it is possible to change the behavior of the Document.normalize( ) method. For example, by setting the "entities" parameter to false, subsequent calls to the Document.normalize( ) method would cause all EntityReference nodes to be replaced with their replacement text and coalesced with adjacent Text nodes. The following table lists the valid parameters for the DOMConfiguration object:

Parameter name	Value	Meaning
canonical-form	true	Canonicalize the document per the Canonical XML specification. Duplicate namespace declarations are removed, and other changes are made to reduce the document to its simplest possible form. Setting this parameter to true automatically sets the following parameters: cdata-sections: false element-content-whitespace: true entities: false namespace-declarations: true namespaces: true normalize-characters: false well-formed: true
	false*	Do not canonicalize.
cdata-sections	true*	Keep CDataSection nodes intact.
	false	Transform CDataSection nodes into Text nodes and coalesce redundant Text nodes as necessary.
check-character-normalization	true	Check that the characters in the document are fully normalized per Appendix B of the XML 1.1 specification.
	false*	Do not check for character normalization.
comments	true*	Keep Comment nodes in document.
	false	Discard Comment nodes.
datatype-normalization	true	Expose the normalized value of a node (i.e., strings with collapsed whitespace) within the tree, per the information from the schema used for validation. For this to occur, the validate parameter must also be set to true.
	false*	Do not perform schema normalization.

Parameter name	Value	Meaning
element-content-whitespace	true*	Keep all whitespace from the original document.
	false	Discard Text nodes that contain element whitespace. See the Text.isElementContentWhitespace attribute for more information.
entities	true*	Keep EntityReference nodes in the document.
	false	Replace EntityReference nodes with their expansions as Text nodes (which will be coalesced as necessary).
error-handler	DOMError-Handler	This property may be set to an object instance that implements the DOMErrorHandler interface. The DOMErrorHandler.handleError( ) method will then be called if errors occur during document operations.
infoset	true	This parameter is a shortcut to force the DOM processor to conform to the XML Information Set specification. Setting this parameter to true automatically sets the following parameters: cdata-sections: false comments: true datatype-normalization: false element-content-whitespace: true entities: false namespace-declarations: true namespaces: true validate-if-schema: false well-formed: true
	false	Setting the infoset parameter to false has no effect.
namespaces	true*	Minimizes the number of namespace declarations throughout the document by assigning elements and attributes to the "nearest" namespace declaration that matches their namespace URI.
	false	No namespace declaration processing is done.
namespace-declarations	true*	Note that this parameter is only effective if the namespaces parameter is set to true. Include all namespace declaration attributes as Attr nodes within the document.
	false	Discard namespace declaration nodes.
normalize-characters	true	Fully normalize the characters in the document per Appendix B of the XML 1.1 Recommendation.
	false*	Do not perform character normalization.
schema-location	DOMString	A space-separated list of URIs of schemas against which the document will be validated. This parameter works in conjunction with the schema-type parameter. The value of this parameter takes precedence over the schema information specified in the document.
schema-type	DOMString	An absolute URI representing what type of schema documents are referenced by the schema-location parameter. The two schema type URIs given in the DOM specification are: XML Schema: http://www.w3.org/2001/XMLSchema XML DTD: http://www.w3.org/TR/REC-xml
split-cdata-sections	true*	Automatically splits a CDATA section whose text value contains the]]> termination marker. The termination marker code will be converted to text and another CDATA section created to follow the new Text node.
	false	Raise an error if a CDATASection contains unrepresentable content.

DOM
Reference

Parameter name	Value	Meaning
validate	true	Require that the document be validated against a schema during the Document.normalization( ) process. The schema may come from the schema-location parameter or from within the document itself.
	false*	Do not validate, including the internal subset, unless the validate-if-schema parameter is set to true.
validate-if-schema	true	Validate only if a schema can be found for the document element.
	false*	Do not validate, unless the validate parameter is set to true.
well-formed	true*	Ensure that the document is well-formed. This includes checking the content of Attr, Element, Comment, Text, CDataSection, and ProcessingInstruction nodes for characters that could not be present in a well-formed XML document. For example, the]]> CDATA termination sequence cannot be present in the text value of a CDataSection node.
	false	Do not enforce character value restrictions within the DOM nodes. This may result in a document that will not be well-formed when saved and reparsed.

* Indicates the parameter's default value. Parameters without a default value are optional.

Attributes

The DOMConfiguration object contains the following attributes:

parameterNames: DOMStringList[3]

Returns the list of parameters supported by the DOMConfiguration object. May include parameters that are not part of the DOM Recommendation. Read-only.

Java binding

```
public DOMStringList getParameterNames( );
```

Methods

The DOMConfiguration object defines the following methods:

canSetParameter: name, value[3]

Returns true if the name parameter could accept the value given. Essentially the same as calling setParameter( ) without actually modifying the value of the parameter.

Arguments

name: DOMString
> The name of a valid parameter (from the parameterNames list) to verify.

value: DOMUserData
> The potential value to verify.

Java binding

```
public boolean canSetParameter(String name, Object value);
```

getParameter: name[(3)]

Returns the value of the parameter given, if it is known. The return value is of the type DOMUserData, and is null if the specified parameter has no value associated or is not recognized.

Argument
name: DOMString
> The name of a valid parameter (from the parameterNames list) to verify.

Exception
NOT_FOUND_ERR
> Raised if the given parameter name is not recognized.

Java binding
```
public Object getParameter(String name) throws DOMException;
```

---

setParameter: name, value[(3)]

Attempts to set the named parameter to the value given.

Arguments
name: DOMString
> The name of a valid parameter (from the parameterNames list) to set.

value: DOMUserData
> The new value of the parameter.

Exceptions
NOT_FOUND_ERR
> Raised if the given parameter name is not recognized.

NOT_SUPPORTED_ERR
> Raised if the given parameter name is recognized but not supported.

TYPE_MISMATCH_ERR
> Raised if the value for this parameter is incompatible with the expected type (e.g., attempting to set the error-handler parameter to an object that doesn't implement the DOMErrorHandler interface).

Java binding
```
public void setParameter(String name, Object value) throws DOMException;
```

Methods
The DOMConfiguration object has no methods.

DOMError[(3)]

This interface defines an object that will contain information regarding errors that might occur during DOM operations. It is used as a parameter to the DOMErrorHandler. handleError( ) callback method.

Attributes

The DOMError object contains the following attributes:

location: DOMLocator[3]

Contains information regarding the location of the error within the original XML document as well as within the DOM tree. Read-only.

Java binding
```
public DOMLocator getLocation( );
```

message: DOMString[3]

A message generated by the DOM implementation describing the error. Read-only.

Java binding
```
public String getMessage( );
```

relatedData: DOMObject[3]

Based on the type attribute, this attribute will most likely contain a reference to the DOM Node object that caused the error.

Java binding
```
public Object getRelatedData( )
```

relatedException: DOMObject[3]

If the error is the result of a platform-dependent exception, this attribute will contain a reference to the exception object in question.

Java binding
```
public Object getRelatedException( )
```

severity: unsigned short[3]

This attribute indicates the severity of the error, which will be one of the constants from the following table:

Severity constant	Value	Meaning
SEVERITY_WARNING	1	This is an "informational" error, and DOM processing may proceed normally.
SEVERITY_ERROR	2	This is a possibly recoverable error (such as a schema validation problem in an otherwise well-formed document).
SEVERITY_FATAL_ERROR	3	An unrecoverable error (such as a well-formedness problem) has occurred.

Java binding
```
public short getSeverity( )
```

type: DOMString[3]

The value of the type attribute determines what type of object reference will appear in the relatedData attribute.

Java binding
```
public String getType( )
```

Methods

The DOMError object has no methods.

DOMErrorHandler[3]

This is a callback interface that allows DOM programmers to register an object to receive notifications when errors occur during DOM operations. The DOMConfiguration.setParameter( ) method is used with the error-handler parameter name to register a DOMErrorHandler for a given implementation.

Attributes

The DOMErrorHandler object has no attributes.

Methods

The following method is defined for this object:

handleError: error[3]

This is the callback method that is invoked by the DOM when an error occurs. Programmers using the DOM are responsible for implementing this method, processing errors, and determining whether processing should continue or be aborted. If this method returns true, processing will continue (unless an error of SEVERITY_FATAL_ERROR has occurred). If it returns false, processing will halt.

Argument
error: DOMError
    The object that describes the error.

Java binding
```
public boolean handleError(DOMError error);
```

DOMException

For languages and runtime platforms that support them, structured exceptions provide a way to separate the code that deals with abnormal or unexpected problems from the normal flow of execution. For languages that don't support exceptions, such as ECMAScript or Perl, these conditions are reported to your program as error codes from the method that recognized the condition.

The ExceptionCode is an integer value that indicates what type of exception was detected. The following ExceptionCodes are defined, with unused numeric codes reserved for future use by the W3C.

INDEX_SIZE_ERR [unsigned short, value: 1]

An index outside the expected range was passed to a method that accepts an index. The expected range for most collections is 0 <= index < collection. length.

Java binding

```
public static final short INDEX_SIZE_ERR = 1;
```

DOMSTRING_SIZE_ERR [unsigned short, value: 2]

The DOMString that would be returned from a method is too large.

Java binding

```
public static final short DOMSTRING_SIZE_ERR = 2;
```

HIERARCHY_REQUEST_ERR [unsigned short, value: 3]

The node insertion you requested violates the document structure's integrity. For example, the insertion would cause a node to become one of its own children.

Java binding

```
public static final short HIERARCHY_REQUEST_ERR = 3;
```

WRONG_DOCUMENT_ERR [unsigned short, value: 4]

An attempt to insert a node from one document directly into another.

Java binding

```
public static final short WRONG_DOCUMENT_ERR = 4;
```

INVALID_CHARACTER_ERR [unsigned short, value: 5]

An invalid character was used in a name—e.g., trying to create an element object with the name my element, as spaces are not allowed.

Java binding

```
public static final short INVALID_CHARACTER_ERR = 5;
```

NO_DATA_ALLOWED_ERR [unsigned short, value: 6]

Data was assigned to a node that doesn't support data, like an Element node.

Java binding

```
public static final short NO_DATA_ALLOWED_ERR = 6;
```

NO_MODIFICATION_ALLOWED_ERR [unsigned short, value: 7]

An attempt was made to modify a read-only node.

Java binding

```
public static final short NO_MODIFICATION_ALLOWED_ERR = 7;
```

NOT_FOUND_ERR [unsigned short, value: 8]

A node was modified in a context in which it could not be found.

Java binding

```
public static final short NOT_FOUND_ERR = 8;
```

NOT_SUPPORTED_ERR [unsigned short, value: 9]

If the specific implementation of the DOM did not implement an optional feature, this exception would be thrown.

Java binding

```
public static final short NOT_SUPPORTED_ERR = 9;
```

INUSE_ATTRIBUTE_ERR [unsigned short, value: 10]

An attempt was made to add an attribute that was already in use elsewhere. This error could occur if you acquired an attribute via the getAttributeNode( ) method and tried to add the same object instance to another element using the setAttributeNode( ) method. You would first need to create a new Attr object, probably using the cloneNode( ) method.

Java binding

```
public static final short INUSE_ATTRIBUTE_ERR = 10;
```

INVALID_STATE_ERR [unsigned short, value: 11][2]

An attempt was made to use an object that is no longer usable.

Java binding

```
public static final short INVALID_STATE_ERR = 11;
```

SYNTAX_ERR [unsigned short, value: 12][2]

An invalid or illegal string was specified.

Java binding

```
public static final short SYNTAX_ERR = 12;
```

INVALID_MODIFICATION_ERR [unsigned short, value: 13][2]

An attempt was made to change the type's underlying object.

Java binding

```
public static final short INVALID_MODIFICATION_ERR = 13;
```

DOM
Reference

NAMESPACE_ERR [unsigned short, value: 14][2]

An attempt was made to use a method that supports XML namespaces in a way that would violate namespace rules. This error could occur if a qualified name were given to a method without a corresponding namespace URI.

Java binding
```
public static final short NAMESPACE_ERR = 14;
```

INVALID_ACCESS_ERR [unsigned short, value: 15][2]

The underlying object does not support a parameter or operation.

Java binding
```
public static final short INVALID_ACCESS_ERR = 15;
```

VALIDATION_ERR [unsigned short, value: 16][3]

An attempted modification to the document tree would result in a validity error.

Java binding
```
public static final short VALIDITY_ERR = 16;
```

TYPE_MISMATCH_ERR [unsigned short, value: 17][3]

Raised if the type of a parameter is not compatible with the expected type.

Java binding
```
public static final short TYPE_MISMATCH_ERR = 17;
```

DOMImplementation

The DOMImplementation interface provides global information about the DOM implementation you currently use. The only way to obtain a reference to the DOMImplementation interface is through the getImplementation() method of the Document object.

Java example
```
// Check for DOM Level 1 support
DOMImplementation di = doc.getImplementation( );
// make sure that DOM Level 1 XML is supported
if (!di.hasFeature("XML", "1.0")) {
    return null;
}
```

Attributes
The DOMImplementation object has no attributes.

Methods
The DOMImplementation object defines the following methods:

createDocument: namespaceURI, qualifiedName, doctype[(2)]

Creates a new, empty Document object with the given document type. It also creates the single, top-level document element using the given qualified name and namespace URI.

Arguments

namespaceURI: DOMString
> The namespace URI used to create the top-level document element. Can be null if no namespace is used.

qualifiedName: DOMString
> The namespace-aware qualified name of the top-level document element to be created. The prefix given in this parameter is associated with the namespace URI given in the namespaceURI parameter.

doctype: DOMString
> The document type definition object to be associated with the new document. If this parameter is not null, the DocumentType node's ownerDocument attribute is set to point to the new document object.

Exceptions

INVALID_CHARACTER_ERR
> Indicates that the qualifiedName parameter has a malformed XML identifier.

NAMESPACE_ERR
> Raised if an inconsistency exists between the values given for the namespaceURI and the qualifiedName parameters. Passing in a qualified name with a namespace prefix and not passing in a namespace URI is illegal. This can also be generated if a reserved namespace prefix, such as xml, is given with an incorrect namespace URI.

WRONG_DOCUMENT_ERR
> Raised if the DocumentType node passed in the doctype parameter is already associated with another document object. New DocumentType objects must be created using the new createDocumentType method of the DOMImplementation interface.

Java binding

```
public Document createDocument(String namespaceURI,
    String qualifiedName, DocumentType doctype) throws DOMException;
```

createDocumentType: qualifiedName, publicId, systemId[(2)]

Creates an empty DocumentType node that is not associated with any document. No entity declarations or notations are available in this new, empty DocumentType object. No support currently exists in the DOM to populate this object.

Arguments

qualifiedName: DOMString
> The qualified name of the document type to be created.

publicId: DOMString
> The external subset's public identifier.

systemId: DOMString
> The system identifier (URI) of the external subset to be created.

Return value

A new DocumentType object with the ownerDocument attribute set to null.

Exceptions

INVALID_CHARACTER_ERR
> Indicates that the qualifiedName parameter has a malformed XML identifier.

NAMESPACE_ERR
> Raised if the qualified name is malformed.

Java binding
```
public DocumentType createDocumentType(String qualifiedName,
        String publicId, String systemId) throws DOMException;
```

---

getFeature: feature, version[3]

Provides a nonbinding–specific way to retrieve an object instance that implements a specific version of a given feature. Primarily used to access features beyond the scope of the DOM Core.

Arguments

feature: DOMString
> The package name of the feature to retrieve.

version: DOMString
> The DOM version level of the specified feature to retrieve.

Return value

Returns an object that implements the APIs for the specified features, or null if no implementation is available.

Java binding
```
public Object getFeature(String feature, String version);
```

---

hasFeature: feature, version

Tests to see if the DOM implementation supports a specific version of a named feature package.

Arguments

feature: DOMString
> The package name of the feature to test. The following feature names (and others listed at *http://www.w3.org/TR/DOM-Level-2-Core/introduction.html-ID-Conformance*) are valid:

> *XML*
>> Supports DOM Level 1.0 or 2.0 Core objects.

> *HTML*
>> Supports DOM Level 1.0 or 2.0 HTML objects.

version: DOMString

Represents the DOM version level of the specified feature to test. If no version number is specified, the function returns true if any version is supported.

Return value

Returns true if the particular version of the specified feature is available; otherwise, it returns false.

Java binding

```
public boolean hasFeature(String feature, String version);
```

Java example

```
// Make sure that DOM Level 1 XML is supported
if (!di.hasFeature("XML", "1.0")) {
    return null;
}
```

The HTML-specific DOM objects are beyond the scope of this book, but they are extremely useful tools for building applications that perform transformations on HTML documents. An excellent reference to the HTML DOM objects can be found in the book *Dynamic HTML: The Definitive Reference*, by Danny Goodman (O'Reilly).

DOMImplementationRegistry[3]

One of the concepts introduced in the Level 3 Core is that of "bootstrapping" a DOM implementation. Prior to Level 3, some language- and implementation-specific code was needed to initially create a DOMImplementation that could be used to create documents and gain access to DOM functionality. The DOMImplementationRegistry object has no formal IDL specification within the DOM recommendation, but every implementation of the Level 3 Core is required to provide an object that implements two methods: getDOMImplementation( ) and getDOMImplementationList( ). These methods are then used to locate a DOMImplementation object that supports the required features for the application.

DOMImplementationSource[3]

This interface supplies an ordered list of DOMImplementation objects that can be accessed via a zero-based index.

Attributes

The DOMImplementationSource object has no attributes.

Methods

The following methods are defined for this object:

getDOMImplementation: features[3]

Used to retrieve a DOMImplementation object that matches the space-separated list of features (and optional version numbers) provided. DOM implementers are free to provide multiple versions of the various DOM components, which developers can query at runtime using this method. Most of the available features are beyond the scope of this book; however, it is possible to request a specific version of XML support by passing in a features string such as the following: "XML 3.0". This string would request that a DOMImplementation object that supports Version 3.0 of the XML Core be returned. If no matching implementation is available, the method returns null.

Argument

features: DOMString
    The space-separated list of requested features and versions.

Java binding
    public DOMImplementation getDOMImplementation(String features);

getDOMImplementationList: features[3]

Used to retrieve a list of DOMImplementation objects that matches the space-separated list of features (and optional version numbers) provided. The list is returned as a DOMImplementationList. For more information on the construction of the features argument, see the getDOMImplementation( ) method.

Argument

features: DOMString
    The space-separated list of requested features and versions.

Java binding
    public DOMImplementationList getDOMImplementation(String features);

DOMLocator[3]

This interface describes an object that can identify a specific location within a document that is being processed by a DOM implementation.

Attributes
The DOMLocator object contains the following attributes:

byteOffset: long[3]

The byte offset into the input source, or -1 if no byte offset is available. Read-only.

Java binding
    public int getByteOffset( );

columnNumber: long[3]

The column number within the line of the input source, or -1 if no column number is available. Read-only.

Java binding
```
public int getColumnNumber( );
```

lineNumber: long[3]

The line number within the line of the input source, or -1 if no line number is available. Read-only.

Java binding
```
public int getLineNumber( );
```

relatedNode: Node[3]

This attribute contains a reference to the DOM Node object that corresponds to the document location in question. Read-only.

Java binding
```
public Node getRelatedNode( )
```

uri: DOMString[3]

The URI of the source document if it is available; otherwise, it is null. Read-only.

Java binding
```
public String getUri( );
```

utf16Offset: long[3]

Similar to the byte offset attribute, but instead of returning an absolute byte reference, it returns a UTF character offset, per the Unicode specification. See Chapter 5 for more information about character encodings and Unicode. Read-only.

Java binding
```
public int getUtf16Offset( );
```

Methods

The DOMLocator object has no methods.

DOMObject[3]

Starting with DOM Level 3, some methods either accept or return a reference to a language-specific object. The DOMObject type provides a generic placeholder to represent these objects in the DOM IDL. For Java and ECMAScript, this type is bound to the Object type.

DOMString

The DOMString type serves as a generic placeholder within the DOM IDL for the native string handling type for a given implementation language. For example, within the Java binding, the DOMString type maps to the java.lang.String type.

DOMStringList[3]

This interface supplies a read-only, ordered list of DOMString objects that can be accessed via a zero-based index.

Attribute

The DOMStringList object contains the following attribute:

length: unsigned long[3]

Gives the number of DOMString objects in the list. Read-only.

Java binding
```
public int getLength( );
```

Methods

The following methods are defined for this object:

contains: str[3]

Returns true if the given string is contained in the list; otherwise, it returns false.

Argument
str: DOMString
The string value to locate.

Java binding
```
public boolean contains(String str);
```

item: index[3]

Used to retrieve strings from the list. Valid values for the index argument are 0 through length - 1. If an invalid index is provided, this method returns null.

Argument
index: unsigned long
The index of the string to retrieve.

Java binding
```
public String item(int index);
```

DOMUserData(3)

The new Node.getUserData( ) and Node.setUserData( ) methods are intended to allow the programmer to store application-specific information within the DOM tree. The DOMUserData type provides a generic placeholder for use within the DOM IDL descriptions. For Java and ECMAScript, this type is bound to the Object type.

Element

The Element interface provides access to the XML document's structure and data. Every XML element is translated into a single Element node. The document's root element is accessible through the documentElement property of the Document object. From this node, it is possible to re-create the full structure of the original XML document by traversing the element tree.

Java example

```
// Get the XML document's root element
Element elem = doc.getDocumentElement( );
```

This interface extends the basic Node interface to allow access to the XML attributes of the document element. Two sets of methods allow access to attribute values, either as Attr object trees or as simple DOMStrings.

Attributes

The Element object contains the following attributes:

schemaTypeInfo: TypeInfo(3)

This property provides a link to any type information that may be available for this element, based on the DTD or Schema associated with the parent document. Read-only.

Java binding

```
public TypeInfo getSchemaTypeInfo( );
```

tagName: DOMString

The XML tag name from the original document.

Java binding

```
public String getTagName( );

// Show the name of the root element tag
Element elem = doc.getDocumentElement( );
System.out.println("This is a " + elem.getTagName( ) + " document.");
```

Methods

The following methods are defined for this object:

getAttribute: name

Returns the attribute specified by the name parameter as a DOMString. See "createElementNS: namespaceURI, qualifiedName(2)" for a complete explanation of how an attribute value is determined. This returns an empty string if no attribute is set and if no default attribute value was specified in the DTD.

Java binding

```
public String getAttribute(String name);
```

Java example

```
// Check for the name attribute
Element elem = doc.getDocumentElement( );

if (elem.getAttribute("name") == "") {
    System.out.println("warning: " + elem.getTagName( ) +
                " element: no name attribute");
}
```

getAttributeNS: namespaceURI, localName(2)

Returns an attribute as a DOMString, based on the namespace URI and local part of the qualified name.

Arguments

namespaceURI: DOMString
    The namespace URI of the attribute to return.

localName: DOMString
    The local name portion of the qualified attribute name to return.

Return value

Returns an empty string if no attribute is set and if no default attribute value was specified in the DTD.

Java binding

```
public String getAttributeNS(String namespaceURI, String localName);
```

getAttributeNode: name

Retrieves the Attr with the given name. Returns a reference to the attribute object if it is found; otherwise, it is null.

Argument

name: DOMString
    Name of the attribute to retrieve.

Java binding

```
public Attr getAttributeNode(String name);
```

Java example

```
// Use the id attribute
Attr attr;

if ((attr = elem.getAttributeNode("id")) == null) {
    System.out.println("warning: element " + elem.getTagName( ) +
                        ": no id attribute provided.");
}
```

getAttributeNodeNS: namespaceURI, localName[2]

Retrieves the Attr object for the attribute specified by the given namespace URI and local name. Returns a reference to the attribute object if it is found; otherwise, it returns null.

Arguments

namespaceURI: DOMString
Namespace URI of the target attribute.

localName: DOMString
Local name of the target attribute. The local name is the part of the name to the right of the : in a qualified name.

Java binding

```
public Attr getAttributeNodeNS(String namespaceURI, String localName);
```

getElementsByTagName: name

Returns a NodeList of all descendant Element nodes whose tagName attribute matches the given name parameter. The nodes are returned in the same order in which they would be encountered in a preorder traversal of the document tree. A preorder traversal conforms to the order in which the XML elements appear in the source document.

Argument

name: DOMString
The name of the tag to use as a filter. The special name * matches any tag.

Java binding

```
public NodeList getElementsByTagName(String name);
```

Java example

```
// Find every address element in the document
Element elem = doc.getDocumentElement( );
NodeList nlAddrs = elem.getElementsByTagName("address");
```

getElementsByTagNameNS: namespaceURI, localName[2]

Like the getElementsByTagName method, returns a list of Element nodes (descendants of the Element node on which the method is called) that match the criteria given in the namespaceURI and localName parameters. The resulting list contains all elements matching the namespace URI and local name restrictions, as they would be encountered in a preorder traversal of the document tree.

DOM
Reference

Arguments

namespaceURI: DOMString
> The namespace URI of elements to be matched. The special * value matches any namespace.

localName: DOMString
> The local name part of elements to be matched. The special value * matches any local name.

Java binding
```
public NodeList getElementsByTagNameNS(String namespaceURI,
                                       String localName);
```

---

hasAttribute: name(2)

Returns true if an attribute with the given name has been set or has a default value. Returns false if the attribute isn't defined.

Argument

name: DOMString
> The name of the attribute to be identified.

Java binding
```
public boolean hasAttribute(String name);
```

---

hasAttributeNS: namespaceURI, localName(2)

Returns true if an attribute with the given namespaceURI and localName has been set or has a default value. Returns false if the attribute isn't defined.

Arguments

namespaceURI: DOMString
> The namespace URI of the attribute to be identified.

localName: DOMString
> The local name of the attribute to be identified.

Java binding
```
public boolean hasAttribute(String namespaceURI, String localName);
```

---

normalize

Traverses the subtree of the current Element, combining adjacent Text nodes into a single node.

 This method was moved to the Node interface as part of the DOM Level 2 specification. It is still accessible from the Element interface, as it inherits from the Node interface.

Java binding
```
public void normalize( );
```

Java example

```
// Merge all adjacent text nodes below this element
elem.normalize( );
```

removeAttribute: name

Removes the named attribute from this element's attributes collection. If the attribute to be removed has a default value declared in the DTD, subsequent attempts to retrieve the attribute value return the default value.

Argument

name: DOMString
    Name of the attribute to remove.

Exception

NO_MODIFICATION_ALLOWED_ERR
    Raised if the element is read-only.

Java binding

```
public void removeAttribute(String name) throws DOMException;
```

Java example

```
// Remove the unique ID
...
elem.removeAttribute("id");
...
```

removeAttributeNS: namespaceURI, localName[2]

Removes the attribute with the given namespace URI and local name from the element's attributes collection.

Arguments

namespaceURI: DOMString
    Namespace URI of the target attribute.

localName: DOMString
    Local name part of the target attribute. The local name is the part to the right of the final : in a qualified name.

Exception

NO_MODIFICATION_ALLOWED_ERR
    Raised if the element is read-only.

Java binding

```
public void removeAttributeNS(String namespaceURI, String localName)
                throws DOMException;
```

DOM
Reference

removeAttributeNode: oldAttr

Removes the referenced attribute node from this element's attributes collection.
If the attribute to be removed has a default value declared in the DTD, subsequent attempts to retrieve the attribute value return the default value.

Argument

oldAttr: Attr
> The attribute node to remove.

Exceptions

NO_MODIFICATION_ALLOWED_ERR
> Raised if the node is read-only.

NOT_FOUND_ERR
> Raised if no attribute name matching the oldAttr parameter is found in the map.

Java binding

```
public Attr removeAttributeNode(Attr oldAttr) throws DOMException;
```

Java example

```
// Find and remove temporary attributes
Attr attr;

if ((attr = elem.getAttributeNode("temp")) != null) {
    // remove it
    elem.removeAttributeNode(attr);
}
```

setAttribute: name, value

Sets the attribute specified by the name parameter to the DOMString passed in the value argument. The string is not parsed for entity references and is set as a Text node child of the corresponding member of the attributes collection. If an attribute with the given name already exists, the value is set to the value argument.

Arguments

name: DOMString
> The attribute name to set or modify.

value: DOMString
> The new attribute value.

Exceptions

INVALID_CHARACTER_ERR
> Indicates that the attribute name you passed in doesn't represent a valid XML attribute name.

NO_MODIFICATION_ALLOWED_ERR
> Raised if the element is read-only.

```
public void setAttribute(String name, String value) throws DOMException;
```

Java example

```
// Check for the name attribute
if (elem.getAttribute("name") == "") {
    // oh well, set a reasonable default
    elem.setAttribute("name", elem.getTagName( ));
}
```

---

setAttributeNS: namespaceURI, qualifiedName, value[2]

This method is the namespace-enabled version of the basic setAttribute method. The namespace URI and the qualified name update the attributes collection of the element in question.

Arguments

namespaceURI: DOMString
The namespace URI of the attribute value to set.

qualifiedName: DOMString
The qualified name (including the namespace prefix) of the new value to set.

value: DOMString
The new attribute value.

Exceptions

INVALID_CHARACTER_ERR
Indicates that the attribute name you passed in is not a legal XML attribute name.

NO_MODIFICATION_ALLOWED_ERR
Raised if the element is read-only.

NAMESPACE_ERR
Raised if the namespaceURI and qualifiedName parameters would violate rules concerning namespaces. If the qualified name includes a prefix, the namespace URI cannot be null or an empty string. If the reserved xml or xmlns prefixes are used, the namespace URI must match the corresponding specified system URI. See Chapter 4 for more information about namespaces and prefixes.

Java binding

```
public void setAttributeNS(String namespaceURI, String qualifiedName,
                           String value) throws DOMException;
```

---

setAttributeNode: newAttr

Sets or replaces the attribute in the Node interface's attributes collection with the given Attr object. The attribute name is retrieved from the name attribute of the new attribute object. If an Attr object with the given name already exists in the attributes collection, this method returns a reference to the old Attr object. Otherwise, it returns null.

Argument

newAttr: Attr
> The new Attr object to set.

Exceptions

WRONG_DOCUMENT_ERR
> Raised if the newAttr node was created in a document different than the parent node.

NO_MODIFICATION_ALLOWED_ERR
> Raised if the new parent node is read-only.

INUSE_ATTRIBUTE_ERR
> Raised if another Element already uses the new Attr node. Each element must have a distinct Attr object.

Java binding

```java
public Attr setAttributeNode(Attr newAttr) throws DOMException;
```

Java example

```java
// Make sure you have an id attribute to work with
Attr attr;

if ((attr = elem.getAttributeNode("id")) == null) {
    // add a default, unique id
    attr = doc.createAttribute("id");

    elem.setAttributeNode(attr);

    // continue processing
}
```

---

setAttributeNodeNS: newAttr(2)

Sets or replaces the attribute in the element's attributes collection that matches the namespace URI and the given Attr object's local name. This operation is identical to the setAttributeNode method, except that it considers namespace differences between attributes. If an Attr object with the given name in the attributes collection already exists, this method returns a reference to the old Attr object; otherwise, it returns null.

Argument

newAttr: Attr
> The new Attr object to set.

Exceptions

WRONG_DOCUMENT_ERR
> Raised if the newAttr node was created in a different document than the parent node.

NO_MODIFICATION_ALLOWED_ERR
> Raised if the new parent node is read-only.

INUSE_ATTRIBUTE_ERR
> Raised if another Element already uses the newAttr node. Each element must have a unique Attr object.

```
public Attr setAttributeNodeNS(Attr newAttr) throws DOMException;
```

setIdAttribute: name, isId[3]

This method provides a way to mark an attribute as a user-determined ID attribute. Although attributes that are marked as ID attributes using this method will show up in searches conducted using the `Document.getElementById()` method, it will not modify any of the type information provided by the `Attr.schemaTypeInfo` attribute. To mark namespace-aware attributes, use the `setIdAttributeNS()` method.

Arguments

name: DOMString
> The attribute name to modify.

isId: boolean
> Set to `true` if the attribute is to be an ID attribute; otherwise, set to `false`.

Exceptions

NO_MODIFICATION_ALLOWED_ERR
> Raised if the element is read-only.

NOT_FOUND_ERR
> Raised if no attribute matching the `name` parameter is found in the attributes collection.

Java binding
```
public void setIdAttribute(String name, boolean isId)
    throws DOMException;
```

setIdAttributeNS: namespaceURI, localName, isId[3]

This method provides a way to mark an attribute that belongs to a namespace as a user-determined ID attribute. Although attributes that are marked as ID attributes using this method will show up in searches conducted using the `Document.getElementById()` method, it will not modify any of the type information provided by the `Attr.schemaTypeInfo` attribute.

Arguments

namespaceURI: DOMString
> The namespace URI of the attribute to modify.

localName: DOMString
> The local part of the name of the attribute to modify.

isId: boolean
> Set to `true` if the attribute is to be an ID attribute; otherwise, it is `false`.

Exceptions

NO_MODIFICATION_ALLOWED_ERR
> Raised if the element is read-only.

NOT_FOUND_ERR
> Raised if no attribute matching the `name` parameter is found in the attributes collection.

```
public void setIdAttributeNS(String namespaceURI, String localName,
                            boolean isId) throws DOMException;
```

setIdAttributeNode: idAttr, isId(3)

This method provides a way to mark an attribute as a user-determined ID attribute. Although attributes that are marked as ID attributes using this method will show up in searches conducted using the Document.getElementById( ) method, it will not modify any of the type information provided by the Attr. schemaTypeInfo attribute. To mark namespace-aware attributes, use the setIdAttributeNS( ) method.

Arguments

idAttr: Attr
> The attribute to modify.

isId: boolean
> Set to true if the attribute is to be an ID attribute; otherwise, set to false.

Exceptions

NO_MODIFICATION_ALLOWED_ERR
> Raised if the element is read-only.

NOT_FOUND_ERR
> Raised if the specified attribute is not an attribute of the element in question.

Java binding
```
public void setIdAttributeNode(Attr idAttr, boolean isId)
throws DOMException;
```

Entity

The Entity object represents a given general XML entity's replacement value. Depending on whether a given DOM implementation is validating or nonvalidating, and whether it chooses to expand entity references inline during parsing, Entity objects may not be available to the DOM user.

Java example
```
// Locate the my_entity entity declaration
Entity ndEnt = (Entity)(doc.getDoctype( ).getEntities( ).
    getNamedItem("my_entity"));
```

Attributes

The following read-only attributes are defined for the Entity object:

inputEncoding: DOMString(3)

Gives the character encoding detected at parse time for external parsed entities. See Chapter 5 for more information about character encodings. Is null for internal parsed entities or if the encoding is not known. Read-only.

```
    public String getInputEncoding( );
```

notationName: DOMString

If this entity is unparsed, the entity's notation name. For parsed entities, this attribute is null.

Java binding
```
    public String getNotationName( );
```

Java example
```
    // Find out if it's a parsed entity
    boolean fParsedEnt = ndEnt.getNotationName( ) == null;
```

publicId: DOMString

The public identifier URL given for this entity, or null if none was specified.

Java binding
```
    public String getPublicId( );
```

systemId: DOMString

The system identifier URL (URI) given for this entity, or null if none was specified.

Java binding
```
    public String getSystemId( );
```

Java example
```
    // Get the Public ID or System ID for this entity
    Entity ndEnt = (Entity)doc.getDoctype( ).getEntities( ).
    getNamedItem("my_ entity");

    String strURL = ndEnt.getPublicId( );

    // if can't find the public URL
    if (strURL == null) {
        // find the system URL
        strURL = ndEnt.getSystemId( );
    }
```

xmlEncoding: DOMString[3]

Returns the character encoding specified in the encoding pseudo-attribute of the text declaration for an external parsed entity. See Chapter 5 for more information about character encodings. Is null if no text declaration is present. Read-only.

Java binding
```
    public String getXmlEncoding( );
```

xmlVersion: DOMString[3]

Returns the value of the version pseudo-attribute of the text declaration of an external parsed entity. Is null if no text declaration is present. Read-only.

Java binding
```
public String getXmlVersion( );
```

Methods
The Entity object has no methods.

EntityReference

EntityReference nodes appear within the document hierarchy wherever an XML general entity reference is embedded within the source document. Depending on the DOM implementation, a corresponding Entity object may exist in the entities collection of the docType attribute of the Document object. If such an entity exists, then the child nodes of both the Entity and EntityReference represent the replacement text associated with the given entity.

Java example
```
// Create a new entity reference
EntityReference ndER = doc.createEntityReference("my_entity");
```

NameList[3]

This interface supplies a read-only, ordered list names and namespace values that can be accessed via a zero-based index.

Attribute
The NameList object contains the following attributes:

length: unsigned long[3]

Gives the number of name/namespace pairs in the list. Read-only.

Java binding
```
public int getLength( );
```

Methods
The following methods are defined for this object:

contains: str[3]

Returns true if the name given by the str parameter is contained in the list; otherwise, it returns false.

Argument

str: DOMString
> The name value to locate.

Java binding
```
public boolean contains(String str);
```

---

containsNS: namespaceURI, name[3]

Returns true if the given name/namespace pair is contained in the list; otherwise, returns false.

Argument

namespaceURI: DOMString
> The namespace URI of the name to locate.

name: DOMString
> The name value to locate.

Java binding
```
public boolean containsNS(String namespaceURI, String name);
```

---

getName: index[3]

Used to retrieve names from the list. Valid values for the index argument are 0 through length - 1. If an invalid index is provided, this method returns null.

Argument

index: unsigned long
> The index of the name to retrieve.

Java binding
```
public String getName(int index);
```

---

getNamespaceURI: index[3]

Used to retrieve the namespace URI associated with a given name from the list. Valid values for the index argument are 0 through length - 1. If an invalid index is provided or the name has no associated namespace URI, this method returns null.

Argument

index: unsigned long
> The index of the name to retrieve.

Java binding
```
public String getNamespaceURI(int index);
```

DOM
Reference

NamedNodeMap

The NamedNodeMap interface provides a mechanism used to retrieve Node objects from a collection by name. Although this interface exposes the same methods and attributes as the NodeList class, they are not related. While it is possible to enumerate the nodes in a NamedNodeMap using the item() method and length attribute, the nodes are not guaranteed to be in any particular order.

Java example

```
// Get an element's attributes
NamedNodeMap nnm = elem.getAttributes( );
```

Attribute

The NamedNodeMap defines one attribute:

length: unsigned long

The total number of Node objects in the list.

Java binding

```
public long getLength( );
```

Java example

```
// Iterate over the attribute list
for (int i = 0; i < nnm.getLength( ); i++) {
    ...
}
```

Methods

The following methods are defined for the NamedNodeMap object:

getNamedItem: name

Returns a reference to the node with the given nodeName property specified by name.

Argument

name: DOMString
    Name of the node to retrieve.

Java binding

```
public Node getNamedItem(String name);
```

Java example

```
// Check to see if an ID attribute exists
// in this map, and add it if necessary
// nnm was created by getting the attributes
// from an element
if (nnm.getNamedItem("id") == null) {
```

```
// get the document
Document doc = elem.getOwnerDocument( );
// create a new attribute Node
Attr attrID = doc.createAttribute("id");

// set the attribute value
attrID.appendChild(doc.createTextNode(makeUniqueID(elem)));
// ... and add it to the NamedNodeMap
nnm.setNamedItem(attrID);
}
```

getNamedItemNS: namespaceURI, localName[2]

Extends the basic getNamedItem method to include support for namespaces. Instead of finding an item in the list based only on the local part of the node name, it is possible to incorporate the namespace URI into the search.

Arguments

namespaceURI: DOMString
Namespace URI of the node to retrieve.

localName: DOMString
Local name of the node to retrieve.

Java binding

```
public Node getNamedItemNS(String namespaceURI, String localName);
```

item: index

Returns a reference to the Node object at position index. If the given index is < 0 or >= the length attribute of the NodeList, this function returns null.

Argument

index: unsigned long
Zero-based index of the list of the node to return.

Java binding

```
public Node item(long index);
```

Java example

```
// Remove the last attribute from the list
if (nnm.getLength( ) > 0) {
    nnm.removeNamedItem(nnm.item(nnm.getLength( )-1).getNodeName( ));
}
```

removeNamedItem: name

Removes the Node object with the nodeName property that matches the name parameter and returns a reference to the removed object. If the node you plan to remove is an Attr node and if it has a defined default value, the node will be replaced immediately with a new Node object set to the default value.

Argument

name: DOMString
> The nodeName value of the node to be removed.

Exception

NOT_FOUND_ERR
> Raised if no node matching the name parameter is found in the map.

Java binding
```
public Node removeNamedItem(String name) throws DOMException;
```

Java example
```
// Remove the ID node attribute
NamedNodeMap nnm = elem.getAttributes( );

if (nnm.removeNamedItem("id") == null) {
    System.err.println("no ID attribute found");
}
```

---

removeNamedItemNS: namespaceURI, localName[2]

Removes the Node object with the matching namespaceURI and localName properties and returns a reference to the removed object. If the node you plan to remove is an Attr node and if it has a defined default value, a new Node object set to the default value will replace the node immediately.

Arguments

namespaceURI: DOMString
> Namespace URI of the node to retrieve.

localName: DOMString
> Local name of the node to retrieve.

Exception

NOT_FOUND_ERR
> Raised if no node matching the namespaceURI and localName parameter is found in the map.

Java binding
```
public Node removeNamedItemNS(String namespaceURI, String localName);
```

---

setNamedItem: arg

Inserts the given Node object into the list, using its nodeName attribute. Since many DOM node types expose the same, hardcoded value for this property, storing only one of them in a single NamedNodeMap is possible. Each subsequent insertion overwrites the previous node entry. See the "nodeName: DOMString" topic for a discussion of these special name values.

This method returns a reference to the Node object that the new node replaces. If no nodes with the same nodeName value are currently in the map, this method returns null.

Argument

arg: Node

The Node object to be stored in the map. The value of the nodeName property is used as the lookup key. A node with the same nodeName value as the new node is replaced with the node referenced by arg.

Exceptions

WRONG_DOCUMENT_ERR

Raised if a document different than the creator of the target NamedNodeMap created the arg node.

NO_MODIFICATION_ALLOWED_ERR

Raised if the NamedNodeMap is read-only.

INUSE_ATTRIBUTE_ERR

Raised if the arg node is an Attr node that is already in use by another element's attributes map.

Java binding

```
public Node setNamedItem(Node arg) throws DOMException;
```

Java example

```
// Check to see if an ID attribute exists
// in this map, and add it if necessary
if (nnm.getNamedItem("id") == null) {
    // get the document
    Document doc = elem.getOwnerDocument( );
    // create a new attribute Node
    Attr attrID = doc.createAttribute("id");

    // set the attribute value
    attrID.appendChild(doc.createTextNode(makeUniqueID(elem)));

    // ... and add it to the NamedNodeMap
    nnm.setNamedItem(attrID);
}
```

---

setNamedItemNS: arg[2]

Identical in function to the basic setNamedItem method, except that it considers namespace properties in the Node object. A reference to the replaced Node object is returned.

Argument

arg: Node

The Node object to be stored in the map. The values of the namespaceURI and localName properties are used as the lookup key. If another node with identical values for these two properties exists, the new node replaces it.

Exceptions

WRONG_DOCUMENT_ERR

Raised if a document different than the creator of the target NamedNodeMap created the arg node.

NO_MODIFICATION_ALLOWED_ERR

Raised if the NamedNodeMap is read-only.

INUSE_ATTRIBUTE_ERR

Raised if the arg node is an Attr node already in use by another element's attributes map.

Java binding

```
public Node setNamedItemNS(Node arg) throws DOMException;
```

Node

The Node interface is the base interface for every member of a DOM document tree. It exposes attributes common to every type of document object and provides simple methods to retrieve type-specific information without resorting to downcasting. For instance, the attributes list provides access to the Element object's attributes, but it would have no meaning for a ProcessingInstruction node. (Extracting pseudo-attributes from a processing instruction requires your application to parse the contents of the processing instruction.)

This interface also exposes all methods for querying, inserting, and removing objects from the document hierarchy. The Node interface makes it easier to build general-purpose tree-manipulation routines that are not dependent on specific document element types.

Attributes

The following attributes provide information about where the Node object is located within the document tree. These attributes are read-only, and methods are provided for inserting and removing nodes within the document tree.

attributes: NamedNodeMap

Has meaning only for Element objects. It provides access to a list of Attr objects in a NamedNodeMap. For all other object types, it returns null.

Java binding

```
public NamedNodeMap getAttributes( );
```

Java example

```
// List the attributes of an Element node
NamedNodeMap nnm = doc.getDocumentElement( ).getAttributes( );

if (nnm != null) {

    for (int i = 0; i < nnm.getLength( ); i++) {
        // print the attribute and value
        System.out.println(nnm.item(i).getNodeName( ) + " = \"" +
                           nnm.item(i).getNodeValue( ) + "\"");
    }
}
```

baseURI: DOMString[3]

Returns the effective base URI for the node in question, or null if none is available. The base URI is the absolute URI that should be used to properly resolve relative links from within an XML document.

Java binding
```
public String getBaseURI( );
```

childNodes: NodeList

Returns a NodeList containing a reference to every child of this Node.

Java binding
```
public NodeList getChildNodes( );
```

Java example
```
// List the text contents of an element
NodeList nlChildren = elem.getChildNodes( );
Node ndChild;

for (int iNode = 0; iNode < nlChildren.getLength( ); iNode++) {
    ndChild = nlChildren.item(iNode);

    if (ndChild.getNodeType( ) == Node.TEXT_NODE) {
        System.out.println(ndChild.getNodeValue( ));
    }
}
```

Dynamic Tree References

Throughout the DOM, several places return lists or collections of nodes that represent the current state of the document tree. These references are all live; any modifications to the document hierarcy, made by inserting or removing nodes, are reflected in the list immediately.

Whether due to multithreading or unforeseen side effects of procedure calls, the contents of the list being used could change. To reduce the likelihood of difficult-to-find bugs resulting from stale values, request values (such as the length of a list) directly from the NodeList or NamedNodeMap objects. This option is safer than storing values in intermediate variables.

firstChild: Node

Points to the head of the linked list of children of this node. If no child nodes exist, it returns null.

Java binding
```
public Node getFirstChild( );
```

Java example

```
// List the contents of a node
for (Node nd = ndDump.getFirstChild( ); nd != null;
    nd = nd.getNextSibling( )) {
    if (nd.getNodeValue( ) != null) {
        System.out.println(nd.getNodeValue( ));
    }
}
```

lastChild: Node

Returns a pointer to the end of a given Node object's linked list of child nodes. If the node does not have children, it returns null.

Java binding

```
public Node getLastChild( );
```

Java example

```
// List the value of a node in reverse order
for (Node nd = ndDump.getLastChild( ); nd != null;
    nd = nd.getPreviousSibling( )) {
    if (nd.getNodeValue( ) != null) {
        System.out.println(nd.getNodeValue( ));
    }
}
```

localName: DOMString[2]

Returns the local part of the fully qualified node name. This part of the name is to the right of the final : in a namespace-qualified name.

Java binding

```
public String getLocalName( );
```

namespaceURI: DOMString[2]

Represents the namespace URI given to this Node object at creation time; returns null if no namespace was given. The value is null if the node has been created by a createNodeType( ) method rather than a createNodeTypeNS( ) method.

Java binding

```
public String getNamespaceURI( );
```

nextSibling: Node

Returns the next node in the sibling list. If this node is the end of the list, nextSibling returns null.

Java binding

```
public Node getNextSibling( );
```

Java example

```
// List the contents of a node
for (Node nd = ndDump.getFirstChild( ); nd != null;
    nd = nd.getNextSibling( )) {
    if (nd.getNodeValue( ) != null) {
        System.out.println(nd.getNodeValue( ));
    }
}
```

nodeName: DOMString

Intended to represent the underlying DOM object's name. Depending on the object type, this attribute may map to another attribute of the object or a constant string, as listed in this table:

Object type	nodeName
Element	Tag name
Attr	Attribute name
Text	"#text"
CDATASection	"#cdata-section"
EntityReference	Name of entity referenced
Entity	Entity name
ProcessingInstruction	Target
Comment	"#comment"
Document	"#document"
DocumentType	Document type name
DocumentFragment	"#document-fragment"
Notation	Notation name

Java binding

```
public String getNodeName( );

// Print the document root tag name
Node ndDoc = (Node)doc.getDocumentElement( );
System.out.println("Document root element type: " + ndDoc.getNodeName( ));
```

nodeType: unsigned short

Contains a value that indicates the true type of the object referenced through the Node interface. The following table lists this attribute's possible values, along with the actual object types they represent:

Constant name	Object type	Constant value
ELEMENT_NODE	Element	1
ATTRIBUTE_NODE	Attr	2
TEXT_NODE	Text	3
CDATA_SECTION_NODE	CDATASection	4

Constant name	Object type	Constant value
ENTITY_REFERENCE_NODE	EntityReference	5
ENTITY_NODE	Entity	6
PROCESSING_INSTRUCTION_NODE	ProcessingInstruction	7
COMMENT_NODE	Comment	8
DOCUMENT_NODE	Document	9
DOCUMENT_TYPE_NODE	DocumentType	10
DOCUMENT_FRAGMENT_NODE	DocumentFragment	11
NOTATION_NODE	Notation	12

The parent-child and sibling relationships between nodes can be visualized as two doubly linked lists. One list links parents to children, while the other links nodes that exist at the same level.

Java binding

```
public short getNodeType( );
```

Java example

```
// Check to see if a node is an Element type node
public boolean isElement(Node nd) {
    return nd.getNodeType( ) == Node.ELEMENT_NODE;
}
```

nodeValue: DOMString

Intended to provide a reasonable string value for the underlying DOM object. Depending on the nodeType, this property may be read-only, read/write, or null. This table lists the values for the object types.

Object type	nodeValue
Element	null
Attr	Attribute value
Text	Text node content
CDATASection	CDATA section content
EntityReference	null
Entity	null
ProcessingInstruction	Entire content, excluding the target
Comment	Comment content
Document	null
DocumentType	null
DocumentFragment	null
Notation	null

Exceptions

NO_MODIFICATION_ALLOWED_ERR
>   Indicates the nodeValue attribute is read-only for this DOM object type.

DOMSTRING_SIZE_ERR
   This exception is raised if the value that would be returned is too large to be contained by a DOMString type in the given implementation.

Java bindings
```
public String getNodeValue( ) throws DOMException;
public void setNodeValue(String nodeValue) throws DOMException;
```

Java example
```
// If this node is a text node, make the value lowercase
if (nd.getNodeType( ) == Node.TEXT_NODE) {
    // make it lowercase
    nd.setNodeValue(nd.getNodeValue( ).toLowerCase( ));
}
```

ownerDocument: Document

Returns a reference to the Document used to create this Node object. Since the Document object is the only mechanism exposed for creating new nodes, even these newly created, empty nodes have the ownerDocument property set. This attribute can be null only for Document nodes and DocumentType nodes that are not yet part of a document. You can't move a node directly to another document; instead, you must import it. This property can be useful for checking where a node came from.

Java binding
```
public Document getOwnerDocument( );
```

Java example
```
// Add my two cents
Document doc = elem.getOwnerDocument( );
Text txtAdd = doc.createTextNode("My $.02");
elem.appendChild(txtAdd);
```

parentNode: Node

Provides a reference to the parent of this node. All node types—except Document, DocumentFragment, and Attr—may have a parent node. Every node within a Document hierarchy has a parent. Nodes that are not part of the document tree, such as new nodes and nodes removed from the document using the replaceChild( ) or removeChild( ) methods, have a parentNode attribute of null.

Java binding
```
Node getParentNode( );
```

Java example
```
// Unlink an element from the document tree
elem.getParentNode( ).removeChild(elem);
```

DOM
Reference

prefix: DOMString[2]

Represents the namespace prefix of this node, used for nodes that support namespace prefixes. For `ELEMENT_NODE` and `ATTRIBUTE_NODE` type nodes, changing the namespace prefix also affects the nodeName, tagName, and name attributes. Since these properties hold the qualified name of the node, changing the prefix also updates it.

Exceptions

INVALID_CHARACTER_ERR
> Raised if the prefix includes an illegal character.

NO_MODIFICATION_ALLOWED_ERR
> Indicates that the prefix attribute is read-only for this DOM object type.

NAMESPACE_ERR
> Raised if the prefix is malformed, according to the rules of namespace identifier formation. This exception is also raised if the namespaceURI attribute is null, or if an attempt was made to violate the XML rules of identifier formation. Such an attempt includes invalid use of the xml or xmlns identifier. For more information about namespaces, see Chapter 4.

Java bindings

```
public String getPrefix( );
public void setPrefix(String prefix) throws DOMException;
```

previousSibling: Node

Returns the preceding node in the sibling list. If this node is the head of the sibling list, it returns null.

Java binding

```
public Node getPreviousSibling( );
```

Java example

```
// List the value of a node in reverse order
for (Node nd = ndDump.getLastChild( ); nd != null;
     nd = nd.getPreviousSibling( )) {
   if (nd.getNodeValue( ) != null) {
       System.out.println(nd.getNodeValue( ));
   }
}
```

textContent: DOMString[3]

This attribute provides a quick method to get and set the textual content of nodes within the document tree. When used to retrieve text, it returns the contents of all descendant Text nodes without any whitespace normalization. Markup nodes (Attr, Element, and so forth) are ignored. When used to set text, it causes any child nodes to be removed and a single Text node to be created and linked in as the only child of the target node. The following table shows how the textContent attribute is constructed for the various node types:

Node type	Value
ELEMENT_NODE ATTRIBUTE_NODE ENTITY_NODE ENTITY_REFERENCE_NODE DOCUMENT_FRAGMENT_NODE	Combines the textContent of all child nodes, excluding nodes of type COMMENT_NODE and PROCESSING_INSTRUCTION_NODE, or an empty string if no child nodes
TEXT_NODE CDATA_SECTION_NODE COMMENT_NODE PROCESSING_INSTRUCTION_NODE	Returns the same value as the nodeValue attribute
DOCUMENT_NODE DOCUMENT_TYPE_NODE NOTATION_NODE	Returns null

Exceptions

NO_MODIFICATION_ALLOWED_ERR
> Thrown on set if node is read-only.

DOMSTRING_SIZE_ERR
> Thrown on get when length of text content would exceed the maximum allowable length of a DOMString on the implementation platform.

Java binding

```
public String getTextContent( );
public void setTextContent(String textContent) throws DOMException
```

Methods

The following methods are defined for Node interface objects:

---

appendChild: newChild

Appends the newChild node to the end of the child list. If newChild is already linked into the document tree, it is unlinked before the append is performed. This method returns a reference to the newChild node.

Argument

newChild: Node
> The node to append. If the node is a DocumentFragment node, the children of newChild are appended in sequence to the end of the node's child list.

Exceptions

HIERARCHY_REQUEST_ERR
> Raised if the insert operation violates at least one document structure rule. For instance, the node doesn't allow children or doesn't allow children of the newChild node type. This exception is also raised if the operation creates a circular reference (i.e., it tries to insert a node's parent as a node's child).

WRONG_DOCUMENT_ERR
> Raised if the newChild node is created in a different document than that of the new parent node.

DOM Reference

NO_MODIFICATION_ALLOWED_ERR
> Raised if the new parent node is read-only.

Java binding
```
public Node appendChild(Node newChild) throws DOMException;
```

Java example
```
// Move the first child to the end of the child node list
if (elem.getFirstChild( ) != null) {
    elem.appendChild( elem.getFirstChild( ) );
}
```

cloneNode: deep

Returns a copy of the node without a parent node. If the cloned node is specified as deep = true, the subtree under the node is also copied. Otherwise, the cloned node does not contain child nodes.

Argument
deep: boolean
> If true, child nodes are copied to the cloned node. If false, only the original node is copied.

Java binding
```
public Node cloneNode(boolean deep);
```

Java example
```
// Make a copy of this element and all children
elem.cloneNode(true);
```

compareDocumentPosition: other[3]

Compares the relative position of the node on which the method is invoked with the position of the other node. The return value is a bit mask that indicates the relative position between the two nodes in document order. The following table lists the bit mask members and their meanings:

Constant name	Value	Meaning
DOCUMENT_POSITION_DISCONNECTED	0x01	The two nodes are disconnected (do not share a common container ancestor) and cannot be compared.
DOCUMENT_POSITION_PRECEDING	0x02	The other node precedes the target node within the document.
DOCUMENT_POSITION_FOLLOWING	0x04	The other node follows the target node.
DOCUMENT_POSITION_CONTAINS	0x08	The other node contains the target node.
DOCUMENT_POSITION_CONTAINED_BY	0x010	The other node is contained by the target node.
DOCUMENT_POSITION_ IMPLEMENTATION_SPECIFIC	0x020	The relative positions are implementation-specific, such as in the case of disconnected nodes.

Argument
other: Node
> The other node to use in the position comparison.

Exception

NOT_SUPPORTED_ERR

Raised if the two nodes are from incompatible DOM implementations and their relative positions cannot be determined.

Java binding

```
public static final short DOCUMENT_POSITION_DISCONNECTED = 0x01;
public static final short DOCUMENT_POSITION_PRECEDING = 0x02;
public static final short DOCUMENT_POSITION_FOLLOWING = 0x04;
public static final short DOCUMENT_POSITION_CONTAINS = 0x08;
public static final short DOCUMENT_POSITION_CONTAINED_BY = 0x10;
public static final short DOCUMENT_POSITION_IMPLEMENTATION_SPECIFIC =
0x20;
public short compareDocumentPosition(Node other) throws DOMException;
```

getFeature: feature, version[3]

Provides a nonbinding–specific way to retrieve an object instance that implements a specific version of a given feature. Primarily used to access features beyond the scope of the DOM Core.

Arguments

feature: DOMString

The package name of the feature to retrieve.

version: DOMString

The DOM version level of the specified feature to retrieve.

Return value

Returns an object that implements the APIs for the specified features, or null if no implementation is available.

Java binding

```
public Object getFeature(String feature, String version);
```

getUserData: key[3]

This method is used to retrieve user-defined data from a node that was placed there using the setUserData( ) method. If no user data with the given key is found, the method returns null.

Argument

key: DOMString

The unique key associated with the user data to retrieve.

Java binding

```
public Object getUserData(String key);
```

hasAttributes( )

Indicates whether an Element node has any attributes. Returns true if the node has attributes; otherwise, it returns false.

```
public boolean hasAttributes( );
```

hasChildNodes( )

Provides a quick way to determine if a node has children. Returns true if the node has any children; otherwise, it returns false.

Java binding
```
public boolean hasChildNodes( );
```

insertBefore: newChild, refChild

Inserts the Node object newChild into the child list of the parent node that invokes it. The refChild parameter allows you to specify where to insert the new node in the list. If refChild is null, the new node is inserted at the end of the child list. (This behavior is the same as appendChild.) If it is not null, the new node is inserted into the list in front of the specified node. If the newChild node is already part of the document tree, it is unlinked before it is inserted in its new position. Also, if the newChild node references a DocumentFragment object, each of its children are inserted, in order, before the refChild node. A reference to the newChild node is returned.

Arguments

newChild: Node
> The new node to insert.

refChild: Node
> The node that follows the new node in the child list, or null if the new node is inserted at the end of the child list.

Exceptions

HIERARCHY_REQUEST_ERR
> Raised if the insert operation would violate at least one document structure rule. For instance, the node doesn't allow children or doesn't allow children of the newChild node type. This exception is also raised if the operation creates a circular reference (i.e., it tries to insert a node's parent as a node's child).

WRONG_DOCUMENT_ERR
> Raised if the newChild node was created in a document different than that of the new parent node.

NO_MODIFICATION_ALLOWED_ERR
> Raised if the new parent node is read-only.

NOT_FOUND_ERR
> Raised if the node pointed to by refChild is not a child of the node performing the insert.

NOT_SUPPORTED_ERR
> Raised if the DOM implementation in question doesn't support inserting DocumentType or Element nodes into a Document node.

```
public Node insertBefore(Node newChild, Node refChild)
            throws DOMException;
```

Java example
```
// Insert a new node at the head of the child list of a parent node
ndParent.insertBefore(ndNew, ndParent.getFirstChild( ));
```

isDefaultNamespace: namespaceURI[3]

This method returns true if the namespace URI given is the default namespace for this node, false if it is not.

Argument

namespaceURI: DOMString
  The namespace URI to check against the default namespace URI.

Java binding
```
public boolean isDefaultNamespace(String namespaceURI);
```

isEqualNode: arg[3]

This method compares the node on which the method is invoked with the node referenced by the other parameter. The two nodes are considered to be equal if:

- They are of the same type
- The following attributes are equal: nodeName, localName, namespaceURI, prefix, nodeValue
- The attributes maps are equal (contain the same number of nodes that are equal to one another)
- The childNodes lists are equal (the child node trees are identical, and each child passes this equality test with its counterpart in the other tree)
- For DocumentType nodes only: the publicId, systemId, internalSubset, entities, and notations attributes must be identical as well

The method returns true if the nodes pass all of the above tests; otherwise, it returns false.

Argument

arg: Node
  The node to use in the comparison.

Java binding
```
public boolean isEqualNode(Node arg);
```

isSameNode: other[3]

This method returns true if the node on which the method is invoked and the node referred to by the other parameter refer to the same Node object, false if they do not.

DOM Reference

Argument

other: Node
> The other node to use in the comparison.

Java binding
```
public boolean isSameNode(Node other);
```

---

isSupported: feature, version[2]

Checks to see if a particular DOM feature is available for this implementation. For more information about the feature names, see the "appendData: arg" method of the "CharacterData" object earlier in this chapter. This method returns true if the feature is available, false if it is not.

Arguments

feature: DOMString
> The name of the feature to test for. See details of the "appendData: arg" method of the "CharacterData" object for a list of this parameter's valid values.

version: DOMString
> The version number of the feature to test. For example, for DOM Level 2, Version 1, this string should be 2.0. If the version is not specified, this method tests for any version of the feature.

Java binding
```
public boolean supports(String feature, String version);
```

---

lookupNamespaceURI: prefix[3]

This method searches for the namespace URI associated with the given namespace prefix, starting with the node on which it is invoked. It then recursively searches parent nodes until the prefix is located. The return value is a DOMString containing the namespace URI associated with the prefix if it is found; otherwise, the method returns null.

Argument

prefix: DOMString
> The namespace prefix to be located.

Java binding
```
public String lookupNamespaceURI(String prefix);
```

---

lookupPrefix: namespaceURI[3]

This method searches for the namespace prefix assigned to the given namespace URI, starting with the node on which it is invoked; it then recursively searches parent nodes until a suitable prefix is located. The return value is a DOMString containing the prefix if it is found; otherwise, the method returns null. If more than one suitable prefix is found, the returned prefix is implementation-specific.

namespaceURI: DOMString
> The namespace URI of the prefix to be located.

Java binding

```
public String lookupPrefix(String namespaceURI);
```

normalize( )[2]

Recursively combines all adjacent Text nodes into a single node. It also removes empty Text nodes from the document tree. This operation is useful for operations that require absolute references within a document or if two documents must be compared.

Java binding

```
public void normalize( );
```

removeChild: oldchild

Unlinks the oldchild node from the child list of a given node and returns a reference to the now detached Node object.

Argument

oldchild: Node
> The node to be removed.

Exceptions

NO_MODIFICATION_ALLOWED_ERR
> Raised if the parent node is read-only.

NOT_FOUND_ERR
> Raised if the oldchild node is not a child of this node.

NOT_SUPPORTED_ERR
> Could be raised if the Document node of a DOM implementation in question doesn't support removing DocumentType or Element nodes.

Java binding

```
public Node removeChild(Node oldChild) throws DOMException;
```

Java example

```
// Unlink an element and all its children
// from the document tree
elem.getParentNode( ).removeChild(elem);
```

replaceChild: newChild, oldchild

Replaces the child node oldchild with newChild. If newChild is currently linked into the document tree, it is removed before the replace is performed. The method returns a reference to the oldchild node.

DOM Reference

Arguments

newChild: Node
> The node to be inserted.

oldchild: Node
> The node being replaced.

Exceptions

HIERARCHY_REQUEST_ERR
> Raised if the insert operation violates at least one document structure rule. For instance, the node doesn't allow children or doesn't allow children of the newChild node type. This exception is also raised if the operation creates a circular reference (i.e., it tries to insert a node's parent as a node's child).

WRONG_DOCUMENT_ERR
> Raised if the newChild node was created in a different document than the new parent node.

NO_MODIFICATION_ALLOWED_ERR
> Raised if the new parent node is read-only.

NOT_FOUND_ERR
> Raised if the node pointed to by oldchild is not a child of the node performing the replacement.

NOT_SUPPORTED_ERR
> Could be raised if the Document node of a DOM implementation in question doesn't support replacing DocumentType or Element nodes.

Java binding

```
public Node replaceChild(Node newChild, Node oldChild)
            throws DOMException;
```

Java example

```
// Replace an old node with a new one
ndOld.getParentNode( ).replaceChild(ndNew, ndOld);
```

---

setUserData: key, data, handler[3]

The setUserData( ) method (in conjunction with the getUserData( ) method) provides a facility for attaching application-specific information to DOM nodes. By using distinct key values, it is possible to attach multiple user objects to a single DOM node. The information to be attached must conform to the DOMUserData type and may include a data handler object that implements the UserDataHandler interface.

Arguments

key: DOMString
> The unique key to associate with the data parameter in the node's list of user data.

data: DOMUserData
> The user data to attach.

handler: UserDataHandler
> An object that will receive notification when various operations are performed on the DOM node in question.

```
public Object setUserData(String key, Object data,
UserDataHandler handler);
```

NodeList

The NodeList interface allows DOM classes to expose an ordered collection of nodes. A NodeList represents a read-only, zero-based array of Node objects. Since no mechanism exists for creating, adding, or removing nodes from a NodeList, DOM users cannot use this class as a general-purpose utility class.

Java example
```
// List the text contents of an element
NodeList nlChildren = elem.getChildNodes( );
Node ndChild;

for (int iNode = 0; iNode < nlChildren.getLength( ); iNode++) {
    ndChild = nlChildren.item(iNode);

    if (ndChild.getNodeType( ) == Node.TEXT_NODE) {
        System.out.println(ndChild.getNodeValue( ));
    }
}
```

Attribute
The NodeList interface defines one attribute:

length: unsigned long

The total number of Node objects in the list.

Java binding
```
public long getLength( );
```

Method
The NodeList interface defines one method:

item:index

Returns a reference to the Node object at position index or returns null if the index is invalid. If the index given is < 0 or >= the length attribute of the NodeList, this function returns null.

Argument
index: unsigned long
Zero-based index into the list of the Node to return.

Java binding
```
public Node item(long index);
```

DOM
Reference

ProcessingInstruction

This interface provides access to the contents of an XML processing instruction. Processing instructions provide a mechanism for embedding commands to an XML processing application that is in line with the XML content.

Java example

```
// Add an application-specific processing instruction
ProcessingInstruction pi = doc.createProcessingInstruction("my_app",
        "action=\"save\"");
```

Attributes

The interface defines two attributes:

---

data: DOMString

Returns the data portion of this processing instruction. The data portion is identified starting at the first nonwhitespace character after the target token and ending at the closing ?>.

Write exception

NO_MODIFICATION_ALLOWED_ERR
    Raised if the node is read-only.

Java bindings

```
public String getData( );
public void setData(String data) throws DOMException;
```

Java example

```
// Check the application's data attribute
if (pi.getTarget( ) == "MY_APPLICATION") {
    // check the data attribute for my own application-specific info
    if (pi.getData( ) == "CHECK_SIBLINGS") {
        // check the siblings
        ...
    }

    pi.setData("SIBLINGS_CHECKED");
}
```

---

target: DOMString

Returns the target portion of this processing instruction. The target is the first whitespace-delimited token within the processing-instruction block.

Processing instructions are meant to embed application-specific instructions for automatic content generation, parsing, etc., within the XML stream. The instruction's target portion is the flag that allows different processing applications to coexist. Applications that use processing instructions for formatting should ignore processing instructions they do not recognize.

```
    public String getTarget( );

    // Check to see if your application is targeted
    if (pi.getTarget( ) == "MY_APPLICATION") {
        // do my application-specific processing here
    }
```

Methods

ProcessingInstruction has no methods.

Text

Text nodes contain the nonmarkup character data contained within the XML document. After the XML document is parsed, exactly one Text node exists for each uninterrupted block of nonmarkup text.

Attributes

The Text interface defines the following attributes:

---

wholeText: DOMString[3]

This is a convenience attribute that returns all of the text from the target node as well as the text from adjacent Text nodes, in document order. For the purposes of this attribute, Text nodes are considered to be adjacent if they can be reached without exiting, entering, or skipping any of the following node types: Element, Comment, and ProcessingInstruction. Read-only.

Java binding
```
    public String getWholeText();
```

---

isElementContentWhitespace: boolean[3]

Returns true if the element contains only whitespace that XML validation has determined to be insignificant. Whitespace is insignificant if it does not belong to an element that has been declared to contain text or mixed content. Read-only.

Java binding
```
public boolean isElementContentWhitespace( );
```

Methods

The following methods are defined for the Text interface:

---

replaceWholeText: content[3]

This is a convenience method for replacing multiple adjacent text nodes with a single node that will contain the text passed in the content argument. The method returns a reference to the Text node that received the new content, or null if content contained a zero-length string.

DOM Reference

Argument

content: DOMString
New text content to be used for replacement.

Exceptions

NO_MODIFICATION_ALLOWED_ERR
Raised if the element is read-only.

---

splitText: offset

Splits a Text node into two adjacent Text nodes. The contents of the original node are divided at the given split offset, with the second substring used as the new node's value. The first substring remains in the original node. If the node is currently linked into the DOM tree, the new node with the split content becomes the next sibling of the original node. A new Text node containing the second part of the split data is returned.

Argument

offset (unsigned long)
Zero-based offset where the split occurs.

Exceptions

INDEX_SIZE_ERR
Raised if the offset given is < 0 and >= the length attribute.

NO_MODIFICATION_ALLOWED_ERR
Raised if the element is read-only.

Java binding

```
public Text splitText(long offset) throws DOMException;
```

Java example

```
// Make one Text node = doc.createTextNode("This text is split.");

// and split it
Text ndSplit = ndText.splitText(9);
```

Text is a subclass of the CharacterData interface. See the "CharacterData" interface section in this chapter for a list of applicable methods for accessing character data in nodes of this type.

TypeInfo[3]

Starting with the DOM Level 3, Element and Attr nodes include a schemaTypeInfo attribute that may reference a TypeInfo object. For valid XML documents, this object is used to provide information about the declared data type for a given element or attribute. Since the DOM is intended to be parser-independent, the contents of this object will vary depending on the type of schema validation that was performed (XML DTD, XML Schema, RELAX NG, and so forth). The DOM Level 3 Core specification includes detailed information about the significance of the typeName and typeNamespace attributes for both DTDs and XML Schemas.

Attributes

The `TypeInfo` object contains the following attributes:

typeName: DOMString[3]

Returns the declared type name of the element or attribute (varies depending on the validation method used). Returns `null` if the type name is unknown. Read-only.

Java binding
```
public String getTypeName( );
```

typeNamespace: DOMString[3]

Returns the namespace URI of the type given in by the `typeName` attribute. For example, an attribute validated against the type `xs:date` will have a namespace of `http://www.w3.org/2001/XMLSchema`. Read-only.

Java binding
```
public String getTypeNamespace( );
```

Method

The following method is defined for this object:

isDerivedFrom: typeNamespaceArg, typeNameArg, derivationMethod[3]

This method provides the capability to determine the relationship between the target data type and another data type (given by the `typeNameArg` and `typeNamespaceArg` arguments). This method returns `true` if the target type is derived from the given data type via one of the methods passed in using the `derivationMethod` bitmask argument; otherwise, it returns `false`. Currently, this method is only defined for use with XML Schema validation. For more information on type derivation methods in XML Schema, see Chapter 17.

Arguments

typeNamespaceArg: DOMString
> The namespace associated with the `typeNameArg` argument.

typeNameArg: DOMString
> The type name to be compared with the target type.

derivationMethod: unsigned long
> A bitmask that restricts which types of derivation the method will recognize. The valid bitmask values are listed below:

Constant name	Value	Meaning
DERIVATION_RESTRICTION	0x00000001	The target type is derived from the other type by restricting its possible values (e.g., a positive integer is derived from a signed integer by restricting it to nonnegative values).
DERIVATION_EXTENSION	0x00000002	The target type is derived from the other type by extending its possible values (e.g., a signed integer type would be an extension of an unsigned integer).

Constant name	Value	Meaning
DERIVATION_UNION	0x00000004	The target type is partially derived from the other type by its inclusion in a union.
DERIVATION_LIST	0x00000008	The target type is a list of items of the other type.

Java binding

```
public boolean isDerivedFrom(String typeNamespaceArg,
        String typeNameArg, int derivationMethod);
```

UserDataHandler[3]

The Node.setUserData() method provides the capability for the programmer to register a callback object that will be notified when various operations are performed on the node in question. These callback objects must implement this interface to receive those notifications.

Attributes

The UserDataHandler interface has no attributes.

Method

The following method is defined for this interface:

handle: operation, key, data, src, dst[3]

This method is called whenever the Node object to which the parent UserDataHandler-derived object is attached is imported or cloned. This method is to be implemented by users of the DOM who wish to receive notifications when watched Node objects are manipulated.

 When implementing the handle() method, it is important to catch any exceptions that might be thrown so that they will not be raised within the calling DOM code. The behavior within the DOM is undefined if an exception is raised within this method.

Arguments

operation: unsigned short
    The type of operation that occurred, based on the following values:

Constant name	Value	Meaning
NODE_CLONED	1	The watched node was cloned using Node.cloneNode( ).
NODE_IMPORTED	2	The watched node was imported using Document.importNode( ).
NODE_DELETED	3	The node was deleted, which is not necessarily reliable in environments that have no explicit delete operator (such as Java).
NODE_RENAMED	4	The node was renamed using Document.renameNode( ).
NODE_ADOPTED	5	The watched node was adopted using Document.adoptNode( ).

key: DOMString
> The user-defined key from the `Node.setUserData()` method for which the `handle()` method is being called.

data: DOMUserData
> The user data corresponding to the key argument that was originally set using the `Node.setUserData()` method.

src: Node
> The node being cloned, adopted, imported, or renamed. This argument will be `null` if the node is being deleted.

dst: Node
> The newly cloned or imported node, or `null` if no new node was created.

Java binding
```
public boolean isDerivedFrom(String typeNamespaceArg,
        String typeNameArg, int derivationMethod);
```

26

SAX Reference

SAX, the Simple API for XML, is an event-based API used to parse XML documents. David Megginson, SAX's original author, placed SAX in the public domain. SAX is bundled with all parsers that implement the API, including Xerces, MSXML, Crimson, the Oracle XML Parser for Java, and Ælfred. However, you can also get it and the full source code from *http://sax.sourceforge.net/*.

SAX was originally defined as a Java API and is intended primarily for parsers written in Java, so this chapter will focus on its Java implementation. However, its port to other object-oriented languages, such as C++, C#, Python, Perl, and Eiffel, is common and usually quite similar.

This chapter covers SAX2 exclusively. In 2004, all major parsers that support SAX support SAX2. The major change from SAX1 to SAX2 was the addition of namespace support. This addition necessitated changing the names and signatures of almost every method and class in SAX. The old SAX1 methods and classes are still available, but they're now deprecated and shouldn't be used.

SAX 2.0.2 is a minor update to SAX2 that add a few extra optional classes, features, and properties without really affecting the core API. They were carefully designed to be backward compatible with SAX 2.0 and 2.0.1. Some, but not all, current parsers support SAX 2.0.2. When something in this chapter is only available in SAX 2.0.2, it will be clearly noted.

The org.xml.sax Package

The org.xml.sax package contains the core interfaces and classes that comprise the Simple API for XML.

The Attributes Interface

An object that implements the Attributes interface represents a list of attributes on a start-tag. The order of attributes in the list is not guaranteed to match the order in the document itself. Attributes objects are passed as arguments to the startElement( ) method of ContentHandler. You can access particular attributes in three ways:

- By number
- By namespace URI and local name
- By qualified name

This list does not include namespace declaration attributes (xmlns and xmlns:*prefix*) unless the http://xml.org/sax/features/namespace-prefixes feature is true. It is false by default.

If the http://xml.org/sax/features/namespace-prefixes feature is false, qualified name access may not be available; if the http://xml.org/sax/features/namespaces feature is false, local names and namespace URIs may not be available.

```
package org.xml.sax;

public interface Attributes {

    public int    getLength( );
    public String getURI(int index);
    public String getLocalName(int index);
    public String getQName(int index);
    public int    getIndex(String uri, String localName);
    public int    getIndex(String qualifiedName);
    public String getType(int index);
    public String getType(String uri, String localName);
    public String getType(String qualifiedName);
    public String getValue(String uri, String localName);
    public String getValue(String qualifiedName);
    public String getValue(int index);

}
```

The ContentHandler Interface

ContentHandler is the key piece of SAX. Almost every SAX program needs to use this interface. ContentHandler is a callback interface. An instance of this interface is passed to the parser via the setContentHandler( ) method of XMLReader. As the parser reads the document, it invokes the methods in its ContentHandler to tell the program what's in the document:

```
package org.xml.sax;

public interface ContentHandler {

    public void setDocumentLocator(Locator locator);
    public void startDocument( ) throws SAXException;
    public void endDocument( ) throws SAXException;
    public void startPrefixMapping(String prefix, String uri)
      throws SAXException;
```

```
    public void endPrefixMapping(String prefix) throws SAXException;
    public void startElement(String namespaceURI, String localName,
      String qualifiedName, Attributes atts) throws SAXException;
    public void endElement(String namespaceURI, String localName,
      String qualifiedName) throws SAXException;
    public void characters(char[ ] text, int start, int length)
      throws SAXException;
    public void ignorableWhitespace(char[ ] text, int start, int length)
      throws SAXException;
    public void processingInstruction(String target, String data)
      throws SAXException;
    public void skippedEntity(String name) throws SAXException;

}
```

The DTDHandler Interface

After passing an instance of the DTDHandler interface to the setDTDHandler( ) method of
XMLReader, the program will receive notification of notation and unparsed entity declarations in the DTD. You can store this information and use it later to retrieve
information about the unparsed entities you encounter while reading the document:

```
package org.xml.sax;

public interface DTDHandler {

    public void notationDecl(String name, String publicID, String systemID)
      throws SAXException;
    public void unparsedEntityDecl(String name, String publicID,
      String systemID, String notationName) throws SAXException;

}
```

The EntityResolver Interface

By passing an instance of the EntityResolver interface to the setEntityResolver( )
method of XMLReader, you can intercept parser requests for external entities, such as
the external DTD subset or external parameter entities, and redirect those requests in
order to substitute different entities. For example, you could replace a reference to a
remote copy of a standard DTD with a local one or find the sources for particular
public IDs in a catalog.

```
package org.xml.sax;

public interface EntityResolver {

    public InputSource resolveEntity(String publicID, String systemID)
      throws SAXException, IOException;

}
```

The ErrorHandler Interface

By passing an instance of the ErrorHandler interface to the setErrorHandler( ) method of XMLReader, you can provide custom handling for particular classes of errors detected by the parser. For example, you can choose to stop parsing when a validity error is detected by throwing an exception from the error( ) method. The SAXParseException passed to each of the three methods in this interface provides details about the specific cause and location of the error:

```
package org.xml.sax;

public interface ErrorHandler {

    public void warning(SAXParseException exception) throws SAXException;
    public void error(SAXParseException exception) throws SAXException;
    public void fatalError(SAXParseException exception)
      throws SAXException;

}
```

Warnings represent possible problems noticed by the parser that are not technically violations of XML's well-formedness or validity rules. For instance, a parser might issue a warning if an xml:lang attribute's value was not a legal ISO-639 language code. The most common kind of error is a validity problem. The parser should report it, but it should also continue processing. A fatal error violates well-formedness. The parser should not continue parsing after reporting such an error. Some parsers report violations of namespace well-formedness as fatal errors. Others report these as nonfatal errors.

The Locator Interface

Unlike most other interfaces in the org.xml.sax package, the Locator interface does not have to be implemented. Instead, the parser has the option to provide an implementation. If it does so, it passes its implementation to the setDocumentLocator( ) method in the ContentHandler instance before it calls startDocument( ). You can save a reference to this object in a field in your ContentHandler class, like this:

```
private Locator locator;

public void setDocumentLocator(Locator locator) {
    this.locator = locator;
}
```

Once you've found the locator, you can then use it inside any other ContentHandler method, such as startElement( ) or characters( ), to determine in exactly which document and at which line and column the event took place. For instance, the locator allows you to determine that a particular start-tag began on the third column of the document's seventeenth line at the URL *http://www.slashdot.org/slashdot.xml*:

```
package org.xml.sax;

public interface Locator {
```

SAX Reference

```
    public String getPublicId( );
    public String getSystemId( );
    public int    getLineNumber( );
    public int    getColumnNumber( );

}
```

The XMLFilter Interface

An XMLFilter is an XMLReader that obtains its events from another parent XMLReader, rather than reading it from a text source such as InputStream. Filters can sit between the original source XML and the application and modify data in the original source before passing it to the application. Implementing this interface directly is unusual. It is almost always much easier to use the more complete org.xml.sax.helpers. XMLFilterImpl class instead.

```
package org.xml.sax;

public interface XMLFilter extends XMLReader {

    public void      setParent(XMLReader parent);
    public XMLReader getParent( );

}
```

The XMLReader Interface

The XMLReader interface represents the parser that reads XML documents. You generally do not implement this interface yourself. Instead, use the org.xml.sax.helpers. XMLReaderFactory class to build a parser-specific implementation. Then use this parser's various setter methods to configure the parsing process. Finally, invoke the parse( ) method to read the document, while calling back to methods in your own implementations of ContentHandler, ErrorHandler, EntityResolver, and DTDHandler as the document is read:

```
package org.xml.sax;

public interface XMLReader {

    public boolean getFeature(String name)
      throws SAXNotRecognizedException, SAXNotSupportedException;
    public void    setFeature(String name, boolean value)
      throws SAXNotRecognizedException, SAXNotSupportedException;
    public Object  getProperty(String name)
      throws SAXNotRecognizedException, SAXNotSupportedException;

    public void           setProperty(String name, Object value)
      throws SAXNotRecognizedException, SAXNotSupportedException;
    public void           setEntityResolver(EntityResolver resolver);
    public EntityResolver getEntityResolver( );
    public void           setDTDHandler(DTDHandler handler);
    public DTDHandler     getDTDHandler( );
```

```
public void            setContentHandler(ContentHandler handler);
public ContentHandler  getContentHandler( );
public void            setErrorHandler(ErrorHandler handler);
public ErrorHandler    getErrorHandler( );

public void parse(InputSource input) throws IOException, SAXException;
public void parse(String systemID) throws IOException, SAXException;

}
```

The InputSource Class

The InputSource class is an abstraction of a data source from which the raw bytes of an XML document are read. It can wrap a system ID, a public ID, an InputStream, or a Reader. When given an InputSource, the parser tries to read from the Reader. If the InputSource does not have a Reader, the parser will try to read from the InputStream using the specified encoding. If no encoding is specified, then it will try to autodetect the encoding by reading the XML declaration. Finally, if neither a Reader nor an InputStream has been set, then the parser will open a connection to the URL given by the system ID.

```
package org.xml.sax;

public class InputSource {

    public InputSource( );
    public InputSource(String systemID);
    public InputSource(InputStream byteStream);
    public InputSource(Reader reader);

    public void            setPublicId(String publicID);
    public String          getPublicId( );
    public void            setSystemId(String systemID);
    public String          getSystemId( );
    public void            setByteStream(InputStream byteStream);
    public InputStream     getByteStream( );
    public void            setEncoding(String encoding);
    public String          getEncoding( );
    public void            setCharacterStream(Reader reader);
    public Reader          getCharacterStream( );

}
```

The SAXException Class

Most exceptions thrown by SAX methods are instances of the SAXException class or one of its subclasses. The single exception to this rule is the parse( ) method of XMLReader, which may throw a raw IOException if a purely I/O-related error occurs; for example, if a socket is broken before the parser finishes reading the document from the network.

Besides the usual exception methods such as getMessage( ) and printStackTrace( ) that SAXException inherits from or overrides in its superclasses, SAXException adds a getException( ) method to return the nested exception that caused the SAXException to be thrown in the first place.

```
package org.xml.sax;

public class SAXException extends Exception {

    public SAXException(String message);
    public SAXException(Exception ex);
    public SAXException(String message, Exception ex);

    public String      getMessage( );
    public Exception getException( );
    public String      toString( );

}
```

SAXParseException

If the parser detects a well-formedness error while reading a document, it throws a SAXParseException, a subclass of SAXException. SAXParseExceptions are also passed as arguments to the methods of the ErrorHandler interface, where you can decide whether you want to throw them.

Besides the methods it inherits from its superclasses, this class adds methods to get the line number, column number, system ID, and public ID of the document where the error was detected:

```
package org.xml.sax;

public class SAXParseException extends SAXException {

    public SAXParseException(String message, Locator locator);
    public SAXParseException(String message, Locator locator,
     Exception e);
    public SAXParseException(String message, String publicID,
     String systemID, int lineNumber, int columnNumber);
    public SAXParseException(String message, String publicID,
     String systemID, int lineNumber, int columnNumber, Exception e);

    public String getPublicId( );
    public String getSystemId( );
    public int      getLineNumber( );
    public int      getColumnNumber( );

}
```

SAXNotRecognizedException

A SAXNotRecognizedException is thrown if you attempt to set a property or feature the parser does not recognize. Besides the constructors, all its methods are inherited from superclasses:

```
package org.xml.sax;

public class SAXNotRecognizedException extends SAXException {

  public SAXNotRecognizedException( );
  public SAXNotRecognizedException(String message);

}
```

SAXNotSupportedException

A SAXNotSupportedException is thrown if you attempt to set a property or feature that the parser recognizes, but either cannot set or get or does not allow the particular value you're trying to set it to. Besides the constructors, all of its methods are inherited from superclasses:

```
package org.xml.sax;

public class SAXNotSupportedException extends SAXException {

  public SAXNotSupportedException( );
  public SAXNotSupportedException(String message);

}
```

The org.xml.sax.helpers Package

The org.xml.sax.helpers package contains support classes for the core SAX classes. These include factory classes used to build instances of particular org.xml. sax interfaces and default implementations of those interfaces.

The AttributesImpl Class

AttributesImpl is a default implementation of the Attributes interface that SAX parsers and filters may use. Besides the methods of the Attributes interface, this class offers manipulator methods so the list of attributes can be modified or reused. These methods allow you to take a persistent snapshot of an Attributes object in startElement( ) and construct or modify an Attributes object in a SAX driver or filter:

```
package org.xml.sax.helpers;

public class AttributesImpl implements Attributes {

  public AttributesImpl( );
  public AttributesImpl(Attributes atts);

  public int      getLength( );
```

SAX Reference

```
    public String getURI(int index);
    public String getLocalName(int index);
    public String getQName(int index);
    public String getType(int index);
    public String getValue(int index);
    public int    getIndex(String uri, String localName);
    public int    getIndex(String qualifiedName);
    public String getType(String uri, String localName);
    public String getType(String qualifiedName);
    public String getValue(String uri, String localName);
    public String getValue(String qualifiedName);
    public void   clear();
    public void   setAttributes(Attributes atts);
    public void   addAttribute(String uri, String localName,
     String qualifiedName, String type, String value);
    public void   setAttribute(int index, String uri, String localName,
     String qualifiedName, String type, String value);
    public void   removeAttribute(int index)
    public void   setURI(int index, String uri)
    public void   setLocalName(int index, String localName)
    public void   setQName(int index, String qualifiedName);
    public void   setType(int index, String type);
    public void   setValue(int index, String value);

}
```

The DefaultHandler Class

DefaultHandler is a convenience class that implements the EntityResolver, DTDHandler, ContentHandler, and ErrorHandler interfaces with do-nothing methods. You can subclass DefaultHandler and override methods for events to which you actually want to respond. You never have to use this class. You can always implement the interfaces directly instead. The pattern is similar to the adapter classes in the AWT, such as MouseAdapter and WindowAdapter:

```
package org.xml.sax.helpers;

public class DefaultHandler
 implements EntityResolver, DTDHandler, ContentHandler, ErrorHandler {

  // Default implementation of the EntityResolver interface.
  public InputSource resolveEntity(String publicID, String systemID)
   throws SAXException {
    return null;
  }

  // Default implementation of the DTDHandler interface.
  public void notationDecl(String name, String publicID, String systemID)
   throws SAXException { }
  public void unparsedEntityDecl(String name, String publicID,
   String systemID, String notationName) throws SAXException{ }
```

```
        // Default implementation of the ContentHandler interface.
        public void setDocumentLocator(Locator locator) { }
        public void startDocument( ) throws SAXException { }
        public void endDocument( ) throws SAXException { }
        public void startPrefixMapping(String prefix, String uri)
          throws SAXException { }
        public void endPrefixMapping(String prefix) throws SAXException { }
        public void startElement(String uri, String localName,
          String qualifiedName, Attributes attributes) throws SAXException { }
        public void endElement(String uri, String localName,
          String qualifiedName) throws SAXException { }
        public void characters(char[ ] text, int start, int length)
          throws SAXException { }
        public void ignorableWhitespace(char[ ] whitespace, int start,
          int length) throws SAXException { }
        public void processingInstruction(String target, String data)
          throws SAXException { }
        public void skippedEntity(String name) throws SAXException { }

        // Default implementation of the ErrorHandler interface.
        public void warning(SAXParseException ex) throws SAXException { }
        public void error(SAXParseException ex) throws SAXException { }
        public void fatalError(SAXParseException ex) throws SAXException {
          throw ex;
        }

    }
```

The LocatorImpl Class

LocatorImpl is a default implementation of the Locator interface for the convenience of parser writers. You probably won't need to use it directly. Besides the constructors, it adds setter methods to set the public ID, system ID, line number, and column number returned by the getter methods declared in Locator:

```
    package org.xml.sax.helpers;

    public class LocatorImpl implements Locator {

        public LocatorImpl( );
        public LocatorImpl(Locator locator);

        public String getPublicId( );
        public String getSystemId( );
        public int    getLineNumber( );
        public int    getColumnNumber( );
        public void   setPublicId(String publicID);
        public void   setSystemId(String systemID);
        public void   setLineNumber(int lineNumber);
        public void   setColumnNumber(int columnNumber);

    }
```

The NamespaceSupport Class

NamespaceSupport provides a stack that can track the namespaces in scope at various points in the document. To use it, push a new context at the beginning of each element's namespace mappings, and pop it at the end of each element. Each startPrefixMapping( ) invocation should call declarePrefix( ) to add a new mapping to the NamespaceSupport object. Then at any point where you need to figure out to which URI a prefix is bound, you can call getPrefix( ). The empty string indicates the default namespace. The getter methods can then tell you the prefix that is mapped to any URI or the URI that is mapped to any prefix at each point in the document. If you reuse the same NamespaceSupport object for multiple documents, be sure to call reset( ) between documents.

```
package org.xml.sax.helpers;

public class NamespaceSupport {

  public final static String XMLNS="http://www.w3.org/XML/1998/namespace";

  public NamespaceSupport( );

  public void        reset( );
  public void        pushContext( );
  public void        popContext( );
  public boolean     declarePrefix(String prefix, String uri);
  public String[ ]   processName(String qualifiedName, String[ ] parts,
    boolean isAttribute);
  public String      getURI(String prefix);
  public Enumeration getPrefixes( );
  public String      getPrefix(String uri);
  public Enumeration getPrefixes(String uri);
  public Enumeration getDeclaredPrefixes( );

}
```

The ParserAdapter Class

The ParserAdapter class uses the adapter design pattern to convert a SAX1 org.xml. sax.Parser object into a SAX2 org.xml.sax.XMLReader object. As more parsers support SAX2, this class becomes less necessary. Note that some SAX2 features are not available through an adapted SAX1 parser. For instance, a parser created with this adapter does not report skipped entities and does not support most features and properties, not even the core features and properties:

```
package org.xml.sax.helpers;

public class ParserAdapter implements XMLReader, DocumentHandler {

  public ParserAdapter( ) throws SAXException;
  public ParserAdapter(Parser parser);

  // Implementation of org.xml.sax.XMLReader.
```

```
public void           setFeature(String name, boolean state)
 throws SAXNotRecognizedException, SAXNotSupportedException;
public boolean        getFeature(String name)
 throws SAXNotRecognizedException, SAXNotSupportedException;
public void           setProperty(String name, Object value)
 throws SAXNotRecognizedException, SAXNotSupportedException;
public Object         getProperty(String name)
 throws SAXNotRecognizedException, SAXNotSupportedException;
public void           setEntityResolver(EntityResolver resolver);
public EntityResolver getEntityResolver();
public void           setDTDHandler(DTDHandler handler);
public DTDHandler     getDTDHandler();
public void           setContentHandler(ContentHandler handler);
public ContentHandler getContentHandler();
public void           setErrorHandler(ErrorHandler handler);
public ErrorHandler   getErrorHandler();
public void parse(String systemID) throws IOException, SAXException;
public void parse(InputSource input) throws IOException, SAXException;

// Implementation of org.xml.sax.DocumentHandler.
public void setDocumentLocator(Locator locator);
public void startDocument() throws SAXException;
public void endDocument() throws SAXException;
public void startElement(String qualifiedName,
 AttributeList qualifiedAttributes) throws SAXException;
public void endElement(String qualifiedName) throws SAXException;
public void characters(char[] text, int start, int length)
 throws SAXException;
public void ignorableWhitespace(char[] text, int start, int length)
 throws SAXException;
public void processingInstruction(String target, String data)
 throws SAXException;

}
```

The XMLFilterImpl Class

XMLFilterImpl is invaluable for implementing XML filters correctly. An instance of this class sits between an XMLReader and the client application's event handlers. It receives messages from the reader and passes them to the application unchanged, and vice versa. However, by subclassing this class and overriding particular methods, you can change the events that are sent before the application gets to see them. You chain a filter to an XMLReader by passing the reader as an argument to the filter's constructor. When parsing, you invoke the filter's parse() method, not the reader's parse() method.

```
package org.xml.sax.helpers;

public class XMLFilterImpl implements XMLFilter, EntityResolver,
DTDHandler, ContentHandler, ErrorHandler {

 public XMLFilterImpl();
 public XMLFilterImpl(XMLReader parent);
```

```
// Implementation of org.xml.sax.XMLFilter
public void        setParent(XMLReader parent);
public XMLReader getParent();

// Implementation of org.xml.sax.XMLReader
public void          setFeature(String name, boolean state)
 throws SAXNotRecognizedException, SAXNotSupportedException;
public boolean       getFeature(String name)
 throws SAXNotRecognizedException, SAXNotSupportedException;
public void          setProperty(String name, Object value)
 throws SAXNotRecognizedException, SAXNotSupportedException;
public Object        getProperty(String name)
 throws SAXNotRecognizedException, SAXNotSupportedException;
public void          setEntityResolver(EntityResolver resolver);
public EntityResolver getEntityResolver();
public void          setDTDHandler(DTDHandler handler);
public DTDHandler    getDTDHandler();
public void          setContentHandler(ContentHandler handler);
public ContentHandler getContentHandler();
public void          setErrorHandler(ErrorHandler handler);
public ErrorHandler  getErrorHandler();
public void parse(InputSource input) throws SAXException, IOException;
public void parse(String systemID) throws SAXException, IOException

// Implementation of org.xml.sax.EntityResolver
public InputSource resolveEntity(String publicID, String systemID)
 throws SAXException, IOException;

// Implementation of org.xml.sax.DTDHandler
public void notationDecl(String name, String publicID, String systemID)
 throws SAXException;
public void unparsedEntityDecl(String name, String publicID,
 String systemID, String notationName) throws SAXException;

// Implementation of org.xml.sax.ContentHandler
public void setDocumentLocator(Locator locator);
public void startDocument() throws SAXException;
public void endDocument() throws SAXException;
public void startPrefixMapping(String prefix, String uri)
 throws SAXException;
public void endPrefixMapping(String prefix) throws SAXException;
public void startElement(String namespaceURI, String localName,
 String qualifiedName, Attributes atts) throws SAXException;
public void endElement(String namespaceURI, String localName,
 String qualifiedName) throws SAXException;
public void characters(char[] text, int start, int length)
 throws SAXException;
public void ignorableWhitespace(char[] text, int start, int length)
 throws SAXException;
public void processingInstruction(String target, String data)
 throws SAXException;
public void skippedEntity(String name) throws SAXException;
```

```
// Implementation of org.xml.sax.ErrorHandler
public void warning(SAXParseException ex) throws SAXException;
public void error(SAXParseException ex) throws SAXException;
public void fatalError(SAXParseException ex) throws SAXException;


}
```

The XMLReaderAdapter Class

XMLReaderAdapter is the reverse of ParserAdapter; it uses the Adapter design pattern to adapt a SAX2 XMLReader to a SAX1 Parser. This lets you use SAX2 parsers for legacy programs written to a SAX1 interface:

```
package org.xml.sax.helpers;

public class XMLReaderAdapter implements Parser, ContentHandler {

    public XMLReaderAdapter( ) throws SAXException;
    public XMLReaderAdapter(XMLReader reader);

    // Implementation of org.xml.sax.Parser.
    public void setLocale(Locale locale) throws SAXException;
    public void setEntityResolver(EntityResolver resolver);
    public void setDTDHandler(DTDHandler handler);
    public void setDocumentHandler(DocumentHandler handler);
    public void setErrorHandler(ErrorHandler handler);
    public void parse(String systemID) throws IOException, SAXException;
    public void parse(InputSource input) throws IOException, SAXException

    // Implementation of org.xml.sax.ContentHandler.
    public void setDocumentLocator(Locator locator);
    public void startDocument( ) throws SAXException;
    public void endDocument( ) throws SAXException;
    public void startPrefixMapping(String prefix, String uri)
      throws SAXException;
    public void endPrefixMapping(String prefix) throws SAXException;
    public void startElement(String namespaceURI, String localName,
      String qualifiedName, Attributes atts) throws SAXException;
    public void endElement(String namespaceURI, String localName,
      String qualifiedName) throws SAXException;
    public void characters(char[ ] text, int start, int length)
      throws SAXException;
    public void ignorableWhitespace(char[ ] text, int start, int length)
      throws SAXException;
    public void processingInstruction(String target, String data)
      throws SAXException;
    public void skippedEntity(String name) throws SAXException;


}
```

SAX Reference

The XMLReaderFactory Class

XMLReaderFactory creates XMLReader instances in a parser-independent manner. The noargs createXMLReader() method instantiates the class named by the org.xml.sax. driver system property. The other createXMLReader() method instantiates the class named by its argument. This argument should be a fully packaged qualified name, such as org.apache.xerces.parsers.SAXParser:

```
package org.xml.sax.helpers;

public final class XMLReaderFactory {

    public static XMLReader createXMLReader() throws SAXException;
    public static XMLReader createXMLReader(String className)
      throws SAXException;

}
```

SAX Features and Properties

Absolute URIs are used to name a SAX parser's properties and features. Features have a Boolean value; that is, for each parser, a recognized feature is either true or false. Properties have object values. SAX 2.0 defines six core features and two core properties that parsers should recognize. SAX 2.0.2 adds nine more. In addition, most parsers add features and properties to this list.

SAX Core Features

All SAX parsers should recognize six core features. Of these six, two (http://xml.org/ sax/features/namespaces and http://xml.org/sax/features/namespace-prefixes) must be implemented by all conformant processors. The other four are optional and may not be implemented by all parsers:

http://xml.org/sax/features/namespaces
> When true, this feature indicates that the startElement() and endElement() methods provide namespace URIs and local names for elements and attributes. When false, the parser provides prefixed element and attribute names to the startElement() and endElement() methods. If a parser does not provide something it is not required to provide, then that value will be set to the empty string. However, most parsers provide all three (URI, local name, and prefixed name), regardless of the value of this feature. This feature is true by default.

http://xml.org/sax/features/namespace-prefixes
> When true, this feature indicates that xmlns and xmlns:*prefix* attributes will be included in the attributes list passed to startElement(). When false, these attributes are omitted. Furthermore, if this feature is true, then the parser will provide the prefixed names for elements and attributes. The default is false unless http://xml.org/sax/features/namespaces is false, in which case this feature

defaults to true. You can set both `http://xml.org/sax/features/namespaces` and `http://xml.org/sax/features/namespace-prefixes` to true to guarantee that local names, namespace URIs, and prefixed names are all available.

`http://xml.org/sax/features/string-interning`
When this feature is true, all element names, prefixes, attribute names, namespace URIs, and local names are internalized using the intern( ) method of `java.lang.String`; that is, equal names compare equally when using ==.

`http://xml.org/sax/features/validation`
When true, the parser validates the documents against its DTD. When false, it doesn't. The default is false for most parsers. If you turn on this feature, you'll probably also want to register an ErrorHandler with the XMLReader to receive notice of any validity errors.

`http://xml.org/sax/features/external-general-entities`
When true, the parser resolves external parsed general entities. When false, it doesn't. The default is true for most parsers that can resolve external entities. Turning on validation automatically activates this feature because validation requires resolving external entities.

`http://xml.org/sax/features/external-parameter-entities`
When true, the parser resolves external parameter entities. When false, it doesn't. Turning on validation automatically activates this feature because validation requires resolving external entities.

SAX 2.0.2 adds eight more standard features, although as with the SAX 2.0 features, parsers are not required to support any of these:

`http://xml.org/sax/features/lexical-handler/parameter-entities`
When true, the parser reports parameter entity boundaries to the LexicalHandler using the startEntity( ) and endEntity( ) methods. The default behavior is implementation-dependent.

`http://xml.org/sax/features/is-standalone`
Indicates whether the document's XML declaration specified standalone="yes". This feature is read-only and can be inspected only after startDocument( ) has returned and before the parser has finished reading the document.

`http://xml.org/sax/features/resolve-dtd-uris`
When true, relative URIs found in notation declarations, unparsed entity declarations, and external entity declarations will be converted to absolute URIs before being reported to the methods of DTDHandler and DeclHandler. When false, relative URIs are not absolutized. The default is true. Relative URIs are never absolutized before being passed to the methods of LexicalHandler or EntityResolver.

`http://xml.org/sax/features/unicode-normalization-checking`
When true, the parser checks that text content is in Unicode Normalization Form C, as recommended by the XML 1.1 specification. Any normalization problems found are reported to the registered ErrorHandler using the nonfatal error( ) method. The default is false, do not check for normalization.

`http://xml.org/sax/features/use-attributes2`
When true, the Attributes object passed to startElement( ) can be cast to Attributes2, a subclass of Attributes with extra methods to determine whether an attribute was declared in the DTD, specified in the instance document, or both.

SAX Reference

http://xml.org/sax/features/use-entityresolver2

When true, the parser will use the extra methods defined in EntityResolver2 if you pass an EntityResolver2 object to setEntityResolver( ).

http://xml.org/sax/features/use-locator2

When true, the Locator object passed to setLocator( ) can be cast to Locator2, with extra methods to determine the character encoding and XML version of the entity or document.

http://xml.org/sax/features/xmlns-uris

When true, this feature indicates that the parser adheres to a backward incompatible revision of the namespaces specification that binds the xmlns prefix to the namespace URI http://www.w3.org/2000/xmlns/. The default is false, do not bind the xmlns prefix to any namespace URI.

SAX Core Properties

SAX defines four core properties, although implementations are not required to support them:

http://xml.org/sax/properties/declaration-handler

This property's value is an org.xml.sax.ext.DeclHandler object to which the parser will report ELEMENT, ATTLIST, and parsed ENTITY declarations found in the document's DTD.

http://xml.org/sax/properties/lexical-handler

This property's value is an org.xml.sax.ext.LexicalHandler object to which the parser reports comments, CDATA section boundaries, and entity boundaries.

http://xml.org/sax/properties/dom-node

This property's value is an org.w3c.dom.Node object that represents the current node the parser is visiting.

http://xml.org/sax/properties/xml-string

This property's value is a java.lang.String object containing the characters that were the source for the current event. As of mid-2004, no parsers are known to implement this property.

SAX 2.0.2 adds one more standard property:

http://xml.org/sax/properties/document-xml-version

This property's value is a java.lang.String containing the version of the XML document. It would normally be either 1.0 or 1.1. This is a read-only property.

The org.xml.sax.ext Package

The org.xml.sax.ext package provides optional interfaces that parsers may use to provide further functionality. Not all parsers support these interfaces, although most major ones do.

The Attributes2 Interface

SAX 2.0.2 adds an `Attributes2` subclass of `Attributes` that provides extra methods to determine whether a given attribute was declared in the DTD and/or specified in the instance document (as opposed to being defaulted in from the DTD). A parser that supports `Attributes2` will pass an `Attributes2` object to `startElement()` instead of a plain `Attributes` object. Using the extra methods requires a cast. Before casting, you may wish to check whether the cast will succeed by getting the value of the `http://xml.org/sax/features/use-attributes2` feature. If this feature is true, the parser passes `Attributes2` objects.

```
package org.xml.sax.ext;

public interface Attributes2 {

    public boolean isDeclared(int index);
    public boolean isDeclared(String qualifiedName);
    public boolean isSpecified(String namespaceURI, String localName);
    public boolean isSpecified(int index);
    public boolean isSpecified(String qualifiedName);
    public boolean isSpecified(String namespaceURI, String localName);

}
```

The DeclHandler Interface

`DeclHandler` is a callback interface that provides information about the `ELEMENT`, `ATTLIST`, and parsed `ENTITY` declarations in the document's DTD. To configure an `XMLReader` with a `DeclHandler`, pass the name `http://xml.org/sax/properties/DeclHandler` and an instance of the handler to the reader's `setProperty()` method:

```
try {
  parser.setProperty(
    "http://xml.org/sax/properties/DeclHandler",
      new YourDeclHandlerImplementationClass());
}
catch(SAXException ex) {
  System.out.println("This parser does not provide declarations.");
}
```

If the parser does not provide declaration events, it throws a `SAXNotRecognizedException`. If the parser cannot install a `DeclHandler` at this moment (generally because it's in the middle of parsing a document), then it throws a `SAXNotSupportedException`. If it doesn't throw one of these exceptions, it will call back to the methods in your `DeclHandler` as it parses the DTD:

```
package org.xml.sax.ext;

public interface DeclHandler {

    public void elementDecl(String name, String model) throws SAXException;
    public void attributeDecl(String elementName, String attributeName,
      String type, String defaultValue, String value) throws SAXException;
```

```
    public void internalEntityDecl(String name, String value)
      throws SAXException;
    public void externalEntityDecl(String name, String publicID,
      String systemID) throws SAXException;

}
```

The EntityResolver2 Interface

SAX 2.0.2 adds an EntityResolver2 subclass of EntityResolver that provides extra methods for more flexible entity resolution. In particular, it lets a program provide an external DTD subset for a document that does not have a document type declaration. It also lets entities be resolved based on the root element name and base URL, as well as the public ID and system ID. Your code can always pass an EntityResolver2 object to setEntityResolver( ). A parser that does not supports EntityResolver2 will simply ignore the extra methods. The http://xml.org/sax/features/use-entity-resolver2 feature tells you whether the parser will use the extra methods in EntityResolver2.

```
    package org.xml.sax.ext;

    public interface EntityResolver2 {

      public InputSource getExternalSubset(String name, String baseURI);
      public InputSource resolveEntity(
        String name, String publicID, String baseURI, String systemID);

    }
```

The LexicalHandler Interface

LexicalHandler is a callback interface that provides information about aspects of the document that are not normally relevant, specifically:

- CDATA sections
- Entity boundaries
- DTD boundaries
- Comments

Without a LexicalHandler, the parser simply ignores comments and expands entity references and CDATA sections. By using the LexicalHandler interface, however, you can read the comments and learn which text came from regular character data, which came from a CDATA section, and which came from which entity reference.

To configure an XMLReader with a LexicalHandler, pass an instance of your handler class to the reader's setProperty( ) method with the name http://xml.org/sax/properties/LexicalHandler:

```
    try {
      parser.setProperty(
        "http://xml.org/sax/properties/LexicalHandler",
        new YourLexicalHandlerClass( )
      );
```

```
      }
      catch(SAXException ex) {
        System.out.println("This parser does not provide lexical events.");
      }
```

If the parser does not provide lexical events, it throws a SAXNotRecognizedException. If the parser cannot install a LexicalHandler at this moment (generally because it's in the middle of parsing a document), then it throws a SAXNotSupportedException. If it doesn't throw one of these exceptions, it calls back to the methods in the LexicalHandler as it encounters entity references, comments, and CDATA sections. The basic content of the resolved entities and CDATA sections are still reported through the ContentHandler interface, as normal:

```
package org.xml.sax.ext;

public interface LexicalHandler {

    public void startDTD(String name, String publicID, String systemID)
     throws SAXException;
    public void endDTD( ) throws SAXException;
    public void startEntity(String name) throws SAXException;
    public void endEntity(String name) throws SAXException;
    public void startCDATA( ) throws SAXException;
    public void endCDATA( ) throws SAXException;
    public void comment(char[ ] text, int start, int length)
     throws SAXException;

}
```

The Locator2 Interface

SAX 2.0.2 adds a Locator2 subclass of Locator that provides extra methods to determine the character encoding and XML version used by the current entity. A parser that supports Locator2 will simply pass a Locator2 object to setLocator( ) instead of a plain Locator object. Using the extra methods requires a cast. Before casting, you may wish to check whether the cast will succeed by getting the value of the http://xml.org/sax/features/use-locator2 feature. If this feature is true, the parser passes Locator2 objects.

```
package org.xml.sax.ext;

public interface EntityResolver2 {

    public String getXMLVersion( );
    public String getEncoding( );

}
```

The getXMLVersion( ) method returns the version of the current *entity*. The http://xml.org/sax/properties/document-xml-version property returns the version of the current *document*. These may be but do not have to be the same.

27

Character Sets

By default, an XML parser assumes that XML documents are written in the UTF-8 encoding of Unicode. However, documents may be written instead in any character set the XML processor understands, provided that there's either some external metadata like an HTTP header or internal metadata like a byte-order mark or an encoding declaration that specifies the character set. For example, a document written in the Latin-5 character set would need this XML declaration:

```
<?xml version="1.0" encoding="ISO-8859-9"?>
```

Most good XML processors understand many common character sets. The XML specification recommends the character names shown in Table 27-1. When using any of these character sets, you should use these names. Of these character sets, only UTF-8 and UTF-16 must be supported by all XML processors, although many XML processors support all character sets listed here, and many support additional character sets besides. When using character sets not listed here, you should use the names specified in the IANA character sets registry at *http://www.iana.org/assignments/character-sets*.

Table 27-1. Character set names defined by the XML specification

Name	Character set
UTF-8	The default encoding used in XML documents, unless an encoding declaration, byte-order mark, or external metadata specifies otherwise; a variable-width encoding of Unicode that uses one to four bytes per character. UTF-8 is designed such that all ASCII documents are legal UTF-8 documents, which is not true for other character sets, such as UTF-16 and Latin-1. This character set is normally the best encoding choice for XML documents that don't contain a lot of Chinese, Japanese, or Korean.
UTF-16	A two-byte encoding of Unicode in which all Unicode characters defined in Unicode 3.0 and earlier (including the ASCII characters) occupy exactly two bytes. However, characters from planes 1 through 14, added in Unicode 3.1 and later, are encoded using surrogate pairs of four bytes each. This encoding is the best choice if your XML documents contain substantial amounts of Chinese, Japanese, or Korean.

Name	Character set
ISO-10646-UCS-2	The Basic Multilingual Plane of Unicode, i.e., plane 0. This character set is the same as UTF-16, except that it does not allow surrogate pairs to represent characters with code points beyond 65,535. The difference is only significant in Unicode 3.1 and later. Each Unicode character is represented as exactly one two-byte, unsigned integer. Determining endianness requires a byte-order mark at the beginning of the file.
ISO-10646-UCS-4	A four-byte encoding of Unicode in which each Unicode character is represented as exactly one four-byte, unsigned integer. Determining endianness requires a byte-order mark at the beginning of the file.
ISO-8859-1	Latin-1, ASCII plus the characters needed for most Western European languages, including Danish, Dutch, English, Faroese, Finnish, Flemish, German, Icelandic, Irish, Italian, Norwegian, Portuguese, Spanish, and Swedish. Some non-European languages, such as Hawaiian, Indonesian, and Swahili, also use these characters.
ISO-8859-2	Latin-2, ASCII plus the characters needed for most Central European languages, including Croatian, Czech, Hungarian, Polish, Slovak, and Slovenian.
ISO-8859-3	Latin-3, ASCII plus the characters needed for Esperanto, Maltese, Turkish, and Galician. Latin-5, ISO-8859-9, however, is now preferred for Turkish.
ISO-8859-4	Latin-4, ASCII plus the characters needed for the Baltic languages Latvian, Lithuanian, Greenlandic, and Lappish. Now largely replaced by ISO-8859-10, Latin-6.
ISO-8859-5	ASCII plus the Cyrillic characters used for Byelorussian, Bulgarian, Macedonian, Russian, Serbian, and Ukrainian.
ISO-8859-6	ASCII plus Arabic
ISO-8859-7	ASCII plus modern Greek.
ISO-8859-8	ASCII plus Hebrew.
ISO-8859-9	Latin-5, which is essentially the same as Latin-1 (ASCII plus Western Europe), except that the Turkish letters İ, I, Ş, ş, Ğ, and ğ replace the less-commonly used Icelandic letters Ý, ý, Þ, þ, Ð, and ð.
ISO-8859-10	Latin-6, which covers the characters needed for the Northern European languages Estonian, Lithuanian, Greenlandic, Icelandic, Inuit, and Lappish. It's similar to Latin-4, but drops some symbols and the Latvian letter, ᚱ adds a few extra letters needed for Inuit and Lappish, and moves various characters around. ISO-8859-13 now supersedes this character set.
ISO-8859-11	Adds the Thai alphabet to basic ASCII. However, it is not well supported by current XML parsers, and you're probably better off using Unicode instead.
ISO-8859-12	Not yet in existence and unlikely to exist in the foreseeable future. At one point, this character set was considered for Devanagari, so the number was reserved. However, this effort is not yet off the ground, and it now seems likely that the increasing acceptance of Unicode will make such a character set unnecessary.
ISO-8859-13	Another character set designed to cover the Baltic languages. This set adds back in the Latvian letter ᚱ and other symbols dropped from Latin-6.
ISO-8859-14	Latin-8; a variant of Latin-1 with extra letters needed for Gaelic and Welsh, such as ċ, ẁ, and ġ. These letters mostly replace punctuation marks, such as × and │.
ISO-8859-15	Known officially as Latin-9 and unofficially as Latin-0; a revision of Latin-1 that replaces the international currency symbol ¤ with the Euro sign €. It also replaces the seldom-used fraction characters 1/4, 1/2, and 3/4 with the uncommon French letters Œ, œ, Ÿ, and the ¬, ¨, and ´ symbols with the Finnish letters Š, š, and Ž. Otherwise, it's identical to ISO-8859-1.
ISO-8859-16	Latin-10; intended primarily for Romanian.
ISO-2022-JP	A seven-bit encoding of the character set defined in the Japanese national standard JIS X-0208-1997 used on web pages and in email; see RFC 1468.
Shift_JIS	The encoding of the Japanese national standard character set JIS X-0208-1997 used in Microsoft Windows.
EUC-JP	The encoding of the Japanese national standard character set JIS X-0208-1997 used by most Unixes.

Some parsers do not understand all these encodings. Specifically, parsers based on James Clark's expat often support only UTF-8, UTF-16, ISO-8859-1, and US-ASCII encodings. Xerces-C supports ASCII, UTF-8, UTF-16, UCS4, IBM037, IBM1140, ISO-8859-1, and Windows-1252. IBM's XML4C parser, derived from the Xerces codebase, adds over 100 more encodings, including ISO-8859 character sets 1 through 9 and 15. However, for maximum cross-parser compatibility, you should convert your documents to either UTF-8 or UTF-16 before publishing them, even if you author them in another character set.

Character Tables

The XML specification divides Unicode into five overlapping sets:

Name characters
> Characters that can appear in an element, attribute, or entity name. These characters are letters, ideographs, digits, and the punctuation marks _, -, ., and :. In the tables that follow, name characters are shown in bold type, such as **A**, **Å**, **Ą**, **Д**, **Ġ**, **1**, **2**, **3**, **α**, **א**, and **_**.

> One of the major differences between XML 1.0 and 1.1 is in which characters are name characters. All XML 1.0 name characters are also XML 1.1 name characters. However, XML 1.1 also promotes many other characters to name characters. Some of these, such as the Burmese and Mongolian letters, reasonably deserve to be name characters. However, XML 1.1 also allows many problematic characters including ligatures such as ij, currency symbols such as the Greek drachma sign, letter-like symbols such as ™, number forms such as Roman numerals, and presentation forms. Finally, it allows all characters not defined as of Unicode 3.1.1 and all characters from beyond the basic multilingual plane, including such strange things as the musical symbol for a six-string fretboard. Unless you are working in a language such as Burmese or Mongolian that requires these new characters, it is recommended that you restrict your markup to characters that are legal in XML 1.0. The tables that follow are based on XML 1.0 rules.

Name start characters
> Characters that can be the first character of an element, attribute, or entity name. These characters are letters, ideographs, and the underscore _. In the tables that follow, these characters are shown with a gray background, such as **A**, **Å**, **Ą**, **Д**, **Ġ**, **α**, **א**, and **_**. Because name start characters are a subset of name characters, they are also shown in bold.

Character data characters
> All characters that can be used anywhere in an XML document, including element and attribute content, comments, and DTDs. This set includes almost all Unicode characters, except for surrogates and most C0 control characters. These characters are shown in a normal typeface. If they are name characters, they will be bold. If they are also name start characters, they'll have a gray background.

Illegal characters

Characters that may not appear anywhere in an XML document, such as in part of a name, character data, or comment text. These characters are shown in italic, such as *NUL* or *BEL*. Most of these characters are either C0 control characters or half of a surrogate pair.

XML 1.1 does allow the C0 control characters, except for NUL, to be included with a character reference such as &#x0B;. XML 1.0 does not allow this. XML 1.1 also requires C1 control characters, except for NEL, to be escaped with character references. XML 1.0 does not require this.

Unassigned code points

Bytes or byte sequences that are not assigned to a character as of Unicode 4.0.1. Theoretically, a program could produce a file containing one of these byte sequences, but their meaning is undefined and they should be avoided. They are represented in the following tables as *n/a*.

Figure 27-1 shows the relationship between these sets. Note that all name start characters are name characters and that all name characters are character data characters.

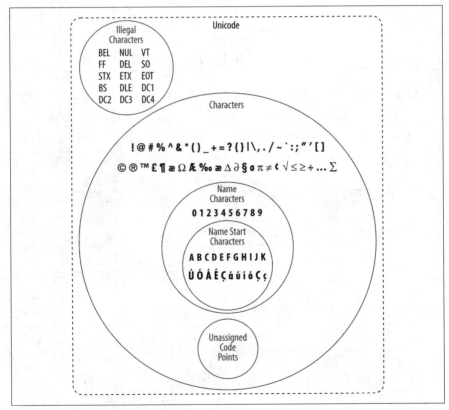

Figure 27-1. XML's division of Unicode characters

In all the tables that follow, each cell's upper lefthand corner contains the character's two-digit Unicode hexadecimal value, and the upper righthand corner contains the character's Unicode decimal value. You can insert a character in an XML document by prefixing the decimal value with &# and suffixing it with a semicolon. Thus, Unicode character 69, the capital letter E, can be written as E. Hexadecimal values work the same way, except that you prefix them with &#x;. In hexadecimal, the letter E is 45, so it can also be written as E.

ASCII

Most character sets in common use today are supersets of ASCII. That is, code points 0 through 127 are assigned to the same characters to which ASCII assigns them. Table 27-2 lists the ASCII character set. The only notable exceptions are the EBCDIC-derived character sets. Specifically, Unicode is a superset of ASCII, and code points 1 through 127 identify the same characters in Unicode as they do in ASCII.

Table 27-2. The first 128 Unicode characters (the ASCII character set)

00 0	01 1	02 2	03 3	04 4	05 5	06 6	07 7
NUL	SOH	STX	ETX	EOT	ENQ	ACK	BEL
08 8	**09** 9	**0A** 10	**0B** 11	**0C** 12	**0D** 13	**0E** 14	**0F** 15
BS	TAB	LF	VTB	FF	CR	SO	SI
10 16	**11** 17	**11** 18	**13** 19	**14** 20	**15** 21	**16** 22	**17** 23
DLE	DC1	DC2	DC3	DC4	NAK	SYN	ETB
18 24	**19** 25	**1A** 26	**1B** 27	**1C** 28	**1D** 29	**1E** 30	**1F** 31
CAN	EM	SUB	ESC	FS	GS	RS	US
20 32	**21** 33	**22** 34	**23** 35	**24** 36	**25** 37	**26** 38	**27** 39
	!	"	#	$	%	&	'
28 40	**29** 41	**2A** 42	**2B** 43	**2C** 44	**2D** 45	**2E** 46	**2F** 47
(	)	*	+	,	–	.	/
30 48	**31** 49	**32** 50	**33** 51	**34** 52	**35** 53	**36** 54	**37** 55
0	1	2	3	4	5	6	7
38 56	**39** 57	**3A** 58	**3B** 59	**3C** 60	**3D** 61	**3E** 62	**3F** 63
8	9	:	;	<	=	>	?
40 64	**41** 65	**42** 66	**43** 67	**44** 68	**45** 69	**46** 70	**47** 71
@	A	B	C	D	E	F	G
48 72	**49** 73	**4A** 74	**4B** 75	**4C** 76	**4D** 77	**4E** 78	**4F** 79
H	I	J	K	L	M	N	O
50 80	**51** 81	**52** 82	**53** 83	**54** 84	**55** 85	**56** 86	**57** 87
P	Q	R	S	T	U	V	W

58	88	59	89	5A	90	5B	91	5C	92	5D	93	5E	94	5F	95
X		Y		Z		[		\		]		^		_	
60	96	61	97	62	98	63	99	64	100	65	101	66	102	67	103
`		a		b		c		d		e		f		g	
68	104	69	105	6A	106	6B	107	6C	108	6D	109	6E	110	6F	111
h		i		j		k		l		m		n		o	
70	112	71	113	72	114	73	115	74	116	75	117	76	118	77	119
p		q		r		s		t		u		v		w	
78	120	79	121	7A	122	7B	123	7C	124	7D	125	7E	126	7F	127
x		y		z		{		|		}		~		DEL	

Characters 0 through 31 and character 127 are nonprinting control characters, sometimes called the C0 controls to distinguish them from the C1 controls used in the ISO-8859 character sets. Of these 33 characters, only the carriage return, line feed, and horizontal tab may appear in XML documents. The other 30 may not appear anywhere in an XML document, including in tags, comments, or parsed character data. In XML 1.1 (but not XML 1.0), 29 of these 30 characters (all of them except NUL) can be inserted with character references, such as &#31;.

ISO-8859-1, Latin-1

Character sets defined by the ISO-8859 standard comprise one popular superset of the ASCII character sets. These characters all provide the normal ASCII characters from code points 0 through 127 and the C1 controls from 128 to 159. They provide different repertoires of characters in the range from 160 to 255.

In particular, many Western European and American systems use a character set called Latin-1. This set is the first code page defined in the ISO-8859 standard and is also called ISO-8859-1. Although all common encodings of Unicode map code points 128 through 255 differently than Latin-1, code points 128 through 255 map to the same characters in both Latin-1 and Unicode. This situation does not occur in other character sets.

C1 controls

All ISO-8859 character sets begin with the same 32 extra nonprinting control characters in code points 128 through 159. These sets are used on terminals like the DEC VT-320 to provide graphics functionality not included in ASCII—for example, erasing the screen and switching it to inverse video or graphics mode. These characters cause severe problems for anyone reading or editing an XML document on a terminal or terminal emulator.

Fortunately, these characters are not necessary in XML documents. Their inclusion in XML 1.0 was an oversight. They should have been banned like the C0 controls. Unfortunately, many editors and documents incorrectly label documents written in the Cp1252 Windows character set as ISO-8859-1. This character set does use the code points between 128 and 159 for noncontrol graphics characters. When documents written with this character set are displayed or edited on a dumb terminal, they can effectively disable the user's terminal. Similar problems exist with most other Windows code pages for single-byte character sets. XML 1.1 corrects this by requiring all of these, except NEL, to be escaped with character references such as š.

In the spirit of being liberal in what you accept and conservative in what you generate, you should never use Cp1252, correctly labeled or otherwise. You should also avoid using other nonstandard code pages for documents that move beyond a single system. On the other hand, if you receive a document labeled as Cp1252 (or any other Windows code page), it can be displayed if you're careful not to throw it at a terminal unfiltered. If you suspect that a document labeled as ISO-8859-1 that uses characters between 128 and 159 is in fact a Cp1252 document, you should probably reject it. This decision is difficult, however, given the prevalence of broken software that does not identify documents sent properly.

Latin-1

Latin-1 covers most Western European languages that use some variant of the Latin alphabet. Characters 0 through 127 in this set are identical to the ASCII characters with the same code points. Characters 128 to 159 are the C1 control characters used only for dumb terminals. Character 160 is the nonbreaking space. Characters 161 through 255 are accented characters, such as è, á, and ö, non-U.S. punctuation marks, such as £ and ¿, and a few new letters, such as the Icelandic þ and ß. Table 27-3 shows the upper half of this character set. The lower half is identical to the ASCII character set shown in Table 27-2.

Table 27-3. Unicode characters between 160 and 255 and the second half of the Latin-1, ISO-8859-1 character set

80	128	81	129	82	130	83	131	84	132	85	133	86	134	87	135
n/a		*n/a*		BPH		NBH		IND		NEL		SSA		ESA	
88	136	**89**	137	**8A**	138	**8B**	139	**8C**	140	**8D**	141	**8E**	142	**8F**	143
HTS		HTJ		VTS		PLD		PLU		RI		SS2		SS3	
90	144	**91**	145	**92**	146	**93**	147	**94**	148	**95**	149	**96**	150	**97**	151
DCS		PU1		PU2		STS		CCH		MW		SPA		EPA	
98	152	**99**	153	**9A**	154	**9B**	155	**9C**	156	**9D**	157	**9E**	158	**9F**	159
SOS		*n/a*		SCI		CSI		ST		OSC		PM		APC	
A0	160	**A1**	161	**A2**	162	**A3**	163	**A4**	164	**A5**	165	**A6**	166	**A7**	167
		¡		¢		£		¤		¥		¦		§	

A8	168	A9	169	AA	170	AB	171	AC	172	AD	173	AE	174	AF	175
¨		©		ª		«		¬		–		®		‾	

B0	176	B1	177	B2	178	B3	179	B4	180	B5	181	B6	182	B7	183
°		±		2		3		´		µ		¶		·	

B8	184	B9	185	BA	186	BB	187	BC	188	BD	189	BE	190	BF	191
¸		1		º		»		¼		½		¾		¿	

C0	192	C1	193	C2	194	C3	195	C4	196	C5	197	C6	198	C7	199
À		Á		Â		Ã		Ä		Å		Æ		Ç	

C8	200	C9	201	CA	202	CB	203	CC	204	CD	205	CE	206	CF	207
È		É		Ê		Ë		Ì		Í		Î		Ï	

D0	208	D1	209	D2	210	D3	211	D4	212	D5	213	D6	214	D7	215
Ð		Ñ		Ò		Ó		Ô		Õ		Ö		×	

D8	216	D9	217	DA	218	DB	219	DC	220	DD	221	DE	222	DF	223
Ø		Ù		Ú		Û		Ü		Ý		Þ		ß	

E0	224	E1	225	E2	226	E3	227	E4	228	E5	229	E6	230	E7	231
à		á		â		ã		ä		å		æ		ç	

E8	232	E9	233	EA	234	EB	235	EC	236	ED	237	EE	238	EF	239
è		é		ê		ë		ì		í		î		ï	

F0	240	F1	241	F2	242	F3	243	F4	244	F5	245	F6	246	F7	247
ð		ñ		ò		ó		ô		õ		ö		÷	

F8	248	F9	249	FA	250	FB	251	FC	252	FD	253	FE	254	FF	255
ø		ù		ú		û		ü		ý		þ		ÿ	

HTML4 Entity Sets

HTML 4.0 predefines several hundred named entities, many of which are quite useful. For instance, the nonbreaking space is . XML, however, defines only five named entities:

&
> The ampersand (&)

<
> The less-than sign (<)

>
> The greater-than sign (>)

"
>   The straight double quote (")

'
>   The straight single quote (')

Other needed characters can be inserted with character references in decimal or hexadecimal format. For instance, the nonbreaking space is Unicode character 160 (decimal). Therefore, you can insert it in your document as either   or . If you really want to type it as , you can define this entity reference in your DTD. Doing so requires you to use a character reference:

```
<!ENTITY nbsp " ">
```

The XHTML 1.0 specification includes three DTD fragments that define the familiar HTML character references:

Latin-1 characters (http://www.w3.org/TR/xhtml1/DTD/xhtml-lat1.ent)
>   The non-ASCII, graphic characters included in ISO-8859-1 from code points 160 through 255, shown in Table 27-3

Special characters (http://www.w3.org/TR/xhtml1/DTD/xhtml-special.ent)
>   A few useful letters and punctuation marks not included in Latin-1

Symbols (http://www.w3.org/TR/xhtml1/DTD/xhtml-symbol.ent)
>   The Greek alphabet, plus various arrows, mathematical operators, and other symbols used in mathematics

Feel free to borrow these entity sets for your own use. They should be included in your document's DTD with these parameter entity references and PUBLIC identifiers:

```
<!ENTITY % HTMLlat1 PUBLIC
    "-//W3C//ENTITIES Latin 1 for XHTML//EN"
    "http://www.w3.org/TR/xhtml1/DTD/xhtml-lat1.ent">
%HTMLlat1;
<!ENTITY % HTMLspecial PUBLIC
    "-//W3C//ENTITIES Special for XHTML//EN"
    "http://www.w3.org/TR/xhtml1/DTD/xhtml-special.ent">
%HTMLspecial;
<!ENTITY % HTMLsymbol PUBLIC
    "-//W3C//ENTITIES Symbols for XHTML//EN"
    "http://www.w3.org/TR/xhtml1/DTD/xhtml-symbol.ent">
%HTMLsymbol;
```

However, we do recommend saving local copies and changing the system identifier to match the new location, rather than downloading them from the *http://www.w3.org* every time you need to parse a file. You may import just one, two, or all three of them, depending on what you need. There are no interdependencies.

Instead, you can just use the character references shown in Tables 27-4, 27-5, and 27-6.

Table 27-4. *The HTML Latin-1 entity set*

Character	Meaning	XHTML entity reference	Hexadecimal character reference	Decimal character reference
	Nonbreaking space	` `	` `	` `
¡	Inverted exclamation mark	`&iexcl;`	`&#xA1;`	`&#161;`
¢	Cent sign	`&cent;`	`&#xA2;`	`&#162;`
£	Pound sign	`&pound;`	`&#xA3;`	`&#163;`
¤	Currency sign	`&curren;`	`&#xA4;`	`&#164;`
¥	Yen sign, Yuan sign	`&yen;`	`&#xA5;`	`&#165;`
¦	Broken vertical bar	`&brvbar;`	`&#xA6;`	`&#166;`
§	Section sign	`&sect;`	`&#xA7;`	`&#167;`
¨	Dieresis, spacing dieresis	`&uml;`	`&#xA8;`	`&#168;`
©	Copyright sign	`&copy;`	`&#xA9;`	`&#169;`
ª	Feminine ordinal indicator	`&ordf;`	`&#xAA;`	`&#170;`
«	Left-pointing double angle quotation mark, left-pointing guillemot	`&laquo;`	`&#xAB;`	`&#171;`
¬	Not sign	`&not;`	`&#xAC;`	`&#172;`
-	Soft hyphen, discretionary hyphen	`&shy;`	`&#xAD;`	`&#173;`
®	Registered trademark sign	`&reg;`	`&#xAE;`	`&#174;`
¯	Macron, overline, APL overbar	`&macr;`	`&#xAF;`	`&#175;`
°	Degree sign	`&deg;`	`&#xB0;`	`&#176;`
±	Plus-or-minus sign	`&plusmn;`	`&#xB1;`	`&#177;`
²	Superscript digit two, squared	`&sup2;`	`&#xB2;`	`&#178;`
³	Superscript digit three, cubed	`&sup3;`	`&#xB3;`	`&#179;`
´	Acute accent, spacing acute	`&acute;`	`&#xB4;`	`&#180;`
µ	Micro sign	`&micro;`	`&#xB5;`	`&#181;`
¶	Pilcrow sign, paragraph sign	`&para;`	`&#xB6;`	`&#182;`
·	Middle dot, Georgian comma, Greek middle dot	`&middot;`	`&#xB7;`	`&#183;`
¸	Cedilla, spacing cedilla	`&cedil;`	`&#xB8;`	`&#184;`
¹	Superscript digit one	`&sup1;`	`&#xB9;`	`&#185;`
º	Masculine ordinal indicator	`&ordm;`	`&#xBA;`	`&#186;`
»	Right-pointing double angle quotation mark, right-pointing guillemot	`&raquo;`	`&#xBB;`	`&#187;`
1/4	Vulgar fraction one-quarter	`&frac14;`	`&#xBC;`	`&#188;`
1/2	Vulgar fraction one-half	`&frac12;`	`&#xBD;`	`&#189;`
3/4	Vulgar fraction three-quarters	`&frac34;`	`&#xBE;`	`&#190;`
¿	Inverted question mark	`&iquest;`	`&#xBF;`	`&#191;`
À	Latin capital letter A with grave	`&Agrave;`	`&#xC0;`	`&#192;`
Á	Latin capital letter A with acute	`&Aacute;`	`&#xC1;`	`&#193;`
Â	Latin capital letter A with circumflex	`&Acirc;`	`&#xC2;`	`&#194;`
Ã	Latin capital letter A with tilde	`&Atilde;`	`&#xC3;`	`&#195;`
Ä	Latin capital letter A with dieresis	`&Auml;`	`&#xC4;`	`&#196;`

Table 27-4. The HTML Latin-1 entity set (continued)

Character	Meaning	XHTML entity reference	Hexadecimal character reference	Decimal character reference
Å	Latin capital letter A with ring above, Latin capital letter A ring	&Aring;	&#xC5;	&#197;
Æ	Latin capital letter AE, Latin capital ligature AE	&AElig;	&#xC6;	&#198;
Ç	Latin capital letter C with cedilla	&Ccedil;	&#xC7;	&#199;
È	Latin capital letter E with grave	&Egrave;	&#xC8;	&#200;
É	Latin capital letter E with acute	&Eacute;	&#xC9;	&#201;
Ê	Latin capital letter E with circumflex	&Ecirc;	&#xCA;	&#202;
Ë	Latin capital letter E with dieresis	&Euml;	&#xCB;	&#203;
Ì	Latin capital letter I with grave	&Igrave;	&#xCC;	&#204;
Í	Latin capital letter I with acute	&Iacute;	&#xCD;	&#205;
Î	Latin capital letter I with circumflex	&Icirc;	&#xCE;	&#206;
Ï	Latin capital letter I with dieresis	&Iuml;	&#xCF;	&#207;
Ð	Latin capital letter eth	&ETH;	&#xD0;	&#208;
Ñ	Latin capital letter N with tilde	&Ntilde;	&#xD1;	&#209;
Ò	Latin capital letter O with grave	&Ograve;	&#xD2;	&#210;
Ó	Latin capital letter O with acute	&Oacute;	&#xD3;	&#211;
Ô	Latin capital letter O with circumflex	&Ocirc;	&#xD4;	&#212;
Õ	Latin capital letter O with tilde	&Otilde;	&#xD5;	&#213;
Ö	Latin capital letter O with dieresis	&Ouml;	&#xD6;	&#214;
×	Multiplication sign	&times;	&#xD7;	&#215;
Ø	Latin capital letter O with stroke	&Oslash;	&#xD8;	&#216;
Ù	Latin capital letter U with grave	&Ugrave;	&#xD9;	&#217;
Ú	Latin capital letter U with acute	&Uacute;	&#xDA;	&#218;
Û	Latin capital letter U with circumflex	&Ucirc;	&#xDB;	&#219;
Ü	Latin capital letter U with dieresis	&Uuml;	&#xDC;	&#220;
Ý	Latin capital letter Y with acute	&Yacute;	&#xDD;	&#221;
Þ	Latin capital letter thorn	&THORN;	&#xDE;	&#222;
ß	Latin small letter sharp s, ess-zett	&szlig;	&#xDF;	&#223;
à	Latin small letter a with grave	&agrave;	&#xE0;	&#224;
á	Latin small letter a with acute	&aacute;	&#xE1;	&#225;
â	Latin small letter a with circumflex	&acirc;	&#xE2;	&#226;
ã	Latin small letter a with tilde	&atilde;	&#xE3;	&#227;
ä	Latin small letter a with dieresis	&auml;	&#xE4;	&#228;
å	Latin small letter a with ring above	&aring;	&#xE5;	&#229;
æ	Latin small letter ae, Latin small ligature ae	&aelig;	&#xE6;	&#230;
ç	Latin small letter c with cedilla	&ccedil;	&#xE7;	&#231;
è	Latin small letter e with grave	&egrave;	&#xE8;	&#232;
é	Latin small letter e with acute	&eacute;	&#xE9;	&#233;
ê	Latin small letter e with circumflex	&ecirc;	&#xEA;	&#234;

Table 27-4. The HTML Latin-1 entity set (continued)

Character	Meaning	XHTML entity reference	Hexadecimal character reference	Decimal character reference
ë	Latin small letter e with dieresis	`&euml;`	`&#xEB;`	`&#235;`
ì	Latin small letter i with grave	`&igrave;`	`&#xEC;`	`&#236;`
í	Latin small letter i with acute	`&iacute;`	`&#xED;`	`&#237;`
î	Latin small letter i with circumflex	`&icirc;`	`&#xEE;`	`&#238;`
ï	Latin small letter i with dieresis	`&iuml;`	`&#xEF;`	`&#239;`
ð	Latin small letter eth	`&eth;`	`&#xF0;`	`&#240;`
ñ	Latin small letter n with tilde	`&ntilde;`	`&#xF1;`	`&#241;`
ò	Latin small letter o with grave	`&ograve;`	`&#xF2;`	`&#242;`
ó	Latin small letter o with acute	`&oacute;`	`&#xF3;`	`&#243;`
ô	Latin small letter o with circumflex	`&ocirc;`	`&#xF4;`	`&#244;`
õ	Latin small letter o with tilde	`&otilde;`	`&#xF5;`	`&#245;`
ö	Latin small letter o with dieresis	`&ouml;`	`&#xF6;`	`&#246;`
÷	Division sign	`&divide;`	`&#xF7;`	`&#247;`
ø	Latin small letter o with stroke	`&oslash;`	`&#xF8;`	`&#248;`
ù	Latin small letter u with grave	`&ugrave;`	`&#xF9;`	`&#249;`
ú	Latin small letter u with acute	`&uacute;`	`&#xFA;`	`&#250;`
û	Latin small letter u with circumflex	`&ucirc;`	`&#xFB;`	`&#251;`
ü	Latin small letter u with dieresis	`&uuml;`	`&#xFC;`	`&#252;`
ý	Latin small letter y with acute	`&yacute;`	`&#xFD;`	`&#253;`
þ	Latin small letter thorn	`&thorn;`	`&#xFE;`	`&#254;`

Table 27-5. The HTML special characters entity set

Character	Meaning	XHTML entity reference	Hexadecimal character reference	Decimal character reference
"	Quotation mark, APL quote	`&quot;`	`&#x22;`	`&#34;`
&	Ampersand	`&amp;`	`&#x26;`	`&#38;`
'	Apostrophe mark	`&apos;`	`&#x27;`	`&#39;`
<	Less-than sign	`&lt;`	`&#x3C;`	`&#60;`
>	Greater-than sign	`&gt;`	`&#x3E;`	`&#62;`
Œ	Latin capital ligature OE	`&OElig;`	`&#x152;`	`&#338;`
œ	Latin small ligature oe	`&oelig;`	`&#x153;`	`&#339;`
Š	Latin capital letter S with caron	`&Scaron;`	`&#x160;`	`&#352;`
š	Latin small letter s with caron	`&scaron;`	`&#x161;`	`&#353;`
Ÿ	Latin capital letter Y with dieresis	`&Yuml;`	`&#x178;`	`&#376;`
ˆ	Modifier letter circumflex accent	`&circ;`	`&#x2C6;`	`&#710;`
~	Small tilde	`&tilde;`	`&#x2DC;`	`&#732;`
	En space	` `	` `	` `
	Em space	` `	` `	` `

Table 27-5. The HTML special characters entity set (continued)

Character	Meaning	XHTML entity reference	Hexadecimal character reference	Decimal character reference
	Thin space	` `	` `	` `
Nonprinting character	Zero width nonjoiner	`&zwnj;`	`&#x200C;`	`&#8204;`
Nonprinting character	Zero width joiner	`&zwj;`	`&#x200D;`	`&#8205;`
Nonprinting character	Left-to-right mark	`&lrm;`	`&#x200E;`	`&#8206;`
Nonprinting character	Right-to-left mark	`&rlm;`	`&#x200F;`	`&#8207;`
–	En dash	`&ndash;`	`&#x2013;`	`&#8211;`
—	Em dash	`&mdash;`	`&#x2014;`	`&#8212;`
'	Left single quotation mark	`&lsquo;`	`&#x2018;`	`&#8216;`
'	Right single quotation mark	`&rsquo;`	`&#x2019;`	`&#8217;`
‚	Single low-9 quotation mark	`&sbquo;`	`&#x201A;`	`&#8218;`
"	Left double quotation mark	`&ldquo;`	`&#x201C;`	`&#8220;`
"	Right double quotation mark	`&rdquo;`	`&#x201D;`	`&#8221;`
„	Double low-9 quotation mark	`&bdquo;`	`&#x201E;`	`&#8222;`
†	Dagger	`&dagger;`	`&#x2020;`	`&#8224;`
‡	Double dagger	`&Dagger;`	`&#x2021;`	`&#8225;`

Table 27-6. The HTML symbol entity set

Character	Meaning	XHTML entity reference	Hexadecimal character reference	Decimal character reference
ƒ	Latin small f with hook, function, florin	`&fnof;`	`&#x192;`	`&#402;`
Α	Greek capital letter alpha	`&Alpha;`	`&#x391;`	`&#913;`
Β	Greek capital letter beta	`&Beta;`	`&#x392;`	`&#914;`
Γ	Greek capital letter gamma	`&Gamma;`	`&#x393;`	`&#915;`
Δ	Greek capital letter delta	`&Delta;`	`&#x394;`	`&#916;`
Ε	Greek capital letter epsilon	`&Epsilon;`	`&#x395;`	`&#917;`
Ζ	Greek capital letter zeta	`&Zeta;`	`&#x396;`	`&#918;`
Η	Greek capital letter eta	`&Eta;`	`&#x397;`	`&#919;`
Θ	Greek capital letter theta	`&Theta;`	`&#x398;`	`&#920;`
Ι	Greek capital letter iota	`&Iota;`	`&#x399;`	`&#921;`
Κ	Greek capital letter kappa	`&Kappa;`	`&#x39A;`	`&#922;`
Λ	Greek capital letter lambda	`&Lambda;`	`&#x39B;`	`&#923;`
Μ	Greek capital letter mu	`&Mu;`	`&#x39C;`	`&#924;`
Ν	Greek capital letter nu	`&Nu;`	`&#x39D;`	`&#925;`
Ξ	Greek capital letter xi	`&Xi;`	`&#x39E;`	`&#926;`
Ο	Greek capital letter omicron	`&Omicron;`	`&#x39F;`	`&#927;`

Table 27-6. The HTML symbol entity set (continued)

Character	Meaning	XHTML entity reference	Hexadecimal character reference	Decimal character reference
Π	Greek capital letter pi	&Pi;	&#x3A0;	&#928;
P	Greek capital letter rho	&Rho;	&#x3A1;	&#929;
Σ	Greek capital letter sigma	&Sigma;	&#x3A3;	&#931;
T	Greek capital letter tau	&Tau;	&#x3A4;	&#932;
Υ	Greek capital letter upsilon	&Upsilon;	&#x3A5;	&#933;
Φ	Greek capital letter phi	&Phi;	&#x3A6;	&#934;
X	Greek capital letter chi	&Chi;	&#x3A7;	&#935;
Ψ	Greek capital letter psi	&Psi;	&#x3A8;	&#936;
Ω	Greek capital letter omega	&Omega;	&#x3A9;	&#937;
α	Greek small letter alpha	&alpha;	&#x3B1;	&#945;
β	Greek small letter beta	&beta;	&#x3B2;	&#946;
γ	Greek small letter gamma	&gamma;	&#x3B3;	&#947;
δ	Greek small letter delta	&delta;	&#x3B4;	&#948;
ε	Greek small letter epsilon	&epsilon;	&#x3B5;	&#949;
ζ	Greek small letter zeta	&zeta;	&#x3B6;	&#950;
η	Greek small letter eta	&eta;	&#x3B7;	&#951;
θ	Greek small letter theta	&theta;	&#x3B8;	&#952;
ι	Greek small letter iota	&iota;	&#x3B9;	&#953;
κ	Greek small letter kappa	&kappa;	&#x3BA;	&#954;
λ	Greek small letter lambda	&lambda;	&#x3BB;	&#955;
μ	Greek small letter mu	&mu;	&#x3BC;	&#956;
ν	Greek small letter nu	&nu;	&#x3BD;	&#957;
ξ	Greek small letter xi	&xi;	&#x3BE;	&#958;
o	Greek small letter omicron	&omicron;	&#x3BF;	&#959;
π	Greek small letter pi	&pi;	&#x3C0;	&#960;
ρ	Greek small letter rho	&rho;	&#x3C1;	&#961;
ς	Greek small letter final sigma	&sigmaf;	&#x3C2;	&#962;
σ	Greek small letter sigma	&sigma;	&#x3C3;	&#963;
τ	Greek small letter tau	&tau;	&#x3C4;	&#964;
υ	Greek small letter upsilon	&upsilon;	&#x3C5;	&#965;
φ	Greek small letter phi	&phi;	&#x3C6;	&#966;
χ	Greek small letter chi	&chi;	&#x3C7;	&#967;
ψ	Greek small letter psi	&psi;	&#x3C8;	&#968;
ω	Greek small letter omega	&omega;	&#x3C9;	&#969;
ϑ	Greek small letter theta symbol	&thetasym;	&#x3D1;	&#977;
ϒ	Greek upsilon with hook symbol	&upsih;	&#x3D2;	&#978;
ϖ	Greek pi symbol	&piv;	&#x3D6;	&#982;
•	Bullet, black small circle	&bull;	&#x2022;	&#8226;
…	Horizontal ellipsis, three-dot leader	&hellip;	&#x2026;	&#8230;

Table 27-6. The HTML symbol entity set (continued)

Character	Meaning	XHTML entity reference	Hexadecimal character reference	Decimal character reference
′	Prime, minutes, feet	&prime;	&#x2032;	&#8242;
″	Double prime, seconds, inches	&Prime;	&#x2033;	&#8243;
‾	Overline, spacing overscore	&oline;	&#x203E;	&#8254;
⁄	Fraction slash	&frasl;	&#x2044;	&#8260;
ℑ	Black letter capital I, imaginary part	&image;	&#x2111;	&#8465;
℘	Script capital P, power set, Weierstrass p	&weierp;	&#x2118;	&#8472;
ℜ	Black letter capital R, real part symbol	&real;	&#x211C;	&#8476;
™	Trademark sign	&trade;	&#x2122;	&#8482;
ℵ	Aleph symbol, first transfinite cardinal	&alefsym;	&#x2135;	&#8501;
←	Leftward arrow	&larr;	&#x2190;	&#8592;
↑	Upward arrow	&uarr;	&#x2191;	&#8593;
→	Rightward arrow	&rarr;	&#x2192;	&#8594;
↓	Downward arrow	&darr;	&#x2193;	&#8595;
↔	Left-right arrow	&harr;	&#x2194;	&#8596;
↵	Downward arrow with corner leftward, carriage return	&crarr;	&#x21B5;	&#8629;
⇐	Leftward double arrow	&lArr;	&#x21D0;	&#8656;
⇑	Upward double arrow	&uArr;	&#x21D1;	&#8657;
⇒	Rightward double arrow	&rArr;	&#x21D2;	&#8658;
⇓	Downward double arrow	&dArr;	&#x21D3;	&#8659;
⇔	Left-right double arrow	&hArr;	&#x21D4;	&#8660;
∀	For all	&forall;	&#x2200;	&#8704;
∂	Partial differential	&part;	&#x2202;	&#8706;
∃	There exists	&exist;	&#x2203;	&#8707;
∅	Empty set, null set, diameter	&empty;	&#x2205;	&#8709;
∇	Nabla, backward difference	&nabla;	&#x2207;	&#8711;
∈	Element of	&isin;	&#x2208;	&#8712;
∉	Not an element of	&notin;	&#x2209;	&#8713;
∋	Contains as member	&ni;	&#x220B;	&#8715;
∏	N-ary product, product sign	&prod;	&#x220F;	&#8719;
∑	N-ary summation	&sum;	&#x2211;	&#8721;
−	Minus sign	&minus;	&#x2212;	&#8722;
∗	Asterisk operator	&lowast;	&#x2217;	&#8727;
√	Square root, radical sign	&radic;	&#x221A;	&#8730;
∝	Proportional to	&prop;	&#x221D;	&#8733;
∞	Infinity	&infin;	&#x221E;	&#8734;
∠	Angle	&ang;	&#x2220;	&#8736;
∧	Logical and, wedge	&and;	&#x2227;	&#8743;
∨	Logical or, vee	&or;	&#x2228;	&#8744;

Table 27-6. The HTML symbol entity set (continued)

Character	Meaning	XHTML entity reference	Hexadecimal character reference	Decimal character reference
∩	Intersection, cap	&cap;	&#x2229;	&#8745;
∪	Union, cup	&cup;	&#x222A;	&#8746;
∫	Integral	&int;	&#x222B;	&#8747;
∴	Therefore	&there4;	&#x2234;	&#8756;
~	Tilde operator, varies with, similar to	&sim;	&#x223C;	&#8764;
≅	Approximately equal to	&cong;	&#x2245;	&#8773;
≈	Almost equal to, asymptotic to	&asymp;	&#x2248;	&#8776;
≠	Not equal to	&ne;	&#x2260;	&#8800;
≡	Identical to	&equiv;	&#x2261;	&#8801;
≤	Less than or equal to	&le;	&#x2264;	&#8804;
≥	Greater than or equal to	&ge;	&#x2265;	&#8805;
⊂	Subset of	&sub;	&#x2282;	&#8834;
⊃	Superset of	&sup;	&#x2283;	&#8835;
⊄	Not a subset of	&nsub;	&#x2284;	&#8836;
⊆	Subset of or equal to	&sube;	&#x2286;	&#8838;
⊇	Superset of or equal to	&supe;	&#x2287;	&#8839;
⊕	Circled plus, direct sum	&oplus;	&#x2295;	&#8853;
⊗	Circled times, vector product	&otimes;	&#x2297;	&#8855;
⊥	Up tack, orthogonal to, perpendicular	&perp;	&#x22A5;	&#8869;
·	Dot operator	&sdot;	&#x22C5;	&#8901;
⌈	Left ceiling, APL upstile	&lceil;	&#x2308;	&#8968;
⌉	Right ceiling	&rceil;	&#x2309;	&#8969;
⌊	Left floor, APL downstile	&lfloor;	&#x230A;	&#8970;
⌋	Right floor	&rfloor;	&#x230B;	&#8971;
⟨	Left-pointing angle bracket, bra	&lang;	&#x2329;	&#9001;
⟩	Right-pointing angle bracket, ket	&rang;	&#x232A;	&#9002;
◊	Lozenge	&loz;	&#x25CA;	&#9674;
♠	Black spade suit	&spades;	&#x2660;	&#9824;
♣	Black club suit, shamrock	&clubs;	&#x2663;	&#9827;
♥	Black heart suit, valentine	&hearts;	&#x2665;	&#9829;
♦	Black diamond suit	&diams;	&#x2666;	&#9830;

Other Unicode Blocks

So far we've accounted for a little over 300 of the more than 90,000 Unicode characters. Many thousands are still unaccounted for. Outside the ranges defined in XHTML and SGML, standard entity names don't exist. You should either use an editor that can produce the characters you need in the appropriate character set or you should use character references. Most of the 90,000-plus Unicode characters are either Han ideographs, Hangul syllables, or rarely used characters. However, we do list a few of the most useful blocks later in this chapter. Others can be found online at *http://www.unicode.org/charts/* or in *The Unicode Standard 4.0* by the Unicode Consortium (Addison Wesley).

In the tables that follow, the upper lefthand corner contains the character's hexadecimal Unicode value, and the upper righthand corner contains the character's decimal Unicode value. You can use either value to form a character reference so as to use these characters in element content and attribute values, even without an editor or fonts that support them.

Latin Extended-A

The128 characters in the Latin Extended-A block of Unicode are used in conjunction with the normal ASCII and Latin-1 characters. They cover most European Latin letters missing from Latin-1. The block includes various characters you'll find in the upper halves of the other ISO-8859 Latin character sets, including ISO-8859-2, ISO-8859-3, ISO-8859-4, and ISO-8859-9. When combined with ASCII and Latin-1, this block lets you write Afrikaans, Basque, Breton, Catalan, Croatian, Czech, Esperanto, Estonian, French, Frisian, Greenlandic, Hungarian, Latvian, Lithuanian, Maltese, Polish, Provençal, Rhaeto-Romanic, Romanian, Romany, Sami, Slovak, Slovenian, Sorbian, Turkish, and Welsh. See Table 27-7.

Table 27-7. Unicode's Latin Extended-A block

100	256	101	257	102	258	103	259	104	260	105	261	106	262	107	263
Ā		ā		Ă		ă		Ą		ą		Ć		ć	
108	264	**109**	265	**10A**	266	**10B**	267	**10C**	268	**10D**	269	**10E**	270	**10F**	271
Ĉ		ĉ		Ċ		ċ		Č		č		Ď		ď	
110	272	**111**	273	**112**	274	**113**	275	**114**	276	**115**	277	**116**	278	**117**	279
Đ		đ		Ē		ē		Ĕ		ĕ		Ė		ė	
118	280	**119**	281	**11A**	282	**11B**	283	**11C**	284	**11D**	285	**11E**	286	**11F**	287
Ę		ę		Ě		ě		Ĝ		ĝ		Ğ		ğ	
120	288	**121**	289	**122**	290	**123**	291	**124**	292	**125**	293	**126**	294	**127**	295
Ġ		ġ		Ģ		ģ		Ĥ		ĥ		Ħ		ħ	
128	296	**129**	297	**12A**	298	**12B**	299	**12C**	300	**12D**	301	**12E**	302	**12F**	303
Ĩ		ĩ		Ī		ī		Ĭ		ĭ		Į		į	
130	304	**131**	305	**132**	306	**133**	307	**134**	308	**135**	309	**136**	310	**137**	311
İ		ı		IJ		ij		Ĵ		ĵ		Ķ		ķ	
138	312	**139**	313	**13A**	314	**13B**	315	**13C**	316	**13D**	317	**13E**	318	**13F**	319
ĸ		Ĺ		ĺ		Ļ		ļ		Ľ		ľ		Ŀ	
140	320	**141**	321	**142**	322	**143**	323	**144**	324	**145**	325	**146**	326	**147**	327
ŀ		Ł		ł		Ń		ń		Ņ		ņ		Ň	

Table 27-7. Unicode's Latin Extended-A block (continued)

148 328	149 329	14A 330	14B 331	14C 332	14D 333	14E 334	14F 335
ň	ʼn	Ŋ	ŋ	Ō	ō	Ŏ	ŏ
150 336	**151** 337	**152** 338	**153** 339	**154** 340	**155** 341	**156** 342	**157** 343
Ő	ő	Œ	œ	Ŕ	ŕ	Ŗ	ŗ
158 344	**159** 345	**15A** 346	**15B** 347	**15C** 348	**15D** 349	**15E** 350	**15F** 351
Ř	ř	Ś	ś	Ŝ	ŝ	Ş	ş
160 352	**161** 353	**162** 354	**163** 355	**164** 356	**165** 357	**166** 358	**167** 359
Š	š	Ţ	ţ	Ť	ť	Ŧ	ŧ
168 360	**169** 361	**16A** 362	**16B** 363	**16C** 364	**16D** 365	**16E** 366	**16F** 367
Ũ	ũ	Ū	ū	Ŭ	ŭ	Ů	ů
170 368	**171** 369	**172** 370	**173** 371	**174** 372	**175** 373	**176** 374	**177** 375
Ű	ű	Ų	ų	Ŵ	ŵ	Ŷ	ŷ
178 376	**179** 377	**17A** 378	**17B** 379	**17C** 380	**17D** 381	**17E** 382	**17F** 383
Ÿ	Ź	ź	Ż	ż	Ž	ž	ſ

Latin Extended-B

The Latin Extended-B block of Unicode is used in conjunction with the normal ASCII and Latin-1 characters. It mostly contains characters used for transcription of non-European languages not traditionally written in a Roman script. For instance, it's used for the Pinyin transcription of Chinese and for many African languages. See Table 27-8.

Table 27-8. The Latin Extended-B block of Unicode

180 384	181 385	182 386	183 387	184 388	185 389	186 390	187 391
ƀ	Ɓ	Ƃ	ƃ	Ƅ	ƅ	Ɔ	Ƈ
188 392	**189** 393	**18A** 394	**18B** 395	**18C** 396	**18D** 397	**18E** 398	**18F** 399
ƈ	Ɖ	Ɗ	Ƌ	ƌ	ƍ	Ǝ	Ə
190 400	**191** 401	**192** 402	**193** 403	**194** 404	**195** 405	**196** 406	**197** 407
Ɛ	Ƒ	ƒ	Ɠ	Ɣ	ƕ	ɩ	Ɨ
198 408	**199** 409	**19A** 410	**19B** 411	**19C** 412	**19D** 413	**19E** 414	**19F** 415
Ƙ	ƙ	ƚ	ƛ	Ɯ	Ɲ	ƞ	Ɵ
1A0 416	**1A1** 417	**1A2** 418	**1A3** 419	**1A4** 420	**1A5** 421	**1A6** 422	**1A7** 423
Ơ	ơ	Ƣ	ƣ	Ƥ	ƥ	Ʀ	Ƨ
1A8 424	**1A9** 425	**1AA** 426	**1AB** 427	**1AC** 428	**1AD** 429	**1AE** 430	**1AF** 431
ƨ	Ʃ	ƪ	ƫ	Ƭ	ƭ	Ʈ	Ư

Table 27-8. The Latin Extended-B block of Unicode (continued)

1B0 432	1B1 433	1B2 434	1B3 435	1B4 436	1B5 437	1B6 438	1B7 439
ư	Ʊ	ʊ	Ʋ	ʋ	Ȥ	ȥ	Ʒ
1B8 440	1B9 441	1BA 442	1BB 443	1BC 444	1BD 445	1BE 446	1BF 447
Ƹ	ƹ	ƺ	ƻ	Ƽ	ƽ	ƾ	ƿ
1C0 448	1C1 449	1C2 450	1C3 451	1C4 452	1C5 453	1C6 454	1C7 455
ǀ	ǁ	ǂ	ǃ	DŽ	Dž	dž	LJ
1C8 456	1C9 457	1CA 458	1CB 459	1CC 460	1CD 461	1CE 462	1CF 463
Lj	lj	NJ	Nj	nj	Ǎ	ǎ	Ǐ
1D0 464	1D1 465	1D2 466	1D3 467	1D4 468	1D5 469	1D6 470	1D7 471
ǐ	Ǒ	ǒ	Ǔ	ǔ	Ǖ	ǖ	Ǘ
1D8 472	1D9 473	1DA 474	1DB 475	1DC 476	1DD 477	1DE 478	1DF 479
ǘ	Ǚ	ǚ	Ǜ	ǜ	ǝ	Ǟ	ǟ
1E0 480	1E1 481	1E2 482	1E3 483	1E4 484	1E5 485	1E6 486	1E7 487
Ǡ	ǡ	Ǣ	ǣ	Ǥ	ǥ	Ǧ	ǧ
1E8 488	1E9 489	1EA 490	1EB 491	1EC 492	1ED 493	1EE 494	1EF 495
Ǩ	ǩ	Ǫ	ǫ	Ǭ	ǭ	Ǯ	ǯ
1F0 496	1F1 497	1F2 498	1F3 499	1F4 500	1F5 501	1F6 502	1F7 503
ǰ	DZ	Dz	dz	Ǵ	ǵ	Ƕ	Ƿ
1F8 504	1F9 505	1FA 506	1FB 507	1FC 508	1FD 509	1FE 510	1FF 511
Ǹ	ǹ	Ǻ	ǻ	Ǽ	ǽ	Ǿ	ǿ
200 512	201 513	202 514	203 515	204 516	205 517	206 518	207 519
Ȁ	ȁ	Ȃ	ȃ	Ȅ	ȅ	Ȇ	ȇ
208 520	209 521	20A 522	20B 523	20C 524	20D 525	20E 526	20F 527
Ȉ	ȉ	Ȋ	ȋ	Ȍ	ȍ	Ȏ	ȏ
210 528	211 529	212 530	213 531	214 532	215 533	216 534	217 535
Ȑ	ȑ	Ȓ	ȓ	Ȕ	ȕ	Ȗ	ȗ
218 536	219 537	21A 538	21B 539	21C 540	21D 541	21E 542	21F 543
Ș	ș	Ț	ț	Ȝ	ȝ	Ȟ	ȟ
220 544	221 545	222 546	223 547	224 548	225 549	226 550	227 551
Ƞ	ȡ	Ȣ	ȣ	Ȥ	ȥ	Ȧ	ȧ
228 552	229 553	22A 554	22B 555	22C 556	22D 557	22E 558	22F 559
Ȩ	ȩ	Ȫ	ȫ	Ȭ	ȭ	Ȯ	ȯ

Table 27-8. The Latin Extended-B block of Unicode (continued)

230	560	231	561	232	562	233	563	234	564	235	565	236	566	237	567
Ō		ō		Ȳ		ȳ		ļ		ɳ		ţ		*n/a*	
238	568	**239**	569	**23A**	570	**23B**	571	**23C**	572	**23D**	573	**23E**	574	**23F**	575
n/a		*n/a*		*n/a*		*n/a*		*n/a*		*n/a*		*n/a*		*n/a*	

IPA Extensions

Linguists use the International Phonetic Alphabetic (IPA) to identify uniquely and unambiguously particular sounds of various spoken languages. Besides the symbols listed in this block, the IPA requires use of ASCII, various other extended Latin characters, the combining diacritical marks in Table 27-11, and a few Greek letters. The block, shown in Table 27-9, only contains the characters not used in more traditional alphabets.

Table 27-9. The IPA Extensions block of Unicode

250	592	251	593	252	594	253	595	254	596	255	597	256	598	257	599
ɐ		ɑ		ɒ		ɓ		ɔ		ɕ		ɖ		ɗ	
258	600	**259**	601	**25A**	602	**25B**	603	**25C**	604	**25D**	605	**25E**	606	**25F**	607
ɘ		ə		ɚ		ɛ		ɜ		ɝ		ɞ		ɟ	
260	608	**261**	609	**262**	610	**263**	611	**264**	612	**265**	613	**266**	614	**267**	615
ɠ		ɡ		ɢ		ɣ		ɤ		ɥ		ɦ		ɧ	
268	616	**269**	617	**26A**	618	**26B**	619	**26C**	620	**26D**	621	**26E**	622	**26F**	623
ɨ		ɩ		ɪ		ɫ		ɬ		ɭ		ɮ		ɯ	
270	624	**271**	625	**272**	626	**273**	627	**274**	628	**275**	629	**276**	630	**277**	631
ɰ		ɱ		ɲ		ɳ		ɴ		ɵ		ɶ		ɷ	
278	632	**279**	633	**27A**	634	**27B**	635	**27C**	636	**27D**	637	**27E**	638	**27F**	639
ɸ		ɹ		ɺ		ɻ		ɼ		ɽ		ɾ		ɿ	
280	640	**281**	641	**282**	642	**283**	643	**284**	644	**285**	645	**286**	646	**287**	647
ʀ		ʁ		ʂ		ʃ		ʄ		ʅ		ʆ		ʇ	
288	648	**289**	649	**28A**	650	**28B**	651	**28C**	652	**28D**	653	**28E**	654	**28F**	655
ʈ		ʉ		ʊ		ʋ		ʌ		ʍ		ʎ		ʏ	
290	656	**291**	657	**292**	658	**293**	659	**294**	660	**295**	661	**296**	662	**297**	663
ʐ		ʑ		ʒ		ʓ		ʔ		ʕ		ʖ		ʗ	
298	664	**299**	665	**29A**	666	**29B**	667	**29C**	668	**29D**	669	**29E**	670	**29F**	671
ʘ		ʙ		ʚ		ʛ		ʜ		ʝ		ʞ		ʟ	

Table 27-9. The IPA Extensions block of Unicode (continued)

2A0	672	2A1	673	2A2	674	2A3	675	2A4	676	2A5	677	2A6	678	2A7	679
ɠ		ʡ		ʢ		dz		dʒ		dʑ		ts		tʃ	
2A8	680	2A9	681	2AA	682	2AB	683	2AC	684	2AD	685	2AE	686	2AF	687
tɕ		fŋ		ls		lz		ʬ		ʭ		ɥ		ʮ	

Spacing Modifier Letters

The Spacing Modifier Letters block, shown in Table 27-10, includes characters from multiple languages and scripts that modify the preceding or following character, generally by changing its pronunciation.

Table 27-10. The Spacing Modifier Letters block of Unicode

2B0	688	2B1	689	2B2	690	2B3	691	2B4	692	2B5	693	2B6	694	2B7	695
h		ɦ		j		r		ɹ		ɻ		ʁ		w	
2B8	696	2B9	697	2BA	698	2BB	699	2BC	700	2BD	701	2BE	702	2BF	703
y		′		″		'		'		'		'		'	
2C0	704	2C1	705	2C2	706	2C3	707	2C4	708	2C5	709	2C6	710	2C7	711
?		ʕ		<		>		^		v		^		v	
2C8	712	2C9	713	2CA	714	2CB	715	2CC	716	2CD	717	2CE	718	2CF	719
'		−		'		`		ˌ		_		`		'	
2D0	720	2D1	721	2D2	722	2D3	723	2D4	724	2D5	725	2D6	726	2D7	727
ː		ˑ		,		᷄		⊥		⊤		+		−
2D8	728	2D9	729	2DA	730	2DB	731	2DC	732	2DD	733	2DE	734	2DF	735
˘		˙		°		˛		~		″		ˇ		×
2E0	736	2E1	737	2E2	738	2E3	739	2E4	740	2E5	741	2E6	742	2E7	743
ɣ		l		s		x		ʕ		˥		˦		˧
2E8	744	2E9	745	2EA	746	2EB	747	2EC	748	2ED	749	2EE	750	2EF	751
˨		˩		L		⊢		v		=		″		v
2F0	752	2F1	753	2F2	754	2F3	755	2F4	756	2F5	757	2F6	758	2F7	759
^		<		>		°		`		``		″		~
2F8	760	2F9	761	2FA	762	2FB	763	2FC	764	2FD	765	2FE	766	2FF	767
∴		⌐		¬		L		⌐		⊔		⊏		←

Combining Diacritical Marks

The Combining Diacritical Marks block contains characters that are not used on their own, such as the accent grave and circumflex. Instead, they are merged with the preceding character to form a single glyph. For example, to write the character Ñ, you could type the ASCII letter N followed by the combining tilde character, like this: Ñ. When rendered, this combination would produce the single glyph Ñ. In Table 27-11, the character to which the diacritical mark is attached is a dotted circle ◌ (Unicode code point &0x25CC;), but of course it could be any normal character.

For compatibility with legacy character sets, there is often more than one way to write accented characters. For example the letter é, e with accent acute, can either be written as the single character 0xE9 or as the letter e (0x65) followed by a combining accent acute (0x301). This can be a problem for naïve algorithms for searching, sorting, indexing, and performing other operations on text. It's also an issue for XML. For instance, the <resumé> start-tag cannot be matched with a </resumé> end-tag if one uses character 0xE9 and the other uses 0x65 followed by 0x301. Where such multiple ways of writing the same character exist, the W3C strongly recommends using the precomposed form; that is, you should use the single character instead of the base character followed by a combining diacritical mark. In XML, these marks are primarily intended for forming characters that do not have precomposed forms.

Table 27-11. The Combining Diacritical Marks block of Unicode

300 768	301 769	302 770	303 771	304 772	305 773	306 774	307 775
◌̀	◌́	◌̂	◌̃	◌̄	◌̅	◌̆	◌̇
308 776	**309** 777	**30A** 778	**30B** 779	**30C** 780	**30D** 781	**30E** 782	**30F** 783
◌̈	◌̉	◌̊	◌̋	◌̌	◌̍	◌̎	◌̏
310 784	**311** 785	**312** 786	**313** 787	**314** 788	**315** 789	**316** 790	**317** 791
◌̐	◌̑	◌̒	◌̓	◌̔	◌̕	◌̖	◌̗
318 792	**319** 793	**31A** 794	**31B** 795	**31C** 796	**31D** 797	**31E** 798	**31F** 799
◌̘	◌̙	◌̚	◌̛	◌̜	◌̝	◌̞	◌̟
320 800	**321** 801	**322** 802	**323** 803	**324** 804	**325** 805	**326** 806	**327** 807
◌̠	◌̡	◌̢	◌̣	◌̤	◌̥	◌̦	◌̧
328 808	**329** 809	**32A** 810	**32B** 811	**32C** 812	**32D** 813	**32E** 814	**32F** 815
◌̨	◌̩	◌̪	◌̫	◌̬	◌̭	◌̮	◌̯
330 816	**331** 817	**332** 818	**333** 819	**334** 820	**335** 821	**336** 822	**337** 823
◌̰	◌̱	◌̲	◌̳	◌̴	◌̵	◌̶	◌̷
338 824	**339** 825	**33A** 826	**33B** 827	**33C** 828	**33D** 829	**33E** 830	**33F** 831
◌̸	◌̹	◌̺	◌̻	◌̼	◌̽	◌̾	◌̿
340 832	**341** 833	**342** 834	**343** 835	**344** 836	**345** 837	**346** 838	**347** 839
◌̀	◌́	◌͂	◌̓	◌̈́	◌ͅ	◌͆	◌͇
348 840	**349** 841	**34A** 842	**34B** 843	**34C** 844	**34D** 845	**34E** 846	**34F** 847
◌͈	◌͉	◌͊	◌͋	◌͌	◌͍	◌͎	CGJ

Table 27-11. The Combining Diacritical Marks block of Unicode (continued)

350	848	351	849	352	850	353	851	354	852	355	853	356	854	357	855
o̔̆		ó		o̔̑		o̗		o̘		o̙		o̚		o̕	
358	856	359	857	35A	858	35B	859	35C	860	35D	861	35E	862	35F	863
n/a		n/a		n/a		n/a		n/a		o͝		o͞		o͟	
360	864	361	865	362	866	363	867	364	868	365	869	366	870	367	871
o͠		o͡		o͢		o^a		o^e		o^i		o^o		o^u	
368	872	369	873	36A	874	36B	875	36C	876	36D	877	36E	878	36F	879
o^c		o^d		o^h		o^m		o^r		o^t		o^v		o^x	

Greek and Coptic

The Greek block of Unicode is used primarily for the modern Greek language. Currently, it's the only option for the Greek-derived Coptic script, but it doesn't really serve that purpose very well, and a separate Coptic block is a likely addition in the future. Extending coverage to classical and Byzantine Greek requires many more accented characters, which are available in the Greek Extended block, shown in Table 27-22, or by combining these characters with the Combining Diacritical Marks in Table 27-11. The Greek alphabet is also a fertile source of mathematical and scientific notation, although some common letters, such as Δ and Σ, are encoded separately in the Mathematical Operators block in Table 27-27 and the Mathematical Alphanumeric Symbols block in Table 27-28 for their use as mathematical symbols. The Greek and Coptic block of Unicode is shown in Table 27-12.

Table 27-12. The Greek and Coptic block of Unicode

370	880	371	881	372	882	373	883	374	884	375	885	376	886	377	887
n/a		n/a		n/a		n/a		ʹ		͵		n/a		n/a	
378	888	379	889	37A	890	37B	891	37C	892	37D	893	37E	894	37F	895
n/a		n/a		ͺ		n/a		n/a		n/a		;		n/a	
380	896	381	897	382	898	383	899	384	900	385	901	386	902	387	903
n/a		n/a		n/a		n/a		΄		΅		Ά		·	
388	904	389	905	38A	906	38B	907	38C	908	38D	909	38E	910	38F	911
Έ		Ή		Ί		n/a		Ό		n/a		Ύ		Ώ	
390	912	391	913	392	914	393	915	394	916	395	917	396	918	397	919
ΐ		Α		Β		Γ		Δ		Ε		Ζ		Η	
398	920	399	921	39A	922	39B	923	39C	924	39D	925	39E	926	39F	927
Θ		Ι		Κ		Λ		Μ		Ν		Ξ		Ο	

Table 27-12. The Greek and Coptic block of Unicode (continued)

3A0 928	3A1 929	3A2 930	3A3 931	3A4 932	3A5 933	3A6 934	3A7 935
Π	P	*n/a*	Σ	T	Υ	Φ	X
3A8 936	**3A9** 937	**3AA** 938	**3AB** 939	**3AC** 940	**3AD** 941	**3AE** 942	**3AF** 943
Ψ	Ω	Ϊ	Ϋ	ά	έ	ή	ί
3B0 944	**3B1** 945	**3B2** 946	**3B3** 947	**3B4** 948	**3B5** 949	**3B6** 950	**3B7** 951
ΰ	α	β	γ	δ	ε	ζ	η
3B8 952	**3B9** 953	**3BA** 954	**3BB** 955	**3BC** 956	**3BD** 957	**3BE** 958	**3BF** 959
θ	ι	κ	λ	μ	ν	ξ	ο
3C0 960	**3C1** 961	**3C2** 962	**3C3** 963	**3C4** 964	**3C5** 965	**3C6** 966	**3C7** 967
π	ρ	ς	σ	τ	υ	φ	χ
3C8 968	**3C9** 969	**3CA** 970	**3CB** 971	**3CC** 972	**3CD** 973	**3CE** 974	**3CF** 975
ψ	ω	ϊ	ϋ	ό	ύ	ώ	*n/a*
3D0 976	**3D1** 977	**3D2** 978	**3D3** 979	**3D4** 980	**3D5** 981	**3D6** 982	**3D7** 983
ϐ	ϑ	ϒ	ϓ	ϔ	φ	ϖ	ϗ
3D8 984	**3D9** 985	**3DA** 986	**3DB** 987	**3DC** 988	**3DD** 989	**3DE** 990	**3DF** 991
Ϙ	ϙ	Ϛ	ϛ	Ϝ	ϝ	Ϟ	ϟ
3E0 992	**3E1** 993	**3E2** 994	**3E3** 995	**3E4** 996	**3E5** 997	**3E6** 998	**3E7** 999
Ϡ	ϡ	Ш	ш	ϥ	ϥ	ħ	ϧ
3E8 1000	**3E9** 1001	**3EA** 1002	**3EB** 1003	**3EC** 1004	**3ED** 1005	**3EE** 1006	**3EF** 1007
Ϩ	ϩ	Ϫ	ϫ	ϭ	ϭ	Ϯ	ϯ
3F0 1008	**3F1** 1009	**3F2** 1010	**3F3** 1011	**3F4** 1012	**3F5** 1013	**3F6** 1014	**3F7** 1015
ϰ	ϱ	ϲ	ϳ	ϴ	ϵ	϶	Ϸ
3F8 1016	**3F9** 1017	**3FA** 1018	**3FB** 1019	**3FC** 1020	**3FD** 1021	**3FE** 1022	**3FF** 1023
ϸ	Ϲ	Ϻ	ϻ	*n/a*	*n/a*	*n/a*	*n/a*

Cyrillic

While the Cyrillic script, shown in Table 27-13, is most familiar to Western readers from Russian, it's also used for other Slavic languages, including Serbian, Ukrainian, and Byelorussian, and for many non-Slavic languages of the former Soviet Union, such as Azerbaijani, Tuvan, and Ossetian. Indeed, many characters in this block are not actually found in Russian but exist only in other languages written in the Cyrillic script. Following the breakup of the Soviet Union, some non-Slavic languages, such as Moldavian and Azerbaijani, are now reverting to Latin-derived scripts.

Table 27-13. The Cyrillic block of Unicode

400 1024 È	**401** 1025 Ë	**402** 1026 Ђ	**403** 1027 Ѓ	**404** 1028 Є	**405** 1029 Ѕ	**406** 1030 І	**407** 1031 Ї
408 1032 J	**409** 1033 Љ	**40A** 1034 Њ	**40B** 1035 Ћ	**40C** 1036 Ќ	**40D** 1037 Ѝ	**40E** 1038 Ў	**40F** 1039 Џ
410 1040 А	**411** 1041 Б	**412** 1042 В	**413** 1043 Г	**414** 1044 Д	**415** 1045 Е	**416** 1046 Ж	**417** 1047 З
418 1048 И	**419** 1049 Й	**41A** 1050 К	**41B** 1051 Л	**41C** 1052 М	**41D** 1053 Н	**41E** 1054 О	**41F** 1055 П
420 1056 Р	**421** 1057 С	**422** 1058 Т	**423** 1059 У	**424** 1060 Ф	**425** 1061 Х	**426** 1062 Ц	**427** 1063 Ч
428 1064 Ш	**429** 1065 Щ	**42A** 1066 Ъ	**42B** 1067 Ы	**42C** 1068 Ь	**42D** 1069 Э	**42E** 1070 Ю	**42F** 1071 Я
430 1072 а	**431** 1073 б	**432** 1074 в	**433** 1075 г	**434** 1076 д	**435** 1077 е	**436** 1078 ж	**437** 1079 з
438 1080 и	**439** 1081 й	**43A** 1082 к	**43B** 1083 л	**43C** 1084 м	**43D** 1085 н	**43E** 1086 о	**43F** 1087 п
440 1088 р	**441** 1089 с	**442** 1090 т	**443** 1091 у	**444** 1092 ф	**445** 1093 х	**446** 1094 ц	**447** 1095 ч
448 1096 ш	**449** 1097 щ	**44A** 1098 ъ	**44B** 1099 ы	**44C** 1100 ь	**44D** 1101 э	**44E** 1102 ю	**44F** 1103 я
450 1104 è	**451** 1105 ё	**452** 1106 ђ	**453** 1107 ѓ	**454** 1108 є	**455** 1109 ѕ	**456** 1110 і	**457** 1111 ї
458 1112 ј	**459** 1113 љ	**45A** 1114 њ	**45B** 1115 ћ	**45C** 1116 ќ	**45D** 1117 ѝ	**45E** 1118 ў	**45F** 1119 џ
460 1120 Ѡ	**461** 1121 ѡ	**462** 1122 Ѣ	**463** 1123 ѣ	**464** 1124 Ѥ	**465** 1125 ѥ	**466** 1126 Ѧ	**467** 1127 ѧ
468 1128 Ѩ	**469** 1129 ѩ	**46A** 1130 Ѫ	**46B** 1131 ѫ	**46C** 1132 Ѭ	**46D** 1133 ѭ	**46E** 1134 Ѯ	**46F** 1135 ѯ
470 1136 Ѱ	**471** 1137 ѱ	**472** 1138 Ѳ	**473** 1139 ѳ	**474** 1140 Ѵ	**475** 1141 ѵ	**476** 1142 Ѷ	**477** 1143 ѷ
478 1144 Ѹ	**479** 1145 ѹ	**47A** 1146 Ѻ	**47B** 1147 ѻ	**47C** 1148 Ѽ	**47D** 1149 ѽ	**47E** 1150 Ѿ	**47F** 1151 ѿ
480 1152 Ҁ	**481** 1153 ҁ	**482** 1154 ҂	**483** 1155 ҃	**484** 1156 ҄	**485** 1157 ҅	**486** 1158 ҆	**487** 1159 *n/a*

Table 27-13. The Cyrillic block of Unicode (continued)

488 1160	489 1161	48A 1162	48B 1163	48C 1164	48D 1165	48E 1166	48F 1167
◌҈	◌҉	Ҋ	ҋ	Ҍ	ҍ	Ҏ	ҏ
490 1168	**491** 1169	**492** 1170	**493** 1171	**494** 1172	**495** 1173	**496** 1174	**497** 1175
Ґ	ґ	Ғ	ғ	Ҕ	ҕ	Җ	җ
498 1176	**499** 1177	**49A** 1178	**49B** 1179	**49C** 1180	**49D** 1181	**49E** 1182	**49F** 1183
Ҙ	ҙ	Қ	қ	Ҝ	ҝ	Ҟ	ҟ
4A0 1184	**4A1** 1185	**4A2** 1186	**4A3** 1187	**4A4** 1188	**4A5** 1189	**4A6** 1190	**4A7** 1191
Ҡ	ҡ	Ң	ң	Ҥ	ҥ	Ҧ	ҧ
4A8 1192	**4A9** 1193	**4AA** 1194	**4AB** 1195	**4AC** 1196	**4AD** 1197	**4AE** 1198	**4AF** 1199
Ҩ	ҩ	Ҫ	ҫ	Ҭ	ҭ	Ү	ү
4B0 1200	**4B1** 1201	**4B2** 1202	**4B3** 1203	**4B4** 1204	**4B5** 1205	**4B6** 1206	**4B7** 1207
Ұ	ұ	Ҳ	ҳ	Ҵ	ҵ	Ҷ	ҷ
4B8 1208	**4B9** 1209	**4BA** 1210	**4BB** 1211	**4BC** 1212	**4BD** 1213	**4BE** 1214	**4BF** 1215
Ҹ	ҹ	Һ	һ	Ҽ	ҽ	Ҿ	ҿ
4C0 1216	**4C1** 1217	**4C2** 1218	**4C3** 1219	**4C4** 1220	**4C5** 1221	**4C6** 1222	**4C7** 1223
Ӏ	Ӂ	ӂ	Ӄ	ӄ	Ӆ	ӆ	Ӈ
4C8 1224	**4C9** 1225	**4CA** 1226	**4CB** 1227	**4CC** 1228	**4CD** 1229	**4CE** 1230	**4CF** 1231
ӈ	Ӊ	ӊ	Ӌ	ӌ	Ӎ	ӎ	*n/a*
4D0 1232	**4D1** 1233	**4D2** 1234	**4D3** 1235	**4D4** 1236	**4D5** 1237	**4D6** 1238	**4D7** 1239
Ӑ	ӑ	Ӓ	ӓ	Ӕ	ӕ	Ӗ	ӗ
4D8 1240	**4D9** 1241	**4DA** 1242	**4DB** 1243	**4DC** 1244	**4DD** 1245	**4DE** 1246	**4DF** 1247
Ә	ә	Ӛ	ӛ	Ӝ	ӝ	Ӟ	ӟ
4E0 1248	**4E1** 1249	**4E2** 1250	**4E3** 1251	**4E4** 1252	**4E5** 1253	**4E6** 1254	**4E7** 1255
Ӡ	ӡ	Ӣ	ӣ	Ӥ	ӥ	Ӧ	ӧ
4E8 1256	**4E9** 1257	**4EA** 1258	**4EB** 1259	**4EC** 1260	**4ED** 1261	**4EE** 1262	**4EF** 1263
Ө	ө	Ӫ	ӫ	Ӭ	ӭ	Ӯ	ӯ
4F0 1264	**4F1** 1265	**4F2** 1266	**4F3** 1267	**4F4** 1268	**4F5** 1269	**4F6** 1270	**4F7** 1271
Ӱ	ӱ	Ӳ	ӳ	Ӵ	ӵ	*n/a*	*n/a*
4F8 1272	**4F9** 1273	**4FA** 1274	**4FB** 1275	**4FC** 1276	**4FD** 1277	**4FE** 1278	**4FF** 1279
Ӹ	ӹ	*n/a*	*n/a*	*n/a*	*n/a*	*n/a*	*n/a*
500 1280	**501** 1281	**502** 1282	**503** 1283	**504** 1284	**505** 1285	**506** 1286	**507** 1287
Ԁ	ԁ	Ԃ	ԃ	Ԅ	ԅ	Ԇ	ԇ
508 1288	**509** 1289	**50A** 1290	**50B** 1291	**50C** 1292	**50D** 1293	**50E** 1294	**50F** 1295
Ԉ	ԉ	Ԋ	ԋ	Ԍ	ԍ	Ԏ	ԏ

Armenian

The Armenian script, shown in Table 27-14, is used for writing the Armenian language, currently spoken by about seven million people around the world.

Table 27-14. The Armenian block of Unicode

530 1328	531 1329	532 1330	533 1331	534 1332	535 1333	536 1334	537 1335
n/a	Ա	Բ	Գ	Դ	Ե	Զ	Է
538 1336	**539** 1337	**53A** 1338	**53B** 1339	**53C** 1340	**53D** 1341	**53E** 1342	**53F** 1343
Ը	Թ	Ժ	Ի	Լ	Խ	Ծ	Կ
540 1344	**541** 1345	**542** 1346	**543** 1347	**544** 1348	**545** 1349	**546** 1350	**547** 1351
Հ	Ձ	Ղ	Ճ	Մ	Յ	Ն	Շ
548 1352	**549** 1353	**54A** 1354	**54B** 1355	**54C** 1356	**54D** 1357	**54E** 1358	**54F** 1359
Ո	Չ	Պ	Ջ	Ռ	Ս	Վ	Տ
550 1360	**551** 1361	**552** 1362	**553** 1363	**554** 1364	**555** 1365	**556** 1366	**557** 1367
Ր	Ց	Ւ	Փ	Ք	Օ	Ֆ	*n/a*
558 1368	**559** 1369	**55A** 1370	**55B** 1371	**55C** 1372	**55D** 1373	**55E** 1374	**55F** 1375
n/a	ՙ	՚	՛	՜	՝	՞	՟
560 1376	**561** 1377	**562** 1378	**563** 1379	**564** 1380	**565** 1381	**566** 1382	**567** 1383
n/a	ա	բ	գ	դ	ե	զ	է
568 1384	**569** 1385	**56A** 1386	**56B** 1387	**56C** 1388	**56D** 1389	**56E** 1390	**56F** 1391
ը	թ	ժ	ի	լ	խ	ծ	կ
570 1392	**571** 1393	**572** 1394	**573** 1395	**574** 1396	**575** 1397	**576** 1398	**577** 1399
հ	ձ	ղ	ճ	մ	յ	ն	շ
578 1400	**579** 1401	**57A** 1402	**57B** 1403	**57C** 1404	**57D** 1405	**57E** 1406	**57F** 1407
ո	չ	պ	ջ	ռ	ս	վ	տ
580 1408	**581** 1409	**582** 1410	**583** 1411	**584** 1412	**585** 1413	**586** 1414	**587** 1415
ր	ց	ւ	փ	ք	օ	ֆ	և
588 1416	**589** 1417	**58A** 1418	**58B** 1419	**58C** 1420	**58D** 1421	**58E** 1422	**58F** 1423
n/a	։	֊	*n/a*	*n/a*	*n/a*	*n/a*	*n/a*

Hebrew

The Hebrew abjad, shown in Table 27-15, is used for Hebrew, Yiddish, and Judezmo. It's commonly used for Phoenician as well, but the Phoenician and Hebrew abjads are arguably different, and a separate Phoenician block is a likely addition in the future. The Hebrew script is also occasionally used for mathematical notation.

Table 27-15. The Hebrew block of Unicode

590 1424	591 1425	592 1426	593 1427	594 1428	595 1429	596 1430	597 1431
n/a	◌	◌̊	◌	◌	◌	◌	◌

598 1432	599 1433	59A 1434	59B 1435	59C 1436	59D 1437	59E 1438	59F 1439
◌	◌	◌	◌	◌	◌	◌	◌

5A0 1440	5A1 1441	5A2 1442	5A3 1443	5A4 1444	5A5 1445	5A6 1446	5A7 1447
◌	◌	n/a	◌	◌	◌	◌	◌

5A8 1448	5A9 1449	5AA 1450	5AB 1451	5AC 1452	5AD 1453	5AE 1454	5AF 1455
◌	◌	◌	◌	◌	◌	◌	◌

5B0 1456	5B1 1457	5B2 1458	5B3 1459	5B4 1460	5B5 1461	5B6 1462	5B7 1463
◌	◌	◌	◌	◌	◌	◌	◌

5B8 1464	5B9 1465	5BA 1466	5BB 1467	5BC 1468	5BD 1469	5BE 1470	5BF 1471
◌	◌	n/a	◌	◌	◌	◌	◌

5C0 1472	5C1 1473	5C2 1474	5C3 1475	5C4 1476	5C5 1477	5C6 1478	5C7 1479
׀	◌	◌	:	◌	n/a	n/a	n/a

5C8 1480	5C9 1481	5CA 1482	5CB 1483	5CC 1484	5CD 1485	5CE 1486	5CF 1487
n/a	n/a	n/a	n/a	n/a	n/a	n/a	n/a

5D0 1488	5D1 1489	5D2 1490	5D3 1491	5D4 1492	5D5 1493	5D6 1494	5D7 1495
א	ב	ג	ד	ה	ו	ז	ח

5D8 1496	5D9 1497	5DA 1498	5DB 1499	5DC 1500	5DD 1501	5DE 1502	5DF 1503
ט	י	ך	כ	ל	ם	מ	ן

5E0 1504	5E1 1505	5E2 1506	5E3 1507	5E4 1508	5E5 1509	5E6 1510	5E7 1511
נ	ס	ע	ף	פ	ץ	צ	ק

5E8 1512	5E9 1513	5EA 1514	5EB 1515	5EC 1516	5ED 1517	5EE 1518	5EF 1519
ר	ש	ת	n/a	n/a	n/a	n/a	n/a

5F0 1520	5F1 1521	5F2 1522	5F3 1523	5F4 1524	5F5 1525	5F6 1526	5F7 1527
װ	ױ	ײ	׳	״	n/a	n/a	n/a

5F8 1528	5F9 1529	5FA 1530	5FB 1531	5FC 1532	5FD 1533	5FE 1534	5FF 1535
n/a	n/a	n/a	n/a	n/a	n/a	n/a	n/a

Arabic

The Arabic script, shown in Table 27-16, is used for many languages besides Arabic, including Kurdish, Pashto, Persian, Sindhi, and Urdu. Turkish was also written in the Arabic script until early in the twentieth century when Turkey converted to a modified Latin alphabet.

Table 27-16. The Arabic block of Unicode

600 1536	**601** 1537	**602** 1538	**603** 1539	**604** 1540	**605** 1541	**606** 1542	**607** 1543
ـٰ	لسم	لسم	حد	*n/a*	*n/a*	*n/a*	*n/a*
608 1544	**609** 1545	**60A** 1546	**60B** 1547	**60C** 1548	**60D** 1549	**60E** 1550	**60F** 1551
n/a	*n/a*	*n/a*	*n/a*	،	،	؎	؏
610 1552	**611** 1553	**612** 1554	**613** 1555	**614** 1556	**615** 1557	**616** 1558	**617** 1559
ؐ	ؑ	ؒ	ؓ	ؔ	ؕ	*n/a*	*n/a*
618 1560	**619** 1561	**61A** 1562	**61B** 1563	**61C** 1564	**61D** 1565	**61E** 1566	**61F** 1567
n/a	*n/a*	*n/a*	؛	*n/a*	*n/a*	*n/a*	؟
620 1568	**621** 1569	**622** 1570	**623** 1571	**624** 1572	**625** 1573	**626** 1574	**627** 1575
Y	ء	آ	أ	ؤ	إ	ئ	ا
628 1576	**629** 1577	**62A** 1578	**62B** 1579	**62C** 1580	**62D** 1581	**62E** 1582	**62F** 1583
Y	ة	ت	ث	ج	ح	خ	د
630 1584	**631** 1585	**632** 1586	**633** 1587	**634** 1588	**635** 1589	**636** 1590	**637** 1591
Y	ر	ز	س	ش	ص	ض	ط
638 1592	**639** 1593	**63A** 1594	**63B** 1595	**63C** 1596	**63D** 1597	**63E** 1598	**63F** 1599
Y	ع	غ	*n/a*	*n/a*	*n/a*	*n/a*	*n/a*
640 1600	**641** 1601	**642** 1602	**643** 1603	**644** 1604	**645** 1605	**646** 1606	**647** 1607
ـ	ف	ق	ك	ل	م	ن	ه
648 1608	**649** 1609	**64A** 1610	**64B** 1611	**64C** 1612	**64D** 1613	**64E** 1614	**64F** 1615
و	ى	ي	ً	ٌ	ٍ	َ	ُ
650 1616	**651** 1617	**652** 1618	**653** 1619	**654** 1620	**655** 1621	**656** 1622	**657** 1623
ِ	ّ	ْ	ٓ	ٔ	ٕ	ٖ	ٗ
658 1624	**659** 1625	**65A** 1626	**65B** 1627	**65C** 1628	**65D** 1629	**65E** 1630	**65F** 1631
٘	*n/a*	*n/a*	*n/a*	*n/a*	*n/a*	*n/a*	*n/a*
660 1632	**661** 1633	**662** 1634	**663** 1635	**664** 1636	**665** 1637	**666** 1638	**667** 1639
٠	١	٢	٣	٤	٥	٦	٧
668 1640	**669** 1641	**66A** 1642	**66B** 1643	**66C** 1644	**66D** 1645	**66E** 1646	**66F** 1647
٨	٩	٪	٫	٬	٭	*n/a*	*n/a*
670 1648	**671** 1649	**672** 1650	**673** 1651	**674** 1652	**675** 1653	**676** 1654	**677** 1655
ٰ	ٱ	ٲ	ٳ	ٴ	ٵ	ٶ	ٷ
678 1656	**679** 1657	**67A** 1658	**67B** 1659	**67C** 1660	**67D** 1661	**67E** 1662	**67F** 1663
ٸ	ٹ	ٺ	ٻ	ټ	ٽ	پ	ٿ

Table 27-16. The Arabic block of Unicode (continued)

680 1664	681 1665	682 1666	683 1667	684 1668	685 1669	686 1670	687 1671
688 1672	689 1673	68A 1674	68B 1675	68C 1676	68D 1677	68E 1678	68F 1679
690 1680	691 1681	692 1682	693 1683	694 1684	695 1685	696 1686	697 1687
698 1688	699 1689	69A 1690	69B 1691	69C 1692	69D 1693	69E 1694	69F 1695
6A0 1696	6A1 1697	6A2 1698	6A3 1699	6A4 1700	6A5 1701	6A6 1702	6A7 1703
6A8 1704	6A9 1705	6AA 1706	6AB 1707	6AC 1708	6AD 1709	6AE 1710	6AF 1711
6B0 1712	6B1 1713	6B2 1714	6B3 1715	6B4 1716	6B5 1717	6B6 1718	6B7 1719
6B8 1720	6B9 1721	6BA 1722	6BB 1723	6BC 1724	6BD 1725	6BE 1726	6BF 1727
6C0 1728	6C1 1729	6C2 1730	6C3 1731	6C4 1732	6C5 1733	6C6 1734	6C7 1735
6C8 1736	6C9 1737	6CA 1738	6CB 1739	6CC 1740	6CD 1741	6CE 1742	6CF 1743
6D0 1744	6D1 1745	6D2 1746	6D3 1747	6D4 1748	6D5 1749	6D6 1750	6D7 1751
6D8 1752	6D9 1753	6DA 1754	6DB 1755	6DC 1756	6DD 1757	6DE 1758	6DF 1759
6E0 1760	6E1 1761	6E2 1762	6E3 1763	6E4 1764	6E5 1765	6E6 1766	6E7 1767
6E8 1768	6E9 1769	6EA 1770	6EB 1771	6EC 1772	6ED 1773	6EE 1774	6EF 1775
6F0 1776 ۰	6F1 1777 ۱	6F2 1778 ۲	6F3 1779 ۳	6F4 1780 ۴	6F5 1781 ۵	6F6 1782 ۶	6F7 1783 ۷
6F8 1784 ۸	6F9 1785 ۹	6FA 1786	6FB 1787	6FC 1788	6FD 1789	6FE 1790	6FF 1791

Devanagari

The Devanagari script is used for many languages of the Indian subcontinent, including Awadhi, Bagheli, Bhatneri, Bhili, Bihari, Braj Bhasa, Chhattisgarhi, Garhwali, Gondi, Harauti, Hindi, Ho, Jaipuri, Kachchhi, Kanauji, Konkani, Kului, Kumaoni, Kurku, Kurukh, Marwari, Mundari, Newari, Palpa, and Santali. It's also used for the classical language Sanskrit. See Table 27-17.

Table 27-17. The Devanagari block of Unicode

900 2304	901 2305	902 2306	903 2307	904 2308	905 2309	906 2310	907 2311
n/a	ँ	ं	ः	ऎ	अ	आ	इ
908 2312	**909** 2313	**90A** 2314	**90B** 2315	**90C** 2316	**90D** 2317	**90E** 2318	**90F** 2319
ई	उ	ऊ	ऋ	ऌ	ऍ	ऎ	ए
910 2320	**911** 2321	**912** 2322	**913** 2323	**914** 2324	**915** 2325	**916** 2326	**917** 2327
ऐ	ऑ	ऒ	ओ	औ	क	ख	ग
918 2328	**919** 2329	**91A** 2330	**91B** 2331	**91C** 2332	**91D** 2333	**91E** 2334	**91F** 2335
घ	ङ	च	छ	ज	झ	ञ	ट
920 2336	**921** 2337	**922** 2338	**923** 2339	**924** 2340	**925** 2341	**926** 2342	**927** 2343
ठ	ड	ढ	ण	त	थ	द	ध
928 2344	**929** 2345	**92A** 2346	**92B** 2347	**92C** 2348	**92D** 2349	**92E** 2350	**92F** 2351
न	ऩ	प	फ	ब	भ	म	य
930 2352	**931** 2353	**932** 2354	**933** 2355	**934** 2356	**935** 2357	**936** 2358	**937** 2359
र	ऱ	ल	ळ	ऴ	व	श	ष
938 2360	**939** 2361	**93A** 2362	**93B** 2363	**93C** 2364	**93D** 2365	**93E** 2366	**93F** 2367
स	ह	n/a	n/a	़	ऽ	ा	ि
940 2368	**941** 2369	**942** 2370	**943** 2371	**944** 2372	**945** 2373	**946** 2374	**947** 2375
ी	ु	ू	ृ	ॄ	ॅ	ॆ	े
948 2376	**949** 2377	**94A** 2378	**94B** 2379	**94C** 2380	**94D** 2381	**94E** 2382	**94F** 2383
ै	ॉ	ॊ	ो	ौ	्	n/a	n/a
950 2384	**951** 2385	**952** 2386	**953** 2387	**954** 2388	**955** 2389	**956** 2390	**957** 2391
ॐ	॑	॒	॓	॔	n/a	n/a	n/a
958 2392	**959** 2393	**95A** 2394	**95B** 2395	**95C** 2396	**95D** 2397	**95E** 2398	**95F** 2399
क़	ख़	ग़	ज़	ड़	ढ़	फ़	य़
960 2400	**961** 2401	**962** 2402	**963** 2403	**964** 2404	**965** 2405	**966** 2406	**967** 2407
ॠ	ॡ	ॢ	ॣ	।	॥	०	१

Table 27-17. The Devanagari block of Unicode (continued)

968	2408	969	2409	96A	2410	96B	2411	96C	2412	96D	2413	96E	2414	96F	2415
२		३		४		५		६		७		८		९	
970	2416	**971**	2417	**972**	2418	**973**	2419	**974**	2420	**975**	2421	**976**	2422	**977**	2423
०		n/a		n/a		n/a		n/a		n/a		n/a		n/a	
978	2424	**979**	2425	**97A**	2426	**97B**	2427	**97C**	2428	**97D**	2429	**97E**	2430	**97F**	2431
n/a		n/a		n/a		n/a		n/a		n/a		n/a		n/a	

Thai

The Thai script is used for Thai and several other Southeast Asian languages, including Kuy, Lavna, and Pali. See Table 27-18.

Table 27-18. The Thai block of Unicode

E00	3584	E01	3585	E02	3586	E03	3587	E04	3588	E05	3589	E06	3590	E07	3591
n/a		ก		ข		ฃ		ค		ฅ		ฆ		ง	
E08	3592	**E09**	3593	**E0A**	3594	**E0B**	3595	**E0C**	3596	**E0D**	3597	**E0E**	3598	**E0F**	3599
จ		ฉ		ช		ซ		ฌ		ญ		ฎ		ฏ	
E10	3600	**E11**	3601	**E12**	3602	**E13**	3603	**E14**	3604	**E15**	3605	**E16**	3606	**E17**	3607
ฐ		ฑ		ฒ		ณ		ด		ต		ถ		ท	
E18	3608	**E19**	3609	**E1A**	3610	**E1B**	3611	**E1C**	3612	**E1D**	3613	**E1E**	3614	**E1F**	3615
ธ		น		บ		ป		ผ		ฝ		พ		ฟ	
E20	3616	**E21**	3617	**E22**	3618	**E23**	3619	**E24**	3620	**E25**	3621	**E26**	3622	**E27**	3623
ภ		ม		ย		ร		ฤ		ล		ฦ		ว	
E28	3624	**E29**	3625	**E2A**	3626	**E2B**	3627	**E2C**	3628	**E2D**	3629	**E2E**	3630	**E2F**	3631
ศ		ษ		ส		ห		ฬ		อ		ฮ		ฯ	
E30	3632	**E31**	3633	**E32**	3634	**E33**	3635	**E34**	3636	**E35**	3637	**E36**	3638	**E37**	3639
ะ		ั		า		ำ		ิ		ี		ึ		ื	
E38	3640	**E39**	3641	**E3A**	3642	**E3B**	3643	**E3C**	3644	**E3D**	3645	**E3E**	3646	**E3F**	3647
ุ		ู		ฺ		n/a		n/a		n/a		n/a		฿	
E40	3648	**E41**	3649	**E42**	3650	**E43**	3651	**E44**	3652	**E45**	3653	**E46**	3654	**E47**	3655
เ		แ		โ		ใ		ไ		ๅ		ๆ		็	
E48	3656	**E49**	3657	**E4A**	3658	**E4B**	3659	**E4C**	3660	**E4D**	3661	**E4E**	3662	**E4F**	3663
่		้		๊		๋		์		ํ		๎		๏	
E50	3664	**E51**	3665	**E52**	3666	**E53**	3667	**E54**	3668	**E55**	3669	**E56**	3670	**E57**	3671
๐		๑		๒		๓		๔		๕		๖		๗	
E58	3672	**E59**	3673	**E5A**	3674	**E5B**	3675	**E5C**	3676	**E5D**	3677	**E5E**	3678	**E5F**	3679
๘		๙		๚		๛		n/a		n/a		n/a		n/a	

Tibetan

The Tibetan script is used to write the various dialects of Tibetan and Dzongkha, Bhutan's main language. Like Chinese, Tibetan is divided into mutually unintelligible spoken languages, although the written forms are identical. See Table 27-19.

Table 27-19. The Tibetan block of Unicode

F00	3840	F01	3841	F02	3842	F03	3843	F04	3844	F05	3845	F06	3846	F07	3847
ༀ		༁		༂		༃		༄		༅		༆		༇	
F08	3848	**F09**	3849	**F0A**	3850	**F0B**	3851	**F0C**	3852	**F0D**	3853	**F0E**	3854	**F0F**	3855
༈		༉		༊		་		༌		།		༎		༏	
F10	3856	**F11**	3857	**F12**	3858	**F13**	3859	**F14**	3860	**F15**	3861	**F16**	3862	**F17**	3863
༐		༑		༒		༓		༔		༕		༖		༗	
F18	3864	**F19**	3865	**F1A**	3866	**F1B**	3867	**F1C**	3868	**F1D**	3869	**F1E**	3870	**F1F**	3871
༘		༙		༚		༛		༜		༝		༞		༟	
F20	3872	**F21**	3873	**F22**	3874	**F23**	3875	**F24**	3876	**F25**	3877	**F26**	3878	**F27**	3879
༠		༡		༢		༣		༤		༥		༦		༧	
F28	3880	**F29**	3881	**F2A**	3882	**F2B**	3883	**F2C**	3884	**F2D**	3885	**F2E**	3886	**F2F**	3887
༨		༩		༪		༫		༬		༭		༮		༯	
F30	3888	**F31**	3889	**F32**	3890	**F33**	3891	**F34**	3892	**F35**	3893	**F36**	3894	**F37**	3895
༰		༱		༲		༳		༴		༵		༶		༷	
F38	3896	**F39**	3897	**F3A**	3898	**F3B**	3899	**F3C**	3900	**F3D**	3901	**F3E**	3902	**F3F**	3903
༸		༹		༺		༻		༼		༽		༾		༿	
F40	3904	**F41**	3905	**F42**	3906	**F43**	3907	**F44**	3908	**F45**	3909	**F46**	3910	**F47**	3911
ཀ		ཁ		ག		གྷ		ང		ཅ		ཆ		ཇ	
F48	3912	**F49**	3913	**F4A**	3914	**F4B**	3915	**F4C**	3916	**F4D**	3917	**F4E**	3918	**F4F**	3919
n/a		ཉ		ཊ		ཋ		ཌ		ཌྷ		ཎ		ཏ	
F50	3920	**F51**	3921	**F52**	3922	**F53**	3923	**F54**	3924	**F55**	3925	**F56**	3926	**F57**	3927
ཐ		ད		དྷ		ན		པ		ཕ		བ		བྷ	
F58	3928	**F59**	3929	**F5A**	3930	**F5B**	3931	**F5C**	3932	**F5D**	3933	**F5E**	3934	**F5F**	3935
མ		ཙ		ཚ		ཛ		ཛྷ		ཝ		ཞ		ཟ	
F60	3936	**F61**	3937	**F62**	3938	**F63**	3939	**F64**	3940	**F65**	3941	**F66**	3942	**F67**	3943
འ		ཡ		ར		ལ		ཤ		ཥ		ས		ཧ	
F68	3944	**F69**	3945	**F6A**	3946	**F6B**	3947	**F6C**	3948	**F6D**	3949	**F6E**	3950	**F6F**	3951
ཨ		ཀྵ		ཪ		*n/a*		*n/a*		*n/a*		*n/a*		*n/a*	
F70	3952	**F71**	3953	**F72**	3954	**F73**	3955	**F74**	3956	**F75**	3957	**F76**	3958	**F77**	3959
n/a		ཱ		ི		ཱི		ུ		ཱུ		ྲྀ		ཷ	

Table 27-19. The Tibetan block of Unicode (continued)

F78	3960	F79	3961	F7A	3962	F7B	3963	F7C	3964	F7D	3965	F7E	3966	F7F	3967
ླྀ		ཹ		ེ		ཻ		ོ		ཽ		ཾ		ཿ	

F80	3968	F81	3969	F82	3970	F83	3971	F84	3972	F85	3973	F86	3974	F87	3975
ྀ		ཱྀ		ྂ		ྃ		྄		྅		྆		྇	

F88	3976	F89	3977	F8A	3978	F8B	3979	F8C	3980	F8D	3981	F8E	3982	F8F	3983
ྈ		ྉ		ྊ		ྋ		n/a		n/a		n/a		n/a	

F90	3984	F91	3985	F92	3986	F93	3987	F94	3988	F95	3989	F96	3990	F97	3991
ྐ		ྑ		ྒ		ྒྷ		ྔ		ྕ		n/a		ྗ	

F98	3992	F99	3993	F9A	3994	F9B	3995	F9C	3996	F9D	3997	F9E	3998	F9F	3999
n/a		ྙ		ྚ		ྛ		ྜ		ྜྷ		ྞ		ྟ	

FA0	4000	FA1	4001	FA2	4002	FA3	4003	FA4	4004	FA5	4005	FA6	4006	FA7	4007
ྠ		ྡ		ྡྷ		ྣ		ྤ		ྥ		ྦ		ྦྷ	

FA8	4008	FA9	4009	FAA	4010	FAB	4011	FAC	4012	FAD	4013	FAE	4014	FAF	4015
ྨ		ྩ		ྪ		ྫ		ྫྷ		ྭ		ྮ		ྯ	

FB0	4016	FB1	4017	FB2	4018	FB3	4019	FB4	4020	FB5	4021	FB6	4022	FB7	4023
ྰ		ྱ		ྲ		ླ		ྴ		ྵ		ྶ		ྷ	

FB8	4024	FB9	4025	FBA	4026	FBB	4027	FBC	4028	FBD	4029	FBE	4030	FBF	4031
ྸ		ྐྵ		ྺ		ྻ		n/a		྽		྾		྿	

FC0	4032	FC1	4033	FC2	4034	FC3	4035	FC4	4036	FC5	4037	FC6	4038	FC7	4039
࿀		࿁		࿂		࿃		࿄		࿅		࿆		࿇	

FC8	4040	FC9	4041	FCA	4042	FCB	4043	FCC	4044	FCD	4045	FCE	4046	FCF	4047
࿈		࿉		࿊		࿋		࿌		n/a		n/a		࿏	

Ethiopic

The Ethiopic script is used by several languages in Ethiopia, including Amharic, Tigre, Oromo, and the liturgical language Ge'ez. See Table 27-20.

Table 27-20. The Ethiopic block of Unicode

1200	4608	1201	4609	1202	4610	1203	4611	1204	4612	1205	4613	1206	4614	1207	4615
ሀ		ሁ		ሂ		ሃ		ሄ		ህ		ሆ		n/a	

1208	4616	1209	4617	120A	4618	120B	4619	120C	4620	120D	4621	120E	4622	120F	4623
ለ		ሉ		ሊ		ላ		ሌ		ል		ሎ		ሏ	

1210	4624	1211	4625	1212	4626	1213	4627	1214	4628	1215	4629	1216	4630	1217	4631
ሐ		ሑ		ሒ		ሓ		ሔ		ሕ		ሖ		ሗ	

Table 27-20. The Ethiopic block of Unicode (continued)

1218	4632	1219	4633	121A	4634	121B	4635	121C	4636	121D	4637	121E	4638	121F	4639
መ		ሙ		ሚ		ማ		ሜ		ም		ሞ		ሟ	
1220	4640	**1221**	4641	**1222**	4642	**1223**	4643	**1224**	4644	**1225**	4645	**1226**	4646	**1227**	4647
ሠ		ሡ		ሢ		ሣ		ሤ		ሥ		ሦ		ሧ	
1228	4648	**1229**	4649	**122A**	4650	**122B**	4651	**122C**	4652	**122D**	4653	**122E**	4654	**122F**	4655
ረ		ሩ		ሪ		ራ		ሬ		ር		ሮ		ሯ	
1230	4656	**1231**	4657	**1232**	4658	**1233**	4659	**1234**	4660	**1235**	4661	**1236**	4662	**1237**	4663
ሰ		ሱ		ሲ		ሳ		ሴ		ስ		ሶ		ሷ	
1238	4664	**1239**	4665	**123A**	4666	**123B**	4667	**123C**	4668	**123D**	4669	**123E**	4670	**123F**	4671
ሸ		ሹ		ሺ		ሻ		ሼ		ሽ		ሾ		ሿ	
1240	4672	**1241**	4673	**1242**	4674	**1243**	4675	**1244**	4676	**1245**	4677	**1246**	4678	**1247**	4679
ቀ		ቁ		ቂ		ቃ		ቄ		ቅ		ቆ		*n/a*	
1248	4680	**1249**	4681	**124A**	4682	**124B**	4683	**124C**	4684	**124D**	4685	**124E**	4686	**124F**	4687
ቈ		*n/a*		ቊ		ቋ		ቌ		ቍ		*n/a*		*n/a*	
1250	4688	**1251**	4689	**1252**	4690	**1253**	4691	**1254**	4692	**1255**	4693	**1256**	4694	**1257**	4695
ቐ		ቑ		ቒ		ቓ		ቔ		ቕ		ቖ		*n/a*	
1258	4696	**1259**	4697	**125A**	4698	**125B**	4699	**125C**	4700	**125D**	4701	**125E**	4702	**125F**	4703
ቘ		*n/a*		ቚ		ቛ		ቜ		ቝ		*n/a*		*n/a*	
1260	4704	**1261**	4705	**1262**	4706	**1263**	4707	**1264**	4708	**1265**	4709	**1266**	4710	**1267**	4711
በ		ቡ		ቢ		ባ		ቤ		ብ		ቦ		ቧ	
1268	4712	**1269**	4713	**126A**	4714	**126B**	4715	**126C**	4716	**126D**	4717	**126E**	4718	**126F**	4719
ቨ		ቩ		ቪ		ቫ		ቬ		ቭ		ቮ		ቯ	
1270	4720	**1271**	4721	**1272**	4722	**1273**	4723	**1274**	4724	**1275**	4725	**1276**	4726	**1277**	4727
ተ		ቱ		ቲ		ታ		ቴ		ት		ቶ		ቷ	
1278	4728	**1279**	4729	**127A**	4730	**127B**	4731	**127C**	4732	**127D**	4733	**127E**	4734	**127F**	4735
ቸ		ቹ		ቺ		ቻ		ቼ		ች		ቾ		ቿ	
1280	4736	**1281**	4737	**1282**	4738	**1283**	4739	**1284**	4740	**1285**	4741	**1286**	4742	**1287**	4743
ኀ		ኁ		ኂ		ኃ		ኄ		ኅ		ኆ		*n/a*	
1288	4744	**1289**	4745	**128A**	4746	**128B**	4747	**128C**	4748	**128D**	4749	**128E**	4750	**128F**	4751
ኈ		*n/a*		ኊ		ኋ		ኌ		ኍ		*n/a*		*n/a*	
1290	4752	**1291**	4753	**1292**	4754	**1293**	4755	**1294**	4756	**1295**	4757	**1296**	4758	**1297**	4759
ነ		ኑ		ኒ		ና		ኔ		ን		ኖ		ኗ	
1298	4760	**1299**	4761	**129A**	4762	**129B**	4763	**129C**	4764	**129D**	4765	**129E**	4766	**129F**	4767
ኘ		ኙ		ኚ		ኛ		ኜ		ኝ		ኞ		ኟ	

Table 27-20. The Ethiopic block of Unicode (continued)

12A0 4768	12A1 4769	12A2 4770	12A3 4771	12A4 4772	12A5 4773	12A6 4774	12A7 4775
ከ	ኩ	ኪ	ካ	ኬ	ክ	ኮ	ኯ
12A8 4776	**12A9** 4777	**12AA** 4778	**12AB** 4779	**12AC** 4780	**12AD** 4781	**12AE** 4782	**12AF** 4783
ኰ	኱	ኲ	ኳ	ኴ	ኵ	኶	*n/a*
12B0 4784	**12B1** 4785	**12B2** 4786	**12B3** 4787	**12B4** 4788	**12B5** 4789	**12B6** 4790	**12B7** 4791
ኸ	*n/a*	ኺ	ኻ	ኼ	ኽ	*n/a*	*n/a*
12B8 4792	**12B9** 4793	**12BA** 4794	**12BB** 4795	**12BC** 4796	**12BD** 4797	**12BE** 4798	**12BF** 4799
ኸ	ኹ	ኺ	ኻ	ኼ	ኽ	ኾ	*n/a*
12C0 4800	**12C1** 4801	**12C2** 4802	**12C3** 4803	**12C4** 4804	**12C5** 4805	**12C6** 4806	**12C7** 4807
ዀ	*n/a*	ዂ	ዃ	ዄ	ዅ	*n/a*	*n/a*
12C8 4808	**12C9** 4809	**12CA** 4810	**12CB** 4811	**12CC** 4812	**12CD** 4813	**12CE** 4814	**12CF** 4815
ወ	ዉ	ዊ	ዋ	ዌ	ው	ዎ	*n/a*
12D0 4816	**12D1** 4817	**12D2** 4818	**12D3** 4819	**12D4** 4820	**12D5** 4821	**12D6** 4822	**12D7** 4823
ዐ	ዑ	ዒ	ዓ	ዔ	ዕ	ዖ	*n/a*
12D8 4824	**12D9** 4825	**12DA** 4826	**12DB** 4827	**12DC** 4828	**12DD** 4829	**12DE** 4830	**12DF** 4831
ዘ	ዙ	ዚ	ዛ	ዜ	ዝ	ዞ	ዟ
12E0 4832	**12E1** 4833	**12E2** 4834	**12E3** 4835	**12E4** 4836	**12E5** 4837	**12E6** 4838	**12E7** 4839
ዠ	ዡ	ዢ	ዣ	ዤ	ዥ	ዦ	ዧ
12E8 4840	**12E9** 4841	**12EA** 4842	**12EB** 4843	**12EC** 4844	**12ED** 4845	**12EE** 4846	**12EF** 4847
የ	ዩ	ዪ	ያ	ዬ	ይ	ዮ	*n/a*
12F0 4848	**12F1** 4849	**12F2** 4850	**12F3** 4851	**12F4** 4852	**12F5** 4853	**12F6** 4854	**12F7** 4855
ደ	ዱ	ዲ	ዳ	ዴ	ድ	ዶ	ዷ
12F8 4856	**12F9** 4857	**12FA** 4858	**12FB** 4859	**12FC** 4860	**12FD** 4861	**12FE** 4862	**12FF** 4863
ዸ	ዹ	ዺ	ዻ	ዼ	ዽ	ዾ	ዿ
1300 4864	**1301** 4865	**1302** 4866	**1303** 4867	**1304** 4868	**1305** 4869	**1306** 4870	**1307** 4871
ጀ	ጁ	ጂ	ጃ	ጄ	ጅ	ጆ	ጇ
1308 4872	**1309** 4873	**130A** 4874	**130B** 4875	**130C** 4876	**130D** 4877	**130E** 4878	**130F** 4879
ገ	ጉ	ጊ	ጋ	ጌ	ግ	ጎ	*n/a*
1310 4880	**1311** 4881	**1312** 4882	**1313** 4883	**1314** 4884	**1315** 4885	**1316** 4886	**1317** 4887
ጐ	*n/a*	ጒ	ጓ	ጔ	ጕ	*n/a*	*n/a*
1318 4888	**1319** 4889	**131A** 4890	**131B** 4891	**131C** 4892	**131D** 4893	**131E** 4894	**131F** 4895
ጘ	ጙ	ጚ	ጛ	ጜ	ጝ	ጞ	*n/a*

Character Sets

Table 27-20. The Ethiopic block of Unicode (continued)

1320 4896	1321 4897	1322 4898	1323 4899	1324 4900	1325 4901	1326 4902	1327 4903
ጠ	ጡ	ጢ	ጣ	ጤ	ጥ	ጦ	ጧ
1328 4904	**1329** 4905	**132A** 4906	**132B** 4907	**132C** 4908	**132D** 4909	**132E** 4910	**132F** 4911
ጨ	ጩ	ጪ	ጫ	ጬ	ጭ	ጮ	ጯ
1330 4912	**1331** 4913	**1332** 4914	**1333** 4915	**1334** 4916	**1335** 4917	**1336** 4918	**1337** 4919
ጰ	ጱ	ጲ	ጳ	ጴ	ጵ	ጶ	ጷ
1338 4920	**1339** 4921	**133A** 4922	**133B** 4923	**133C** 4924	**133D** 4925	**133E** 4926	**133F** 4927
ጸ	ጹ	ጺ	ጻ	ጼ	ጽ	ጾ	ጿ
1340 4928	**1341** 4929	**1342** 4930	**1343** 4931	**1344** 4932	**1345** 4933	**1346** 4934	**1347** 4935
ፀ	ፁ	ፂ	ፃ	ፄ	ፅ	ፆ	*n/a*
1348 4936	**1349** 4937	**134A** 4938	**134B** 4939	**134C** 4940	**134D** 4941	**134E** 4942	**134F** 4943
ፈ	ፉ	ፊ	ፋ	ፌ	ፍ	ፎ	ፏ
1350 4944	**1351** 4945	**1352** 4946	**1353** 4947	**1354** 4948	**1355** 4949	**1356** 4950	**1357** 4951
ፐ	ፑ	ፒ	ፓ	ፔ	ፕ	ፖ	ፗ
1358 4952	**1359** 4953	**135A** 4954	**135B** 4955	**135C** 4956	**135D** 4957	**135E** 4958	**135F** 4959
ፘ	ፙ	ፚ	*n/a*	*n/a*	*n/a*	*n/a*	*n/a*
1360 4960	**1361** 4961	**1362** 4962	**1363** 4963	**1364** 4964	**1365** 4965	**1366** 4966	**1367** 4967
n/a	፡	።	፣	፤	፥	፦	፧
1368 4968	**1369** 4969	**136A** 4970	**136B** 4971	**136C** 4972	**136D** 4973	**136E** 4974	**136F** 4975
፨	፩	፪	፫	፬	፭	፮	፯
1370 4976	**1371** 4977	**1372** 4978	**1373** 4979	**1374** 4980	**1375** 4981	**1376** 4982	**1377** 4983
፰	፱	፲	፳	፴	፵	፶	፷
1378 4984	**1379** 4985	**137A** 4986	**137B** 4987	**137C** 4988	**137D** 4989	**137E** 4990	**137F** 4991
፸	፹	፺	፻	፼	*n/a*	*n/a*	*n/a*

Latin Extended Additional

The Latin Extended Additional characters are single code-point representations of letters combined with diacritical marks. This block is particularly useful for modern Vietnamese. See Table 27-21.

Table 27-21. The Latin Extended Additional block of Unicode

1E00 7680	1E01 7681	1E02 7682	1E03 7683	1E04 7684	1E05 7685	1E06 7686	1E07 7687
Ḁ	ḁ	Ḃ	ḃ	Ḅ	ḅ	Ḇ	ḇ
1E08 7688	1E09 7689	1E0A 7690	1E0B 7691	1E0C 7692	1E0D 7693	1E0E 7694	1E0F 7695
Ḉ	ḉ	Ḋ	ḋ	Ḍ	ḍ	Ḏ	ḏ
1E10 7696	1E11 7697	1E12 7698	1E13 7699	1E14 7700	1E15 7701	1E16 7702	1E17 7703
Ḑ	ḑ	Ḓ	ḓ	Ḕ	ḕ	Ḗ	ḗ
1E18 7704	1E19 7705	1E1A 7706	1E1B 7707	1E1C 7708	1E1D 7709	1E1E 7710	1E1F 7711
Ḙ	ḙ	Ḛ	ḛ	Ḝ	ḝ	Ḟ	ḟ
1E20 7712	1E21 7713	1E22 7714	1E23 7715	1E24 7716	1E25 7717	1E26 7718	1E27 7719
Ḡ	ḡ	Ḣ	ḣ	Ḥ	ḥ	Ḧ	ḧ
1E28 7720	1E29 7721	1E2A 7722	1E2B 7723	1E2C 7724	1E2D 7725	1E2E 7726	1E2F 7727
Ḩ	ḩ	Ḫ	ḫ	Ḭ	ḭ	Ḯ	ḯ
1E30 7728	1E31 7729	1E32 7730	1E33 7731	1E34 7732	1E35 7733	1E36 7734	1E37 7735
Ḱ	ḱ	Ḳ	ḳ	Ḵ	ḵ	Ḷ	ḷ
1E38 7736	1E39 7737	1E3A 7738	1E3B 7739	1E3C 7740	1E3D 7741	1E3E 7742	1E3F 7743
Ḹ	ḹ	Ḻ	ḻ	Ḽ	ḽ	Ḿ	ḿ
1E40 7744	1E41 7745	1E42 7746	1E43 7747	1E44 7748	1E45 7749	1E46 7750	1E47 7751
Ṁ	ṁ	Ṃ	ṃ	Ṅ	ṅ	Ṇ	ṇ
1E48 7752	1E49 7753	1E4A 7754	1E4B 7755	1E4C 7756	1E4D 7757	1E4E 7758	1E4F 7759
Ṉ	ṉ	Ṋ	ṋ	Ṍ	ṍ	Ṏ	ṏ
1E50 7760	1E51 7761	1E52 7762	1E53 7763	1E54 7764	1E55 7765	1E56 7766	1E57 7767
Ṑ	ṑ	Ṓ	ṓ	Ṕ	ṕ	Ṗ	ṗ
1E58 7768	1E59 7769	1E5A 7770	1E5B 7771	1E5C 7772	1E5D 7773	1E5E 7774	1E5F 7775
Ṙ	ṙ	Ṛ	ṛ	Ṝ	ṝ	Ṟ	ṟ
1E60 7776	1E61 7777	1E62 7778	1E63 7779	1E64 7780	1E65 7781	1E66 7782	1E67 7783
Ṡ	ṡ	Ṣ	ṣ	Ṥ	ṥ	Ṧ	ṧ
1E68 7784	1E69 7785	1E6A 7786	1E6B 7787	1E6C 7788	1E6D 7789	1E6E 7790	1E6F 7791
Ṩ	ṩ	Ṫ	ṫ	Ṭ	ṭ	Ṯ	ṯ
1E70 7792	1E71 7793	1E72 7794	1E73 7795	1E74 7796	1E75 7797	1E76 7798	1E77 7799
Ṱ	ṱ	Ṳ	ṳ	Ṵ	ṵ	Ṷ	ṷ
1E78 7800	1E79 7801	1E7A 7802	1E7B 7803	1E7C 7804	1E7D 7805	1E7E 7806	1E7F 7807
Ṹ	ṹ	Ṻ	ṻ	Ṽ	ṽ	Ṿ	ṿ
1E80 7808	1E81 7809	1E82 7810	1E83 7811	1E84 7812	1E85 7813	1E86 7814	1E87 7815
Ẁ	ẁ	Ẃ	ẃ	Ẅ	ẅ	Ẇ	ẇ

Table 27-21. The Latin Extended Additional block of Unicode (continued)

1E88 7816	1E89 7817	1E8A 7818	1E8B 7819	1E8C 7820	1E8D 7821	1E8E 7822	1E8F 7823
Ẉ	ẉ	Ẋ	ẋ	Ẍ	ẍ	Ẏ	ẏ
1E90 7824	**1E91** 7825	**1E92** 7826	**1E93** 7827	**1E94** 7828	**1E95** 7829	**1E96** 7830	**1E97** 7831
Ẑ	ẑ	Ẓ	ẓ	Ẕ	ẕ	ẖ	ẗ
1E98 7832	**1E99** 7833	**1E9A** 7834	**1E9B** 7835	**1E9C** 7836	**1E9D** 7837	**1E9E** 7838	**1E9F** 7839
ẘ	ẙ	ẚ	ẛ	n/a	n/a	n/a	n/a
1EA0 7840	**1EA1** 7841	**1EA2** 7842	**1EA3** 7843	**1EA4** 7844	**1EA5** 7845	**1EA6** 7846	**1EA7** 7847
Ạ	ạ	Ả	ả	Ấ	ấ	Ầ	ầ
1EA8 7848	**1EA9** 7849	**1EAA** 7850	**1EAB** 7851	**1EAC** 7852	**1EAD** 7853	**1EAE** 7854	**1EAF** 7855
Ẩ	ẩ	Ẫ	ẫ	Ậ	ậ	Ắ	ắ
1EB0 7856	**1EB1** 7857	**1EB2** 7858	**1EB3** 7859	**1EB4** 7860	**1EB5** 7861	**1EB6** 7862	**1EB7** 7863
Ằ	ằ	Ẳ	ẳ	Ẵ	ẵ	Ặ	ặ
1EB8 7864	**1EB9** 7865	**1EBA** 7866	**1EBB** 7867	**1EBC** 7868	**1EBD** 7869	**1EBE** 7870	**1EBF** 7871
Ẹ	ẹ	Ẻ	ẻ	Ẽ	ẽ	Ế	ế
1EC0 7872	**1EC1** 7873	**1EC2** 7874	**1EC3** 7875	**1EC4** 7876	**1EC5** 7877	**1EC6** 7878	**1EC7** 7879
Ề	ề	Ể	ể	Ễ	ễ	Ệ	ệ
1EC8 7880	**1EC9** 7881	**1ECA** 7882	**1ECB** 7883	**1ECC** 7884	**1ECD** 7885	**1ECE** 7886	**1ECF** 7887
Ỉ	ỉ	Ị	ị	Ọ	ọ	Ỏ	ỏ
1ED0 7888	**1ED1** 7889	**1ED2** 7890	**1ED3** 7891	**1ED4** 7892	**1ED5** 7893	**1ED6** 7894	**1ED7** 7895
Ố	ố	Ồ	ồ	Ổ	ổ	Ỗ	ỗ
1ED8 7896	**1ED9** 7897	**1EDA** 7898	**1EDB** 7899	**1EDC** 7900	**1EDD** 7901	**1EDE** 7902	**1EDF** 7903
Ộ	ộ	Ớ	ớ	Ờ	ờ	Ở	ở
1EE0 7904	**1EE1** 7905	**1EE2** 7906	**1EE3** 7907	**1EE4** 7908	**1EE5** 7909	**1EE6** 7910	**1EE7** 7911
Ỡ	ỡ	Ợ	ợ	Ụ	ụ	Ủ	ủ
1EE8 7912	**1EE9** 7913	**1EEA** 7914	**1EEB** 7915	**1EEC** 7916	**1EED** 7917	**1EEE** 7918	**1EEF** 7919
Ứ	ứ	Ừ	ừ	Ử	ử	Ữ	ữ
1EF0 7920	**1EF1** 7921	**1EF2** 7922	**1EF3** 7923	**1EF4** 7924	**1EF5** 7925	**1EF6** 7926	**1EF7** 7927
Ự	ự	Ỳ	ỳ	Ỵ	ỵ	Ỷ	ỷ
1EF8 7928	**1EF9** 7929	**1EFA** 7930	**1EFB** 7931	**1EFC** 7932	**1EFD** 7933	**1EFE** 7934	**1EFF** 7935
Ỹ	ỹ	n/a	n/a	n/a	n/a	n/a	n/a

Greek Extended

The Greek Extended block, shown in Table 27-22, contains mostly archaic letters and accented letters that are used in classical and Byzantine Greek but not in modern Greek.

Table 27-22. The Greek Extended block of Unicode

1F00 7936	1F01 7937	1F02 7938	1F03 7939	1F04 7940	1F05 7941	1F06 7942	1F07 7943
ἀ	ἁ	ἂ	ἃ	ἄ	ἅ	ἆ	ἇ
1F08 7944	1F09 7945	1F0A 7946	1F0B 7947	1F0C 7948	1F0D 7949	1F0E 7950	1F0F 7951
Ἀ	Ἁ	Ἂ	Ἃ	Ἄ	Ἅ	Ἆ	Ἇ
1F10 7952	1F11 7953	1F12 7954	1F13 7955	1F14 7956	1F15 7957	1F16 7958	1F17 7959
ἐ	ἑ	ἒ	ἓ	ἔ	ἕ	n/a	n/a
1F18 7960	1F19 7961	1F1A 7962	1F1B 7963	1F1C 7964	1F1D 7965	1F1E 7966	1F1F 7967
Ἐ	Ἑ	Ἒ	Ἓ	Ἔ	Ἕ	n/a	n/a
1F20 7968	1F21 7969	1F22 7970	1F23 7971	1F24 7972	1F25 7973	1F26 7974	1F27 7975
ἠ	ἡ	ἢ	ἣ	ἤ	ἥ	ἦ	ἧ
1F28 7976	1F29 7977	1F2A 7978	1F2B 7979	1F2C 7980	1F2D 7981	1F2E 7982	1F2F 7983
Ἠ	Ἡ	Ἢ	Ἣ	Ἤ	Ἥ	Ἦ	Ἧ
1F30 7984	1F31 7985	1F32 7986	1F33 7987	1F34 7988	1F35 7989	1F36 7990	1F37 7991
ἰ	ἱ	ἲ	ἳ	ἴ	ἵ	ἶ	ἷ
1F38 7992	1F39 7993	1F3A 7994	1F3B 7995	1F3C 7996	1F3D 7997	1F3E 7998	1F3F 7999
Ἰ	Ἱ	Ἲ	Ἳ	Ἴ	Ἵ	Ἶ	Ἷ
1F40 8000	1F41 8001	1F42 8002	1F43 8003	1F44 8004	1F45 8005	1F46 8006	1F47 8007
ὀ	ὁ	ὂ	ὃ	ὄ	ὅ	n/a	n/a
1F48 8008	1F49 8009	1F4A 8010	1F4B 8011	1F4C 8012	1F4D 8013	1F4E 8014	1F4F 8015
Ὀ	Ὁ	Ὂ	Ὃ	Ὄ	Ὅ	n/a	n/a
1F50 8016	1F51 8017	1F52 8018	1F53 8019	1F54 8020	1F55 8021	1F56 8022	1F57 8023
ὐ	ὑ	ὒ	ὓ	ὔ	ὕ	ὖ	ὗ
1F58 8024	1F59 8025	1F5A 8026	1F5B 8027	1F5C 8028	1F5D 8029	1F5E 8030	1F5F 8031
n/a	Ὑ	n/a	Ὓ	n/a	Ὕ	n/a	Ὗ
1F60 8032	1F61 8033	1F62 8034	1F63 8035	1F64 8036	1F65 8037	1F66 8038	1F67 8039
ὠ	ὡ	ὢ	ὣ	ὤ	ὥ	ὦ	ὧ
1F68 8040	1F69 8041	1F6A 8042	1F6B 8043	1F6C 8044	1F6D 8045	1F6E 8046	1F6F 8047
Ὠ	Ὡ	Ὢ	Ὣ	Ὤ	Ὥ	Ὦ	Ὧ
1F70 8048	1F71 8049	1F72 8050	1F73 8051	1F74 8052	1F75 8053	1F76 8054	1F77 8055
ὰ	ά	ὲ	έ	ὴ	ή	ὶ	ί
1F78 8056	1F79 8057	1F7A 8058	1F7B 8059	1F7C 8060	1F7D 8061	1F7E 8062	1F7F 8063
ὸ	ό	ὺ	ύ	ὼ	ώ	n/a	n/a

Table 27-22. The Greek Extended block of Unicode (continued)

1F80 8064	1F81 8065	1F82 8066	1F83 8067	1F84 8068	1F85 8069	1F86 8070	1F87 8071
ᾀ	ᾁ	ᾂ	ᾃ	ᾄ	ᾅ	ᾆ	ᾇ
1F88 8072	**1F89** 8073	**1F8A** 8074	**1F8B** 8075	**1F8C** 8076	**1F8D** 8077	**1F8E** 8078	**1F8F** 8079
ᾈ	ᾉ	ᾊ	ᾋ	ᾌ	ᾍ	ᾎ	ᾏ
1F90 8080	**1F91** 8081	**1F92** 8082	**1F93** 8083	**1F94** 8084	**1F95** 8085	**1F96** 8086	**1F97** 8087
ᾐ	ᾑ	ᾒ	ᾓ	ᾔ	ᾕ	ᾖ	ᾗ
1F98 8088	**1F99** 8089	**1F9A** 8090	**1F9B** 8091	**1F9C** 8092	**1F9D** 8093	**1F9E** 8094	**1F9F** 8095
ᾘ	ᾙ	ᾚ	ᾛ	ᾜ	ᾝ	ᾞ	ᾟ
1FA0 8096	**1FA1** 8097	**1FA2** 8098	**1FA3** 8099	**1FA4** 8100	**1FA5** 8101	**1FA6** 8102	**1FA7** 8103
ᾠ	ᾡ	ᾢ	ᾣ	ᾤ	ᾥ	ᾦ	ᾧ
1FA8 8104	**1FA9** 8105	**1FAA** 8106	**1FAB** 8107	**1FAC** 8108	**1FAD** 8109	**1FAE** 8110	**1FAF** 8111
ᾨ	ᾩ	ᾪ	ᾫ	ᾬ	ᾭ	ᾮ	ᾯ
1FB0 8112	**1FB1** 8113	**1FB2** 8114	**1FB3** 8115	**1FB4** 8116	**1FB5** 8117	**1FB6** 8118	**1FB7** 8119
ᾰ	ᾱ	ᾲ	ᾳ	ᾴ	*n/a*	ᾶ	ᾷ
1FB8 8120	**1FB9** 8121	**1FBA** 8122	**1FBB** 8123	**1FBC** 8124	**1FBD** 8125	**1FBE** 8126	**1FBF** 8127
Ᾰ	Ᾱ	Ὰ	Ά	ᾼ	᾽	ι	᾿
1FC0 8128	**1FC1** 8129	**1FC2** 8130	**1FC3** 8131	**1FC4** 8132	**1FC5** 8133	**1FC6** 8134	**1FC7** 8135
῀	῁	ῂ	ῃ	ῄ	*n/a*	ῆ	ῇ
1FC8 8136	**1FC9** 8137	**1FCA** 8138	**1FCB** 8139	**1FCC** 8140	**1FCD** 8141	**1FCE** 8142	**1FCF** 8143
Ὲ	Έ	Ὴ	Ή	ῌ	῍	῎	῏
1FD0 8144	**1FD1** 8145	**1FD2** 8146	**1FD3** 8147	**1FD4** 8148	**1FD5** 8149	**1FD6** 8150	**1FD7** 8151
ῐ	ῑ	ῒ	ΐ	*n/a*	*n/a*	ῖ	ῗ
1FD8 8152	**1FD9** 8153	**1FDA** 8154	**1FDB** 8155	**1FDC** 8156	**1FDD** 8157	**1FDE** 8158	**1FDF** 8159
Ῐ	Ῑ	Ὶ	Ί	*n/a*	῝	῞	῟
1FE0 8160	**1FE1** 8161	**1FE2** 8162	**1FE3** 8163	**1FE4** 8164	**1FE5** 8165	**1FE6** 8166	**1FE7** 8167
ῠ	ῡ	ῢ	ΰ	ῤ	ῥ	ῦ	ῧ
1FE8 8168	**1FE9** 8169	**1FEA** 8170	**1FEB** 8171	**1FEC** 8172	**1FED** 8173	**1FEE** 8174	**1FEF** 8175
Ῠ	Ῡ	Ὺ	Ύ	Ῥ	῭	΅	`
1FF0 8176	**1FF1** 8177	**1FF2** 8178	**1FF3** 8179	**1FF4** 8180	**1FF5** 8181	**1FF6** 8182	**1FF7** 8183
n/a	*n/a*	ῲ	ῳ	ῴ	*n/a*	ῶ	ῷ
1FF8 8184	**1FF9** 8185	**1FFA** 8186	**1FFB** 8187	**1FFC** 8188	**1FFD** 8189	**1FFE** 8190	**1FFF** 8191
Ὸ	Ό	Ὼ	Ώ	ῼ	´	῾	*n/a*

General Punctuation

The General Punctuation block, shown in Table 27-23, contains punctuation characters used across a variety of languages and scripts that are not already encoded in Latin-1. Characters 0x2000 through 0x200B are all varying amounts of whitespace ranging from zero width (0x200B) to six ems (0x2007). 0x200C through 0x200F and 0x206A through 0x206F are nonprinting format characters with no graphical representation.

Table 27-23. The General Punctuation block of Unicode

2000 8192	2001 8193	2002 8194	2003 8195	2004 8196	2005 8197	2006 8198	2007 8199
NQSP	*MQSP*	*ENSP*	*EMSP*	*3/MSP*	*4/MSP*	*6/MSP*	*FSP*
2008 8200	2009 8201	200A 8202	200B 8203	200C 8204	200D 8205	200E 8206	200F 8207
PSP	*THSP*	*HSP*	*ZWSP*	*ZWNJ*	*ZWJ*	*LRM*	*RLM*
2010 8208	2011 8209	2012 8210	2013 8211	2014 8212	2015 8213	2016 8214	2017 8215
-	-	-	–	—	—	‖	=
2018 8216	2019 8217	201A 8218	201B 8219	201C 8220	201D 8221	201E 8222	201F 8223
‘	’	‚	‛	“	”	„	‟
2020 8224	2021 8225	2022 8226	2023 8227	2024 8228	2025 8229	2026 8230	2027 8231
†	‡	•	‣	․	‥	…	‧
2028 8232	2029 8233	202A 8234	202B 8235	202C 8236	202D 8237	202E 8238	202F 8239
LSEP	*PSEP*	*LRE*	*RLE*	*PDF*	*LRO*	*RLO*	*NNBSP*
2030 8240	2031 8241	2032 8242	2033 8243	2034 8244	2035 8245	2036 8246	2037 8247
‰	‱	′	″	‴	‵	‶	‷
2038 8248	2039 8249	203A 8250	203B 8251	203C 8252	203D 8253	203E 8254	203F 8255
‸	‹	›	※	‼	‽	‾	‿
2040 8256	2041 8257	2042 8258	2043 8259	2044 8260	2045 8261	2046 8262	2047 8263
⁀	⁁	⁂	⁃	⁄	⁅	⁆	⁇
2048 8264	2049 8265	204A 8266	204B 8267	204C 8268	204D 8269	204E 8270	204F 8271
⁈	⁉	⁊	⁋	⁌	⁍	⁎	⁏
2050 8272	2051 8273	2052 8274	2053 8275	2054 8276	2055 8277	2056 8278	2057 8279
⁐	⁑	⁒	⁓	⁔	*n/a*	*n/a*	⁗

Currency Symbols

The Currency Symbols block includes a few monetary symbols not already encoded in other blocks, such as the Indian rupee, the Italian lira, and the Greek drachma. See Table 27-24.

Table 27-24. The Currency Symbols block of Unicode

20A0 8352	20A1 8353	20A2 8354	20A3 8355	20A4 8356	20A5 8357	20A6 8358	20A7 8359
₠	₡	₢	₣	₤	₥	₦	₧
20A8 8360	**20A9** 8361	**20AA** 8362	**20AB** 8363	**20AC** 8364	**20AD** 8365	**20AE** 8366	**20AF** 8367
₨	₩	₪	₫	€	₭	₮	₯
20B0 8368	**20B1** 8369	**20B2** 8370	**20B3** 8371	**20B4** 8372	**20B5** 8373	**20B6** 8374	**20B7** 8375
₰	₱	n/a	n/a	n/a	n/a	n/a	n/a

Letter-Like Symbols

The Letter-Like Symbols block covers characters that look like letters but really aren't, such as the **R** symbol used to represent a prescription. See Table 27-25.

Table 27-25. The Letter-Like Symbols block of Unicode

2100 8448	2101 8449	2102 8450	2103 8451	2104 8452	2105 8453	2106 8454	2107 8455
℀	℁	ℂ	℃	℄	℅	℆	ℇ
2108 8456	**2109** 8457	**210A** 8458	**210B** 8459	**210C** 8460	**210D** 8461	**210E** 8462	**210F** 8463
℈	℉	ℊ	ℋ	ℌ	ℍ	ℎ	ℏ
2110 8464	**2111** 8465	**2112** 8466	**2113** 8467	**2114** 8468	**2115** 8469	**2116** 8470	**2117** 8471
ℐ	ℑ	ℒ	ℓ	℔	ℕ	№	℗
2118 8472	**2119** 8473	**211A** 8474	**211B** 8475	**211C** 8476	**211D** 8477	**211E** 8478	**211F** 8479
℘	ℙ	ℚ	ℛ	ℜ	ℝ	℞	℟
2120 8480	**2121** 8481	**2122** 8482	**2123** 8483	**2124** 8484	**2125** 8485	**2126** 8486	**2127** 8487
SM	TEL	TM	℣	ℤ	℥	Ω	℧
2128 8488	**2129** 8489	**212A** 8490	**212B** 8491	**212C** 8492	**212D** 8493	**212E** 8494	**212F** 8495
ℨ	℩	K	Å	ℬ	ℭ	℮	ℯ
2130 8496	**2131** 8497	**2132** 8498	**2133** 8499	**2134** 8500	**2135** 8501	**2136** 8502	**2137** 8503
ℰ	ℱ	Ⅎ	ℳ	ℴ	ℵ	ℶ	ℷ
2138 8504	**2139** 8505	**213A** 8506	**213B** 8507	**213C** 8508	**213D** 8509	**213E** 8510	**213F** 8511
ℸ	ℹ	℺	℻	n/a	γ	Γ	Π
2140 8512	**2141** 8513	**2142** 8514	**2143** 8515	**2144** 8516	**2145** 8517	**2146** 8518	**2147** 8519
Σ	⅁	⅂	⅃	⅄	ⅅ	ⅆ	ⅇ
2148 8520	**2149** 8521	**214A** 8522	**214B** 8523	**214C** 8524	**214D** 8525	**214E** 8526	**214F** 8527
ⅈ	ⅉ	⅊	⅋	n/a	n/a	n/a	n/a

Arrows

The Arrows block contains commonly needed arrow characters, as shown in Table 27-26.

Table 27-26. The Arrows block of Unicode

2190	8592	2191	8593	2192	8594	2193	8595	2194	8596	2195	8597	2196	8598	2197	8599
←		↑		→		↓		↔		↕		↖		↗	
2198	8600	**2199**	8601	**219A**	8602	**219B**	8603	**219C**	8604	**219D**	8605	**219E**	8606	**219F**	8607
↘		↙		↚		↛		↜		↝		↞		↟	
21A0	8608	**21A1**	8609	**21A2**	8610	**21A3**	8611	**21A4**	8612	**21A5**	8613	**21A6**	8614	**21A7**	8615
↠		↡		↢		↣		↤		↥		↦		↧	
21A8	8616	**21A9**	8617	**21AA**	8618	**21AB**	8619	**21AC**	8620	**21AD**	8621	**21AE**	8622	**21AF**	8623
↨		↩		↪		↫		↬		↭		↮		↯	
21B0	8624	**21B1**	8625	**21B2**	8626	**21B3**	8627	**21B4**	8628	**21B5**	8629	**21B6**	8630	**21B7**	8631
↰		↱		↲		↳		↴		↵		↶		↷	
21B8	8632	**21B9**	8633	**21BA**	8634	**21BB**	8635	**21BC**	8636	**21BD**	8637	**21BE**	8638	**21BF**	8639
↸		↹		↺		↻		↼		↽		↾		↿	
21C0	8640	**21C1**	8641	**21C2**	8642	**21C3**	8643	**21C4**	8644	**21C5**	8645	**21C6**	8646	**21C7**	8647
⇀		⇁		⇂		⇃		⇄		⇅		⇆		⇇	
21C8	8648	**21C9**	8649	**21CA**	8650	**21CB**	8651	**21CC**	8652	**21CD**	8653	**21CE**	8654	**21CF**	8655
⇈		⇉		⇊		⇋		⇌		⇍		⇎		⇏	
21D0	8656	**21D1**	8657	**21D2**	8658	**21D3**	8659	**21D4**	8660	**21D5**	8661	**21D6**	8662	**21D7**	8663
⇐		⇑		⇒		⇓		⇔		⇕		⇖		⇗	
21D8	8664	**21D9**	8665	**21DA**	8666	**21DB**	8667	**21DC**	8668	**21DD**	8669	**21DE**	8670	**21DF**	8671
⇘		⇙		⇚		⇛		⇜		⇝		⇞		⇟	
21E0	8672	**21E1**	8673	**21E2**	8674	**21E3**	8675	**21E4**	8676	**21E5**	8677	**21E6**	8678	**21E7**	8679
⇠		⇡		⇢		⇣		⇤		⇥		⇦		⇧	
21E8	8680	**21E9**	8681	**21EA**	8682	**21EB**	8683	**21EC**	8684	**21ED**	8685	**21EE**	8686	**21EF**	8687
⇨		⇩		⇪		⇫		⇬		⇭		⇮		⇯	
21F0	8688	**21F1**	8689	**21F2**	8690	**21F3**	8691	**21F4**	8692	**21F5**	8693	**21F6**	8694	**21F7**	8695
⇰		⇱		⇲		⇳		⇴		⇵		⇶		*n/a*	
21F8	8696	**21F9**	8697	**21FA**	8698	**21FB**	8699	**21FC**	8700	**21FD**	8701	**21FE**	8702	**21FF**	8703
n/a		*n/a*		*n/a*		*n/a*		*n/a*		*n/a*		*n/a*		*n/a*	

Mathematical Operators

The Mathematical Operators block, shown in Table 27-27, contains a wide variety of symbols used in higher mathematics. A few of these symbols superficially resemble letters in other blocks. For instance, in most fonts, character 2206, ∆, is virtually identical to the Greek capital letter delta. However, using characters in this block is preferable for mathematical expressions, as it allows software to distinguish between letters and mathematical symbols. Fonts may use the same glyph to represent different code points in cases like this.

Table 27-27. The Mathematical Operators block of Unicode

2200 8704	2201 8705	2202 8706	2203 8707	2204 8708	2205 8709	2206 8710	2207 8711
∀	⊂	∂	∃	∄	∅	∆	∇
2208 8712	2209 8713	220A 8714	220B 8715	220C 8716	220D 8717	220E 8718	220F 8719
∈	∉	∊	∋	∌	∍	∎	∏
2210 8720	2211 8721	2212 8722	2213 8723	2214 8724	2215 8725	2216 8726	2217 8727
∐	∑	−	∓	∔	∕	∖	∗
2218 8728	2219 8729	221A 8730	221B 8731	221C 8732	221D 8733	221E 8734	221F 8735
∘	∙	√	∛	∜	∝	∞	∟
2220 8736	2221 8737	2222 8738	2223 8739	2224 8740	2225 8741	2226 8742	2227 8743
∠	∡	∢	∣	∤	∥	∦	∧
2228 8744	2229 8745	222A 8746	222B 8747	222C 8748	222D 8749	222E 8750	222F 8751
∨	∩	∪	∫	∬	∭	∮	∯
2230 8752	2231 8753	2232 8754	2233 8755	2234 8756	2235 8757	2236 8758	2237 8759
∰	∱	∲	∳	∴	∵	∶	∷
2238 8760	2239 8761	223A 8762	223B 8763	223C 8764	223D 8765	223E 8766	223F 8767
∸	∹	∺	∻	∼	∽	∾	∿
2240 8768	2241 8769	2242 8770	2243 8771	2244 8772	2245 8773	2246 8774	2247 8775
≀	≁	≂	≃	≄	≅	≆	≇
2248 8776	2249 8777	224A 8778	224B 8779	224C 8780	224D 8781	224E 8782	224F 8783
≈	≉	≊	≋	≌	≍	≎	≏
2250 8784	2251 8785	2252 8786	2253 8787	2254 8788	2255 8789	2256 8790	2257 8791
≐	≑	≒	≓	≔	≕	≖	≗
2258 8792	2259 8793	225A 8794	225B 8795	225C 8796	225D 8797	225E 8798	225F 8799
≘	≙	≚	≛	≜	≝	≞	≟
2260 8800	2261 8801	2262 8802	2263 8803	2264 8804	2265 8805	2266 8806	2267 8807
≠	≡	≢	≣	≤	≥	≦	≧

Table 27-27. The Mathematical Operators block of Unicode (continued)

Code	Dec	Char	Code	Dec	Char	Code	Dec	Char	Code	Dec	Char
2268	8808	≨	2269	8809	≩	226A	8810	≪	226B	8811	≫
226C	8812	≬	226D	8813	≭	226E	8814	≮	226F	8815	≯
2270	8816	≰	2271	8817	≱	2272	8818	≲	2273	8819	≳
2274	8820	≴	2275	8821	≵	2276	8822	≶	2277	8823	≷
2278	8824	≸	2279	8825	≹	227A	8826	≺	227B	8827	≻
227C	8828	≼	227D	8829	≽	227E	8830	≾	227F	8831	≿
2280	8832	⊀	2281	8833	⊁	2282	8834	⊂	2283	8835	⊃
2284	8836	⊄	2285	8837	⊅	2286	8838	⊆	2287	8839	⊇
2288	8840	⊈	2289	8841	⊉	228A	8842	⊊	228B	8843	⊋
228C	8844	⊌	228D	8845	⊍	228E	8846	⊎	228F	8847	⊏
2290	8848	⊐	2291	8849	⊑	2292	8850	⊒	2293	8851	⊓
2294	8852	⊔	2295	8853	⊕	2296	8854	⊖	2297	8855	⊗
2298	8856	⊘	2299	8857	⊙	229A	8858	⊚	229B	8859	⊛
229C	8860	⊜	229D	8861	⊝	229E	8862	⊞	229F	8863	⊟
22A0	8864	⊠	22A1	8865	⊡	22A2	8866	⊢	22A3	8867	⊣
22A4	8868	⊤	22A5	8869	⊥	22A6	8870	⊦	22A7	8871	⊧
22A8	8872	⊨	22A9	8873	⊩	22AA	8874	⊪	22AB	8875	⊫
22AC	8876	⊬	22AD	8877	⊭	22AE	8878	⊮	22AF	8879	⊯
22B0	8880	⊰	22B1	8881	⊱	22B2	8882	⊲	22B3	8883	⊳
22B4	8884	⊴	22B5	8885	⊵	22B6	8886	⊶	22B7	8887	⊷
22B8	8888	⊸	22B9	8889	⊹	22BA	8890	⊺	22BB	8891	⊻
22BC	8892	⊼	22BD	8893	⊽	22BE	8894	⊾	22BF	8895	⊿
22C0	8896	⋀	22C1	8897	⋁	22C2	8898	⋂	22C3	8899	⋃
22C4	8900	⋄	22C5	8901	⋅	22C6	8902	⋆	22C7	8903	⋇
22C8	8904	⋈	22C9	8905	⋉	22CA	8906	⋊	22CB	8907	⋋
22CC	8908	⋌	22CD	8909	⋍	22CE	8910	⋎	22CF	8911	⋏
22D0	8912	⋐	22D1	8913	⋑	22D2	8914	⋒	22D3	8915	⋓
22D4	8916	⋔	22D5	8917	⋕	22D6	8918	⋖	22D7	8919	⋗
22D8	8920	⋘	22D9	8921	⋙	22DA	8922	⋚	22DB	8923	⋛
22DC	8924	⋜	22DD	8925	⋝	22DE	8926	⋞	22DF	8927	⋟
22E0	8928	⋠	22E1	8929	⋡	22E2	8930	⋢	22E3	8931	⋣
22E4	8932	⋤	22E5	8933	⋥	22E6	8934	⋦	22E7	8935	⋧

Table 27-27. The Mathematical Operators block of Unicode (continued)

22E8 8936	22E9 8937	22EA 8938	22EB 8939	22EC 8940	22ED 8941	22EE 8942	22EF 8943
⋨	⋩	⋪	⋫	⋬	⋭	⋮	⋯
22F0 8944	**22F1** 8945	**22F2** 8946	**22F3** 8947	**22F4** 8948	**22F5** 8949	**22F6** 8950	**22F7** 8951
⋰	⋱	⋲	⋳	⋴	⋵	⋶	⋷
22F8 8952	**22F9** 8953	**22FA** 8954	**22FB** 8955	**22FC** 8956	**22FD** 8957	**22FE** 8958	**22FF** 8959
⋸	⋹	⋺	⋻	⋼	⋽	⋾	⋿

Unicode 3.1 added one more block of mathematical alphanumeric symbols in Plane 1 between 0x1D400 and 0x1D7FF, as shown in Table 27-28. Mostly these are repetitions of the ASCII and Greek letters and digits in what would normally be considered font variations. For instance, 0x1D400 is mathematical bold capital **A**. The justification for these is that when used in an equation, they really aren't the same characters as the equivalent glyphs in text.

Table 27-28. The Mathematical Alphanumeric Symbols block of Unicode

1D400 119808	1D401 119809	1D402 119810	1D403 119811	1D404 119812	1D405 119813	1D406 119814	1D407 119815
A	**B**	**C**	**D**	**E**	**F**	**G**	**H**
1D408 119816	**1D409** 119817	**1D40A** 119818	**1D40B** 119819	**1D40C** 119820	**1D40D** 119821	**1D40E** 119822	**1D40F** 119823
I	**J**	**K**	**L**	**M**	**N**	**O**	**P**
1D410 119824	**1D411** 119825	**1D412** 119826	**1D413** 119827	**1D414** 119828	**1D415** 119829	**1D416** 119830	**1D417** 119831
Q	**R**	**S**	**T**	**U**	**V**	**W**	**X**
1D418 119832	**1D419** 119833	**1D41A** 119834	**1D41B** 119835	**1D41C** 119836	**1D41D** 119837	**1D41E** 119838	**1D41F** 119839
Y	**Z**	**a**	**b**	**c**	**d**	**e**	**f**
1D420 119840	**1D421** 119841	**1D422** 119842	**1D423** 119843	**1D424** 119844	**1D425** 119845	**1D426** 119846	**1D427** 119847
g	**h**	**i**	**j**	**k**	**l**	**m**	**n**
1D428 119848	**1D429** 119849	**1D42A** 119850	**1D42B** 119851	**1D42C** 119852	**1D42D** 119853	**1D42E** 119854	**1D42F** 119855
o	**p**	**q**	**r**	**s**	**t**	**u**	**v**
1D430 119856	**1D431** 119857	**1D432** 119858	**1D433** 119859	**1D434** 119860	**1D435** 119861	**1D436** 119862	**1D437** 119863
w	**x**	**y**	**z**	*A*	*B*	*C*	*D*
1D438 119864	**1D439** 119865	**1D43A** 119866	**1D43B** 119867	**1D43C** 119868	**1D43D** 119869	**1D43E** 119870	**1D43F** 119871
E	*F*	*G*	*H*	*I*	*J*	*K*	*L*
1D440 119872	**1D441** 119873	**1D442** 119874	**1D443** 119875	**1D444** 119876	**1D445** 119877	**1D446** 119878	**1D447** 119879
M	*N*	*O*	*P*	*Q*	*R*	*S*	*T*
1D448 119880	**1D449** 119881	**1D44A** 119882	**1D44B** 119883	**1D44C** 119884	**1D44D** 119885	**1D44E** 119886	**1D44F** 119887
U	*V*	*W*	*X*	*Y*	*Z*	*a*	*b*
1D450 119888	**1D451** 119889	**1D452** 119890	**1D453** 119891	**1D454** 119892	**1D455** 119893	**1D456** 119894	**1D457** 119895
c	*d*	*e*	*f*	*g*	*n/a*	*i*	*j*

1D458 119896	1D459 119897	1D45A 119898	1D45B 119899	1D45C 119900	1D45D 119901	1D45E 119902	1D45F 119903
k	*l*	*m*	*n*	*o*	*p*	*q*	*r*
1D460 119904	1D461 119905	1D462 119906	1D463 119907	1D464 119908	1D465 119909	1D466 119910	1D467 119911
s	*t*	*u*	*v*	*w*	*x*	*y*	*z*
1D468 119912	1D469 119913	1D46A 119914	1D46B 119915	1D46C 119916	1D46D 119917	1D46E 119918	1D46F 119919
A	*B*	*C*	*D*	*E*	*F*	*G*	*H*
1D470 119920	1D471 119921	1D472 119922	1D473 119923	1D474 119924	1D475 119925	1D476 119926	1D477 119927
I	*J*	*K*	*L*	*M*	*N*	*O*	*P*
1D478 119928	1D479 119929	1D47A 119930	1D47B 119931	1D47C 119932	1D47D 119933	1D47E 119934	1D47F 119935
Q	*R*	*S*	*T*	*U*	*V*	*W*	*X*
1D480 119936	1D481 119937	1D482 119938	1D483 119939	1D484 119940	1D485 119941	1D486 119942	1D487 119943
Y	*Z*	*a*	*b*	*c*	*d*	*e*	*f*
1D488 119944	1D489 119945	1D48A 119946	1D48B 119947	1D48C 119948	1D48D 119949	1D48E 119950	1D48F 119951
g	*h*	*i*	*j*	*k*	*l*	*m*	*n*
1D490 119952	1D491 119953	1D492 119954	1D493 119955	1D494 119956	1D495 119957	1D496 119958	1D497 119959
o	*p*	*q*	*r*	*s*	*t*	*u*	*v*
1D498 119960	1D499 119961	1D49A 119962	1D49B 119963	1D49C 119964	1D49D 119965	1D49E 119966	1D49F 119967
w	*x*	*y*	*z*	𝒜	n/a	𝒞	𝒟
1D4A0 119968	1D4A1 119969	1D4A2 119970	1D4A3 119971	1D4A4 119972	1D4A5 119973	1D4A6 119974	1D4A7 119975
n/a	n/a	𝒢	n/a	n/a	𝒥	𝒦	n/a
1D4A8 119976	1D4A9 119977	1D4AA 119978	1D4AB 119979	1D4AC 119980	1D4AD 119981	1D4AE 119982	1D4AF 119983
n/a	𝒩	𝒪	𝒫	𝒬	n/a	𝒮	𝒯
1D4B0 119984	1D4B1 119985	1D4B2 119986	1D4B3 119987	1D4B4 119988	1D4B5 119989	1D4B6 119990	1D4B7 119991
𝒰	𝒱	𝒲	𝒳	𝒴	𝒵	𝒶	𝒷
1D4B8 119992	1D4B9 119993	1D4BA 119994	1D4BB 119995	1D4BC 119996	1D4BD 119997	1D4BE 119998	1D4BF 119999
𝒸	𝒹	n/a	𝒻	n/a	𝒽	𝒾	𝒿
1D4C0 120000	1D4C1 120001	1D4C2 120002	1D4C3 120003	1D4C4 120004	1D4C5 120005	1D4C6 120006	1D4C7 120007
𝓀	𝓁	𝓂	𝓃	n/a	𝓅	𝓆	𝓇
1D4C8 120008	1D4C9 120009	1D4CA 120010	1D4CB 120011	1D4CC 120012	1D4CD 120013	1D4CE 120014	1D4CF 120015
𝓈	𝓉	𝓊	𝓋	𝓌	𝓍	𝓎	𝓏
1D4D0 120016	1D4D1 120017	1D4D2 120018	1D4D3 120019	1D4D4 120020	1D4D5 120021	1D4D6 120022	1D4D7 120023
𝓐	𝓑	𝓒	𝓓	𝓔	𝓕	𝓖	𝓗
1D4D8 120024	1D4D9 120025	1D4DA 120026	1D4DB 120027	1D4DC 120028	1D4DD 120029	1D4DE 120030	1D4DF 120031
𝓘	𝓙	𝓚	𝓛	𝓜	𝓝	𝓞	𝓟
1D4E0 120032	1D4E1 120033	1D4E2 120034	1D4E3 120035	1D4E4 120036	1D4E5 120037	1D4E6 120038	1D4E7 120039
𝓠	𝓡	𝓢	𝓣	𝓤	𝓥	𝓦	𝓧

Table 27-28. The Mathematical Alphanumeric Symbols block of Unicode (continued)

1D4E8 120040	1D4E9 120041	1D4EA 120042	1D4EB 120043	1D4EC 120044	1D4ED 120045	1D4EE 120046	1D4EF 120047
$\mathcal{Y}$	$\mathcal{Z}$	a	b	c	d	e	f
1D4F0 120048	**1D4F1** 120049	**1D4F2** 120050	**1D4F3** 120051	**1D4F4** 120052	**1D4F5** 120053	**1D4F6** 120054	**1D4F7** 120055
g	h	i	j	k	l	m	n
1D4F8 120056	**1D4F9** 120057	**1D4FA** 120058	**1D4FB** 120059	**1D4FC** 120060	**1D4FD** 120061	**1D4FE** 120062	**1D4FF** 120063
o	p	q	r	s	t	u	v
1D500 120064	**1D501** 120065	**1D502** 120066	**1D503** 120067	**1D504** 120068	**1D505** 120069	**1D506** 120070	**1D507** 120071
w	x	y	z	A	B	*n/a*	D
1D508 120072	**1D509** 120073	**1D50A** 120074	**1D50B** 120075	**1D50C** 120076	**1D50D** 120077	**1D50E** 120078	**1D50F** 120079
E	F	G	*n/a*	*n/a*	J	K	L
1D510 120080	**1D511** 120081	**1D512** 120082	**1D513** 120083	**1D514** 120084	**1D515** 120085	**1D516** 120086	**1D517** 120087
M	N	O	P	Q	*n/a*	S	T
1D518 120088	**1D519** 120089	**1D51A** 120090	**1D51B** 120091	**1D51C** 120092	**1D51D** 120093	**1D51E** 120094	**1D51F** 120095
U	V	W	X	Y	*n/a*	a	b
1D520 120096	**1D521** 120097	**1D522** 120098	**1D523** 120099	**1D524** 120100	**1D525** 120101	**1D526** 120102	**1D527** 120103
C	d	e	f	g	h	i	j
1D528 120104	**1D529** 120105	**1D52A** 120106	**1D52B** 120107	**1D52C** 120108	**1D52D** 120109	**1D52E** 120110	**1D52F** 120111
K	l	m	n	o	p	q	r
1D530 120112	**1D531** 120113	**1D532** 120114	**1D533** 120115	**1D534** 120116	**1D535** 120117	**1D536** 120118	**1D537** 120119
S	t	u	v	w	x	y	z
1D538 120120	**1D539** 120121	**1D53A** 120122	**1D53B** 120123	**1D53C** 120124	**1D53D** 120125	**1D53E** 120126	**1D53F** 120127
$\mathbb{A}$	$\mathbb{B}$	*n/a*	$\mathbb{D}$	$\mathbb{E}$	$\mathbb{F}$	$\mathbb{G}$	*n/a*
1D540 120128	**1D541** 120129	**1D542** 120130	**1D543** 120131	**1D544** 120132	**1D545** 120133	**1D546** 120134	**1D547** 120135
$\mathbb{I}$	$\mathbb{J}$	$\mathbb{K}$	$\mathbb{L}$	$\mathbb{M}$	*n/a*	$\mathbb{O}$	*n/a*
1D548 120136	**1D549** 120137	**1D54A** 120138	**1D54B** 120139	**1D54C** 120140	**1D54D** 120141	**1D54E** 120142	**1D54F** 120143
n/a	*n/a*	$\mathbb{S}$	$\mathbb{T}$	$\mathbb{U}$	$\mathbb{V}$	$\mathbb{W}$	$\mathbb{X}$
1D550 120144	**1D551** 120145	**1D552** 120146	**1D553** 120147	**1D554** 120148	**1D555** 120149	**1D556** 120150	**1D557** 120151
$\mathbb{Y}$	*n/a*	a	b	c	d	e	f
1D558 120152	**1D559** 120153	**1D55A** 120154	**1D55B** 120155	**1D55C** 120156	**1D55D** 120157	**1D55E** 120158	**1D55F** 120159
g	h	i	j	k	l	m	n
1D560 120160	**1D561** 120161	**1D562** 120162	**1D563** 120163	**1D564** 120164	**1D565** 120165	**1D566** 120166	**1D567** 120167
o	p	q	r	s	t	v	v
1D568 120168	**1D569** 120169	**1D56A** 120170	**1D56B** 120171	**1D56C** 120172	**1D56D** 120173	**1D56E** 120174	**1D56F** 120175
w	x	y	z	$\mathfrak{A}$	$\mathfrak{B}$	$\mathfrak{C}$	$\mathfrak{D}$
1D570 120176	**1D571** 120177	**1D572** 120178	**1D573** 120179	**1D574** 120180	**1D575** 120181	**1D576** 120182	**1D577** 120183
$\mathfrak{E}$	$\mathfrak{F}$	$\mathfrak{G}$	$\mathfrak{H}$	$\mathfrak{I}$	$\mathfrak{J}$	$\mathfrak{K}$	$\mathfrak{L}$

1D578 120184	1D579 120185	1D57A 120186	1D57B 120187	1D57C 120188	1D57D 120189	1D57E 120190	1D57F 120191
𝕸	𝕹	𝕺	𝕻	𝕼	𝕽	𝕾	𝕿
1D580 120192	**1D581** 120193	**1D582** 120194	**1D583** 120195	**1D584** 120196	**1D585** 120197	**1D586** 120198	**1D587** 120199
𝖀	𝖁	𝖂	𝖃	𝖄	𝖅	𝖆	𝖇
1D588 120200	**1D589** 120201	**1D58A** 120202	**1D58B** 120203	**1D58C** 120204	**1D58D** 120205	**1D58E** 120206	**1D58F** 120207
𝖈	𝖉	𝖊	𝖋	𝖌	𝖍	𝖎	𝖏
1D590 120208	**1D591** 120209	**1D592** 120210	**1D593** 120211	**1D594** 120212	**1D595** 120213	**1D596** 120214	**1D597** 120215
𝖐	𝖑	𝖒	𝖓	𝖔	𝖕	𝖖	𝖗
1D598 120216	**1D599** 120217	**1D59A** 120218	**1D59B** 120219	**1D59C** 120220	**1D59D** 120221	**1D59E** 120222	**1D59F** 120223
𝖘	𝖙	𝖚	𝖛	𝖜	𝖝	𝖞	𝖟
1D5A0 120224	**1D5A1** 120225	**1D5A2** 120226	**1D5A3** 120227	**1D5A4** 120228	**1D5A5** 120229	**1D5A6** 120230	**1D5A7** 120231
A	B	C	D	E	F	G	H
1D5A8 120232	**1D5A9** 120233	**1D5AA** 120234	**1D5AB** 120235	**1D5AC** 120236	**1D5AD** 120237	**1D5AE** 120238	**1D5AF** 120239
I	J	K	L	M	N	O	P
1D5B0 120240	**1D5B1** 120241	**1D5B2** 120242	**1D5B3** 120243	**1D5B4** 120244	**1D5B5** 120245	**1D5B6** 120246	**1D5B7** 120247
Q	R	S	T	U	V	W	X
1D5B8 120248	**1D5B9** 120249	**1D5BA** 120250	**1D5BB** 120251	**1D5BC** 120252	**1D5BD** 120253	**1D5BE** 120254	**1D5BF** 120255
Y	Z	a	b	c	d	e	f
1D5C0 120256	**1D5C1** 120257	**1D5C2** 120258	**1D5C3** 120259	**1D5C4** 120260	**1D5C5** 120261	**1D5C6** 120262	**1D5C7** 120263
g	h	i	j	k	l	m	n
1D5C8 120264	**1D5C9** 120265	**1D5CA** 120266	**1D5CB** 120267	**1D5CC** 120268	**1D5CD** 120269	**1D5CE** 120270	**1D5CF** 120271
o	p	q	r	s	t	u	v
1D5D0 120272	**1D5D1** 120273	**1D5D2** 120274	**1D5D3** 120275	**1D5D4** 120276	**1D5D5** 120277	**1D5D6** 120278	**1D5D7** 120279
w	x	y	z	A	B	C	D
1D5D8 120280	**1D5D9** 120281	**1D5DA** 120282	**1D5DB** 120283	**1D5DC** 120284	**1D5DD** 120285	**1D5DE** 120286	**1D5DF** 120287
E	F	G	H	I	J	K	L
1D5E0 120288	**1D5E1** 120289	**1D5E2** 120290	**1D5E3** 120291	**1D5E4** 120292	**1D5E5** 120293	**1D5E6** 120294	**1D5E7** 120295
M	N	O	P	Q	R	S	T
1D5E8 120296	**1D5E9** 120297	**1D5EA** 120298	**1D5EB** 120299	**1D5EC** 120300	**1D5ED** 120301	**1D5EE** 120302	**1D5EF** 120303
U	V	W	X	Y	Z	a	b
1D5F0 120304	**1D5F1** 120305	**1D5F2** 120306	**1D5F3** 120307	**1D5F4** 120308	**1D5F5** 120309	**1D5F6** 120310	**1D5F7** 120311
c	d	e	f	g	h	i	j
1D5F8 120312	**1D5F9** 120313	**1D5FA** 120314	**1D5FB** 120315	**1D5FC** 120316	**1D5FD** 120317	**1D5FE** 120318	**1D5FF** 120319
k	l	m	n	o	p	q	r
1D600 120320	**1D601** 120321	**1D602** 120322	**1D603** 120323	**1D604** 120324	**1D605** 120325	**1D606** 120326	**1D607** 120327
s	t	u	v	w	x	y	z

Table 27-28. The Mathematical Alphanumeric Symbols block of Unicode (continued)

1D608 120328	1D609 120329	1D60A 120330	1D60B 120331	1D60C 120332	1D60D 120333	1D60E 120334	1D60F 120335
A	B	C	D	E	F	G	H
1D610 120336	1D611 120337	1D612 120338	1D613 120339	1D614 120340	1D615 120341	1D616 120342	1D617 120343
I	J	K	L	M	N	O	P
1D618 120344	1D619 120345	1D61A 120346	1D61B 120347	1D61C 120348	1D61D 120349	1D61E 120350	1D61F 120351
Q	R	S	T	U	V	W	X
1D620 120352	1D621 120353	1D622 120354	1D623 120355	1D624 120356	1D625 120357	1D626 120358	1D627 120359
Y	Z	a	b	c	d	e	f
1D628 120360	1D629 120361	1D62A 120362	1D62B 120363	1D62C 120364	1D62D 120365	1D62E 120366	1D62F 120367
g	h	i	j	k	l	m	n
1D630 120368	1D631 120369	1D632 120370	1D633 120371	1D634 120372	1D635 120373	1D636 120374	1D637 120375
o	p	q	r	s	t	u	v
1D638 120376	1D639 120377	1D63A 120378	1D63B 120379	1D63C 120380	1D63D 120381	1D63E 120382	1D63F 120383
w	x	y	z	A	B	C	D
1D640 120384	1D641 120385	1D642 120386	1D643 120387	1D644 120388	1D645 120389	1D646 120390	1D647 120391
E	F	G	H	I	J	K	L
1D648 120392	1D649 120393	1D64A 120394	1D64B 120395	1D64C 120396	1D64D 120397	1D64E 120398	1D64F 120399
M	N	O	P	Q	R	S	T
1D650 120400	1D651 120401	1D652 120402	1D653 120403	1D654 120404	1D655 120405	1D656 120406	1D657 120407
U	V	W	X	X	Z	a	b
1D658 120408	1D659 120409	1D65A 120410	1D65B 120411	1D65C 120412	1D65D 120413	1D65E 120414	1D65F 120415
c	d	e	f	g	h	i	j
1D660 120416	1D661 120417	1D662 120418	1D663 120419	1D664 120420	1D665 120421	1D666 120422	1D667 120423
k	l	m	n	o	p	q	r
1D668 120424	1D669 120425	1D66A 120426	1D66B 120427	1D66C 120428	1D66D 120429	1D66E 120430	1D66F 120431
s	t	u	v	w	x	y	z
1D670 120432	1D671 120433	1D672 120434	1D673 120435	1D674 120436	1D675 120437	1D676 120438	1D677 120439
A	B	C	D	E	F	G	H
1D678 120440	1D679 120441	1D67A 120442	1D67B 120443	1D67C 120444	1D67D 120445	1D67E 120446	1D67F 120447
I	J	K	L	M	N	O	P
1D680 120448	1D681 120449	1D682 120450	1D683 120451	1D684 120452	1D685 120453	1D686 120454	1D687 120455
Q	R	S	T	U	V	W	X
1D688 120456	1D689 120457	1D68A 120458	1D68B 120459	1D68C 120460	1D68D 120461	1D68E 120462	1D68F 120463
Y	Z	a	b	c	d	e	f
1D690 120464	1D691 120465	1D692 120466	1D693 120467	1D694 120468	1D695 120469	1D696 120470	1D697 120471
g	h	i	j	k	l	m	n

1D698 120472	1D699 120473	1D69A 120474	1D69B 120475	1D69C 120476	1D69D 120477	1D69E 120478	1D69F 120479
o	p	q	r	s	t	u	v
1D6A0 120480	1D6A1 120481	1D6A2 120482	1D6A3 120483	1D6A4 120484	1D6A5 120485	1D6A6 120486	1D6A7 120487
w	x	y	z	*n/a*	*n/a*	*n/a*	*n/a*
1D6A8 120488	1D6A9 120489	1D6AA 120490	1D6AB 120491	1D6AC 120492	1D6AD 120493	1D6AE 120494	1D6AF 120495
A	B	Γ	Δ	E	Z	H	Θ
1D6B0 120496	1D6B1 120497	1D6B2 120498	1D6B3 120499	1D6B4 120500	1D6B5 120501	1D6B6 120502	1D6B7 120503
I	K	Λ	M	N	Ξ	O	Π
1D6B8 120504	1D6B9 120505	1D6BA 120506	1D6BB 120507	1D6BC 120508	1D6BD 120509	1D6BE 120510	1D6BF 120511
P	Θ	Σ	T	Y	Φ	X	Ψ
1D6C0 120512	1D6C1 120513	1D6C2 120514	1D6C3 120515	1D6C4 120516	1D6C5 120517	1D6C6 120518	1D6C7 120519
Ω	∇	α	β	γ	δ	ε	ζ
1D6C8 120520	1D6C9 120521	1D6CA 120522	1D6CB 120523	1D6CC 120524	1D6CD 120525	1D6CE 120526	1D6CF 120527
η	θ	ι	κ	λ	μ	ν	ξ
1D6D0 120528	1D6D1 120529	1D6D2 120530	1D6D3 120531	1D6D4 120532	1D6D5 120533	1D6D6 120534	1D6D7 120535
o	π	ρ	ς	σ	τ	υ	φ
1D6D8 120536	1D6D9 120537	1D6DA 120538	1D6DB 120539	1D6DC 120540	1D6DD 120541	1D6DE 120542	1D6DF 120543
χ	ψ	ω	∂	ε	ϑ	ϰ	Φ
1D6E0 120544	1D6E1 120545	1D6E2 120546	1D6E3 120547	1D6E4 120548	1D6E5 120549	1D6E6 120550	1D6E7 120551
ρ	ϖ	*A*	*B*	*Γ*	*Δ*	*E*	*Z*
1D6E8 120552	1D6E9 120553	1D6EA 120554	1D6EB 120555	1D6EC 120556	1D6ED 120557	1D6EE 120558	1D6EF 120559
H	*Θ*	*I*	*K*	*Λ*	*M*	*N*	*Ξ*
1D6F0 120560	1D6F1 120561	1D6F2 120562	1D6F3 120563	1D6F4 120564	1D6F5 120565	1D6F6 120566	1D6F7 120567
O	*Π*	*P*	*Θ*	*Σ*	*T*	*Y*	*Φ*
1D6F8 120568	1D6F9 120569	1D6FA 120570	1D6FB 120571	1D6FC 120572	1D6FD 120573	1D6FE 120574	1D6FF 120575
X	*Ψ*	*Ω*	∇	*α*	*β*	*γ*	*δ*
1D700 120576	1D701 120577	1D702 120578	1D703 120579	1D704 120580	1D705 120581	1D706 120582	1D707 120583
ε	*ζ*	*η*	*θ*	*ι*	*κ*	*λ*	*μ*
1D708 120584	1D709 120585	1D70A 120586	1D70B 120587	1D70C 120588	1D70D 120589	1D70E 120590	1D70F 120591
ν	*ξ*	*o*	*π*	*ρ*	*ς*	*σ*	*τ*
1D710 120592	1D711 120593	1D712 120594	1D713 120595	1D714 120596	1D715 120597	1D716 120598	1D717 120599
υ	*φ*	*χ*	*ψ*	*ω*	*∂*	*ε*	*ϑ*
1D718 120600	1D719 120601	1D71A 120602	1D71B 120603	1D71C 120604	1D71D 120605	1D71E 120606	1D71F 120607
ϰ	*φ*	*ρ*	*ϖ*	*A*	*B*	*Γ*	*Δ*
1D720 120608	1D721 120609	1D722 120610	1D723 120611	1D724 120612	1D725 120613	1D726 120614	1D727 120615
E	*Z*	*H*	*Θ*	*I*	*K*	*Λ*	*M*

1D728 120616	1D729 120617	1D72A 120618	1D72B 120619	1D72C 120620	1D72D 120621	1D72E 120622	1D72F 120623
N	Ξ	O	Π	P	Θ	Σ	T
1D730 120624	**1D731** 120625	**1D732** 120626	**1D733** 120627	**1D734** 120628	**1D735** 120629	**1D736** 120630	**1D737** 120631
Y	Φ	X	Ψ	Ω	∇	α	β
1D738 120632	**1D739** 120633	**1D73A** 120634	**1D73B** 120635	**1D73C** 120636	**1D73D** 120637	**1D73E** 120638	**1D73F** 120639
γ	δ	ε	ζ	η	θ	ι	κ
1D740 120640	**1D741** 120641	**1D742** 120642	**1D743** 120643	**1D744** 120644	**1D745** 120645	**1D746** 120646	**1D747** 120647
λ	μ	ν	ξ	o	π	ρ	ς
1D748 120648	**1D749** 120649	**1D74A** 120650	**1D74B** 120651	**1D74C** 120652	**1D74D** 120653	**1D74E** 120654	**1D74F** 120655
σ	τ	υ	φ	χ	ψ	ω	∂
1D750 120656	**1D751** 120657	**1D752** 120658	**1D753** 120659	**1D754** 120660	**1D755** 120661	**1D756** 120662	**1D757** 120663
ε	ϑ	$\varkappa$	ϕ	ρ	ϖ	A	B
1D758 120664	**1D759** 120665	**1D75A** 120666	**1D75B** 120667	**1D75C** 120668	**1D75D** 120669	**1D75E** 120670	**1D75F** 120671
Γ	Δ	E	Z	H	Θ	I	K
1D760 120672	**1D761** 120673	**1D762** 120674	**1D763** 120675	**1D764** 120676	**1D765** 120677	**1D766** 120678	**1D767** 120679
Λ	M	N	Ξ	O	Π	P	Θ
1D768 120680	**1D769** 120681	**1D76A** 120682	**1D76B** 120683	**1D76C** 120684	**1D76D** 120685	**1D76E** 120686	**1D76F** 120687
Σ	T	Y	Φ	X	Ψ	Ω	∇
1D770 120688	**1D771** 120689	**1D772** 120690	**1D773** 120691	**1D774** 120692	**1D775** 120693	**1D776** 120694	**1D777** 120695
α	β	γ	δ	ε	ζ	η	θ
1D778 120696	**1D779** 120697	**1D77A** 120698	**1D77B** 120699	**1D77C** 120700	**1D77D** 120701	**1D77E** 120702	**1D77F** 120703
ι	κ	λ	μ	ν	ξ	o	π
1D780 120704	**1D781** 120705	**1D782** 120706	**1D783** 120707	**1D784** 120708	**1D785** 120709	**1D786** 120710	**1D787** 120711
ρ	ς	σ	τ	υ	φ	χ	ψ
1D788 120712	**1D789** 120713	**1D78A** 120714	**1D78B** 120715	**1D78C** 120716	**1D78D** 120717	**1D78E** 120718	**1D78F** 120719
ω	∂	ε	ϑ	ϰ	φ	ρ	ϖ
1D790 120720	**1D791** 120721	**1D792** 120722	**1D793** 120723	**1D794** 120724	**1D795** 120725	**1D796** 120726	**1D797** 120727
A	*B*	*Γ*	*Δ*	*E*	*Z*	*H*	*Θ*
1D798 120728	**1D799** 120729	**1D79A** 120730	**1D79B** 120731	**1D79C** 120732	**1D79D** 120733	**1D79E** 120734	**1D79F** 120735
I	*K*	*Λ*	*M*	*N*	*Ξ*	*O*	*Π*
1D7A0 120736	**1D7A1** 120737	**1D7A2** 120738	**1D7A3** 120739	**1D7A4** 120740	**1D7A5** 120741	**1D7A6** 120742	**1D7A7** 120743
P	*Θ*	*Σ*	*T*	*Y*	*Φ*	*X*	*Ψ*
1D7A8 120744	**1D7A9** 120745	**1D7AA** 120746	**1D7AB** 120747	**1D7AC** 120748	**1D7AD** 120749	**1D7AE** 120750	**1D7AF** 120751
Ω	*∇*	*α*	*β*	*γ*	*δ*	*ε*	*ζ*
1D7B0 120752	**1D7B1** 120753	**1D7B2** 120754	**1D7B3** 120755	**1D7B4** 120756	**1D7B5** 120757	**1D7B6** 120758	**1D7B7** 120759
η	*θ*	*ι*	*κ*	*λ*	*μ*	*ν*	*ξ*

Table 27-28. The Mathematical Alphanumeric Symbols block of Unicode (continued)

1D7B8 120760	1D7B9 120761	1D7BA 120762	1D7BB 120763	1D7BC 120764	1D7BD 120765	1D7BE 120766	1D7BF 120767
ο	π	ρ	ς	σ	τ	υ	φ
1D7C0 120768	**1D7C1** 120769	**1D7C2** 120770	**1D7C3** 120771	**1D7C4** 120772	**1D7C5** 120773	**1D7C6** 120774	**1D7C7** 120775
χ	ψ	ω	∂	ε	ϑ	ϰ	φ
1D7C8 120776	**1D7C9** 120777	**1D7CA** 120778	**1D7CB** 120779	**1D7CC** 120780	**1D7CD** 120781	**1D7CE** 120782	**1D7CF** 120783
ρ	ϖ	n/a	n/a	n/a	n/a	0	1
1D7D0 120784	**1D7D1** 120785	**1D7D2** 120786	**1D7D3** 120787	**1D7D4** 120788	**1D7D5** 120789	**1D7D6** 120790	**1D7D7** 120791
2	3	4	5	6	7	8	9
1D7D8 120792	**1D7D9** 120793	**1D7DA** 120794	**1D7DB** 120795	**1D7DC** 120796	**1D7DD** 120797	**1D7DE** 120798	**1D7DF** 120799
0	1	2	3	4	5	6	7
1D7E0 120800	**1D7E1** 120801	**1D7E2** 120802	**1D7E3** 120803	**1D7E4** 120804	**1D7E5** 120805	**1D7E6** 120806	**1D7E7** 120807
8	9	0	1	2	3	4	5
1D7E8 120808	**1D7E9** 120809	**1D7EA** 120810	**1D7EB** 120811	**1D7EC** 120812	**1D7ED** 120813	**1D7EE** 120814	**1D7EF** 120815
6	7	8	9	0	1	2	3
1D7F0 120816	**1D7F1** 120817	**1D7F2** 120818	**1D7F3** 120819	**1D7F4** 120820	**1D7F5** 120821	**1D7F6** 120822	**1D7F7** 120823
4	5	6	7	8	9	0	1
1D7F8 120824	**1D7F9** 120825	**1D7FA** 120826	**1D7FB** 120827	**1D7FC** 120828	**1D7FD** 120829	**1D7FE** 120830	**1D7FF** 120831
2	3	4	5	6	7	8	9

Miscellaneous Technical

The Miscellaneous Technical block, shown in Table 27-29, contains an assortment of symbols taken from electronics, quantum mechanics, the APL programming language, the ISO-9995-7 standard for language-neutral keyboard pictograms, and other sources.

Table 27-29. The Miscellaneous Technical block of Unicode

2300 8960	2301 8961	2302 8962	2303 8963	2304 8964	2305 8965	2306 8966	2307 8967
⌀	⌁	⌂	⌃	⌄	⌅	⌆	⌇
2308 8968	**2309** 8969	**230A** 8970	**230B** 8971	**230C** 8972	**230D** 8973	**230E** 8974	**230F** 8975
⌈	⌉	⌊	⌋	⌌	⌍	⌎	⌏
2310 8976	**2311** 8977	**2312** 8978	**2313** 8979	**2314** 8980	**2315** 8981	**2316** 8982	**2317** 8983
⌐	⌑	⌒	⌓	⌔	⌕	⌖	⌗
2318 8984	**2319** 8985	**231A** 8986	**231B** 8987	**231C** 8988	**231D** 8989	**231E** 8990	**231F** 8991
⌘	⌙	⌚	⌛	⌜	⌝	⌞	⌟
2320 8992	**2321** 8993	**2322** 8994	**2323** 8995	**2324** 8996	**2325** 8997	**2326** 8998	**2327** 8999
⌠	⌡	⌢	⌣	⌤	⌥	⌦	⌧

Table 27-29. *The Miscellaneous Technical block of Unicode (continued)*

Code	Dec	Code	Dec	Code	Dec	Code	Dec	Code	Dec	Code	Dec	Code	Dec	Code	Dec
2328	9000	2329	9001	232A	9002	232B	9003	232C	9004	232D	9005	232E	9006	232F	9007
2330	9008	2331	9009	2332	9010	2333	9011	2334	9012	2335	9013	2336	9014	2337	9015
2338	9016	2339	9017	233A	9018	233B	9019	233C	9020	233D	9021	233E	9022	233F	9023
2340	9024	2341	9025	2342	9026	2343	9027	2344	9028	2345	9029	2346	9030	2347	9031
2348	9032	2349	9033	234A	9034	234B	9035	234C	9036	234D	9037	234E	9038	234F	9039
2350	9040	2351	9041	2352	9042	2353	9043	2354	9044	2355	9045	2356	9046	2357	9047
2358	9048	2359	9049	235A	9050	235B	9051	235C	9052	235D	9053	235E	9054	235F	9055
2360	9056	2361	9057	2362	9058	2363	9059	2364	9060	2365	9061	2366	9062	2367	9063
2368	9064	2369	9065	236A	9066	236B	9067	236C	9068	236D	9069	236E	9070	236F	9071
2370	9072	2371	9073	2372	9074	2373	9075	2374	9076	2375	9077	2376	9078	2377	9079
2378	9080	2379	9081	237A	9082	237B	9083	237C	9084	237D	9085	237E	9086	237F	9087
2380	9088	2381	9089	2382	9090	2383	9091	2384	9092	2385	9093	2386	9094	2387	9095
2388	9096	2389	9097	238A	9098	238B	9099	238C	9100	238D	9101	238E	9102	238F	9103
2390	9104	2391	9105	2392	9106	2393	9107	2394	9108	2395	9109	2396	9110	2397	9111
2398	9112	2399	9113	239A	9114	239B	9115	239C	9116	239D	9117	239E	9118	239F	9119
23A0	9120	23A1	9121	23A2	9122	23A3	9123	23A4	9124	23A5	9125	23A6	9126	23A7	9127
23A8	9128	23A9	9129	23AA	9130	23AB	9131	23AC	9132	23AD	9133	23AE	9134	23AF	9135
23B0	9136	23B1	9137	23B2	9138	23B3	9139	23B4	9140	23B5	9141	23B6	9142	23B7	9143

Table 27-29. The Miscellaneous Technical block of Unicode (continued)

23B8	9144	23B9	9145	23BA	9146	23BB	9147	23BC	9148	23BD	9149	23BE	9150	23BF	9151
│		│		─		─		─		─		⌐		∟	
23C0	9152	23C1	9153	23C2	9154	23C3	9155	23C4	9156	23C5	9157	23C6	9158	23C7	9159
⏀		⏁		⏂		⏃		⏄		⏅		⏆		⏇	
23C8	9160	23C9	9161	23CA	9162	23CB	9163	23CC	9164	23CD	9165	23CE	9166	23CF	9167
⏈		⏉		⏊		⏋		⏌		⏍		⏎		⏏	
23D0	9120	23D1	9121	23D2	9122	23D3	9123	23D4	9124	23F5	9125	23A6	9126	23A7	9127
│		n/a		n/a		n/a		n/a		n/a		n/a		n/a	

Optical Character Recognition

The Optical Character Recognition (OCR) block, shown in Table 27-30, includes the OCR-A characters that are not already encoded as ASCII and magnetic-ink character-recognition symbols used on checks.

Table 27-30. The Optical Character Recognition block of Unicode

2440	9280	2441	9281	2442	9282	2443	9283	2444	9284	2445	9285	2446	9286	2447	9287
⑀		⑁		⑂		⑃		⑄		⑅		⑆		⑇	
2448	9288	2449	9289	244A	9290	244B	9291	244C	9292	244D	9293	244E	9294	244F	9295
⑈		⑉		⑊		n/a		n/a		n/a		n/a		n/a	

Geometric Shapes

The Geometric Shapes block combines simple triangles, squares, circles, and other shapes found in various character sets Unicode attempts to superset. See Table 27-31.

Table 27-31. The Geometric Shapes block of Unicode

25A0	9632	25A1	9633	25A2	9634	25A3	9635	25A4	9636	25A5	9637	25A6	9638	25A7	9639
■		□		▢		▣		▤		▥		▦		▧	
25A8	9640	25A9	9641	25AA	9642	25AB	9643	25AC	9644	25AD	9645	25AE	9646	25AF	9647
▨		▩		▪		▫		▬		▭		▮		▯	
25B0	9648	25B1	9649	25B2	9650	25B3	9651	25B4	9652	25B5	9653	25B6	9654	25B7	9655
▰		▱		▲		△		▴		▵		▶		▷	
25B8	9656	25B9	9657	25BA	9658	25BB	9659	25BC	9660	25BD	9661	25BE	9662	25BF	9663
▸		▹		►		▻		▼		▽		▾		▿	
25C0	9664	25C1	9665	25C2	9666	25C3	9667	25C4	9668	25C5	9669	25C6	9670	25C7	9671
◀		◁		◂		◃		◄		◅		◆		◇	

Table 27-31. The Geometric Shapes block of Unicode (continued)

25C8 9672	25C9 9673	25CA 9674	25CB 9675	25CC 9676	25CD 9677	25CE 9678	25CF 9679
◈	◉	◊	○	◌	◍	◎	●
25D0 9680	**25D1** 9681	**25D2** 9682	**25D3** 9683	**25D4** 9684	**25D5** 9685	**25D6** 9686	**25D7** 9687
◐	◑	◒	◓	◔	◕	◖	◗
25D8 9688	**25D9** 9689	**25DA** 9690	**25DB** 9691	**25DC** 9692	**25DD** 9693	**25DE** 9694	**25DF** 9695
◘	◙	◚	◛	◜	◝	◞	◟
25E0 9696	**25E1** 9697	**25E2** 9698	**25E3** 9699	**25E4** 9700	**25E5** 9701	**25E6** 9702	**25E7** 9703
◠	◡	◢	◣	◤	◥	◦	◧
25E8 9704	**25E9** 9705	**25EA** 9706	**25EB** 9707	**25EC** 9708	**25ED** 9709	**25EE** 9710	**25EF** 9711
◨	◩	◪	◫	◬	◭	◮	◯
25F0 9712	**25F1** 9713	**25F2** 9714	**25F3** 9715	**25F4** 9716	**25F5** 9717	**25F6** 9718	**25F7** 9719
◰	◱	◲	◳	◴	◵	◶	◷
25F8 9720	**25F9** 9721	**25FA** 9722	**25FB** 9723	**25FC** 9724	**25FD** 9725	**25FE** 9726	**25FF** 9727
◸	◹	◺	◻	◼	◽	◾	◿

Miscellaneous Symbols

The Miscellaneous Symbols block contains mostly pictographic symbols found in vendor and national character sets that preceded Unicode. See Table 27-32.

Table 27-32. The Miscellaneous Symbols block of Unicode

2600 9728	2601 9729	2602 9730	2603 9731	2604 9732	2605 9733	2606 9734	2607 9735
☀	☁	☂	☃	☄	★	☆	☇
2608 9736	**2609** 9737	**260A** 9738	**260B** 9739	**260C** 9740	**260D** 9741	**260E** 9742	**260F** 9743
☈	☉	☊	☋	☌	☍	☎	☏
2610 9744	**2611** 9745	**2612** 9746	**2613** 9747	**2614** 9748	**2615** 9749	**2616** 9750	**2617** 9751
☐	☑	☒	☓	☔	☕	☖	☗
2618 9752	**2619** 9753	**261A** 9754	**261B** 9755	**261C** 9756	**261D** 9757	**261E** 9758	**261F** 9759
n/a	☙	☚	☛	☜	☝	☞	☟
2620 9760	**2621** 9761	**2622** 9762	**2623** 9763	**2624** 9764	**2625** 9765	**2626** 9766	**2627** 9767
☠	☡	☢	☣	☤	☥	☦	☧
2628 9768	**2629** 9769	**262A** 9770	**262B** 9771	**262C** 9772	**262D** 9773	**262E** 9774	**262F** 9775
☨	☩	☪	☫	☬	☭	☮	☯
2630 9776	**2631** 9777	**2632** 9778	**2633** 9779	**2634** 9780	**2635** 9781	**2636** 9782	**2637** 9783
☰	☱	☲	☳	☴	☵	☶	☷
2638 9784	**2639** 9785	**263A** 9786	**263B** 9787	**263C** 9788	**263D** 9789	**263E** 9790	**263F** 9791
☸	☹	☺	☻	☼	☽	☾	☿

Table 27-32. The Miscellaneous Symbols block of Unicode (continued)

2640 9792	2641 9793	2642 9794	2643 9795	2644 9796	2645 9797	2646 9798	2647 9799
♀	♁	♂	♃	♄	♅	♆	♇
2648 9800	**2649** 9801	**264A** 9802	**264B** 9803	**264C** 9804	**264D** 9805	**264E** 9806	**264F** 9807
♈	♉	♊	♋	♌	♍	♎	♏
2650 9808	**2651** 9809	**2652** 9810	**2653** 9811	**2654** 9812	**2655** 9813	**2656** 9814	**2657** 9815
♐	♑	♒	♓	♔	♕	♖	♗
2658 9816	**2659** 9817	**265A** 9818	**265B** 9819	**265C** 9820	**265D** 9821	**265E** 9822	**265F** 9823
♘	♙	♚	♛	♜	♝	♞	♟
2660 9824	**2661** 9825	**2662** 9826	**2663** 9827	**2664** 9828	**2665** 9829	**2666** 9830	**2667** 9831
♠	♡	♢	♣	♤	♥	♦	♧
2668 9832	**2669** 9833	**266A** 9834	**266B** 9835	**266C** 9836	**266D** 9837	**266E** 9838	**266F** 9839
♨	♩	♪	♫	♬	♭	♮	♯
2670 9840	**2671** 9841	**2672** 9842	**2673** 9843	**2674** 9844	**2675** 9845	**2676** 9846	**2677** 9847
♰	♱	♲	♳	♴	♵	♶	♷
2678 9848	**2679** 9849	**267A** 9850	**267B** 9851	**267C** 9852	**267D** 9853	**267E** 9854	**267F** 9855
♸	♹	♺	♻	♼	♽	*n/a*	*n/a*
2680 9856	**2681** 9857	**2682** 9858	**2683** 9859	**2684** 9860	**2685** 9861	**2686** 9862	**2687** 9863
⚀	⚁	⚂	⚃	⚄	⚅	⚆	⚇
2688 9864	**2689** 9865	**268A** 9866	**268B** 9867	**268C** 9868	**268D** 9869	**268E** 9870	**268F** 9871
⚈	⚉	⚊	⚋	⚌	⚍	⚎	⚏
2690 9872	**2691** 9873	**2692** 9874	**2693** 9875	**2694** 9876	**2695** 9877	**2696** 9878	**2697** 9879
⚐	⚑	*n/a*	*n/a*	*n/a*	*n/a*	*n/a*	*n/a*
2698 9880	**2699** 9881	**269A** 9882	**269B** 9883	**269C** 9884	**269D** 9885	**269E** 9886	**269F** 9887
n/a	*n/a*	*n/a*	*n/a*	*n/a*	*n/a*	*n/a*	*n/a*
26A0 9888	**26A1** 9889	**26A2** 9880	**26A3** 9881	**26A4** 9882	**26A5** 9883	**26A6** 9884	**26A7** 9885
⚠	⚡	*n/a*	*n/a*	*n/a*	*n/a*	*n/a*	*n/a*

Dingbats

The Dingbats block, shown in Table 27-33, is based on characters in the popular Adobe Zapf Dingbats font.

Table 27-33. The Dingbats block of Unicode

2700 9984 n/a	2701 9985 ✁	2702 9986 ✂	2703 9987 ✃	2704 9988 ✄	2705 9989 n/a	2706 9990 ✆	2707 9991 ✇
2708 9992 ✈	2709 9993 ✉	270A 9994 n/a	270B 9995 n/a	270C 9996 ✌	270D 9997 ✍	270E 9998 ✎	270F 9999 ✏
2710 10000 ✐	2711 10001 ✑	2712 10002 ✒	2713 10003 ✓	2714 10004 ✔	2715 10005 ✕	2716 10006 ✖	2717 10007 ✗
2718 10008 ✘	2719 10009 ✙	271A 10010 ✚	271B 10011 ✛	271C 10012 ✜	271D 10013 ✝	271E 10014 ✞	271F 10015 ✟
2720 10016 ✠	2721 10017 ✡	2722 10018 ✢	2723 10019 ✣	2724 10020 ✤	2725 10021 ✥	2726 10022 ✦	2727 10023 ✧
2728 10024 n/a	2729 10025 ✩	272A 10026 ✪	272B 10027 ✫	272C 10028 ✬	272D 10029 ✭	272E 10030 ✮	272F 10031 ✯
2730 10032 ✰	2731 10033 ✱	2732 10034 ✲	2733 10035 ✳	2734 10036 ✴	2735 10037 ✵	2736 10038 ✶	2737 10039 ✷
2738 10040 ✸	2739 10041 ✹	273A 10042 ✺	273B 10043 ✻	273C 10044 ✼	273D 10045 ✽	273E 10046 ✾	273F 10047 ✿
2740 10048 ❀	2741 10049 ❁	2742 10050 ❂	2743 10051 ❃	2744 10052 ❄	2745 10053 ❅	2746 10054 ❆	2747 10055 ❇
2748 10056 ❈	2749 10057 ❉	274A 10058 ❊	274B 10059 ❋	274C 10060 n/a	274D 10061 ❍	274E 10062 n/a	274F 10063 ❏
2750 10064 ❐	2751 10065 ❑	2752 10066 ❒	2753 10067 n/a	2754 10068 n/a	2755 10069 n/a	2756 10070 ❖	2757 10071 n/a
2758 10072 ❘	2759 10073 ❙	275A 10074 ❚	275B 10075 ❛	275C 10076 ❜	275D 10077 ❝	275E 10078 ❞	275F 10079 n/a
2760 10080 n/a	2761 10081 ❡	2762 10082 ❢	2763 10083 ❣	2764 10084 ❤	2765 10085 ❥	2766 10086 ❦	2767 10087 ❧
2768 10088 ❨	2769 10089 ❩	276A 10090 ❪	276B 10091 ❫	276C 10092 ❬	276D 10093 ❭	276E 10094 ❮	276F 10095 ❯
2770 10096 ❰	2771 10097 ❱	2772 10098 ❲	2773 10099 ❳	2774 10100 ❴	2775 10101 ❵	2776 10102 ❶	2777 10103 ❷
2778 10104 ❸	2779 10105 ❹	277A 10106 ❺	277B 10107 ❻	277C 10108 ❼	277D 10109 ❽	277E 10110 ❾	277F 10111 ❿
2780 10112 ➀	2781 10113 ➁	2782 10114 ➂	2783 10115 ➃	2784 10116 ➄	2785 10117 ➅	2786 10118 ➆	2787 10119 ➇

Table 27-33. The Dingbats block of Unicode (continued)

2788	10120	2789	10121	278A	10122	278B	10123	278C	10124	278D	10125	278E	10126	278F	10127
⑨		⑩		❶		❷		❸		❹		❺		❻	
2790	10128	**2791**	10129	**2792**	10130	**2793**	10131	**2794**	10132	**2795**	10133	**2796**	10134	**2797**	10135
❼		❽		❾		❿		→		*n/a*		*n/a*		*n/a*	
2798	10136	**2799**	10137	**279A**	10138	**279B**	10139	**279C**	10140	**279D**	10141	**279E**	10142	**279F**	10143
↘		→		↗		→		→		→		→		➠	
27A0	10144	**27A1**	10145	**27A2**	10146	**27A3**	10147	**27A4**	10148	**27A5**	10149	**27A6**	10150	**27A7**	10151
➡		➡		➢		➣		➤		➥		➦		➧	
27A8	10152	**27A9**	10153	**27AA**	10154	**27AB**	10155	**27AC**	10156	**27AD**	10157	**27AE**	10158	**27AF**	10159
➨		⇨		⇨		⇨		⇦		⇨		⇨		⇨	
27B0	10160	**27B1**	10161	**27B2**	10162	**27B3**	10163	**27B4**	10164	**27B5**	10165	**27B6**	10166	**27B7**	10167
n/a		⇨		➲		➳		➴		➵		➶		➷	
27B8	10168	**27B9**	10169	**27BA**	10170	**27BB**	10171	**27BC**	10172	**27BD**	10173	**27BE**	10174	**27BF**	10175
➸		➹		➺		➻		➼		➽		➾		*n/a*	

Index

Symbols

( ) (parentheses)
  in element declarations, 39
  grouping operator, 383
& (ampersand)
  entity reference for (&), 49,
    374, 601
  escaping in element character
    data, 20
  in CDATA sections, 21
<? and ?>, delimiting processing
    instructions, 22
<!-- and -->, delimiting X ML
    comments, 22
< (angle bracket, left), escaping in
    element character data, 20
' (apostrophe)
  entity reference for ('), 20, 49,
    602
    XML specification, 374
* (asterisk)
  CSS universal selector, 225
  node test, 461
  suffix for element names, 38, 383
  XPath arithmetic operator, 176
  XPath wildcard, 169
@ (at sign), selecting an attribute, 167,
    458
]]> (CDATA end delimiter), 21
: (colon), in XML names, 64, 373

:: (double colon), in unabbreviated
    location paths, 173
// (double forward slash)
  building compound location
    paths, 458
  selecting from context node
    descendants, 170
.. (double period)
  selecting parent element, 171
  selecting parent node, 458
= (equals sign)
  CSS attribute value selector, 226
  separating attribute name-value
    pairs, 16
/ (forward slash)
  combining location steps with, 170
  combining XPath location steps, 458
  root location path, 165
> (greater-than sign)
  CSS child element selector, 225
  entity reference for (>), 20, 49,
    374, 601
  escaping, need for, 21
< (less-than sign)
  entity reference for (<), 20, 49,
    374, 601
  hexadecimal escape in URIs
    (%3C), 202
  in CDATA sections, 21
  not allowed in attribute values, 390

We'd like to hear your suggestions for improving our indexes. Send email to *index@oreilly.com*.

events (XHTML DTD module), 123
exceptions
  SAX, 349
    features not provided by
      parser, 359
  SAXException class, 579
  SAXNotRecognizedException
    class, 580
  SAXNotSupportedException
    class, 581
  SAXParseException class, 580
exclusive min and max facets, 295
expat parser, 596
expressions, XPath, 151, 175–177
  Booleans, 177
  data types, 456
  numbers, 176
  predicates, 461
  strings, 176
  (see also location paths; location
    steps)
Extended Backus-Naur Form (EBNF)
    grammar, 399
  for XML 1.1, 405
Extended Interfaces (DOM Core), 327
extended links, 188–195
  arcs, 190–193
    multiple arcs from one arc
      element, 191–193
    role attributes, 193
    title attributes, 193
  local resources, 194
  locator elements, 189
  title elements, 194
  XPointers and, 203
Extensible Linking Language (see
    XLinks)
Extensible Messaging and Presence
    Protocol (XMPP), 267
Extensible Stylesheet Language (see XSL;
    XSL-FO; XSLT)
Extensible Stylesheet Language
    Transformations (see XSLT)
extension element, 421
  deriving new type from, 303
extension elements in XSLT, 470
extent attributes (XSL-FO nonbody
    regions), 238
external declarations
  including, 301
  modifying, 302

external DTD subsets, 34
  general entity references and, 83
  parameter entity references and, 55
  text declarations and, 74
  XML processing and, 316
  XML specification for, 381, 389
external general entities
  parsed, 50–52, 380
    attribute values and, 390
    no recursion allowed, 391
    SAX core feature, 589
    text declarations and, 73
    text declarations of, 380
  unparsed, 52, 380
    declaring notations, 398
external parameter entity references, 55
  SAX core feature, 589

F

facet elements, 293
  enforcing format, 296
  enumeration, 295, 421
  fixed, 306
  fractionDigits, 422
  length, 424
  length-restriction, 294
  list, 296
  maxExclusive, 424
  maxInclusive, 425
  maxLength, 425
  minExclusive, 426
  minInclusive, 426
  minLength, 426
  numeric, 295
  pattern, 427–429
  totalDigits, 433
  union, 297
  whiteSpace, 294, 434
fallback element, 216, 477
false( ) function (XPath), 177, 182, 463
features, DOM
  getFeature( ) (Node), 561
  support of, checking, 564
features, SAX, 358
  SAXCoreFeatures class, 588
  turning on, 359
Feynman, Richard, 163, 166, 172
  XML document describing, 144
field element, 421
file formats, XML and, 269
filesystems, MIME types in, 72

filters
  event-based parsers and, 312
  SAX, 360–363
    for processing instructions, 361
    steps in using, 363
    well-formedness, problems
      with, 362
    XMLFilter interface, 578
    XMLFilterImpl class, 361, 585
final attribute, 306
firstChild attribute (Node), 553
first-letter pseudo-element, CSS, 227
first-line pseudo-element, CSS, 227
fixed attribute, 306
#FIXED attributes (XLink), 196
#FIXED default declaration, 48, 384
  explicit value must match default
    value, 397
float type, 441
floating-point doubles (in XPath), 176
floating-point numbers (in XPath), 457
floor( ) function (XPath), 182, 463
flow element (XSL-FO), 240
%Flow.mix; entity reference, 125
fo prefix (XSL-FO), 237
focus pseudo-class, CSS, 227
fo:flow element (XSL-FO), 240
fo:layout-master-set element, 237
following axis, 173, 460
following-sibling axis, 173, 460
font properties
  CSS, 230
  XSL-FO, 244
fo:page-sequence elements, 237
for-each element, 477
format-number( ) function (XSLT), 180,
  492
formatting objects, 234
formatting program (FOP, Apache XML
  Project), 243
forms, XHTML DTD modules for, 123
fo:root element, 237
fractionDigits facet element, 296, 422
fragment identifiers, 200
  XPointer href attributes and, 217
frames modules (XHTML DTD), 123
frameset DTD (XHTML), 116
French language, subcodes for
  dialects, 84
functionality, removing from XML
  applications, 277

function-available( ) function, 493
functions
  XPath, 178, 462–468
    Boolean, 182
    node-set, 179
    number, 182
    string, 180
  XSLT, 490–494
Fundamental Interfaces (DOM
  Core), 327

G

gDay type, 441
general entities
  external parsed, 50–52
    attribute values and, 390
    no recursion allowed, 391
    text declarations and, 73
  external unparsed, 52, 380
    declaring notations, 398
  internal, 380
  parsed, 380
  unparsed, 380
general entity declarations, 49, 380
  declaring, 397
general entity references, 318
  XML specification for, 376
General Punctuation Unicode
  block, 635
generate-id( ) function, 493
generating XML documents for other
  applications, 322
Geometric Shapes Unicode block, 649
getAttribute( ) (Element), 536
getAttributeNode( ) (Element), 536
getAttributeNodeNS( ) (Element), 537
getAttributeNS( ) (Element), 536
getElementById( ) (Document), 514
getElementsByTagName( )
  Document interface, 514
  Element interface, 537
getElementsByTagNameNS( )
  Document interface, 514, 516
  Element interface, 537
getException( ) (SAXException), 580
getFeature( )
  DOMImplementation, 339
  Node, 561
  XMLReader, 359
getNamedItem( )
  (NamedNodeMap), 548

getNamedItemNS( )
    (NamedNodeMap), 549
getProperty( ) (SAX), 359
getTextContent( ) method (DOM), 330
getUserData (Node), 561
global elements in schemas, 281
glyph areas (XSL-FO), 236
gMonth type, 442
gMonthDay type, 442
Goldfarb, Charles F., 8, 89
Goodman, Danny, 531
grammar for XML documents
    XML 1.0, 399–405
    XML 1.1, 405–410
Greek language, 595
    Greek Extended Unicode block, 632
    Greek Unicode block, 616
Gregorian calendar, 441–443
group element, 299, 422
GUI programs for XML document
    validation, 36
gYear type, 443
gYearMonth type, 443

H

handle( ) (UserDataHandler), 572
handleError( )
    (DOMErrorHandler), 342
hasAttribute( ) (Element), 538
hasAttributeNS( ) (Element), 538
hasAttributes( ) (Node), 561
hasChildNodes( ) (Node), 562
hasFeature( )
    (DOMImplementation), 339,
    530
head element, 305
Hebrew language, 595
Hebrew Unicode block, 620
here( ) function, 210
hexadecimals
    character references, 20, 81
    CSS color numbers, 233
    escaping XPointer characters not
        allowed in URIs, 202
hexBinary type, 444
hidden elements (CSS display
    property), 229
HIERARCHY_REQUEST_ERR
    exception (DOM), 526
hover pseudo-class, CSS, 227

href attribute
    include element, 213
    XPointer, URLs used in, 217
href pseudo-attribute, 118, 224
HTML
    a link in rddl:resource element, 255
    converting document to
        XHTML, 111–115
    entity sets (Version 4.0), 601–609
        Latin-1, 602–605
        special characters, 605
        symbols, 606–609
    malformed markup, correcting, 320
    serving XML pages in, 122
    SGML and, 9
    structure of documents, 91
    XPointer fragment identifiers in URLs
        used in elements, 202
    (see also XHTML)
HTML forms, XHTML DTD
    modules, 123
HTML module, DOM, 325
HTTP
    Content-Type field in headers, 72
    XML over, 263

I

IANA (Internet Assigned Numbers
    Authority)
    character sets registered with, 74
    MIME types for XSLT
        stylesheets, 118
IBM
    character sets, 78
    XSL Formatting Objects
        Composer, 244
id( ) function (XPath), 179, 204, 463
ID attribute type, 45
    default for, 395
    generate-id( ), 493
    in element type declarations, 383
    only one per element type, 394
    values must be unique, 394
    in XPointer shorthand pointers, 203
ID type, 444
IDL (Interface Definition Language) and
    DOM, 325, 496
IDREF attribute type, 46
    in element type declarations, 383
    matching IDs in document, 395
IDREF type, 444

OpenOffice, 98–101
   file format developed by
      OpenOffice.org, 269
Opera, support for XHTML, 117
Optical Character Recognition Unicode
      block, 649
org.xml.sax package, 574–581
org.xml.sax.ext package, 590–593
org.xml.sax.helpers package, 581–588
origin( ) function (XPointer), 210
otherwise element, 482
outbound links, 195
output element, 482
output formats for XML
      documents, 107
ownerDocument attribute (Node), 557
ownerElement attribute (Attr
      interface), 507, 508, 535

P

page-sequence element (XSL-FO), 237
page-sequence elements (XSL-FO), 237
param element, 483
param module (XHTML DTD), 123
parameter entities, 53–56
   connecting XHTML DTD
      modules, 122
   syntax of, 54
   XML specification for, 379
parameter entity references, 54, 376
   connecting XHTML modules, 122
   defining, with document model
      modules, 133
   in DTD only, 391
   external DTD subsets and, 55
   including declarations in, 389
   internal subsets and, 388
   mixing XHTML into
      applications, 125
   for namespace prefixes, 69
   preceding with parameter entity
      declarations, 397
   proper nesting
      with conditional sections, 397
      with markup declarations, 392
      with parenthesized groups, 394
   redefining, 55
   XLink elements and, 196
parent axis, 173, 460
parent elements, 14
   selecting with .. (double period), 458

parentheses in element declarations, 39
parentNode attribute (Node), 557
parse( ) (XMLReader), 349
parse attribute (xi:include), 215
parsed character data (#PCDATA), 31,
      37
parsed general entities, 380
   attribute values and, 390
   no recursion allowed, 391
   text declarations and, 73
ParserAdapter class (SAX), 584
parsers, 7
   Apache Xerces XML DOM
      parser, 343
   billion laugh attacks, 319
   checking documents for well-
      formedness, 26
   checking the character set, 80
   comparing namespace URIs, 67
   determining character encoding, 72
   event-based, 311
   handling of namespaces, 68
   SAX XMLReader interface, 578
   support for XInclude, 214
   validating, 8, 281, 343
      comparing document to its
         DTD, 28
      validity constraints
         enforced, 392–398
   whitespace, treatment of, 317
   Xerces Java Parser, 347
   XML-defined character sets, 74
   (see also DOM; SAX)
PassiveTeX library, 243
pattern facet element, 296, 427–429
pattern matching
   match attribute (xsl:template), 148
   text( ) node test, 154
#PCDATA keyword, 31, 37
PCs, Mac-specific character sets on, 79
PDF format for XSL-FO
      documents, 249
permanence of XML documents, 105
Phoenician (Unicode block for), 620
PHP, processing instructions in, 23
pictographic symbols, Unicode block
      for, 650
Pinard, François, 80
pixels (CSS unit of length), 230
platform-dependent character sets, 78

About the Authors

Elliotte Rusty Harold is originally from New Orleans, to which he returns periodically in search of a decent bowl of gumbo. However, he currently resides in the Prospect Heights neighborhood of Brooklyn with his wife Beth and cats Charm (named after the quark) and Marjorie (named after his mother-in-law). He's an adjunct professor of computer science at Polytechnic University, where he teaches Java and object-oriented programming. His Cafe au Lait web site (*http://www.cafeaulait.org*) has become one of the most popular independent Java sites on the Internet; and his spinoff site, Cafe con Leche (*http://www.cafeconleche.org*), has become one of the Internet's most popular XML sites. Elliotte's previous books for O'Reilly include *Java I/O* and *Java Network Programming*.

W. Scott Means began his career as a software developer with Microsoft in 1988, joining the company at age 17. Scott was one of the original developers on both Microsoft's OS/2 and Windows NT operating systems. He was also involved in the early design and development stages of the Microsoft Network for the Advanced Technology and Business Development Group. Scott has been a consultant on XML and Internet topics since 1998. He has authored and co-authored three books on XML topics. He is currently serving as President and CEO of Enterprise Web Machines, a South Carolina–based Internet software product and services company.

Colophon

Our look is the result of reader comments, our own experimentation, and feedback from distribution channels. Distinctive covers complement our distinctive approach to technical topics, breathing personality and life into potentially dry subjects.

The animal on the cover of *XML in a Nutshell*, Third Edition, is a peafowl, the largest bird in the Phasianinae family, which also includes pheasants and turkeys. People often incorrectly call peafowl peacocks. Peacocks are actually male peafowl; the females are called peahens. Two wild peafowl species exist today: the Indian peafowl (*Pavo cristatus*) and the Green peafowl of Southeast Asia (*Pavo muticus*), which may be endangered. These wild peafowl live in musters of 8 to 12 birds in dense forest near water. Though they do not fly very well, and do so only for short distances, they do manage to escape most predators and roost peacefully at night, high up in treetops.

The peafowl's most famous characteristic, of course, is its beautiful fan of feathers, known as a "train." Each blue-green train feather has a dark spot on its tip that looks much like an eye. Peacocks develop especially brilliant plumage, an indicator of sexual maturity, by age three. A healthy peacock has a full and vibrant train each year during the spring mating season. During this period, peacocks strut their stuff—display their "breeding plumage," as it is called—to attract peahens. Scientists theorize that the peacock's performance plays upon the peahen's instinctive drives to find healthy mates in the hope of producing hardy offspring. Each summer after the mating season, peafowl shed their train feathers, which are often collected by humans as eye-catching souvenirs.

Marlowe Shaeffer was the production editor and copyeditor for *XML in a Nutshell*, Third Edition. Jane Ellin was the proofreader. Sarah Sherman and Claire Cloutier provided quality control. James Quill provided production assistance. Ellen Troutman-Zaig wrote the index.

Ellie Volckhausen designed the cover of this book, based on a series design by Edie Freedman. The cover image is an original illustration created by Susan Hart. Clay Fernald produced the cover layout with QuarkXPress 4.1 using Adobe's ITC Garamond font.

Melanie Wang designed the interior layout, based on a series design by David Futato. This book was converted by Joe Wizda to FrameMaker 5.5.6 with a format conversion tool created by Erik Ray, Jason McIntosh, Neil Walls, and Mike Sierra that uses Perl and XML technologies. The text font is Linotype Birka; the heading font is Adobe Myriad Condensed; and the code font is LucasFont's TheSans Mono Condensed. The tables in Chapter 27 were produced using Code2000, Code2001, Arial Unicode MS, Tibetan Machine Web, Tibetan Machine Uni, Doulos SIL, and PakType Naqsh fonts. The illustrations that appear in the book were produced by Robert Romano and Jessamyn Read using Macromedia FreeHand 9 and Adobe Photoshop 6. The tip and warning icons were drawn by Christopher Bing. This colophon was written by Sarah Jane Shangraw and Molly Shangraw.

Better than e-books

Search
inside electronic versions of thousands of books

Browse
books by category. With Safari researching any topic is a snap

Find
answers in an instant

Read books from cover to cover. Or, simply click to the page you need.

Search Safari! The premier electronic reference library for programmers and IT professionals

Related Titles Available from O'Reilly

O'REILLY®

Our books are available at most retail and online bookstores.
To order direct: 1-800-998-9938 • *order@oreilly.com* • *www.oreilly.com*
Online editions of most O'Reilly titles are available by subscription at *safari.oreilly.com*

Keep in touch with O'Reilly

1. Download examples from our books

To find example files for a book, go to:

www.oreilly.com/catalog

select the book, and follow the "Examples" link.

2. Register your O'Reilly books

Register your book at *register.oreilly.com*

Why register your books? Once you've registered your O'Reilly books you can:

* Win O'Reilly books, T-shirts or discount coupons in our monthly drawing.
* Get special offers available only to registered O'Reilly customers.
* Get catalogs announcing new books (US and UK only).
* Get email notification of new editions of the O'Reilly books you own.

3. Join our email lists

Sign up to get topic-specific email announcements of new books and conferences, special offers, and O'Reilly Network technology newsletters at:

elists.oreilly.com

It's easy to customize your free elists subscription so you'll get exactly the O'Reilly news you want.

4. Get the latest news, tips, and tools

http://www.oreilly.com

* "Top 100 Sites on the Web"—PC Magazine
* CIO Magazine's Web Business 50 Awards

Our web site contains a library of comprehensive product information (including book excerpts and tables of contents), downloadable software, background articles, interviews with technology leaders, links to relevant sites, book cover art, and more.

5. Work for O'Reilly

Check out our web site for current employment opportunities:

jobs.oreilly.com

6. Contact us

O'Reilly & Associates
1005 Gravenstein Hwy North
Sebastopol, CA 95472 USA

TEL: 707-827-7000 or 800-998-9938
(6am to 5pm PST)

FAX: 707-829-0104

order@oreilly.com
For answers to problems regarding your order or our products.
To place a book order online, visit:

www.oreilly.com/order_new

catalog@oreilly.com
To request a copy of our latest catalog.

booktech@oreilly.com
For book content technical questions or corrections.

corporate@oreilly.com
For educational, library, government, and corporate sales.

proposals@oreilly.com
To submit new book proposals to our editors and product managers.

international@oreilly.com
For information about our international distributors or translation queries. For a list of our distributors outside of North America check out:

international.oreilly.com/distributors.html

adoption@oreilly.com
For information about academic use of O'Reilly books, visit:

academic.oreilly.com

O'REILLY®

Our books are available at most retail and online bookstores.
To order direct: 1-800-998-9938 • *order@oreilly.com* • *www.oreilly.com*
Online editions of most O'Reilly titles are available by subscription at *safari.oreilly.com*